GROUP PSYCHOTHERAPY
AND GROUP FUNCTION

GROUP PSYCHOTHERAPY AND GROUP FUNCTION

edited by

MAX ROSENBAUM, Ph.D.

MILTON BERGER, M.D.

Basic Books, Inc., Publishers
NEW YORK
LONDON

Fourth Printing

© 1963 by Basic Books, Inc., Publishers
Library of Congress Catalog Card Number 63–12841
Manufactured in the United States of America
DESIGNED BY JOAN WALL

Ac ne forte roges,
quo me duce,
quo lare tuter.
(Nullius addictus iurare
in verba magistri.)
—HORACE

And do not ask, by chance,
what leader I follow
or what godhead guards me.
(I am not bound to revere
the word of any particular master.)

CONTENTS

Preface   xi
List of Authors   xiii
Introduction   1

Part 1   SOCIAL PSYCHOLOGY AND SMALL GROUP
        THEORY   29

1. Group Psychotherapy in Our Society, GARDNER MURPHY   33
2. Opinions and Social Pressure, SOLOMON E. ASCH   42
3. Experiments in Group Conflict, MUZAFER SHERIF   52
4. Status and Conformity to Pressures in Informal Groups,
   O. J. HARVEY AND CONRAD CONSALVI   61
5. Emotional Dynamics and Group Culture, DOROTHY STOCK AND
   HERBERT A. THELEN   71
6. Quiet and Vocal Groups, ANDIE L. KNUTSON   92

Part 2   HISTORICAL SURVEY   109

7. The Tuberculosis Class: An Experiment in Home Treatment,
   JOSEPH H. PRATT   111
8. The Use of Dejerine's Methods in the Treatment of the
   Common Neuroses by Group Psychotherapy, JOSEPH H. PRATT   123
9. Group Therapy and the Psychiatric Clinic, L. CODY MARSH   131
10. The Group Method of Analysis, TRIGANT BURROW   143
11. A Summary Note on the Work of Trigant Burrow, HANS SYZ   154
12. A New Theory of Neuroses, D. H. LAWRENCE (A Review of The
   Social Basis of Consciousness by TRIGANT BURROW)   162
13. Group Psychotherapy from the Point of View of Adlerian
   Psychology, RUDOLF DREIKURS   168
14. C. G. Jung on the Present Trends in Group Psychotherapy,
   HANS A. ILLING   180

15. *Some Applications of Harry Stack Sullivan's Theories to Group Psychotherapy*, GEORGE D. GOLDMAN   188
16. *Horney Concepts in Group Psychotherapy*, SIDNEY ROSE   195

Part 3   THEORY AND TECHNIQUE   207

17. *The Dynamics of Group Psychotherapy and Its Application*, LOUIS WENDER   211
18. *Results and Problems of Group Psychotherapy in Severe Neuroses*, PAUL SCHILDER   218
19. *Group Therapy Special Section Meeting*, LAWSON G. LOWREY, CHAIRMAN; S. R. SLAVSON   228
20. *Scientific Foundations of Group Psychotherapy*, J. L. MORENO   242
21. *Psychoanalysis and Group Psychotherapy*, NATHAN W. ACKERMAN   250
22. *Description of a Project in Group Therapy*, DOROTHY W. BARUCH   261
23. *The Psychoanalysis of Groups*, ALEXANDER WOLF   273
24. *The Case for Didactic Group Psychotherapy*, J. W. KLAPMAN   328
25. *Mechanisms of Group Psychotherapy: Processes and Dynamics*, RAYMOND J. CORSINI AND BINA ROSENBERG   340
26. *The Relationship of Group Therapy to Other Group Influence Attempts*, SAUL SCHEIDLINGER   352
27. *The Challenge of Group Psychoanalysis*, MAX ROSENBAUM   362
28. *Psychoanalytic Applications to Levels of Group Psychotherapy with Adults*, BENJAMIN KOTKOV   370
29. *Group Counseling with Parents*, HANNA GRUNWALD AND BERNARD CASELLA   381
30. *Multiple Psychotherapy*, HERMAN H. SPITZ AND SHELDON B. KOPP   391
31. *Homogeneous Versus Heterogeneous Groups*, WILLIAM FURST   407
32. *Concerning the Size of Therapy Groups*, JOSEPH J. GELLER   411
33. *An Approach to the Selection of Patients for Group Psychotherapy*, J. E. NEIGHBOR, MARGARET BEACH, DONALD T. BROWN, DAVID KEVIN, AND JOHN S. VISHER   413
34. *Nonverbal Communications in Group Psychotherapy*, MILTON MILES BERGER   424
35. *Coordinated Meetings in Group Psychotherapy*, ASYA L. KADIS   437

Part 4   APPLICATIONS TO PARTICULAR DIAGNOSTIC ENTITIES   451

36. *Group Therapy in the Mental Hospital*, JEROME D. FRANK   453
37. *Group Analysis in a Military Neurosis Center*, S. H. FOULKES   469

38. Group Psychotherapy with Psychotics, CHRISTOPHER T.
    STANDISH AND ELVIN V. SEMRAD   477
39. A Review of Some Recent Group Psychotherapy Methods for
    Elderly Psychiatric Patients, MATHEW ROSS   487
40. Group Therapy of Alcoholics with Concurrent Group Meet-
    ings of Their Wives, LESTER H. GLIEDMAN, DAVID ROSENTHAL,
    JEROME D. FRANK, AND HELEN T. NASH   510
41. An Experimental Study of Directive Group Therapy with De-
    fective Delinquents, ROBERT SNYDER AND LEE SECHREST   525
42. Group Therapy with Retarded Readers, BERNARD FISHER   534

Part 5 TRAINING   543

43. The Utilization of a Therapy Group in Teaching Psycho-
    therapy, SAMUEL B. HADDEN   545
44. Training in Group Psychotherapy: A Symposium, CORNELIUS
    BEUKENKAMP; MILTON M. BERGER   553
45. The Training of the Group Psychotherapist, AARON STEIN   558
46. An Experience in Teaching Psychotherapy by Means of Group
    Therapy, JOHN WARKENTIN   577

Part 6 NEW TRENDS IN GROUP PSYCHOTHERAPY   587

47. Status Denial in Group Psychoanalysis, HUGH MULLAN   591
48. Dialogue and the "Essential We"—The Bases of Values in the
    Philosophy of Martin Buber, MAURICE FRIEDMAN   604
49. Beyond Transference Behavior, CORNELIUS BEUKENKAMP   614
50. The Role of Psychotropic Drugs in Group Therapy,
    R. A. SANDISON   618
51. Recent Advances in Family Group Therapy, JOHN ELDERKIN
    BELL   635

An Exhortation—Group Process Analysis: Past Is Prologue,
EUGENE L. HARTLEY   653

Index   659

PREFACE

This volume has a dual aim—first, to give some idea of the vastness and historical roots of group psychotherapy, and second, to encourage all who work with groups to begin to share with one another their experiences. Hopefully, this should lead to some conceptualizations and finally to hypotheses that may be systematically studied. There is a great deal of dogma in the field of psychotherapy. While it is not our intent to criticize assumptions or opinions, it is our hope that assumptions and opinions will not be confused with facts. Perhaps the very humanness and authenticity of intensive psychotherapy will preclude systematic research, but in the absence of data to deny the possibility of research we can still make efforts to formulate and test research hypotheses.

Many scientists in different major fields of interest share with us the common goal of seeking to know man. To the degree that we do know man we may be in a better position not only to help our fellow man and ourselves therapeutically but also to help man singly and in groups to more completely develop and fulfill his healthy potential for his own good and the good of that larger group referred to as mankind. We can influence our own evolution through the knowledge of people in groups.

We have attempted to select articles and excerpts that are truly representative. On occasion, an author of an article would feel that the work chosen was not truly representative of his effort. Our purpose was to note the historical importance of such an article at a particular point in the evolution of group psychotherapy and group function. Unfortunately, a few authors refused consent unless an article was reprinted in its entirety or was brought "up to date." Due to space limitations we were unable to reprint some articles which we believe to be valuable. Originally, the collection of readings was envisioned as a two-volume work, but practical considerations put this plan to rest. It is our hope that in the near future we may be able to publish a second volume which will serve as part of a continuing series devoted to the rapprochement between group psychotherapy and group dynamics.

We are grateful for the generous cooperation of the numerous contributors to this volume, as well as to the publishers and professional societies who granted consent for reprinting.

We are deeply appreciative to all those who participated with us in our multiple group experiences, which ranged from our own family groups to our current research, teaching, and therapy groups. All group experiences are valuable and the knowledge gained in these experiences, if shared with the "influentials" of the world, can be utilized to clarify man's relationship with his fellow man and to constructively improve these relationships.

We wish particularly to thank Eugene L. Hartley, who gave so freely of his time and experience. While the opinions expressed are our own, we thank him for much of the stimulus.

We give special thanks to the groups we live with—our families, and to the groups we work with—our patients and colleagues.

Last, our thanks to Belle Rosenbaum for pinch-hitting at the many times we needed extra help, and to Myra Dolin for her expert secretarial help.

M. R.
M. M. B.

January 1963

LIST OF AUTHORS

Nathan W. Ackerman, M.D.
Solomon E. Asch, Ph.D.
Dorothy W. Baruch, Ph.D.
Margaret Beach, M.S.W.
John Elderkin Bell, Ed.D.
Milton Miles Berger, M.D.
Cornelius Beukenkamp, M.D.
Donald T. Brown, M.D.
Trigant Burrow, M.D., Ph.D.
Bernard Casella, Ph.D.
Conrad Consalvi, M.A.
Raymond J. Corsini, Ph.D.
Rudolf Dreikurs, M.D.
Bernard Fisher, Ph.D.
S. H. Foulkes, M.D.
Jerome D. Frank, M.D., Ph.D.
Maurice Friedman, Ph.D.
William Furst, M.D.
Joseph J. Geller, M.D.
Lester H. Gliedman, M.D.
George D. Goldman, Ph.D.
Hanna Grunwald, Ph.D.
Samuel B. Hadden, M.D.
Eugene L. Hartley, Ph.D.
O. J. Harvey, Ph.D.
Hans A. Illing, Ph.D.
Asya L. Kadis
David Kevin, M.S.W.
J. W. Klapman, M.D.
Andie L. Knutson, Ph.D.
Sheldon B. Kopp, Ph.D.
Benjamin Kotkov, Ph.D.

D. H. Lawrence
Lawson G. Lowrey, M.D.
L. Cody Marsh, M.D.
J. L. Moreno, M.D.
Hugh Mullan, M.D.
Gardner Murphy, Ph.D.
Helen T. Nash, M.S.
J. E. Neighbor, M.D.
Joseph H. Pratt, M.D.
Sidney Rose, M.D.
Max Rosenbaum, Ph.D.
Bina Rosenberg, M.D.
David Rosenthal, Ph.D.
Mathew Ross, M.D.
R. A. Sandison, M.D.
Saul Scheidlinger, Ph.D.
Paul Schilder, M.D.
Lee Sechrest, Ph.D.
Elvin V. Semrad, M.D.
Muzafer Sherif, Ph.D.
S. R. Slavson
Robert Snyder, M.S.
Herman H. Spitz, Ph.D.
Christopher T. Standish, M.D.
Aaron Stein, M.D.
Dorothy Stock, Ph.D.
Hans Syz, M.D.
Herbert A. Thelen, Ph.D.
John S. Visher, M.D.
John Warkentin, M.D., Ph.D.
Louis Wender, M.D.
Alexander Wolf, M.D.

INTRODUCTION

Philosophic tradition in the United States stresses the ethic of individual responsibility, with, historically, little emphasis on the group and its relationship to the individual. Nevertheless, the country is in fact group oriented. Certainly, although the pioneers who settled our frontiers stressed the rights of the individual, they were dependent upon group functioning to carry out their ambitious goals of settlement. With the turbulent passage of the nation from an agrarian to an industrial life, one of the problems of American reformers during the early 1900's was that in fighting for individual values they had to use techniques of organization. As the homogeneous, rural, Protestant Yankee community felt the impact of industrialization and of new waves of immigration, individualistic forms of living were supplanted by highly organized forms of group living. The image of the independent and extremely self-reliant man was rapidly disappearing. Today the student of human behavior, however deeply concerned with the individual, must also be concerned with the individual within the group.

Symptomatic of this shift in emphasis has been the expansion of group psychotherapy since the end of World War II. Much of this growth was stimulated by the problems of the large numbers of people in need of psychiatric treatment and the limited number of professional personnel. Thus, group psychotherapy made it possible for one therapist to increase treatment facilities by seeing a group of patients at one time. However, group psychotherapy before long was seen as having intrinsic value of its own. Today many therapists prefer to prescribe group treatment even for the patient who is financially able to obtain individual psychotherapy.

Meanwhile, in settings such as universities, religious groups, labor unions, and settlement houses, the study of group dynamics was growing. With increasing awareness of the development of the individual personality within a group-cultural setting, students of human behavior became more and more interested in studying the group's impact upon the growing person. For some time these two streams—group dynamics, the study of the unique ways in which a work or recreation or family group functions, and

1

group psychotherapy, in which individual patients with emotional difficulties could meet together and clarify their personal problems in living while experiencing their problems in this group setting—have been running parallel to one another. The streams then began to converge. Some practitioners in each field began to share and profit from one another's experiences. In one instance there were ostensibly "normal" individuals working within a group framework. In another setting there was a group of neurotic or psychotic individuals led by a group psychotherapist. Were there any principles of group structure common to both settings? Could the psychotherapist who was working with a group of troubled patients apply any of the knowledge gained by the student of the so-called normal group?

Psychotherapists as a group have been remarkably ignorant of the various relevant studies by "academic" psychologists and sociologists. Not until World War II did psychologists discover that they were often talking about the same thing that interested the sociologists. Some sociologists who study groups consider themselves social psychologists. These *sociological* social psychologists study groups from the basic orientation of the study of society, in which a society is seen as a group. The *psychological* social psychologists, coming from a tradition where the individual is studied, are oriented toward the group as a society. To further complicate matters, the psychologist has been bound by a tradition of studying the individual apart from groups. Biologically oriented psychologists, on the other hand, tend to be skeptical of the notion of the cultural impact upon personality. There are even many who question the existence of the field called "social psychology." * Inkeles[1] writes, in the book *Sociology Today:*[1] "I find it extremely difficult to understand just what social psychology is today. . . ." This sounds like semantic bedlam. Nevertheless, there has been a constant attempt to delineate fields of study.

Gardner Murphy[2] considers the psychology of perception the keystone for modern social psychology. This research in perception followed upon the studies of viewpoints, values, and folkways carried out by sociologists and anthropologists. The work in perception was helped immeasurably in the late 1920's and early 1930's by the work of two psychologists, F. C. Bartlett,[3] who carried on research in England, and Muzafer Sherif,[4] a young

---

* The first modern coverage of social psychology was published in 1902, written by Charles Horton Cooley, and titled, *Human Natures and the Social Order.* The first two textbooks in the field, both titled *Social Psychology,* were published in 1908. They were written by the psychologist William McDougall and the sociologist Edward A. Ross.

Sociologists teach approximately one half of the courses in social psychology (see W. B. Cameron, P. Lasley, and R. Dewey, "Who Teaches Social Psychology?" *American Sociological Review,* 15:554, 1950). The American Sociological Association has organized a section on social psychology. One fourth of this association's membership allied themselves with social psychology (see M. W. Riley, "Membership of the American Sociological Association," *American Sociological Review,* 25:925, 1960).

Turkish scholar who came to the United States during the early 1930's. Sherif studied the autokinetic effect and the group's influence upon the individual observer of this phenomenon. In the autokinetic effect, subjects are exposed to an ambiguous stimulus situation. An individual in a totally darkened room, with no visible perceptual standards—anchorages—by which to orient himself, will perceive a fixed point of light as moving. The subject is instructed to look into a box in this darkened room. Nothing can be seen except a light from a pinhole in the box which shines briefly and then goes out. Without prompting, the subject will invariably see the light as moving. When questioned, the subject will describe how much the light moves. Each subject appears to have a certain order about his judgments. Sherif then placed his subjects in groups of two or three. Each subject was asked to give his judgment of the light while the other subjects were present. Very quickly the subject became a member of a group and a group norm began to evolve. A group pattern developed, with a leader and followers. When the group was dissolved it was found that the individual carried the group norm into the setting where he was asked to give his judgment privately. Sherif has continued his basic research schema in many complex group settings, studying the impact of membership in a group upon perception.

Murphy[5] credits Sherif with developing the experimental and conceptual model of the *new* social psychology in contrast with the older behavioristic social psychology.[6] Murphy himself, together with his wife, Lois Murphy, had written an encyclopedic text in social psychology.[7] Six years later, a revised edition of this text could be only a synthesis, for the field had grown so rapidly that it was impossible to summarize studies.[8]

A BRIEF HISTORY OF GROUP PSYCHOTHERAPY

The Early Period

Group psychotherapy has been described as uniquely American. It is indeed a consequence of the pragmatism of American psychiatry, which appeared willing to explore any new and possibly helpful technique.

Viewed in perspective, group psychotherapy's historical roots go back to the beginning of recorded time. Every great religious movement from Moses on has been psychotherapeutic and has reached masses of people. The Greek dramatists of the Hellenic era were deeply concerned about family relationships. The day-long performances of the Grecian classics were a form of mass psychotherapy in that the audience watched actors interpret many of the themes of family involvement. The dramas of Shakespeare, although set in the Elizabethan era, are concerned with many of the same themes. Formal group psychotherapy as such may be traced to Anton Mesmer's group hypnotic sessions of the early 1700's.

Today, most observers credit Joseph Hersey Pratt, a Boston internist,

with the beginning of group psychotherapy. It is believed that Pratt originated the technique in 1905, when he organized tuberculosis patients into
groups in class-type settings.[9]

Most of these patients were seriously ill and discouraged. They were
suffering from a disease that then had a poor prognosis. Pratt was interested in helping his patients establish sound practices of physical hygiene.
He lectured to them and conducted group discussions. He utilized an inspirational approach as he reassured them and tried to help them to overcome their discouragement and pessimism, to relinquish secondary gains
from their illness, and to develop increasing self-confidence and self-esteem.

One can doubt that Pratt was entirely clear as to what he was doing.
His first theoretical awareness seemed to develop in 1913, after he had
been practicing his early version of group psychotherapy for a few years.
Though self-taught in the area of emotional reeducation, he maintained a
limited contact with a few psychiatrists who answered some of his questions. However, the psychiatrists were for the most part uninterested. Possibly the struggle of psychiatry to develop as a specialty in the field of medicine led to an overreaction on the part of many practitioners so that they
were unwilling to explore anything which was not strictly "scientific." In
1876, Beard had first publicly proposed his theory that the mind might be
the cause of disease, which led to fears that psychiatry might become part
of theology. In 1908, an editorial in a leading medical journal attacked the
clergy who had become active in psychotherapy.[10] Pratt, who had received
financial support for his work from one of these clergymen, came under
criticism because of this and had to point out that he had no involvement
with the work of these clergymen.

During his early group work, Pratt was largely left to his own devices.
He believed that most patients with emotional difficulties should be treated
by the internist and general practitioner and that the physician should
treat both the inner and outer man. Psychiatrists were too busy fighting
their own battle for recognition to be concerned with one busy internist
and his problems. The psychiatrists gave him little encouragement, and the
psychologists were involved with problems of introspection.

During this first decade of the twentieth century, Freud's new concepts were attracting the interest and attention of some very aware psychologists, but nothing in his theories related specifically to the group.

Although Moreno has stated that from 1910 to 1914 he carried on experiments with groups of children, displaced persons, and prostitutes in
Vienna, and classifies this work with Pratt's class method as the beginning
of modern group psychotherapy, he too has described group psychotherapy
as an "American product."

Dreikurs and Corsini[11] have stated that in the early period of group
psychotherapy, from 1900 to 1930, a group method called "collective counseling" was being used by German and Austrian psychotherapists to treat

stammerers, neurotic patients, alcoholics, and patients with sexual disturbances. Russian and Danish psychiatrists also employed group methods.

Alfred Adler is credited with being the first European psychiatrist to use group methods. Combining his interest in intensive psychotherapy with his political philosophy of socialism, Adler was concerned with ways of bringing psychotherapy to the working class. The group method of treatment seemed to be an excellent solution to the problem, since psychoanalysis, which stemmed from the environment of the Viennese intellectual elite, had little impact upon the working people of that time.

Most traditional European psychoanalysts, bound by their own class and status needs, expressed opposition and hostility to group psychotherapy (an observation that seems to confirm recent studies[12] indicating that psychotherapists are often drawn to patients who reflect their own class and status needs and mirror the psychotherapist's value system). Consequently, those European psychiatrists who used the group method worked in relative ignorance of one another. In later years, the growth of fascism in Europe discouraged the group method which seemed to flourish in a climate of political freedom.

In the United States, before World War I, there were few physicians, other than Pratt who used a group method of psychological treatment, although in New England of the early 1900's some inspirational group psychotherapy was carried on by ministers, within a religious setting.[13] At the end of World War I, Edward Lazell established lecture classes for patients at the St. Elizabeth Psychiatric Hospital in Washington, D.C.[14] Aware of group influences, he was enthusiastic about the group method in his therapy, which was essentially didactic.

About ten years later, L. Cody Marsh, a minister who later became a psychiatrist, described in some detail his use of the group method of psychotherapy.[15] Marsh combined his treatment with everything that he believed might be helpful to the psychological well-being of his patients. He employed techniques such as art classes, dance classes, and so on. A good deal of this work evolved from the theory that patients could be supportive to one another. Marsh worked with psychotic patients on an active level as contrasted with Lazell's series of didactic lectures to schizophrenics. When Louis Wender practiced group therapy with borderline patients in a mental hospital, he began using psychoanalytic concepts. This work, begun in 1929, was reported in 1935.[16]

Although Jacob L. Moreno is supposed to have coined the term *group psychotherapy* in 1931, in 1920 Trigant L. Burrow had used the term *group analysis*. In the history of psychotherapy there has been little attention given to Burrow—a great and original thinker of the early years of psychoanalysis who has been oddly neglected in surveys of contemporary psychotherapy. His pioneer group analytic studies were largely ignored and only currently is he receiving some recognition.

Burrow wrote sixty-eight articles and five books which summarized much of his research and concepts. His work is today carried on by his son-in-law, Hans Syz, a physician and psychiatrist. Burrow, after he obtained his medical degree and a doctorate in psychology, began to work in psychiatry under Adolf Meyer. After meeting Freud and Jung in 1909, in the United States, Burrow went to Switzerland to study psychoanalysis with Carl Jung. He returned in 1910 and began the practice of psychoanalysis. In 1911, he was one of the founding members of the American Psychoanalytic Association. Clarence Oberndorf, in his book *History of Psychoanalysis in America* cites Burrow as one of the four most original contributors to the science of psychoanalysis before 1920. From 1923 to 1932, Burrow engaged upon research in group dynamics, which he later called phyloanalysis. This group behavioral exploration stemmed from Burrow's dissatisfaction with the psychoanalytic emphasis on the individual—an emphasis which, he felt, excluded social forces. He believed that behavioral disorders should be traced back to social relatedness and that such research could best be carried out in the group setting. Burrow believed that in a therapeutic group, the emotionally troubled person would find his distorted self-image clarified as he observed others and their reaction to him. In 1923, Burrow and some twenty other persons—associates, students, patients—lived and worked together at a summer camp in the Adirondacks. From this group, the Lifwynn (Joy of Life) Foundation was formed. As Burrow studied groups, he moved more and more to an exploration of *his underlying concept*—the biological principles of behavior underlying the "group." He finally discarded the term "group analysis" in favor of the term "phyloanalysis." Burrow's position with regard to groups was essentially exploratory, although he was concerned with psychotherapy as carried out in the group setting. His work estranged him from the psychoanalytic community, and in 1933, when the American Psychoanalytic Association was reorganized, he was dropped from membership. It has been conjectured that Burrow's impact upon D. H. Lawrence, who admired Burrow, indirectly came through to Fromm and Horney, who were familiar with Lawrence's writings. Toward the end of his life Burrow complained that Harry Stack Sullivan, whom he knew, had never properly acknowledged Burrow's contribution to Sullivanian theory. In the years prior to his death Burrow was almost solely concerned with physiological studies of human behavior.

Another American pioneer was Paul Schilder, who introduced group psychotherapy at the Bellevue Psychiatric Hospital in New York City. He based his group psychotherapy on psychoanalytic concepts, and in 1939 he described the results of his pioneering efforts.[17] In this same period Moreno was developing and refining his concepts of psychodrama.[18] During the 1930's, Samuel Slavson, an engineer who later entered group work, established activity group therapy at the Jewish Board of Guardians. He worked with emotionally disturbed youngsters and encouraged them to work out their conflicts within a controlled play setting. He used psychoanalytic concepts in exploring the difficulties of these children but did not interpret directly for the youngsters. Essentially, Slavson's method of activity group therapy was not designed for severely disturbed children. The method encourages the acting out of conflicts and behavior problems in the setting of a play group, a relatively permissive environment. The interaction of the children as well as their relationship to the activity group therapist is carefully studied. The activity group is usually composed of eight children, about the same age and same sex. The group is carefully structured to achieve some sort of balance. Thus, the withdrawn child would be a balance to the aggressive child.[19] In 1943, at a symposium meeting of the American Orthopsychiatric Association, he reported his work in detail.[20] A briefer report by him was published in 1940.[21]

Contemporary Group Psychotherapy

At the end of World War II, group psychotherapy was being used in many different settings. It had received a tremendous stimulus during World War II, when, largely due to the limitations of trained personnel and the number of psychiatric casualties who could not be treated, there was a strong effort to explore newer and briefer treatment methods. By 1943, Giles Thomas was ready to compile a relatively extensive review of the literature.[22]

Every school of psychotherapy was involved in group psychotherapy by 1945. The continuum ranged from the frankly repressive-inspirational, where group psychotherapy was used supportively, to the psychoanalytic, where group psychotherapy was used reconstructively. Carl Rogers, while not directly interested in group psychotherapy, encouraged students of his "client-centered psychotherapy" to apply his techniques in the group.[23] Reports came to the United States of the English psychiatrists who had begun to use group techniques. Joshua Bierer used Adlerian concepts in organizing his social club groups in England.[24] Foulkes was using a direct psychoanalytic technique in his work with groups in England.[25]

In 1949, in the United States, Alexander Wolf published a lengthy paper in which he described in much detail his work on the "psychoanalysis of groups."[26] Both in 1948 and 1949 he had reported his work at conferences of the American Group Psychotherapy Association. Wolf has directly applied the principles of individual psychoanalysis to the group setting, using the major tools of the psychoanalytic method such as the transference, free association, dreams, and historical development. Wolf describes his group as the re-creation of the original family wherein the patient works through his unresolved problems. This is similar to the primary group that the sociologist is concerned with. Wolf had begun his work in 1938, stimulated by the reports of Wender and Schilder. Within one year, he was so excited and optimistic about his results, that he telescoped most of his private practice, and in 1940 he was working with five groups of eight to ten patients each. During four years of Army service, he continued his active interest in group psychotherapy and gained more insights into his work. He has stimulated and trained many psychiatrists, psychologists, and social workers in the technique of group psychoanalysis.

By the time Wolf reported his findings, many were ready to report their clinical experiences with group psychotherapy. Since then, there has been conflict as to who is entitled to recognition as a pioneer in the field of group psychotherapy. Since World War II, the literature on group psychotherapy has grown tremendously. At the end of 1955, there was a bibliography of 1,700 items. There are approximately 200 items—books, articles, and so on—written each year. Bach,[27] with a background and interest in the field of group dynamics, and heavily influenced by Kurt Lewin, the social and child psychologist, attempted to graft Lewin's concepts of group dynamics to the practice of group psychotherapy. His work is provocative, but at times he seems too speculative. A major problem apparently confronting the student of human behavior who attempts to relate group psychotherapy and group dynamics is the resistance to Freud's biology-based instinct theory of human behavior. Many group dynamics researchers feel more comfortable with a concept such as Harry Stack Sullivan's theory of interpersonal relations, which is provocative but quite vague at times. Leary,[28] in a study primarily centered on clinical diagnosis, has described the types of exchanges different personality types will look for. He has developed a very elaborate schematic system where his *principle of reciprocal relationships* is charted. Leary worked with an eight dimensional multilevel system to predict the individual's behavior in group therapy and the effectiveness of the group as a whole. Each of the eight variables covered the adaptive to pathological range:

(1) competitive—narcissistic
(2) managerial—autocratic
(3) responsible—hypernormal
(4) cooperative—overconventional
(5) docile—dependent
(6) self-effacing—masochistic
(7) rebellious—distrustful
(8) aggressive—sadistic

However, Leary's report is not specific as to data analysis, the samples of subjects for his research, or how certain conclusions are drawn from certain observations.

Group Dynamics and Group Psychotherapy

One English psychiatrist, W. R. Bion, has attempted through the last decade, to formulate a relationship between group dynamics and group psychotherapy. His work has attracted the interest of American researchers in the field of group dynamics but has been in the main ignored by most group psychotherapists in the United States. Bion, unlike most group psychotherapists, has concerned himself with an understanding of what the group context is. Most group psychotherapists, in their emphasis on the individual, have neglected the group variables at work in group psychotherapy. Bion, in a series of articles, attempted to set forth a theory of group culture and social structure which would apply to group psychotherapy.[29] Bion's work has been studied by group dynamics researchers at Teachers College, Columbia University and researchers working under the direction and stimulus of Herbert Thelen at the University of Chicago. Thelen has presented an excellent summary of Bion's speculations concerning group processes which are included in our volume of readings. To evaluate Bion it is important to first note that Bion has been trained and influenced in his psychoanalytic development by Melanie Klein. She was an English psychoanalyst whose influence is apparently minimal amongst American psychoanalysts but who carries great weight in Europe and in South America. While Bion has not specifically advanced Klein's controversial theories, her thinking is imbedded in much of his conceptualizations. To summarize Klein's position we would say that Klein has modified the orthodox Freudian concept of personality. She believed that the *ego exists from birth*. Good and bad emotions come from the infant's contact with the mother, who represents the external world. The capacity to love and feelings of persecution stem from these early contacts, which in turn are influenced by constitutional and environmental forces. As the infantile ego develops, two major processes come to the fore—introjection and projection. The people and situations that the infant encounters are taken up in the inner life of the infant—thus introjection. The infant attributes to others different feelings—thus projection. The interplay of these two processes is basic to the infant's perception of the world. The ego splits, dividing objects into good and bad. This splitting occurs in the early months of living. The ego growth is accompanied by anxiety and destructive impulses which Klein labeled the paranoid-schizoid position. With healthy development, the infant is increasingly able to understand reality, but from the sixth to the twelfth month of his life, he enters a depressed period related to his guilt and anxiety about his destructive impulses. The infant never fully recovers from this depressive period, and all this plays a part in the child's concept of social relationships. Human relationships can then be interpreted, according to Klein, in terms of introjection and projection and splitting, with the individual accepting his good feelings and denying his bad impulses. This is an individual-centered concept of group phenomena.

Bion has related group formations to type of leadership, but essentially he has expanded upon Freud's limited ideas concerning group psychology. Like almost all group psychotherapists, Bion has ignored the influence of group structure. There is no attention given to the new social roles that the patient may take on when he enters a group therapy situation, as the patient responds to the group interaction. Bion has been aware that there are group goals which are often not overtly expressed by group members. In this area, he draws our attention to the nonverbal aspect of group processes, which has been detailed by Berger with reference to group psychotherapy (see our collected papers). Herbert Thelen (see our collected papers), in his work with groups, became aware of how often his findings touched upon Bion's speculations. From that point, he began to use these speculations as hypotheses which could be systematically researched. For example, Stock and Thelen,[30] working with training groups, used the sentence completion test to characterize each group member as preferring one of Bion's six valences of behavior toward others. The six valences are:

pairing—counterpairing (movement toward intimacy or a desire to remain isolated)
dependency—counterdependency (reliance on or rejection of external authority)
fight—flight (fighting or fleeing from stress)

They related these individual characterizations to group behavior that too was conceptualized in these terms. The results showed a relatively weak relationship between the personal patterns as derived from the reactions to the Group Situation Test (a sentence completion test) and behavior in the group. It can be stated, therefore, that the group behavior of any individual cannot be predicted from this test. In this way, we may begin to study the relationship between group goals and group function. The clinical, subjective experience of the practitioner in the field of group psychotherapy—the one great stream—is finally joined with the other great stream—the objective researcher in group dynamics.

Before the group dynamics researcher and the group therapist practitioner join hands too firmly, they will have to include the researcher in child development. This is because the student of child development will inform us as to how the child socializes or learns "the rules of the game." The outstanding student in this area is Jean Piaget, who is largely summarized and rarely read in the original in the United States. Piaget has described the child's first orientation to learning the "rules of the game." [31] To clarify his presentation, Piaget discussed the concepts of the sociologist Emile Durkheim (one of the first students of the group) regarding the individual's relationship with the group,[32] as well as the evolution of moral realities.

THE HISTORY OF SMALL GROUP RESEARCH

The Primary Group

The concept of the primary group was discussed both extensively and intensively by the American sociologist Charles H. Cooley[33] in the early 1900's. He defined the primary group as the "face to face" group characterized by intimate cooperation. A basic primary group is the family. It is a primary group that some group psychotherapists attempt to recreate in clinical practice. This group is primary in the sense that it gives the individual the early and complete experience of social unity. Furthermore, the primary group does not change in the same degree as more elaborate relationships. It forms a comparatively permanent source out of which the latter are ever springing. Cooley's writing had a marked impact upon the American social philosophers of his day. At about the same time as Cooley set forth his observations, over sixty years ago, Emile Durkheim,[34] in France, was also noting the importance of the group in human behavior. In Germany, during the same period, the sociologist Simmel [35] was similarly concerned about the interaction amongst individuals.

The concern for the primary group, which occupied Cooley, later found expression in the writings and teachings of George Herbert Mead,[36] the philosopher and student of human behavior who, independent of psychoanalytic thinking, expressed the view that the primary group is the group which essentially trains the individual and provides him with the emotional and psychological developments that he will need in his functioning in human society. Mead developed in great detail Aristotle's basic premise—man is a *social* animal. Quite removed geographically from the Chicago of George Herbert Mead, Sigmund Freud had been speculating about the different aspects of the individual's functioning in the primary group called the family and about the importance of the early familial experience in the psychological and emotional development of the individual. Freud pointed out the necessity of recognizing the important figures who influenced the child in his development in the primary group. There is no evidence to indicate that either Mead or Freud was influenced by the other, although Mead knew of Freud's work. Freud pondered about the primary group in his book, "Group Psychology and the Analysis of the Ego," [37] a work which is highly speculative and influenced by the concept of Le Bon, the French sociologist who described the group as a collective entity—a distinct being.[38] Freud's speculations concerning group psychology are even today apparently highly valued by many practitioners of psychoanalytic group psychotherapy. He noted that a group is held together by a common identification with a leader, and in his book he commented upon the primary group. He stated:

We may further emphasize, as being specially instructive, the relation that holds between the contrivance by means of which an artificial group is held together and the constitution of the primal horde. We have seen that with an army and a church this contrivance is the illusion that the leader loves all of the individuals equally and justly. But this is simply an idealistic remodelling of the state of affairs in the primal horde, where all of the sons knew that they were equally persecuted by the primal father, and feared him equally. This same recasting upon which all social duties are built up is already presupposed by the next form of human society, the totemistic clan. The indestructible strength of the family as a natural group formation rests upon the fact that this necessary pre-supposition of the father's equal love can have a real application in the family.

Freud's basic point, that a group is formed by the identification of group members with the leader, represents one view. Although Freud's ruminations were little more than that, many contemporary group psycho-analysts tend to base all theory of group functioning on this early text of Freud. A survey of Freud's writings, published after his book on group psychology, indicates his optimism concerning the possibilities of group treatment.

Mead's students at the University of Chicago carried his concepts into many academic settings. He made a tremendous impact upon the social sciences with his writing and teaching about the development of self and the awareness of social relationships. His writing and his apparent effectiveness as a teacher stimulated an entire generation of sociologists. His work and that of Cooley are of prime significance in the early history of group dynamics. During this period, the sociologists were apparently more aware of the impact of interpersonal relationships and social roles than the psychologists. Park,[39] with his emphasis on research, was also an outstanding teacher during this time and influenced much sociological research in the area of community interaction. A group of sociologists who were students at this time at the University of Chicago, amongst them Zorbaugh and Thrasher,[40] carried out studies of the Chicago Gold Coast and the slums of the city and during these studies observed primary group formation in boys' gangs. Thrasher in his study did not assume that primary group relations are inevitably affective or nonlogical or consistently solid. William Foote White continued studies of the gang.[41] During the late 1920's and early 1930's, a series of studies was carried out in the Hawthorne plant, located in Chicago.[42] This plant, a division of Western Electric, was the scene of continuing studies of incentives and work productivity amongst groups of employees. It was found that *increased output was very much related to the interaction of the members of a working group.* Workers in the plant would increase or restrict productivity, and this was related to group pressures. From these studies it was recognized that workers who are in close contact with one another over a period of time tend to develop a primary group organization with loyalties, codes of behavior, and value systems. The pioneer and leader in this research was Elton Mayo* and the research studies of the group in industry have continued through the years.[43] During the 1920's, Edward Sapir set forth his observations of the group and the cultural scene.[44] He observed that there are basic principles underlying the formation of a group. The casual group and the structured and more permanent group are subject to the same principles. To illustrate, he cited two groups, the crowd at an automobile accident and the Senate:

> There is in reality no definite line of division anywhere along the gamut of group forms which connect these extremes. If the automobile accident is serious and one of the members of the crowd is a doctor, the informal group may with comparatively little difficulty resolve itself into something like a medical squad with an implicitly elected leader. On the other hand, if the government is passing through a great political crisis, if there is little confidence in the representative character or honesty of the senators or if an enemy is besieging the capitol and likely at any moment to substitute entirely new forms of corporate authority for those legally recognized by the citizens of the country, the Senate may easily become an unimportant aggregation of individuals who suddenly and with unexpected poignancy feel their helplessness as mere individuals.

Sapir did not delineate the basic principles of group formation but merely stated that these could be ascertained at some future time. His observations influenced the theoretical formulations of the early cultural psychoanalysts such as Harry Stack Sullivan. However, outside of atypical occurrences such as Sapir's influence upon Sullivan, there was little intermingling of the streams of academic thinking and psychiatric practice. An example of an atypical analyst who attempted to integrate studies of the individual and the group is Trigant Burrow, discussed earlier, one of the first American psychoanalysts.

Jacob L. Moreno, the psychiatrist and group psychotherapist, has been consistently interested in the individual's relationship to the group. He welcomed the cooperation of social scientists when he arrived in the United States in the 1930's. During the late 1920's in Europe and in the early 1930's in the United States he developed the concept of sociometry. This concept is essentially a recognition of the group membership needs

---

* It is interesting to note that Elton Mayo taught Joseph Pratt, the pioneer in modern group therapy, techniques of hypnosis, modifications of which Pratt used with "classes" of patients. Most industrial psychologists and students of human behavior in industry are unaware of the "other side" of Mayo, who served as a professor at the Harvard School of Business Administration. He was friendly with Pierre Janet, the physician and psychologist who pioneered dynamic psychiatry in France. Mayo was intrigued by Janet's concepts and wrote a book, published posthumously, in which he attempted to relate Janet's concepts to problems of industrial employees (*The Psychology of Pierre Janet*, Routledge and Kegan Paul, 1952).

of the individual and is based upon a measurement of group relation-ships. Members of a group are asked to list which members of the group they would like best or least to engage with in given activities. Generally three to five choices are requested. For example, in a boys' club, a member may be asked: "With which three boys would you like most to go to a ball game?" The spontaneous likes and dislikes are then charted out on "socio-grams," graphic representation as to who is liked most or least and by which individuals. This technique of studying to whom an individual reaches out has been related by Moreno to his theory of spontaneity. Further, Moreno has been concerned with role-playing, the capacity of an individual to take another's role. This concept is related to how individuals perceive one an-other. It is of interest to note that role-playing had been discussed in the writings of Mead and Cooley. Moreno integrated role-playing into the group psychotherapy technique known as psychodrama in which an in-dividual plays the role of another person and thereby gains awareness and insight into that person's expectations and anxieties. Psychodrama is a val-uable reeducative technique in clarifying interpersonal distortions.

When Moreno established his journal, *Sociometry*, which has been re-cently turned over to the American Sociological Association, he encour-aged psychologists and sociologists to join him in his work. Over the years, many students of the behavioral sciences have tended to dismiss him as too strongly partisan and as a result have tended to overlook his contributions to group psychology.[45]

The Group and Individual Change

The German Gestalt psychologist, Kurt Lewin, before his arrival in the United States in the early 1930's, had, in Germany, been a psychologist in an academic and theoretic setting, interested in the analysis of the child's social behavior. The tremendous upheaval and the rise of Nazism apparently dislodged him quite thoroughly from his earlier interests. He be-came acutely aware of the social problems of the day and began to devote his genius to the solution of these problems from a psychologist's perspec-tive. He died in 1947, but during the decade or more that he spent in the United States he stimulated and led the field of group dynamics and left his impact upon a generation of students and colleagues. He worked first at Cornell, then at the University of Iowa Child Welfare Research Station and stimulated students and colleagues, among them, Ronald Lippitt and Dorwin Cartright. He moved briefly to Massachusetts Institute of Technol-ogy under the sponsorship of Douglas MacGregor.[46] His influence was felt in the establishment of the Research Center for Group Dynamics at the University of Michigan. This research center carries on his work with small groups and other problems in the field of social psychology.

Lewin was active in many projects and stimulated research in a variety of problems. Prior to World War II, Lewin and two of his students, Ronald

Lippitt and Ralph K. White, carried on an experimental study of leader-ship and group life.[47] Both a summary of the research and a fuller report of the original study are worth reading. Although the original study has been criticized on the grounds of experimental design and ideological bias, its basic contribution remains—*the investigation of the impact of the leader upon the structure and functioning of the group as well as the climate of the group and its relationship to productivity.* Lewin was increasingly aware toward the end of his life of the impact of group decision upon social change. He wrote in some detail about this. A brief excerpt from one of his writings is pertinent at this point. Lewin stated:

> Group decision is a process of social management or self-management of groups. It is related to social channels, gates and gate keepers—to the problem of social perception and the planning and to the relation be-tween motivation and action between individuals and the group. . . . The effect of group decision can probably best be understood by relating it to a theory of quasi-stationary social equilibria to social habits and resistance to change and to the various problems of unfreezing, changing and freezing social levels.[48]

In this same article Lewin generalized that it is "usually easier to change individuals formed into a group than to change any one of them separately." This generalization, independently derived from studies of group function, is a basic tenet of the practice of group psychotherapy. During World War II, he embarked on a series of studies in which he was interested in increasing productivity, exploring problems of prejudice, changing food habits of individuals so that in a wartime economy they would eat foods which they previously were averse to, as well as many other related areas where social and individual change were concerned. In a sum-mary of these studies he made the following statement:

> The prevalent theory in psychology assumes action to be the direct result of motivation. I am inclined to think that we will have to modify this theory. We will have to study the particular conditions under which a motivating constellation leads or does not lead to a decision or to an equivalent process through which a state of "considerations" (indecisive-ness) is changed into a state where the individual has "made up his mind" and is ready for action although he may not act at that moment. The act of decision is one of those transitions.[49]

It would appear that Lewin, if anything, overemphasized the influ-ence of social forces, but he certainly stimulated research in the area of group processes. Toward the end of his life, Lewin became an ardent Zionist and was deeply concerned with the creation of the state of Israel. He was particularly interested in the problems of minority group identifica-tion and the relationship to the majority group. His theme was "action research"—research that could be put into use—a far cry from the very academic Gestalt psychologist who first came to the United States.

Since then, the National Education Association, as well as other groups, have stimulated further research in group functioning. The National Training Laboratories have awarded grants for study of group processes, and almost every major industrial, labor union, religious as well as educational group is interested in group processes in relationship to their particular field of interest.

Group Pressure and Individual Change

The most significant breakthrough at this time would appear to be in the area of social perception. How an individual perceives others, in what context the percept is made and the influence of the setting upon the perceptual process, has major significance in delineating group goals and working through hostilities between antagonistic groups who are composed of individuals. This perceptual research has been largely stimulated by the work of Muzafer Sherif in the mid-1930's. Its earlier structure was also based upon the perceptual studies of the English psychologist Bartlett in the late 1920's and the early 1930's. Through the years, Sherif has stimulated his students to more and more provocative research concerning the relationship between group membership and social perception. A good deal of research along this line has been carried out by Solomon E. Asch.[50] Asch, in a series of experiments, has found that when an individual is confronted with a majority group opinion that is contrary to his own as well as to fact, he will commonly change his opinions to conform with those of the group. However, there are some individuals who do not give in to group pressure and maintain their own opinions. The study of such people—who they are and what they are or whether they find the need to be in opposition to the group or whether they are truly "independent" personalities—will reveal much that is valuable to students of human behavior.

CURRENT RESEARCH AND THEORY

Since World War II, small group theory and research has expanded tremendously.

A Mathematical Approach

Von Neumann and Morgenstern introduced the modern game theory approach in 1944.[51] They analyzed some fundamental questions of economic theory in terms of a mathematical theory of games. The common elements of economic behavior and such factors as strategy in games were presented. The interrelated concepts were analyzed around a more or less central problem of utility. When the theory was introduced, many economists and sociologists felt that it might aid in the development of a theory of human behavior and group function and decision. Since then, the band wagon feeling has terminated. Modern statistical decision theory has been helpful to many researchers in conceptualizations. However, we are dealing with a *human* organism when we begin to explore the nature of rational choice. This fact apparently eludes some researchers. In 1957, the game theory was surveyed by Luce and Raiffa.[52] They were still moderately enthusiastic about its usefulness. Solomon[53] edited a readings book in 1960, titled *Mathematical Thinking in the Measurement of Behavior.* In this volume are three distinct monographs. The monograph of particular interest to the student of group function was written by James S. Coleman. It is called "The Mathematical Study of Small Groups." This 150-page monograph was prepared as part of the program of the Bureau of Applied Social Research at Columbia University. The research was initiated during the years 1952-1956. In the monograph, Coleman discusses the relative paucity of mathematical models for behavior of small groups. He then examines in great detail several models which have been proposed. His systematic analysis of the pros and cons of each model are extremely discerning.

In 1959, Thibaut and Kelley[54] wrote a book on group behavior. Although the book includes references to 314 pieces of research on small group behavior, its main value lies in its theoretical constructs. In the book, Thibaut and Kelley try very strongly to introduce the game theory approach to group dynamics. While they do deal with interaction between two or more persons, rather than simple behavior in a social context, in common with the many psychologists who are researchers in group dynamics, they pay minimal attention to personality variables as they may be related to interaction in a group. This is one of the real problems of the statistical approach.

Group Life and Personality Variables

Homans, in setting forth his concepts of group life, has attempted to pay attention to the personality variables. He distinguishes between the internal and external systems of a group which make up the total social system. Thus, the internal system is "group behavior that is an expression of the sentiments towards one another developed by the members of the group in the course of their life together." The external system is conditioned by the environment and is the solution to the group's problem—how to survive in the environment.[55]

In 1954, an encyclopedic handbook devoted to social psychology appeared,[56] a handbook that may be a helpful reference to the student of social groups. Before his premature death at the age of 37, Olmsted wrote an introductory text to small group theory. The text stemmed from his doctoral dissertation, which was concerned with small group interaction and social norms.[57] This work is valuable, but it is still somewhat cursory.

The Problem-Solving Approach

Currently, one of the most systematic investigators of the small group is Robert Bales and his many associates and students. He has studied, for the most part, problem solving groups, among them several psychotherapy groups. These studies are devoted to the process of interaction and communication in the group as well as group size. The studies depend mainly upon the spoken word, as the group observer records on a moving tape who says what to whom in terms of one of twelve types of interaction. The Bales system of categorizing group interaction involves twelve possible ratings:

(1) shows solidarity, raises other's status, gives help
(2) shows tension-release, jokes, shows satisfaction
(3) agrees, shows passive acceptance, understands
(4) gives suggestion, implying autonomy for others
(5) gives opinion, evaluation, analysis
(6) gives orientation, information, clarifies
(7) asks for orientation, information, confirmation
(8) asks for opinion, evaluation, expression of feeling
(9) asks for suggestion, direction, possible ways of action
(10) disagrees, shows passive rejection, withholds help
(11) shows tension, asks for help, withdraws out of field
(12) shows antagonism, deflates other's status, defends or asserts self

Each participant's response, whether a few words or lengthy, would be considered a unit and scored as a unit as long as the major theme and attitude expressed remained essentially the same. Within one speech, if one or more noteworthy shifts occurred, an appropriate second or third score would be indicated. The observer would rely on the inflection and modulation of speech, the words that made up the verbalization and the body and face mannerisms that accompanied each statement, in addition to the content. All this in order to evaluate a response. Gestures and movements without verbalization are not part of a scorable response.

The Bales system may be considered useful in preliminary investigations, but it is not a very adequate measure. It conceptualizes social interaction as a problem-solving sequence and categories are overgeneralized. The rating method appears overly atomistic. There appears to be a major emphasis on a verbal approach, and the nonverbal aspects of communication are not given sufficient recognition.[58]

In April, 1960, one organization, under a U.S. Air Force contract, compiled a bibliography of small group research. This bibliography is part of an over-all program designed to provide integration of small group research knowledge. The bibliography contains some 2,200 items and is comprehensive for the period 1950-1959 but not as complete for preceding years, since there are existing bibliographies. This bibliography included only *selected* group psychotherapy studies and omitted masters' and doctoral theses as well as studies written in languages other than English.[59] It is understandable that even the devoted student of small group research will be hard put today to keep abreast of the deluge of studies. The practitioner of group psychotherapy will probably end up reading only selected studies or summaries of research with small groups.

THE MEETING POINTS

Today, every piece of research on the conforming or nonconforming member of the group studied by the academic psychologist or sociologist can find its counterpart in the clinical experiences of the group psychotherapist who describes the resistant or compliant group patient. We may not always see the immediate impact of academic research, but the practitioner of group therapy does finally and hopefully look for some plausible reason as to *why*. He observes that an intensive psychotherapy group should optimally be composed of not more than eight or nine members. He cannot indefinitely state that the reason is because it works best. Why do some patients improve in a group while others do not? Is it all to be found in the dynamics of the individual, or can modification of group structure make the difference? Hopefully the hypotheses will come from the clinical hunches and inferences that are capable of operational testing.

It is necessary for the practitioner to have a frame of reference. Otherwise he cannot deal with his patients. He cannot afford to be insensitive to their needs, whether he functions in private practice or in an outpatient clinic. He has to have some way of getting started. However, he should conceive of his principles in psychotherapy as a sort of hypothesis. There should not be rigidity. There should be a willingness to orient toward research, toward the possibility of alternative theories giving a reasonable accounting of a particular clinical phenomenon. This may perhaps help him to improve his practice. He cannot take a complete research orientation toward his practice; but there is research, and it is increasing in quantity, quality, and scope. Researchers do not talk quite the same language as therapy practitioners or therapy theoreticians do. That does not mean that any one is wrong. It doesn't mean that there is trouble. It simply means that some way has to be found for these things to be reconciled—what goes on and what is found on the couch or in the group with what is found in the laboratory. If the psychotherapists do not interest themselves in research, the research workers may waste a lot of time. They may go along on a lot of problems that are of no earthly use to the psychotherapist. If, however, the therapist keeps alert and keeps communication open with the line of research, the possibility of having the research relate to the therapeutic question is increased. In our introduction we have reviewed development and changes in group psychotherapy, and we have reviewed research. These are two independent quests. A few people have come ahead and attempted to reconcile these two quests. There is more to be done, and we believe that every therapist should try his own system of reconciliation.

A major problem that will confront the researcher is that the psychotherapy group is not a laboratory problem-solving group. There is no neat problem set up for a solution which has to be reached by the end of the meeting. The free, spontaneous discussion of the psychotherapy group is still quite different from the task-directed laboratory group. There is a difference between the transient involvement of the group member in the laboratory problem-solving group and the deep emotional involvement of patients who are in the same psychotherapy group, where they expose their deepest fantasies and feelings about themselves and toward one another, session after session, over a prolonged period.[60] While the goal of the group psychotherapist is individual psychological change, and he is concerned about maintaining a shifting and ever-changing group to achieve that goal, he does use group relationships to change the personalities of group members. The therapeutic group is one example of a group in which the therapist or leader uses principles of group dynamics—in this case group influence and interaction to induce individual change.

We offer to the practicing psychotherapist a positive philosophy of openmindedness, nonrigidity and nondoctrinairism. For the practice of psychotherapy, we present material about the practice of group psychotherapy. But for the sake of the psychotherapist's insight and understanding we offer research findings so that there may be new emergence. Do the research findings concerning cohesiveness and leadership or other processes (see the Harvey and Consalvi article) jibe with what goes on in the therapy group? Can we extrapolate what we have learned about the psychodynamics of family structure as we observe it in the therapy group (see the Alexander Wolf article) and translate this into observations of all social behavior?

The reader may state, "Is this a series of questions?" Yes, this is what we suggest—that therapists transform doctrine into questions. Remember that Freud's individual psychology started with his patients and in a short time was extrapolated to all of mankind, all cultures, all ages. Some therapists speak of schizophrenic nations. While the soundness of this statement may be questioned, the statement is nevertheless made. It is as good a hypothesis and a way of beginning to structure the complex data that we have on social groups as any that we know about from other points of view.

The present writers are sympathetic with the work of Sherif, but once you have the concept of frames of reference, what does the therapist do with it? Does the group therapy experience and its norms change the patient because he responds to group pressure? Does he really change? The phrase "ego involvement" is often used, but what do you do with it? We must go beyond phrases and explore ways of applying or extending them. (See Stock and Thelen's research with Bion's concepts.)

Sapir's comments regarding the group and Freud's belief that the leader was the crucial factor in group function are speculations. Consider the following. When nine young men meet to play baseball they are drawn together by a common goal. This serves to regulate the behavior and structure the group. When nine young men are brought together by a psychotherapist, there is no common goal other than the therapist's opinion that the group experience will be beneficial for each patient and the patient's hope that this opinion is valid. In this situation, does the group psychotherapist set this goal? Is this absurd, or are there common principles at work? Many therapists have observed that in psychotherapy we largely explore the patient's fantasy about reality. What brings the person to psychotherapy is mainly fantasy. Does fantasy bring together the nine young men who play baseball? The exploration of group fantasy may conceivably be a research problem that concerns the student of group function.

As practicing psychotherapists, we make our approach to our groups and our patients as we see fit. However, at this point, a true synthesis of the approaches that we make in a therapeutic setting with the approaches that are made in the laboratory is premature. There are many directions in which the research people have moved and had interesting findings. There are many areas where psychotherapists do not know the answers. We have many questions, and each therapist can raise questions. There will not always be the same questions because therapists obtain their patients from different sources, and they work with them in different ways. However, unless the questions are asked, will we ever get answers?

This, therefore, is a book to stimulate therapists to ask questions and to stimulate social psychologists to be aware of the many questions that therapists are asking them. It is also a book that reviews the approaches that have been made to the findings of answers. The section on social psychology gives some picture of social psychology that is particularly meaningful to psychotherapists—convergence, group pressure on the individual, status, productivity in different kinds of groups, and the beginning of research in social psychology and group psychotherapy. As the reader goes on, he may at different points have many questions. For example, when there is convergence in the group, status problems come up. If you have a relatively unsophisticated and naïve subject in an experiment, the convergence will be from the naïve to the high prestige position. Perhaps we are dealing with a situation which is somewhat comparable in the psychotherapy group. The group therapist may serve as an anchorage and get convergence, if not to what he says, at least to the value system which he represents. Is the group an extension of these values?

Group psychotherapy offers a unique and important setting for the student of small groups. While the line-judging group of college sopho-mores is artificially created and somewhat unreal, the therapy group be-comes very real to the patient who is deeply involved in it. It might be rea-sonable to ask why the academician cannot be involved in the study of therapy groups. Until recently there were few students of small groups who had sufficient therapeutic awareness or clinical experience to be aware of the complexities of psychotherapy. The patient must be consistently seen as an individual in distress and not as an experimental subject. There-fore the patient's interest must always come first, no matter how much this upsets the usual research patterns.

The practicing group psychotherapist has fumbled along with the little established theory of group functioning to guide him. He has generally learned through experience to solve such problems as the optimal size of a therapy group and the various clinical entities with whom he can best work. The various theories of psychoanalytic psychology have been helpful as the group psychotherapist gropes along. For the most part, the language of psychoanalysis has been used as a framework for group psychotherapy theory and in the formulation of hypotheses. Until recently, there has been little systematic attention paid to the *group* variables which operate specifi-cally in the group psychotherapy setting.

Some fifteen years ago, Murphy, in an introduction to Sherif's text on social psychology, wrote:

> What a society does when it molds the individual into membership in the group is first of all to insist upon his learning to see the world in one way rather than another.[61]

Murphy further noted:

> . . . a sound psychological analysis will discover in laboratory situations and in life situations the same fundamental dynamics of human life and conduct, because being human, one cannot ever function without display-ing these basic principles from which every sound interpretation proceeds. It is the task of the laboratory to discover the essentials of the "real life" situations, and to throw light upon them, just as it is the task of the study of life situations to see where a given principle may be systematically explored in laboratory terms.[62]

It is to this theme that these collected papers are dedicated.

REFERENCES

1. A. Inkeles, "Personality and Social Structure," in R. K. Merton, L. Broom, L. S. Cottrell (eds.), *Sociology Today* (New York: Basic Books, 1959), p. 274.
2. G. Murphy, "Social Psychology," in *American Handbook of Psychiatry,* Vol. 2 (New York: Basic Books, 1959), pp. 1738-1739.

3. F. C. Bartlett, *Remembering* (Cambridge: Cambridge University Press, 1932).
4. M. Sherif, *The Psychology of Social Norms* (New York: Harper & Brothers, 1936).
5. Murphy, *loc. cit.*
6. F. H. Allport, *Social Psychology* (Boston: Houghton Mifflin Company, 1924).
7. G. Murphy and Lois B. Murphy, *Experimental Social Psychology* (New York: Harper & Brothers, 1931).
8. G. Murphy, Lois B. Murphy, and T. M. Newcomb, *Experimental Social Psychology* (revised ed.; New York: Harper & Brothers, 1937).
9. J. H. Pratt, "The Class Method of Treating Consumption in the Homes of the Poor," *J. A. M. A.*, 49:755-759, 1907.
10. Editorial, "The Emmanuel Church Movement in Boston," *N. Y. Med. J.*, 87:947-1048, 1908.
11. R. Dreikurs and R. Corsini, "Twenty Years of Group Psychotherapy," *Am. J. Psychiat.*, 8:567-575, 1954.
12. A. B. Hollingshead and F. C. Redlich, *Social Class and Mental Illness* (New York: John Wiley & Sons, 1958).
13. Editorial, "The Emmanuel Church Movement in Boston," *loc. cit.*
14. E. W. Lazell, "The Group Treatment of Dementia Praecox," *Psychoanalyt. Rev.*, Vol. 8, pp. 168-179, April 1921.
15. L. C. Marsh, "Group Therapy and the Psychiatric Clinic," *J. Nerv. & Ment. Dis.*, Vol. 82, pp. 381-392, 1935.
16. L. Wender, "Current Trends in Group Psychotherapy," *Am. J. Psychother.*, 3:381-404, 1951.
17. P. Schilder, "Results and Problems of Group Psychotherapy in Severe Neurosis," *Ment. Hyg.*, Vol. 23, pp. 87-98, 1939.
18. J. L. Moreno, "Psychodrama and Group Therapy," *Sociometry*, Vol. 9, pp. 249-253, 1946.
19. S. R. Slavson, *An Introduction to Group Therapy* (New York: International Universities Press, 1954).
20. L. Lowrey (Chairman), S. R. Slavson, Dorothy Spiker, H. B. Peck, Mrs. Helen Glauber, N. W. Ackerman, "Group Therapy Special Section Meeting, 1943," *Am. J. Orthopsychiat.*, Vol. Xiii, No. 4, 1943.
21. S. R. Slavson, "Group Therapy," *Ment. Hyg.*, Vol. 24, pp. 36-49, January 1940.
22. G. W. Thomas, "Group Psychotherapy. A Review of the Recent Literature," *Psychosomat. Med.*, Vol. V, pp. 166-180, 1943.
23. N. Hobbs, "Group Centered Psychotherapy," in C. R. Rogers (ed.), *Client Centered Psychotherapy* (Boston: Houghton Mifflin Company, 1951).
24. J. Bierer (ed.), *Therapeutic Social Clubs* (London: H. K. Lewis, 1948).
25. S. H. Foulkes, *Introduction to Group-Analytic Psychotherapy* (London: Wm. Heineman Medical Books Limited, 1948).
26. A. Wolf, "The Psychoanalysis of Groups," *Am. J. Psychother.*, 4:16-50, 1949; 1:525-558, 1950.

27. G. R. Bach, *Intensive Group Psychotherapy* (New York: Ronald Press, 1954).

28. T. Leary, *Interpersonal Diagnosis of Personality* (New York: Ronald Press, 1957).

29. W. R. Bion, "Experiences in Groups, I-VII," *Hum. Relat.*, 1:314-320, 487-496, 1948; 2:13-22, 295-303, 1949; 3:3-14, 395-402, 1950; 4:221-227, 1951; "Group Dynamics: A Re-View," *Int. J. Psychoanal.*, Vol. 33, pp. 235-247, 1952.

30. Dorothy Stock and H. A. Thelen, *Emotional Dynamics and Group Culture*, No. 2 of Research Training Series of the National Training Laboratories, National Education Association of the U.S. (New York: New York University Press, 1958).

31. J. Piaget, *The Moral Judgment of the Child* (New York: Harcourt, Brace & Company, 1932; Glencoe, Ill.: Free Press, 1952).

32. E. Durkheim, *The Division of Labor in Society* (Glencoe, Ill.: Free Press, 1947).

33. C. Cooley, *Social Organization* (New York: Charles Scribner's Sons, 1909).

34. Durkheim, *op. cit.*

35. G. Simmel, *Soziologie* (Leipzig: Duncker and Humblot, 1908).

36. G. H. Mead, *Mind, Self and Society* (Chicago: University of Chicago Press, 1934).

37. S. Freud, *Group Psychology and the Analysis of the Ego* (London: Hogarth Press, 1948), p. 80.

38. G. Le Bon, *The Crowd: A Study of the Popular Mind* (*La Psychologie des Foules*) (New edition; London: T. Fisher Unwin, 1922).

39. R. E. Park, E. W. Burgess, and R. D. McKenzie, *The City* (Chicago: University of Chicago Press, 1925); R. E. Park, *Human Communities* (Glencoe, Ill.: Free Press, 1952).

40. F. Thrasher, *The Gang* (Chicago: University of Chicago Press, 1927).

41. W. F. White, *The Streetcorner Society* (Chicago: University of Chicago Press, 1943).

42. F. J. Roethlisberger and W. J. Dickson, *Management and the Worker* (Hawthorne Studies; Cambridge, Mass.: Harvard University Press, 1939).

43. E. Mayo, *Human Problems of Industrial Civilization* (Cambridge, Mass.: Harvard University Press, 1933).

44. E. Sapir, "Group," in E. R. A. Seligman and A. Johnson (eds.), *Encyclopedia of the Social Sciences*, Vol. VII-VIII (New York: The Macmillan Company, 1932).

45. J. L. Moreno, *Who Shall Survive? A New Approach to the Problems of Human Interrelations* (Washington, D.C.: Nervous and Mental Disease Publishing Company, 1934); "Psychodrama and Group Therapy," *Sociometry*, Vol. 9, pp. 249-253, 1946; Helen H. Jennings, *Leadership and Isolation* (2nd ed.; New York: Longmans, Green & Company, 1950).

46. K. Lewin, "The Research Center for Group Dynamics at Massachusetts Institute of Technology," *Sociometry*, Vol. VIII, pp. 126-136, 1945.

47. K. Lewin, R. Lippitt, and R. K. White, "Patterns of Aggressive Behavior in Experimentally Created Social 'Climate,'" *J. Soc. Psychol.*, Vol. 10, pp. 271-299, 1939; R. Lippit and R. K. White, "An Experimental Study

of Leadership and Group Life," in T. M. Newcomb and E. L. Hartley (eds.), *Readings in Social Psychology* (New York: Henry Holt & Co., 1947), pp. 315-330.

48. K. Lewin, "Group Decision and Social Change," in T. M. Newcomb and E. L. Hartley (eds.), *Readings in Social Psychology* (New York: Henry Holt & Co., 1947), p. 344.

49. Lewin, *ibid.*, p. 336.

50. S. E. Asch, *Social Psychology* (New York: Prentice-Hall, 1952).

51. J. Von Neumann and O. Morgenstern, *Theory of Games and Economic Behavior* (Princeton, N.J.: Princeton University Press, 1944).

52. R. D. Luce and H. Raiffa, *Games and Decisions: Introduction and Critical Survey* (New York: John Wiley & Sons, 1957).

53. H. Solomon (ed.), *Mathematical Thinking in the Measurement of Behavior* (Glencoe, Ill.: Free Press, 1960), pp. 314.

54. J. W. Thibaut and H. H. Kelley, *The Social Psychology of Groups* (New York: John Wiley & Sons, 1959).

55. G. Homans, *The Human Group* (New York: Harcourt, Brace & Company, 1950).

56. G. Lindzey (ed.), *Handbook of Social Psychology*, Vols. I and II (Reading, Mass.: Addison-Wesley Publishing Company, 1954).

57. M. S. Olmsted, *The Small Group* (New York: Random House, 1959).

58. R. F. Bales, *Interaction Process Analysis* (Cambridge, Mass.: Addison-Wesley Publishing Company, 1950).

59. Anita Terauds, I. Altman, and J. E. McGrath, *A Bibliography of Small Group Research* (Arlington, Va.: Human Sciences Research, 1960).

60. G. A. Talland, "Task and Interaction Process: Some Characteristics of Therapeutic Group Discussion," *J. Abnorm. and Soc. Psychol.*, 1:105-109, 1955.

61. M. Sherif, *An Outline of Social Psychology* (New York: Harper and Brothers, 1948), p. ix.

62. *Ibid.*, p. x.

Part 1

SOCIAL PSYCHOLOGY AND SMALL GROUP THEORY

THIS SECTION INCLUDES PAPERS that relate social psychology to group process. According to the classical psychoanalytic approach, all of the social values, as well as ego values, which remain primary are derivatives of basic drives. This appears to be a denial of the emergences in group interaction. People associate and interact primarily to secure satisfaction of their basic psychobiogenic needs. After this original interaction has occurred and continued, there emerge values and norms which, in turn, begin to have a validity of their own and act as primary factors in the determination of individual or group behavior. This important issue is often overlooked by students of human behavior who are entirely motivational in their approach to group function. The philosopher Ralph Barton Perry has referred to the classical psychoanalytic concept as the atavistic fallacy. He states that psychoanalysis is founded on this fallacy and quotes Freud, "This oldest portion of the mental apparatus [the id] remains the most important throughout life." * "The fallacy [according to Perry] consists in supposing that despite his racial evolution and personal history man remains at heart a fetus or a rat." † Perry points out that through the process of conditioning and learning the individual's behavior is varied, and new motivations are engrafted, and he states that supporters of the atavistic fallacy believe these new motivations remain on the original stem of human behavior. Perry believes that later experiences and influences may count far more than the earlier ones in mature behavior, the primary drives having been succeeded by secondary drives and psychogenic drives. Perry's position and his concern with the influence of the atavistic fallacy in the behavioral sciences is highly relevant.‡ When individuals begin to be to-

* From *Outline of Psychoanalysis*, trans. by J. Strachey (New York: W. W. Norton & Co., 1949), p. 14.

† Perry, *Realms of Value* (Cambridge, Mass.: Harvard University Press, 1954), p. 21.

‡ We do not deny the importance of instinctive behavior; the behavior of man cannot be understood without study of instinct and evolution. See in this regard K. Breland and M. Breland, "The Misbehavior of Organisms," *Am. Psychol.*, Vol. 16, No. 11, November 1961.

gether within a group structure, new configurations become apparent. Some students of group process criticize advocates of motivational theory and state that these people have consistently ignored the intellective processes that are at work in group formation. For example, Asch, one of the authors we have included in the papers in this section, stresses the cognitive or intellective approach in his study of social interaction and group function. He has criticized many social psychologists for stressing the emotional in their studies of social interaction.

In the early days of social psychology, as far back as the 1920's, there were great debates over the concept of the group mind. This concept, briefly stated, is that a group continues to exist even if there has been a complete change in membership; that a group has properties such as a system of values and a certain structure which cannot be conceived of as being properties of individuals and that there are specific laws governing this group functioning. Some contemporary psychotherapists still perceive the student of group process as working along this concept of the group mind. That is to say, they are suspicious of any feelings of students of group dynamics that these people are postulating a group mind and are therefore denying any individual approach to group behavior.

On the other extreme of this controversy is the position that only individuals are real and that groups are repeated in each individual mind and exist only in these minds. Groups are conceived of as abstractions from collections of individuals, and the group mind is considered fallacious, since it is nothing but the similarities among individual minds. Therefore, a group exists only in the minds of men. The studies of social interaction which are presented in this group of papers touch this area but relate specifically to the concepts of the social norm. Murphy notes the interplay between the work of social psychologist and student of group behavior and the work of the group psychotherapist when he discusses the question of group thinking. Asch questions what happens when groups of individuals get together. How important is it for individuals to conform in a group? Is there really individual difference? Is the prime motivation of the individual to be liked and to be accepted by the group? Could this conceivably play a part in the thinking of patients who come for a therapeutic experience within a group structure?

Asch, in his paper, stresses the cognitive aspect. A paper that would be more toward the frame of reference of the individual psychotherapist is the paper by Sherif, which is a summary of some of his studies of group process and group conflict. Sherif, for years, as noted in the introduction, has worked on the feasibility of subjecting group behavior to experimental investigation. He first started by forming groups in laboratory settings and observing how these groups begin to set up artificial but, for them, valid social norms. By subjecting this concept of a social norm to psychological analysis, he helped to break down the barrier that existed, the artificial categorization and separation of the individual and the group. His research was instrumental in establishing among psychologists the belief that groups may have certain properties, including the development of social norms. He suggested that there may be a valid psychological basis in the contention of some social psychologists that new and supra-individual qualities arise in group situations. In the research that is reported in this collection of readings, Sherif has moved on to studying the natural history of groups. He expresses great enthusiasm for changing human behavior within group structure and feels that group therapy is more effective than the one-to-one psychotherapeutic relationship.*

The articles that we have selected in this section are in keeping with our position as editors in terms of an approach to group behavior. When we speak of the group here, we do not speak of a collection of individuals. For example, a collection of advertising men may not be considered a group. They may properly be referred to as a class of people. When we speak of a group, we refer to two or more people who bear a definite psychological relationship to one another. This means that for each member of the group, the other group members exist in some psychological way, so that the behavior and the characteristics of the other members of the group influence a particular member of a group. One of the problems that plagues many students of group behavior is that, in doing away with the concept of the group mind, the concept that many lay people still accept, the social psychologist is left with the individual as the unit of analysis. Yet he gropes for a unit that is larger than that of the individual. He begins to speak in terms of a series of social behaviors, and he exchanges the word "group" for the word "individual" in setting up what he believes to be certain valid psychological laws. From this he deduces what he feels are valid laws of group dynamics. This does not appear to be either fair or possible. Sherif and the workers who have followed him appear to be more systematic in their treatment. They explore the social variable and demonstrate the group influence on personality functioning. The work by Harvey and Consalvi in this section follows upon the original studies of Sherif and continues to explore the effect of membership in a group upon individual differences.

This is relevant to the rather lengthy presentation in this section of the abstract from the carefully reported study by Stock and Thelen. Thelen is a student of child development and personality development, and primarily an educational psychologist. Though he was influenced by the work of the social psychologists at the University of Michigan, he attempted in his own work at the University of Chicago to do systematic studies of group formation and group structure. He became aware of the work of Bion, the English psychiatrist and psychoanalyst, who was formulating an approach

---

* Personal communication.

to group behavior along analytic lines. Bion feels that his psychoanalytic approach through the individual and his approach through the group are essentially facets of the same phenomena. Bion attempted to apply psycho-analytic principles to the study of natural groups.

The paper by Stock and Thelen is the beginning of a bridge between group function and group psychotherapy. They describe the results of re-search which had tested the culture, or what Bion and others have called the "work-emotionality" of specific groups. It is a valuable study for the group psychotherapist because it indicates how certain approaches to indi-vidual behavior can be subjected to systematic research. It is a valuable study for the student of group dynamics and the social psychologist and sociologist because it indicates the direction they may turn to if they begin to systematically test or research the particular clinical experiences and concepts of psychotherapists who practice both individually and in the group setting.

We have included a paper by Knutson to indicate how the phenom-ena of verbal and nonverbal participation can be explored in great detail in a nontherapeutic setting. The valuable research design arranged by Knutson can be of great aid to the practicing psychotherapist. It is also of value in confirming from a quite independent source, outside of the thera-peutic setting, certain of the clinical observations of practicing psychother-apists. His article indicates that the student of ego psychology and self-image may receive aid from the group researcher.

Eugene Hartley's treatment of the field of group psychotherapy from the viewpoint of an active researcher and social psychologist should prop-erly be read after most of these readings have been studied. However, the reader may want to jump immediately to Hartley's postscript to this col-lection of readings to study more the interrelationship between group psy-chotherapy and group function.

GROUP PSYCHOTHERAPY IN OUR SOCIETY

Gardner Murphy

There is not, I suppose, anything essentially new about small groups which exert fundamental directive influences on their members in educational and therapeutic directions.

In many periods like that of the "mystery religions" of the Greeks or the guilds of the Medieval Period, special interests and skills permitted a strongly inculcated sense of identification. The informal groups that gathered at a bridge on the river Cam in the thirteenth century developed a fellow feeling and gave strength and discipline to individual members. We can readily imagine that the therapeutic and the educational tended to coalesce. I should not, therefore, urge that there is anything absolutely new about the use of groups, led or unled, in the service of therapy and personal reeducation. The two things that are new are first the *secular*, rather than the religious, spirit in which individual aims are redirected, and secondly the sense of *skill* or technique. This emphasis on skill is a part of the scientific, technological movement which began in the seventeenth and eighteenth centuries, underlying the growth of science on the one hand and the Industrial Revolution on the other. From this point of view we move away from "Mark Hopkins on a log," conveying personal inspiration to a student, all the way to the modern teacher armed with many years of formal educational theory and "practice teaching" under supervision, which gives a sense of professional identity and professional competence. Many students speak of such experiences as therapeutic.

Along with this the point has often been made that a group can convey at least three things which the individual therapist cannot accomplish:

This article is based upon a speech delivered at the Seventeenth Annual Conference of the American Group Psychotherapy Association, New York City, January, 1960.

It can supply the warmth and cohesion of a sort of family solidarity, with which the suffering individual can identify; without any change of role the individual patient can immerse himself in and become deeply identified with the other group members. This is in itself a form of support, characteristic of men and women of all periods but refurbished with the sense of professional identity which pervades all who lead in such movements. Secondly, the group can sometimes prepare for life by giving opportunities in the group itself to exemplify forms of social adaptation, such as love and friendly competition, which can perhaps be directly carried over to other and larger groups. The process of transfer from the polarized situation of individual psychotherapy to living one's daily life in the group may perhaps, in some cases, be simplified and its sharp edges rounded off and made bearable; in other cases, of course, this is not true. Third, groups can make possible for the individual, from the very beginning, the experience of giving as well as receiving help. There is therefore a direct and fundamental ego fulfillment in being capable of directed love and support, controlled by the individual for the benefit of other group members.

It is fundamental in our modern way of living, let us say in the growth of America since the disappearance of the frontier, that we have preferred to solve our problems in a group rather than individually. This is the theme of David Riesman's impelling analyses of Western culture, and of American life in particular, in his volume on *The Lonely Crowd*; it is the theme of Holly Whyte's *The Organization Man* and of many studies of "suburbia," of families of young executives, and of the lost quality of those who must find solidarity in groups, however tenuous, because they are no one by themselves alone. There is, however, a tremendous difference between the group in which one is *lost* and the group in which one is *found*. It is partly a question of the size of the group, partly a question of its aim, its organization, and its leadership. We have been groping for a century or more in our churches, fraternal orders, college fraternities, and sororities for something to keep going the spirit of brotherhood and of sisterhood which the Roman Catholic Church maintained and today so vigorously maintains as a way of building a bridge between the isolated individual and the vast community of the Church as a whole. The Church has needed familylike small groups built into scattered groups known as Orders. The development of groups for therapeutic and educational purposes can, within definite limits, reflect this response to loneliness, helplessness in the face of the vastness of today, and at the same time the use of a somewhat familylike organization, with a leader in the role of father or mother, or big brother or sister. The psychoanalytic conception of the family is rich in thoughts for the understanding of group therapy. Let us now use our psychoanalytic approach against the backdrop of a broad sociocultural definition of group life.

THE SOCIOCULTURAL APPROACH TO
GROUP PSYCHOTHERAPY

Viewing the situation in terms of a psychoanalytic model, we may certainly assume that the child who has *all* of the father's attention has something very precious which cannot be equaled in a *diffuse* family situation, no matter how strong and well knit the family group may be. It is something to have the priest's full attention in absolution, to have the attorney's full attention in consultation, to be one who seeks out and gets a chance to communicate with the teacher on a personal basis. These are valuable and fundamental in themselves. They do not in themselves have anything to do with economic considerations as such. If, however, it proves to be economical as well as expedient and practical to work with patients in groups, there is a further factor enormously enhancing the difference between individual therapy and group therapy. But the very fact that one does not pay as much may sometimes mean that the therapy is not regarded as having the same value. Everyone knows that classes with just a few members are expensive for colleges to organize and that a highly focused group-person situation, as in the Sarah Lawrence classes of ten, can do something personally, educationally, emotionally, and spiritually, which it is very difficult to do with even the most brilliant of classes where there are 35 to 40 students. In a society so quick to assign monetary value to social relationships, it is not surprising that group psychotherapy should be regarded as cheaper both in the direct economic sense and in the sense in which we say that anything that belongs to the market place is vulgar or cheap.

Here, however, is a basic contradiction. What we want is not just the support of the father figure, but the support of the family as a whole. This is true not only of the extended family, as in India or China or Japan; it is also true of the small biological family. It is wonderfully precious to have mother's and father's full attention, but there are many times when it is even more precious to have the family participation and support in one's deepest intellectual and emotional ventures, as when one starts a new and difficult task, assuming responsibilities and emotional ties with which one would wish to weave together all the family members so that one remains a part of their collective unity and has their corporate support. Group psychotherapy against this background becomes for some persons a symbol of a kind of family support. It is suggested that it offers father and mother, big brother and big sister relationships yet maintains the collectivity, the *esprit de corps*, without which we should feel isolated, lonely, polarized in the presence of the superior or austere therapist. Not only is it easier, we are sometimes reminded, to communicate one's intimate problems when others are communicating their own intimate problems and getting dispassionate and friendly understanding and support; one also has the sense of being important to each member and to the group in its entirety. Consequently, the feeling of intimate exchange with the strong and beloved leader might be compared with another kind of intimate exchange in which the sharing of problems makes the group almost religious in its merging of individuals in a network of interpersonal realities. But this parallel may be challenged, and in general we must study the wide range of individual differences.

Ansbacher has reminded us that the appeal of psychoanalysis from the very beginning was largely to the elite, economically, intellectually, and socially. Psychoanalysis was a rich, intricate, and demanding conceptual system. Individual psychology, on the other hand, was simple, crude, rough-and-ready. Adler's slouching, or even slovenly, manner, his delight in working-class associations and socialist affiliations, his establishment of lower middle-class kinds of clinics in the Vienna schools led Ansbacher to paraphrase the old cliché "What this country needs is a good five-cent cigar" with the phrase that what this country needs is a good five-dollar psychiatrist. There can be no doubt at all that these factors even among the very democratic and very conscientious can lead to many confused ideas about group psychotherapy, interfering with the factual examination of the situation which is so urgently necessary both for the welfare of the patient and for the long-run evaluation of what is really sound and effective in our culture. Let us prejudge no issues.

EXPERIMENTS IN GROUP THINKING

Another type of co-working group that may have some relevance to our problem is the group which has been asked to find the answer to an experimentally posed problem or to find a creative solution of a difficulty. These experiments which have been under way now for some forty years have yielded a very considerable fund of information about the kind of thinking which the group situation permits and encourages. It is a waste of time to ask abstractly whether groups think more effectively than the individuals who compose the groups, by the classical method of working with matched problems and having some of them solved by the individual method and others by the group method. The trouble with the traditional question as to superiority of the groups is that it ignores all the particulars which make the problem significant and meaningful. In some situations, one individual has the necessary information or skill or both and can do better than any other individual or than any arrangement of individuals in the group. Under other circumstances there are scattered bits of information and potential insight which can become integrated in the group setting, so that the group thinks a good deal more efficiently than any other individual members.

In some cases the beneficial result of the group setting lies not so much in the creative accumulation of potential contributions scattered in the mind of the various members, but rather in the enhancement of a critical capacity; a capacity to see the false assumptions and blind alleys which have arisen in the early attempts to solve the problem. A can criticize B and C for omitting essential issues, and if the group atmosphere is at all congenial for serious work, other individuals, let us say, D and E, see where the implications lie and develop out of the criticisms a constructive possibility. But the individual himself may actually see his own mistakes in the situation, because, as George Herbert Mead never tired of pointing out, the individual sees himself reflected in the awareness of the others. There is a "looking-glass" personality, an awareness of the "generalized other" and the way in which the "generalized other" perceives one. These kinds of experiences profoundly recast our notion that the group is merely an additive collection of fragmentary bits of information. The group experience may recast our images of ourselves and enable us to think more effectively. How much of all this is directly relevant to group psychotherapy will, I think, be clear if one refers to the writings in the twenties and thirties, in which the influence of Mead was beginning to be clear. What began as a normal part of the social science analysis of group life was taken over by the therapist.

These studies were not unrelated to the comparable studies of propaganda and resistance to propaganda which likewise made their first great advent during the 1920's. It became clear that the resistance offered to vigorously formulated public communications lay very largely in the group support which each individual shared with others when an authoritative figure went further than the psychological structure of the situation permitted. Individual resistance to propaganda, as we are led to understand it by reference to the study of psychoanalysis, and particularly the theory of ego structures, may overlook the *shared* nature of social resistance. This, despite the fact that Freud's *Group Psychology and the Analysis of the Ego* made clear that the affective bonds which tie the group together are in some ways similar to a system of affective bonds in the family and should make us ready for awareness of the fact that the resistance of the group to the strong leader is of an utterly different order from the cumulative resistances of separate individuals. The public-opinion poller neglects (to his peril) the relation of the individual response of acceptance or rejection to public communication, as if each individual were bottled up within a separate cell. Even the recent brilliant studies of Richard S. Crutchfield on the conformity responses seem to begin with the assumption that the individual, pocketed off and made immune to communication from others, except through a highly artificial and channelized system of beamed communications, could give us a picture of social cohesion and the act of resisting. Studies by John French and others in laboratory situations in which experimental panic has been induced through a realistic simulation of a fire with smoke, alarm, and so on, and studies by Grinker and Spiegel of the mass response of bombing crews in World War II to strong or weak leadership in their commanding officer, have taught us to see how intensely social is the response of the individual to the abuse of confidence or the inappropriate utilization of authority. One responds not to panic in general, but concretely to companions whose strength and weaknesses one knows and to leaders whose strengths and weaknesses one knows.

EXPERIMENTS IN CLASSROOM ATMOSPHERES

There is an experiment of Everett Bovard at the University of Michigan which I believe has enormous theoretical and practical value for us who are interested in group psychotherapy. I shall take the liberty of streamlining the account from various scattered publications. Bovard and a colleague at the University of Michigan undertook to teach elementary psychology to equated classes by two fundamentally different methods, each instructor utilizing each of the two methods with separate groups. One method, which we would ordinarily call the individual-centered method, involved the usual teacher-student interaction through question and answer; that is, assuming that the students had familiarized themselves with the basic required material, each student had his chance to ask questions. The instructor answered him as well as he could. In this way each student had his turn. This sounds democratic and effective. The other method, however, called the group-centered method, involved the instructor's standing back and taking as little part as possible in the proceedings. He started the ball rolling but then encouraged the various members of the class to pitch their problems at one another in a process of continuous cross fires. In this way there was no polarization of the individual student toward the instructor. Rather, there was a network of constantly shifting polarizations, all of which were fluid, unstable, and susceptible of constant redefinition. There was, moreover, a group morale which was easily observed, a collective learning process.

Now when the time came for an examination the students were tested not at all in terms of true-false or multiple choice propositions covering the content of the class work. On the contrary, they were shown motion pictures prepared by the Canadian mental health authorities. The *Feeling of Rejection* is a particularly well-known one. In these films the emotional problems of disturbed, anxious, and lonely persons are depicted, so that those with some degree of empathy and sympathy latch on, understand, and have a glimmering of possible ways of helping. We find now that when tested by their understanding and their practical remedial responses to these films, the group-centered students did substantially better. They had, in other words, learned what was emotionally significant from these films depicting a social situation, because they had learned something about empathy and social interaction in the classroom teaching situation. This, at least, is Bovard's aim and the gist of his report.

Such studies, of course, require replication. My theme is not to offer final and dogmatic evidence regarding a teaching method; rather, my aim is to arouse you to a number of important research and practical issues regarding how we actually learn in group settings. These are experiences of the sort which Daniel Prescott at the University of Maryland has emphasized for many years; experiences described by T. M. Newcomb in his Bennington College Study; by Lois Murphy and Henry Ladd in the Sarah Lawrence Study; and paralleled in some respects by J. L. Moreno's early studies at the New York State Training School at Hudson, New York. We seem to encounter here many experiences in which there is a realignment, reorganization of the affective ties of each person with his fellow, so that as the subject matter becomes meaningful to him, his social relationships to those who are coping with the same subject matter become more precious to him, and he himself, as a learner, identifies with others who are learning at the same time.

I believe that the group psychotherapy situation has much in common with this kind of educational practice, which has been going on, of course, since the laboratory school of John Dewey in 1902 and since the progressive school research efforts of George A. Coe and others before and after World War I. The whole vast field of group dynamics as defined by Kurt Lewin, especially at the University of Iowa in the mid-thirties, was an expression of this conception of the social definition of the *learning process*. This is as fresh today as it was in the time of John Dewey and in this Dewey centennial year may again be emphasized.

The work of Kurt Lewin's students on authoritarian and democratic groups are likewise relevant here. Group psychotherapy may at times involve a redefinition of the group learning situation in the best progressive educational setup. Instead of asking whether group psychotherapy is derived from the group method as used in education or derived from Kurt Lewin's group dynamics, I should be inclined, rather, to ask whether all of these are not expressions of a Whitman-like fellow feeling, a need of comradeship, which took shape as a reaction against the excessive individualism of American pioneer and frontiersman life and as a way of blunting the shock of an impersonal industrialization which swept over our country from east to west during the nineteenth and early twentieth centuries. I would ask, in other words, whether group psychotherapy is a form of sharing of personal experiences which arose as individualism and whether its counterpart—loneliness—proved to need some sort of counterpart or balance wheel. Are these not *three* trends, one toward impersonal group life, the second toward a protesting individualism, the third toward small group efforts to find companionship free of the difficulties both of mass living and of solitary living? This emotional craving joined with the technical progress of psychotherapy itself in the formulation of the very natural question: "If we have here two good things, namely, solidarity on the one hand and, on the other hand, high professional competence in dealing with people's personal difficulties, is it not possible to fuse at high temperature the best of the two movements?"

This focuses the issue where it belongs, namely, on the question of what is best in the two movements. I think we have here a good historical model for the rise of group psychotherapy as a way of carrying out one of the healing arts. I think, however, that from this point on the question is the objective evaluation of the kinds of personal and social goals which can best be reached by this kind of psychotherapy in comparison with the others now available.

SOME FINAL REFLECTIONS

1. Society itself is a "therapeutic community," making and breaking us all the time. We have become aware of the breaking function and only slowly the making function.

2. A fundanental principle in therapy enunciated by Freud—namely, that of transference—means inevitably that basic transference models established by the child in growing up are carried into the community. It also means, however, that there is a transfer from the community into the home. Hereford, at the University of Texas, has some interesting observations regarding the role of P.T.A.'s in implementing community decisions and of families in influencing children's behavior in such a way that this carries back into school.

3. The much-discussed issue whether fundamental group or personal psychotherapy can be done with an individual person in a direction which is opposed by the basic values and life rules of the society around him has to be reconsidered. In this connection, how deep into unconscious personality dynamics can we go if we really believe that there is a fundamental opposition between the therapeutic and the daily given cultural values? Is it realistic to believe that a small number of persons in therapy can in some real way change the larger society in which they are members? Are there perhaps palliative or compromise solutions? Are we perhaps involved in a sort of third step toward social reconstruction every time we carry out group psychotherapy?

4. For myself, I believe in the very fundamental possibilities for the remaking of personality, as I have tried to define this in a recent volume on *Human Potentialities*. My own feeling is that realistic thinking through of the way in which group therapy can modify deeper cultural interactions is fundamental before effective therapy can be done. Mere day by day or

even year by year "adjustment" will not do the job. Perhaps, being an outsider, I can go much further with this than your own professional conscience could let you go. But I shall claim this privilege and conclude by claiming a belief of group therapy, that it offers principles and modes truly prophetic for other types of group structures in a society to which small groups will have massive importance in competition with the impersonal forces of a technological society.

I have already hinted a few directions in which group psychotherapy research might move:

(1) It might emphasize the kinds of personality changes that occur in group psychotherapy as such, as contrasted with those which are concerned simply with group dynamics, group cohesion, and effective learning in group situations.

(2) It might emphasize the economic, political, and cultural contrasts in which the public image of psychotherapy is developing today, with attention to economic, cultural, and other factors which, whether rational or irrational, predispose toward acceptance or resistance.

(3) It might emphasize the potential impacts of today's group psychotherapy upon larger cultural phenomena in a lonely yet impersonal world.

2

OPINIONS AND SOCIAL PRESSURE

Solomon E. Asch

That social influences shape every person's practices, judgments, and beliefs is a truism to which anyone will readily assent. A child masters his "native" dialect down to the finest nuances; a member of a tribe of cannibals accepts cannibalism as altogether fitting and proper. All the social sciences take their departure from the observation of the profound effects that groups exert on their members. For psychologists, group pressure upon the minds of individuals raises a host of questions they would like to investigate in detail.

How, and to what extent, do social forces constrain people's opinions and attitudes? This question is especially pertinent in our day. The same epoch that has witnessed the unprecedented technical extension of communication has also brought into existence the deliberate manipulation of opinion and the "engineering of consent." There are many good reasons why, as citizens and as scientists, we should be concerned with studying the ways in which human beings form their opinions and the role that social conditions play.

Studies of these questions began with the interest in hypnosis aroused by the French physician Jean Martin Charcot (a teacher of Sigmund Freud) toward the end of the nineteenth century. Charcot believed that only hysterical patients could be fully hypnotized, but this view was soon challenged by two other physicians, Hyppolyte Bernheim and A. A. Liébault, who demonstrated that they could put most people under the hypnotic spell. Bernheim proposed that hypnosis was but an extreme form of a normal psychological process which became known as "suggestibility." It was shown that monotonous reiteration of instructions could induce in normal persons in the waking state involuntary bodily changes such as swaying or rigidity of the arms and sensations such as warmth and odor.

From *Scientific American*, Vol. 193, No. 5, November 1955, pp. 31-35. Reprinted with permission.

It was not long before social thinkers seized upon these discoveries as a basis for explaining numerous social phenomena, from the spread of opinion to the formation of crowds and the following of leaders. The sociologist Gabriel Tarde summed it all up in the aphorism: "Social man is a somnambulist."

When the new discipline of social psychology was born at the beginning of this century, its first experiments were essentially adaptations of the suggestion demonstration. The technique generally followed a simple plan. The subjects, usually college students, were asked to give their opinions or preferences concerning various matters; some time later they were again asked to state their choices, but now they were also informed of the opinions held by authorities or large groups of their peers on the same matters. (Often the alleged consensus was fictitious.) Most of these studies had substantially the same result: Confronted with opinions contrary to their own, many subjects apparently shifted their judgments in the direction of the views of the majorities or the experts. The late psychologist Edward L. Thorndike reported that he had succeeded in modifying the esthetic preferences of adults by this procedure. Other psychologists reported that people's evaluations of the merit of a literary passage could be raised or lowered by ascribing the passage to different authors. Apparently the sheer weight of numbers or authority sufficed to change opinions, even when no arguments for the opinions themselves were provided.

Now the very ease of success in these experiments arouses suspicion. Did the subjects actually change their opinions, or were the experimental victories scored only on paper? On grounds of common sense, one must question whether opinions are generally as watery as these studies indicate. There is some reason to wonder whether it was not the investigators who, in their enthusiasm for a theory, were suggestible, and whether the ostensibly gullible subjects were not providing answers which they thought good subjects were expected to give.

The investigations were guided by certain underlying assumptions, which today are common currency and account for much that is thought and said about the operations of propaganda and public opinion. The assumptions are that people submit uncritically and painlessly to external manipulation by suggestion or prestige and that any given idea or value can be "sold" or "unsold" without reference to its merits. We should be skeptical, however, of the supposition that the power of social pressure necessarily implies uncritical submission to it: Independence and the capacity to rise above group passion are also open to human beings. Further, one may question on psychological grounds whether it is possible as a rule to change a person's judgment of a situation or an object without first changing his knowledge or assumptions about it.

In what follows I shall describe some experiments in an investigation of the effects of group pressure which was carried out recently with the help of a number of my associates. The tests not only demonstrate the operations of group pressure upon individuals but also illustrate a new kind of attack on the problem and some of the more subtle questions that it raises.

A group of seven to nine young men, all college students, are assembled in a classroom for a "psychological experiment" in visual judgment. The experimenter informs them that they will be comparing the lengths of lines. He shows two large white cards. On one is a single vertical black line—the standard whose length is to be matched. On the other card are three vertical lines of various lengths. The subjects are to choose the one that is of the same length as the line on the other card. One of the three actually is of the same length; the other two are substantially different, the difference ranging from three quarters of an inch to an inch and three quarters.

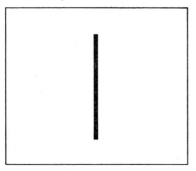 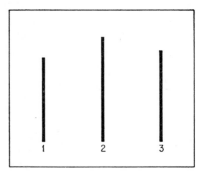

Fig. 2–1. *Subjects were shown two cards. One bore a standard line. The other bore three lines, one of which was the same length as the standard. The subjects were asked to choose this line.*

The experiment opens uneventfully. The subjects announce their answers in the order in which they have been seated in the room, and on the first round every person chooses the same matching line. Then a second set of cards is exposed; again the group is unanimous. The members appear ready to endure politely another boring experiment. On the third trial there is an unexpected disturbance. One person near the end of the group disagrees with all the others in his selection of the matching line. He looks surprised, indeed incredulous, about the disagreement. On the following trial he disagrees again, while the others remain unanimous in their choice. The dissenter becomes more and more worried and hesitant as the disagreement continues in succeeding trials; he may pause before announcing his answer and speak in a low voice, or he may smile in an embarrassed way.

What the dissenter does not know is that all the other members of the group were instructed by the experimenter beforehand to give incorrect answers in unanimity at certain points. The single individual who is not a party to this prearrangement is the focal subject of our experiment. He is placed in a position in which, while he is actually giving the correct answers, he finds himself unexpectedly in a minority of one, opposed by a unanimous and arbitrary majority with respect to a clear and simple fact. Upon him we have brought to bear two opposed forces: the evidence of his senses and the unanimous opinion of a group of his peers. Also, he must declare his judgments in public, before a majority which has also stated its position publicly.

The instructed majority occasionally reports correctly in order to reduce the possibility that the naïve subject will suspect collusion against him. (In only a few cases did the subject actually show suspicion; when this happened, the experiment was stopped and the results were not

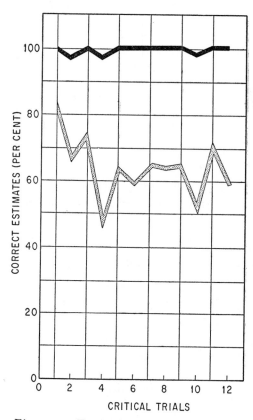

Fig. 2–2. *Error of 123 subjects, each of whom compared lines in the presence of six to eight opponents, is plotted in the shaded curve. The accuracy of judgments not under pressure is indicated in black.*

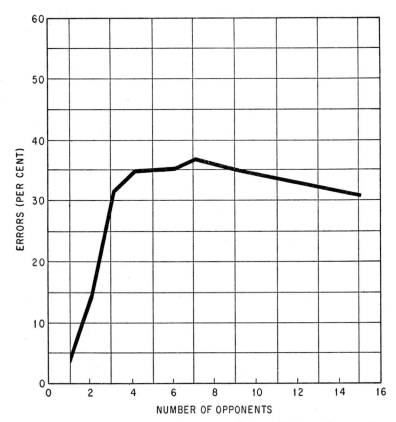

Fig. 2–3. Size of majority which opposed them had an effect on the subjects. With a single opponent the subject erred only 3.6 per cent of the time; with two opponents he erred 13.6 per cent; three, 31.8 per cent; four, 35.1 per cent; six, 35.2 per cent; seven, 37.1 per cent; nine, 35.1 per cent; 15, 31.2 per cent.

counted.) There are 18 trials in each series, and on 12 of these the majority responds erroneously.

How do people respond to group pressure in this situation? I shall report first the statistical results of a series in which a total of 123 subjects from three institutions of higher learning (not including my own, Swarthmore College) were placed in the minority situation described above.

Two alternatives were open to the subject: he could act independently, repudiating the majority, or he could go along with the majority, repudiating the evidence of his senses. Of the 123 put to the test, a considerable percentage yielded to the majority. Whereas in ordinary circumstances individuals matching the lines will make mistakes less than 1 per cent of the time, under group pressure the minority subjects swung to acceptance of the misleading majority's wrong judgments in 36.8 per cent of the selections.

Of course individuals differed in response. At one extreme, about one quarter of the subjects were completely independent and never agreed with the erroneous judgments of the majority. At the other extreme, some individuals went with the majority nearly all the time. The performances of individuals in this experiment tend to be highly consistent. Those who strike out on the path of independence do not, as a rule, succumb to the majority even over an extended series of trials, while those who choose the path of compliance are unable to free themselves as the ordeal is prolonged.

The reasons for the startling individual differences have not yet been investigated in detail. At this point we can only report some tentative generalizations from talks with the subjects, each of whom was interviewed at the end of the experiment. Among the independent individuals were many who held fast because of staunch confidence in their own judgment. The most significant fact about them was not absence of responsiveness to the majority but a capacity to recover from doubt and to re-establish their equilibrium. Others who acted independently came to believe that the majority was correct in its answers, but they continued their dissent on the simple ground that it was their obligation to call the play as they saw it.

Among the extremely yielding persons we found a group who quickly reached the conclusion: "I am wrong, they are right." Others yielded in order "not to spoil your results." Many of the individuals who went along suspected that the majority were "sheep" following the first responder or that the majority were victims of an optical illusion; nevertheless, these suspicions failed to free them at the moment of decision. More disquieting were the reactions of subjects who construed their difference from the majority as a sign of some general deficiency in themselves, which at all costs they must hide. On this basis they desperately tried to merge with the majority, not realizing the longer-range consequences to themselves. All the yielding subjects underestimated the frequency with which they conformed.

Which aspect of the influence of a majority is more important—the size of the majority or its unanimity? The experiment was modified to examine this question. In one series the size of the opposition was varied from one to 15 persons. The results showed a clear trend. When a subject was confronted with only a single individual who contradicted his answers, he was swayed little: He continued to answer independently and correctly in nearly all trials. When the opposition was increased to two, the pressure became substantial: Minority subjects now accepted the wrong answer 13.6 per cent of the time. Under the pressure of a majority of three, the subjects' errors jumped to 31.8 per cent. But further increases in the size of the majority apparently did not increase the weight of the pressure substantially. Clearly the size of the opposition is important only up to a point.

Disturbance of the majority's unanimity had a striking effect. In this experiment the subject was given the support of a truthful partner—either another individual who did not know of the prearranged agreement among the rest of the group or a person who was instructed to give correct answers throughout.

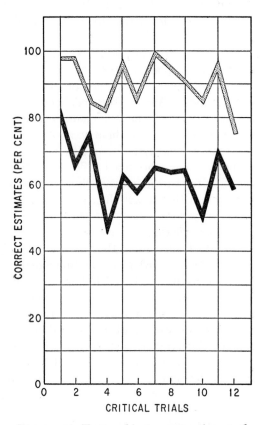

Fig. 2–4. Two subjects supporting each other against a majority made fewer errors (shaded curve) than one subject did against a majority (black curve).

The presence of a supporting partner depleted the majority of much of its power. Its pressure on the dissenting individual was reduced to one fourth: That is, subjects answered incorrectly only one fourth as often as under the pressure of a unanimous majority. (See Figure 4.) The weakest persons did not yield as readily. Most interesting were the reactions to the partner. Generally the feeling toward him was one of warmth and close-ness; he was credited with inspiring confidence. However, the subjects re-pudiated the suggestion that the partner decided them to be independent.

Was the partner's effect a consequence of his dissent, or was it related to his accuracy? We now introduced into the experimental group a person who was instructed to dissent from the majority but also to disagree with the subject. In some experiments the majority was always to choose the worst of the comparison lines and the instructed dissenter to pick the line that was closer to the length of the standard one; in others the majority was consistently intermediate and the dissenter most in error. In this man-ner we were able to study the relative influence of "compromising" and "extremist" dissenters.

Again the results are clear. When a moderate dissenter is present, the effect of the majority on the subject decreases by approximately one third, and extremes of yielding disappear. Moreover, most of the errors the sub-jects do make are moderate, rather than flagrant. In short, the dissenter largely controls the choice of errors. To this extent the subjects broke away from the majority even while bending to it.

On the other hand, when the dissenter always chose the line that was more flagrantly different from the standard, the results were of quite a dif-ferent kind. The extremist dissenter produced a remarkable freeing of the subjects; their errors dropped to only 9 per cent. Furthermore, all the er-rors were of the moderate variety. We were able to conclude that dissent per se increased independence and moderated the errors that occurred, and that the direction of dissent exerted consistent effects.

In all the foregoing experiments each subject was observed only in a single setting. We now turned to studying the effects upon a given indi-vidual of a change in the situation to which he was exposed. The first ex-periment examined the consequences of losing or gaining a partner. The instructed partner began by answering correctly on the first six trials. With his support the subject usually resisted pressure from the majority: 18 of 27 subjects were completely independent. But after six trials the partner joined the majority. As soon as he did so, there was an abrupt rise in the subjects' errors. Their submission to the majority was just about as fre-quent as when the minority subject was opposed by a unanimous majority throughout.

It was surprising to find that the experience of having had a partner and of having braved the majority opposition with him had failed to strengthen the individuals' independence. Questioning at the conclusion of the experiment suggested that we had overlooked an important cir-cumstance; namely, the strong specific effect of "desertion" by the partner to the other side. We therefore changed the conditions so that the partner would simply leave the group at the proper point. (To allay suspicion it was announced in advance that he had an appointment with the dean.)

In this form of the experiment, the partner's effect outlasted his presence. The errors increased after his departure, but less markedly than after a partner switched to the majority.

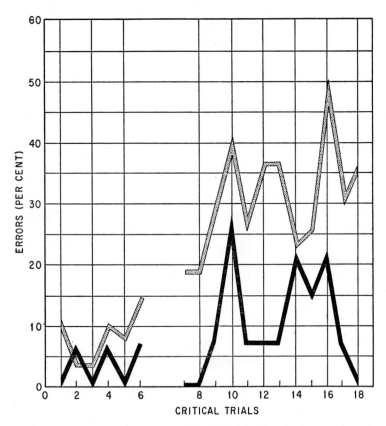

Fig. 2–5. *Partner left subject after six trials in a single experiment. The shaded curve shows the error of the subject when the partner "deserted" to the majority. Black curve shows error when partner merely left the room.*

In a variant of this procedure the trials began with the majority unanimously giving correct answers. Then they gradually broke away until on the sixth trial the naïve subject was alone and the group unanimously against him. As long as the subject had anyone on his side, he was almost invariably independent, but as soon as he found himself alone, the tendency to conform to the majority rose abruptly.

As might be expected, an individual's resistance to group pressure in these experiments depends to a considerable degree on how wrong the majority is. We varied the discrepancy between the standard line and the other lines systematically with the hope of reaching a point where the error of the majority would be so glaring that every subject would repudiate it and choose independently. In this we regretfully did not succeed. Even when the difference between the lines was seven inches, there were still some who yielded to the error of the majority.

The study provides clear answers to a few relatively simple questions, and it raises many others that await investigation. We would like to know the degree of consistency of persons in situations which differ in content and structure. If consistency of independence or conformity in behavior is shown to be a fact, how is it functionally related to qualities of character and personality? In what ways is independence related to sociological or cultural conditions? Are leaders more independent than other people, or are they adept at following their followers? These and many other questions may perhaps be answerable by investigations of the type described here.

Life in society requires consensus as an indispensable condition. But consensus, to be productive, requires that each individual contribute independently out of his experience and insight. When consensus comes under the dominance of conformity, the social process is polluted and the individual at the same time surrenders the powers on which his functioning as a feeling and thinking being depends. That we have found the tendency to conformity in our society so strong that reasonably intelligent and well-meaning young people are willing to call white black is a matter of concern. It raises questions about our ways of education and about the values that guide our conduct.

Yet anyone inclined to draw too pessimistic conclusions from this report would do well to remind himself that the capacities for independence are not to be underestimated. He may also draw some consolation from a further observation: Those who participated in this challenging experiment agreed nearly without exception that independence was preferable to conformity.

3

EXPERIMENTS IN GROUP CONFLICT

Muzafer Sherif

Conflict between groups—whether between boys' gangs, social classes, "races," or nations—has no simple cause, nor is mankind yet in sight of a cure. It is often rooted deep in personal, social, economic, religious, and historical forces. Nevertheless it is possible to identify certain general factors which have a crucial influence on the attitude of any group toward others. Social scientists have long sought to bring these factors to light by studying what might be called the "natural history" of groups and group relations. Intergroup conflict and harmony is not a subject that lends itself easily to laboratory experiments. But in recent years there has been a beginning of attempts to investigate the problem under controlled yet life-like conditions, and I shall report here the results of a program of experimental studies of groups which I started in 1948. Among the persons working with me were Marvin B. Sussman, Robert Huntington, O. J. Harvey, B. Jack White, William R. Hood, and Carolyn W. Sherif. The experiments were conducted in 1949, 1953, and 1954; this article gives a composite of the findings.

We wanted to conduct our study with groups of the informal type, where group organization and attitudes would evolve naturally and spontaneously, without formal direction or external pressures. For this purpose we conceived that an isolated summer camp would make a good experimental setting, and that decision led us to choose as subjects boys about 11 or 12 years old, who would find camping natural and fascinating. Since our aim was to study the development of group relations among these boys under carefully controlled conditions, with as little interference as possible from personal neuroses, background influences or prior experiences, we selected normal boys of homogeneous background who did not know one another before they came to the camp.

From *Scientific American*, Vol. 195, No. 5, November 1956, pp. 54-58. Reprinted with permission. Copyright © 1956 by Scientific American, Inc. All rights reserved.

They were picked by a long and thorough procedure. We interviewed each boy's family, teachers, and school officials, studied his school and medical records, obtained his scores on personality tests, and observed him in his classes and at play with his schoolmates. With all this information we were able to assure ourselves that the boys chosen were of like kind and background: All were healthy, socially well-adjusted, somewhat above average in intelligence and from stable, white, Protestant, middle-class homes.

None of the boys was aware that he was part of an experiment on group relations. The investigators appeared as a regular camp staff—camp directors, counselors, and so on. The boys met one another for the first time in buses that took them to the camp, and so far as they knew it was a normal summer of camping. To keep the situation as lifelike as possible, we conducted all our experiments within the framework of regular camp activities and games. We set up projects which were so interesting and attractive that the boys plunged into them enthusiastically without suspecting that they might be test situations. Unobtrusively we made records of their behavior, even using "candid" cameras and microphones when feasible.

We began by observing how the boys became a coherent group. The first of our camps was conducted in the hills of northern Connecticut in the summer of 1949. When the boys arrived, they were all housed at first in one large bunkhouse. As was to be expected, they quickly formed particular friendships and chose buddies. We had deliberately put all the boys together in this expectation, because we wanted to see what would happen later after the boys were separated into different groups. Our object was to reduce the factor of personal attraction in the formation of groups. In a few days we divided the boys into two groups and put them in different cabins. Before doing so, we asked each boy informally who his best friends were and then took pains to place the "best friends" in different groups so far as possible. (The pain of separation was assuaged by allowing each group to go at once on a hike and camp-out.)

As everyone knows, a group of strangers brought together in some common activity soon acquires an informal and spontaneous kind of organization. It comes to look upon some members as leaders, divides up duties, adopts unwritten norms of behavior, develops an *esprit de corps*. Our boys followed this pattern as they shared a series of experiences. In each group the boys pooled their efforts, organized duties, and divided up tasks in work and play. Different individuals assumed different responsibilities. One boy excelled in cooking. Another led in athletics. Others, though not outstanding in any one skill, could be counted on to pitch in and do their level best in anything the group attempted. One or two seemed to disrupt activities, to start teasing at the wrong moment, or to offer useless suggestions. A few boys consistently had good suggestions and showed ability to coordinate the efforts of others in carrying them through. Within a few days one person had proved himself more resourceful and skillful than the rest. Thus, rather quickly, a leader and lieutenants emerged. Some boys sifted toward the bottom of the heap, while others jockeyed for higher positions.

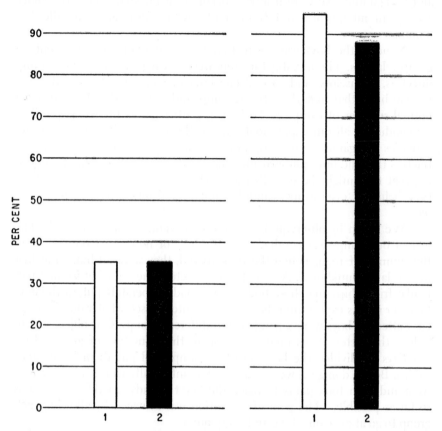

Fig. 3–1. *Friendship choices of campers for others in their own cabin are shown for Red Devils (white) and Bulldogs (black). At first a low percentage of friendships were in the cabin group (left). After five days, most friendship choices were within the group (right).*

We watched these developments closely and rated the boys' relative positions in the group, not only on the basis of our own observations, but also by informal sounding of the boys' opinions as to who got things started, who got things done, who could be counted on to support group activities.

As the group became an organization, the boys coined nicknames. The big, blond, hardy leader of one group was dubbed "Baby Face" by his admiring followers. A boy with a rather long head became "Lemon Head." Each group developed its own jargon, special jokes, secrets, and special ways of performing tasks. One group, after killing a snake near a place where it had gone to swim, named the place "Moccasin Creek" and thereafter preferred this swimming hole to any other, though there were better ones nearby.

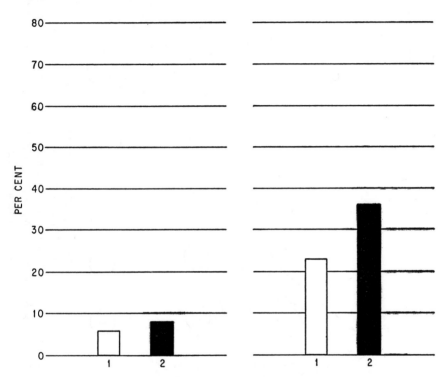

Fig. 3–2. During conflict between the two groups in the Robber's Cave experiment there were few friendships between cabins (left). After cooperation toward common goals had restored good feelings, the number of friendships between groups rose significantly (right).

Wayward members who failed to do things "right" or who did not contribute their bit to the common effort found themselves receiving the "silent treatment," ridicule, or even threats. Each group selected symbols and a name, and they had these put on their caps and T shirts. The 1954 camp was conducted in Oklahoma, near a famous hideaway of Jesse James called Robber's Cave. The two groups of boys at this camp named themselves the Rattlers and the Eagles.

Our conclusions on every phase of the study were based on a variety of observations, rather than on any single method. For example, we de-

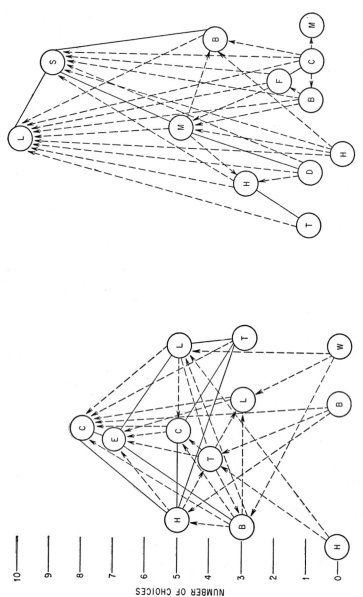

Fig. 3–3. Sociograms represent patterns of friendship choices within the fully developed groups. One-way friendships are indicated by broken arrows; reciprocal friendships, by solid lines. Leaders were among those highest in the popularity scale. Bulldogs (left) had a close-knit organization with good group spirit. Low-ranking members participated less in the life of the group but were not rejected. Red Devils (right) lost the tournament of games between the groups. They had less group unity and were sharply stratified.

vised a game to test the boys' evaluations of one another. Before an important baseball game, we set up a target board for the boys to throw at, on the pretense of making practice for the game more interesting. There were no marks on the front of the board for the boys to judge objectively how close the ball came to a bull's-eye, but, unknown to them, the board was wired to flashing lights behind so that an observer could see exactly where the ball hit. We found that the boys consistently overestimated the performances by the most highly regarded members of their group and underestimated the scores of those of low social standing.

The attitudes of group members were even more dramatically illustrated during a cookout in the woods. The staff supplied the boys with unprepared food and let them cook it themselves. One boy promptly started to build a fire, asking for help in getting wood. Another attacked the raw hamburger to make patties. Others prepared a place to put buns, relishes, and the like. Two mixed soft drinks from flavoring and sugar. One boy who stood around without helping was told by the others to "get to it." Shortly the fire was blazing and the cook had hamburgers sizzling. Two boys distributed them as rapidly as they became edible. Soon it was time for the watermelon. A low-ranking member of the group took a knife and started toward the melon. Some of the boys protested. The most highly regarded boy in the group took over the knife, saying, "You guys who yell the loudest get yours last."

When the two groups in the camp had developed group organization and spirit, we proceeded to the experimental studies of intergroup relations. The groups had had no previous encounters; indeed, in the 1954 camp at Robber's Cave the two groups came in separate buses and were kept apart while each acquired a group feeling.

Our working hypothesis was that when two groups have conflicting aims—i.e. when one can achieve its ends only at the expense of the other —their members will become hostile to each other even though the groups are composed of normal well-adjusted individuals. There is a corollary to this assumption which we shall consider later. To produce friction between the groups of boys we arranged a tournament of games: baseball, touch football, a tug-of-war, a treasure hunt, and so on. The tournament started in a spirit of good sportsmanship. But as it progressed good feeling soon evaporated. The members of each group began to call their rivals "stinkers," "sneaks," and "cheaters." They refused to have anything more to do with individuals in the opposing group. The boys in the 1949 camp turned against buddies whom they had chosen as "best friends" when they first arrived at the camp. A large proportion of the boys in each group gave negative ratings to all the boys in the other. The rival groups made threatening posters and planned raids, collecting secret hoards of green apples for ammunition. In the Robber's Cave camp the Eagles, after a defeat in a tournament game, burned a banner left behind by the Rattlers;

the next morning the Rattlers seized the Eagles' flag when they arrived on the athletic field. From that time on name-calling, scuffles, and raids were the rule of the day.

Within each group, of course, solidarity increased. There were changes: One group deposed its leader because he could not "take it" in the contests with the adversary; another group overnight made something of a hero of a big boy who had previously been regarded as a bully. But morale and cooperativeness within the group became stronger. It is noteworthy that this heightening of cooperativeness and generally democratic behavior did not carry over to the group's relations with other groups.

We now turned to the other side of the problem: How can two groups in conflict be brought into harmony? We first undertook to test the theory that pleasant social contacts between members of conflicting groups will reduce friction between them. In the 1954 camp we brought the hostile Rattlers and Eagles together for social events: going to the movies, eating in the same dining room, and so on. But far from reducing conflict, these situations only served as opportunities for the rival groups to berate and attack each other. In the dining hall line they shoved each other aside, and the group that lost the contest for the head of the line shouted "Ladies first!" at the winner. They threw paper, food, and vile names at each other at the tables. An Eagle bumped by a Rattler was admonished by his fellow Eagles to brush "the dirt" off his clothes.

We then returned to the corollary of our assumption about the creation of conflict. Just as competition generates friction, working in a common endeavor should promote harmony. It seemed to us, considering group relations in the everyday world, that where harmony between groups is established, the most decisive factor is the existence of "superordinate" goals which have a compelling appeal for both but which neither could achieve without the other. To test this hypothesis experimentally, we created a series of urgent, and natural, situations which challenged our boys.

One was a breakdown in the water supply. Water came to our camp in pipes from a tank about a mile away. We arranged to interrupt it and then called the boys together to inform them of the crisis. Both groups promptly volunteered to search the water line for the trouble. They worked together harmoniously, and before the end of the afternoon they had located and corrected the difficulty.

A similar opportunity offered itself when the boys requested a movie. We told them that the camp could not afford to rent one. The two groups then got together, figured out how much each group would have to contribute, chose the film by a vote, and enjoyed the showing together.

One day the two groups went on an outing at a lake some distance away. A large truck was to go to town for food. But when everyone was hungry and ready to eat, it developed that the truck would not start (we had taken care of that). The boys got a rope—the same rope they had used in their acrimonious tug-of-war—and all pulled together to start the truck.

These joint efforts did not immediately dispel hostility. At first the groups returned to the old bickering and name-calling as soon as the job in hand was finished. But gradually the series of cooperative acts reduced friction and conflict. The members of the two groups began to feel more friendly to each other. For example, a Rattler whom the Eagles disliked for his sharp tongue and skill in defeating them became a "good egg." The boys stopped shoving in the meal line. They no longer called each other names, and sat together at the table. New friendships developed between individuals in the two groups.

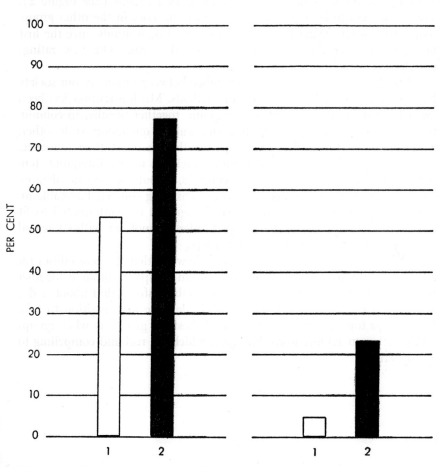

Fig. 3–4. *Negative ratings of each group by the other were common during the period of conflict (left) but decreased when harmony was restored (right). The graphs show per cent who thought that all (rather than some or none) of the other group were cheaters, sneaks, etc.*

In the end the groups were actively seeking opportunities to mingle, to entertain, and to "treat" each other. They decided to hold a joint campfire. They took turns presenting skits and songs. Members of both groups requested that they go home together on the same bus, rather than on the separate buses in which they had come. On the way the bus stopped for refreshments. One group still had five dollars which they had won as a prize in a contest. They decided to spend this sum on refreshments. On their own initiative they invited their former rivals to be their guests for malted milks.

Our interviews with the boys confirmed this change. From choosing their "best friends" almost exclusively in their own group, many of them shifted to listing boys in the other group as best friends (See Figure 2). They were glad to have a second chance to rate boys in the other group, some of them remarking that they had changed their minds since the first rating made after the tournament. Indeed they had. The new ratings were largely favorable (See Figure 4).

Efforts to reduce friction and prejudice between groups in our society have usually followed rather different methods. Much attention has been given to bringing members of hostile groups together socially, to communicating accurate and favorable information about one group to the other, and to bringing the leaders of groups together to enlist their influence. But as everyone knows, such measures sometimes reduce intergroup tensions and sometimes do not. Social contacts, as our experiments demonstrated, may only serve as occasions for intensifying conflict. Favorable information about a disliked group may be ignored or reinterpreted to fit stereotyped notions about the group. Leaders cannot act without regard for the prevailing temper in their own groups.

What our limited experiments have shown is that the possibilities for achieving harmony are greatly enhanced when groups are brought together to work toward common ends. Then favorable information about a disliked group is seen in a new light, and leaders are in a position to take bolder steps toward cooperation. In short, hostility gives way when groups pull together to achieve overriding goals which are real and compelling to all concerned.

4

STATUS AND CONFORMITY
TO PRESSURES
IN INFORMAL GROUPS

O. J. Harvey
Conrad Consalvi

The primary focus of this study was on the differential reactions of the leader, the second ranking member, and the lowest status member of an informal group to pressures from other members of the group. The reciprocal side of this question, the differential influence of members in these three status positions on the evaluations of the other members, was also investigated together with the relative weight of each in determining the group norm.

A member's striving to gain and maintain status in one of his more important reference groups should be among the key determinants of his conformity to conflicting group judgments. The higher his motivation to attain these ends, and hence the greater his dependency on the group for motive satisfaction, the greater should be his susceptibility to group influence. This possibility assumes the status system of the group to be sufficiently open that a member perceives as real the possibility of either moving up the status hierarchy or of being displaced from his present station by other aspirants to his position. Viewed this way, the central question of this study becomes that of whether or not the three selected status occupants are differentially motivated to improve and maintain their positions in their reference group. These three members were selected as the main figures of the study because there exist plausible reasons for attributing greatest striving and conformity to each of them.

The hypothesis that motivation is a simple function of the magnitude

Reprinted from *Journal of Abnormal and Social Psychology*, Vol. 60, No. 2, 1960, pp. 182-187.

of distance from the goal would favor the possibility of greatest striving and conformity on the part of the lowest status man, in line with results of Fenchel, Monderer, and Hartley[1] in their test of Benoit-Smullyan's[2] status equilibration hypothesis. In their study, the reference groups in which subjects displayed the greatest status striving were those in which they perceived their status as lowest. And yet, the very remoteness of the lowest status man from the top position might result in his being less motivated to move up the status ladder and consequently less sensitive to group pressures, especially if his position were a secure one. If, on the other hand, his position is a tenuous one, and if, as Thrasher[3] long ago averred, ". . . any status in the group is better than none . . . ," then the lowest status man might manifest greatest conformity, since any further status loss would jeopardize his membership in the group.

The second ranking person could prove to be the member on whom the goal of the top position exercises greatest motivational pull. Studies relating to goal gradient, level of aspiration, and class mobility seem consistent with this possibility, as is William James' observation on ". . . the paradox of a man shamed to death because he is only the second pugilist or the second oarsman in the world. That he is able to beat the whole population of the globe minus one is nothing; he has 'pitted' himself to beat that one; and as long as he doesn't do that nothing else counts." [4]

The findings of Dittes and Kelley[5] suggest the greatest conformity for the second status man, if the degree of one's perceived acceptance in a group can be assumed to relate highly to his status in the group. These authors found the highest incidence of conformity to group evaluations to occur among those individuals who had been led to believe that their degree of acceptance by the other members was average, which in this case was next to the highest of the four degrees of induced acceptance.

The leader's behavior should be less affected by striving for the top position than that of either of the other two status members by virtue of his having attained that goal. To the extent that conformity relates to striving for the goal, his need for conforming behavior should be at a minimum. The attainment of the top position, however, exposes the leader to pressures from a new source, that of maintaining his leadership status. If his position is secure, the leader can perhaps afford to deviate further from the behavior of the other members[6]; but if insecure in his position, the leader might be the most conforming to pressures from the group because of the greater psychological distance he could fall if displaced from the top of the hierarchy.

The studies of Sundby[7] and Harvey and Rutherford[8] also bear on this problem. Higher status members were found to be more yielding than those of lower status to majority opinion when the issue involved was relevant to the group.[9] But higher status persons were less influenced by devi-

ant evaluations of other high status members on an issue of minor significance to the group.[10] However, in neither of these studies were leaders'
responses separated in the analyses from those of other higher ranking
members.

The differential influence of the leader, the second ranking member,
and the lowest status member in both the formation and the change of
group norms was also investigated. The results of studies concerned with
the importance of status to source effectiveness, in the informal group[11]
and in larger social units[12] led to the simple assumption that the relative influence exerted in both these instances would follow the status positions
directly. The design of the study was not ideally suited, however, for answering the latter questions.

METHOD

Subjects

Twenty-seven informal cliques (122 Ss in all) were selected sociometrically from a state training school for delinquent boys. Nine groups,
each with an average of 4-5 members, served in each of three conditions of
source influence. Each group served only in one source condition.

Cliques in the training school were selected for study because of the
assumption that status within them was very important to the members
and that the resulting pressures against the deviant would be pronounced.
The cliques were ascertained by a four-item sociometric questionnaire
which asked for preferences from among all the boys in the school as team-
mates and as team captains for a baseball team and for the team in which
they preferred to perform the experimental task. Only the responses on
the two items having to do with preferred captains or leaders were considered in determining status within the group.

Task and Apparatus

The experimental task was the judgment of the distance between two
simultaneous flashes of light in a completely dark room. Two sets of such
stimuli were used for each group. The leader or the second or the lowest
ranking member (*source*) was exposed at appropriate stages to one set of
stimuli while the remaining members of the group (*members*) were being
presented with the other pair of light flashes. In all conditions, the distance
between the stimulus lights was 12 in. for the members, while for the source
the distance between the lights was either 12 or 48 in., depending on the
condition. Unknown to the Ss, a partition separated the two sets of stimulus lights so that the source and members could be exposed to different
stimuli while assuming they were seeing the identical stimulus. The use
of the partition avoided the need for collaborators, thus leaving Ss free to
interact naturally and to impose the pressures normally applied in their

particular group. Special caution was exercised by E throughout the experiment to prevent Ss' bumping into the partition and becoming suspicious of the procedure of the study.

Activation of the lights was controlled by circuits in two Hunter Decade Interval Timers. The two lights, on the same circuit, flashed on and off at the same time. Exposure time was .4 sec. and the time between trials was either 15 or 30 secs., 15 secs. for private and 30 secs. for public judgments.

Procedure

The sociometric questionnaire was administered in the boys' own dormitory approximately two weeks before the selected groups participated in the experiment. The questionnaire was introduced with the explanation that its purpose was to pick groups of friends who would like to participate in a forthcoming experiment. The experiment was described as a study being sponsored by the Navy and concerned with the visual accuracy of individuals working in small groups in complete darkness. Cash prizes were promised for the three groups that made the most accurate judgments on the experimental task. The cash awards promised for the first, second, and third most accurate groups were six, four, and two dollars, respectively, for each person in the group. It was emphasized that the scores would be based upon judgments of the entire group so that no single individual could win a prize without his whole group having won. The offer of cash awards and emphasis upon the group as the winner was intended to increase the likelihood that the boys would take the study seriously, make careful selections in the sociometric choices, and hence be more prone to apply group pressures against persons who made deviant judgments in the subsequent experimental situation.

The conditions according to which the cash prizes would be awarded were re-emphasized to each group as it came to take part in the experiment. Prior to going into the experimental room, each person within a group was assigned a number that represented the order in which judgments of the light distance were to be called out. The source, one of the three selected status occupants, was always assigned the highest number so his judgment would be made last. Ss were then led into the experimental room, a large room in one of the dormitories, and seated in the reverse order. The source, always seated first, was placed on one side of the partition and the members were seated on the other side of the partition so that neither could see the stimulus lights of the other.

Ss were then instructed that their task was simply to judge the distance between the two flashes of light. The source and members, after being advised correctly of the 12-ft. distance between them and the lights, were then presented the 12-in. stimulus lights and told the actual distance between them in order to reduce further the intersubject variability in scales of judgment. To prevent the sample presentation from stereotyping the Ss' responses, E pointed out that the pairs of lights that were to follow might all be the same distance apart, or no two pairs might be the same.

The procedure from here on was divided into three phases:

1. This phase was concerned with the *differential contribution* of the highest, middle, and lowest status members to the formation of a group norm. The aim was to have each person first reach an individual standardization in his judgments of the stimulus and then have a group norm formed in which these personal norms would be differentially reflected. To form the personal norm all Ss were presented the same stimulus, the light flashes of 12-in. distance, for 20 trials with a time interval of 15 secs. between trials. In this stage Ss recorded their own judgments on small pads without knowledge of any other member's judgment. The group norm was formed by presenting the same stimulus for 10 more trials with only one judgment acceptable to all members allowed for each trial and with an interval of 30 secs. between trials for discussion and joint decision. A score of zero, represented to the Ss as harmful to their chances of winning a prize, was recorded if a group decision was not reached within the 30-sec. period. Group pressures consequently were applied to the point that a zero score rarely occurred, and when it did it was always only for the first trial.

2. This was the phase critical to the main problem. It was concerned with the extent to which the occupants of the selected status positions would deviate from the judgments of the other members; and if there was deviation, with the differential influence of the three sources on shift in judgments by the other members. This objective was approached in two steps. To provide a control measure for both source and members for the subsequent influence situation, all Ss once again made 20 private judgments of the presented stimuli, which they recorded without discussion. In this block of trials, however, the source and members were presented different stimuli. The source was exposed to the pair of lights 48 in. apart from one side of the partition, while from the other side the members continued to be presented with the 12-in. stimulus lights. Following the 20 private judgments, the same stimuli were judged for 20 more trials under influence conditions in which, instead of being forced to reach a common group norm, each S gave his own judgment aloud after each trial. An interval of 30 secs. between trials allowed enough time for Ss to give their judgments of what they assumed erroneously to be a common stimulus and to register their reaction of approval or disapproval of the evaluations of the others.

3. This last phase was concerned with the *continuation* of the effects of social influence in a situation free of external pressures, or in current terminology, the correspondence between *public* and *private* conformity.

For this purpose, the source and other members rendered 10 private judgments of the same stimuli that they had judged publicly in the preceding phase.

One E remained in the experimental room with the Ss during the experiment, while a second E, seated in an adjoining room, controlled the presentation of the stimuli.

RESULTS

Differential Influence of Status in Formation of Group Norm

This result was determined by subtracting the personal norm of the leader and of the second and lowest status members in each group, represented by the mean of his first 20 private judgments of the 12-in. stimulus, from the group norm, represented by the mean of the 20 unanimous judgments of the same stimulus by the entire group. The assumption was that the smaller the difference the greater the weight of the respective source judgments in forming the group norm. Results in Table 1 show the

Table 4–1   Difference between the Personal Norm of Leader, Second Ranking, and Lowest Status Member and Subsequent Group Norm for the 12-In. Stimulus

Status[a]	Group Norm— Source's Personal Norm	Comparison of Differences		
			Diff.	t	P
Leader	3.67	Leader-Second	1.04	1.28	> .20
Second	4.71	Leader-Lowest	1.57	1.39	> .10
Lowest	5.24	Second-Lowest	.45	.30	> .60

[a] N = 27 for each of the three sources, a source of each status from each of the total 27 groups which were combined in this comparison.

Table 4–2   Sources' Mean Judgments of the 48-In. Stimulus before and during Members' Influence

Source[a]	Before Influence	During Influence	Diff.	Comparison of Differences		
					Diff.	t	P
Leader	47.70	32.08	15.62	Leader-Second	− 23.53	3.21	< .01
Second	56.67	17.52	39.15	Leader-Lowest	− 4.02	.58	> .50
Lowest	46.87	27.20	19.68	Lowest-Second	− 19.47	22.94	< .001

[a] N = 9 for each of the three sources, one source from each of the nine groups in each of the three experimental conditions.

Table 4–3   Sources' Mean Judgments of the 48-In. Stimulus during and after Members' Influence

	During Influence	After Influence	Diff.	Comparison of Differences			
Source[a]					Diff.	t	P
Leader	32.08	40.53	8.45	Leader-Second	1.11	.14	> .50
Second	17.52	24.86	7.34	Leader-Lowest	− 1.23	.16	> .50
Lowest	27.20	36.88	9.68	Lowest-Second	2.34	.37	> .50

[a] $N = 9$ for each of the three sources, one source from each of the nine groups in each of the three experimental conditions.

difference to have been smaller, but not significantly so, the higher the status of the source.* Thus, while the data suggest that contribution to norm formation may be a positive function of status, the lack of statistical significance does not permit the difference in subsequent conformity to group pressures to be attributed to the differential weight of different status members in the initial formation of the norm, as some have supposed.

Differential Conformity of the Three Sources

Conformity of sources' to members' judgments was measured by the difference between the sources' mean judgments of the 48-in. stimulus before and during the phase that public judgments of the 12-in. lights were being made by the members. Results in Table 2 show the second ranking source to have been influenced significantly more by members' judgments than was either the leader or lowest status member. The leader was least influenced, but not significantly less than the lowest status source.

Conformity of Sources in the Private Situation Following Members' Influence

It can be inferred from Table 3 that the influence exerted by the members on sources' evaluations continued even when the external pressures were removed. The three sources tended to shift their judgments of the 48-in. stimulus toward the veridical when judging it in private, but none did so significantly nor to an extent significantly different from the others.

Differential Effects of Sources on Members' Judgments

The fact that the three sources differed in the extent to which their judgments deviated from the members' necessitated an analysis of member change in terms of proportions rather than absolute magnitudes: the ratio of member change to the amount of change advocated by the source. The

* All t tests reported in this study are based on the formula for correlated samples. See J. E. Wert, C. O. Neidt, and J. S. Ahmann, *Statistical Methods in Educational and Psychological Research* (New York: Appleton-Century-Crofts, 1954), p. 141.

change in each member's judgment of the 12-in. stimulus from the second private to the immediately subsequent influence condition was divided by the difference between the mean of that member's judgment of the 12-in. stimulus in the second private condition and the mean of the source's judgment of the 48-in. stimulus during influence.

In Table 4 is presented a comparison of the relative effectiveness of the somewhat discrepant evaluations of the three sources in changing members' judgments. The higher the status of the source the greater his proportionate influence on members' judgments, although the only significant difference in source effectiveness was between the leader and lowest ranking member $(t = 2.01; P < .05)$.

Latent Source Effects Following Influence

In Table 5 are presented data concerning changes in members' judgments of the 12-in. stimulus in the third private condition, the condition that followed the members' experience of the more discrepant evaluations by the source. The leader's influence on members' judgments increased when the members were removed from the restraints of the public condi-

Table 4–4   Effects of Discrepant Source Evaluations on Changing Members' Judgments of the 12-In. Stimulus

Source Condition	Members N	Mean Source Discrepancy	Mean Member Change	Member Change: Source Deviation
Leader	31	10.20	1.53	.15
Second	34	4.65	.35	.08
Lowest	30	6.63	−3.50	−.53

Table 4–5   Latent Effects of Sources on Members' Private Judgments Following Public Influence

Status of Source	Members N	Mean Change		Mean Diff.	t	P
Leader	31	1.27	Leader-Second	1.51	2.01	< .05
Second	34	−.24	Leader-Lowest	1.72	2.12	< .05
Lowest	30	−.45	Lowest-Second	−.21	.38	> .50

tion, whereas the influence of the other two sources was less in the private than in the preceding public condition. The second-order difference between measures of differential leader influence on members' judgments under conditions of private vs. public judgment, on the one hand, and corresponding measures of differential influence by the second and lowest ranking sources, on the other, was statistically significant, but the difference between the latent effects of the latter sources was not significant.

DISCUSSION

The most important of the foregoing results is probably the demonstration of greatest conformity to group pressures on the part of the second ranking persons, those only one step removed from the leadership position. This finding is compatible with goal gradient theory and the concept of relative deprivation, both of which underlie certain phenomena of level of aspiration, including greater status strivings and conformity of members of the middle class.

The failure of the study to show any clear-cut differences in the influence of the highest, second, and lowest status members in the formation and change of group judgments could well be due to the small size of the sample and to limitations of the experimental design inherent in the focus of the study. An adequate test of the effects of different sources would require their judgments to be made at a controlled and constant distance from the judgments of the other members, a requirement not met in this study because of the differential effects of the group on the sources.

The tendency for the three sources to continue to give decreased judgments after removal of external group pressures suggests that the changes in sources' judgment were due to something other than just public yielding to group pressure, a point similarly illustrated in Sherif's[13] early experiment. Such change might be unwitting, or the interesting possibility exists that, even though a person may have knowingly modified his judgments to agree with another's, pride may not allow him to switch back immediately to his initial evaluation even when he is free to do so.

An unpredicted but not surprising finding was the tendency for the effects of leaders on members' judgments to increase when the latter were rendered subsequently in private conditions in which the restraints of public surveillance were lessened.

SUMMARY

This study was concerned primarily with the differential conformity of the leader, the second ranking member and the lowest ranking member to pressures in the informal group. The informal groups were 27 cliques sociometrically selected from a training school for delinquent boys.

Under the incentive of a financial reward for the group most accurate in the experimental task, members of each group judged the distance between two simultaneous flashes of light in a dark room. While the other members were judging the distance between two flashes of light 12 inches apart, the leader (or second ranking or lowest status members, depending on the experimental condition) estimated the distance between two flashes of light 48 inches apart, which unknown to the Ss were separated from the other lights by a partition. In this condition, under the assumption all were seeing the same lights, Ss made their judgments aloud and brought verbal pressures against the person who rendered the deviant judgments.

The main finding of the study was that the second status member, the one only one step from the top, was significantly more conforming to judgments of the other members than was either the leader or lowest status man. The leader was least conforming, but not reliably less than the lowest status person.

REFERENCES

1. G. H. Fenchel, J. H. Monderer, and E. L. Hartley, "Subjective Status and the Equilibration Hypothesis," *J. Abnorm. Soc. Psychol.*, 46:476-479, 1951.
2. E. Benoit-Smullyan, "Status, Status Types and Status Inter-relations," *Am. Socio. Rev.*, 9:151-161, 1944.
3. F. M. Thrasher, *The Gang* (Chicago: University of Chicago Press, 1927), p. 332.
4. M. Knight (*ed.*), *William James* (London: Pelican Books, 1950), pp. 103-104.
5. J. E. Dittes and H. H. Kelley, "Effects of Different Conditions of Acceptance Upon Conformity to Group Norms," *J. Abnorm. Soc. Psychol.*, 53:100-107, 1956.
6. H. H. Kelley, "Communication in Experimentally Created Hierarchies," *Hum. Relat.*, 4:39-56, 1951.
7. E. Sundby, Unpublished doctoral study, Vanderbilt University, 1959.
8. O. J. Harvey and Jeanne Rutherford, "Relationship of Status in the Informal Group to Influence and Influencibility," *Child Developm.*, 31:377-385, 1960.
9. Sundby, *op. cit.*
10. Harvey and Rutherford, *op. cit.*
11. *Ibid.*
12. C. L. Hovland, I. Janis, and H. H. Kelley, *Communication and Persuasion* (New Haven: Yale University Press, 1953).
13. M. Sherif, "A Study of Some Social Factors in Perception," *Arch. Psychol.*, No. 187, 1935.

OVERVIEW OF BION'S THEORETICAL CONCEPTS

- 5 -

EMOTIONAL DYNAMICS
AND GROUP CULTURE

Dorothy Stock
Herbert A. Thelen

The theoretical position described here is the product of a series of investigations into the functioning of small groups carried on at the Human Dynamics Laboratory of the University of Chicago during the years 1947 to 1955. Under the direction of Herbert A. Thelen a number of investigators conducted studies on group issues as composition, subgroup formation, developmental phases, sociometric choice, group culture, and individual learning and change.[1] Much effort was devoted to developing appropriate methodology for studying sequential group interaction, group-relevant aspects of personality, and member perceptions of self and others.[2] Especially composed work-groups and training-groups were utilized as settings for the research.[3]

In the course of its work the research team became interested in the theoretical writings of W. R. Bion, which seemed to fit its thinking about group interaction as a functional process, about the relevance of cognitive and emotional factors in group life, and about relationships between individual personality and group culture. Thus, at about 1950 or 1951, research became focused around attempts to understand various aspects of group functioning in terms of this theoretical approach. As substantive findings accumulated and progress was made on methodological issues, a theoretical position emerged which was based heavily on Bion's work, but included some modifications and extensions.

This chapter presents, first, an overview of Bion's theoretical approach, and then discusses implications for individual behavior and per-

Reprinted from *Emotional Dynamics and Group Culture* by Dorothy Stock and Herbert A. Thelen, No. 2 of the Research Training Series, National Training Laboratories, Division of Adult Education Service, National Education Association of the United States, Washington, D.C. (New York: New York University Press, 1958).

sonality, sociometric choice and subgroup operation, group composition, group development, and individual change.

OVERVIEW OF BION'S THEORETICAL CONCEPTS

W. R. Bion[4] dealt with small groups of neurotic patients. As therapist, he provided the group with no direction or structure. The patients' reactions to this lack of structure constituted the initial material for therapy. As the group moved along, its content might derive from personal experiences of members or from group events, including members' feelings about the therapist or one another. The therapist's interpretations focused on two kinds of phenomena: the group's mood and individual members' reactions to the group situation. For example, Bion might indicate to the group that the members were banding together to misunderstand his comments or that Member X wanted to speak but felt he would be rejected by the rest of the group if he did so. One has the impression, from his articles, that Bion interpreted to the group its emotional state immediately as he became aware of it. The two major and perhaps distinguishing characteristics of Bion's approach as therapist are thus (1) an emphasis on the interpretation of group rather than individual phenomena and (2) a rather immediate interpretation of the group situation to the group.

As Bion observed his groups of patients, he noticed certain massive emotional reactions in the group. At times, for example, the group appeared to be *unanimously* expressing a need to run away from the group situation or to demand that the therapist provide more direction. From this kind of observation Bion developed the idea that a group could be thought of in terms of a series of emotional states or basic assumption cultures in which some affective need was inextricably associated with the work the group was trying to do. He saw individuals as contributing toward, acquiescing in, or reacting against, these cultures. Members also formed relationships with one another on the basis of their affinities for the various cultures. The particular relationship between the individual and the culture is accounted for by what Bion called "valency."

These two concepts—the basic assumption culture and valency—are fundamental in this theoretical approach. The first pertains to the situation in the group as a whole; the second refers to the individual member and his tendencies toward interaction in the total group.

In developing his concept of the basic assumption culture, Bion perceived that work and emotional components of group life are so interrelated that one never occurs without the other and that an understanding of group experience can come about only when both are studied in their dynamic and changing relationships to each other. The work aspects of group operation are the consciously determined, deliberative, reality-bound, goal-seeking aspects of the group's activities. While task activity can always be perceived in the group, there are times when an analysis of this kind of activity alone cannot explain what is happening. At times, for example, although the group may say it is interested in solving some problem, all its behavior seems to lead it farther and farther away from coming to grips with it. Or a group may seem to engage in apparently illogical activity, which becomes understandable only if one sees that it is preoccupied with (for example) its relation to its leader. As a result of this kind of observation, Bion came to see that the work activity of a group is always influenced to some extent by certain emotional states or concerns. In contrast to work, the emotional preoccupations of the group are nonpurposive, "instinctual," and not under conscious control. He felt that the emotional aspect of group operation could be described in terms of three rather comprehensively defined emotional states, which he called "cultures." These are dependency, pairing, and fight-flight. That is, a group can be described at any given time as operating in a work-dependency culture, a work-pairing culture, a work-fight-flight culture, or as being in some transitional phase. In each case the work aspects of the group's activities are suffused and influenced by the emotional state or concern.

In defining these group cultures, Bion[4] says that when the group is operating in a dependency-work culture it is acting "as if" (that is, on the basic assumption that) the group exists in order to find support and direction from something outside itself—the leader, external standards, or its own history. When it is operating in pairing-work it acts "as if" its function is to find strength from within its own peer group. When it is operating in fight-flight-work it is operating "as if" its purpose is to avoid something by fighting or running away from it. The "as if's" in these definitions are important, since they indicate what Bion does *not* mean when he describes a group as operating in a certain work-emotionality culture. He does not mean that when a group is operating in dependency-work, for example, nothing but dependency is expressed, or that the group is consciously aware of its preoccupation with dependency, or that the dependency can necessarily be directly observed. What he does mean is that if one makes the assumption that the group is acting as if it needs support and direction from something outside itself, then the diverse and apparently illogical and contradictory behaviors of the members of the group can be understood and will take on a certain coherence and order.

The concept of group culture is one that is applied globally to the total group process. It provides a means for understanding such problems as climate, group development, and overt and covert aspects of group functioning. It illuminates aspects of group operation that refer to the group as a whole rather than those involving the individual member.

Bion developed the concept of "valency" to pertain particularly to the relation between the individual and the group culture. He defines valency as ". . . a capacity for instantaneous and involuntary combination of one individual with another for sharing and acting on a basic assumption." [5] Thus valency is an inherent property of the individual that accounts for the nature of his participation in the emotional aspects of group life. It refers to the particular way in which the individual interacts with the group culture and appears to involve two interrelated aspects: expressive behavior and combining with others. Expressive behavior refers to the kind of affect the individual is most likely to express behaviorally in the group.

By "combining with others" Bion means the capacity of individuals to support or cooperate with others in developing, maintaining, or moving away from the various work-emotionality cultures. He uses the possibly obscure term "combining" because he does not want to imply that such activity is at all purposive, conscious, or planned in character. That is, the individual contributions to the affectual aspects of the group's life are in keeping with the nature of emotionality in the total group and are also essentially nonpurposive in character. Taken together, the two concepts of group culture and valency form a theoretical frame within which many problems of group operation can be described and studied.

INDIVIDUAL BEHAVIOR AND PERSONALITY

In his original formulation, Bion suggested that at any given time the group-as-a-whole acts as if it were operating on one of three basic assumptions: that it will maintain itself through developing intimacy (pairing), through reliance on external authority (dependency), or through fighting or fleeing from stress (fight-flight). During each phase members can be seen either as accepting and expressing the basic assumption or as reacting in some other way to its existence in the culture of the group. It was supposed that these individual ways of reacting to the various basic assumptions operating in the group culture might reveal basic tendencies in personality. Thus, when the group appeared to have the purpose of establishing dependency on the leader, one individual might respond with hostility (fight) and another with efforts to deepen his relationships to other individuals (pairing). Thus the question arose as to whether these basic assumption categories of modalities, meaningful for studying the group as a whole, might also be applicable to individual behavior.

Successful characterization of individual behavior in these terms should permit one to describe the individual's over-all pattern of behavior expected in group situations and to identify the way in which the individual would behave when the group was in different kinds of emotional or basic assumption situations. It should open the way to description of such roles as spokesmen for the various emotionality cultures and to identification of specific ways in which individuals respond affectively to the group situation. In short, it should help to identify the particular ways in which each group member would contribute to the development, maintenance, and dissolution of a variety of work-emotion cultures of the group.

We assume that the actual behavior observable in a group is a product of an individual's "valency pattern" plus the character of the group situation in which he finds himself. The concept of valency implies that each individual has differentiated preferences for participating with others who express the various emotional modalities and that he himself has predispositions to express these modalities in overt action. These differentiated preferences would constitute the individual's valency pattern and would throw light on his expressive behavior and his relationships with other members.

In its most simple terms, an individual who has a strong valency for fight tends to express hostility freely in the group; a strong valency for pairing indicates a tendency to express warmth freely and to wish to establish close relationships with others; a strong valency for dependency indicates a tendency to rely on others for support and direction; and a strong valency for flight indicates a tendency to avoid, in some way, the interactive situation. Every person possesses some valency, in varying degrees, for each of these emotional modalities. Such tendencies reside in the individual and form part of an habitual or stable approach to group interaction.

In applying this idea of valency pattern to a characterization of a specific individual, we find that valencies for fight, flight, pairing, and dependency are often very complexly related. (For example, an individual may pair in order to satisfy dependency needs; or he may take refuge in flight because he is so concerned about his own impulses to fight.) In order to help deal with these complexities it has seemed to us that valency—as an organized set of emotional predispositions residing in the individual—can profitably be differentiated into three related but distinguishable elements: area of concern, culture preference, and affective approach.

Area of concern is the most basic of these, yet it is most elusive and most difficult to observe directly. By area of concern we mean an affect-laden problem that, on some internal, possibly unconscious, level is felt to be significant by the individual and mobilizes his psychic energies. For example, a certain group member may be particularly sensitive to problems concerning dependency—any problem of relating to an authority figure lies within this area of concern. Another member's particular sensitivities may lie in the area of pairing—establishing close relationships with others; another may be concerned with handling his own hostility. Additional areas of concern may be important for other members. Clues to these basic or underlying concerns *may* be found in the person's behavior—either directly or as a break in his more typical pattern. But oftentimes the underlying concern is so deeply hidden or so well defended that behavioral clues are obscured. For the moment, however, let us assume that such areas of concern do exist for many individuals. In some cases they correspond somewhat to the emotional categories we have used in defining the group culture; in other cases these concerns either emphasize some one aspect of these emotionalities, cut across our categories, or fall outside them entirely.

Culture preference refers to the fact that a group member seems to prefer certain work-emotionality cultures to others. This preference may be indicated in a number of ways. He is more comfortable, more free, more relevant, more spontaneously and less compulsively active, more able to work in certain specific group-cultural environments. Some persons may express this preference directly ("I don't like it when everyone is fighting." "Why do we always have to ask the leader what to do next?"); while in other cases the preference must be inferred. The individual may or may not be aware of his own preferences.

Affective approach refers to the ways in which the individual responds expressively to the various group cultures: that is, the ways in which he behaves and does not behave. To illustrate: A certain individual may typically express fight more readily than any other affect, but when the group as a whole is in a dependency culture, he is likely to flight. He may find it easiest to express warmth toward individuals who are themselves rather withdrawn. Such a pattern can become complex, but when it is thoroughly defined for an individual it can provide a comprehensive picture of his affective approach under a variety of conditions in the group.

These three aspects of total valency pattern may, for different individuals, be related to each other in a variety of ways. For some persons the same emotionality may be dominant in all three aspects. For example, the area of concern may be dependency—that is, the individual is most alerted to dependency conditions. He is ambivalent and anxious about accepting or rejecting dependency, and he puts proportionately more of his energies into this area. At the same time he is most comfortable when the group as a whole is in a dependency state—that is, when the responsibility for group activity lies in the leader or in some external element. His habitual approach to interaction is one of appeal—a need for external limitation and goal-setting, willingness to comply with the wishes of others, and so on. This kind of uniformity is rare. Usually area of concern involves more conflict than this would imply, and the other two aspects of valency pattern are likely to be organized at least partially as a defense. There always will be a relationship among the three, such that each becomes understandable in terms of the others, but the particular relationship will be unique for each person. The total pattern may vary in the specificity of the area of concern, the extent of conflict, the character and degree of organization of the defense, and the person's awareness of his own pattern.

It should be pointed out that delineating a group member's valency pattern does not provide a complete picture of the individual's personality structure. It does, however, define in an organized way aspects of personality particularly relevant to behavior in groups.[6]

SOCIOMETRIC CHOICE AND SUBGROUP OPERATION

In addition to its relevance for individual personality, the concept of valency suggests a basis for understanding the positive and negative feelings group members develop about one another and subgroup interaction within the total group.

If an individual perceives another member as having similar needs and interests and as working toward establishing group conditions congenial to him, he is likely to feel friendly toward that person. If, on the other hand, he perceives someone else as interfering with his interests in the group and as working to establish group conditions that he finds uncongenial, he is likely to dislike that person. To illustrate: An individual who characteristically withdraws from close personal contact with others is likely to prefer others with similar needs, since these members together can meet one another's needs in this respect. The same person is likely to reject those members who are constantly urging the group to become more intimate and reveal more personal material, since these are the members who are, in effect, forcing him to enter into a kind of relationship distasteful to him.

To translate this common-sense illustration into our theoretical terms, we would say that this flight member (who flees intimacy) is likely to prefer other flight members and to reject pairing members. It is possible to imagine other flight members who might reject flight persons as well as pairing persons. This might happen, for example, when the member is so disturbed or conflicted about his own flight needs that he is equally threatened by members who wish to escape close contact with others, since these would keep his conflict in the foreground. Counterdependency members might be expected to reject (rather than accept) one another, since each member can satisfy his own needs to control the group only by competing against others with similar needs.

Several studies were conducted which taken together suggest some of the dynamic bases of sociometric choice.[7] For example, certain affective approach types do not simply or necessarily make choices among their own membership; nor do they necessarily choose specific other types. Whether a member's active participation is elicited by conditions of warmth and friendliness or by conditions of conflict influences his participation or nonparticipation with the persons he chooses sociometrically. Choice is influenced *both* by considerations of who will provide support in creating a need-satisfying milieu *and* by considerations of who can help support or maintain defensive needs. Total group composition and emotional state are also influencing factors, since preoccupations of the group as a whole may focus the attention of members on certain individuals.

Our current hypothesis is that group composition has a limiting or focusing influence on the choices made, but that within this context individual valency characteristics are operative.

A related assumption is that individuals with similar needs form a special kind of subgroup within the total group. That is, individuals who have in common a need (let us say) for fight are likely to act together to establish conditions in the group that will permit hostile interchanges, aggressive approaches to problem solving, and so on. Or, to state this more generally, a group can be seen as being made up of a limited number of subgroups, each of which shares certain need characteristics and may act together to establish group conditions which are congenial, comfortable, and nonthreatening.

When the members of a subtype are described as "acting together" we do not mean that they *consciously* cooperate or that they are necessarily aware of common needs. We simply mean that because they do share certain needs they can be expected (at least under interactive conditions) to express similar attitudes and to attempt to influence the group toward similar emotionality-work states.

When groups are viewed as an interacting collection of subtypes they may be seen to vary in several ways: A group might be composed of subtypes whose needs are compatible or incompatible with one another. There may be much or little communality among the subtypes. Certain needs and approaches characteristic of a particular subtype may be present in one group and not in another. The designated leader may, by his personal characteristics, reinforce one subtype and not the others. A specific member may be part of the majority subtype in one group and isolated in another. These possibilities illustrate ways in which groups may be differentiated by knowledge of subtype composition. These and other conditions may be useful in accounting for the kinds of learning opportunities the group offers its members, the extent and nature of conflict in the group, and its course of development.[8]

VALENCY COMPOSITION AND GROUP PROBLEM-SOLVING

As is implied in the previous section, the concept of "individual valency pattern" seems to offer a profitable conceptual approach to group composition.

To illustrate: Suppose an individual is reluctant to become involved in a group's activities and, more particularly, tries to avoid involvement in disagreements and feels uncomfortable when others become involved. Clinical analysis shows that he has impulses to fight, but that he attempts to suppress them. Suppose further that this general approach to group interaction is habitual with this person. In our terminology, such a person would be described as having a strong valency for flight and a weak valency for fight. He would be expected to behave in certain ways in the group: When the group is fighting he may be one of the members who tries (possibly ineffectually) to urge the group toward some other mode of emotional expression. When the group is in flight he may take the lead and act to prolong the flight situation. He is likely to go along with others who express similar needs to avoid fight and express flight. Because these members support his own inclinations and needs he may feel more friendliness toward them than toward others.

A group in which most of the members can be described in this way will take on a certain character that is an expression of the interaction of members with strong valencies for flight. Groups composed differently with respect to the valency characteristics of the members can be expected to show different over-all characteristics that are, in turn, an expression of the interaction among the valency types included in *their* composition.

The valency pattern of an individual is likely to involve very intricate relationships between tendencies to act (affective approach), preferences for pairing, fight, flight, dependency, and work (culture preference), and area of concern. All three levels of valency are important to an understanding of a particular individual's interaction in a group. When discussing a collection of individuals, however, affective approach may be the most relevant. For purposes, then, of studying the group as a whole, each member can be generally characterized as having a predominant valency for expressing one or two of the modalities.

The possibility of describing each individual in valency terms makes it possible to consider the group-as-a-whole in terms of (1) the valency type or types predominantly represented in the group and/or (2) the range of valency types present in the group.

Let us now consider the kinds of information that can be deduced from knowledge of the two aspects of group valency composition indicated above.

1. Groups may differ with respect to the valency type preponderantly represented in the group composition. Depending on the dominant modality, groups should differ in the kind of work-emotionality culture they most often establish, in the way they operate within the various work-emotionality cultures, and in their characteristic attack on task problems. To make this a little more concrete, consider two groups: one having a preponderance of members who express fight readily and who act together to maintain a fight culture in the group; and one which can similarly be characterized as predominantly "pairing." We might expect such differences as the following to exist between these two groups:

a. The groups will differ in their efficiencies when dealing with any particular task problem. Each will be more efficient than the other with respect to different kinds of problems.

b. Both groups will be able to deal adequately with certain task problems but will show differences in the way they attack these problems.

c. The two groups will have different capabilities for dealing with "process" or interpersonal problems. In the second group, ambiguities in the limits to expression and/or management of hostility might never be dealt with, since when fight situations arise the pairing members will tend to move the group out of the fight modality.

d. Considering the individual member, a person with strong predispositions toward pairing will be somewhat isolated in the first group and find little support for his needs. The same will be true of a fight person in the second group.

e. The two groups will differ in the standards they develop with respect to the tolerance and encouragement of fight and pairing. In the first group the limits imposed on fight will be much broader than in the second group. The second group will show higher tolerance for pairing than will the first group.

One would not generally expect to find compositions in which *all* members show strong predispositions for fight or for dependency, etc. Yet it is not unusual for a group to tend toward a preponderance of one or another of the emotional modalities; and such a tendency will have a significant influence on the course of group operation.

2. Groups may differ with respect to the range of valency types included in their composition. A group whose composition includes a wide range of valency types would presumably be able to deal explicitly with a wide range of emotional issues. The theoretical rationale for this may be formulated as follows: An individual whose valency pattern leads him to express a certain emotional modality readily and to feel most comfortable when this modality is predominant in the group culture may be thought of as a spokesman for that particular modality. As spokesman he might be expected to introduce that affective mode into the group and to attempt to influence the group as a whole to move into or to maintain this culture or to terminate cultures that may be antithetical to it. If the group includes spokesmen for emotional cultures opposed to each other, for example dependency and counterdependency, then both these needs are likely to be expressed overtly in the group. Moreover, the way in which this problem is eventually dealt with is likely to be settled by means of interaction between these spokesmen. If spokesmen for only one end of the dependency-counterdependency continuum appear in the group, then only that affective mode would be expressed overtly, and since there is no one to express opposition to it, the group is likely to accept this mode implicitly as its standard.

Our prediction, then, is that a group that includes a wide range of valency types will deal more explicitly with a wider range of emotional issues. A group whose range of valency types is narrower will deal with a more restricted range of emotional issues, and it will tend to deal with them in a less explicit way. If this is true, it follows that a group of the first type will provide opportunities for a wider range of learning than will a group of the second type.[9]

DYNAMICS OF GROUP GROWTH

Our theoretical position states that a group can be seen as operating successively in a series of work-emotionality cultures, each differing from the one preceding or succeeding it in the relative dominance of the work or the emotional aspects of the culture and/or in the particular emotional state with which the work is associated. A group may operate in a work-pairing culture (work-dominant) for a time, then shift to a work-dependency culture (work-dominant), and then to a fight-flight-work culture (fight-flight-dominant), and so on. This is, of course, a stylized view and provides only a generalized model for the characterization of a group's development. There may be many times when the group is operating in some mixed or transitional state or when the situation is so confused that the basic assumptions on which the group is operating cannot be identified. A particular work-emotionality state or culture may last only a few minutes, or it may go on over several meetings or even dominate a group's entire existence.

In considering the problem of how a group moves from one work-emotionality culture to another, Bion suggests that unique satisfactions and anxieties may be associated with each emotional state. For example, group members operating in work-dependency may find satisfaction in the fact that they can relax, rely on someone else for direction, and not have to assume responsibility for their own operation. At the same time they may feel anxious because of the implied immaturity, lack of control over their own interaction, and, perhaps, denial of many individual needs.

The second of the two basic concepts, individual valency, seems operative here. For example, when a group is operating in a fight culture, certain individuals in the group who are particularly sensitive to the threats and anxieties involved in this culture (i.e. for whom fight is an area of concern) may so act as to communicate these anxieties to others or to attempt to move the group into some other work-emotionality culture. Presumably, when these anxieties build up to some crucial level for the group as a whole, a shift will occur. The new culture will be maintained for a while because of the particular satisfactions associated with it and because of relief from the anxieties associated with the previous culture. As time goes on, other members, particularly sensitive to the anxieties associated with the new culture, may be expected to initiate another shift. Similarly, one can expect certain members to fight a kind of rear guard action. Just as some members are especially threatened by a particular work-emotionality situation, some others may be especially rewarded by it and can be expected to influence the group to remain in that culture. It is through the interaction of these kinds of forces that shifts from culture to culture occur.

This approach to group development leads to speculations about the probable sequence of development and about the work-emotionality characteristics of the "mature" and the "immature" group. One possibility is that preoccupation with one kind of emotional issue is followed by preoccupation with another in some predictable sequence. For example, groups may typically operate in a work-dependency culture during their first meetings and move toward work-pairing or work-fight cultures during later meetings. Another possibility is that the particular way in which work and emotionality are related within a culture changes over time. For example, in early work-dependency cultures the preoccupation with dependency might disrupt the work efforts of the group, while in later work-dependency cultures the group may use its preoccupation with dependency more constructively. It is our impression that the latter is a more accurate statement of what is likely to occur. In general, we do not expect the particular sequence of work-emotionality cultures to be constant from group to group, but to depend on such factors as the particular valency characteristics of the members, the leader's personal needs and leadership approach, and the task demands to which the group is subject. Rather than a fixed sequence, the same underlying emotional preoccupations may recur from time to time in the same group, but the manner in which work and emotionality are integrated may shift. Movement toward maturity involves an increased integration of emotionality with work such that the emotional needs of the group are progressively more stimulating to and supportive of the work needs.

This view of group development includes the possibility that changes may occur in the group without, necessarily, having changes occur in the valency characteristics of individual members. That is, group growth may be a matter of a more strategic activation or use of members of particular valency types, such that specific kinds of contributions are introduced more appropriately into the discussion.

To summarize this view of group development:

1. Group interaction can be described in terms of two aspects: work and emotionality.

2. The significant emotional categories of group interaction are dependency, pairing, and fight-flight.

3. At any given time a group is operating in a work-emotionality culture in which work is associated with one or another of the above emotional states.

4. The development of a group can be described in terms of successive phases of varying duration in which one work-emotionality culture

gives way to another. Successive work-emotionality states or cultures differ in the particular emotionality associated with the work and/or in the relative dominance of work over emotionality or vice versa.

5. Anxiety and need gratification account for the shift from one work-emotionality culture to another.

6. As the group develops, there is a trend toward integration of work and emotional activity such that neither is denied and both are mutually supportive.[10]

READINESS FOR AND CHARACTERISTICS OF INDIVID-UAL CHANGE

Research at the Human Dynamics Laboratory has been done principally with training groups, and we have therefore been particularly concerned with the sorts of individual changes ordinarily expected from such groups. Thus the kinds of changes we have studied represent only a limited sampling of the many kinds of changes possible as a result of experiences in groups.

The training group is a small one, having 15 to 20 members, including a leader and, possibly, an associate leader. The group typically meets from 12 to 20 times. The group is brought together in order that members may learn about group operation and about their own behavior and feelings in a group situation. Discussion is exploratory, informal, and relatively free. The curriculum emerges from diagnosis of concerns revealed during discussion. The role of the leader is usually to suggest and interpret rather than to direct. These groups ordinarily deal with such problems as the identification of authority in the group, the nature of limits to expression of feeling, the manner of organization of efforts toward problem solving or decision making, etc. These kinds of problems are dealt with much more explicitly than in a group upon which specific task demands are imposed. For the training group-as-a-whole, the major purpose is to establish, through study of its problems, a set of agreements that will enable discussion to be profitable. For the individual, goals include increased understanding of group operation; increased awareness of one's own roles, needs, and effects on others; and increased personal effectiveness in a group situation. It is assumed that these changes or learnings will lead to increased effectivness in the back-home work situation; and this, rather than change per se, is the *raison d'être* for the training group.

The concepts of "individual valency" and "group culture," of central importance to the understanding of group phenomena, are also relevant to the problem of individual change. The following postulates seem most pertinent:

1. Individual change can be described in terms of shifts in valency pattern.

2. The group culture can be seen as the context within which change takes place.

3. The nature of change is determined by the particular interaction between the individual's valency characteristics and the nature of the group culture.

1. Individual Change in Relation to Shifts in Valency Pattern

Valency, as a property of the individual, includes the three related aspects of affective approach, culture preference, and area of concern. These three aspects of valency may be diagnosed by an observer or clinician. To some extent they are also available to the subject himself as the content of self-perceptions.

It is possible to imagine the independent occurrence of each of four kinds of change: affective approach (the way the individual behaves), culture preference (the kinds of group situations in which he prefers to operate), area of concern (the affective areas with which he is concerned or preoccupied or in conflict), or self-percept (the ways in which he thinks of his own operation in a group situation). More commonly, however, one would expect concurrent changes: change in affective approach accompanied by change in self-percept; change in area of concern accompanied by shifts in the preferred culture; and so on.

The most rigorous and thorough understanding of change would take into account all four factors. For example, a change in affective approach (behavior) in one individual might reflect a strengthening of defenses against the awareness of some more basic conflict. A change in affective approach in another member might indicate an increased freedom to express certain affective needs. A change in self-percept might indicate temporary conformity to the standards of the training group, or it might represent a shift that is also reflected in complementary modifications in behavior and culture preferences.

The "real meaning" of change is communicated as an interpretation of relationships among the four factors. Problems can be defined in such a way that one is interested in only one of these factors: only behavior or only self-percept. But it is our feeling that a consideration of the dynamic relationship among all four factors is required, first to clarify the kind of change one really is talking about and second to interpret the psychological meaning of the change for the individual.

2. The Group Culture as the Context Within Which Individual Change Takes Place

According to our conceptual approach, the continuity of interaction in the total group can be described as a series of constantly shifting and alternating work-emotionality cultures. We assume that a training group is always engaged in work: That is, it is always engaged in some rationally definable activity involving planning, making, or acting on decisions, or the like. At the same time we assume that the group is moving through a succession of emotional phases in which the atmosphere may be dominated in turn by fight (hostility, attack), by flight (withdrawal, silliness, irrelevance), by pairing (warmth, feelings of relatedness), by dependency (a wish to be led or directed), by certain combinations of these, or by transitional phases leading from one to another. At any given time the emotional aspects of the group's life have specific relationships to the work aspects of its operation. At times work may seem to be almost completely in abeyance and the group largely engulfed by its emotional preoccupations. At other times the emotional atmosphere and the affect expressed may seem to fit in constructively with the work activities and support and further the task goals of the group.

These various phases, combinations, and sequences of phases constitute a way of characterizing the ongoing group situation. Whatever change takes place in the individual results from the impact of these phases on him—the ways in which he participates in them and reacts to them.

3. *Change as an Effect of Interaction Between the Individual's Valency Characteristics and the Nature of the Group-Cultural Context*

It is possible that certain kinds of group environments are more conducive to change than others. We would imagine, for example, that in general more members are likely to have an opportunity to learn in a group that offers a wide variety of experiences to its members. In contrast, in a group where discussion is limited to one or a few issues, the possible learnings are more likely to be restricted. Another general characteristic of groups that may influence learning is the relative clarity or confusion of the group situation. It seems reasonable that under very confused conditions members would be less likely to learn because of the difficulty in understanding either what is going on or their own reactions to the situation.

Turning to the individual, it is likely that some persons are more ready to make use of a training experience for personal change than are others. In our terms, it is possible that certain affective approach types are more likely to change than others. It is also possible that an affective approach type is not as relevant as the interrelations among affective approach, culture preference, and basic concern within the individual's total valency pattern. In the latter case we would expect such factors as extent of conflict, adequacy of defenses, rigidity or flexibility, and so on, to be influential.

To understand change thoroughly in the case of any one individual, it is probably necessary to consider the *interaction* between total valency pattern and the nature of the group situation. A group-cultural situation that is a good learning environment for one individual may not be equally effective for another. For example, an individual whose valency pattern shows a strong need for external control or reliance on an authority figure (dependency) might simply be immobilized or driven into unproductive defensive maneuvers in a group where the leader denies or rejects his own authority. This same member might be very responsive to a group in which the designated leader supplies more structure and direction. What is meaningful and insight-producing to one member may be irrelevant or disturbing to another. It is possible to imagine the probable conduciveness to learning of many combinations of individual valency and group conditions.

In considering the problem of how and why change takes place for a particular individual, it appears that the interaction between individual valency and group culture can be viewed either macroscopically or microscopically.

The macroscopic or general approach involves assessing the over-all valency characteristics of the individual and the over-all work-emotionality characteristics of the group and then predicting change in terms of the relationship between these two factors. Thus a group might be considered a potentially profitable experience for a certain member if it offers a range of experiences relevant to his problems, if it provides an atmosphere sufficiently permissive or protected (whatever he needs) to permit the member to experiment freely in his behavior, and if it offers opportunity for the member to look clearly at what he is doing and at the effects of his behavior on others. In contrast, a group is likely to provide an unprofitable learning experience if the situations that develop in the group are essentially irrelevant to the member's needs, or if they do not cover a sufficient range, or if they are so threatening that they preclude any experimentation or looking at the self.

A more microscopic and specific approach is required to trace the specific experiences and interactions that account for change in the individual. One is required to look more concretely into the group experience, identifying those situations in which the individual was active and also those in which he did not participate but which can be assumed to be important to him. These psychologically meaningful situations must then be examined systematically for the ways in which he responded, the range of his responses, his feelings of anxiety or adequacy communicated in his behavior, and any tendencies for his responses to change through time.[11]

SOME MAJOR UNANSWERED QUESTIONS

The relation of the designated leader to other members and his influence on group events is both a theoretical and a practical problem. In a training group, the two most relevant factors may well be his approach to training and certain personal characteristics. Training approach includes his image of what the group "should be like," the directions in which he would like it to move, his assumptions about appropriate limits, the directiveness or nondirectiveness of his leadership, and the extent to which he acts as an authority or assumes responsibility for group events. By personal characteristics we mean his valency pattern: the interrelationships of affective approach, culture preference, and basic concern. His valency pattern may not have a direct relationship with his behavior as leader because the expectations of that office impose their own performance criteria. Even so, it is more than likely that his training approach is subtly influenced by his personal needs. If he is rendered uncomfortable by close contact with others, he may in subtle ways impose on his group barriers to contact; and he may incorporate this personal need within a training approach emphasizing strict work orientation and focus on theoretical issues. A group characteristic which is intolerable on a personal level becomes intolerable on a level of training philosophy.

If the designated leader influences the group through interpretation of process, the character and timing of his interpretations are crucial. It seems reasonable to study the *character* of interpretation in terms of the leader's valency pattern in relation to the current group culture. The *timing* of an interpretation might be studied in terms of its location within an established work-emotionality culture or at some point in a transitional phase. It is proposed that the effect of leader interventions in delaying or facilitating shifts may be due to their alleviation or reinforcement of anxieties inherent in the cultural alternatives.

Further *study of the operation of "natural" leadership* would extend the applicability of our concepts. Bion proposed that at certain times particular individuals may "speak for" the prevailing group culture. At another point he suggests that a particular kind of leader may be associated with each of the work-emotionality cultures. For example, when a group is in a fight culture one of its characteristics is that it needs to attack something or someone. Bion has observed that at such times the group may "follow" (that is, pay special attention to, encourage to talk) a member with paranoid tendencies, because such a member can justify the fight tendencies by assuring the group that it is beset by "enemies"; or a group wishing to avoid meaningful discussion may listen with rapt attention for considerable periods of time to a member who is dull, irrelevant, or incoherent. If challenged, the group will claim that they were completely interested and absorbed. In Bion's terms, such a member is leading the group in flight.

The "basic assumption leader" is similar to Redl's "central person" [12] in that he becomes the focus around whom the group organizes itself. This process can sometimes be seen very clearly in a group; at other times whole meetings may go by without such a person being identifiable.

EVALUATION OF THE THEORY

Perhaps the most fundamental theoretical proposition is that group interaction involves a complex interrelationship between work and emotionality. Since most of our work has been with groups in which there is no imposed task, we have perhaps emphasized emotionality over work. However, Glidewell's work with decision-making groups demonstrates that the emotional character of task groups influences the problem-solving characteristics of the group. Additional work with task groups, perhaps paralleling some of the work already done, is needed. Subsequent work by one of the authors (Stock) on therapy groups has suggested that while the concepts of work and emotionality remain relevant, "work" must be redefined in terms of the specific goals of the group being investigated. The four levels of work defined in the original series of studies for application to training groups were not relevant to therapy groups. It now seems likely that the concept of "work" is generally meaningful, but one's notion of what constitutes work activity must be specifically defined for problem-solving, training, and therapy groups.

Almost as indispensable for understanding group interaction is some way of characterizing the total group and also the relations among individual members' tendencies, predispositions, and group events (behaviors). The concepts of the basic assumption culture and of valency fill these needs for us. Their effectiveness lies in their utilization of the same affective categories.

Our research has indicated the range of conditions under which a generalized concept of individual valency pattern is useful. Individuals "typed" as having different "most characteristic" affective approaches also show differences in relationships between their perceptions of the self and of the total group and in sociometric choice. The over-all operating characteristics of a group are consistent with the patterning of affective approach types of which they are composed.

Yet the limitations of this kind of generalized "single variable" approach are also clear. An attempt to predict sociometric choice from modality preference showed that such predictions held for some members but not for others, depending on the nature of the underlying conflict. It was found that particular changes in individuals were not specifically related to affective approach type. These studies suggest that prediction of the behavior of an individual requires a thorough assessment of all three aspects of valency. The case studies presented demonstrate such an approach for one individual and suggest that it is feasible to hunt for relationships between valency pattern and perceptions in given group situations.

Our research has tested the usefulness of the concepts of flight, fight, pairing, and dependency for characterizing the work-emotionality state or culture of training groups. There are times when the group can very clearly be described in terms of a single modality. At other times the group culture is more confused; two or more modalities may be operating or competing simultaneously, but such characterizations of the state of affairs result in loss of meaning; they do not "really fit." Some more fundamental assumption that integrates the modalities within a simple theme is needed. Moreover, one often sees illustrations of one modality being used to express concern over another. For example, periods of general expressions of warmth and friendliness may be used to avoid getting at real issues; pairing is used to express flight. In this case, the pairing and flight are sensed at different levels of consciousness, and this further complicates interpretation.

Further differentiation within the general concept of group culture may be required. To illustrate what might be involved: There are many situations that can be characterized, on the level of the basic assumption, as dependency. Yet in order to understand fully the meaning of this phase for the group one may well need to know the kind of dependency, the context in which it occurs, and the affective modes being used to express or react to dependency.

This theoretical approach seems especially useful in studying group composition, subgroup functioning, and certain characteristics of group development. When applied to individual personality the concepts of valency and of the emotional and work modalities seem relevant when the various aspects of an individual's valency pattern are defined in some detail; less useful when only one aspect of the valency pattern is utilized as a general measure. When applying the emotional modalities to either the total group or the individual, there is need to differentiate behavior and motivation, and preconscious and conscious levels.

REFERENCES

1. Substantive findings are summarized in Dorothy Stock and H. A. Thelen, *Emotional Dynamics and Group Culture*, No. 2 of the Research Training Series, National Training Laboratories, Washington, D.C. (New York: New York University Press, 1958). Specific studies are reported in: S. Ben-Zeev, "The Formulation and Validation of a Method for Unitizing Group Interaction." Unpublished Ph.D. dissertation, Department of Education, University of Chicago, 1951; R. DeHaan, "Graphic Analysis of Group Process." Unpublished Ph.D. dissertation, Committee on Human Development, University of Chicago, 1951; J. C. Glidewell, "Group Emotionality and Productivity." Unpublished Ph.D. dissertation, Department of Psychology, University of Chicago, 1953; Bettie Belk Sarchet, "Prediction of Individual Work Role in Two Adult Learning Groups." Unpublished Ph.D. dissertation, Committee on Human Development, University of Chicago, 1952; W. F. Hill, "The Influence of Subgroups on Participation

in Human Relations Training Groups." Unpublished Ph.D. dissertation, Committee on Human Development, University of Chicago, 1955; M. A. Lieberman, "The Relationship Between Group Emotional Culture and Individual Change." Unpublished research, Department of Psychology, University of Chicago, June 1957; A. G. Mathis, "Development and Validation of a Trainability Index for Laboratory Training Groups." Unpublished Ph.D. dissertation, Department of Education, University of Chicago, 1955; Dorothy McPherson, "An Investigation into the Nature of Role Consistency." Unpublished Ph.D. dissertation, Department of Education, University of Chicago, 1951; J. McPherson, "A Method for Describing the Emotional Life of a Group and the Emotional Needs of Group Members." Unpublished Ph.D. dissertation, Department of Education, University of Chicago, 1951.

2. Methodology is summarized in Stock and Thelen, *op. cit.*, and described in greater detail in S. Ben-Zeev, Ida Heintz Gradolph, P. Gradolph, W. F. Hill, Dorothy Stock, and H. A. Thelen, "Methods for Studying Work and Emotionality in Group Operation" (planographed) (Human Dynamics Laboratory, University of Chicago, 1954), p. 208.

3. The training group is a special educational opportunity for adults which has been developing over a period of years in Human Relations Workshops conducted by the National Training Laboratories of the N.E.A. It was regarded as an especially appropriate setting for the study of many issues related to group development and functioning because of its initial lack of structure and the absence of a previous history or externally imposed goals. See L. P. Bradford and J. Gibb (eds.), *Theory of T-Group Training.* In Press.

4. W. R. Bion, "Experiences in Groups, I," *Hum. Relat.*, I:314-320, 1948; "Experiences in Groups, II," *Hum. Relat.*, I:487-496, 1948; "Experiences in Groups, III," *Hum. Relat.*, II:13-22, 1949; "Experiences in Groups, IV," *Hum. Relat.*, II:295-304, 1949; "Experiences in Groups, V," *Hum. Relat.*, III:3-14, 1950; "Experiences in Groups, VI," *Hum. Relat.*, III:395-402, 1950; "Experiences in Groups, VII," *Hum. Relat.*, IV:221-228, 1951; "Group Dynamics: A Re-View," *Int. J. Psychoanal.*, 33:235-247, 1952.

5. W. R. Bion, "Group Dynamics: A Re-View," *Int. J. Psychoanal.*, 33:235-247, 1952.

6. The elaboration of valency pattern into the three elements of affective approach, culture preference, and area of concern developed in response to some early research efforts and were then utilized in later work. A sentence completion test (the Reactions to Group Situations Test) was developed to identify an individual's valency pattern. It has been used as a clinical instrument to assess individual learning and change. Ben-Zeev used it as an objective instrument in a study relating valency tendencies to behavior. Lieberman studied relationships between the emotionality predominant in the members' valency patterns and their perceptions of their own roles and of the character of the total group. Lieberman also related valency pattern to sociometric choice. These studies, as well as others to be referred to later are reported in Stock and Thelen, *op. cit.*

7. In separate studies, Morton A. Lieberman and Dorothy Stock explored

the relation between valency pattern and sociometric choice. Lieberman found that group composition and culture were mediating factors. Ben-Zeev related sociometric choice and the extent to which members participated in the group, showing that a mediating factor was individual valency pattern.

8. Studies by William F. Hill examined subtype formation in training groups, exploring their relation to behavior, intermember perception, and group development.

9. John C. Glidewell conducted research on the relation between the valency composition of small groups and their problem-solving styles. Ida Heintz Gradolph studied the problem-solving and interactive characteristics of groups which were homogeneously composed with reference to the predominant affective approach of members. Lieberman compared a group composed of a wide range of valency types with a group composed of a narrower range.

10. Dorothy Stock and Saul Ben-Zeev traced the development of a single training group in work-emotionality terms. Stock and William F. Hill related the developmental characteristics of this and a second group to compositional factors.

11. Studies of individual change have been conducted by Andrew G. Mathis and Dorothy Stock. Mathis developed a "trainability index" which incorporated personality factors found to be conducive to and inhibitory of change. Stock studied changes in self-percept and valency pattern which occurred during the course of a training group experience.

12. Fritz Redl, "Group Emotion and Leadership," *Psychiat.*, 5:573-596, 1942.

6

QUIET AND VOCAL·GROUPS

Andie L. Knutson

There is a rapidly growing body of research on the influence of group structure on group identification and performance. Emphasis on leadership training has focused attention toward the differential effects groups have on the attitudes and behavior of individual participants. Of particular interest to clinicians and psychologically oriented researchers is the relationship between the effectiveness of the group in influencing individual behavior change and the personality characteristics of those individuals. More recently the question has arisen as to whether groups of individuals "compatible" or "incompatible" in terms of certain personal characteristics are more effective in solving problems.

The present study is concerned with two questions of significant theoretical and clinical interest emerging from these lines of research:

1. When compatible groups of quiet and vocal members are assigned similar tasks, what are the effects in terms of membership satisfaction, group identification, and performance?
2. Will assigning members who are low-verbal in behavior to groups compatible in terms of verbal ability lead to an increase in their verbal behavior in these and other groups?

The first question, which concerns the relative effectiveness of vocal and quiet groups in problem solving, is of considerable interest, since several researchers have found that verbal output is significantly related to leadership status as measured by peer or observer judgments.[1] Bass, for example, found a correlation of .93 between the time a member of a leadership group spent talking and the votes he received from observers for having demonstrated leadership. Caudill noted a similar correspondence between the evaluations given resident physicians by their senior officers in a mental hospital and verbal participation in staff meetings.[2] From a peer judgmental point of view, then, grouping members in terms of their verbal

Reprinted from *Sociometry*, Vol. 23, No. 1, March 1960, pp. 36-48.

output may mean grouping them in terms of leadership status as perceived by themselves and their peers. What effect does this have on group functioning, membership identification, and performance?

The second question, which is concerned with increasing the participation of nonvocal group members, deals with a problem that has baffled many leaders in group process. Educators and therapists alike tend to feel that active participation is necessary for individual growth in the group situation. Their feelings are supported by much clinical and theoretical evidence and by some research.[3]

While some group leaders and therapists make special efforts to bring the nonverbal member actively into the group as early as possible, so he may profit from his experience, others seem to feel that certain individuals are emotionally oriented in such a way that they will gain little from the group experience. Stock and Thelen, along with Mathis, have been concerned with developing a trainability index, to apply in screening out individuals who are not likely to profit from the group process experience.[4]

How to assure that every member of a group process class has a profitable experience becomes a matter of real concern when it is not possible to select out those who tend to be passive group members and where the experience in the group is an important part of the educational program.

The Setting

Two laboratory courses in the School of Public Health provided an ideal situation in which to investigate these questions. The student body included 31 Master of Public Health candidates who were concurrently enrolled in the group process laboratory and the mass communications laboratory. While all members of the group had had some orientation in the behavioral sciences, the range among members was from a single elementary course to a Master's degree in anthropology. All students had had at least two years' experience beyond the baccalaureate degree in some field of public health. Several held doctoral degrees. Ten were foreign students, some of whom, while able to speak English, were not expert in the language and hence, perhaps, insecure in the group situation.

The group process laboratory was organized into three separate sections—each with a faculty member serving as a nondirective consultant. At the time the study was initiated, six weeks after the beginning of the course, it had been observed that in each section a few members of the group were low participants, whereas some members were very active participants. The low-participant group was of primary concern to all consultants who wished to find some way of bringing them more actively into the group.

The mass communications laboratory, in which the students were concurrently enrolled, was organized in such a way that small groups were used from time to time for the purpose of working on specific research problems. For each project, a different pattern of small-group organization was used so that all members of the class could become closely acquainted with one another and use fellow members as resource persons. It was observed that the same members who were low participants in group process also tended to be low participants in the communications laboratory sessions.

The experiment was initiated to test whether regrouping the students according to verbal ability for work in the mass communications laboratory would help to solve the problem of nonparticipant behavior. The regrouping was to be tried out experimentally over a three-session period to see whether it would bring the nonverbal members more actively into the discussions. At the time this approach was initially considered, the possibility of measuring the relative production of the four groups was not recognized. Fortunately, however, the tasks were similar and were randomly distributed among the four groups, so that the measure of productivity could be included in the research, this possibility having been recognized at the first session of the groups.

The three faculty members responsible for the two courses participated in ranking students in terms of their verbal fluency as judged by participation in the two laboratory courses. Students were assigned to four groups, three of seven members each and one with ten members. Little difficulty was experienced in first splitting the total group into a quieter group and a more vocal one, and the faculty agreed that the least vocal member of the more vocal group was more verbal in behavior than the most vocal member of the quieter group. Agreement was also reached in separating out the most vocal members of the vocal group and in separating out the very quiet members of the quiet group, but these decisions were more difficult to make. Therefore, some overlapping between the two vocal groups and some overlapping between the two quiet groups may have occurred.

Several minor changes were made in the distributions to assure equal representation in terms of foreign residence and intellectual ability insofar as this could be judged. Information available for judging intellectual ability included grades in previous courses and on the papers submitted during the school year. Honor students and other students were about equally distributed among the four groups; there was no evidence of intellectual superiority for members of any one of the four groups. It was later possible to check these groups against final grades available for the year.

The Task

The purpose of the communications laboratory sessions used for the experiment was to provide experience in the pretesting of a public health pamphlet. This was a topic of considerable interest to the group. The content materials were four pamphlets prepared for public distribution by the

California State Health Department. The Department planned to revise these pamphlets and the students were advised that any suggestions coming out of their studies would be considered in preparing the revision. Insofar as could be judged, the pamphlets provided an equal opportunity for carrying out the task designated for the three-week group session. The pamphlets were randomly distributed, with each group responsible for the pretest of one of the four pamphlets. The instructions were as follows:

> A. Outline a preliminary plan for making a pretest of the public health pamphlet assigned to your group. Then try using your exploratory pretest on at least one person prior to coming to class. Come to class prepared to use these exploratory findings in working with other members of your group in completing a sound pretest plan.
> B. Complete pretest of the pamphlet using the plan developed in class. Hand in a brief written report of your findings and what you have learned using this approach.

Several references on methods of pretesting had been provided prior to making this assignment.[5] Once the assignment had been given, the class was broken up into the four groups. Four faculty members served as nondirective resources to the groups. The groups were advised that this was a three-week group assignment and that group reports were desired.

Group Reaction to the Task

Initial reactions of members of the four groups to the group placements were a surprise to the faculty. In the very quiet group, the members seemed astounded to find themselves together without a vocal member. Members of the group kept their eyes on the distributed written assignment and no one spoke for fifteen minutes; after the project, one member observed that he had timed this first interval of silence as seventeen minutes long. The first member of the group to raise a question concerning the task was looked to as leader. During the first session, this group was very slow in moving and seemed to ponder endlessly over the mechanics of getting started. Following the session, the group leader sought consultation on how to be a leader. It was the first time this person had found herself in a leadership role, and she was quite disturbed that she did not know how to handle the role.

On the other hand, the very vocal group set immediately to the task and scarcely took the time to read the assignment or consider its meaning. They moved along rapidly, competing with one another for leadership. Good suggestions may have been lost because of the eagerness of the group members to express their individual points of view.

The degree of active participation in other groups also seemed to be related to the group's ranking as to verbal facility.

Hypotheses and Research Questions

It was recognized after the first session that the group reports would provide objective evidence of achievement, so that a comparative evaluation of group performance could be made. The opportunity for research was unique, since the groups were closely matched except for the variable "verbal fluency" and such unknown factors as might be related to it and also since similar tasks were performed by the different groups.

The behavior of the four groups, as observed during the first session, was in the direction expected—the quiet groups were quiet and the noisy groups were noisy—but the degree of the difference between the quiet and verbal groups was more marked than had been anticipated. To understand the situation it was necessary to learn how the participants perceived the experience and their attitudes regarding the experience. Several hypotheses were posed and plans were made to test these hypotheses systematically.

It was hypothesized:

(1) That members of the more vocal groups would be happier with their group assignments than would members of the quieter groups. The research question posed was: How did members of the different groups react to their being included in the particular group to which they were assigned?

(2) That members of the more vocal groups would be more satisfied with their early progress than would members of the quieter groups. Overt differences in group behavior had been observed, as already mentioned, and it was expected that these would be reflected in the feelings of the members. The research question posed was: How did members of the different groups evaluate their own progress during the initial session?

(3) That members of the more vocal groups would be more satisfied than members of the quieter groups with their production, participation, leadership, and group spirit and hence with their evaluation of the total experience. It was hoped that this would be a good learning experience for all, but it was expected to be particularly good for members of the quieter group. The research question posed was: How did members of the different groups evaluate the total experience?

(4) That there would be no systematic difference between the groups in the quality of the task performance. The research question posed was: How did the groups compare in terms of the quality and usefulness of the product produced?

(5) That the nonparticipating member in the group process laboratory would profit from the experience of being put in a group with others of his own kind where he would be forced to take a more active role and that this would lead him to take a more active role in other group situations. The research question posed was: What changes in group behavior were observed following the demonstration for the experimental project?

Method of Collecting Data

The data were collected by means of a questionnaire at the first class session following the end of the project. At this session three members of the group were absent, and since it was not desirable to obtain these data at a later date, the final groups included in the study consisted of ten for the most vocal group and six for each of the other three groups.

The first page of the questionnaire included three questions concerned with attitudes toward the group assignment. These were open questions, and the group was asked to complete this page of the questionnaire before looking at the remaining questions. Cooperation was excellent. Every member completed every question adequately from the standpoint of analysis. The group was advised that it would receive a feedback of the findings of the study and an explanation of its purpose at a later date.

FINDINGS

Hypothesis 1

It was hypothesized that members of the more vocal groups would be happier in their group assignments than would be members of the quieter groups. Data were therefore gathered regarding the reactions of the members of the different groups to their assignments. These data have been summarized in Table 1.

Table 6–1   Reaction to Group Assignment by Members of Quiet and Vocal Groups

	Very Vocal Group	Vocal Group	Quiet Group	Very Quiet Group	Significance*
Q2. Description of own group membership					P < .01
Very positive terms	8	5			
Indifferent or neutral terms	2	1	2	3	
Negative terms			4	3	
Q3. Satisfaction with group assignment					P < .01
Satisfied, pleased	9	6	1	1	
Indifferent, dissatisfied	1	0	5	5	
Q4. Group preference					P < .01
Preferred own group to other groups	10	5	2		
Preferred own group, but defensive	0	0	2	3	
Preferred other group to own group	0	1	2	3	
Number in group	10	6	6	6	

* For purposes of testing significance of differences, the two vocal groups were combined and the two quiet groups were combined, since the individual groups were small. The median test was employed.

Subjects were asked, "How would you describe this group to someone who was not present?" In response to this question, nearly all the members of the most vocal group and the next most vocal group expressed satisfaction and indicated strong positive reaction to other group members. On the other hand, the members of the quiet and very quiet groups tended to be either indifferent or negative in their reactions.

The terms used by members of the most vocal group to describe their fellow members included "a group of possible leaders who might have bogged down because of competition for leadership, but didn't," "quite cohesive," "active, ambitious, task-oriented, cooperative, industrious, scholarly," "cooperative, cohesive, easy to work with," "quite verbal, active, jovial, cooperative, strong, made up of people who represent the kinds of power," "one of the most active and effective groups," "capable, highly motivated people with good intellectual capacity," "most verbal members of the class," "the cream of the crop in terms of positive and effective contributions."

The terms used by the members of the quiet group to describe their fellow members were far less self-laudatory. The most favorable observation was, "It was a nice group who worked together and found out many good points"; others described themselves in more timid terms; "generally of the milquetoast variety," "nonparticipators," "reluctant of the entire problem," "slow in getting started," "most verbally reticent members."

Members of the quiet group tended to compare themselves in terms quite similar to the very quiet group; likewise, members of the vocal group tended to describe themselves in terms somewhat similar to those used by the very vocal group.

In response to the question, "How did you feel about being assigned to this group?" nearly all members of the two most vocal groups expressed high satisfaction with the assignment. They said it was fine, the best group they had worked with; they felt comfortable, found it challenging, were pleased to be in it, and enjoyed it.

In contrast, the members of the quiet and very quiet groups did not like to be considered as "reticent," wondered why everybody seemed to be of the same caliber, felt that the group had been assembled to represent the more reticent, asked if the assignments were loaded, and "wondered why I had been grouped with these . . . ," "was this the mousiest, or what?" Two members were somewhat apologetic: "no unusual feeling, the personalities were adequate," "one group is as good as another—no real anticipations or disappointments."

The vocal and very vocal groups were almost unanimous in responding "no" to the question, "Would you rather have been placed in some other group at the time?" On an open question, they backed up their response with the reaffirmation of their satisfaction with the opportunity of working with the group in which they were placed.

Members of the quiet and very quiet groups were about evenly split in their responses to the question regarding their preference for some other group. In the open question following, even those who said "no" (they would not have preferred some other group) indicated that they were not wholly satisfied but felt that it was a reflection on the group to speak otherwise: "Nothing against any of the members, but I thought the group could have been divided a little more equally," "No, because I felt *any* group was worth my effort," "No, I felt this was a good working group, though some more aggressive individuals were in others," "No, having worked previously with other members, their traits and characteristics were acceptable," "No, at first I was perturbed, but. . . ."

Thus, data from all three questions tends to support strongly the hypothesis that members of the more vocal groups were happier with their group assignments than were members of the quieter groups. The responses of members of both groups suggest a value placement upon verbal facility and identified the more vocal groups as groups of greater status.

Hypotheses 2 and 3

It was hypothesized that the vocal groups would be more satisfied both with their first session and with their total experience during the proj-

Table 6–2   Self-Evaluation of Project by Members of Quiet and Vocal Groups

	Median Rankings of Members				
	Very Vocal Group	Vocal Group	Quiet Group	Very Quiet Group	Significance*
Production of group †					
During 1st session	6	5.5	3	2	P < .01
During total project	6	6	3.5	5	P < .01
Satisfaction with own participation					
During 1st session	5.5	5.5	3	3.5	P < .01
During total project	5.5	6	4.5	5	P < .05
Satisfaction with leadership	5.5	6	3	4	P < .05
Value of project as learning experience	5	5	5	6	N.S.
Prefer own group for another project	5	5	4.5	4	N.S.
Number in group	10	6	6	6	

* See footnote, Table 1.
† Rank of 6 indicates most productive, most satisfied, most successful, and preference of own group to any other. Rank of 1 indicates least productive, least satisfied, least successful, and preference of other group to own group.

ect than would members of the less vocal groups. It was expected that they would be more satisfied with their production, their participation, and their leadership and would prefer to work with the same group on other projects.

Table 2 summarizes the data from seven questions used to obtain the reactions of the groups in terms of these factors. It will be noted that the vocal groups were more satisfied with their own participation and with their leadership than were members of the quiet groups. In response to a question concerning the choice of groups for another project, there was a tendency for members of the more vocal groups to express a higher preference for their own group than for some other group, but the differences were not significant.

It will be recalled that the initial purpose of the project was to provide a new type of learning experience for members of the quiet groups. All members of the very quiet group rated the project as their most successful learning experience. Members of the other three groups also rated it very high as a learning experience.

The reactions to these questions tend to support hypotheses 2 and 3 in that the more vocal groups tended to express greater satisfaction with their production, participation, and leadership. It tends also to support the hypothesis regarding the success of the project as a learning experience for the quiet groups, as judged by personal ratings. An individual's own estimate of learning may not, of course, be supported by other data.

Hypothesis 4

It was hypothesized that there would be no difference in the quality of task performance by the four groups. This hypothesis was not strongly expressed because there was some feeling among the faculty that the more vocal groups might turn out better products.

Each of the four groups completed a plan for pretesting the pamphlet assigned to them, carried out this plan, and prepared a report of findings and recommendations. Members of the staff felt too deeply involved in this project to make a valid judgment as to the quality of the final reports. Outside evaluation seemed indicated. Accordingly, the Chief of Health Education in the State Health Department was requested to assign this responsibility to two top members of her staff. These members were asked to rank the group reports in terms of the quality and usefulness of the product.

Before the reports were submitted for evaluation, all personal references were removed. Furthermore, in order to make the reports appear as similar as possible, they were put in like folders along with a copy of the pamphlet subjected to pretest.

The findings of these consultants are presented in Table 3. Their independent rankings were similar and in full agreement with the expectations

*Table 6–3   Consultants' Rankings of Groups in Terms of Quality and Usefulness of Product ***

	Very Vocal Group	Vocal Group	Quiet Group	Very Quiet Group
Consultant A	1	2	3	4
Consultant B	1	2	4	3

* Highest ranking (4) indicates best quality and usefulness.

of members of the staff after they had looked over the papers. The quiet and very quiet groups had produced the most integrated reports, and these reports reflected careful thought and planning. They also reflected an organized and interrelated approach to the gathering of essential data and to the drawing up of pertinent conclusions. This was less true of the reports of the vocal groups. The very vocal group revealed in its report the degree to which competition for leadership and individual expression must have influenced its group process. The report lacked coordination. Included in it was a page of the personal observations of each member of the team; members of the group had failed to reach complete agreement and each may have felt the need for personal identification with the part of the final product to which he had contributed.

Hypothesis 4 is, therefore, not confirmed. There was a distinct difference between the less vocal and more vocal groups in terms of the quality of performance.

Follow Up: The Feedback

There was considerable concern among members of the faculty as to how these findings should be reported back to the class. After discussion, it was agreed that the best thing to do was to present the data straightforwardly, with the expectation that the more vocal members would be able to handle the situation. Accordingly, a feedback situation was planned in such a way that the individual groups could meet immediately after the feedback to discuss among themselves, with no one else present, the implications of the findings.

The more vocal members of the group were highly satisfied with the early findings of the study. The less verbal members were somewhat embarrassed to find that they had described themselves in this way, and yet they found others in sympathy with their descriptions.

When the findings from the evaluation of the final report were presented, the vocal groups were stunned, and could scarcely believe what had happened. The discussions that followed continued for about an hour. Members of the faculty were not present at these sessions, but they gradually received "feedback."

At first, many members of the vocal groups rejected the findings outright. Later, several of them came to look over the papers and draw their own conclusions. It appeared that no one in the most vocal group had read the complete report as it was turned in. Each member had been responsible for a part, but no one had taken the role of coordinating. They became fully aware in their discussions of the lack of coordination between their findings and reporting. The quiet groups, on the other hand, were pleased with themselves and with the considerable status achieved in the total group.

During the several weeks following the experiment, it was observed, both in the group process laboratory and in the communications laboratory, that members of the more vocal groups were less active participants in the discussion, and during this short period of time, several members of the quiet groups assumed leadership roles. These roles were not given up when the vocal members recovered and started to take more active parts. By the end of the year, several members of the quiet groups had assumed active leadership roles in various activities of the school. The long-term effect on the more vocal members of the class was less observable.

Discussion

Findings concerned with the relative effectiveness of quiet and vocal groups in performance of the present task, while interesting, cannot safely be generalized to other situations. There is need for replication of the study, using different tasks and a control group or two including both quiet and vocal members. Such a study might be focused toward learning under what conditions, and with what tasks, quiet groups function more effectively than vocal groups; with what kinds of problems the reverse occurs; and when the heterogeneous group is more effective.

Several avenues of research are suggested by the fact that the findings regarding performance are in conflict with what seems to be a generally held norm, that vocal members function more effectively than quiet members.[6] Riecken's research on this problem shows a tendency on the part of the group to rank a high-talking member as having contributed more than a low-talking member, even when the group accepted the solution of the low-talking member.[7] Does holding such a norm influence the levels of aspiration of quiet and vocal group members? Does it influence their self-images as group members? How is performance in this situation influenced by expectation? If the project had been perceived as competition between groups, how might this have influenced the findings?

Of particular interest are questions this study raises regarding the concept of leadership as it applies in small-group situations. The data support the viewpoint that leadership in groups is neither a unitary quality nor a set pattern of role behaviors that apply similarly in all situations. Rather, a particular type of group seems to require for its direction a certain pattern of leadership roles and individuals with both the abilities and initiative to carry out these roles. The leadership characteristics required for effective group functioning may not be the same for all groups. Successful leadership in a very quiet group seems to require a set of leadership characteristics different from those required for effective leadership in a very vocal group.

Ordering the groups in terms of quiet and verbal members selectively removed persons with certain verbal leadership qualities from the quiet groups. Their absence was immediately apparent, for the group could not move toward its goal until some member stepped forward to fill the verbal leadership role.

The vocal group had an abundance of members with verbal leadership qualities but seemed to lack members able and willing to perform other leadership roles. Verbal fluency seemed to be identified as the *sole* mark of leadership. No one took responsibility for recording suggestions and decisions, for summarizing discussion and reviewing progress, for planning the report, for coordinating the ideas and findings of others in preparing the final report. The present study does not tell us whether the qualities necessary for performing these leadership functions were lacking, or whether the high premium placed on verbal leadership resulted in these other roles being ignored.

The two groups seem to have had different types of leadership needs. The retiring members comprising the quiet group needed a leader capable of eliciting their ideas without threat and helping them to move with security. The fast-speaking members of the vocal group needed a leader who could hold them back until sound decisions were reached, help them to evaluate progress and make necessary changes in plans, coordinate ideas and findings, and make sure that an integrated product resulted.

To the extent that this observation holds, it may have significant implications for leadership selection and training. Is it reasonable to expect the same group leader to perform effectively the two different sets of roles described above? Should recognition of the leadership needs of different types of groups be included in leadership training courses? Should leaders in training be provided with opportunities for experience in groups of various composition, and concerned with different types of problems, so they will learn to identify the special leadership requirements of different situations?

The initial reaction of group members in identifying verbal fluency with leadership is consistent with findings already mentioned. Discussion with students after the experiment suggests that they believed this was a norm held by both peers and faculty. Being identified with the quiet group tended to be damaging to the ego; being identified with the vocal group seemed to be ego-enhancing.

The study suggests that some quiet and some vocal members held unrealistic self-images in the group situation before being assigned to a group similar to themselves in behavior. Several quiet members later expressed the opinion that they had felt shocked to find themselves grouped with persons they had seen as quiet and retiring. They had not previously identified themselves as quiet in the group situation. The experience must have been particularly disturbing for those members of the quiet group with leadership strivings. The experience of being so grouped seems to have shocked them into a more realistic perception of their own behavior patterns and led them to take steps to change. Further research may provide additional information on the value of this type of approach in influencing behavior change. It may identify also other means available in the teaching situation for reality testing with respect to self-image.

The value of the present research would have been greatly enhanced if it had been possible to obtain some measure of self-image prior to the experiment so that a more objective estimate of change could have been obtained. An objective index of verbal behavior for use in grouping members would be an improvement over faculty rating, which, while successful in this particular situation, might be more difficult to carry out with agreement in other situations. It would have been also most desirable to have a large number of groups, including some control groups with heterogeneous distribution of quiet and vocal members. Measures of aspiration and expectation regarding performance would be of interest, but obtaining such measures would probably introduce the factor of competition, which did not seem to play a role in the present research. A replication of the study with such improvements in design would be useful in answering some of the questions posed regarding the relative effectiveness of quiet, vocal, and heterogeneous groups and regarding the effects of assignment to such groups on self-image and behavior in other groups.

REFERENCES

1. B. M. Bass, "An Analysis of Leaderless Group Discussion," *J. Appl. Psychol.*, 33:527-533, 1949; P. M. Blau, "Patterns of Interaction Among a Group of Officials in a Government Agency," *Hum. Relat.*, 7:337-348, 1954; R. L. French, "Verbal Output and Leadership Status in Initially Leaderless Discussion Groups," *Am. Psychol.*, 5:310-311, 1950.
2. W. Caudill, *The Psychiatric Hospital as a Small Society* (Cambridge, Mass.: Harvard University Press, 1958), p. 252.
3. Dorothy Stock and H. A. Thelen, *Emotional Dynamics and Group Culture* (New York: New York University Press, 1958); D. A. Shaskan, "Evolution and Trends in Group Psychotherapy," *Am. J. Orthopsychiat.*, 18:447-454, 1948; H. Perez, "An Investigation of Non-Directive Group Therapy," *J. Consult. Psychol.*, 11:4, 1947.
4. Stock and Thelen, *op. cit.*
5. A. Knutson, "Pretesting; A Positive Approach to Evaluation," *Public Health*

Reports, Reprint 3192, Washington, D.C., Supt. of Documents, 1952; G. R. Klare and B. Buck, *Know Your Reader* (New York: Hermitage House, 1954); "Pretesting and Evaluating Health Education," *Public Health Monograph No. 8,* Washington, D.C., Supt. of Documents, 1952; *Ten Checkpoints for Better Booklets* (New York: Council of National Organizations, 1956).

6. R. F. Bales, "The Equilibrium Problem in Small Groups," in T. Parsons, R. F. Bales, and E. A. Shils, *Working Papers in the Theory of Action* (Glencoe, Ill.: The Free Press, 1953); H. Riecken, "The Effect of Talkativeness on Ability to Influence Group Solutions to Problems," *Sociometry,* 21:309-321, 1958.

7. Riecken, *op. cit.*

Part 2

HISTORICAL SURVEY

Part 2 is an historical survey for the reader and an overview of most of the theoretical positions to be found in group psychotherapy. Joseph Pratt is presented here as being the founder of group psychotherapy in the United States. Because his original article is not particularly specific in terms of what he actually did with the groups he formed for his tuberculosis classes, the editors have selected for this collection of readings an article which we believe to be a more detailed statement of his work at that time. The second article included in this section was written by Pratt toward the end of his life. It is a statement of his later experiences and how he ventured into the field of psychotherapy. It is a much clearer overview of Pratt's thinking.

Marsh's article is a statement by one of the pioneers in the field of group psychotherapy. It is an interesting example of a revival-inspirational approach to group psychotherapy. We have dealt at some length in this historical survey with the work of Trigant Burrow, whom we feel to have been a significant figure in the entire development of psychotherapy in the United States. Unfortunately, Burrow has written in such a complex and often esoteric language that it is "tough sledding" for the reader. His son-in-law, Hans Syz, who carries on the tradition of Burrow, has written a detailed statement of Burrow's work and an excellent summary of Burrow's philosophy and approach to psychotherapy. One of the clearest statements of Burrow's own approach to psychotherapy in the group treatment of the individual is the article on the group method of analysis which we have included. It is a rare article because it is specific as a statement and is different from the often obscure language that Burrow later used to describe his work.

We have included a review of Burrow, written by D. H. Lawrence, for three major reasons. One, it is a precursor to much of what is currently called "existential psychotherapy." Two, it shows the many currents that were at work during the early years of psychoanalytic psychotherapy and the awareness of the group by some major figures in the culture. Three, it is a beautiful statement of the importance of the group experience for the individual, as perceived by one of the great novelists of contemporary culture who was also a gifted psychologist.

The remaining articles in this section are statements of the theoretic positions of group psychotherapists who stem from various analytic persuasions. They seem to confirm what Fred Fiedler has concluded in his research at the University of Chicago. Experienced therapists apparently are much more similar to one another in clinical practice than they are aware. They often find a good deal of difficulty in fitting their everyday clinical practice to the theoretical persuasions by which they were originally influenced and which they attempt to hold on to in the course of their professional development.

The series of letters that Illing exchanged with Jung are interesting, as they are a specific statement of a pioneer psychoanalyst's approach to the group method of treatment.

7

THE TUBERCULOSIS CLASS:
AN EXPERIMENT
IN HOME TREATMENT

Joseph H. Pratt

The topic assigned to me is the Convalescent Care of Tuberculosis Patients, but the term "convalescence" cannot properly be applied to tuberculosis as it can be to such diseases as pneumonia and typhoid fever. I accepted the invitation to speak, because I appreciated greatly the honor of coming here, to a city that has taken the lead in so much good work along the lines of public health, and, although I cannot talk to you about convalescent care, in speaking of my experiments in the home treatment of tuberculosis I shall lay special reference on the after care.

The after care of tuberculosis depends a good deal upon the treatment the patient has had during the active stage of the disease. As I just said, we cannot speak of a patient with tuberculosis as being convalescent any more than we can speak of a patient who has syphilis as being convalescent. Those of you who are social workers among tuberculosis individuals must realize the truth of this. A man may appear perfectly well who a short time before presented symptoms of tuberculosis. The disease may show no signs of activity, the temperature and pulse may be normal, and yet, a day after some trifling overexertion he may have a hemorrhage and a return of symptoms. Recently I saw a patient who had been free from symptoms for several months, with no fever, no cough, and yet such slight exertion as dressing and going down one flight of stairs to dinner was followed by a return of cough, elevation of temperature, and a feeling of general malaise. Therefore, it is very important in dealing with tuberculosis to remember the distinction between this disease and such diseases as

Reprinted from *Proceedings*, New York Conference on Hospital Social Service, Vol. IV, 1917, pp. 49-68. Some statistical tables accompanying this article were omitted for reasons of space.

typhoid fever and pneumonia, for example, which have definite convalescent stages.

In the spring of 1905 I formulated a plan for the treatment of consumption in the homes of poor patients. The organization was called a tuberculosis class. Sanatorium methods were to be employed and supervision obtained (1) by visits to the home by the class nurse; (2) a record book in which the details of the daily life were noted down by the patient—the value of this I had learned from Dr. Charles L. Minor of Asheville—and (3) weekly meetings of the patients.

It was the intention from the outset to give a great deal of care to a small number of patients. My project did not find favor with the existing organizations to which I appealed for financial support, but finally I obtained from Dr. Elwood Worcester, the rector of Emmanuel Church, the sum of $500 with which to begin the experiment.

In organizing the class I had the able assistance of Dr. John B. Hawes and of Miss Isabel Strong, a graduate nurse of unusual ability and well suited to carry on work along original lines. Miss Strong became the first class visitor and gave her entire time without pay.

Before the class started on July 1, I spent a week with Dr. Lawrason Brown, at that time resident physician of the Adirondack Cottage Sanatorium at Trudeau. From him I learned much of value. From the monograph of Moeller, which had recently appeared in the Deutsche Klinik, I became familiar with the details of the rest cure as carried out by Dettweiler and his followers. I was deeply impressed by Moeller's statement that all his patients found the rest cure extremely beneficial. I remember well my surprise when I read on the train coming home from Saranac this sentence: "I have still to hear of a single patient who found the rest cure irksome. On the other hand, many have said to me that the hours of the 'Liegekur' are to them the pleasantest of the day."

I mused over this a long time, and when the class started, the rest cure on roof, yard, or balcony was our chief reliance in treatment. Every fever-free patient was provided with a reclining chair.

From the outset exercise was regarded as dangerous, and, when taken, the duration of the walks was always exactly prescribed.

We began with one patient, whom Dr. Hawes had discovered in the outpatient department of the Massachusetts General Hospital, where she had been under treatment for more than six months, and in spite of her faithful efforts was slowly but steadily getting worse. She has now been well and working for ten years.

I have preserved the report written by Miss Strong, the class nurse, of the first visit to the first patient in 1905. This patient had received the ordinary treatment as carried out in a tuberculosis dispensary. The letter is as follows:

I visited the first member of the class this morning and everything goes well. I think I showed her how to take her temperature, and taught her her lesson thoroughly, I hope. She is being cared for by an aunt, and therefore has no money. Could we buy a chair for her? She says she cannot. I went to Paine's and they carry the $2.00 chair. I found she could not sit out on the little piazza in the afternoon because of the sun, so I visited a neighbor and made arrangements for her chair to be placed under a tree. I find she is going in to Boston and taking electric car rides, etc. Will you give explicit directions about the amount of exercise? I told her absolute rest for the first week anyway. Her temperature at 12 noon was 98.8 and pulse 80. I also told her to take it every two hours. I find she is taking cold sponge baths every day. I believe you said twice a week. She had a chest protector on, in fact two, which I asked her to remove; also she is taking olive oil, three teaspoonfuls in twenty-four hours. Yesterday she vomited curdled milk, and as I could give no other cause I suggested diminishing the oil to see if that was the trouble. She sleeps very well, and is faithful to the outdoor orders. She asked me when she could come again to the dispensary, and if she could join the Parker Day Camp Hill. I believe they spend the day in tents, and are gathered from the different dispensaries. It seems to me she is quite well situated now. I told her I would bring a record book to her later on when you have them.

I feel rather doubtful about the baths and exercise, not knowing exactly what you would say. Perhaps we could have a rule for all patients for the first week or ten days.

Waban, July 6, 1905.

I quote this in full to show that from the beginning we realized the importance of careful supervision of the individual patient and to let you see that I had a very good supporter in Miss Strong. Much of the success in organizing our work was due to her.

This class was the beginning of the social service work at the Massachusetts General Hospital. Three months later Dr. Richard C. Cabot broadened the work there to cover the investigation and, where possible, the solution of the various social problems of the outpatients by trained and by volunteer workers. At Dr. Cabot's request a second tuberculosis class was organized by Dr. Hawes for the treatment of patients who lived in the suburbs of Boston. Within the next few years many classes were formed in various parts of the country. Most of them, like the seed sown on thin soil, sprang up quickly, but quickly withered away, as adequate financial support was lacking and the vital elements underlying the success in our work were not understood. One class, an off-shoot of ours, organized by one of my assistants, Dr. N. K. Wood, is still in existence after ten years of successful work. The nurse in this class for the entire period has been our first class member.

In New York City in 1906 a tuberculosis class was established by Dr.

Walter L. Niles, called the Christ Church Tuberculosis Class. It had an efficient, friendly visitor, and our methods were carried out by Dr. Niles most successfully. He demonstrated clearly and conclusively that it was possible to treat tuberculosis by substantially the same methods in the heart of New York City. That experiment should be known to all of you. It was very successful, and Dr. Niles deserves great credit. It was abandoned in a few years because money for its support was discontinued.

Shortly after the Christ Church Class was formed, a class was organized at St. George's Church in New York and was carried on successfully by Dr. N. Gilbert Seymour and Dr. Tasker Howard for a period of three years or more. It is important to emphasize the success of these classes, because of the impression that has gone out throughout the country that the class method had been tried but had been given up as unsuccessful. I hope very much that these physicians in New York will publish reports and state the advantages and difficulties of class work. I believe that Dr. Landis who organized and conducted the class at the Phipps Institute in Philadelphia is planning to issue such a report. I know of no class that has carefully followed the same methods we have employed that has not been successful. Dr. Hawes, who was my first assistant, has lost his faith in the class method. Some of you may have been at New Haven and heard his criticism. He considered my success a matter of personality rather than of method. When Dr. Hawes was associated with me in the Emmanuel Church Class, much of the detail work was in his hands. This he did with enthusiasm and success. His own experiment with the Suburban Tuberculosis Class he now regards as a failure. I think I should have failed had I attempted, as he did, to treat 88 patients in one year—to say nothing of the fact that he had no funds at his disposal and that he depended on volunteer visitors to give instructions in the homes, while we had a trained visiting nurse from the start.

In the beginning we sought only far-advanced cases that were refused admission to the only public sanatorium in the state—that of Rutland. Of the 17 patients admitted to the class in the first six months, one was incipient, six advanced, and ten far-advanced. The next year, 1906, 15 of the 31 patients taken into the class were in the far-advanced stage of the disease. That answered the criticism that we selected our cases.

At first we had our weekly meetings in my consulting room. Later we moved to a dispensary on Washington Street, supported by Dr. Haynes, and after that to the Massachusetts General Hospital, where we still have our headquarters. A few years ago we were forced by lack of space in the growing outpatient department to the basement, where we meet in a rather cheerless room. Nevertheless, we are very thankful to the hospital authorities for the aid they have given us.

I wish to emphasize the one point: We are not a church class in the sense that we meet in a church; the only connection comes through financial support. The St. George's Class was a true church class. They met in the parish house.

Our path even at the start was not wholly smooth. When Miss Strong made the second visit to the first patient two or three days after the one described in her letter, she found that her explicit instructions regarding rest had not been followed, as the patient had been to church on Sunday.

One day that hot first summer the visitor came to me in a discouraged hour and said: "Why insist that these poor consumptives with far advanced disease follow the strict rest treatment out-of-doors, when you know that they cannot recover?" Speaking with the wisdom of hope, if not of experience, I assured her that it was my conviction that some would get well, and they did. We allowed a few patients to go to the day camp that year, but I learned from observations that the exertion of the trips to and from the camp were so injurious as to offset any advantage to be found there. The first member failed to gain for several months, and some who died, I believe, might have been saved if I had kept them in bed for a long period of time.

Within two years my ideas regarding rest were definitely formed, and in a paper read before the National Association for the Study and Prevention of Tuberculosis, in the spring of 1907, I write as follows regarding the rest treatment:

> The chief reason that so many of our moderately advanced cases have recovered seems to lie in the fact that we have insisted on absolute rest in every instance. Even in cases without fever, rest in the recumbent position is continued until symptoms have disappeared. I find less difficulty in keeping a patient quiet all the time than half the time. The rest treatment simplifies wonderfully the management of the case. It saves the patient from many dangers. Each patient is provided with a comfortable canvas reclining chair. The friendly visitor at her first visit selects the exact spot out-of-doors where the cot bed and chair are to be placed. The chair must not be moved without permission. Many of the members spend the greater part of the day on their cot beds. This is encouraged. The patients are never allowed to take any of the prescribed rest in a sitting position or in any form of rocking chair. No sewing or other hand work is allowed, and only a moderate amount of reading. The "cure" consists simply in keeping in the recumbent posture all the time, except that members free from fever are allowed to dress themselves and to take their meals at the table. The members do not find the enforced hours of rest irksome. It is, of course, hard to keep quiet for the first week or two of treatment—much harder for some than for others. But the rest habit is soon acquired. In the past year not a single member has begged me for exercise. It is rare, indeed, that they ask for it after the treatment is fairly begun.

In the years that have passed since this was written I have used more rest rather than less, as a study of the records show. The average time at which exercise in the form of walking was begun in 30 cases admitted from 1905 to 1907 was 7 weeks. In a second group of 30 cases covering the years from 1908 to 1911 it was four months, and in a third series, 1911 to 1913, it was again four months. The average duration of treatment in the first group was 8 months, in the second 8½, and in the third 11 months.

In a paper read in Dublin, Ireland, 1908, I stated my belief "that a case of pulmonary tuberculosis during the active state should be given the same form of rest treatment that is employed in typhoid fever."

My ideal has been immobilization of the patient, and this word gives perhaps a clearer idea of our form of treatment than the word rest. Unfortunately in this work among the poor, with the limited facilities at our disposal, the immobilization has been far from complete. Many of the patients have been obliged to walk to the bathroom and to take their meals at the table. Furthermore, the visits to the class have involved an amount of exercise that has doubtless been distinctly harmful in some cases, but the class meetings have proved so helpful to the members in keeping up their courage and their determination to persevere in the rest treatment that the physical work entailed upon attendance has seemed a necessary evil. Some patients have attended only once in three or four weeks, and none except those who are nearly ready for discharge, and for whom walking and work in considerable amount are prescribed, are allowed to come to the class meetings oftener than once in two weeks. The rest treatment is now carried out in cot beds, and very few of the patients during the past five years have used reclining chairs. The only chair that we can recommend—Dr. Brown's Adirondack model—which is patterned after that of Dettweiler, is too expensive for our patients.

When we discovered that the rest treatment at home was giving better immediate results than those obtained in the sanatorium open to wage earners in Massachusetts, we no longer advised patients in the early stages of the disease who sought admission to the class to go to a sanatorium in preference to taking the treatment at home. The end results of home treatment in the class were better than those obtained at Rutland, although this is a sanatorium limited to favorable cases, while patients in all stages of the disease have been admitted to our class, and no one has been refused because the outlook seemed hopeless. The percentage of Rutland ex-patients able to work after a period of 8 to 10 years was less than 25, while 42 per cent of our class members were working after this length of time.

The class meeting has been described in earlier papers. The patients bring their record books for inspection. Each one is weighed and the temperature and pulse taken and recorded. The gains in weight are posted on a blackboard. After a few words of commendation and cheer, or a brief talk, the members in turn come forward to my desk or to that of my assistant. The record book is carefully inspected, advice given, and an entry made on the clinical history of the patient's condition. If a candidate for membership is present one of the "star" patients is frequently asked to testify what the rest treatment has done for him, and this is done with the enthusiasm that exerts a powerful influence on the newcomer. But the healthy appearance of most of the patients probably makes a deeper impression than anything that is said. At least this was true in the case of James M., who is often requested to tell his experience at the class meeting.

Soon after the death of his wife, James, who was a longshoreman of middle age, and a free user of alcohol, developed a severe cough and rapidly lost weight and strength. At the dispensary at Burrough's Place tubercle bacilli were found in his sputum. His lungs were extensively diseased, and he was advised to go to the city tuberculosis hospital for advanced cases at Mattapan, but he refused. A nurse called several times but he remained obdurate and insisted on staying at home.*

Finally, in despair, his brother having gotten my name somewhere as one who knew something about tuberculosis, brought him to me as a private patient. I explained to James the seriousness of his condition, and the importance of taking the rest treatment, but he remained taciturn and unmoved. On leaving my consulting room he told his brother frankly that he didn't think much of me. I did not make any impression upon him. My personality did not work that time. He said to his brother: "I don't think he is a doctor: he didn't say anything about medicine. He is more like a Christian Scientist, or a professor of physical culture, or something like that." The idea of lying down all day out-of-doors just as though he were a log of wood did not appeal to him at all.

He sought out a doctor who gave him medicine, but he felt that it did him no good. Finally he heeded the persuasions of my class visitor, herself a former member of the class, and came rather reluctantly to one of the meetings. He saw there two or three men who had made good progress, and who had followed the rest treatment faithfully for months. Out of complete discouragement, a hope arose in his mind that he, too, might recover. At the end of the meeting he accepted at once the invitation to join the class, and a more faithful patient in following out the rest treatment we have never had.

To the question often asked by doctors "How do you induce your patients to take the strict rest treatment?" the answer is: the class meeting.

Results obtained 1905-1915. These were briefly reported at the last meeting of the National Association for the Study and Prevention of Tu-

---

* Long afterwards we learned the reason for his refusal. He had known sixteen or seventeen men who had been sent to Mattapan. All but one had died. "They made a quick cure of that patient," James said, "he left in forty-eight hours and is well today." In this experience is a lesson for all who think the segregation of advanced cases in hospitals devoted to this purpose is the essential feature in the tuberculosis campaign. Many, like James, will refuse to go to a hospital for advanced cases when they know of many deaths there and no recoveries. The solution of this difficulty is the care of early and advanced cases in the same institution, although not in the same ward.

berculosis. Of all patients discharged from 1906 to 1913, 58.2 per cent were well and working in 1915, two to nine years after their discharge.

Few sanatoriums publish detailed reports of the after-history of their patients. This is most regrettable, and it has often raised the suspicion that the end results are so poor that those in authority do not care to go to the expense of collecting and publishing data that will have a discouraging effect on workers in the tuberculosis campaign. Among the few sanatoriums that have published excellent reports of the after-histories, the Gaylord Farm Sanatorium and the Adirondack Cottage Sanatorium in this State deserve special mention.

One of the most detailed reports of results was published in 1914 by the Brompton Hospital Sanatorium located at Frimley, in England. This institution was opened only a year before our class was formed. There, various forms of graduated labor have been employed as the essential element in treatment. At first the patient is given walking exercises, varying from one to six miles daily. After two or three weeks a small basket is carried or light gardening is begun. The after-histories of their cases are given in sufficient detail to permit the construction of tables placing side by side results obtained by two radically different methods of treatment.

In comparing results it should be remembered that we were dealing with unselected cases and that the Brompton Hospital was dealing with selected cases. To quote from the Brompton official report: "The cases sent here have been carefully selected, only those patients being chosen who were free from fever or other serious constitutional symptoms, who possessed considerable vitality and had already begun to show signs of improvement. So far as possible, also, patients with signs of limited disease have been preferred, although it was early found that patients with the disease extensive, but of a quiescent type, often did remarkably well. The presence of pulmonary symptoms, such as cough, expectoration and occasional slight haemoptysis has not excluded the patient from this class, provided the general condition has remained good and the capacity for work has been maintained."

In this report the staff of Brompton admits that the end results are disappointing. "In view of the careful selection of cases for the Frimley Sanitorium, it was hoped that a larger percentage would have retained their health." They point out that their results compare not unfavorably with the German Sanatoria established under the insurance law. But Cornet has clearly shown that the end results in these sanatoria are bad—so bad, in fact, as to bring the sanatorium treatment for wage-earners largely into discredit in Germany. He found that among 19,938 persons who received treatment in the German sanatoria for working men, 13,891, or 70 per cent, were either dead or invalided at the end of four years.

68.4 per cent of those with positive sputum were dead or invalided four years after discharge from Brompton. Our form of home treatment has given better results, as 21 per cent less, 46.7 per cent instead of 68.4 per cent, of the patients with positive sputum treated by the class method were dead or invalided four to ten years after their discharge.

Of 416 patients discharged from the Brompton Hospital Sanatorium 112 were well and able to work five to seven years after their discharge. Deducting the 147 untraced, the percentage is 41.6.

At the end of five to seven years following their discharge from the class 40 of the 59 patients were well and able to work. Deducting the two untraced, the percentage is 70.

Of the 55 patients discharged from Brompton in 1905, only 8 were well seven years later, while of the 21 discharged from the tuberculosis class in 1908, 14 were well seven years later. Patients who were in the sanatorium less than two months are not considered.

The Frimley method found almost instant favor in America. On all sides one heard that work, not rest, was the proper treatment for tuberculosis. Yet Brehmer,* the father of the sanatorium treatment, was convinced after years of clinical observation that labor was injurious in the active stages of the disease; he would not let his patients play croquet or billiards, and he warned them against the danger of breathing exercises. It is strange that all his teaching and that of Dettweiler and Cornet should have been cast aside in favor of the Frimley method, without any evidence except that some carefully selected consumptives, without fever, who had had three months of rest treatment at the Brompton Hospital, could do hard work without any immediate ill effects.

The class method is sometimes criticized as too limited in its scope, because we find it necessary to spend so much time, energy, and money on a single patient. Miss La Motte in her book on the *Tuberculosis Nurse* says that the tuberculosis class "deals with so few people that it makes no real impression on the situation." She adds that the tuberculosis problem is what can be done for a thousand patients, not for twenty. With these statements I cannot agree, and I am convinced that the view widely held that little can be done for the individual patient explains in large part the disappointing results obtained thus far in the tuberculosis campaign. The tuberculosis problem as it presents itself to the practicing physician and the nurse is, or should be, the individual patient. Give him the proper treatment, whether he be the sole consumptive in a small hamlet, a member of a tuberculosis class of twenty, or a patient in a sanatorium for a thousand patients, and the tuberculosis problem will be largely solved.

---

* It should be made clear that Brehmer did employ exercise in the form of walking. He held the mistaken idea that the disease was due to weakness of the heart, and he maintained that walks of increasing length, by strengthening the heart, brought about the cure of the disease. Great care was taken to avoid fatigue which he recognized as injurious. The following was one of his dictums: "The healthy person sits down when he is tired; the consumptive sits down that he may not get tired."

Not only may one tuberculosis class make a real impression on the tuberculosis situation, but the efforts of one nurse expended on a single patient may exert a widespread influence. The history of Robert D. illustrates the truth of this statement. To many nurses it might have seemed that efforts to make a poor ignorant Negro with far-advanced consumption take the proper treatment were a waste of time, especially as the patient was unwilling to heed her advice. He might readily have been placed in the group of unteachable consumptives. Mrs. Green, the class nurse, was unwilling to admit that this man was unteachable, although she made a dozen visits before he agreed to follow the treatment. After he had yielded, she persuaded the landlord to build a balcony at the cost of $11.50. The picture of this simple porch is familiar to many. It appears in the pamphlet on outdoor sleeping published by the National Association for the Study and Prevention of Tuberculosis and in the widely distributed pamphlet issued by the Metropolitan Life Insurance Company. It is also to be found in Dr. Knopf's "Prize Essay" and Dr. Hawes' two books on tuberculosis. The porch itself is still used as a sleeping place by the patient, although he has been at work for nearly nine years. In the neighborhood in which he lives it serves the purpose of a permanent tuberculosis exhibit. He tells his own story in the following letter:

Cambridge, August 3, 1911.

Dear Doctor:

Please excuse Long Delay. I am all so Sleepy at night after the Days work I culdent keep wake Long enough. this is my after noon of So I have a good chance to write after 5 or 6 years of continuous Sleeping out of dose I am thorley convinced that your way of living in the fresh air is the onley way for me. I have allso convinced my meny Collard Friends who come around after the Nurse had gorn and Beg me not to take that treatment as it would give me more Cold. what I wanted was a warm Room and Some thing that would loosen the Sputum and bring it up all this Seamed just the thing for me expecially the medison which was rum and molasses your Friendly visitor was coming every day telling me of her wonderfull treatment all of her treatment seamed hard Sleep out in the Backyard where the cats was fighting all Night. take cold watter bath that I never did while in the South wher it was warm and this was February. I allmost Beleaved what my Friends had told me that they was trying to kill me so I would not be exspence to the city of Camb or they was experimenting on me So the would know how to cure the nex fellow.

Your friendly visitor Miss Orieon exsplained the treatment to me in Such a way that I Beleaved if I could take the treatment and do every thing just as She wand me to do I would be cured. I desided with my Self I would do everything She want me to do exactly the way She want it don. One month be for the month was up She gave me a Chest Bath in a cold Room before a open window in month of Feb. and Bandaved my Body with wet Bandages. I desided I would not take the treatment enny Longer. When she came her kind and earnest talk perswaded me to keep on. thank god to-day I am feeling better than I felt for years Befor I was Sick god bless you and you Class. Just think where would I been now if you had not taken me in you class. I remain

R—— D——

R.D. admitted to class Jan. 6, 1906. Far advanced. Positive sputum. Unable to work since July, 1904. Wt. 145 lbs. Wife and 2 children slept in room with patient. Porch built by landlord. Photograph appears in Knopf's Prize Essay, and Carrington's Pamphlet on Open Air Sleeping. Allowed to work May to Nov., 1907. Resumed treatment Nov., 1907. Discharged March, 1908. Wt. 209. Well and working 8 years. (July, 1915.)

Many of the discharged patients that had learned any sort of trade before their sickness have followed the same occupation since returning to work. When indoor workers have taken out-of-door jobs they have rarely held them. It is usually far less fatiguing for ex-patients to do work to which they are accustomed than to take up some unfamiliar employment. It is most encouraging to find that those who have recovered their health at home are able in the majority of cases to work full time month after month and year after year.

Of 124 patients the occupations when taken ill were as follows: housewives 38, schoolchildren 14, engaged in various sewing trades 11, tailors, machinists and laborers, and factory operatives 4 each, clerks, teamsters, printers, and stenographers 3 each, shoe factory operatives, sales girls, tinsmiths, and designers 2 each, and 1 of each of the following: store owner, traveling salesman, peddler, barber, deaconess, letter carrier, comedian, confectioner, electrotype molder, scrub woman, lawyer, watchmaker, jeweler, conductor, detective, note broker, cobbler, Pullman car cleaner, milliner, waitress, bindery worker, telephone operator, tobacco stripper, boardinghouse keeper, school teacher. Two had no occupation, and of two the occupations are not known.

The occupations of the same 124 patients in 1915 were: housewives 46, nine of whom had had children since leaving the class; engaged in sewing trades and store owners 6, schoolchildren and tailors 4 each, machinists, clerks, teamsters, shoe factory operatives, traveling salesmen, peddlers, foremen, farmers, janitors, attendant nurses, social workers, and bookkeepers 2 each, and 1 of each of the following: printer, designer, barber, deaconess, letter carrier, comedian, confectioner, die forger, scrub woman, collector, forester, writer and photographer, stewardess, hotel checker, music teacher, ticket seller. Two changed occupations too frequently to be classified. One was a patient in a sanatorium; three were still class members. Five had no occupation, and of five the occupation was not known.

Space permits only two examples of what has been done in the way of family rehabilitation. The first patient who returned to work was a tailor. During the period of class treatment the family resources reached such a low point that his wife, without our knowledge, pawned her wedding ring. This man was rated on admission as a third stage case with signs of a cavity at the apex of the right lung. He was paid by Dr. Cabot to attend one of his clinical exercises as a subject for demonstration in physical diagnosis. I mention this as an indication that he had definite physical signs. After he was thought ready for work we were loath to send him back to a sweatshop, so an appeal was made to one of the generous friends of the class, who gave him enough money to start in business in a tiny shop of his own. He later moved to a larger place on a busier street and has supported himself and family for more than ten years. At the time of his illness his only child was a little boy of four. The boy now is a first year student in the English High School with a good record in scholarship, and his father is planning to send him to college.

At Christmas 1907 one of the Church workers learned of a family that were without money or food. Investigation brought the fact to light that both husband and wife were sick with pulmonary tuberculosis. There were three children, the oldest of which was only 11. The children were placed in families. After long search, a boarding place for the two patients was found in a colored family. A tent was purchased and the treatment was taken on the flat roof. Both recovered. The family was reunited. The woman has been doing her own housework for years, and the man has been self-supporting for seven years. He is a motorman.

It is often stated that the consumptive should not be treated at home because of the danger that others of his family may become infected. Our experience confirms the opinion expressed many years ago by Cornet that "the consumptive in himself is almost harmless, and only becomes harmful through bad habits." We have statistics on the health of all members of 131 families who had representatives in the Class between 1905 and 1915. Although 83 (41 per cent) of our 200 patients had a family history of pulmonary tuberculosis, since their connection with our class, only 3 new cases of pulmonary tuberculosis (2.3) have developed among the 131 families of which the subsequent report is complete. There have been two cases of tuberculous meningitis and two of tuberculosis of the lymph nodes. In these 131 families there were 220 children.

8

THE USE OF DEJERINE'S METHODS IN THE TREATMENT OF THE COMMON NEUROSES BY GROUP PSYCHOTHERAPY

Joseph H. Pratt

A simple form of psychotherapy that has been successfully employed in the treatment of the common neuroses requires no special training in psychology or psychiatry yet is unfamiliar to most physicians because it is rarely taught in the schools.

Nearly forty years ago, on the street one day I chanced to meet Dr. Isadore Coriat, the late well-known psychiatrist, as he was coming from the Boston Medical Library. He had just been reading Dejerine's new book on the treatment of the psychoneuroses by psychotherapy and recommended it so enthusiastically that I at once obtained a copy. It was a revelation to me.

Sir Arthur Hurst, in his recently published reminiscences, writes of Dejerine as follows: "At a time when in England and America neurotic patients received either no treatment at all or were treated by isolation, rest, overfeeding, and massage according to the routine invented by the poet physician Weir Mitchell, Dejerine had discarded purely physical treatment for a form of psychotherapy which differs little from the best methods practised today. He summarized his methods in these words: 'Expliquer au malade, après lui avoir fait confesser sa vie, comment et pourquoi il est tombé malade, comment et pourquoi il arrivera à se guérir.' "

Joseph Jules Dejerine's book *Les Manifestations Fonctionnelles des Psychonévroses; Leur Traitement par la Psychothérapie** was published in 1911. About the book, Sir Arthur wrote, "It is in my opinion the wisest ever written on the subject, and even today it gives a better introduction to

Reprinted from the *Bulletin of the New England Medical Center*, Vol. XV, March 1953, pp. 1-9.
* E. Gauckler, coauthor.

psychotherapy than any more modern book, except perhaps T. A. Ross's *The Common Neuroses*, which, as Ross acknowledged in his preface, was largely based on Dejerine's teaching. Every medical student should read these two books before going into practice, as they will help him to deal with almost any patient who seeks his advice."

Before writing the account of his methods and the results he had obtained, Dejerine had developed methods of emotional reeducation and employed them in hundreds of cases over a period of fifteen years. He was the first to recognize that the neuroses are of emotional origin and that emotional training and reeducation are the essential elements in their treatment. I have followed Dejerine's methods ever since reading his book and can pay no greater tribute to this great master of medicine than to acknowledge the gratifying success that has followed my efforts.

Dejerine's book was translated into English by Dr. Smith Ely Jelliffe and published in 1913. It attracted little attention and has apparently remained almost unknown to American psychiatrists and internists, since it is rarely referred to by American writers. When the book could no longer be obtained from dealers in medical books and I wrote the publishers suggesting that it be reprinted, they replied that the book had had such a poor sale the plates had been destroyed. A number of recent medical school graduates have told me they never heard the works of Dejerine or Ross referred to by their teachers. Ross' *The Common Neuroses* is listed by Dr. Edward A. Strecker in Musser's *Textbook of Medicine* and by Dr. Thomas A. C. Rennie among the references given at the end of his article on the psychoneuroses in the eighth edition of Cecil's *Textbook of Medicine*; Dejerine's book is not mentioned by either author.

The milder neuroses occur chiefly in patients whose emotional maladjustment is slight. They complain only of physical symptoms such as fatigue, headache, and indigestion. Convinced as these patients are that their trouble is wholly physical, they would not think of consulting a psychiatrist—and they should not be treated by a psychiatrist. They should be treated by internists and general practitioners. The general physician usually knows better than the psychiatrist the means of distinguishing between functional and organic disease of the physical organism. He needs, however, to study the effect of injurious emotions on the bodily functions and learn how to correct them. I talked with recent graduates of six medical schools, and all of them told me they had received no instruction on the use of psychotherapy in the treatment of the everyday complaints of emotional origin.

Even in 1953, in our best hospitals, great harm is done to patients by members of the treatment staff who see them as cases instead of as sick human beings. As Dr. Jerome D. Frank of the Phipps Neuropsychiatric Institute, Johns Hopkins Hospital, stated in a paper read at a meeting of the American Group Psychotherapy Association, the result is that the patient thinks "the purpose of a general hospital . . . is to treat patients' bodies exclusively." He added, ". . . it is a fact of the unwritten hospital code that members of the treatment staff are not expected to be concerned with patients' personal problems . . ." and ". . . the duties of the physician are so organized that there is little time for such matters." These are strong statements, but I believe they apply to all hospitals. Dr. Sara Dubo, in a psychiatic study of children with pulmonary tuberculosis, found that it was the disease and not the children that received treatment. In one ward in which she interviewed the children she found they were afraid of the interns, called them "ghosts," and referred to the attending physician as the "head ghost."

There have been voices crying in the wilderness for nearly a century at least, and probably longer, proclaiming that hospital patients are persons and should be treated as such. Let us listen to a few of these. In 1855, in his "Letters to a Young Physician," the leading Boston physician Dr. James Jackson pointed out that the original sense of the word *cure*, which comes from the Latin *cura*, is "to take care." "The priest had the parish for his cure, the physician the sick for his." In the original sense of the word, the duty of the physician to his patients is to cure all of them.

Ernest Wagner, professor of medicine in the University of Leipzig, wrote, "We do not treat diseases, but sick human beings." This statement was made about seventy-five years ago. It is all the more remarkable because Wagner had previously been professor of pathology in Leipzig, in his work therefore dealing with the structural changes in the body wrought by disease, yet uninfluenced by his materialistic background into thinking that treatment dealt exclusively with patients' bodies.

The same criticism on the attitude of hospital physicians that Dr. Frank makes today, Dr. Francis W. Peabody made in his famous lecture "The Care of the Patient" nearly a quarter of a century ago. "When a patient enters a hospital," he wrote:

> the first thing that commonly happens to him is that he loses his personal identity. He is generally referred to, not as Henry Jones, but as "that case of mitral stenosis in the second bed on the left." . . . The trouble is that it leads, more or less directly, to the patient's being treated as a case of mitral stenosis and not as a sick man. The disease is treated but Henry Jones, lying awake nights while he worries about his wife and children, represents a problem that is more complex than the pathologic physiology of mitral stenosis. . . . But if teachers and students are inclined to take a limited point of view even toward interesting cases of organic disease, they fall into much more serious error in their attitude toward a large group of patients who do not show objective, organic, pathologic conditions and who are generally spoken of as having "nothing the matter with them." Up to a certain point, as long as they are regarded as diagnostic problems, they command attention; but as soon as the physician has assured himself that they do not have organic disease, he passes them over lightly.

The other day it was reported to me that the chief of a medical out-patient clinic said that all neurotic patients should go to the psychiatric clinic for treatment. He should have known better. The treatment of the simple neuroses belongs in the field of general medicine. As Peabody so well pointed out, "In the first place, the differential diagnosis between organic disease and pure functional disturbance is often extremely difficult, and it needs the broad training in the use of general clinical and laboratory methods which forms the equipment of the internist. Diagnosis is the first step in treatment." I might add that the psychiatrist is often confused as to the significance of bodily symptoms such as severe pain in the chest or abdomen. Not long ago, a woman suffering from anxiety was referred by me to a psychiatrist for confirmation of the diagnosis. A thorough examination had shown that the patient was free from organic disease, although she complained bitterly of severe pain in the region of the gall bladder. It was a simple case of anxiety neurosis, yet the psychiatrist reported to me that he would like to have another X-ray examination of the gall bladder before making a diagnosis. The average internist is no more ignorant of what goes on in his patient's head than the average psychiatrist is of the functional disturbances located below the collar.

Peabody told me he had not read Dejerine's work but had learned and taught the simple method of psychotherapy described by T. A. Ross in *The Common Neuroses*. It was his conviction that the majority of the emotionally maladjusted patients "can be helped by the internist without highly specialized psychologic technique, if he will appreciate the significance of functional disturbances and interest himself in their treatment. The physician who does take these cases seriously—one might say scientifically—has the great satisfaction of seeing some of his patients get well not as a result of drugs or as the result of the disease having run its course, but as the result of his own individual efforts."

Every medical student should have instilled in his heart and mind the truth so well stated by that leading German internist and teacher Rudolf Krehl when he wrote that the physician "is only a true physician when he seeks to know and to influence the inner life of the patient." Lord Horder defines successful medicine as "understanding touched with sympathy."

Dr. Merrill Moore, visiting neurologist at the Boston City Hospital, states in a recently published paper that "there are already hundreds of psychiatric problems on the wards of the Boston City Hospital that are not being adequately cared for."

The word *psychiatry* comes from words meaning "mind" and "healing." Since a physician is "one skilled in healing," it is the duty of the physician to practice psychiatry—his skill in healing—to treat the mind as well as the body, for to do otherwise is to neglect the whole man. To establish close, friendly, personal relations with a patient is an elementary form of psychiatric therapy.

When the Medical Clinic of the Boston Dispensary was reorganized in 1927, the staff took a special interest in the symptoms and diagnosis of the psychoneuroses. Kaplan and Davis found by actual count that such cases constituted 36 per cent of 2,000 consecutive admissions to the clinic. Several studies were made. In one of these, Ayman showed that the early symptoms in hypertension were identical with those in the psychoneuroses. Later, an experimental study of pain of psychic origin was conducted by Golden, Rosenthal, and Pratt.

Even if the young physicians had been trained in the use of psychotherapy, effectual individual treatment would have been impossible, the number of cases was so great. To cope with the situation, group therapy was begun. This was in April, 1930. Within a few weeks it was apparent that this form of treatment was worth while. It has been continued to the present time, a period of 23 years. I determined at the outset that I would use the methods I had learned from the writings of Dejerine and which I had employed successfully with private patients for many years. Dejerine held that:

> reasoning by itself is indifferent. It does not become a factor of energy or creator of effort; but the moment an emotional element appears, the personality of the subject whose mentality one is seeking to modify is moved and affected by it. . . . Psychotherapy depends wholly and exclusively upon the beneficial influence of one person on another. One does not cure an hysteric or a neurasthenic, nor change their mental condition, by reasoning or by syllogisms. They are only cured when they come to believe in you.

At the outset, I had no plan for conducting the meetings except to address the group as if talking to a single patient. I decided that I would make no preparation for the meetings in the form of a formal lecture or address of any kind. If that had to be necessary for success, no busy internist could give the time required week after week. The plan would therefore not be practicable unless psychiatrists or psychologists were available; and in the majority of medical outpatient clinics, they would not be available.

I spoke to the group informally on the nature of their emotional maladjustments and how to rectify them. It was a short talk, lasting about ten or fifteen minutes. I was appealing primarily to the emotions of the members; I did not reason by argument, which, as Dejerine has pointed out, is not sufficient in itself to change the state of mind.

We soon adopted a plan of procedure which has been followed ever since. The meeting begins with a roll call. Each member gives his name and states the number of sessions attended. A slip of paper is given him by a "floor secretary," and on it he writes a signed statement of his present condition. These reports are collected, and the leader reads them to the group without indicating the name of the writer. The slips are then arranged by him in three piles. If the member is feeling well, the slip is placed in the pile to the right; if the condition is stationary or "a little better," in the center pile; and if symptoms are still present, in the one to the left. The number in each lot is then announced. The great majority of the reports are usually favorable. The leader knows how many of the twenty or more present need individual help and how many are doing well. Appointments for personal interviews are made for those whose symptoms persist. This procedure thus serves as a screening process.

A relaxation exercise with eyes closed follows the reading of the reports of the present condition of the members. The short talk given by the leader is followed by testimonies of improvement or by a question period.

We were amazed at the speed with which a change in the emotional state was often effected. This was apparent soon after the group was organized. One of the three women who were the first members of the class got a job within three weeks although she had not worked for the previous five years owing to her ill health.

I have looked over the reports handed in at the last meeting. Twelve members are doing well, five are somewhat improved, and eight are still complaining. This is an unusually large number with symptoms still persisting. The previous week there were thirteen doing well, five stationary, and only three who needed individual help. Typical reports handed in that week were: "Good morning, I am feeling fine and I look forward to coming to this wonderful class." From the middle pile: "Feel good this morning, but have not learned yet to cope with my anger and to control my mind." And from the left-hand column: "Could it be possible, subconsciously, I do not want to get well?"

In the twenty-two years from 1930 to 1952, 3,434 patients have been admitted to the class. There were 566 who attended only one session, indicating by their failure to return that they did not wish to follow this form of treatment. Most of them insisting that their symptoms were due to organic disease, they were referred back to the Medical Clinic. In these cases, the symptoms persisted.

Persons returning for a second meeting are entered as members of the class. These now total 2,868 (84 per cent). New members are urged to come five times before concluding that group therapy is not improving their condition. Those who have attended five times or more number 1,469, 51 per cent of all those enrolled as members.

A large percentage of the members report that they are much improved. Many state that their symptoms have entirely disappeared. To our astonishment, a large number continue to attend the meetings after their recovery. Our records show that 185 members have attended 25 meetings or more, and 62 have attended more than 100 times. The presence and testimony of those who have regained their health in the class is great encouragement to new members. There is a remarkable spirit of comradeship among the members in spite of differences in race and religion. They say that they like to come to a place where they are understood and appreciated and that they continue to profit from the meetings.

One member who entered the class in the summer of 1930 has attended 619 times. She had suffered from severe manifestations of hysteria. Her condition had been mistaken for chronic arthritis, as she had severe pain in the joints on even slight movement. She recovered within a few weeks after entering the class. During World War II her four sons were in the military service, but in spite of natural anxiety for their safety she remained well.

Giles W. Thomas, in a historical review of the development of group psychotherapy, published a chart in which our method was placed midway between the pure analytical and the pure repressive inspirational procedures. A better designation of our method would be emotional reeducation and persuasion, terms used by Dejerine in describing his method of individual therapy.

During the past 17 years our work in group psychotherapy has been carried on by men of outstanding ability. Winfred Rhoades, consulting psychologist, was a full-time worker for ten years. He organized an evening group for day workers and conducted the morning class after my retirement. Out of his experience he wrote *The Self You Have to Live With*, which was reprinted fifteen times, and other helpful books. Outpatients of the Medical Clinic of the Boston Dispensary were referred to him in all cases diagnosed as a psychoneurosis. He would take a detailed history of their emotional life and invite them to enter the class for group therapy. When he retired, this part of the work was taken over by Dr. Rose Hilferding, whose help has been acknowledged by hundreds of the patients that have been referred to her. The classes were conducted by Dr. Paul E. Johnson, professor of the psychology of religion in the Graduate School of Theology, Boston University, who for over five years worked with striking success.

The present director of the group is the psychiatrist, Dr. David Landau, a member of the Dispensary staff. He is assisted by Dr. Joseph H. Kaplan, an internist with large experience in the treatment of the neuroses. In recent years the Monday evening class has been under the consecutive direction of two clergymen with advanced training in therapeutic counseling and group therapy: Rev. Robert E. Leslie and Rev. James H. Burns. The former is now chaplain of the Boston State Hospital for mental patients, and the latter is chaplain of the Massachusetts General Hospital. The present director of our evening group is the Rev. Donald L. Colburn. I believe that clergymen who have done graduate work in psychology can carry on group psychotherapy successfully if associated with a physician trained in psychotherapy.

In addition to the weekly morning and evening classes, there was for a short time an afternoon class, successfully conducted by Dr. Herbert L. Harris of our staff, which was terminated only when he entered the military service. Dr. Harris has published an excellent study of group psychotherapy.

The distinguished psychiatrist, Dr. Alfred Hauptmann, formerly director of the neuropsychiatric clinic at the University of Halle, Germany, served us as consulting psychiatrist from his arrival in America until his untimely death. After a thorough study of the method and the patients at the Boston Dispensary, he wrote "there is convincing proof that at least 90 per cent of the neurotic patients who fill the offices of physicians of all specialties and who throng outpatient departments of our hospitals . . . can be successfully treated by the Pratt method."

- 9 -

GROUP THERAPY AND
THE PSYCHIATRIC CLINIC

L. Cody Marsh

Two previous communications[1] described certain projects in an attempt to treat frankly psychotic individuals by the use of group therapy. In the latter communication on this subject, brief reference was made to group therapy projects with psychoneurotics in the open community.

I now wish to give a more detailed description of these experiments and those which have been performed since the writing of that report.

Private psychiatry is available to very few persons, principally on account of its necessarily high cost. Whereas physicians in other specialties see four or five and even more persons in an hour, a psychiatrist ordinarily requires an hour for each patient. We are constantly being asked, "When are you going to develop a type of psychiatric therapy which is financially within the reach of the average patient with the average sized purse?"

Those who cannot afford to pay the fees of a private psychiatrist have ordinarily but one alternative, and that is the psychiatric clinic. These clinics leave much to be desired. In the first place, they have a morbid taste to them, a taste which has been built up in the mind of the community and for which we psychiatrists are not entirely responsible. Then it is not always possible to have psychiatrists for these clinics who can give regular attention throughout the treatment history of all cases.

To be sure there is the psychopathic ward of a growing number of general hospitals, but these suffer from unsavory reputations built up principally by the fact that the psychopathic ward is too often the place where the community's inebriates are sobered. What is far worse, it is the place where the criminals and near criminals and other notorious characters are housed for "observation." Thanks to the energy of the press for morbid stories, the psychopathic ward of the general hospital is about as inviting

Reprinted from the *Journal of Nervous and Mental Diseases*, Vol. 82, 1935, pp. 381-392.

to the twentieth-century public as the Bridge of Sighs was to the medieval populace. Another objection to the psychopathic ward is that it has the setup and general coloring of a typical hospital ward, and so called "nervous people" and others who require psychiatric care do not feel that they are *sick* and do not wish to be treated as such.

The private sanatorium for nervous diseases is also beyond the reach of the average purse, and very few of them have an Outpatient Department.

Lastly there is the State Hospital, and many of our large cities have these. To be sure, an all too few of them are becoming interested in maintaining an Outpatient Department, but the average citizen, no matter how pressing his emotional conflicts may be, certainly does not wish to admit to himself, much less to his friends, that he is going to the Outpatient Department of "Such and Such an *Insane Asylum*."

In psychiatry, we are dealing with a group of people who, consciously or unconsciously, cling to their maladies because they are serving a very definite purpose, whether they are aware of this or not. The result is that it is only with the greatest difficulty that they can be induced to take any form of treatment. Persons suffering from other maladies than those grouped under psychiatry generally seek treatment energetically and are more or less glad to cooperate. For this reason it is all the more important that we, in psychiatry, offer not only a form of treatment which is financially accessible to patients but which is so adroitly and cleverly presented that this therapy becomes attractive and disarms the sufferer of his forebodings.

THE GROUP APPROACH

Group therapy is not a new thing. The students who clustered about such ancients as Pythagoras, Socrates, Zoroaster, and probably most of the classic philosophers were partly seekers for knowledge, but they were also seekers for emotional help. Many of those early teachers conducted the so-called peripatetic schools, wherein the students walked about with the teacher as he taught. The physical effort involved in these walks, together with the interesting sights encountered, probably combined with the instructor's teachings, to make a form of group therapy as well as a form of education.

Religion has utilized the forces bound up in crowd psychology to produce cures, both alleged and real.

At the Boston Dispensary, Dr. Pratt has successfully treated psychoneurotics in whom organic lesions could not be demonstrated, by the class method.

I have reported certain values of this type of approach for those who are frankly psychotic. It is freely granted that there are types of psychoneurotics whose sufferings are said to be made worse by being placed in a group. However, I have found that where the class work is supplemented with individual attention that this objection is overcome.

There is a compulsion at work in the group which is rarely at work with equal force when the physician meets the patient privately. Another advantage of the group treatment is that the transference is a group transference and a less impersonal one than is made in private treatment. The patient not only makes the transference to the physician but to the group. The transference is more readily broken.

The patient comes to regard the proceeding as an educational one and takes a more sunny attitude toward it. Since he sees that others in the group whom he can respect do not differ greatly from himself, he concludes that he is not in a morbid situation.

The class also takes on a certain enthusiasm which one rarely gets in a private contact. Because of this enthusiasm and the compulsion at work in the group, the case seems to move on more rapidly toward betterment, if not recovery. It is my experience that patients seem more willing to accept a new point of view in the group than they do when approached singly.

In going over some five hundred private cases, I believe that most psychiatrists will agree with me that something like seventy-five per cent of the material which is offered to the patient is material which could be embodied into a course of lectures. That being so, it occurred to me to devise a course of lectures which included this material and supplement this with individual work for the more intimate and specific matters which persons naturally dislike to discuss in an open class.

It has seemed to me that patients also liked the *impersonality* of the class situation. In spite of one's success in developing the so-called objective or psychiatric attitude in the task of psychiatric therapy, private consultation necessarily constitutes a very intimate and personal situation. This very situation seems to act as a fearsome thing, against which the patients build up a whole congerie of defenses.

The descriptive matter following is drawn from the writer's experience with:

(1) *Mental Hygiene Classes Conducted at Worcester State Hospital.* These classes were primarily for the relatives of patients, but in time they came to include many others from the community, clergymen, school teachers, nurses, parents, and a various assortment of persons who could be classed as psychoneurotics and prepsychotics. Of this last group, most of them sought the help of the Group Clinic of their own accord, although there were several who were referred to the Clinic by physicians in the city of Worcester, social service agencies, Y.M.C.A., Y.W.C.A., district nurses, clergymen, and others. Of course no charge was made, although I believe that one should have been made.

In spite of the fact that most of these people had at some time taken a firm but silent vow that they would never enter the doors of what they called "the insane asylum," they seemed to enjoy coming to the classes because of their educational accent and certain other features which they considered attractive. For one thing, the psychoneurotic and psychotic recognized at a glance many persons who occupied substantial places in the community and instantly he identified himself with them, so that membership in the class gave him a tone feeling of comfort and a certain degree of pride. In short it did not strike him as a *clinic* for *queer* people or "crazy" people. Furthermore it was never called a clinic. Many of the class members were given private attention and in most instances, they sought this private attention.

(2) *A Group Class for Normal and Psychoneurotic Persons in the City of Worcester.* This class had a membership of sixteen. All were school teachers, females, and of one religious faith. The religious and sex homogeneity seemed to have certain advantages. This was also an intelligent group and they were taken into the writer's confidence as to what he was trying to do. Because of their splendid cooperation, much was learned about what to do and what not to do in the group approach.

(3) *The Reeducational Institute in Boston.* This was founded by the author in June 1932. A large, high-ceiled studio with two small entrance rooms was engaged for the purpose. The studio was furnished with chairs, blackboard, grand piano, and attractively decorated, and gave the atmosphere of a classroom rather than of a cold treatment room. Twelve series of classes were held in this studio in the course of a year. Classes contained normal persons, physicians, clergymen, educators, teachers, nurses, college students, and so on, and also others who were frankly psychoneurotic, prepsychotic, and others definitely psychotic. This particular experiment, which I have called the Reeducational Institute, gave very gratifying results. Certain social agencies referred cases, but only five physicians in Boston referred cases, although announcements were sent to some two thousand. In this connection I have often wondered what the average physician does with those cases which should be referred to a psychiatrist. In a previous paper I once mentioned that of a long series of patients I had admitted to a State Hospital, and all of whom had family physicians, only in a scant half dozen had these physicians referred the case to a psychiatrist. Certainly the psychiatric clinics are few, and they also are not overcrowded, so I wonder again what the medical profession does about cases which are referable to a psychiatrist.

PROCEDURE

(1) *Enrollment.* Patients were enrolled as *students.* In the case of some of the classes, these students signed a pledge to give their fullest cooperation in the course, to do the assigned homework, and to be regular

and prompt in attendance. The pledge went into some detail as to what was to be accomplished in the course and was, in fact, called the "Psychiatric Pledge." Ordinarily tuition was payable in advance, the understanding being that time taken privately with the instructor was to be an additional cost.

(2) *The Lecture Course.* The course consisted of four lectures. The following is a brief outline of the lecture material:

Family Situation. A constructive sociological study of one's own family to obtain a sunny and sympathetic understanding of family relationships and the role of each member in the family drama. The meaning of "good family" and "good birth."

Foundations of Personality in Childhood. Formation of habits of feeling and thinking which condition us throughout life. Beginnings of play life and dissipation trends. School life. Significance of the Intelligence Quotient. The orderly use of the mind.

Economic Equipment. Job integration, aptitudes, and ambitions. Job behavior. Production drive.

Emotional Life. Understanding one's emotional pattern. The conflict between love and fear. Emotional Agility, the measure of one's modifiability. "Monkey Wrenches" in the emotional machinery. Emotional outlets.

Social Life. Social assets and liabilities. The development of charm and "personality." Sex attraction. Small talk. Free association.

Religious Life. The conflict between religion and modern needs. The new ethics. A psychiatric interpretation of sin, conscience, faith, and so on.

Sex Life. A short history of the philosophies of sex. Influence of sex glands on behavior. Dangers of adolescent period. Values and dangers of sex repression and sex indulgence. Love life and marriage at the juvenile, adolescent, and adult levels.

Abnormal People. Beginnings of "mental trouble" in the rigid, shut-in, and selfish personalities. Common types of nervousness, their meaning and management.

Normal Adult Personality. Health without fads, control over environment, healthy emotional mechanisms, thrift, happiness, the open mind, integrated reaction to life, free association, fact-facing, self-understanding, ability to play, articulacy, social ease, success in small things, security feeling, sense of freedom, satisfactory family and love life, independence without pugnacity, lovableness, push.

In several instances students repeated the lecture course, a few of them three and four times. In the deeply seated neuroses, patients even in classwork put up formidable resistances to instruction. However, this is not so marked in the class approach as in the individual approach. The group compulsion tends to overcome these resistances. It may be said, parenthetically, that neurotics tend to put up resistances to any type of instruction. This accounts in part for the difficult time that most neurotics have in all educational institutions.

(3) *Questions and Answers.* When the lecture was concluded, opportunities were given for asking questions. At first students had to be encouraged by writing out questions and leaving them on the instructor's desk. After the first session, however, few questions were written and, in general, students tended to become amazingly frank in asking the most intimate and personal questions which were clearly descriptive of their own difficulties. Oftentimes the instructor asked for answers from class members, and occasionally a consensus of opinion would be taken. It was not long before each class developed a sound mental hygiene point of view. The class thus became a democratic, educational project wherein the instructor was rather a moderator than a lord.

(4) *Class Atmosphere.* The instructor was always careful to maintain an atmosphere of academic dignity. The language used was rarely scientific, that is, the writer rarely indulged in the "slang," "lingo," or "neologisms" of psychiatry. On the other hand, popular slang was not used, except rarely with apologies. On the other hand, the atmosphere was kept sunny, and the subject matter was handled with a certain lightness of touch. The writer believes that there are great dangers in presenting mental hygiene or the subject matter of psychiatry, unless an air of sunniness and lightness of touch is maintained. Students in this type of a setup must be impressed from the outset that they are not queer, that the subject is not queer, but that, on the other hand, they are people like any other group of persons and that the subject matter is just as normal, sunny, informative, and valuable as any other subject.

The emphasis in the class atmosphere is on *teaching* rather than on *treating.* During the actual lecture period, the atmosphere was distinctly dignified, moderately formal, and academic. But before and after class, the students were encouraged to be sociable, and if they showed a tendency here and there to be rowdyish, this was ignored. Flowers were always placed in the classroom, and the writer generally saw to it that there was someone who could play the grand piano or sing before and after class, but always in a spontaneous fashion. If the group or any part of it wanted to sing, they did so, but the initiative came from the students and not from the instructor, who stood apart from all of these activities. It was remarkable, at times, how these spontaneous social activities socialized the whole group, including two incipient, paranoid praecox young men who looked quite hopeless on admission. This latter situation suggested that there may be great therapeutic values in hazing, for oftentimes students seem to have the ability, by means of hazing, of correcting situations which the "prof" would rarely reach. At least some mild hazing did great things for these two paranoid young men. It is suggested that in attempting to do or improve upon this experiment that this particular feature be encouraged, perhaps with some backstage instruction. Neither the psychiatrist nor the teacher can haze. But students may haze their fellows.

(5) *Organization.* Students were assigned to various tasks, so that by the time the lecture course was completed, each one had done something which gave him or her a sense of ownership in the project. They were assigned to such special tasks as being monitors, "greeters," "introducers," to arrange chairs, care for the flowers, clean the blackboard or write thereon the lecture outline, and in keeping the roll. These activities tended also to dispel the atmosphere of morbidity which is apt to cling to things psychiatric, especially the clinic.

(6) *Notes.* Students were always asked to take notes, and whether they took them or not, they were always given pencils and paper if they did not bring notebooks. The art of taking notes, like the art of studying, is something that very few people learn. It was observed that even college people would, oftentimes, prefer to listen without note-taking. There should be some place in our education plan to teach students how to listen to a lecture, how to take notes, and how to study. After all, these are tokens of our powers of attention and concentration. Neuroses often develop from failures, and failure may be due to an inability to listen, or to observe, or to take notes, or to study. Some attention was given to this with some of the groups, and with profit. However, the notes are not an end in themselves, and it is granted that most of the notes should be taken in the head.

(7) *Grading.* In certain of the courses, each student was given a grade on the following points:

(a) Attendance
(b) Punctuality
(c) Attentiveness
(d) General cooperation
(e) Standing with class members
(f) Evident improvement
(g) Avowed improvement
(h) Insight and judgment

These grades were discussed with the student when he came for the private interview after the lecture course was completed. In one class the students were asked to grade each other on most of these points. In this one instance, it was valuable.

(8) *Outside Reading.* At one time I was rather enthusiastic about giving outside reading to those who have so-called mental difficulties. I am beginning to feel now, however, that it is like certain drugs which we use in medicine, that is, they are very valuable if given under the direction of a physician but never ought to be self-administered. It may be that we have not yet developed the right kind of mental hygiene literature. At least my

feelings are mingled about the advisability of giving outside reading in psychiatry or related subjects. Anyone familiar with the general type of person who registers for "Abnormal Psych" in our colleges must agree that study of these things is only an intellectual achievement and not an emotional one. Some of the best authorities I know on the subjects of mental hygiene and psychiatry are also the unhappiest people I know.

I found it more valuable to send students to the library to work up a little outline on some cultural but unrelated subject as a test of their powers of attention and concentration.

(9) *Treating Each Other.* In most of the classes some of the students were asked to assist the instructor in "teaching" some classmate. In most of these cases the assistant so deputized was one of the outstanding class problems. But in helping a confrere, he was inspired to make an effort which he would not otherwise make. This also gave the instructor an opportunity to give experience to certain ones who were interested in the project. Of these, two were clergymen, a physician in general practice, a young psychiatrist, two social service workers, two mothers with problem children, and a Salvation Army official.

Oftentimes when the instructor noted a flagging interest in a student, an assignment to assist "teaching" another student restored his interest.

(10) *Class Exercises.* First of all there were the exercises which bore directly upon the subject matter. The first one was the preparation of the family case history. The class members were asked to make a family case study of their own families, but with the objective point of view rather than the usual, carpingly critical point of view, which ordinarily characterizes the family member. A form for these studies was put on the blackboard, discussed, and questions answered. Other and similar group tasks were:

(a) My Earliest Memory
(b) Ingredients of My Inferiority Complex
(c) Things I Am Afraid Of
(d) Emotional Monkey Wrenches
(e) Disarmament Conference of the Human Heart
(f) Social Assets and Liabilities
(g) Sources of Inspiration and Happiness
(h) Night and Day Dreams

These classroom tasks, if one made contribution to them, gave an opportunity for a good deal of laughter and also for each one to see that most of the material in the secret recesses of his heart was not sinful, or morbid, or abnormal and that he was quite like anybody else. These tasks also assisted the class members in making out their own private tabulations under the above headings.

In addition to this purely academic work and apart from the spontaneous stunts in which students indulged before and after class, they were required to do certain socializing things under the direction of the instructor:

(a) Class was required to organize within five minutes at the third lecture.

(b) Occasionally the class was given tap dancing instruction en masse. This was found most valuable and would have been used more had the finances of the Institute permitted it. The writer knows of nothing that is better calculated to limber up an individual or a group. It served as an emotional stramonium.

(c) In a few instances the class was conducted as an informal dramatic group. This is also very helpful. The shyest person, for example, is willing "to play" the part of the gayest social lion, and this eventually gives him the courage to *live* something approaching that.

(11) *Homework.* Each student was asked to write out and hand in his own personal tabulations under the headings listed in paragraph (10) above. In addition he wrote a "mood history," so that I could ascertain what his favored emotional mechanisms were and thus help him make a better selection of these mechanisms, if necessary, planning and developing new and better ones. He was also asked to make a list of his problems, first of all to find out what they were. They are ordinarily profound secrets to most people. In some instances, class members were asked to make a brief outline of their love life history, their job history, and a simple description of their physical development and illnesses.

(12) *"Private Consultation."* The writer believes it is highly important in psychiatric work to rid ourselves of this expression for reasons which have been given. The expression was not used at the Institute, and this particular task was always referred to as "tutoring" or "coaching." As a rule, the students sought this, and this was a valuable bit of psychology. If the instructor suggested to the student that he had better have some private tutoring, he was quite apt to put up defenses which had to be overcome. If he asked the instructor for it, he brought to the task a genuine interest and at least some enthusiasm. However, he was not given the tutoring until he had completed the lecture course. In most cases, he came to this private hour with a definite list of questions and problems written out. He knew most of his needs and was ready to receive suggestions about them. Most of this did not require more than two or three hours of private consultation. They were charged a reduced coaching fee, where they had limited finances. Cases referred by welfare organizations were charged five dollars an hour. In several instances my assistants took over this task, and with credit to themselves. Certain agencies advised me that, whereas they had been lugging along for months, at considerable expense, problem people referred to the Institute, the work we had done at very slight expense had relieved the welfare agency of any further responsibility and cost.

Doubtless the great majority of people who are ordinarily being carried on the backs of our welfare agencies are people who need a constructive job in mental hygiene, rather than food, clothing, and money allowances.

(13) *Physical Examination.* In most cases, the physical examination was included "among the privileges for which tuition was paid." The examination given was rather thorough and disclosed many things which needed correction, mostly mistaken ideas. The outstanding need here was to reassure the student that he did *not* have a bad heart, that he was *not* about to die of tuberculosis, that she did *not* have cancer of the breast, or that the snapping feeling felt in the head was not disintegrating nerves in the brain. Thus the value of the physical examination was more for reassurance than as an excuse for some medical treatment.

(14) *The Progress Card.* Students were asked to keep a record of their progress or lack of progress and show this frequently to the instructor. It was a single card, ruled into three columns. The first one named briefly a life situation which was a source of discomfort or unhappiness. The second column listed, quite as briefly, the usual response of the individual to this situation. In the third column the student indicated a newly planned but improved response to the situation described in the first column.

Unfortunately the finances of the Institute did not permit of a staff of social service workers, occupational therapists, and many others the writer could name who would be most helpful in the project. In a few instances, volunteer workers helped with some of these special activities, but only enough to demonstrate the great need of well-trained workers.

We indulged in one type of follow-up which was pleasurable and helpful, and that was the student reunion. These were held occasionally, and all past students were invited. They were allowed to indulge their own spontaneous activities, compare notes about progress, show each other their cards, to tell proudly of achievements of which they had previously despaired, and otherwise renew auld acquaintance. The instructor gave a brief lecture on some mental hygiene topic, suggested by what was being reported in the press, for example, "The Psychiatric Slant of the New Deal." Sometimes we had simple refreshments.

CASES TREATED

(1) Psychoneuroses
(2) Prepsychotic conditions
(3) Psychoses
    (a) Epilepsy with schizoid behavior
    (b) Postencephalitic psychoses
    (c) Involutional melancholia
    (d) Hypomanic state
    (e) Dementia praecox, simple type

    (f) Dementia praecox, hebephrenic type
    (g) Dementia praecox, paranoid type
    (h) Traumatic psychoses
(4) Organic states with neuroses
    (a) Cardiac states
    (b) Gastric ulcer
    (c) Hay fever
    (d) Asthma
    (e) Orthopedic conditions
(5) Stammerers

Occasionally there were persons in the class who spoke little English, Italians, Russians, e.g., but they seemed to derive as much benefit as the others. The classes generally represented varying social strata and varying intellectual levels. However the lecture material was presented in the simplest language, and even those not well favored intellectually seemed to grasp nearly all of the material. The psychology of the group levels off human distinctions, and very shortly the group takes on a uniformity of interests as well as of progress.

The writer is especially enthusiastic however about "teaching" special and homogeneous groups. It is suggested that physicians dealing with such groups as cardiac, orthopedic, asthmatic, and hay fever, gastric ulcer, and diabetic cases have them taught by a consulting psychiatrist or mental hygienist in groups. This will make more certain the purely medical task of the respective specialist.

A group of stammerers, consisting of fourteen men and two women, was a special case in point. One of the secrets of the group psychology is that the group share some one great and common need. This was certainly true of the stammerers, and they were helped a great deal by the group work. Already specialists dealing with diabetes and tuberculosis, to mention but two examples, have found the value of teaching their patients in groups. Here, however, they have, for the most part, dealt with purely medical aspects of the situation. The class has been found to be not only a timesaver but a progress maker.

RESULTS

It is most difficult to appraise results in the field of psychiatry. We do not have the palpable evidences of improvement or failure of improvement which other branches of medicine enjoy. However, both the writer and those students who attended the classes feel that psychiatric patients may be treated successfully by the class method, followed by individual consultation.

It is certain that this method cuts down the expense to the patient considerably, and the method is offered as a contribution toward the solution of the problem: How shall we offer an acceptable plan for psychiatric treatment which is within reach of the average purse?

SUMMARY

1. Attention is called to the fact that facilities for private treatment of psychiatric cases, at the present time, are quite limited.

2. Attention is called to some of the shortcomings of our present facilities for psychiatric treatment.

3. Very few persons can afford the services of a private psychiatrist.

4. The group treatment of psychiatric patients has certain special advantages over individual treatment, particularly in providing a therapeutic compulsion, a helpful transference which is easily broken, an educational and attractive setup; resistances of patients are more easily overcome; enthusiasms are engendered which are not so prominent in private treatment; and the impersonality of the situation makes the patient more amenable to treatment.

5. It has been found, by experience, that at least seventy-five per cent of the material covered in private treatment of patients could be embodied in a course of lectures.

6. The author's experience with the group treatment of psychiatric patients is described.

7. It is believed that the plan, as described, is superior to the psychiatric or mental hygiene clinic, and would enable us, with present facilities, to handle a great many more patients.

8. Emphasis is placed on the belief that patients should be regarded rather as *students* than *patients*, and the process should be an *educational* one rather than a *medical* procedure.

REFERENCE

1. L. Cody Marsh, "The Group Treatment of the Psychoses," *Ment. Hyg.*, April 1931; "An Experiment in Group Therapy," *Ment. Hyg.*, July 1933.

- 10 -

THE GROUP METHOD OF ANALYSIS

Trigant Burrow

A paper that sets out with a paradoxical title can hardly be expected to invite one's confidence unless we can somehow get square with this initial misnomer. An analysis presupposes, of course, the isolation and examination of a part or element representing the structure of a system, combination, or group of elements. But biologically, a group represents a synthesis, and only its parts are susceptible of analysis. So that a group method of analysis is of its nature self-contradictory. One could as consistently speak of a synthetic method of analysis as of a group method of analysis. And yet there is in fact the group material to be confronted, and there is, as I see it, only the analytic method of confronting it. And so, in attempting to reconcile processes that are so obviously opposed—the one group or synthetic, the other individual or analytic—there is clearly some consistent explanation called for. It is this explanation for which it is difficult for me to find words. If, however, as far as may be, you will participate with me in this endeavor, I think that we may together arrive at some common interpretation that will reconcile this seeming contradiction—a contradiction that has for a long time, I confess, been too little clear in my own mind.

I think we do not realize to what extent we have come to employ the term *group* or combination in an entirely artificial and conventional sense. The landscape gardener arranges a group of trees, the historian a group of chronological events. The educator will form a group of students, the sociologist a group of welfare workers. There may be a group of scientists or ironworkers or artists. But such grouping is entirely external and arbitrary. There is no organic inherency uniting the several elements composing such groups. Where elements are assembled in such manner, what is really represented is but a collection or placing together of elements. On the

Reprinted from *The Psychoanalytic Review*, Vol. XIV, No. 3, July 1927, pp. 268-280.

contrary, when we come to speak of such a group as is represented in a colony of ants, let us say, or a herd of deer or a tribe of primitive men, we are at once connoting an assemblage of elements that is grouped into one integral whole by reason of an inner organic bond common to the several elements of which it is composed. It is this type of group that unites the elements of the species. In such organic groups the connecting link among them is an essential and instinctive one. It is not one that is separable by any arbitrary or external process of arrangement.[1]

The life of man today in the midst of his complex civilization embodies still the organic bonds of this instinctive racial unity. The essential biology of the race is not in the least altered from that of the days of man's early primitive societies. Organic principles do not vary under the variations of external circumstance. Racial instincts do not wear out with time. But something has interposed itself unconsciously within the group life of man. Unlike the groups or colonies occurring within the lower orders, man's societal life has been arbitrarily affected by this unconscious factor, and he has not been allowed to group or colonize in response to the natural behest of primary instinctive bonds. On the contrary, man has gathered or disposed himself in various forms of groupings and affiliations—social, political, economic, national, religious—that have been wholly superficial and utterly alien to him from the point of view of his instinctive group life. And so it is necessary that the synthetic and instinctive group life of primitive tribal man be very clearly distinguished from the collective or pseudogroup formations into which man has entered at the dictates of social and conventional tradition or authority.

Naturally in a group that embodies but an arbitrary collection of individuals the part or element within such an assemblage may, without jeopardy to organic instinct, be readily drawn aside and subjected to a process of isolation and examination—the process we know as analysis. Isolating the individual or part of such a conventional association of elements entails no organic breach—not any more than would the disturbance of the landscapist's arrangement of trees or the school principal's distribution of pupils. But tearing the leaves or petals from their stalk in order to analyze them is a process that necessarily severs the part under examination from functional continuity with the organic whole of which it is a part. The continuity of the organism as a whole is instantly destroyed. So with the ants removed from their colony or the deer withdrawn from their herd. But, after all, the operation of this organic group law within the life of gregarious animals is not an observation restricted by any means to the biological expert. It is a circumstance of practical utility among all intelligent keepers of wild animals. Hagenbeck was not less familiar than Darwin or Kropotkin[2] with the significance of this organic principle uniting the individuals of a species. But while we all tacitly admit that there is this tribal or racial instinct extending throughout and binding together the elements or individuals of a species, we have yet to recognize it within ourselves as *an organic principle of consciousness*. We have yet to see that this societal principle, observable in the spontaneous clusters of primitive man, exerts its instinctive and biological sway equally today within the life of civilized communities.

From these considerations I have come to an altered outlook in my analytic work. I have come to the position that, with respect to the organism of man, an analysis, which presupposes the isolation and private examination of the individual elements apart from their instinctive racial congeners, leaves out of account the larger societal organism of which the individuals are a part and without which it is not possible for them to survive in their coherent unitary life. Such an isolated process of analysis, when applied to the individual of the species man, destroys the organic integrity of the organism as a group or race as truly as we destroy the integrity of the organism composing the flower when we isolate its petal or leaf in order to examine it apart from its structural continuity with the whole. The organic principle uniting the group or societal aggregate represents functional solidarity; the isolated element represents its disruption. So that the analysis of the individual element is contradictory to the preservation of the whole. In other words, the continuity of the group and the isolation of the individual are processes which are of their nature exclusive of one another.

In order to offset this inexorable breach as it operates within the system represented by our own psychoanalytic method, with its inevitable isolation of the single individual, the group of students with whom I have in the last years been working in association have undertaken, through a long and exacting experimental method, a process of analysis that takes account of reactions as they pertain to the species as a whole. This comprehensive scheme of analysis has the merit of leaving intact the material of our societal and instinctive group life, while at the same time it proceeds from this group background to examine analytically the social as well as the personal substitutions and repressions embodied in the arbitrary collective sum or pseudo group represented in this selfsame societal organism.

In order to accept with scientific sympathy the analytic basis of this group technique, it is necessary that as analysts we forego, at least tentatively, certain personal and pseudogroup convictions—convictions that rest rather upon the artificial covenants of single individuals in their merely collective expressions than upon the organic bonds of their essential group biology. We need to rid ourselves of the idea that the neurotic individual is sick and that we psychopathologists are well. We need to accept a more liberal societal viewpoint that permits us to recognize without protest that the individual neurotic is in many respects not more sick than we ourselves. For we quite lose count of the circumstance that the neurotic in his private substitutions and distortions has merely failed to ingratiate himself in the collective confederacy of substitutions and distortions which you and I,

with no less an eye to our self-protection, have had the cunning to sub
scribe to under the cover of our arbitrary, pseudogroup symptomatology. It
begins to be clearer to me that only in this inclusive outlook shall we be
prepared to take account of factors which otherwise are quite closed to us
as social individuals thinking only of our social self-protection.

If we will make a disinterested survey of our psychoanalytic work
upon its present personalistic and confidential basis of technique—a technique that concerns itself solely with the isolated element or individual—
I think it must become evident that, from the point of view of science, our
attitude is quite sadly in arrears. The esoteric practice of closeting a patient
in our private consultation room in order to hear a story of ineptitudes
and maladjustments that are due to social interpositions and substitutions
common to the race and therefore identical with one's own, has, I think,
nowhere its counterpart in any sphere of scientific procedure. We make no
secret of the various physical anomalies to which man is subject. Cardiac
and digestive disorders are willingly submitted to medical investigation.
Likewise diseases due to the abuse of our organisms, such as overeating,
excess of alcohol, or even venereal disease, we accept quite openly in the
clinic or laboratory. The reason is not far to seek. The individual no longer
holds himself morally responsible for such conditions. Today he no longer
regards them as providential visitations. He does not think of them as in
any sense reflecting upon his personal integrity. And yet the no less organic distortions represented in our emotional and sexual inadvertences
and pathologies we treat in a wholly moral and semireligious manner,
and in compliance with the attitude of mind we now hold toward these
conditions we invite patients to meet us in secret conferences that are out
of all relation to their medical and scientific significance.

Were we observing data presented in the chemical or biological laboratory, surely none of us would think of attempting to observe such processes in any other than in a consensual scientific attitude of approach.[3]
Consensual observation is synonymous with scientific precision of technique. The noting of immediate data under conditions of observation
that establish a correspondence of sense perceptions among the several observers is the acknowledged prerequisite of the laboratory criterion. And so
I think we must come to see that it is only our unconscious social resistances that have all this while kept us psychoanalysts from adhering to the
same basis of scientific procedure that has been the acknowledged criterion
in every other sphere of scientific investigation. I think we must bring a
social analysis to our own social resistances and gradually recognize that
in the sphere of our mental observations we have adhered to an esoteric
and imprecise basis of determination which we would not for a moment
have employed regarding data pertaining to any other field of observation.[4]

In the laboratory or group work of my associates and myself, such
factors as sexual fantasies, the unseemliness of family conflicts, the incon-

gruities and deceptions that mark many of our social or pseudogroup contacts become the materials of our laboratory observation. These ineptitudes, to which not only the moralist or preacher but also the layman generally holds himself, at least by implication, superior and which the psychoanalyst concedes mention of only behind closed doors, are openly presented and observed by us in sessions composed at times of as many as twenty people. After all, the point that we psychoanalysts have missed, because unconsciously we like to miss it, is not at all that an individual is a victim of sexual conflicts but that *all individuals under our present social system of repression are equally the victims of equal sexual conflicts.* The reason that the nervous patient wishes to make so deep a secret of the inadvertences of his sex life is not at all because these matters are really private to him but because society says to him "do not dare to presume that these matters are *not* private to you." And we psychoanalysts have unconsciously fallen in with the prevalent attitude of the social system that blindly bullies the so-called neurotic into inviolable self-concealment and isolation. And so we invite in him this absurdly timorous and isolated attitude toward the social system because our own social attitude is equally timorous and isolated.

I have stated what seems to me the inadequate basis of the private method of analysis. In various writings I have made as clear as I can the altered position to which I have been brought through the researches of my students and myself during recent years. It may seem to some that I have not placed sufficient emphasis upon the results of our work in the usual sense of an objective tabulation. But results in the subjective field cannot possibly have more than a theoretical meaning to those who through circumstances have felt obliged to leave entirely to others the task of securing these results. It is experimentally demonstrable that people who show most theoretical interest in the social processes which others have taken the pains to collaborate in understanding are precisely those who stand in greatest need of participating in the same group study of their own social processes. So that I would remind the reader that the spirit of the mere onlooker at processes common to all of us as social beings is very far removed from that of the direct investigator of those processes as they may be witnessed within oneself, and that "results" must of necessity have a very different connotation according as they are perceived from within or without. There have been results—very definite results—but the results people have in mind, who merely want to look at them, are results which imply something objectively pat and conclusive, like an experiment in chemistry, for instance, with its postulate and conclusion expressed in set terms of mathematical exactness. But the course and development of man's life is a process. It is a condition of continuous flow, of uninterrupted movement. It is not a static, fixed condition. So that in the sense of a neat pharmaceutical remedy, obtainable upon application, one cannot speak of results as they pertain to the instinctive and evolutionary processes of man's growth.

The reader will readily understand, though, how much more thorough and effective is the result of an analysis that stirs to the bottom not only a patient's individual situation but also whatever pseudogroup situation a patient finds himself a social participant in. This new process of analysis has the merit of uncovering complexes which are socially sustained under the covenant of the secret family-cluster as well as those occurring in the individual neurosis. Under these conditions we have experienced again and again how much more readily the schizoid, for example, resting in his intrauterine lethargy, is roused from his dreaming inactions and learns to enter into the objective immediacy of the surrounding actualities; how much more radically the hysteric is ousted from his egocentric reveries and at length lends himself to the day's constructive demands; and, finally, with what greater dispatch the cyclothymic surrenders his bidimensional mood-alternatives in favor of an adaptation to life that represents a symmetrical, unitary effort. The result of this more encompassing program, therefore, has assisted toward a rapid technique of restoration in our neurotic subjects and furthered the freeing not alone of individual but also of mass reactions as a whole, whether represented in families or in other unconscious community clusters.

In summary, certain of the outstanding results among those of us who have been dealing at first hand with our own immediate reactions are as follows:

1. The disclosure socially of a universally unconscious social suggestion (the condition first recognized scientifically by Freud in its individual expression under the term "transference").

2. The phyletic dissolution of the bipolar fixation comprising the mother-child relationship such as underlies this social hypnosis or transference as represented in each individual.

3. The determination of the completely vicarious and socially unconscious reaction represented in the factor of "sublimation."

In addition the following mechanisms have been observed and studied by us in their social setting:

1. The "vicious" alternative of the image-fixation underlying the composite mother-child relationship as it exists within the personality of each individual and the bipolar impasse of this image basis.

2. The social extension of this private image basis leading to the substitution unconsciously of social images for reality—"God," "love," "virtue," together with "marriage" and "family" regarded as "institutions." [5]

3. The social mechanism of projection as a universal manifestation and its gradual resolution into its ontogenetic source.[6]

4. The ambivalent irreconcilability of personal mood reactions within the "normal" as well as in the neurotic individual and their compulsively

alternating phases of good and bad, love and hate, praise and blame, as shown in the interreaction of these moods within the social milieu.[7]

5. The psychological identity of the pseudosexual images now commonly divided as "homo-" and "heterosexual" and the complete dissociation socially of both these components from man's societal or organic sex instinct.

6. The presence of distorted states existing in social clusters, such as paranoia, homosexuality, hysteria, and the like, but heretofore commonly regarded in clinical isolation as disease entities peculiar to the "neurotic" individual.[8]

7. The experimental evidence for *the principle of primary identification*[9] of the individual with the mother and the demonstration of a preconscious mode in its phylogenetic or societal significance that is comparable to this primary subjective phase of the infant psyche hitherto posited in regard to its ontogenetic basis.

The foregoing categories, I fully realize, cannot possibly be wholly clear to the reader in the absence of a laboratory background of experience in the study of subjective social reactions. Students of conditions which are the result of objective laboratory findings would not think of attempting to reckon with the processes leading to those findings in the absence of familiarity with the objective laboratory technique requisite to their understanding. But because of the factor of social resistances involved in the study of subjective processes those who have not as yet participated in the group study of these processes, notwithstanding their lack of training and experience, too commonly hold the subjective laboratory answerable for making a clear presentation of its findings. While the inadequacy of the preceding statements may be attributable in part to my own ineptness in formulating them, certainly the responsibility for the understanding of our methods and aims cannot rest wholly with me as long as the reader lacks familiarity with the processes and technique of the laboratory from which these results have sprung.

What the scientific inquirer is really interested to learn primarily, after all, are the advantages, if any, of the group method of analysis as compared with the restricted method that limits the analysis to conferences between the physician and his individual patient. First it should be pointed out that the group method of analysis by no means excludes individual conferences between physician and patient. In point of fact every patient's analysis begins with such personal interviews, and he is at liberty to return to them as his need demands. But it is of significance that such interviews do not rest upon the arbitrary and pseudogroup basis that presupposes only the neurosis of the patient while the physician stands as a mere onlooker in respect to it. The patient is at once expected to look at his own disorder as part of a neurosis shared very generally by a social community in which his physician is, along with him, also an integral part. From this organic group basis composed thus of two persons the patient later comes into conference with three or four individuals and gradually into the larger group conferences which may be composed of as many as eight to twelve. A significant aspect of these group sessions lies in the circumstance that the patient is from the outset observer as well as observed. He becomes at once a responsible student of our common human problems, personal and social. Besides, there is this further advantage in a patient's entering upon the group analysis. In his association with a group whether as individuals or as a whole, quite apart from the analytic sessions, he becomes part of a societal plexus, as it were, along with people pursuing an interest common with his own. Still preserving these biological amalgamations inherent to his organism he has the opportunity to form social relationships with maturer, more experienced students upon a basis that preserves throughout the day their mutually analytic aims. This means that the hysteric and paranoidal types have opportunities for social contact without being forced up against the vicarious accommodation of our socially galvanized pseudo-group adaptations. It means that the psychasthenic or precoid type of personality comes into group relationships which, while in no sense critical of his ingrowing habits of self-accommodation, do not permit him to regress into the privacy of his own introversion.

In the personal analysis the consummation upon which the analysis depends from the outset is the transference. This must be brought about and preserved at all costs. *Keine Uebertragung, keine Psychoanalyse.* In our group procedure this condition of a patient's dependence upon his physician is from the outset precluded. We know very well that the essence of the neurosis is the mother-child relationship, that this is the neurotic patient's unconscious impasse, that fixation is his unremitting quest. But, in the group, the mother-child relationship is from the very beginning submitted to consensual observation and study, and no surrogate for this relationship such as obtains in the usual technique of analysis is permitted to creep in unconsciously and defeat the real purpose of a psychoanalysis. I do not mean for a moment that there is not in each patient the tendency toward such a fixation or transference in the group situation. It is constantly present. But under conditions of group association naturally there is not the opportunity favorable to its secret lodgment and entertainment as is the case in the private work involving months of solitary confinement with the individual analyst. What would be the individual transference in a private analysis becomes neutralized in the social participation of many individuals in their common analysis.

There is further inherent in the group method the opportunity for each student to see disinterestedly the elements composing his own neurosis as they are directly reflected to him in the neurosis of another. For in a group analysis the manifestations in another are repeatedly shown to be identical with one's own. This factor of our group method is of the greatest significance in its influence upon the central factor of resistance. I recall so well Freud's words at the Second International Psychoanalytic Congress in Nuremberg in the year 1911. It was in reference to a statement of Jung's. And I remember Freud's saying that the task of psychoanalysis lay not at all in the discovering of complexes but in the dissolving of resistances. It is precisely here, it seems to me, that the group technique offers its most distinctive advantage. For the essence of resistance is undoubtedly one's sense of isolation in one's own conflicts. Where conditions allow the individual to recognize the common nature of his conflicts, naturally a sense of isolation is gradually resolved and with it the resistances which are the backbone of his neurosis.

It must be remembered that our group work is still in its very beginning. There have been in all but four years of actual group analysis. The two years prior to that consisted simply of experimental variations upon the original analytic theme and in mere tentative adaptations of it. Naturally with a method that is as young as ours and still in the process of its growth other aspects are from time to time coming to light which yet remain to be tested in their fuller implication. But the outstanding interest of our work has been the realization of what is man's commonly neglected societal or essential group basis and its challenge of our commonly accepted or pseudogroup amalgamations. From this essential group basis the careful analytic study of the manifest content of our so-called social consciousness has revealed, and is daily revealing, latent elements in which there is not less contrast with our manifest social adaptations than that which Freud first discovered to be the contrast between the dream life of the individual patient and his actual or manifest adaptation as expressed in his daily life.

I do not wish to be understood as repudiating our conventional social forms of association. They undoubtedly have their place in the process of man's conscious evolution, precisely as our primitive societies had their place in the structural or organic sphere of our evolutionary scheme. I have in mind only to repudiate the substitutive factors whereby such external social groupings are made to replace the organic feelings and instincts which unite man as an integral colony, species, or race.

Persons who have become acquainted with our group method of analysis tend to think of it as an innovation in the psychoanalytic method. They seem to think that my thesis offers a departure from the original aims of Freud. I do not share their view. For this is to judge Freud upon wholly external and accidental grounds. It is to miss the internal significance of Freud's original direction of inquiry. In my interpretation the group method of analysis is but the application in the phylogenetic sphere of the individual analysis as first applied by Freud within the ontogenetic sphere.[10] In a just appraisement of the work of Freud one must not fail to recognize the essentially laboratory spirit of procedure that was Freud's approach to the study of consciousness. From the very beginning Freud attempted to replace personal prejudice with scientific observation. He observed what he saw in human consciousness not only as it exists in his patients but in himself, and he reported faithfully what he saw. This was the application to the field of consciousness of the same precision of laboratory technique that had hitherto characterized our scientific attitude of observation in respect to the biological sciences. In brief, Freud raised the study of consciousness to the sphere of the biological sciences. The result was an outrage to social sensibilities and the social mind with all the weight of its traditional social unconscious has opposed itself so compellingly to Freud's laboratory method that its extension to include the social organism was promptly intercepted.

Instead of receiving the support of a consensual group of co-workers Freud was met by an unconscious resistance that was social and pertained to the collective, pseudogroup reaction. He was alone in his position, and alone he was powerless to meet this reaction in its uncoordinated social form. This was inevitable. In the absence of a consensual societal group of co-workers it was not possible for Freud's work to proceed to the inclusion of the generic social unconscious. Though it was inherent in the very nature of Freud's discovery that a consensual laboratory spirit of observation is alone competent to envisage the problems of consciousness, the social resistance with which Freud was confronted from the very beginning is still unrecognized and unresolved within our psychoanalytic ranks. It is the position of my associates and myself, working as a group, that the pseudogroup prejudices that are the unconscious basis of our social resistance will not be resolved until we have recognized that they are as definitely unconscious a manifestation on the part of the social mind as the individual resistances that are met in the individual analysis. The condition which our group investigations have led us to emphasize is that this resistance within the social mind can no more be resolved in the absence of a social analysis than in the absence of an analysis it is possible to resolve the private resistances of the individual patient.[11] In any other recourse we become Freud's followers merely in the sense of collective, arbitrary, pesudogroup participants, and the spirit of the discoverer and of the laboratory becomes submerged under the mass weight of an imitative or competitive social unconscious. Far from being a departure from the essential significance of Freud's basic discoveries the results that are now issuing from our group analysis are simply the results which with Freud were temporarily intercepted through an absence of a consensual collaboration on the part of his social congeners.

The sum of our findings resolves itself into this. The prevailing view that man is an individual is one which the psychopathologist needs bring into serious question. Man is not an individual. He is a societal organism. Our individual analyses based upon differentiations, which along with others of our kind we have assumed to rest upon legitimate scientific ground, rest in fact upon very transient social artifices and lack the support of a true biological basis. Man's analysis as an element is his isolation as an element. And his isolation is an essential affront to an organic group principle of consciousness.

REFERENCES

1. T. Burrow, *An Ethnic Aspect of Consciousness*. Paper read at the mid-year meeting of The American Psychoanalytic Association, New York City, December 28, 1924.
2. P. Kropotkin, *Mutual Aid* (New York: Alfred A. Knopf, 1921).
3. T. Burrow, "Psychiatry as an Objective Science," *Psychoanal. Rev.*, Vol. XIII, No. 2, 1926.
4. T. Burrow, *The Need of an Analytic Psychiatry*. Paper read before the joint session of The American Psychiatric and The American Psychoanalytic Associations, New York, June 10, 1926.
5. T. Burrow, "Social Images versus Reality," *J. Abnorm. Psychol. Soc. Psychol.*, Vol. XIX, No. 3, 1924.
6. T. Burrow, *The Reabsorbed Affect and Its Elimination*. Paper read at the Sixteenth Annual Meeting of The American Psychopathological Association, New York City, June 11, 1926.
7. T. Burrow, "Our Mass Neurosis," *Psychol. Bull.*, Vol. 23, No. 6, 1926.
8. T. Burrow, "Insanity a Social Problem," *Am. J. Sociol.*, Vol. XXXII, No. 1, Part I, 1926.
9. T. Burrow, "The Genesis and Meaning of Homosexuality," *Psychoanal. Rev.*, Vol. IV, No. 3, 1917.
10. T. Burrow, "The Laboratory Method in Psychoanalysis," *Am. J. Psychiat.*, Vol. V, No. 3, 1926.
11. Just as no one has ever yet really understood the significance of the individual analysis except as he himself entered upon the individual anaylsis, so no one will by any process understand the group analysis except as he himself enters upon it. From the first Freud emphasized the futility of knowledge *about* or *in regard to* psychoanalysis. Knowledge of psychoanalysis is not an intellectual process. Resistances which are the barrier to an understanding of psychoanalysis do not reside in the intellect. Only as one submits one's own feeling, personal or social, to the process of analysis does one truly come into an understanding of psychoanalysis in the only true sense of understanding—namely, into an internal acceptance of the significance of man's unconscious processes.

11

A SUMMARY NOTE ON THE WORK
OF TRIGANT BURROW

Hans Syz

The concepts and procedures introduced by Trigant Burrow represent a pioneer undertaking in the field of social psychiatry.[1] He early took the unorthodox position that "an individual discord is but the symptom of a social discord," [7] and that "it is futile to attempt to remedy mental disease occurring within the individual mind as long as psychiatry remains blind to the existence of mental disease within the social mind." [8] He suggested that "the psycho-pathologist must awaken to his wider function of clinical sociologist and recognize his obligation to challenge the neurosis in its social as well as in its individual intrenchments." [5]

Kurt Goldstein wrote Burrow in 1948: "You are one of the few scientists who make one feel that for him life and work are closely related." [20] This comment gives a clue to Burrow's endeavors. Applying theory to life, he questioned accustomed self-identity and its elaborate security devices which impede basic capacities for freedom and creativity. Acting upon this altered insight, Burrow included in his observation his own behavior as enacted in family, social, and professional situations.

We may distinguish four periods in Burrow's life and activities: (1) 1875-1909: youth, medical and psychological studies; (2) 1909-1920: training with Jung, charter member of the American Psychoanalytic Association, psychoanalytic practice, activity in psychoanalytic and psychological societies, beginning emphasis on social as well as physiological aspects of behavior disorders; (3) 1920-1932: development of group- or phylo-analysis, focusing investigation on socially sanctioned forms of destructive trends (*the social neurosis*),[9, 25] organizing The Lifwynn Foundation for Laboratory Research in Analytic and Social Psychiatry; (4) 1932-1950: inten-

This article will appear, in somewhat different form, in the *International Journal of Social Psychiatry*; it appears here with the permission of the author and the publisher.
154

sive group work with increasing emphasis on proprioceptive aspects of man's behavioral health and illness, differentiation of contrasting attentional patterns, and instrumental recording of associated physiological changes.

With regard to Burrow's psychoanalytic background, although he had studied with Jung, he did not side with him when it came to Jung's break with Freud. Rather he considered the positions of Freud, Jung, and Adler[3] as complementary and not mutually exclusive. Burrow thus anticipated the trend to recognize converging principles in various behavior theories—a trend that has come to the fore in recent years. Throughout, he showed the highest regard for Freud's work, and wrote him in 1925 that he had tried to extend and apply "the principles first enunciated by you to the social as well as to individual repressions." [20]

Even in his early psychoanalytic papers Burrow drew attention, not only to harmful environmental influences occurring in a patient's early family situation, but also to the close interrelation of the individual's neurosis with noxious processes embodied in the customary norm of behavior. In the years before he entered upon his group-analytic studies, Burrow referred repeatedly to "the hideous distortion of human values embodied in the repressive subterfuge and untruth of our so-called moral codes and conventions"; "normality" was in his view "nothing else than an expression of the neurosis of the race." [4]

Along with his emphasis upon "the social neurosis," Burrow early proposed concepts which for him were basic in understanding the human organism as an inherent element in the social and phylic setting, and in interpreting behavior pathology. That is, he drew attention to the "preconscious" * phase of development and to the infant's "primary identification" with the mother. For Burrow, the recognition of the "preconscious" and preconative phase of prenatal and postnatal existence with its psychophysiological continuity with the mother, entailed "no dissent whatsoever from Freud and the unconscious as envisaged by him"; in fact, it was "not only not incompatible with Freud, but . . . a requisite correlate of his teaching." [3]

The evaluation of this early stage of development was essential to Burrow's interpretation of neurotic reactions. While still engaged in psychoanalysis, he suggested that the neurosis is an accentuation and fixation of the original subjective mode of continuity which has not been brought to

---

* Burrow's "preconscious" is to be distinguished from the concept of the preconscious as generally used in present-day psychoanalysis for those phases of psychological function which are not conscious but not repressed and to a large extent capable of becoming conscious.

Clarence P. Oberndorf wrote that one of the four "most noteworthy and original among American contributions before 1920" in the field of psychoanalysis was "Trigant Burrow's emphasis of a 'primary subjective phase' in the infant chronologically preceding the Oedipus situation." [21]

mature social expression. Thus homosexuality was not interpreted as result-ing from the repression of love for the mother on the objectifying level of the Oedipus situation, but rather as a direct outgrowth or extension into adult life of the pre-objective feeling identification with the mother. That is, mother fixation, narcissism, and latent homosexuality were seen as dif-ferent aspects of a single basic principle.[2]

A second, but interrelated, phase of interpretation was the concept that the organism's basic physiological harmony and feeling-continuity with the mother-organism and with the world has been interfered with by the processes of objectivation and cognition, leading to oppositeness, ob-sessive desire, and neurotic self-defense on an individual and social scale. Burrow considered incest-awe as an expression of this inherent protest against the encroachment of the cognitive, objective process upon the spontaneous, subjective process of the "preconscious," prelibidinal phase —as a reaction against the affront to the basic psychobiological principle of unity. "Incest in not forbidden, it forbids itself." [4]

During his psychoanalytic period Burrow assembled much evidence from everyday life, from dreams and pathological conditions, from the phenomena of creative, aesthetic, and religious experience, to show the significance of this powerfully unifying and integrative urge which is com-monly expressed in incomplete, distorted, or symbolically substitutive forms.*

In these early formulations we find also an emphasis upon physiology which characterized Burrow's work throughout. The principle of the in-fant's "preconscious" identification with the mother lays stress, of course, on physiological foundations. From these conceptions Burrow advanced consistently toward his later neurophysiological interpretations, and toward the practical procedure in which proprioceptive awareness of motor activa-tions plays an important role.

These interpretations embody a far-going change in perspective. As mentioned above, Burrow considered neurotic disorders not primarily as individual events but rather as symptoms of a general social or phylic dis-turbance. Conflict was not traced primarily to society's interdiction of instinctive and aggressive trends, to an antagonism between primitive im-pulses and supposedly mature and socially coordinated forces. The essen-tial conflict was seen to consist rather in the internal imposition of the objectivating, symbolizing function upon the early unitary mode of exist-ence. This basic interference, as Burrow increasingly emphasized, consti-tutes a pathogenic complication which, aggravated by social conditioning, is a source of antagonism, detachment, and image-preoccupation, thus causing repression, neurotic developments, and social conflict. That is, to-gether with his challenge of "the social neurosis," there was with Burrow

* Burrow's unpublished material on the "Preconscious" has been collected and edited by the late W. E. Galt; it is now being prepared for publication.

a consistent recognition of an integrative matrix for individual growth and phylic cohesion. The individual was always considered as an interreactive part of the larger sociobiological structure, an entity whose growth and freedom springs from its integration within the phyloörganism. This positive emphasis represents a significant departure from Freud's concept that antisocial forces are basic in human organization. Burrow's discrimination between an organismically-rooted feeling continuity and image-dependent, egocentric complications which characterize "transference" relations throughout[11] is important for the understanding of behavioral pathology as well as for the therapeutic or reconstructive process.

Burrow's group-analytic studies had their start in 1918 when he accepted the challenge of his student-assistant, Clarence Shields, that they reverse the roles of analyst and student.[10] This mutual analysis later included other participants, both normal and neurotic. The *group analysis*[13, 22] which thus developed took place in everyday activities as well as in formal laboratory meetings. The approach was a phenomenological one and at the same time revaluative, uncovering affects and motives existing in group interactions at the moment of exploration. It meant dealing directly with a social situation in which the psychiatrist's, the observer's, own perceptions, attitudes, and concepts were inquired into as part of the social reaction tissue. The attempt was made to relinquish the restrictions of outlook and feeling due to established roles and status, and to get in closer touch with dependencies, moralistic pretenses, self-justifications, and defenses, as they are commonly enacted. The purpose was to determine the latent content of these manifestations which could be observed in the individual's self-structure, in the interactions of the participants, and in the mood pervading the group as a whole. After consistent and long-continued observation, these interrelated phenomena appeared increasingly as variations of a common theme, as interreactive components of a total constellation in which the defensive emphasis upon the symbolically isolated self plays a major role (Burrow's *social images*[5] and *"I"-persona*).[12] The investigative group effort centered upon clarification of this socio-individual problem[23] of autistic image-bondage[31] and its relation to clinically neurotic as well as overtly antisocial behavior.

A development of this social analysis was the incorporation of The Lifwynn Foundation (1927), which was established by Burrow and a few of his co-workers to give a community setting to their group- or phylo-analytic studies. A distinguishing mark of the foundation's function was that its own administrative activities were material for the study which it was organized to sponsor. Thus a modest beginning was made in investigating, by specific procedures, distortions of community organization.

In the course of this investigation, it gradually became evident that behavior analysis had definite limitations in dealing with the socially patterned autistic trend. The frustration of accustomed self-identity and its socially sanctioned value systems led to an unforeseen development: with consistent challenging of habitual affect-reactions, attention shifted to the perception of tensions related to specific neuromuscular activations.[14, 17, 26] Local strain in the forepart of the head (Burrow's *affecto-symbolic segment*) came to awareness which seemed to be directly related to self-referent affect-imagery. With continued experimentation, this oculo-facial stress was increasingly sensed against the tensional pattern perceptible throughout the organism as a whole. This proprioceptive reconstellation was found to go along with a dissipation of self-reflective and affect-laden images of others and oneself, and with the affirmation of an inclusive feeling attitude, with more objective observation, and with more direct application to immediate tasks. While the shift of attention from behavioral imagery to the "feeling sensation" of endorganismic patterns was at first only momentary, it gradually became possible to maintain the integrative orientation for longer periods and to carry it into everyday activities.

These observations led Burrow to distinguish between two modes of attention, between *ditention*, the usual self-reflexive attitude, and *cotention*, in which a more direct and organismically-oriented contact is established with the world. Instrumental recordings indicated that changes in respiration, eye-movements, and electrical brain-wave patterns accompany the shift from ditention to cotention, further supporting the conclusion that we are dealing with a deep-seated organismic reorientation.[16]

The sweeping discrimination between two major attentional modes cuts across academic and conventional classifications, and implies a unifying interpretation of behavior disorder. Viewing the social neurosis always from the background of the organism's inherent capacity for coordination and species solidarity, Burrow introduced the terms *phylobiology, phylopathology*, and *phyloanalysis*.[15, 18, 27] These concepts take full account of the pervasive character of the defective biosocial dynamics which in Burrow's view could not be relegated to any specific type or phase of personality or culture. Biology and the behavior sciences provide increasing evidence for this phyloörganismic basis.[19, 24, 29] Burrow proposed that the integrated mode of attention (cotention) be investigated further with regard to its potential significance as a criterion of behavioral health. The altered perspective thus developed by practical measures seemed to substantiate the common denominator to which Burrow, in his group-analytic studies, had related important dynamics of behavior disorder. While in his later formulations Burrow continued to emphasize the noxious implications linked to man's use, or rather misuse, of image-symbol and language, the recourse in this dilemma was not seen as a return to a primordial state of unity. The aim was rather to submit the problem to "consensual observation"[6] and to apply measures which would reinstate basic, "phylic" integration on a mature and culturally advancing level.[28]

It is evident that Burrow's early studies in group analysis had considerable influence upon the later developing group psychotherapies, though this influence often remained unacknowledged. In fact, his investigation of the individual's neurotic deviation as part of the deflection within the interrelational structure of groups, was the only forerunner in the United States of dynamic group psychotherapy. However, there are distinguishing marks, in that Burrow's group- or phylo-analysis was (1) essentially an investigative procedure; (2) it included in its scope the behavior defect in community life, as well as in the observer himself; and (3) it made use of specific proprioceptive measures for bringing about constructive behavioral modifications on the socio-individual level.

I should like to mention that these behavior studies, especially in their later phases, were not without reintegrative influence upon individual participants, and in my own therapeutic work with neurotic patients I find this background most valuable.[24, 29, 30] However, the essential goal of the phylobiological studies continues throughout to be concerned with the release of healthy function within the community.

It may be in order to add a few remarks regarding the reaction to the concepts and procedures introduced by Burrow. The breaking down of established formulations, which is a prerequisite to scientific advance, is especially difficult where these formulations are tied in with our socially validated self-structure. Although there has been a thorough revision of concepts during the last fifty years in other fields of science, notably in physics, we are confronted in the field of human behavior with an especially intricate situation. I know from my own experience as a participant in group analysis how intensely the socially patterned self tends to cling to its prejudices and emotional defenses. On a social scale these resistances are indeed formidable—in the writer, the reader, and in the community generally. With regard to Burrow's formulations, several scholars have commented on what have been called "conspiracies of silence"—an almost neurotic hesitation to acknowledge one's involvement in man's behavioral predicament, and a failure to recognize the urgent need to approach it by scientific methods. Freud himself acknowledged in a letter to Burrow[20] that his irritation with some of the latter's statements had led him to misinterpretation. Perhaps the complexity of Burrow's style was an expression of this same resistance—at least he himself thought so. In any case there was lack of response on the part of Burrow's colleagues to the specific issues to which he drew attention when he presented his observations and concepts at psychiatric and psychoanalytic meetings. However, certain of Burrow's ideas reappeared later in the writings of others, and many of his formulations seem to be particularly applicable to the community problems with which we are confronted today.

It is true, we are faced with a seemingly insoluble dilemma. But while the individual investigator may feel that he can make hardly a dent in the vast problem of human discord, he can perhaps realize that he is a part of a sociobiological process to which he may make a positive contribution. A generic conception of behavior disorder does not necessarily imply that we are dealing with unalterably set dynamic formations. Rather we may have reached a stage of development in which man, as individual and group, can take an active and constructive hand in guiding his own evolution.

REFERENCES

1. Trigant Burrow, "The Psychoanalyst and the Community," *J.A.M.A.* 62:1876-1878, 1914.
2. Trigant Burrow, "The Genesis and Meaning of 'Homosexuality' and its Relation to the Problem of Introverted Mental States," *Psychoanal. Rev.* 4:272-284, 1917.
3. Trigant Burrow, "Notes with Reference to Freud, Jung and Adler," *J. Abnorm. Psychol.* 12:161-167, 1917.
4. Trigant Burrow, "The Origin of the Incest-Awe," *Psychoanal. Rev.* 5: 243-254, 1918.
5. Trigant Burrow, "Social Images versus Reality," *J. Abnorm. Psychol. & Soc. Psychol.* 19:230-235, 1924.
6. Trigant Burrow, "Psychiatry as an Objective Science," *Brit. J. Med. Psychol.* 5:298-309, 1925.
7. Trigant Burrow, "Insanity a Social Problem," *Amer. J. Sociol.* 32:80-87, 1926.
8. Trigant Burrow, "Our Mass Neurosis," *Psychol. Bul.* 23:305-312, 1926.
9. Trigant Burrow, "Psychoanalytic Improvisations and the Personal Equation," *Psychoanal. Rev.* 13:173-186, 1926.
10. Trigant Burrow, *The Social Basis of Consciousness—A Study in Organic Psychology* (New York: Harcourt, Brace; London: Kegan Paul, Trench, Trubner, 1927).
11. Trigant Burrow, "The Problem of the Transference," *Brit. J. Med. Psychol.* 7:193-202, 1927.
12. Trigant Burrow, "The Autonomy of the 'I' from the Standpoint of Group Analysis," *Psyche* (London) 8:35-50, 1958.
13. Trigant Burrow, "The Basis of Group-Analysis, or the Analysis of the Reactions of Normal and Neurotic Individuals." *Brit. J. Med. Psychol.* 198-206, 1928.
14. Trigant Burrow, "Physiological Behavior-Reactions in the Individual and the Community—A Study in Phyloanalysis." *Psyche* (London) 11:67-81, 1930.
15. Trigant Burrow, *The Biology of Human Conflict—An Anatomy of Behavior, Individual and Social* (New York: Macmillan, 1937).
16. Trigant Burrow, *The Neurosis of Man—An Introduction to a Science of Human Behavior* (London: Routledge & Kegan Paul; New York: Harcourt, Brace, 1949). Full text is included in *Science and Man's Behavior—The Contribution of Phylobiology*, by William E. Galt, ed. (New York: Philosophical Library, 1953).
17. Trigant Burrow, "Prescription for Peace—The Biological Basis of Man's

Ideological Conflicts," in *Explorations in Altruistic Love and Behavior*, by Pitirim A. Sorokin, ed. (Boston: Beacon Press, 1950).

18. William E. Galt, "Phyloanalysis—A Brief Study in Trigant Burrow's Group or Phyletic Method of Behavior Analysis," *J. Abnorm. & Soc. Psychol.* 27:411-429, 1933.

19. William E. Galt, "The Principle of Cooperation in Behavior." *Quar. Rev. Biol.* 15:401-410, 1940.

20. William E. Galt, *et al.*, eds., *A Search for Man's Sanity—The Selected Letters of Trigant Burrow, with Biographical Notes* (New York: Oxford University Press, 1958).

21. Clarence P. Oberndorf, *A History of Psychoanalysis in America* (New York: Grune & Stratton, 1953).

22. Hans Syz, "Remarks on Group Analysis," *Amer. J. Psychiat.* 8:141-148, 1928.

23. Hans Syz, "Socio-individual Principles in Psychopathology," *Brit. J. Med. Psychol.* 10:329-343, 1930.

24. Hans Syz, "The Concept of the Organism-as-a-Whole and its Application to Clinical Situations," *Human Biol.* 8:489-507, 1936.

25. Hans Syz, "The Social Neurosis," *Amer. J. Sociol.* 42:895-897, 1937.

26. Hans Syz, "Burrow's Differentiation of Tensional Patterns in Relation to Behavior Disorders," *J. Psychol.* 9:153-163, 1940.

27. Hans Syz, "Phylopathology," in *Encyclopedia of Psychology*, Philip L. Harriman, ed. (New York: Philosophical Library, 1946).

28. Hans Syz, "New Perspectives in Behavior Study—A Phylobiological Re-orientation," *J. Psychol.* 31:21-27, 1951.

29. Hans Syz, "An Experiment in Inclusive Psychotherapy" in *Experimental Psychopathology*, by Paul H. Hoch and Joseph Zubin, eds. (New York: Grune & Stratton, 1957).

30. Hans Syz, "Trigant Burrow's Thesis in Relation to Psychotherapy," in *Progress in Psychotherapy*, II, Jules H. Masserman and J. L. Moreno, eds. (New York: Grune & Stratton, 1957).

31. Hans Syz, "Problems of Perspective from the Background of Trigant Burrow's Group-Analytic Researches," *Int. J. Group Psychother.* 11:143-165, 1961.

12

A NEW THEORY OF NEUROSES

D. H. Lawrence

(A review of
THE SOCIAL BASIS OF CONSCIOUSNESS
by Trigant Burrow)

Dr. Trigant Burrow is well known as an independent psychoanalyst through the essays and addresses he has published in pamphlet form from time to time. These have invariably shown the spark of original thought and discovery. The gist of all these essays now fuses into this important book, the latest addition to the International Library of Psychology, Philosophy and Scientific Method.

Dr. Burrow is that rare thing among psychiatrists, a humanly honest man. Not that practitioners are usually dishonest. They are intellectually honest, professionally honest, all that. But that other simple thing, human honesty, does not enter in, because it is primarily subjective; and subjective honesty, which means that a man is honest about his own inward experience, is perhaps the rarest thing, especially among professionals. Chiefly, of course, because men, and especially men with a theory, don't know anything about their own inward experiences.

Here Dr. Burrow is a rare and shining example. He set out, years ago as an enthusiastic psychoanalyst and follower of Freud, working according to the Freudian method, in America. And gradually, the sense that something was wrong, vitally wrong, both in the theory and in the practice of psychoanalysis, invaded him. Like any truly honest man, he turned and asked himself what it was that was wrong, with himself, with his methods and with the theory according to which he was working?

This book is the answer, a book for every man interested in the human consciousness to read carefully. Because Dr. Burrow's conclusions,

Reprinted from *The Bookman*, November 1927, by permission of Laurence Pollinger, Ltd., and the estate of the late Mrs. Frieda Lawrence.

sincere, almost naïve in their startled emotion, are far-reaching, and vital.

First, in his criticism of the Freudian method, Dr. Burrow found, in his clinical experience, that he was always applying a *theory*. Patients came to be analysed, and the analyst was there to examine with open mind. But the mind could not be open, because the patient's neurosis, all the patient's experience, *had* to be fitted to the Freudian theory of the inevitable incest-motive.

And gradually Dr. Burrow realised that to fit life every time to a theory is in itself a mechanistic process, a process of unconscious repression, a process of image-substitution. All theory that has to be applied to life proves at last just another of these unconscious images which the repressed psyche uses as a substitute for life, and against which the psychoanalyst is fighting. The analyst wants to break all this image business so that life can flow freely. But it is useless to try to do so by replacing in the unconscious another image—this time, the image, the fixed motive, of the incest-complex.

Theory as theory is all right. But the moment you apply it to *life*, especially to the subjective life, the theory becomes mechanistic, a substitute for life, a factor in the vicious unconscious. So that while the Freudian theory of the unconscious and of the incest-motive is valuable as a *description* of our psychological condition, the moment you begin to *apply* it, and make it master of the living situation, you have begun to substitute one mechanistic or unconscious illusion for another.

In short, the analyst is just as much fixed in his vicious unconscious as is his neurotic patient, and the will to apply a mechanical incest-theory to every neurotic experience is just as sure an evidence of neurosis, in Freud or in the practitioner, as any psychologist could ask.

So much for the criticism of the psychoanalytic method.

If then, Dr. Burrow asks himself, it is not sex-repression which is at the root of the neurosis of modern life, what is it? For certainly, according to his finding, sex-repression is not the root of the evil.

The question is a big one and can have no single answer. A single answer would only be another "theory." But Dr. Burrow has struggled through years of mortified experience to come to some conclusion nearer the mark. And his finding is surely much deeper and more vital, and also, much less spectacular than Freud's.

The real trouble lies in the inward sense of "separateness" which dominates every man. At a certain point in his evolution, man became cognitively conscious: he bit the apple: he began to know. Up till that time his consciousness flowed unaware, as in the animals. Suddenly his consciousness split.

It would appear that in his separativeness man has inadvertently fallen a victim to the developmental exigencies of his own consciousness. Captivated by the phylogenetically new and unwonted spectacle of his own image, it would seem he has been irresistibly arrested before the mirror of his own likeness and that in the present self-conscious phase of his mental evolution he is still standing spell-bound before it. That such is the case with man is not remarkable. For the appearance of the phenomenon of consciousness marked a complete severance from all that was his past. Here was broken the chain of evolutionary events whose links extended back through the nebulous aeons of our remotest ancestry, and in the first moment of his consciousness man stood, for the first time, *alone*. It was in this moment that he was "created," as the legend runs, "in the image and likeness of God." For breaking with the teleological traditions of his age-long biology, man now became suddenly *aware*.

Consciousness is self-consciousness. "That is, consciousness in its inception entails the fallacy of *a self as over against other selves*."

Suddenly aware of himself, and of other selves over against him, man is a prey to the division inside himself. Helplessly he must strive for more consciousness, which means, also, a more intensified aloneness or individuality: and at the same time he has a horror of his own aloneness, and a blind, dim yearning for the old togetherness of the far past, what Dr. Burrow calls the preconscious state.

What man really wants, according to Dr. Burrow, is a sense of togetherness with his fellow men, which shall balance the secret but overmastering sense of separateness and aloneness which now dominates him. And therefore, instead of the Freudian method of personal analysis, in which the personality of the patient is pitted against the personality of the analyst in the old struggle for dominancy, Dr. Burrow would substitute a method of group analysis, wherein the reactions were distributed over a group of people, and the intensely personal element eliminated as far as possible. For it is only in the intangible reaction of several people, or many people together, on one another that you can really get the loosening and breaking of the me-and-you tension and contest, the inevitable contest of two individualities brought into connection. What must be broken is the egocentric absolute of the individual. We are all such hopeless little absolutes to ourselves. And if we are sensitive, it hurts us, and we complain, we are called neurotic. If we are complacent, we enjoy our own petty absolutism, though we hide it and pretend to be quite meek and humble. But in secret, we are absolute and perfect to ourselves, and nobody could be better than we are. And this is called being normal.

Perhaps the most interesting part of Dr. Burrow's book is his examination of normality. As soon as man became aware of himself, he made a picture of himself. Then he began to live according to the picture. Mankind at large made a picture of itself, and every man had to conform to the picture, the ideal.

This is the great image or idol which dominates our civilization, and which we worship with mad blindness. The idolatry of self. Consciousness should be a flow from within outwards. The organic necessity of the human being should flow into spontaneous action and spontaneous awareness, consciousness.

But the moment man became aware of himself he made a picture of himself, and began to live from the picture: that is, from without inwards. This is truly the reversal of life. And this is how we live. We spend all our time over the picture. All our education is but the elaborating of the picture. "A good little girl"—"a brave boy"—"a noble woman"—"a strong man"—"a productive society"—"a progressive humanity"—it is all the picture. It is all living from the outside to the inside. It is all the death of sponaneity. It is all, strictly, automatic. It is all the vicious unconscious which Freud postulated.

If we could once get into our heads—or if we once dare admit to one another—that we are *not* the picture, and the picture is not what we are, then we might lay a new hold on life. For the picture is really the death, and certainly the neurosis of us all. We have to live from the outside in, idolatrously. And the picture of ourselves, the picture of humanity which has been elaborated through some thousands of years, and which we are still adding to, is just a huge idol. It is not real. It is a horrible compulsion over all of us.

Individuals rebel: and these are the neurotics, who show some sign of health. The mass, the great mass, goes on worshipping the idol, and behaving according to the picture: and this is the normal. Freud tried to force his patients back to the normal, and almost succeeded in shocking them into submission, with the incest-bogey. But the bogey is nothing compared to the actual idol.

As a matter of fact, the mass is more neurotic than the individual patient. This is Dr. Burrow's finding. The mass, the normals, never live a life of their own. They cannot. They live entirely according to the picture. And according to the picture, each one is a little absolute unto himself, there is none better than he. Each lives for his own self-interest. The "normal" activity is to push your own interest with every atom of energy you can command. It is "normal" to get on, to get ahead, at whatever cost. The man who does disinterested work is abnormal. Every Johnny must look out for himself: that is normal. Luckily for the world, there still is a minority of individuals who do disinterested work, and are made use of by the "normals." But the number is rapidly decreasing.

And then the normals betray their utter abnormality in a crisis like the late war. There, there indeed the uneasy individual can look into the abysmal insanity of the normal masses. The same holds good of the bolshevist hysteria of today: it is hysteria, incipient social insanity. And the last great insanity of all, which is going to tear our civilization to pieces, the insanity of class hatred, is almost entirely a "normal" thing, and a "social" thing. It is a state of fear, of ghastly collective fear. And it is absolutely a mark of the normal. To say that class hatred *need not exist* is to show abnormality. And yet it is true. Between man and man, class hatred hardly exists. It is an insanity of the mass, rather than of the individual.

But it is part of the picture. The picture says it is horrible to be poor, and splendid to be rich, and in spite of all individual experience to the contrary we accept the terms of the picture, and thereby accept class war as inevitable.

Humanity, society, has a picture of itself, and lives accordingly. The individual likewise has a private picture of himself, which fits into the big picture. In this picture he is a little absolute and nobody could be better than he is. He must look after his own self-interest. And if he is a man, he must be very male. If she is a woman, she must be very female.

Even sex, today, is only part of the picture. Men and women alike, when they are being sexual, are only acting up. They are living according to the picture. If there is any dynamic, it is that of self-interest. The man "seeketh his own" in sex, and the woman seeketh her own: in the bad, egoistic sense in which St. Paul used the words. That is, the man seeks himself, the woman seeks herself, always and inevitably. It is inevitable, when you live according to the picture, that you seek only yourself in sex. Because the picture is your own image of yourself: your *idea* of yourself. If you are quite normal, you don't have any true self, which "seeketh not her own, is not puffed up." The true self, in sex, would seek a *meeting*, would seek to meet the other. This would be the true flow; what Dr. Burrow calls the "Societal consciousness" and what I would call the human consciousness, in contrast to the social, or "image-consciousness."

But, today, all is image-consciousness. Sex does not exist, there is only sexuality. And sexuality is merely a greedy, blind self-seeking. Self-seeking is the real motive of sexuality. And therefore, since the thing sought is the same, the self, the mode of seeking is not very important. Heterosexual, homosexual, narcissistic, normal or incest, it is all the same thing. It is just sexuality, not sex. It is one of the universal forms of self-seeking. Every man, every woman just seeks his own self, her own self, in the sexual experience. It is the picture over again, whether in sexuality or self-sacrifice, greed or charity, the same thing, the self, the image, the idol: the image of me, and norm!

The true self is not aware that it is a self. A bird, as it sings, sings itself. But not according to a picture. It has no idea of itself.

And this is what the analyst must try to do: to liberate his patient from his own image, from his horror of his own isolation, and the horror of the "stoppage" of his real vital flow. To do it, it is no use rousing sex bogeys. A man is not neurasthenic or neurotic because he loves his mother. If he desires his mother, it is because he is neurotic, and the desire is merely a symptom. The cause of the neurosis is further to seek.

And the cure? For myself, I believe Dr. Burrow is right: the cure would consist in bringing about a state of honesty and a certain trust among a *group* of people, or many people—if possible all the people in the world. For it is only when we can get a man to fall back into his true relation to other men and to women, that we can give him an opportunity to be himself. So long as men are inwardly dominated by their own isolation, their own absoluteness, which after all is but a picture or an idea, nothing is possible but insanity more or less pronounced. Men must get back into *touch*. And to do so they must forfeit the vanity, and the *noli me tangere* of their own absoluteness: also they must utterly break the present great picture of a normal humanity: shatter that mirror in which we all live grimacing: and fall again into true relatedness.

I have tried more or less to give a *résumé* of Dr. Burrow's book. I feel that there is a certain impertinence in giving these *résumés*. But not more than in the affectation of "criticizing" and being superior. And it is a book one should read and assimilate, for it helps a man in his own inward life.

13

GROUP PSYCHOTHERAPY FROM THE POINT OF VIEW OF ADLERIAN PSYCHOLOGY

Rudolf Dreikurs

It can be assumed that the practice of group psychotherapy is to a large extent the same, regardless of the psychological orientation of the therapist. There are certain procedural differences which emanate from the theoretical orientation and varying technical approaches characteristic for each school of thought. However, the greatest and most significant difference between the various practitioners of group psychotherapy is probably their different interpretation of the observed phenomena. The clearest example is the assumption by analytically oriented therapists that transference is the basis for all therapeutic results. Therapists who are not psychoanalytically indoctrinated would not consider this factor at all but would attribute the effects of the therapy to entirely different mechanisms.

The formulation of the theoretical premises can then explain both the technique used in group psychotherapy and the therapeutically effective factors seen from each point of view. I will try to present the Adlerian position, being fully aware of the difficulty to clarify in a short presentation the complexity of Adlerian psychology.

THE PRINCIPLES OF ADLERIAN PSYCHOLOGY

The "individual psychology" of Alfred Adler can be characterized as a *socioteleological* approach to an understanding of human motivation. It is in contrast to the physiologic-mechanistic concept of Watson's behaviorism, which considers all human qualities as the result of stimulus-response reflexes, or to Freud's biological-instinctual concept of man, ac-

Reprinted from the *International Journal of Group Psychotherapy*, Vol. VII, No. 4, October 1957, pp. 363-375.

cording to which the individual is primarily driven by instincts which then are repressed or transformed by superimposed cultural demands. Adler perceived man as a social being, primarily and exclusively. He was the first to emphasize that human behavior is *goal-directed*, purposive. These two basic principles in Adlerian psychology distinguished it from any other school of thought until recently when the various psychoanalysts abandoned the original biologic-instinctual premise for a more social orientation.

These two basic principles deserve some further clarification, since neither of them is easily understood in our present cultural and scientific setting. It is rather paradoxical that the social nature of man should require clarifying comments 2,400 years after man has been called by Aristotle a *zoon politicon*, a social animal. It must be admitted, however, that the assumption of the truly social nature of man is difficult to defend at a time when his obviously antisocial behavior offers convincing proof to the contrary. Conflict, tension, and the threat of all-engulfing war characterize our contemporary cultural scene; they do not testify to man's fundamentally social nature. Yet all human conflicts are essentially social, although the structure of our society does not facilitate the solution of interpersonal conflicts and antagonisms.

Adler described an "ironclad logic of social living" as a basis for prevention and solution of conflicts. This inner logic of social living presupposes the recognition of a fundamental human *equality*, which has first been described by the Greek Stoics, then made into law by the Roman legislators, and put into practice by the early Christians. However, human equality, greatly increased in the democratic evolution of the last few centuries, has not been recognized yet in its significance. While the individual in certain countries, especially in the United States, has gained an unequaled degree of social equality, people have not yet learned to live with each other as equals and solve their problems on the basis of mutual respect. The obvious antisocial behavior of most individuals and groups does not, therefore, require the assumption of fundamentally antisocial elements within human nature.

Opponents of the social orientation may say that man could live without society but not without air, water, and food. Does this not prove that biological concepts are more accurate? True enough, man could live without society, but he would also stop being human. It is not always easy to evaluate properly the relationship of several coexisting factors. Let us take as an example the role of sex in the total human personality. No one can deny that sex exists; but we say "man has sex," rather than "sex has man." From our point of view, all human faculties, needs, and desires are subordinated to the *social* needs and outlook of the individual. All human qualities are expressions of social interaction, all human problems are of social nature. The *desire to belong* is the prime human motivation. The individual may develop devious means to find a place, and he may have a distorted concept of his possibilities to do so; but he never loses his desire to belong. According to Adler, social interest—the ability to participate and the willingness to contribute—is an innate human potentiality. The development of sufficient social interest is a prerequisite for adequate social functioning; its lack is the cause of deficiency and social maladjustment.

The second fundamental principle of Adlerian psychology, the teleo-analytical approach to human behavior, was even more difficult to comprehend in Adler's contemporaries, steeped as they were in the mechanistic tradition of nineteenth-century science. True enough, the teleological mechanisms were described before him by the neovitalists in medicine who recognized the purpose of physiological processes and by philosophers like Bergson and others who recognized basic finalistic perspectives. However, it was still considered unscientific in Adler's time to assume self-determination. Limitations of mechanistic determinism, of the causal principle on which the great scientific progress of the last few centuries has been based, were hardly recognized. Adler was fifty years ahead of his time. Only in the last few years has science discovered the teleological mechanism as a universal principle, applicable not only to an understanding of an individual human being but of physical processes as well. Not until physicists realized the limitations of strict determinism and replaced it with the law of "statistical probability" did Adler's concept of man have a chance to become accepted scientifically.

The struggle between a causal-deterministic orientation and a teleological point of view which perceives the possibility of self-determination will not be waged primarily in the fields of psychiatry and psychology. It seems probable that the necessary changes in epistemology will be brought about by research in the basic and not in the applied sciences. However, these changes are already taking place; they favor Adler's concepts of man, and not the heretofore accepted mechanistic-deterministic ones characteristic of constitutional-hereditary, behavioristic, or psychoanalytic postulates.

According to Adler, all human actions have a purpose, and purpose is primarily of social nature. All human qualities express movement, movement in relationship to others. The individual sets his own goals, both the immediate goals in his present field of action and the over-all goals for his whole life, which form the basis for his personality, his *life style*. Even within the once established general frame of reference of his life style, the individual is free to choose his immediate objectives. He acts at any given moment according to his dominant goals which he sets himself. It does not make any difference whether he is aware of his goals or not; he always acts accordingly. Most often the individual is not aware of his goals and intentions. Consciousness is also self-determined. The individual knows only what he wants or needs to know. And the need for conscious awareness is highly overrated. Most emotional, mental, psychological, and physiological processes take place without any awareness, which has only too often an inhibitive effect. The same principle explains the function of memory. While all experiences are retained cerebrally, the recall depends on the needs of the individual. He takes from the vast filing system of his engrams only what he needs for the moment. His conscious intention may not coincide with his actual goal, and therefore he may find himself forgetting what he seemingly wants to know, or be unable to push out of his mind what he would "like to forget." In either case, a close analysis reveals that he is doing only what he really intends to do, although he does not admit his true intentions to himself and operates on pretense.

Our contemporary picture of man is not inducive to self-understanding. Prevalent psychological constructs prevent us from knowing what we could know about ourselves, although nobody ever will be able to know himself fully. Subjectivity, spontaneity, and creativity are not yet recognized in their full social significance at a time when objectivity and rationality are overrated. The crucial factor which deserves attention and reconsideration is the functions of *emotions*. Adler recognized their purposiveness. We create our own emotions for our own purposes while we subjectively feel driven by them. They seem to be our master while they are actually only our tools. Naturally, we cannot admit to ourselves the purpose for which we create our emotions, otherwise they could no longer serve us. We need emotions to act forcefully, to support our self-determined goals, to fortify them against obstacles. Without emotions, we could not act forcibly. They are the steam which we generate to increase and maintain our movement. They come and go as we need them. Emotions are not irrational; they express our *private logic*, what we really think and believe. Reason and emotions only seem opposed to each other, like the left hand "opposes" the right one when both try to hold an object. Reason and emotions are tools which we use alternately as they best fit our purpose. When they seem to oppose each other, this seeming opposition serves merely as an excuse for our actions, "explained" by our emotions. Any conscious opposition to our emotional impulses is a false pretense—but this is difficult to comprehend. Guilt feelings too are only pretenses, pretenses of good intentions which we do not have. They emerge only when we do not want to amend or change, but to demonstrate our good intentions. We feel guilty only if we are not willing to do what we know we should do. In this sense, guilt feelings too have an obvious social purpose.

Similarly, *dreams* are purposive. Adler called them "the factory of emotions." In our dreams we create situations which stimulate those emotions which we may need for the coming day. Through dream analysis we can recognize a patient's plans, his attitudes, and preparation for his coming problem. Neurotic symptoms too have a purpose. They safeguard the individual against failure, they permit him to withdraw or to gain special privileges and services. Freud also recognized such mechanisms. In his *Psychopathology of Everyday Life,* written while under the influence of Alfred Adler, he describes more than anywhere else the social purpose of actions and deficiencies. However, he relegated them later to be merely "secondary gains" since the primary dynamics were considered within the unconscious. It seems to us that no human action can be understood unless we recognize its purpose. It does not make any difference whether this action is socially acceptable or not, productive or destructive, on the "useless side" or helpful—it always has a purpose.

The third basic principle in Adlerian psychology, which is responsible for its name, is the *unity of the personality.* For Adler, the individual is indivisible, a whole. The holistic concept of man, which in theory is generally approved, is far from being understood today, and was less so in Adler's time. At that time his only support came from Gestalt psychologists who also realized that the whole is more than the sum total of its parts. In the meantime, Smuts developed his theory of holism, which is gaining acceptance. Despite this scientific trend, most references to the totality or unity of the personality give merely lip service to this concept. All mechanistic approaches in psychology, be they experimental, behavioristic, or psychoanalytic, try to understand the individual through an exploration of isolated psychological mechanisms and processes under the assumption that their analysis may lead to an understanding of the whole person. True enough, many helpful insights have been gained in such scientific research; but the individual himself cannot be explained nor understood in this way.

Adler indicated the only way in which the totality of personality can be perceived, not merely theoretically, but in practice, be it in psychotherapy, in education, or in any other field where an objective understanding of the total individual is attempted. It is the *movement* of the individual, the goals which he has set for himself, which indicate his total personality and permit a recognition of it. The direction in which the person moves encompass his whole past, all his shortcomings and assets, abilities and deficiencies, and at the same time his perception of the future. He uses all his faculties, his mind and his body, his thinking, feeling, and physiological functions to pursue his goals. Only in his goals can he be recognized in his uniqueness. Without looking at the individual phenomenologically, one cannot see him as a whole. What makes him move are not any parts operating in him, be they emotions, drives, complexes, or other phenomena within him. The force that makes him move is *he* himself, his own determination, his pursuit in line with his goals.

Adler developed a technique which permits a clear recognition of the goals of the individual. It is not difficult to detect them if the individual is *observed in action;* the result of his actions are usually in line with his immediate goals. The individual may be convinced that he does not want what he brings about, but then he is merely not aware of the objectives he set for himself. It is more difficult to recognize his *basic* goals which are the foundation of his life style, the fictitious goals, as Adler calls them. They represent a scheme of action by which the individual hopes to find his place in society, a set of convictions about himself and life which underlie his social movements. The exploration of the *family constellation*, the interaction of the patient with all the members of the family during the formative years of early childhood, permits a clear picture of the pattern according to which he moves. The *early recollections* indicate the concept of life which he has developed and maintained since childhood. We remember from our early childhood only those incidents which fit into our concept of life. Once we have developed such a concept, we perceive only what fits into the scheme. Our "biased apperception" fortifies our "private logic" and permits us to maintain our basic convictions regardless of how wrong they may be. The "guiding lines" which we have set up in our childhood separate the desirable from the undersirable, the possible from the impossible, the superior from the inferior. Masculine superiority may be such a guiding principle, although the individual, man and woman alike, may rebel against the assumption that a man has to be superior. Adler called this rebellion "masculine protest." Moral or intellectual superiority may be other sets of guiding principles. They indicate the safeguards which the individual may set up for himself when his idea of superiority cannot be realized, when he is confronted with failure.

The question has often been posed why Adler considered the inferiority feeling as the main source of deficiencies, of social and emotional maladjustment. How could one psychological mechanism be at the root of all the manifold disturbances? To understand this assumption one must keep in mind that the individual, as a social being, is primarily concerned with finding his place in the group. A feeling of belonging is essential for social and emotional well-being. It permits the endurance of all hardships and adversities. Not belonging is the worst contingency man can experience; it is worse than death. This explains the supreme significance of status. Feeling deficient and inferior deprives the individual of the realization that he has a place. His "social interest" is restricted by the development of inferiority feelings. The extent of his social interest can be clearly measured by the areas where he feels belonging. The smaller his area is, the more vulnerable becomes the individual. As long as he can move in a field where he feels belonging, where his adequacy is not questioned—at least in his own mind—no safeguards, which are the real defense mechanisms, are necessary. But as soon as he is impressed with his inadequacy and inferiority, be they real or assumed, he seeks detours and compensations, either through socially useful means, or—if he is too discouraged—on the useless side of life.

ADLERIAN GROUP PSYCHOTHERAPY

This orientation of Adlerian psychology explains why Adler and his co-workers were among the first to conduct group psychotherapy. Since man's problems and conflicts are recognized in their social nature, the group is ideally suited, not only to highlight and reveal the nature of a person's conflicts and maladjustments, but to offer corrective influences. Inferiority feelings cannot be more effectively counteracted than in a group setting. Furthermore, at the root of social deficiencies and emotional maladjustments are mistaken concepts and values. The group is a value-forming agent; it influences the convictions and beliefs of its members. For this reason, Adler and his co-workers used a group approach in their child guidance centers in Vienna since 1921. My first experience with group psychotherapy—at that time called "collective therapy"—was, besides in child guidance, in the treatment of alcoholics. In 1929 I began to use group psychotherapy in my private psychiatric practice, and I have continued to do so ever since. Our particular orientation permits specific approaches in group psychotherapy and leads to an interpretation of the observed phenomena which may offer some insight to other group psychotherapists in their own dealings with their patients.

Describing the characteristic dynamics of group psychotherapy in the light of Adlerian psychology, we may use the scheme of the four phases of psychotherapy which seem to be present in any form of uncovering therapy. I have described these four phases, which overlap, as consisting of (1) the establishment and maintenance of the proper therapeutic relationship; (2) the exploration of the dynamics operating in the patient (analysis in the wider sense); (3) communicating to the patient an understanding of himself (insight); and finally, (4) a reorientation.

The establishment and maintenance of a proper therapeutic relationship implies more than a good relationship in general. More important and more difficult is the alignment of goals of patient and therapist so that both work toward the same end, which unfortunately is neither self-evident nor implicit in every case. It is obvious that the therapist wishes the patient to get well, and through a process which he, the therapist, deems necessary. The patient who comes for help, may either not want to get well and merely demonstrate his good intention; he may be determined to prove that he is hopeless. Or he may wish to get well but without doing anything about it, expecting the therapist to do the job, or without acceding to the need for a change in personality.

The therapy group can contribute greatly to fortify the patient's *relationship* to the therapist and to overcome disturbances as they are inevitable in any therapeutic procedure. Confidence in the therapist and his ability may be easily impaired by a hostile group, but is equally enhanced in a well-functioning group. Whatever distrust the patient may have, either due to his general personal inclination or due to his disbelief in psychiatry and the effectiveness of therapy, it may vanish under the impact of the faith exhibited by other patients. The group can undermine as well as build up the morale of the therapeutic setting. An individual patient may feel not understood, or he may be in rebellion against any authority figure and regard the therapist as such. Consequently, he might find it easier to participate fully in the therapeutic process as a member of a group than being alone with the therapist. Many patients who can hardly be reached in individual therapy respond in the group; many who oppose psychological investigation, often because they refuse to consider their condition as anything but organically determined, begin to realize the need for a psychotherapeutic approach which they had resented previously.

The group does not only influence each member in his attitude to psychotherapy and to the therapist, but also to the possible outcome of the procedure. We experimented recently with a group which was almost entirely composed of depressed patients, each of whom felt utterly hopeless. It was interesting to note how each one was equally convinced how wrong the others were in their pessimism and how right he was in his. Each one was sure that *he* did not belong in the group, that *he* did not need it and could not benefit from it, but all the others could. The effect of this recognition was dramatic on all participants. Several patients who for a long period of time maintained a distant, reserved, and defeatist attitude to therapy responded within a short period of time after this group experience.

The *analysis* of the psychodynamic forces operating in the patient, the methods which we use to determine the life style of each patient, can be applied in an individual session as well as in the group setting. However, the patient's goals and movements become much more obvious in the interaction with his fellow group members than in the limited interaction between him and the therapist. Furthermore, the therapist no longer depends entirely on the verbal reports by the patient about his interaction with others outside of the therapeutic session; he sees him in action during the session. Not infrequently, the patient appears in a quite different light when confronted by other members of the group than when he is alone with the therapist. Certain façades of his personality may become more pronounced, or visible.

The greatest benefit of the group is in phases three and four. In individual therapy it is relatively difficult to provide *insight* for the patient, particularly in regard to his goals. We are so used to rationalize that we all find it difficult to recognize our own goals and true intentions. This is the more so when the patient is ambitious and overconscientious, as many neurotics are. The group facilitates the process of gaining insight; for many, it is almost a prerequisite without which they never are able to learn about themselves what they need to know. How is this greater ability to understand oneself achieved in the group?

Interestingly enough, the individual patient may show the same blocking to interpretations in the group as in private consultation. What helps him to overcome his resistance is the similar resistance observed in his fellow patients. There he can clearly see the validity of the psychological interpretation and the difficulties of the patient to recognize the obvious. Most psychological disclosures and interpretations in the group are not for the benefit of the patient to whom they are directed, but for the benefit of the others who learn from it. There is sufficient fundamental similarity in faulty motivations and mistaken approaches among all participants so that each one can, time and again, recognize himself in others. This is particularly true if the members of the group are selected because of their similar problems, a group of mothers, of teenagers, of obese women, of executives, of patients with depression, and so on. We try to arrange our groups in such a way that some common element of either personalities, psychopathology, interests, age, or education is evident. After all, patients learn from each other. This seems to be a fundamental principle, explaining the therapeutic efficiency of group psychotherapy.

In this sense, it is characteristic for all group psychotherapy that the patients help each other. What they tell each other is often much more significant to them than what the therapist has to say. They accept each other more in their corrective endeavors, because they feel equal to each other. This is the reason why some patients can only benefit from group psychotherapy and less so from individual therapy, like juvenile delinquents, alcoholics, drug addicts, the crippled and the blind, and other groups which perceive themselves as a minority. The therapist, regardless of how acceptable he may be to them, is still a member of the hostile or at least different majority. His influence depends on his ability to win the active support of some group members.

Insight is not necessarily a strictly personal matter. Certain psychological dynamics, which operate in all of us alike, are hardly known. While man probably never will be able to understand himself, he will, before long, learn a great deal more about human nature. The significance of inferiority feelings, of guilt feelings, the fallacy of prestige and of the desire for self-elevation, they all are still unknown to most. The patients in the group learn not only about themselves, but about people. As they begin to understand people, they begin to understand themselves. Psychotherapy, as we understand it, is primarily an educational process, the intellectual stimulation being supported by strong and impressive emotional experiences. It seems that the group as such facilitates all learning. A seasoned teacher often prefers a small group to individual instruction. Similarly, the learning process called psychotherapy is greatly facilitated by the group.

Insight is not the basis for cure, improvement, or adjustment; it is merely a step toward it, and not even a necessary prerequisite. Many forms of therapy do not use any analysis and insight and still can be highly effective, like hypnosis, suggestive therapy, and many other nonanalytic forms of therapy. They proceed directly from phase 1, the establishing of the proper relationship, to phase 4, the reorientation. The experience in the therapy group provides stimulations which are highly conducive to *reorientation*.

The most decisive change necessary for a lasting therapeutic effect is relinquishing the faulty premises on which each patient had operated heretofore; this implies a change in the life style, in the fundamental attitude to life. These changes are not only expressed in improvement of functions, amelioration of symptoms, and general well-being; they can be tested by characteristic changes in the early recollections of the patient, since these recollections always represent the basic outlook on life. The group facilitates these changes due to the general improvement of the therapeutic relationship, the greater opportunity to recognize oneself, and above all, through the increased awareness of the patient in the group that his concept of himself and the premises which he had found for himself in his childhood are incorrect and unjustified.

Even greater is the stimulation by the group to recognize faulty value systems on which most of its members have operated and which were induced by our culture. Psychotherapy, to a large extent, offsets certain social stimulations within the community. They induce the patient to consider self-evaluation as most important. This concern with personal prestige limited the patient's ability to cooperate, to take life in his stride, and made him vulnerable to incidents which spelled for him defeat and personal worthlessness. Counseling and psychotherapy lead the patient to a sounder approach to social living, enable him to cooperate, and provide him with healthier and more practical sources of satisfaction and security than those which he previously had considered necessary. Individual psychotherapy may not always be recognized as a means for social reorientation and acceptance of new and better social values; in group psychotherapy this aspect of every psychotherapy cannot be overlooked and becomes obvious. Every group develops its own conventions, its own rules. And the therapy group, dealing with human relationships and with the task to offset or remedy disturbed relationships, cannot escape concerning itself with morals and values conducive to better social functioning.

The most important therapeutic factor in our concept of psychotherapy is the removal of inferiority feelings, or to say it in a positive way, the increase in self-respect. This process can justifiably be called *encouragement*. It is our contention that the effectiveness of *any* corrective procedure, be it called analytic, therapeutic, or educational, rests with the degree of encouragement which it entailed. Without increased self-confidence, without restored faith in his own worth and ability, the patient cannot improve and grow. This aspect of therapy may not be recognized by the therapist, or be minimized by him as constituting mere "supportive" assistance; however, it seems to be the essential factor in all cures and improvement.

In which way does the group contribute to the encouragement of each of its members? To understand this all-important aspect of group psychotherapy, one must take into consideration the peculiar social structure of the therapy group. It is quite unique and different from any other group found in our society. It is characterized by a status of social equality which each member enjoys. Unlike any other group, here, individual differences and particularly deficiencies do not lower the patient's status. Conversely, leadership qualities and personal assets do not necessarily give the patient a status of superiority or envy, since this very envy can be openly expressed by less fortunate members of the group who then see to it that the patient's attempts to achieve elevation is thwarted.

It is this social atmosphere of equality which characterizes a therapy group and which exerts one of the most effective therapeutic influences on each one of its members. First of all, it removes the need for distance. The highly competitive atmosphere of our civilization produces a state of emotional isolation for everybody; revealing oneself as one is entails the danger of ridicule and contempt. In the therapy group this danger is eliminated. For the first time the individual can be himself without fear and danger. This is an utterly new experience and counteracts the basic fears and anxiety which are usually concerned with possible personal failure and defeat.

In this sense, the group provides subtle but all-persuasive encouragement for each member. It permits an unrestricted feeling of belonging without necessary personal bonds or attachments. Unlike personal and close relationships based on friendship or love, the feeling of solidarity is not based here on a union of personal aspirations. It is truly a feeling of human fellowship without any ulterior motives of personal benefits or advantages, which characterize the relationship of friends and lovers. Accordingly, the desire to help each other in the group springs from the deepest source of human empathy and fellowship, from a feeling of solidarity, of genuine humaneness. We have seen patients who never concerned themselves with anyone's interests or needs and who were moved in the group to give assistance and support without any one of the attributes which those acts usually have in our society, namely the demonstration of personal superiority.

It seems necessary to state clearly that all these strong therapeutic factors operating in the therapy group do not make it a cure-all, by any means. No therapeutic procedure guarantees success. Unfortunately, it is a tacit assumption in many quarters that any form of psychiatric treatment is inadequate if it does not bring full success in all cases. In no other branch of medical practice are such demands made. Methods of medication, surgery, and treatment are acceptable and esteemed even if they provide cure only in a small percentage of cases. The advent of group psychotherapy has certainly improved psychiatric effectiveness. It permitted reaching patients who previously were not accessible; it brought often dramatic progress in heretofore refractory cases. It promises new avenues for providing help actually to millions who are in need of emotional adjustment. Particularly its aspect of mutual help of the patients themselves may lead to new experimentations in line with the model which Alcoholics Anonymous has provided and with the pattern of Self-Help which Dr. A. A. Low has established.

14

C. G. JUNG ON THE PRESENT TRENDS
IN GROUP PSYCHOTHERAPY

Hans A. Illing

For the purpose of research in connection with an article concerning a new perspective in group psychotherapy[1] the writer communicated with Professor Jung in order to clarify certain points that, in the writer's mind, were ambiguous. The correspondence ensuing from the initial communication was made in German, and the letters have been translated into English essentially, although not completely.

Los Angeles, California
January 14, 1955

Dear Dr. Jung,

For some time I have been engaged with a psychologist in preparing a historical survey of group psychotherapy at the request of a German medical journal.

While my collaborator and I belong to different schools of thought and while each of us is taking different parts of the subject, both of us agree on one point fully: our admiration of the school founded and headed by you, your creation of the theory of the Unconscious, and the vast potentialities of your theories relative to group psychotherapy, which you don't seem to have appreciated so far as we could ascertain from the literature.

As I understand your conception of the *Wandlungserlebnis*, it centers around the identification of the individual with several individuals, who, as a *group*, undergo a collective *Wandlungserlebnis*. In such an experience it can happen that a deeper level of consciousness is excited than in the ordinary experience of the individual. If I understand you correctly, a species of common *Tierseele* (animal soul) is born when the group is

Reprinted from *Human Relations*, Vol. X, No. 1, 1957, pp. 77-83.

large enough. It seems that you draw the conclusion from this that the "morale" of large organizations is always low. In my opinion, however, some therapies can be much more effective in the group because the togetherness of many produces virtually a mass suggestibility. Certainly I will admit that inevitably psychological regressions may take place in a group; however, these regressions are partially checked by ritual, i.e. cultic action. Cultic action seizes the attention of the individual and, simultaneously, makes it possible for him to experience his own catharsis in the group and to become conscious of his catharsis. If, on the other hand, a connection with the center is missing, a connection which symbolizes the unconscious, then the *Massenseele* (group-soul) will inevitably become the center and will absorb individual instinct or initiative.

Having studied your writings much and long, I note that you repeatedly emphasize that there are positive experiences which inspire the individual to good deeds or, as you call it, *ein positives Gefühl der menschlichen Solidarität*, a positive feeling of human solidarity, to me, perhaps, the finest piece of expression I have ever come across in the literature, especially if applicable to group psychotherapy. On the other hand, my collaborator and I believe that, conceivably, you are in error to equate the group with the loss of the ego. To us, this is a generalization, since the belonging to a group per se does not constitute regression but rather a greater understanding of the ego! As we shall point out in our paper, "as the therapist applies clinically both factors, heightened suggestibility and group pressure, the methods of group psychotherapy will become particularly effective in the exploration of the unconscious of *every* member of the group."

Our paper is not yet completed. I am turning to you with the request to submit some personal comments on the question whether your antipathy to group psychotherapy derives from the general logic of your theory of the maturing of the individual or from other causes. We have attempted to be as objective as possible in the description of the various schools of thought in our paper; yet it seems to me that nothing could be more "objective," more scientifically accurate, than an explanation, however brief, from the inaugurator of a school himself.

May I add that I have just received a copy of the first English translation of your *Answer to Job*,[2] which I was asked to review. I also received the German edition of your contribution to *Der Göttliche Schelm*.[3] After a hasty examination of both books I feel that these are superb works, worthy of their author and a fitting present for your forthcoming (80th) birthday on 26 July.

Thanking you in advance for your courtesy,

Very respectfully,
Hans A. Illing.

Dr. Jung's answer to the above letter was as follows:

Kuesnacht bei Zürich
January 26, 1955

Dear Dr. Illing,

As a physician, I consider any psychic disturbance, whether neurosis or psychosis, to be an individual illness; the patient has to be treated accordingly. The individual can be treated in the group only if he is a member of it. If he is, this should be a great help, since, being submerged in the group, he apparently escapes his self to some degree. The feeling of security is increased and the feeling of responsibility is decreased when one is part of a group. Once I ran into a thick fog, while crossing over a treacherous glacier with a company of soldiers. The situation was so dangerous that everybody had to stop wherever he happened to be. Yet there was no trace of panic, but rather the spirit of a private party! If only one or two persons had been there, the danger of the situation would probably not have been recognized. Now, however, the brave and the experienced in the company found the opportunity to show off. The timid ones were able to lean on the strength of their brave comrades, and nobody said a word about the possibility of having to camp unprepared on the glacier, which could hardly have been done without some limbs being frozen, let alone the chances of death in attempts to climb from the glacier. This is typical of the mind of the group.

Younger people, in larger groups, often do mischief, which they would never undertake alone. So, in war as a result of group pressure, neuroses disappeared in our soldiers overnight. The group experiences of sects, e.g. the so-called Oxford Movement, are well known; likewise the cures of Lourdes, which were unthinkable without an admiring audience. Groups cause not only astonishing cures but just as astonishing psychic "changes" and conversions, *because the suggestibility is increased*. This was recognized a long time ago by the totalitarian dictators; hence the mass parades, noise, etc. Hitler inspired the greatest group experience of change which Germany has undergone since the Reformation; it cost Europe millions of dead.

Increased suggestibility means the individual's bondage, because he has been delivered to the influences of his environment, be these good or bad. The capacity to differentiate is diminished, also the feeling of individual responsibility, which, as in the Oxford Movement, is left to the "Lord Jesus." People have wondered about the psychology of the German Army. It was no wonder: Every single soldier and officer was just a mass product of suggestion, stripped of moral responsibility.

A small group, too, may be controlled by a suggestive *mind of the whole group* (*Gruppengeist*), which, if it is a good one, may have socially favorable influences, though at the expense of the mental and moral independence of the individual. The group *increases the ego;* i.e. the individual becomes more courageous, more impertinent and assertive, more secure, fresher, and less cautious; the *self*, however, is reduced and is pushed into the background in favor of the average. For this reason all weak and insecure persons wish to belong to clubs and organizations, even to a nation of 80 million! In this relationship the individual feels important, because he identifies himself with everybody else; on the other hand, he loses his self (which is the soul the devil is after and wins!) and his individual judgment. But the ego will only be pushed into the background by the group if it is not in accord with the opinion of the group. For this reason there is always the tendency of the individual in the group to give his assent to the majority opinion to the largest possible degree or, if this be possible, to attempt to impose his opinion on the group.

The annihilating influence of the group on the individual will be compensated for by one member, who identifies himself with the *Gruppengeist* and thus becomes the *leader*. For this reason there are always conflicts over prestige and power in the group, springing from the increase of the ego and the egotism of the mass. The ego's social self, so to speak, is multiplied by the number of members in the group.

I do not have any practical objections to group therapy, as I do not have any to Christian Science, the Oxford Movement, and other therapeutically effective sects. I myself founded a group almost forty years ago; however, that group was composed of "analyzed" persons, whose purpose was to define the social position of the individual. This group is still active today. For social position does not function in the dialectic relationship between the patient and the physician and, therefore, is unadjusted, which was the case with the majority of my patients. This misfortune became only apparent when the group was formed and therefore called for a mutual adjustment.

In my opinion, group therapy is only capable of educating the *social* human being. Attempts in this regard are being made in England, particularly with "unanalyzed" persons, on the basis of psychological theories inaugurated by me. Mr. P. W. Martin, Talboys, Hall Hill, Oxted, Surrey, England, could give you detailed information. I welcome these attempts positively. However, what I have said above about group therapy should not be taken to mean that it can replace individual analysis, i.e. the dialectic process between two individuals and the subsequent intrapsychic catharsis, the dialogue with the unconscious. Since the only bearer of life and the absolutely essential element of any kind of community is the individual, it follows that he and his quality are of consummate importance. The individual must be complete and must endure; otherwise, nothing can exist, since any number of zeros still do not amount to more than zero. A group of inferior people is never better than any one of them, i.e. the group is also inferior; and the state which is composed of sheep only is never anything else but a herd of sheep, even though the herd is led by a shepherd with a biting dog.

In our time, a time which puts so much weight on the socialization of the individual because a special capacity for adjustment is needed, the psychologically oriented group formation is of even greater importance. In view of the notorious inclination of people, however, to lean on others and on isms rather than on inner security and independence, which should have first place, there is the danger that the individual will equate the group with father and mother and will, thereby, remain as dependent, insecure, and infantile as before. He may become adjusted socially. But what of his individuality, which alone gives meaning to the social fabric? Surely, if society consisted of superior individuals only, such an adjustment would be profitable; but, in reality, society is composed mainly of unintelligent and morally weak human beings, so that their *niveau* lies beneath that of one of its superior representatives, let alone the fact that the mass naturally suppresses the values of individuality. When a hundred clever heads join in a group, one big nincompoop is the result, because every individual is trammeled by the otherness of the others. There used to be a funny question: Which are the three largest organizations, the morale of which is the lowest? Answer: Standard Oil, the Catholic Church, and the German Army. Especially in a Christian organization one should expect the highest morality, but the necessity to bring into harmony various factions requires compromises of the most questionable kind. (Jesuitic casuistry and distortion of the truth in the interest of the institution!) The worst examples of recent date are National Socialism and Communism, in which the *lie* became the *raison d'être*.

Real virtues are relatively rare and constitute usually the achievements of individuals. Mental and moral laziness, cowardice, prejudice, and unconsciousness are dominant. I have behind me fifty years of pioneer work and, therefore, could tell a few things about these: there is, perhaps, scientific and technical progress. However, one has not heard yet that people in general have become more intelligent or morally better.

Individuals can be improved because they let themselves be treated. Societies, however, let themselves be seduced and deceived, temporarily even for the good. This refers only to temporary and morally weakening effects of suggestion (*Suggestiveffekte*). (It is for this reason that, with few exceptions, medical psychotherapists a long time ago abandoned any real therapy of suggestion.) One can never achieve the good easily; the more it costs, the better it is. Thus the socially good effects have to be paid for, usually later; but then with interest (e.g. the era of Mussolini in Italy and its catastrophic end). Summing up these reflections I arrive at the following conclusions:

1. Group therapy is necessary for the education of the social human being.

2. Group therapy does not replace individual analysis.

3. Both types of therapy complement each other.

4. The danger of group therapy lies in a standstill on a collective basis.

5. The danger of individual analysis lies in the neglect of social adjustment (*Anpassung*).

With kindest regards,
C. G. Jung.

Most of Professor Jung's points seemed to be well taken. However, the writer still did not feel that some of the points were clarified, points over which he had communicated with Dr. Jung initially. His answer to Jung's detailed letter is as follows:

Los Angeles, California
February 3, 1955

Dear Dr. Jung,

Your prompt and detailed reply to my recent inquiry relative to your attitude toward group psychotherapy was greatly appreciated and I shall treat it accordingly. My associate and I believe that your statements were of such importance that we intend to quote your letter in our article to be published soon, provided that you won't object.

Much of your letter's contents was already familiar to me through your books and, therefore, did not come as a surprise; yet you have admirably achieved your purpose to expose the quintessence of today's *societäre Gesellschaft*.

It seems to me immodest to engage in a dispute with a man who can look back "at 50 years of pioneer labor," as I am considerably younger in years and experience as a therapist than you. However, if I, nevertheless, undertake such a correspondence, I do so only because I was encouraged by your expressions of contempt for *unseren lieben Pöbel*, the great mass; you seem to esteem only nobility of soul and the solitude of the creative mind. I sympathize with you the more because I, too, have often had similar notions about *die Minderwertigen*, the inferior, as you choose to call them. However, in my case I could only say: "*Quod licet Iovi non licet bovi*," for the *Pöbel* did not think, rightly, that I was another "Jung." You seem to be an outspoken protagonist of individuality, which, according to Goethe, is *das höchste Gut der Erdenkinder*. Yet although I share your zeal to uphold the dignity and freedom of the individual, I would also venture to cross swords with you on behalf of the "discriminated" group, of which the individual is an integral part.

Firstly, I wish to emphasize my complete agreement on the Five Points with which you sum up the applicability of group psychotherapy. I even agree where I have some reservations, which are probably due to the fact that some words have different meanings to both of us.

One of these words is your term *Individualanalyse*, probably intended as a contrast to *Gruppenanalyse*. Although there is a faction of psycho-analysts who adhere to the school of thought that the psychoanalysis of groups is possible, I never considered it possible, finding myself, I might say, on the side of the majority of group therapists everywhere. No! I meant to say group *therapy* or psychotherapy, terms which are used syn-onymously in America, being applied to the patient as an adjunct or sub-stitute for individual psychotherapy. Analysis may often be therapy—though not necessarily so—but, in my opinion, psychotherapy can never be equated with psychoanalysis. To the best of my knowledge, based on the analytical literature of Freud and his pupils, Fenichel, Abraham, Reik, Jones, *et al.*, the *principles* of psychotherapy are alike whether they are ap-plied in individual or in group psychotherapy. You speak of suggestibility as a heightened risk in the group, since "one is delivered to the influences of the environment." If I have understood you *and* Freud correctly, it is the suggestibility of the individual therapist (in contrast to the free associ-ation in analysis) which is much greater, more dangerous, and more de-pendent on the temperament and personality of the therapist than on that of the group, the therapist's "influence" on which is virtually modified or even cancelled! Is not the person of the therapist in individual psychother-apy the symbol of the *Umweltseinfluss* for the patient?

If I remember correctly, you once said—I believe in *Spirit and Nature*[4]—that, the more unconscious the human being is, the more he integrates into the circle of the general psychic behavior. But the more conscious he becomes of his self, the stronger is his feeling of the differentia-tion from others. . . . And the more the single consciousness is emanci-pated from the rules of society, the stronger becomes the empirical free-dom of the will in comparison to the growth of a larger consciousness. In this connection I would like to make a point: Those who are not familiar with the methods of group psychotherapy (according to which groups are being used *de facto* to further individuation, to stimulate and to complete it) can easily be mistaken about it. For instance, you state that, by equating the group, a loss of the self will result. This appears to me a generalization. Belonging to a group *per se* does not constitute a regression, i.e. does not require of the individual an involuntary expression of his self, an expres-sion which may derive from archetypal and unconscious rites. On the contrary! Participation in well-prepared groups will lead to a greater under-standing of the ego and to a greater toleration of individual differentia-tions. In the fact that the therapist applies clinically both factors, namely the heightened suggestibility and the group pressure, the group psycho-therapeutic methods will become particularly effective, as, above all, *in the exploration of the unconscious of every member of the group.*

Perhaps you are right when you speak of the instinct of the herd (I think you used the analogy of sheep). Perhaps, too, you made a point in stating that the "reality consists mostly of nincompoops and moral weaklings" (Schiller said: "Majority is nonsense; sense is but with a few"). However, it seems to me that we have to live together with these "nincompoops and moral weaklings" unless those of us who do not qualify as nincompoops can manage to live aside as hermits, in "splendid isolation."

With best wishes,
Hans A. Illing.

Replying to the above, Jung wrote:

February 10, 1955

Dear Dr. Illing,

I fully approve of the integration of the individual into society. However, I want to defend the inalienable rights of the individual; for the individual alone is the bearer of life and is, in these times, gravely threatened by degradation. Even in the smallest group, the individual is acceptable only if he appears to be acceptable to the majority. He has to be content with toleration. But mere toleration does not improve the individual; on the contrary, toleration causes a sense of insecurity, by which the lonely individual who has something to champion may be seriously hindered. I am no advocate of solitude; I have to make the greatest effort to shield myself from the demands of people. Without intrinsic value social relations have no importance.

Sincerely,
C. G. Jung.

REFERENCES

1. G. R. Bach and H. A. Illing, "Historische Perspektive zur Gruppenpsychotherapie," *Z. Psychosom. Med.*, I:131-147, 1956.
2. C. G. Jung, *Answer to Job* (London: Routledge and Kegan Paul, 1954).
3. C. G. Jung, K. Kerényi, and P. Radin, *The Trickster* (London: Routledge and Kegan Paul, 1956).
4. C. G. Jung, *Spirit and Nature* (London: Routledge and Kegan Paul, 1955).

15

SOME APPLICATIONS OF HARRY STACK SULLIVAN'S THEORIES TO GROUP PSYCHOTHERAPY

George D. Goldman

A brief summary of how I view psychoanalytic theory and Sullivan's place in it[1] seems to be in order before I proceed to his specific formulations. Psychoanalysis originated in a nineteenth-century Vienna to help the people of that day and place with their specific problems in living. In these earliest days it dealt primarily with problems of sexual and love frustrations that were experienced in growing up in this particular, rather restricting, setting. These conflicts seemed to be handled by the patients in fairly specific common ways—mainly through the development of hysterical symptoms. The therapy was therefore geared to peel back the layers protecting the patient's disrupting sexual memory and allow for a more effective solution to this experience. After Freud discovered that these "memories" were oft more fancied than real, a different theory to account for the patient's problems in living had to be formed. The advent of libido theory and renunciation of the recall method necessitated interpreting the patient's experiences in terms of this new theory. Soon one was not said to be doing psychoanalysis unless one was making the patient's unconscious conscious and accomplishing it through "analysis of the transference." It appears to me as though the patient's memory of events had been replaced by his being educated to use a new and exclusive system of words and ideas to explain himself to himself.

This brief, not too complete, characterization of Freudian theory is not meant to minimize Freud's monumental contributions to the field but to point out factors that underlie the limitations of using any one frame of reference. This theory is in many ways outmoded, specifically, to name a

Reprinted from the *International Journal of Group Psychotherapy*, Vol. VII, No. 4, October 1957, pp. 385-391.

few of these ways, in the areas of infantile sexuality, libido theory, and structure of the personality.

In the years since Freud formulated his theories of personality our economic, political, and social worlds have changed greatly, and with these changes have come concomitant changes in the people in it. Vienna of the nineteenth century is not New York of 1956. Perhaps this can in some way help us to understand that our present-day patients are different and have different ways of handling their problems. This theme is amplified in a previous paper[2] so I will not discuss it further at this time.

Sullivan was a product of our present-day American culture, he was exposed to and influenced by the scientists and social scientists of our time. Meyer's influence was most strongly felt in his early ideas of psychiatry.[3] Cooley's work was seen in Sullivan's formulations of the self-system.[4] Lewin's field theory and Moreno's situational approach parallel his work.[5] I have tried to apply these theories of group dynamics to group psychotherapy in an approach utilizing Sullivanian principles in a study previously reported.[6]

As a man, he appears to have used "the obsessional dynamism" more than most, and his theories with their intricacies of language and thought reflect this as well. The various major theoreticians had to, by the very nature of their being human beings, focus on specific core problems in a specific way which not only characterized the patients they met in their practice but characterized their own individuality and personal view of life and the major problems human beings face. This paper presents an approach that I have found consistent with my view of life and one which I can use effectively with the patients in my practice.

I see Sullivan as having been quite concerned with what are psychiatric problems and what are not.[7] While it surely is one's task to help people and, more specifically, to help people understand their behavior, there are many ways in which this can be done. One could give direct advice or even be the warm, loving, giving parental substitute who would make up for all the deprivation the patient had suffered. Sullivan, however, felt that the most respectful role, as well as the most scientifically and empirically correct role, was that of an expert at understanding those events which would clarify for patients the processes that involve or go on between people. The patient, of course, was the expert on his specific history of significant interrelationships. Sullivan felt that the analyst could function most effectively by *sampling* those events that are characteristic of the patient's interactions with other people. What better laboratory to observe and document these dynamic events than in the therapy group, where the analyst is, in the fullest sense of Sullivan's usage, participant observer of human interaction?

Interaction, characteristic of the patient's interpersonal operations, is thus constantly under observation for its anxiety-laden overtones and for awareness of what else might have been going on other than what the patient assumed was happening.

Having mentioned the patient and his anxiety I feel I cannot go any further without briefly outlining both how the patient got to be first a person and then a patient, and how and why his anxiety appears. Sullivan did not see patients as being different in kind from other human beings; it was rather a matter of degree.[8] The human animal with its biologically determined substratum becomes a distinct person through an infinitely complex series of interactions throughout its developing years with a multitude of significant persons ranging from parents to chums. To be a bit more specific: The "self-system" comes into being very early in the child's education and socialization as the developing human copes with the complex demands, expectations, limitations, appraisals, and security operations of the parents. The self-system controls the patient's awarenesses to his environmental pressures, to the specific demands and attitudes of significant others that are intolerable, by specific dynamisms. The overuse of a specific dynamism, whether it be selective inattention or obsessionalism, differentiates *the patient* from other persons. The self-system develops through the various eras from infancy through late adolescence, learning from the social heritage passed on by the developing human's parents, teachers, and friends. This learning has to take place since humans in their humanness have characteristically certain tendencies to interact and integrate interpersonally. These interactions are governed by the nature of the "need systems," the goals, or integrating tendencies of human beings. These can be classified under two main headings: those having to do with the individual in his culture, his comfort, belongingness, apartness, his security or insecurity with others are called the "pursuit of security"; those that have to do with his more biologically derived needs are grouped under the "pursuit of satisfactions." The person, in his living with other people, is thus constantly striving to avoid anxiety in the pursuit of these two universal needs.

Sullivan saw the vast majority of the work we do in therapy as having to do with acquainting the patient with the various processes and techniques which are his maneuvers for minimizing or avoiding anxiety. Anxiety responses are derived from antecedent historical events involving earlier human situations. These earlier human situations occurred as interaction with *all* significant persons as the developing person with his biologically given substrata progressed (through the stages of development) from infancy to adulthood. Mental illness can be defined as interference with this progression and in the attainment of satisfactions and security.

As an example of what I have been saying, let me illustrate by telling an event that recently took place in one of my groups, showing how it was handled and relating it to the above theoretical framework.

About twenty minutes after one of my group sessions had started,

Ann timidly poked her head in the doorway of my office, looked around, and scurried to a seat. Within the next five minutes she had verbally lashed out at three different group members, especially the analyst. Joe, who had been in the group with Ann for some time, observed that this was a fairly typical way of behaving for Ann when she felt she had done something wrong. Focusing on Ann in this event, let us examine her behavior as the group interaction highlighted it. As the group members confronted Ann with their reactions to her conduct, she became vividly aware of her anxiety. Our initial task was to understand what her behavior was geared to do for her in relation to minimizing anxiety and later to understand the historical perspective of her behavior in the safety of the analytic relationship. This, parenthetically, is my therapeutic method in individual treatment as well. The interpersonal operation involved was delineated as follows: When Ann felt she had done something that would be thought of as bad, wrong, or incorrect by those around her she anticipated a rebuke of such severe intensity that it would destroy her self-esteem. To block the expected attack Ann attacked first at what she felt were the weak spots in those around her. In her framework she was neutralizing those in the group who might hurt her. If they were shown to be weak they were not to be feared. In reality she was acting in direct opposition to her wish to be accepted and was provoking the very behavior she feared most.

Our next task was to explore the historical perspective of this interpersonal operation in order to understand the parataxes involved and advance toward a more mature integration. By parataxes I mean the carryovers into the present of her personalized childhood fantasies about a situation. Thus, as a child, to be yelled at disapprovingly was seen by her as being destroyed, and to err ever so slightly was the invitation to be yelled at. The developing self-system could not tolerate the destructive criticism of Ann's mother (in this case). The dynamism used in adjusting could keep the disruptive appraisal of her mother out of her awareness and thus avoid the anxiety. This approach is both Sullivanian and a distinct contribution in its awareness of personality being studied only in an interaction with another human being; in its realization that it is the adult Ann that gets into difficulty as an adult from using an adaptation of a childhood pattern (rather than exact repetition); in its understanding of dynamisms to keep unfavorable appraisals by others out of our awareness; and finally that these appraisals historically could have come from any significant person. I am going to omit the specific details of Ann's history since my emphasis is only on presenting an example of Sullivan's method.

To apply this method specifically to further our understanding of group therapy theory, I want to mention that this same behavior had been previously brought to Ann's attention in our individual session with little apparent effect. I feel it was the *immediacy* and *vividness* of her being confronted with behavior that had been acted out in a life situation, analo-

gous to the original childhood situation, helped her accept the present interpretation. For this lonely and isolated girl, the security that came from
belonging to a group and the knowledge some part of her had that she was
really accepted by the group gave her the strength to "look at herself" in
the group. Also operating for Ann as a support to go on to explore her
problem was the experience she had had in the group of how similar exploration had helped others. The group in this case was a valuable adjunct
to Ann's individual treatment.

More generally speaking, the group is an ideal place vividly to act out
patterns of interaction that are characteristic of the patient's particular relatedness; in turn, the relatedness of specific group members often stirs up
unique reactions in fellow patients. Consensual validation can indicate the
parataxic elements in the various reactions. To clarify this, let me illustrate
more of the various forces and pulls going on interpersonally during "an
event" and how this is characteristically handled in my groups. The patients in the group all have concomitant individual treatment. The group
interaction therefore can center around the various group members interrelating with each other. These interactions are seen as representative of
their relations in general and are used to spark further exploration of patterns of operation. A specific event, then, could potentially affect each of
the ten patients in the group and enable them to learn something about
their feelings, reactions, attitudes, and so on. Turning once more to the
event previously used as an illustration, we could have focused on Joe and
tried to understand what was behind his sensitivity to Ann. What was
there in him that was awakened by this angry woman? Was he defending
the analyst? If so, what did this mean? Why did he remember that Ann attacked when she felt she was wrong? To clarify Ann's behavior, four members of the group gave identical reactions to her being destructively belittling. It is this consensual validation by a group of significant peers that
made her realize her behavior. The importance of the people and strength
of their reactions was too great to have been kept out of awareness by the
dynamism of selective inattention. Once vividly aware of what she was doing, Ann could and did analyze her behavior. As Ann talked of her feelings in anticipation of being criticized, a strong reaction was stirred up in
Art, another group member, who spoke of his perfectionistic music teacher
and his demands. In this way the group members' characteristic interpersonal operations are highlighted, thus giving each the opportunity to feel
the anxiety concomitant with the reaction and to become aware of acts
and feelings that he has been perhaps totally unaware of.

In the group situation the patient can become aware of unsatisfied
strivings that are typical of some early developmental stage. He can re-
experience the pain of the frustration of his desires in as close to the original situation as his chronological age allows with a minimum loss of self-
esteem, for the group is a place where his imaginary or fantasied people

come to life and are most vividly felt. This re-experiencing with its con-comitant bringing to awareness the feelings that have been dissociated makes for growth. The patient in his group treatment can relive, in a symbolic way, all his life experience, and can experience the unique opportunity to live his psychic life over again.

Let me amplify this point. The groups that I have are heterogeneous in composition, with all age ranges represented. It is possible in the group situation to relive and work through feelings and attitudes that are typical of infancy, childhood, the juvenile era, preadolescence, early or late adolescence. At one time for one or more patients the group is a peer group, and we would find cooperation, banding together of peers against authority, competition, and conformity. Another patient may see the group as the family, and he may be experiencing some of the somatic feelings of anxiety that had their origins at a preverbal level in infancy. If the patient had never had the experience of finding one person who was particularly important to him, a chum, he might start this type of relationship in the group. It is through the development of this relationship that Sullivan felt that one's capacity to love matures. From the above it is clear that I believe the group is not necessarily either a family or a peer group, but will become for the patient what his and his therapist's parataxes demand and allow respectively.

In terms of directly handling a patient's needs for satisfactions and security, group membership gives one the feeling of being part of something and belonging that is often so hard to find in our present-day urban society. His emptiness and loneliness are more directly alleviated in his contact with other people, who are, after all his fears and expectations, human and therefore more similar to than different from himself.

I do not feel that I can conclude this paper without a brief word on this last point—humanness and the respect of it that characterized Sullivan, the man, and his technique. For it is not only the expertness of the analyst that helps the patient to grow and change. Rather it is his personality and the respect for other human beings and feelings for their suffering that he communicates. In the group situation by his gestures, facial expression, or nonverbal acceptance, as well as his verbalizations, the therapist communicates his respect for others. This is sensed by all and helps in the formulation of the group atmosphere, an atmosphere where each can without humiliation and with dignity expose his specific patterns of interpersonal relations. It is in such an atmosphere that parataxes can be pointed out without overwhelming anxiety and their resolution can take place.

In summary, we have attempted to show the relevance of Sullivanian principles to meet the challenge of working with patients in our present-day practice. These principles were shown to be based on the concept of an ever-interacting, constantly changing human being evolving from the human animal through absorbing the social and cultural perspective of those around him. The developing self-system was shown to have used certain dynamisms to protect itself. Through the example of an event in the group used to make the patients vividly and dramatically aware of their interpersonal operations, Sullivan's theory was applied to group practice. Group treatment was thus seen as an effective laboratory to explore and vividly verify one's patterns of interpersonal reaction as a prelude to learning their historical perspective and eventually changing one's behavior.

REFERENCES

1. For their invaluable teachings in this area, I thank Drs. Mary White Hinckley, Meyer Maskin, and Clara Thompson.
2. G. D. Goldman, "Group Psychotherapy and the Lonely Person in Our Changing Times," *Group Psychother.*, 8:247-253, 1955.
3. *The Common Sense Psychiatry of Adolf Meyer*, edited and with biographical narrative by Alfred Lief (New York: McGraw-Hill Book Co., 1948).
4. C. H. Cooley, *Human Nature and the Social Order* (1902), in one volume with *Social Organization* (Glencoe, Ill.: The Free Press, 1955).
5. K. Lewin, *A Dynamic Theory of Personality* (New York: McGraw-Hill Book Co., 1935); J. L. Moreno, *Who Shall Survive?* (Washington, D.C.: Nervous and Mental Disease Publishing Co., 1934).
6. J. L. Singer and G. D. Goldman, "An Experimental Investigation of Contrasting Social Atmospheres in Group Psychotherapy with Chronic Schizophrenics," *J. Soc. Psycho.* 40:23-37, 1954.
7. H. S. Sullivan, *The Psychiatric Interview* (New York: W. W. Norton & Co., 1954).
8. H. S. Sullivan, *The Interpersonal Theory of Psychiatry* (New York: W. W. Norton & Co., 1953).

16

HORNEY CONCEPTS IN GROUP PSYCHOTHERAPY

Sidney Rose

Horney was interested in group psychotherapy, and two years before her death she encouraged several psychoanalysts to begin work with groups. On October 7, 1951, after hearing some preliminary reports, she expressed high hopes for its further development. "Group analysis is not only valuable socially but also for the promise it holds out as a short therapy. . . . It is of such high promise that it should be continued not only for adults but also for younger people such as adolescents." She also warned against overoptimism. "There are also difficulties and dangers. New technical problems arise. . . . The composition of the group . . . the difficulty of evaluating results, of what trends to take up. . . . How to preserve continuity. . . . The danger of behavioristic changes (without character change) . . . the danger of arousing too much anxiety prematurely . . . etc."[1]

Her concepts, which are based on clinical experience, furnish the group therapist with a means of rapidly sizing up a fluid group situation so that he can properly conduct therapy. Quick judgment, which is so important for a group therapist, is not to be equated with superficiality but with a deep feeling for what is essential at any moment in directing the flow of the group process. This is psychological depth in the therapeutic sense.

Rigid adherence to theory determines too much what one selects from the group process, so that what is observed confirms one's theoretical bias. Horney was able to move on with ever new formulations as old concepts were not supported by her clinical observations. She repeatedly reminded us that theory is to be learned but is to be kept in the background

Reprinted from the *International Journal of Group Psychotherapy*, Vol. VII, No. 4, October 1957, pp. 376-384.

when dealing with a therapeutic situation in order not to tailor events to fit one's theoretical preconceptions.

For a restructuring of the personality, neurotic blocking to growth must be worked through. There can be lesser goals such as symptom improvement and better adjustment for which group therapy may be indicated, but we are interested in deep and permanent character change. Horney describes the goal as self-realization, which means the capacity to feel free and independent, to have a sense of inner direction and unity. It means developing one's talents and unique gifts, recognizing one's limitations, having a sense of responsibility to oneself and others, and to relate to them as they are on a mutual basis and undistorted by neurotic needs. These goals are achievable as neurotic patterns are worked through and are replaced by healthy integrating patterns, which are in the background as potentialities. When the healthy patterns become uppermost, they permit an awareness of the values in our present culture that are at odds with basic human values. The therapy group process is a way of fostering, encouraging, and developing those human values that supply an inner-directedness without which there is a gnawing sense of emptiness and loneliness often concealed by neurotic defenses.

To Horney, the personality was not a static structure but an intricate, alive, flowing process with many systems and subsystems. Self-realization is hindered by self-defeating character patterns which originate in childhood and are maintained by the self-perpetuating nature of neurotic processes. The growing child is immersed in his surrounding and immediately responsive to it. Environmental emotional deficits, anxiety, and excessive conflict inhibit the development of full-scale emotional patterns and lead to rigid reactive behavior patterns. Since the latter are inappropriate, they activate other difficulties and conflicts which require new defensive measures to avoid anxiety and escape from compulsive conflict. The developing self-system is always involved in this process. The child's feeling for self is part of the human capacity to symbolize. As the symbolizing function develops, there is a reorganizing and reintegrating of everything that went before. When there is much "basic anxiety," i.e. "the feeling a child has of being isolated and helpless in a potentially hostile world," it permeates the developing self-system, causing rigidity and an overstructuralization with little reserve capacity for meeting new challenges. It results in an exaggerated self-idealization which gives him an unearned significance, a false sense of unity, and a spurious identity. This has a decisive effect on his entire being, his philosophy of life, his relations to self and others. Therapy of children aims at supplying the emotional deficits and breaking the vicious circle between the child and his former environment before the interpersonal conflicts become structured intrapsychically in the distorted idealized self-system.

Neurotic reactions are seen in terms of the *present* character structure.

Horney's emphasis is on the "here and now." Childhood memories are important in establishing a feeling of a common background within the group and enabling each one to have feeling for the origin of some neurotic tendencies. They are also of value in providing a vehicle for the expression of present feelings. The group interactions are not seen in terms of the "repetition compulsion" wherein the individual repeats childhood patterns of behavior. Neither does Horney use the term of "transference," wherein feelings to other individuals supposedly duplicate feelings to significant people in childhood. Her concept is that the repetitive behavior of the neurotic is due to the abnormal character structure best described in terms of a distorted concept of self and the world which comes from disturbances in childhood. This also explains the distorted relatedness to others which is not called a "transference," but designated by a neutral term like "doctor-patient relationship" and in group work "patient-patient" relationship. Identification of neurotic patterns comes from the noting of their rigidity and compulsiveness, which stems from the ever-underlying anxiety, and their being inappropriate and out of proportion to the precipitating factor.

On the interpersonal level, we can go back to Horney's three basic moves which she describes in *Our Inner Conflicts* as "towards," "against," and "away from," compliance, aggressiveness, and detachment, respectively, which are exaggerations of the normal cooperation, assertiveness, and need for solitude. The neurotic has compulsive elements of all three and is pulled in contradictory directions. Such a basic conflict can be solved when one is a member of any hierarchical group where as a result of his position there are those to whom he can submit, those whom he can dominate, and at the same time also maintain a degree of detachment. The analytical therapy group uses democratic values, works against any hierarchical status, and does not permit such an interpersonal solution of conflict.

As a result of the manifestation of these contradictory compulsive needs, different kinds of interpersonal group reactions occur. In her last book, *Neurosis and Human Growth*, Horney focused on the intrapsychic meanings of such interpersonal reactions. She described in great detail the need to idealize the self-concepts as one of the most important ways of resolving conflict and alleviating anxiety. Her description of different "types" is helpful to the beginner in illustrating the most frequent "clusters" of neurotic behavior and patterns: The individual who behaves in a compliant way has an idealized image with predominating self-effacing trends; the aggressive has an idealized image with predominating expansive trends; and the detached has an idealized image with predominating resigned trends.

While one set of trends tend to predominate, the others are in the background. With the idealized image, the individual tries to harmonize the three contradictory trends. He is always trying to be a unit and avoid conflicting feelings. One common way is to repress what is undesirable and does not fit in with his idealized image. Horney retains the concept that certain personality aspects are repressed and kept out of awareness. Another way of avoiding conflicting feelings is by externalization, wherein the contradictory feeling is experienced outside oneself. Another solution is by withdrawing from inner feelings altogether, a self-numbing. Therapy encourages experiencing those personality aspects which are unconscious, recognizing their consequences, and appreciating their connectedness with other personality facets. She describes the nature of the forces that pull the individual in conflicting directions, how they operate in the present, and their dynamic interrelatedness.

Horney describes in great detail how the "pride system" alienates the individual from real feelings and human values, so that instead of a wide range of varied feelings, the neurotic lives in a narrow zone of feeling dominated by an undercurrent of insecurity and anxiety from which he protects himself with his pride system. He tends to experience elation when his pride is fulfilled, or defeat when he fails, or the numbness of noninvolvement. Her detailed descriptions of the various pride manifestations and those of self-hate and their connectedness broadens one's grasp of what goes on in the group. Many of the facets of character structure have been described by Freud and others in different ways. Horney's contribution is the way these are viewed and linked together in a meaningful way which ebb and flow as the neurotic attempts to meet life. Horney is optimistic in her belief that there are basic healthy strivings that can be freed to develop into constructive integrating patterns as neurotic patterns are worked through.

What I found of immense value in group therapy is her concept of the multidimensional nature of personality processes, how they prove inadequate to resolve conflict and relieve anxiety and in the long run become reinforced and self-perpetuating. As has been said, the original anxiety leads to self-idealization. This is a constant source of self-hate whenever the neurotic is faced with the reality of himself. By externalizing he tends to feel that others hate him, reinforcing the original basic anxiety. Feeling the world is more hostile means that he has to resort to renewed defenses which further remove him from reality. The types of defenses resorted to will vary but tend to go in one of three directions. In persons with expansive solutions, the feeling that the world is hostile will increase. Those who tend to use self-effacing solutions will experience an increase in the helpless facet of the basic anxiety, and those who are resigned will go in the direction of increased isolation, with possibly greater self-numbing and living in the imagination.

Briefly, the neurotic's efforts to seek security serve in the long run to make him more insecure, and he then resorts to the same unrealistic, ill-adapted, defensive measures. He is alienated from real feelings and values and relates to others with his compulsive, integrating patterns. Since they are defensive, they tend to activate similar defensive patterns in others, leading to mutual reinforcement.

How can the above concepts be useful in group therapy? First of all, we assume there is a group-unifying process going on, and that under the influence of the therapist it can be turned in a healthy direction. This means the therapist must be sensitive to group atmosphere. Here is where Horney's concept of "basic anxiety" is of help since group cohesiveness can be misused in a neurotic way to relieve basic anxiety, i.e., the feelings of weakness, isolation, and that others are hostile. The obverse of basic anxiety is the feeling of belonging, and this is an important group-integrating force. This concept alerts the therapist to cohesiveness and group unity which caters merely to the relief of anxiety. Against this of course, one must be on guard. The ultimate direction is a healthy feeling of belonging based on the essential humaneness of each. On the group level, the therapist encourages conflict and the emergence of anxiety, and he has to be sensitive to the group's breaking point (the point at which individuals have to leave the group).

As the group strives toward a cooperative mutuality, there is a constant ebb and flow, disorganization and disintegration, which is followed by reorganization and reintegration in new directions. This ebb and flow results from all kinds of interrelatedness in various combinations within the group. The task of the analyst is to feel the pulse of group movement, and when the normal corrective processes fail to operate, he must act. Temporary phases of disharmony always occur and their recognition is important. The therapist rapidly scans the group process, shifting focus from the group atmosphere to interpersonal relatedness, to intrapsychic dynamisms. Intervention can be done on any of these three levels.

He must be able to sense group direction, identify the intrapsychic patterns and the interpersonal effects which have determined the neurotic group direction so that influence can be exerted at the pivotal point. The multidimensional nature and the self-perpetuating effects of neurotic patterns is illustrated repeatedly in the group process, and the aim of therapy is to permit the experiencing of these patterns, and their consequences, and the encouragement of new ways.

It is the interpersonal reactions occurring against the group background which reveal the vicious, self-perpetuating nature of neurotic patterns and expose the neurotic facets of each one. The group process is most sensitive to interpersonal difficulties. In facing an aspect of his behavior which is responsible for excessive group friction, the individual is thrown into conflict, and the false unity, based on his idealized image, is threatened.

The neurotic is not only estranged from his real self but also from his actual conflicted self. The responses of others to him may be contradictory and alert him to conflicting self-aspects. The group also gives him the opportunity to observe disowned self-aspects in others and his repetitive emotional reactions to them. They may vary from intense hatred to admiration, depending on the predominating trends. An individual with contempt for his self-effacing side may react against another with similar trends. As he progresses, he will be able to observe, speculate, and later experience these in himself, at the same time reacting to others more as they are and less in terms of his neurotic needs. He reinternalizes conflicting aspects of his self-image and experiences conflict within himself. Only as he can own more of his actual self can he gain the strength to give up defensiveness, approach wholeness, and move in the direction of self-fulfillment.

A thirty-three-year-old woman at the age of twenty-five years gave up a promising career when she married a capable engineer. She pushed her own expansive, ambitious self to the background and depended on her husband for fulfillment. She brought her self-effacing idealization to the foreground as the always understanding, uncomplaining wife and mother, and was ready to play a dependent role. Her husband's lack of business success frustrated her claims on him for the success she could not achieve. The resentment that was stirred up could not be permitted into awareness because of her need to be supporting and understanding. Instead of a dependent role, she found the roles reversed, with her husband dependent on her. Repressing the resentment increased the anxiety, which she controlled with a greater determination to be still more understanding. After several years of marriage she developed psychosomatic symptoms and had difficulties with her children, for which she sought therapy.

At the group her need to be self-sacrificing was repeatedly pointed out, and she began to experience the intense resentment toward her husband which previously she repressed. In one group session she expressed these feelings of resentment in association with a very significant dream. This touched off similar feelings in a musician who complained that his father had neglected him and that a present-day society failed to give artists a fair deal. She immediately assumed her usual supportive and protective role and sympathized with him. In this sympathetic manner she was controlling the musician and dominating the group scene. This was just what she had been doing with her husband, as she had related to the group earlier in the session. Her behavior was repetitious and encouraged an abused reaction in the musician similar to her husband's. If she had been allowed to continue in the group, a vicious circle would have been set up wherein they would mutually satisfy each one's neurotic needs, reinforcing and perpetuating the neurotic patterns similar to those in their families.

Intrapsychically, it was apparent that the musician was externalizing his self-hate for his failures as a musician, attacking his father and society. Her support of him relieved his self-hate as well as her own self-hate because she was acting out her idealized, saintly role. After she revealed the resentment toward her husband in the group she felt an increasing self-hate which she had to alleviate. This at that moment fitted in with the musician's need for motherly support. The moves to each other in this symbiotic relating were compulsive and the interpersonal results of their intrapsychic needs. On the group level it tended to produce a disruptive effect because the alliance went against the healthy group cohesiveness. If all group members had joined together in an attack on society for its treatment of artists, then it would have been a group unity based on neurotic needs.

In this session, these two members were involved with each other and the rest were silent. My questioning as to what was going on galvanized the group into action. They expressed their feelings of annoyance at having been excluded by the two. The group then proceeded to indicate neurotic aspects in their behavior.

This example illustrates how interpersonal neurotic symbiosis interferes with a group. The group current and influence went against this mutual satisfaction of neurotic needs, preventing the formation of a vicious circle. It illustrates the "here and now" as shown in the interaction process. It shows the actual experiencing of unconscious needs, the full meaning of which was brought to their attention by the group. It illustrates how behavior can be understood in terms of the self-concept of each participant.

Each was attempting to solve his intrapsychic conflicts in the temporary alliance. What the group process did was to help each one become involved in intrapsychic conflict. The woman came closer to her need to be the self-sacrificing mother and ultimately experience and accept herself as she actually was. Much later she was faced with the expansive, ambitious, competitive side of herself, and after experiencing these conflicting elements she was able to shift to healthier motivations.

The path of therapy leads to gradual awareness of disowned aspects of the self, often first observed in other group members. As one is able to own these, one experiences internal conflicts. Vicious interpersonal and intrapsychic perpetuating reactions are ultimately converted into beneficent ones. The neurotic identity which tries to harmonize contradictory superhuman self-concepts is eventually undermined with the emergence of a more whole, human identity.

The film *Troubled People Meet*[2] shows a group session in which an emotional crisis developed between two women and how it was temporarily resolved. The older, middle-aged woman had complained bitterly about her daughter's ingratitude. Hadn't she borne her, washed and scrubbed floors, and given her everything? Everyone in the group seemed sympathetic and attentive, but a young woman casually quoted a sermon in which self-sacrificing women were criticized. Immediately, the older woman sat bolt upright, felt accused, became angry, burst into tears, and threatened to walk out. She was stopped by the young woman, who rushed over and reassured her. This apparently mollified her. To escape feelings of self-contempt she had to idealize herself as the self-sacrificing mother yet at the same time control and dominate her daughter. The daughter's rebellion undermined her feeling of unity through identifying herself in this particular role and awakened self-hate.

What she sought from the group was sympathy and support which would help her re-establish this image of herself and relieve self-hate. The group felt her claims on them for sympathy and her need to dominate the group, and the young woman by means of her oblique remark may have expressed the sentiment of the group. This frustrated the older woman's search for unity. She was thrown into conflict, and showed much exaggerated suffering. By this tactic she succeeded in making the young woman feel guilty and compelled her to come to her support. Her neurotic pattern re-established control over the situation, and it was evident that it was too strong to be tampered with at that time. Sooner or later this pattern had to be undermined through the group process. For her to continue on this level would eventually disrupt the group; either they would leave or she would have to go. What happened at this particular group session could be useful later on when she is stronger and more likely to accept it. She eventually will see the consequences of these patterns in the group response to her and will have to make a choice.

On the group level, the therapist could see the group functioning as a unit. There was group anxiety and danger of disruption for a brief moment after the younger woman made her mild criticism. The disruption was prevented by the appeasing move of the younger woman, and the group came together. The whole experience may have growth value for the members in varying degrees. How much value it had for the older woman could only be determined later. Certainly an important beginning was made, and it may be possible for the therapist or the group to bear this reaction in mind for later reference. In this particular episode the therapist took no overt action, which may have been for the best, since the group was kept together.

The above brief description of psychodynamics is not by any means meant to be a comprehensive psychological survey. It is mentioned here to illustrate the use of Horney concepts in ordering events in the group process for immediate determination of group direction for possible therapeutic intervention. Diagnosis of the situation and therapy go hand in hand. For purposes of long-range diagnosis and prognosis other facets of the personality must be tapped, but for psychotherapy, especially in the group situation, her concepts are admirably suited.

SUMMARY

Horney is optimistic in her belief that there are basic healthy strivings which can be freed to develop into constructive integrating patterns as neurotic patterns are worked through. This I have found feasible in groups. It manifests itself in the group in the mutuality and the group spirit that eventually emerges. Horney's concept of human growth determines the therapeutic aims. She deals with the "here and now" and uses childhood memories in a different sense, which leads to an altered position of what was called "transference," and the distorted interrelatedness of the group is referred to simply as patient-patient and patient-therapist relationships.

The "here and now" manifests itself in the interaction process within the group and can be examined on three different levels: the group, the interpersonal, or the intrapsychic. Underlying all these is the basic anxiety. She describes certain characteristics of neurotic behavior which make identification and prediction possible.

Her concepts in her most recent work have been reformulated from the vantage point of the self-system, which in the neurotic is idealized as a defense against insecurity and anxiety. Her identification of neurotic patterns enables an ordering of events in a living way and alerts the therapist to many possibilities for intervention in the group process.

REFERENCES

1. K. Horney, "Values and Promises of Group Psychoanalysis," *Am. J. Psychoanal.*, XII:80-81, 1952.
2. J. Frank, "Troubled People Meet," a film on group psychotherapy. Phipps Psychiatric Institute.

Part 3

THEORY
AND TECHNIQUE

ALTHOUGH THIS SECTION IS LABELED "Theory and Technique," close inspection of its contents would indicate that we have presented here essentially a collection of papers on a variety of techniques used to treat individuals in group therapy. The theory behind these techniques leaves a great deal to be desired. This is the weakness in group therapy. The original papers by Wender, Schilder, Lowrey and Slavson, Moreno, and Ackerman communicate some of the history of the development of group psychotherapy. A study of the papers makes it more and more obvious that technique came first and theory later. Many techniques used by the earlier practitioners of group psychotherapy were based on psychoanalytic concepts. For the most part emphasis, in working with groups, was on the individual, and at times there was a denial of certain concepts advanced by social psychologists. We have included papers to illustrate the varied evolving approaches to group psychotherapy and technique.

The paper by Moreno has been included because he feels "it should be of value to the readers because it contains the first comprehensive table of the basic categories of group psychotherapy, a tabulation which has hardly been surpassed in the course of years." *†

We have included a nonanalytically oriented paper by Dr. Baruch which stems from her Rogerian phenomenological approach to psychotherapy. The longest paper in this section is the paper written by Wolf on the psychoanalysis of groups. His paper may be considered representative of much of the thinking of group psychotherapists who stem from a psychoanalytic tradition. In another setting, he has expressed his concern that social theory will not give the answer to resolving individual psychopathology. For example, Wolf has expressed the belief that "the group qua group cannot become the means by which its members resolve intrapsychic

* Personal communication from Moreno.

† The editors believe a more basic article is the paper by Moreno entitled "Psychodrama and Group Psychotherapy," which appeared in *Sociometry*, Vol. IX, 249-253, 1946. We were unable to secure the right to reprint it here.

difficulty. The need for such differentiation led us to change our concept of the psychoanalysis of groups [Wolf, 1949-1950] to that of psychoanalysis in groups [Wolf, 1959]. We do not treat a group. We must still analyze the individual in interaction with other individuals." (This is taken from page 137, E. Schwartz and A. Wolf, "Psychoanalysis in Groups: The Mystique of Group Dynamics," in *Topical Problems of Psychotherapy, Volume II, Sources of Conflict in Contemporary Group Psychotherapy* [Basel: S. Karger, 1960], pp. 119-154.) Wolf and some of the people currently associated with him recognize the early pessimism which Freud expressed toward the psychotherapy of individuals in a group setting. This point has previously been noted by the editors in relationship to Le Bon's concept of the mob and Le Bon's influence on Freud. Wolf also recognizes Freud's unwillingness to see the healing potential within the group of individuals. Yet he expresses a very strong point of view when he states, "There is as yet no clinical evidence demonstrating that attention to these phenomena [group dynamics] is useful to the understanding and treatment of the patient in a group setting. How do group dynamics help achieve a healing objective?" (Page 126 of the cited article.) The opinion that Wolf expresses indicates the confusion that many analysts have regarding group dynamics. It is very much related to the desire to root all psychotherapy in the group setting to a psychoanalytic base. It does not recognize the possibility that psychotherapy in a group setting goes beyond analytic concepts and thinking. The fact that patients are brought together and treated psychoanalytically within a group setting does not deny the current relevant findings of the students of group dynamics.

Sherif, White, and Harvey (M. Sherif, B. J. White, and O. J. Harvey, "Status in Experimentally Produced Groups," *American Journal of Sociology*, Volume 60, pp. 370-379, 1955) found in working with a group of boys that even on a task of supreme importance to them, in this case handball throwing, boys base their predictions and judgments of another boy's performance mainly on his status in the group. This kind of observation is extremely valuable when we work with a *group* of patients. If we deny the influence of status in the group setting, we deny the possibility of ascertaining a perceptual base for another patient's functioning. Many firmly psychoanalytically oriented practitioners of group therapy deny the social variable and discount the group influence on personality function. Wolf, for example, is strongly oriented toward the family concept in his perception of the psychotherapy group. The group becomes the historic recreation of the original family milieu. Yet if this concept is too rigidly held, there is a denial of the evolutionary aspects of group psychotherapy and its roots in sociology, psychology, education, and philosophy. There is denial too that group psychotherapy may be essentially different from individual psychotherapy, that the individual in a group is considered unique as well as ill, that there is an immediacy and spontaneity in the face-to-face relationship of patient to patient and patient to therapist within the group experience which is entirely different from the somewhat intellectual and impersonal therapeutic relationship which often occurs when the patient is alone with the therapist. The group experience encourages a sense of equality and commonality. Overemphasis on the individual denies an important facet of human behavior, that the group is both a conforming force and an impelling force. (See Maurice Friedman's article and his discussion of Martin Buber in this volume, Part 6, "New Trends in Group Psychotherapy.") It is unnecessary to deny the closeness of the familial or parafamilial ties, but we also do depend on the group we are closest to, whether it be the family, the squad, or the team. It is conceivable that in the emphasis on the *individual*, the therapist may deny the growth of the *person*—of the "mensch." The potential to become a real person is only fulfilled in relationships with other persons.

Corsini and Rosenberg's article, on the mechanisms of group psychotherapy (included in this section), indicates that many of the terms that are used in attempting to find basic mechanisms are terms that are to be found in the literature of social psychology and group dynamics.

In his article, Scheidlinger, a practitioner who is firmly rooted in orthodox psychoanalytic theory, tries to relate group therapy to other group influence attempts. He recognizes that one of the essential differences between group therapy and group dynamics may be the specific aim of the practitioner for each group member in each particular group, but he is flexible in his awareness that there is a tremendous commonality between group dynamics and group psychotherapy. The excerpt from Rosenbaum's article that is included in this section emphasizes the resistance mechanisms of analysts working with groups, and while the focus in this article is upon the individual analyst, the resistance mechanisms may certainly be applicable in all group settings where leaders have difficulty relating to a group because of what the group represents for them.

The other articles continue the techniques of treating individuals within the group setting, as well as the selection and classification of patients.

Berger's article on nonverbal communications in group psychotherapy recognizes the different sets of symbol systems that may be used as individuals communicate with one another. For example, some students of semantics differentiate between the linguistic (phonemes) and the paralinguistic (sighs, drawls, slurs, inhalations, loudness and softness, breathiness, speech coughs) and note that these communicate something about the behavior of each speaker, as well as what the total impact of a message is to another individual.

The last paper in this section, by Kadis, "Coordinated Meetings in Group Psychotherapy," stresses for patients' growth the importance of encouraging them to meet, interact, and assess themselves, so that they may clarify their difficulties in living without the professionally trained therapist. We note that Kadis' paper and her position stem originally from the work of Wolf, who, while he is opposed to group dynamics in group psychotherapy, would still encourage patients to meet with one another outside of regularly scheduled psychotherapy settings. Such meetings are called alternate meetings. This concept of peer relationship would appear to accept the validity of group functioning, of the importance of group membership for the individual, and the importance of allegiance to a group. It stresses the fact that the stronger and more cohesive the group is, the more impact and influence it has upon each individual member. Interestingly enough, it also communicates something about the importance of a leaderless group. Mullan has stimulated interest in this concept (see Part 6) in his paper on status denial. Some therapists have obscured Mullan's comments on the clearly leader-led group. They interpret him as fostering a denial of the function of the therapist, and have concluded that the therapist is "behaving like a patient" in the group. However, the same therapists who question Mullan's observations do at times themselves encourage the idea of a certain degree of role denial by the therapist. They do so when they inform the members of a group that the responsibility for what happens in alternate (coordinated) meetings belongs to them.

Reading of the papers in this section indicates that many leading group psychotherapists scarcely acknowledge that students of group dynamics can contribute to the effective practice of group psychotherapy.

17

THE DYNAMICS OF GROUP PSYCHOTHERAPY AND ITS APPLICATION

Louis Wender

Group psychotherapy has been practiced at the Hastings Hillside Hospital for nearly six years. Initial experimentation with this method was prompted by the need for devising forms of therapy adapted to meeting the peculiar problems created by the segregation of mild mental patients and psychoneurotics under one roof. Carefully tested experience with this method has convinced the writer that this form of therapy is efficacious in selected situations and that it merits much wider application in hospitals where patients amenable to psychotherapy receive care.

In distinction to the method of extramural group analysis described by Trigant Burrow, which is psychoanalytic in technique and carries large sociological and philosophic implications, group psychotherapy is a method confined to the intramural treatment of certain types of mild mental disease.

In the ensuing material the writer will attempt to review some of the conditions that prompted the adoption of this approach, to define this method of therapy, to show its ideologic basis, to describe its application and scope, and to evaluate its results.

In considering the treatment of patients within a hospital, one has to bear in mind that the choice between extramural and intramural care is not arbitrary. Hospitalization is the last resort, after efforts at extramural care have failed, and it is usually the severity of the patient's condition that precludes continued treatment on the outside. To the patient himself hospitalization is a crisis. His sporadic efforts in the direction of adjustment need no longer be maintained, since not only has his illness been

Reprinted from the *Journal of Nervous and Mental Diseases*, Vol. 84, No. 1, July 1936, pp. 54-60.

acknowledged to himself, but there has been a corresponding certification to society and a meting out of "punishment." Hospitalization also deprives the patient of the attention he received from his family group and of the power he exercised over them because of his illness. He compensates for this loss by identifying the hospital with his family group (home) and proceeds to seek recognition in the new milieu. Since he no longer competes for supremacy with normal people, who accede to his demands because of the illness which distinguishes him from the rest, he resorts to an intensification of his complaints in order to focus attention on himself in the new setting, where he has to endure the competition of other sick people.

Another condition prevailing in hospitals, as in other assemblies, which requires recognition in considering approaches to therapy is the formation of friendships and cliques and the choice of "buddies." Problems are frequently analyzed and discussed among patients with greater candor than with the physician, and it is a common occurrence to learn the problems and conflicts of a patient through his confidant.

McDougall's theory "that the gregarious impulse receives the highest degree of satisfaction from the presence of human beings who most closely resemble the individual, who behave in like manner and respond to the same situations with similar emotions" is amply demonstrated in hospital life. One encounters daily a group interaction, with its resultant infectiousness of symptoms and suggestibility of moods, that demands the diverting of these impulses and the utilization of group interaction into positive therapeutic channels, if we are not to promote "symptoms orgies."

In viewing intramural methods of therapy, one is impressed by the gap between the profound influence psychoanalytic thinking has exerted on our understanding of the individual patient and the barriers to the wide application of individual analysis to hospital patients. In this connection one must remember that as a therapeutic method psychoanalysis has a limited field of application. Hospitalization still further restricts the use of this method for the following reasons: (a) the difficulty of establishing transference where separation of patients cannot be maintained as in private practice and where patients have opportunities to compare physicians and to develop jealousies of one another while sharing a therapist; (b) the prohibitive financial cost; (c) the dearth of patients with a suitable intellectual and cultural equipment; (d) the practical barrier of extending the length of hospitalization to make possible the completion of an analysis.

The conditions enumerated, as well as many minor ones into a discussion of which we have not the time to enter, make clear the need for seeking and crystallizing methods of approach that are applicable to wider groups of patients, that are shorter in duration, and that are realistically adapted to prevailing hospital conditions. To meet these requirements a proposed method of therapy would have to take cognizance not only of the individual through a psychoanalytic approach but also of the psychology of the group with its common reactions, its individual-to-individual identifications, and its responses to the therapist.

(Group psychotherapy is based on the assumption that the application of some of the hypotheses and methods of psychoanalysis, in combination with intellectualization, when applied to a group for the purposes of treatment under conditions of active therapeutic control, will lead to the release of certain emotional conflicts and a partial reorganization of the personality and ultimately to an increased capacity for social amalgamation.) In distinction to individual psychoanalysis this method places greater emphasis on sociological factors (group interaction) and on intellectual comprehension of behavior. The material for this form of therapy is elicited through theoretical discussions with a group of patients, affording a natural tie-up with the individual participants' experiences and problems. The base, or meeting ground, for these patients is established through what Giddings calls "consciousness of kind." He says "that this consciousness is the basis of alliance, of rules of intercourse, of peculiarities of policy and that our conduct toward those whom we feel to be most like ourselves is instinctively and rationally different from our conduct toward others who are different from ourselves." These patients are in the same predicament; they have diminished need for concealment; in a sense, they are temporarily in a different state of society, with different mores, and their resistance to a relatively intimate sharing of problems is reduced by prevailing attitudes in the new setup. These comments are not hypothetical. They are deductions from extended observation of patients and the progressive changes in their perspective and attitudes during hospitalization. These changes are inevitable; the only question that arises is whether one is to permit them to lie fallow or whether they are to be utilized and released through some method such as this form of therapy.

Experience has shown that group psychotherapy is applicable only to disorders in which intellectual impairment is absent and in which some degree of affect is retained. It is believed that the following groups lend themselves to this type of treatment: (a) early schizophrenics where the delusional trends are not fully systematized and in which hallucinatory phenomena are completely absent; where the splitting of the personality is not marked and there is no blocking; (b) depressions without marked retardation and those who libidinize their ideation—depression *sine* depression; (c) psychoneuroses, with the exception of severe compulsion neuroses of long duration.

The application of this method does not preclude the continuance of individual treatment. As a matter of fact, individual interviews are undertaken in conjunction with the patient's participating in a group, and in many instances it has been found that the group stimulated the patient's desire for individual treatment and that during these interviews such patients spoke readily of experiences the discussion of which they had avoided previously.

A group consists of six to eight patients of the same sex. Attendance is entirely voluntary. The procedure is elastic. No patient is introduced into a group immediately upon his arrival in the hospital, as some degree of adaptation to the hospital is considered essential. A new patient learns soon after his arrival that this form of therapy is an established procedure and that some of his fellow patients participate in a group. Frequently requests for this form of treatment come from the patients and great tact and patience have to be exercised in explaining the exclusions. A group has two or three one-hour sessions each week and continues for a period which varies according to the needs of its members and the objectives of the therapist (usually four to five months). New patients are not admitted to a group already in session. At early meetings the group is instructed not to discuss the content of sessions with patients outside the group, but they are encouraged to discuss the material freely with one another.

Sessions are begun with what is almost lecture material: a simple exposition of why we behave as we do, a description of primitive instinctual drives, conscious and unconscious elements, significance of dreams, early infantile traumata, reaction formations, repressions, rationalizations, and so on. The material is presented in elementary form, with simple, everyday illustrations, the intellectual content and method of presentation being adapted to the general cultural and emotional tenor of the group, and varying accordingly. Presentations are planned with a view to arousing sincere interest in the background of everyday life without inculcating a "psychology hobby." This pitfall can be avoided by the therapist, and the response obtained from groups has always been on the level desired. The use of theoretical material in the beginning stimulates intellectual interest and serves to divert patients from their immediate problems. It also serves as an instrument of facilitating a kind of intimacy and social good will that is analogous to the reaction which we experience after spending an evening with a group in stimulating and vital conversation that gives us a feeling of closeness to people toward whom we have never felt this previously.

Even in the early period of the group's existence, there are individual members who have established a transference to the therapist and there are others who have identified themselves with patients who have this transference. What occurs progressively is a common rapport, patient-to-patient transference and patient-to-therapist transference. A sense of intimacy within the group develops, greater freedom from inhibitions is observed in theoretical discussions and is followed by a spontaneous readiness on the part of some patients to discuss their own problems in relation to the theoretical material. Beginning with illustrations of individual incidents in their own lives which they regard as traumatic or significant, the patients go on to a discussion of their own and one another's symptoms and adjustments. They discuss dreams, which are interpreted on a superficial level with some of the patients participating in the interpretation. The therapist exercises no pressure, and when the term "active control" is used, it is in the sense of active awareness, in distinction to any form of manipulation. Whenever resistances are observed in any particular patient, skillful guidance can divert the discussion into safe and still theoretical waters until such a time as the patients wish to resume the subject. Moreover, the use of this more generic approach minimizes resistance and trauma, since the patient is left free to accept as much as he is ready to accept as applying to him, and to the degree necessary for him is also able to project explanations painful to him on to other patients. Nevertheless, the most carefully gauged awareness as to the individual and collective reactions of the group is essential. Both the theoretical material and the guidance of the patients' own discussions have to be adapted to the changing attitudes and receptivity of the group so that even the tempo of discussion and the duration of a group will be determined accordingly.

It is the writer's intention to make available at a later date the complete material of one group throughout its entire duration so that the techniques may be more intensively scrutinized and evaluated. At the present time it seems expedient to summarize briefly some of the dynamics operating in group psychotherapy.

1. *Intellectualization.* In our awareness of how prominent and destructive a role the conscious can play, we may have neglected it too completely as a factor in the healing process. While there may be no pure intellectual acceptance and everything that may seem like logical acceptance is accompanied by emotional tone, the fact remains that a synthesis of intellect and emotion dominates every phase of our lives and is the basis of all social adjustment. Nor can we overlook entirely the fact that there are intellectual disciplines like the yogi philosophy, the application of which results in the regulation of emotional responses through a self-determined intellectual discipline. What we term "insight" or emotional acceptance may have similar components of self-discipline. While group therapy in no way professes or strives to be an intellectual discipline, it does tend to a comprehension of emotional reactions that enables the patient to meet new situations with greater awareness and skill. The writer is convinced that intellectual awareness is a therapeutic aid as indisputable as the fact that while we may be panic-stricken at an unexpected noise coming from behind, we accept such a noise calmly when we know its origin.

2. *Patient-to-Patient Transference.* The influence exerted by one individual on another may contain elements corresponding to the psychoanalytic transference. In group psychotherapy this patient-to-patient transference is made use of in several ways. It is used to facilitate transference to the therapist through the identification of one patient with another who

has established such transference. This type of transference is encouraged, since it serves to meet the needs of the patients more permanently than the transference to the therapist which has to be abrogated for practical reasons as well as for the purpose of sustaining the patient's independence. It is also believed that the relationship which is established between patients in time takes an outward course, embracing a wider area of interests and activities (socialization).

3. *Catharsis-in-the-Family*. In the group there is undoubtedly a transference of tendencies originally directed toward the parents and siblings. There is a possibility that the entire group setup provides a kind of "Catharsis-in-the-Family," with an accompanying resolvement of conflicts and the displacement of parent love on to new objects. The patient finds himself sitting on terms of equality with the therapist (symbolic of the parent) and the other patients (who represent the siblings). He experiences (it may be for the first time in his life) the receiving of understanding from the just parent whom he shares with siblings who are equal in the eyes of that parent. He is not only receiving understanding but is also free to rebel openly, thus averting repression with its concomitant sense of guilt. In the writer's opinion this experience serves as a means of effecting a degree of emotional release, particularly in situations where the early traumata in child-parent relationships have remained unresolved. The fact that the actual setup is on an adult level and that the patient is conscious of it only as a treatment process makes it acceptable to him.

4. *Group Interaction*. Group interaction is a phenomenon to which every patient was exposed prior to his hospitalization. His development, his ego ideal, and his sense of values had their roots in his societal experience. In this method the patient's association with other patients, his new group experience, is made use of. Inevitably this association will influence his mode of thinking and his reactions, as manifested by the patients' competing with their respective complaints during their early sojourn. Under guidance this interaction results in the development of a changed perspective on behavior, which in turn gives rise to new ego ideals and strivings. In the group the patient develops criteria for evaluating his own problem against the problems of others in a way that is not feasible in individual treatment. An individual who prior to his hospitalization regarded his problems as unique and peculiar to himself learns through exchange with the group that many of his fellows have similarly predicated ego conflicts and begins to view his own problems with greater detachment. The individual experiences a resultant lessening of personal tensions, his attitudes undergo modification, and his whole outlook on behavior changes. In this entire experience he is reinforced by the experience of his group.

The patient's drive to get well derives greater impetus through this method than when only individual treatment is undertaken. This drive is motivated in part by the new ego ideal which the individual has adopted and is strengthened by the apparent feasibility of attaining health, since the recovery of other members of the group presents convincing evidence.

It may be argued that suggestion is a major factor in the results gained through group interaction. If by suggestion we mean the concepts as defined by MacDougall or Freud, these types of suggestion play no greater role in this method than in any other technique. In no sense is there acceptance without logical basis or a continued infantile emotional dependence, implicit in suggestion. In the use of group psychotherapy, the patient derives an understanding of the nature and direction of his unconscious trends, experiencing simultaneously an emotional release. This is accompanied by his being exposed to observation and experience which involve himself and others, ultimately leading to a partial reorganization of his personality. In this unified process it is not an outside agent like suggestion which accomplishes the change but the saturation of the individual with the forces of his own experience.

The results yielded by this method, which has been used in the treatment of about seventy-five patients over a period of six years, cannot be computed statistically. Interpretation on the basis of follow-up (in some cases for four to five years), since that is the only form of evaluation open to us in analyzing material of this nature, shows fairly conclusively that this form of therapy carries positive values for social adjustment. It has been observed repeatedly that friendships formed while groups were in session persist on the outside; that these patients retain a common bond of mutual interest, helpfulness, and understanding which is a source of strength to them; and that their drive to remain well is more dynamic and characterized by a competitive quality. While the recovered patients' opinions cannot be interpreted as having scientific validity, it is significant that they attach importance to this form of therapy and attribute to the group experience their continued capacity to discuss their problems freely and their enhanced ability to deal successfully with new and difficult emotional material and experience.

18

RESULTS AND PROBLEMS OF GROUP PSYCHOTHERAPY IN SEVERE NEUROSES

Paul Schilder

The problem of adequate psychotherapeutic care for neurotic patients who frequent the outpatient departments of public hospitals is an urgent one. Psychoanalysis is undoubtedly an efficient therapeutic weapon, but it makes great demands on the time both of the physician and of the patient. Thus it has become in our economic structure a method employed only for the wealthy. In addition, the general trend in psychoanalytic technique is to prolong the treatment; indeed, daily treatments for two or three years are not considered unusual. If psychoanalysis is the best treatment available at the present time, the community should utilize it; but if this be impracticable, experiments should be conducted in an attempt to find an alternative. In public hospitals surgical cases receive care that is in no way inferior to that given the private case. It is our social duty to set up the same standards in the care of the neurotic patient.

Psychoanalysis is based upon a definite and well-studied relationship between two human beings—the analyst and the patient. Other human beings appear in a way suggestive of ghosts during the analysis. The patient confides in an analyst whom he trusts not to divulge his secrets. To be sure, the analyzed person, reëxperiencing his past life with the analyst, finally finds his way back to the social continuum in which he lives. There is no doubt but that the transference situation, carefully as it has been studied, is still full of pitfalls. When one considers that isolation and secrecy are basic factors in the psychology of the neurotic, one is tempted to discard both of them in the therapeutic situation. In group psychotherapy, a number of patients are seen simultaneously by the physician, and each patient is

Reprinted from *Mental Hygiene*, Vol. XXIII, No. 1, 1939, pp. 87-98.

aware of the problems of the others. A second physician may join the group and add his interpretations.

A year and a half ago, I began an experiment in group psychotherapy in the Outpatient Department of the Psychiatric Division of Bellevue Hospital. Up to the present time about fifty cases of severe neuroses and mild psychoses have been treated. Only severe cases have been taken into this group. Most of the neuroses were of long standing and had been previously treated by other methods. A definite therapeutic plan was followed.

Human beings live not only in a group—they live also as comparatively independent entities. A therapy dealing only with the group would be as one-sided as a purely individualistic treatment. Every patient was seen individually before he joined the group, and these personal interviews were continued throughout the treatment. The groups meet once or twice a week, from two to seven patients participating. This type of therapy emphasizes the leadership of the physician, through the mere fact that he directs the group. Patients should have insight into this relationship. They should not be blind believers. The physician should be not an authority, but a leader, and it should be clear that his leadership is based not upon any intrinsic superiority, but upon the particular task to be solved by the group. Basically, he is a fellow human being confronted with the same problems as any other member of the group.

The various forms of psychotherapy emphasize specific sides of interhuman relations. If a physician gives orders to patients without giving them any insight into the nature of these orders, his therapy is based upon the necessity for authority in human life. In hypnosis, therapy is based upon the human relationship of erotic submission. In cathartic hypnosis, the patient is forced into insight. Again, one may treat a patient as a sensible fellow human being with whom problems can be discussed. An attitude of friendly helpfulness may be added.

In psychoanalysis the semblance of an impersonal relationship may be insisted upon, but the patient is in reality in a state of submission which is more or less one of complete surrender. In the further course of analysis, insight accrues with the revival of significant childhood attitudes. The therapeutic situation, if in any way valuable, is based upon a human relationship of fundamental importance. Hypnosis, for instance, which stresses submission and surrender to a magic power of love, reveals at least one important side of human relations. The technique immediately reaches a higher level if the patient has insight into this. The part truth of the hypnotic attitude and of any psychotherapeutic attitude should be seen at its real value. The final aim of psychotherapy can only be insight. Psychoanalysis comes nearest to this goal. Insight means more than verbalization. It means the ability to see the structures of the real world and to act accordingly.

Psychoanalytic insight was utilized in this group treatment. In every case the life history of the patient was discussed and elucidated in detail and early infantile material was particularly studied. A written report was asked of the patient after he had gained partial insight. Not only had he to write his life history, but he also had to discuss his relationship with father, mother, siblings, and nurses. In addition, a report of his sexual development was required. Further reports were called for according to the needs of the therapeutic situation. Dream interpretation and so-called free associations were used both in the individual treatments and in the group treatments. Sexual development was studied as completely as possible. Besides an historical approach to the personality, the ideologies of the patients and their general orientation to life were investigated. No individual can be understood unless his objective is known—his goal and his life plan. One must know his expectations for the future. The individual, too, must gain deeper insight into his own needs and wishes. He must learn to understand the social setting and his social and sexual ambitions.

These basic problems may be formulated briefly as follows: (1) body and beauty; (2) health, strength, efficiency, superiority, and inferiority in a physical sense; (3) aggressiveness and submission; (4) masculinity and femininity; (5) the relationship between sex and love; (6) the expectation for the future; and (7) the meaning of death. Particular attention must be given to the language in which the patient expresses his attitudes toward these basic problems. Certain phrases are very often used in order to enable the patient to hide his real attitudes from himself. Phrases not fully understood in their true meaning are very often found at the turning point of an individual's life. It is necessary that the individual's conscious and unconscious goals come into full light with insight. Modern psychology has all too often forgotten the social nature of human experiences. I have been able to show that even the experience of one's own body, the body image, acquires its final expression only in a continuous interplay with the body images of other human beings.

Hartshorne has justly emphasized the social character of every sensation. Any problem of money, occupation, and sex that may be met has its true meaning only in a social setting of which it is a part, and cannot even be thought of apart from this social setting. Obviously, then, the significance of any detail of an individual life history will be clearer if it is brought forward in a group and appraised by a group. In one discussion, for example, a patient remembered an attempted sexual assault against his sister. It was astonishing how many members of the group recalled similar experiences in their own lives, so that a correct appreciation of such an event became possible. On Mother's Day one of the patients brought forth bitter complaints against his mother, who had curtailed his freedom, had not given him enough love, and had had a sex life of her own. This outcry provoked a whole series of similar associations from the other patients. The deeper social meaning of the Oedipus situation revealed itself, and the patients experienced their specific attitudes merely as variations of a general attitude. The relief patients experience when they no longer feel excluded from the community because of urges and desires that society does not openly tolerate is remarkable. To be sure, in the strictly analytic situation, the analyst offers a like relief, but there he is merely the representative of a group, whereas in the group treatment the patient actually experiences the breaking through of similar or identical impulses in others. Group treatment is in this respect a step nearer to reality.

Feelings of guilt result from sexual drives and actions and from aggressiveness. Both seem to excommunicate the individual from a society that sets up for him a system of ideals that cannot be fulfilled. Mothers are supposed always to love their children and children are expected always to love their parents. There should be no destructive impulses against any one; good deeds from the individual are not enough—the demand is also that he think only good thoughts. Morally we live in a state that punishes not only actions, but thoughts as well. In a general way we feel that the authorities of a country should permit liberty of thought. But the unwritten ideologies and prejudices, the demands of misunderstood morality are much more tyrannical than written laws, since the former punish for thoughts. Thoughts must come out into the open quite in the same way as ideologies if individuals are to be liberated from their feelings of guilt.

In a group, the patients realize with astonishment that the thoughts which have seemed to isolate them are common to all of them. This enables them clearly to see their aggressive instincts and helps them to understand that aggressive instincts and social conduct are compatible.

The thoughts and ideologies of one patient become the common medium for the group in their continuous emotional interplay. Most of the threads are united in the person of the analyst, who enters into the discussions, the language analysis, and even into the free associations of the patients. The definite interpretation of a symptom or of an action of a patient is the work not merely of the analyst, but of the whole group.

The phenomena of positive and negative transference to the analyst are not less outspoken in the group than in the usual psychoanalytic treatment. They express themselves in generally known terms. The reaction of one patient to the transference situation of another patient is very often remarkable. The patient in a state of positive transference feels a need to defend the analyst against the negative transference of another patient. In the negative transference, the group particularly stress that the physician is not sufficiently interested in their fate, that as a public employee he must spend his hours with them regardless, and that he is less interested in the fate of the patients than in the scientific problems they offer. Very often discussions of problems of this type have a very important effect upon the fate of a group. They can be shown that nobody has the right to expect the complete emotional surrender of another person—that the other person has to live his own life even if he does happen to be one's father or one's relative or one's physician.

The patients brought together in one group are not particularly selected, but men and women have been treated separately. It has been my general plan to bring every patient who is at a given time under treatment into contact with the other patients of the same sex. I hope that it will be possible to have persons of both sexes in the same group when we have gained a deeper understanding of this method.

The method I have described will not escape the reproach of being too intellectual and putting too much emphasis upon the factor of insight. Skepticism may be increased when I confess that I do not refrain from using an elaborate system of questionnaires. These contain such questions as what the patient remembers about his father, what he thinks about him, and what fantasies he has had about him. These questions are concerned not only with the sexual problems relating to the father, but with every phase of the father's life, as whether he was considered strong, healthy, gifted, clever, successful, and so on. Similar questions are elaborated about the mother, siblings, nurses, and teachers. A further series relates to ideas about one's own body. Others probe the castration complex, masturbation, intercourse, breasts, urination, defecation, the attitude of the family and of the patient toward disease, food habits, and so forth. A different set sought to discuss aggressiveness and attitudes toward death, the opinions the individual has about himself, his goals in life, and, finally, the general attitude of human beings toward one another. At least one should try to discover the basic attitude of an individual in the following spheres of experience: (1) the need to love and be loved (according to Watson, love means stroking); (2) the tendency to maintain one's own support (in childhood, against gravitation); (3) the tendency to maintain the integrity of the body (sudden noise, sudden impressions are a threat in this respect); (4) the tendency to eat and drink and to get as much property as possible, to acquire and to retain; (5) the tendency to expel what the organism can no longer use and to push away that which is threatening; (6) the tendency to handle and to destroy objects and human beings and to get an insight into their structure; (7) the tendency to help others in the pursuit of the same aims.

This is a reformulation of the problems that we considered as most important in an individual's life.

One of the discussions arising out of the individual problems of the patients is here reproduced in a slightly altered form.*

B., twenty-one years old, had a severe social neurosis which caused him to withdraw from contact with others and to suffer from severe feelings of

---

* I have added the brief remarks on the history of each patient. Every one in the group knew the histories of the others.

inadequacy; his speech was actually hesitant. He stammered when he checked impulses of rage directed against those who he believed were ridiculing him. Excessive ambitions had developed to overcompensate for his sense of being threatened. In school games he did not want to be on the losing team. He was interested in auto races and in all speed races involving motor-driven vehicles, seeming to feel that their force was added to his. He did not like sports in which he was dependent only upon his own ability.

E., twenty-one years old, with a basal metabolism of minus 23, had felt that he had no energy and no drive. Accordingly he would exert himself too much, feel bewildered, and then give up almost completely, until he really had become inefficient. His sexual energy seemed to have little vitality. There were no sex fantasies or sex impulses when he came for treatment. In spite of a rise in the basal metabolic rate to minus 8 under the influence of thyroid medication, he did not change until psychotherapy had given him insight into his problems. Sexuality then awakened. The question is, Where did he get the energy with which to drive himself forward? One may draw the conclusion that human beings should gaily acknowledge their shortcomings. They should be taught neither to overcompensate for them nor to brush them out of consciousness. Every one should be aware of the necessity of having shortcomings. The ideal of general efficiency and of striving to be blameless is a wrong one. If one is a minus variant as a personality, one should accept the fact. Minus qualities in ourselves and in others make us human, and the attempt to be perfect only makes us into caricatures.

F., twenty-one years old, an anxiety neurotic with the fear of sudden death, had no problems of this kind. He lived in an emotional attachment to his mother and brother and expected protection from them against the dangers connected with his own lack of strength. It did not matter whether this attachment to the mother was sexual or not, but it was important that he have no inferiority feelings in the ordinary sense. There is no reason to believe that there is only one fundamental problem lying at the base of neuroses. One should evaluate life situations as human problems in their varieties of expression.

C., twenty-four years old, suffered from inferiority and guilt feelings because of obsessional sex drives against children and men, and obsessional aggressions, such as kicking and pushing. He had been forced into this situation by his mother, who overpowered him. If there were feelings of inferiority, they were the result of a complicated sexual development. He was very much frightened by his impulses, whose strength he overestimated. Perhaps too much is expected of us in a moral way, and it should be acknowledged that there are impulses which go against the standards of society. One should be lenient to one's own morality, especially if it harms no one. It is probable that tolerance of one's own impulses does not strengthen them, but reveals them as inefficient and weak—that is, if they do not fit into the structure of the personality and into society.

In the case of W., nineteen years old, the fight against the father and the protection of the mother against the father (also sexually) were prominent. In W.'s attempt to substitute for the father he cultivated intellectuality. He denied himself sexuality because he condemned it in his father and mother. Since he wanted to convince himself and others that he was superior to his father, he was concerned only in having others acknowledge his superiority. He was shy and self-conscious with people who he believed gave him exaggerated attention.

Modern men suffer from the idea that they should be perfect. They expect perfect health and are unduly perturbed and excited by minor symptoms. W., for example, has palpitations when in bed. One should have patience with one's own body and not be afraid of being weak and tired. People want to be highly efficient, to show speed and energy, when they should have the courage to be slow and adynamic. It is easier to be tolerant toward one's self if no comparison is made with others. Humanity should be considered as consisting of varied types, and those who are not highly gifted are still an important part of society as a whole. The imperfect human being is needed as well as the one approaching perfection, and one should be tolerant toward one's own stupidities. The stupid person is more than a mere background for the intelligent.

If humans ask of themselves speed of movement and of speech and strength, why should they not ask to be beautiful in all the parts of their bodies? The perfection sought for oneself is demanded of others, and intolerance ensues. This intolerance is greater toward the members of one's own family, and they are expected to be ideal figures without blemish. Of course, they can't live up to these images. Parents have to pay dearly for every perfectionistic ideal they put into their children's minds. The child will soon measure his parents against the ideals implanted in him and find them wanting. When parents teach children suppression of sex, children retaliate by fighting against the sexuality of their parents. Asexuality belongs to the perfectionistic ideal. Sometimes it is expected that sexuality shall awaken only at the conventional signal. Perfectionistic ideals exist not only for physical functions, but also for one's strivings, and can be positive as well as negative. They demand, for instance, from one's self and from others (1) absence of hate, (2) a continuous flow of love toward one's love object, (3) continuous sexual impulses toward a socially acknowledged love object, and (4) absence of promiscuous impulses or sexual impulses.

The foregoing paragraphs summarize the record of one group treatment. The objection of intellectuality may again be raised. The account given here does not indicate how closely these general remarks were related to definite experiences of the patients. The discussion shows in detail how the patient developed his attitude. It should not be forgotten either that this is only one of the phases in the treatment. The truth of the formulation is considered only as partial truth which must be completed by the other aspects of the situation. In connection with this specific record, for instance, a discussion would be necessary to show how the individual fits his impulses into society.

In modern psychopathology, the difference between intellectual and emotional processes is too greatly emphasized. To be sure, though it has never been formulated, there is an underlying assumption that intellectual processes are pale and without strength, and this at a time when everybody speaks of the personality as a whole. Attitudes express themselves in thinking as well as in emotions, and emotions also have goals and aims. A separation of intellect and emotion is artificial and is justified only if one considers them as two sides of the unified attitude of an individual, one or the other facet scintillating more strongly according to circumstances.

One might further object to the procedure as recorded because it involved a more or less definite stand on the part of the physician, while psychoanalysis has attempted an attitude of neutrality on questions of morals and values. But as I have stated, Freud is deceiving himself in holding that he is purely scientific and has no *"Weltanschauung."* Psychoanalysis has in fact a definite attitude toward certain moral problems. A body of definite knowledge contains in itself a definitely moral point of view and invites definite actions. One should know this. If one is practicing psychotherapy, and especially group psychotherapy, one should know what to expect from life.

As one would suppose, group psychotherapy is especially effective in cases of what I should characterize as social neuroses. These are cases that do not feel comfortable in the presence of others. They feel that they cannot concentrate, they cannot think, or they are merely embarrassed and uncomfortable. Physical symptoms, such as palpitation or discomfort in the gastrointestinal tract, may be present. Sweating, blushing, awkwardness in movement, may become obvious signals of this discomfort. The individual feels that he is the center of attention, that not only is something wrong with him, but that others realize it. Every object becomes, in this respect, an important object on a sado-masochistic level. To be seen and to be observed means to be hurt and to be pushed into an inferior position.

Twelve cases of social neurosis have been treated by our group method. Three can be considered as cured. In the case of E., mentioned above, sexuality, which had been dormant, appeared in spite of the organic background in the situation. Only two cases showed no improvement. The remaining seven were decidedly improved, and some of them are still under treatment.

In one case of stammering, the stammering was not overcome, but there was an improvement in social attitude.

Nine cases of obsession neurosis have been treated. There has been no complete failure in this series. Two severe cases were cured. In a third an involuntary bromide intoxication led to a complete disappearance of the symptoms. Two cases with slight encephalitic signs showed a very decided improvement. Two other cases, both severe and of long standing, were mildly improved; both were still under treatment at the time this paper was written. The two remaining cases improved to the point where they are adapting well to society and enjoying themselves.

Of three cases of anxiety neurosis, two were cured and one was improved.

Of four hysterias, two were cured, one was unchanged, and one ceased treatment too early.

Three cases of hypochondriasis were not influenced by the treatment.

Two cases with organic vegetative symptoms adapted better, but the organic symptoms did not disappear.

Of three cases of character problems, one was discharged and was well adjusted at the time of writing; the other two were considerably improved and are still under treatment.

Of six depersonalization cases, one was cured and one decidedly improved; one who did not come back for treatment was slightly improved at the time the treatment was broken off. Three were unimproved. One of these three was a schizophrenia and another a depression.

Two cases of depression (in addition to the depersonalization case) were unimproved. One of them committed suicide. The family had been warned.

Among four cases of schizophrenia in which treatment was attempted (besides the depersonalization case) two cases were not influenced. One case, in which the diagnosis was dementia simplex, adjusted much better. The fourth case completely recovered, and was socially and sexually adapted at the time of writing. Fear of homosexuality and homosexual ideas of reference had been in the foreground. I was in no doubt about the diagnosis of schizophrenia when I started the treatment, which lasted several months. The possibility of an atypical depression might have been considered, but I adhered to my original diagnosis.

Many of the cases treated in this group could not have been treated individually even with the classical analysis. They reacted only in the group. This is especially true of social neuroses.

This is only a very brief report of the experiment. It is difficult to judge therapeutic results after so comparatively short a time, and perhaps I have been too optimistic. If this should be so, it lies in the nature of the psychotherapeutic approach. It is probable that not all of the results are permanent and there may be relapses sooner or later. But I believe, as do the patients, that they have been helped to get a better orientation to life. I have had an opportunity to compare the results of this method with those of others. In some cases the approach is preferable to the strictly analytic technique, and again there are cases in which the psychoanalytic approach is doubtlessly superior. However, one will have to learn. A definite technique has been utilized. I hope that this technique can be taught and can be learned.

SUMMARY

A method of group psychotherapy has been developed which attempts to give the patient a deeper insight into his individual life history, his ideologies, his problems, and his expectations for the future. The basis of this treatment is a written report of the patient concerning the various phases and aspects of his life and of his relationships to the persons in his world. Sexual development is elucidated. Dream interpretation and free association are utilized. The patient must understand how much he has been under the influence of merely verbal formulations in his life plan. In individual interviews and in group discussions various aspects of the personality come into the foreground. The analyst as a member of the group is compelled to greater activity. The patients gain a new direction and new orientation in life.

The therapeutic results so far are promising, especially in the social neuroses and obsession neuroses. This truly social method, though it, too, requires much time, enables the physician to treat a relatively large number of cases and to help them in the development of their personalities.

19

GROUP THERAPY
SPECIAL SECTION MEETING

Lawson G. Lowrey, Chairman
*S. R. Slavson**

CHAIRMAN: My interest in the utilization of procedures involving a group has been developing over the past twenty years. Our first efforts in this direction—recreational groups for our "problem" cases, family councils, mothers' and parents' discussion groups—were certainly not specifically planned to be directly therapeutic in the sense in which we would use that term today. But, although primarily thought of as recreation, education, and socializing experiences, there were important therapeutic effects as well—as indeed there may be and frequently are in all sorts of interpersonal relationships.

My first experience with a sort of group therapy—again not precisely viewed that way—was with a special camp setup for "problem" boys in Cleveland during the summer of 1926. That first summer, when I spent weekends at the camp, was really one of groping experimentation. The work was later carried on from the psychiatric side much more effectively by Doctors E. S. Rademacher and A. T. Childers. Mr. Newstetter, in his report on this work,[1] stated three major practical considerations which led to the initiation of the project. These were: the lack of generalized knowledge of the primary group; the problem of adjusting individuals referred by caseworkers for group adjustment; and the problem of practical utilization of mental hygiene contributions.

At our 1939 meeting, in reviewing *Trends in Therapy,*[2] mention was

Reprinted from the *American Journal of Orthopsychiatry*, Vol. XIII, No. 4, October 1943, pp. 648-690.
* *Editors' note:* Because of space limitations, we have not included here all of the papers presented at this meeting. The other contributors were Dorothy Spiker, H. B. Peck, Helen Glauber, and N. Ackerman.

made of several *group therapy* approaches, and there was a brief discussion of the "open approach" as I had seen it in operation abroad and as used in this country, notably by Ira Wile in the Mental Health Class at Mt. Sinai Hospital in New York. It is clear to me now that I then had only an imperfect realization of the potential group psychotherapeutic values of the open approach. From recent correspondence with Dr. Wile (who is unable, I regret to say, to be present at this meeting), it is clear that he regards the methodology in his clinic as *group psychotherapy*. In one letter he states regarding this program:

> We have always had papers [in the programs] on music, puppets, play and all sorts of group activities. . . . It is interesting to note . . . that the common factor in almost all of these therapies *inheres in the group* [italics mine]. This group reflects the factors of interplay, intercommunication, interfeeling, interstimulation, interdependence, with heightened suggestibility, both from active and passive participation. . . . The moment a child meets a medical attendant, a psychologist, or a social worker, particularly if they form a group, active therapy is under way, even though little is said. The theory of work with Scouts, Big Brothers, and Big Sisters, has always involved group therapy. The development of associations and the concept of socialized education involve principles entering into group therapy.

These concepts refer to therapy only in a very broad sense. In another letter, Wile narrows the field somewhat. "Inasmuch as therapy has been based upon conscious and unconscious and even hypnagogic reactions, one must distinguish the effects sought for, the effects secured and known, the effects registered but not expressed. Whether we give a child a toy that can be torn apart or one that cannot, helps to determine a play therapy." He then makes some comments on technique and "reducing terminology to what one wishes to have it mean and appropriating it," and raises interesting questions regarding objective measurements of group therapy and play therapy.

We propose today to discuss not the open approach but group work specifically and consciously planned as therapy, with a background of theory and a body of practice, which has been studied objectively, at least to a degree, and where the dynamic role of the group as such is the important therapeutic tool. This is a much more definitely oriented and circumscribed use of technique than is true in the more general situations mentioned above.

A leading characteristic of modern life is the large number of groups in which an individual lives and functions. Each of these affects the individual, as the latter also affects the group. In this reciprocal relationship, the group is quick to take steps to conserve its own interests, protect itself from hostile aggression, develop its prosperity, maintain its inertia, and so on, at the expense of the individual, who, in turn, exploits the group.[3]

Why, then, should not the specific impact of the group upon the individual's attitudes and behavior be utilized in consciously planned therapy, as it is used more vaguely in education and "socialization"? Speaking broadly, the treatment of mental disorders and delinquency by the use of specially organized and controlled environments is an example of a basic general principle of therapy from which use of the group as a therapeutic tool may be said roughly to stem. Many variations and refinements and considerable differences in theory and practice usually operate under different names.

Turning now to the topic of the day, my first contact with this therapy program of the Jewish Board of Guardians was during the first half of 1941, in the course of a survey of the clinical facilities of that organization and those of the New York Association for Jewish Children. Then, this past year, by special invitation and arrangement, I made a study of the procedures, techniques, and results of group therapy as practiced at JBG, under Mr. Slavson's direction, since 1934. It is not my purpose to review that study at this time, but certain conclusions reached explain my interest in this meeting, which was suggested and arranged by Mr. Slavson.

In my study, a total of 176 children (of 500-550 who had been in groups) were identified in reading 19 of 72 available group records, 55 case records of the child guidance department . . . , and 34 group therapy "individual" records. In a total of 101 cases there were data enough in the records read to permit a *personal* judgment of the results of the group therapy. There were 74 cases with good results, and 27 with poor or no results. These results were in cases taken from all the seven years studied, in groups conducted by 14 different workers, included both sexes, and covered all age ranges. The material therefore represents an adequate random sample, the analyses were rigorous, and the findings must be regarded as significant.

Accordingly, it is obvious that here is a technique which is as effective as is individual therapy. Questions promptly arise concerning the nature of the technique and the types of situations and cases to which it is applicable. For, if the technique can be defined, described, and transmitted and the limitations of its applicability determined, we shall have added a most important instrumentality to our therapeutic armamentarium.

With the final comment that this type of treatment is therapy *by* the group, rather than therapy *in* the group, we pass to descriptions and analyses by the speakers of the day.

The first speaker, Mr. S. R. Slavson, is the Director of the Department of Group Therapy at the Jewish Board of Guardians and the one who developed the technique and analyses of procedures there. He is a Lecturer in Education at New York University. His concepts of group therapy stem from group work, progressive education, and psychoanalysis. Many in this audience will be familiar with his books, *Creative Group Education* (1937) and *Character Education in a Democracy* (1939). Mr. Slavson will present the *Principles and Dynamics of Group Therapy*, which is the general subject of his book.[4]

S. R. SLAVSON: This paper is based on the experience of about nine years in group therapy with approximately 800 children, 63 distinct groups, and 96 group years. It deals with a type of interpersonal therapy for young children developed at the Jewish Board of Guardians and has since been tried in many centers in the United States.

The idea of treatment of adults in groups is not altogether new. It has for some years been employed by Doctors Trigant Burrow, Paul Schilder, Louis Wender, James Sennett Greene, and others. Treatment is carried on through interviews in groups in which the patients' problems are ventilated, inner pressures and anxieties released, and guidance given by the therapist as well as the patient participants.

We, on the other hand, deal with children of the ages from 8 to 15, through activity (rather than interview), and with the resultant interpersonal interactions and their therapeutic effect. It must be made clear that activity therapy which is emphasized here is not the only type of group therapy being employed either at our agency or in similar efforts at other agencies. Because of different treatment needs of clients, we introduced "group interview treatment" or *collective psychotherapy* for adolescents, a combination of activity and interview for younger children, group treatment with mothers, and *transitional* groups for children.

Activity group therapy here described is a type of noninterpretive therapy in which no interview is held during the treatment period. If interview therapy is required, it is given by a caseworker or psychiatrist at another time. Thus, among our clients are children who receive individual treatment concurrently with group treatment (cooperative cases), and children who are treated in groups only (exclusive cases).

The general setting for activity group therapy is work in simple arts and crafts for an hour or an hour and a half. This is followed by a period during which the clients and the group therapist cook, serve, and eat together. They then clean up the room. The meetings are varied by occasional trips, picnics, and excursions, in accordance with the needs and readiness of the members and the seasonal opportunities offered. It will be readily seen that the group is a substitute family with the positive elements a family should have and that the worker is a substitute parent. In fact, many of our children refer to the workers as mama, pop, and "unk."

The clients accepted for treatment have all experienced destructive or undesirable relations with people. We therefore aim to correct attitudes and perceptions through a new type of experience so that the children can enter into constructive personal relations. In addition to the total friendly and permissive atmosphere of the group, the materials and tools serve to prevent mutual invasion on the part of the members before they are ready to accept one another. They work on materials rather than on each other. This is a rather important phase in the treatment, for it serves to redirect aggression and, in some instances, is also a means of sublimating it.

Group therapy is *situational therapy* as differentiated from interview and treatment by interpretation. We have evidence, however, that insight is acquired by our young clients as a result of their own thinking and comparing their abilities and attitudes with each other and their own in the past. "I used to fight all the time," says a boy. "Now I work and am too busy to fight." Another addresses one of his fellow members thus: "You remember when we were enemies? Now we are friends." And still another: "I used to think my little sister was a pest. Now I think she is kind of cute." With security and self-acceptance comes also acceptance of others and a more friendly and relaxed attitude toward the world.

To young children, experience as understood in terms of subjective response and adjustment to an external occurrence, is often more telling than verbal formulations. In fact, in individual treatment, skill is most manifest where the interview is made an emotional experience. This inevitably proceeds from a well-adjusted relation between therapist and client.

The *situational configuration* of a therapy group can be said to consist of (1) the client, (2) the therapist, (3) the situation, and (4) the activities. We shall discuss these elements at different points, but it will be necessary to keep in mind that they are functionally one and inseparable.

What type of problem child can best be served by group therapy? What is it that a child with personality difficulties and social maladjustments needs to get from such a group? By and large, we can say that in order to gain from any group experience, it is necessary that the individual have some initial capacity to relate himself to others; he must have a desire to be with other people, to belong, to be a part of. This we designate as *social hunger*. Whatever the psychologic syndrome or personality problem, clients assigned to groups have some measure of social hunger, latent or overt, for without it no contact with them is possible.

Since eventually satisfactions must come from constructive activity rather than from destruction, and people must become sources of gratification rather than of pain and threat, the child must give up his need to resent or fight the world. Instead, he needs to develop a desire to be a part of it. Psychotherapy can help in this, but it can be successful only when there is a foundation for it within the personality of the client. We found that only children who have this initial capacity and some degree of social hunger respond to treatment. Thus, intensely psychopathic clients and those with some forms of behavior disorders are not suitable for group therapy. Social hunger in group therapy corresponds to the transference relation in individual therapy. Just as a patient who is unable to establish a transference with the therapist is not accessible in individual treatment, so is a client with no social hunger inaccessible in group treatment.

We have found that even narcissistic children gain from a nonrepressive group. They take, however, a very long time and improvement is first observable in other relations—the home, the school, the play group—even though their behavior is not affected in the group itself.

We are dealing with the child whose ego structure is defective. Our clients are those who were directly infantilized by anxious or overprotective mothers or whose infancy was prolonged by rejecting, rigid, hard, unloving parents. They are also children whose identifications had been established with wrong models or images in the persons of the parents or parent surrogates. It is therefore necessary to supply them with opportunities for corrective identifications. This is done through the group therapist and the other children in the group. It becomes clear even from this brief statement how important is the personality of the therapist as well as the choice and grouping of clients.

In many of our clients the superego is either overintense and tyrannical, as in the neurotic child, or it exerts inadequate control over impulses and primary narcissism, as in the child with a behavior disorder and in the child with prolonged infancy. In the one case, the child must find release from the emotional pressure under which he lives; in the other, he must internalize restraints and controls. The authority, restraint, and controls that arise spontaneously and naturally from the group relationships and working conditions are, in most instances, acceptable to the client. He submits because he derives basic satisfactions from the situation. Here we rely on the child's social hunger and the *supportive ego*. This supportive person may be the therapist or a comember whom the client naturally likes or who meets his emotional needs at a given period in his growth.

In the initial stages of our treatment, and as a result of the permissive atmosphere of the group, group therapy temporarily suspends the child's superego. He can act out his problems and difficulties; he can reveal his true nature and his hidden impulses without fear of retaliation, criticism, or punishment. This may create considerable confusion, aggression, and turmoil at the meetings, but *activity catharsis* is essential to equilibrate the personality of each of the participants. The withdrawn child remains quietly at his task; the assertive and aggressive gains release through action, until balance is attained.

We see how important is the choice and grouping of patients. If grouping is incorrect, the anxious and neurotic child grows too frightened to come to the meetings, or when he comes, his anxieties are further increased. He is thus traumatized. The overaggressive provokes and instigates aggression to a point where no group equilibrium is possible and therefore no therapy can occur.

Because the child is plastic, and because he absorbs from experience at a greater rate than do adults, his total personality is affected through the release, control, and relationships in the group. One of the results (and we consider this a major outcome of group treatment) is that his superego is extended and, to a varying degree, also transformed. The early superego is derived from the fear and anxiety of being abandoned, punished, or maltreated. As he matures, the average person learns restraint, not because of fear of punishment, but because of identification with the desires and needs of other people. This growing awareness of others engenders a superego which can be designated the *group superego*, as differentiated from the *infantile superego*. It proceeds from satisfying group experience, growing identifications and associations with individuals, and finally leads to integration into groups. Thus, the child no longer perceives other people as a danger and a threat, and can therefore establish relationships without fear.

In the disturbed and maladjusted child, identifications and strivings toward the group have not supplanted, as it were, the fear-laden, infantile superego. A therapy group, such as we have described, helps in the process of extending the early fears of mature self-restraint. Hyperactive children have gained greatly through the free, unimpeded release in our groups. Some attach themselves to a satisfying interest such as carpentry and canalize their energies in sublimitory, *libido-binding activity*. Children who are too inhibited to communicate their problems to a caseworker are freed from their inhibitions, and as a result, there is greater movement in individual therapy as well.

Then there is the child who is nonverbal—with language limitations, either constitutional or cultural. He may be inhibited, distrustful, frightened, of low intelligence. These conditions would impede communication and understanding in individual treatment. Group therapy is evidently indicated in these cases.

Through the work in arts and crafts, eating together, trips and excursions, and the accepting and permissive atmosphere in the group, the schizoid child is activated. He need not use his self-protective withdrawal in an environment that is friendly and nonthreatening. The mildly schizophrenic child, too, has here a conditioned and attenuated situation of things, occupations, an adult, and the other children to lead him back to reality. Children whose compensatory fantasies interfere with their social adjustment and with the development of an adequate sense of reality, have actualized some of these flights into unreality through their free, undirected work with art and other materials. The recognition they receive from the group therapist, fellow members, at home and at school reduces their need for self-maximation and grandeur. Many children in this category have entirely given up this mechanism. As they gained status, they substituted achievement for fantasy. Children with prolonged infancy and the over-protected child gain much from the experience provided by a free group life with the emergent restraints and graded group pressures. The most perfect attendance is found in this group of clients. The neurotic child can act out his anxieties without fear of retaliation or threat. With security gained through this, he is able to talk out his problems with his caseworker or psychiatrist.

Perhaps the group of clients with whom we were most successful are the emasculated boys who had overdominating mothers, who grew up in an exclusively or predominantly feminine environment, or have been in competition with sisters. Such boys acquire feminine characteristics, become submissive or ingratiating, and are commonly known as sissies. They build up fantasies about the danger and destructiveness of masculinity and some express a wish to be girls and actually imagine themselves as girls. The improvement in these children as a result of a nonthreatening masculine group environment and relations is really quite remarkable.

The primary and most essential element in a therapy group is that it must be a carefully planned and a consciously organized body. A therapy group stands or falls on the insight and skill in grouping. Essentially, the group must consist of children who potentially have therapeutic value to one another. Obviously, a beaten down and rejected child would only be more traumatized if he were to be assigned to a group where he would be beaten and persecuted. A frightened, withdrawn, and sensitive child becomes only more frightened and withdrawn in a tumultuous and aggressive environment. If these children are each to be helped to make better social adaptations and overcome their personality problems, they must have an environment in which their particular difficulties are counteracted and their needs are met. This is accomplished through a planned group in which the interpersonal relations have, in the long run, positive values for every participant.

The difficulties that arise in fitting together seven or eight children who would be useful to each other in treatment are apparent. Luckily, there is no need to fit in all of the children in this manner. In a group of eight, there emerge a number of subgroups of two and three who are suited to each other. A weak and dependent child will attach himself to another member who gives him security, or he may lean upon the group therapist for such support. In either case, this supportive ego functions only for a brief period. The friendly and comforting environment and relations soon make the child secure enough to go on his own and to interact freely with others in the group.

The aggressive child whose aggressiveness does not proceed from serious pathology, and whose social hunger is adequately strong, soon curbs himself because of group pressure. Children gang up on him, demand that he conform and not interfere with their comfort and activities. If this restraint does not arise from the group spontaneously, which is usually the case, we place in the group an equally aggressive or an older child. The conflict for power is then confined to these two and is usually resolved as they become fast friends. The danger here lies in that these two together may tyrannize over the group. If this occurs, a third aggressive child is added. Three children do not act in unison because rivalry is set up among them. Sometimes nothing can be done to check such hostility, and in our experience so far, thirteen children have had to be removed from groups as inoperable despite all our strategies. Restraint may come from the group therapist as well as from the group.

We are able to identify, so far, four types of clients as related to their function in the group: *instigators, neutralizers, social neuters,* and *isolates*. Children of various clinical syndromes and diagnostic categories are found in each of these classifications. Hyperactivity and withdrawal may be neurotic symptoms; they may also be character manifestations more or less normal to the particular individual temperament, or they may be behavior disorders. In assigning clients for interpersonal therapy, the child's function picture rather than the clinical diagnosis is important. However, one must be aware of the latter in order to anticipate future developments. Free expression of hostility may be in some cases not only bad for the group, but destructive to the client as well. One must at all times know the meaning of each child's behavior, as well as understand the effect of that behavior upon the child himself, other children, and the total group atmosphere.

Another major element of the group setting is that it is a *permissive environment*. In the early stages, the child can use the environment in whatever way he wishes. He can make friends or withdraw, work or idle, construct or break, quarrel, fight or fraternize. This free use of the environment by the client in accordance with his own particular needs is of utmost importance. The child is convinced that he is loved, since he is allowed to do whatever he wishes. He discovers that the world is not necessarily frustrating, denying, and punitive. The client gains in his feeling of autonomy, and because of the friendly and accepting attitude of the adult, he relates himself to people. Inability to relate is the predominant cause of our clients' maladjustments, and when they can find their own way into a group at their own pace in their own particular manner, we have a truly therapeutic medium.

The neurotic patient finds in this permissiveness relief from his feelings of guilt concerning his behavior and impulses. He discovers that hilarity, aggressiveness, and destructiveness do not destroy one. He feels reassured. For a long time he watches from a distance the play and aggressiveness of his fellow members, but cannot bring himself to take part. Gradually he begins to participate vicariously by looking, laughing, turning lights on and off, or tripping another child. After some months, he takes part furtively at first, and quite freely later, in all the activities of the other children. Display of hostility makes these children very anxious, and some may not return for a number of weeks. In some cases release through individual treatment must precede group treatment. Almost all of the neurotic clients have overcome the fear of their impulses, with constructive effects upon their total adjustment. In fact, one study of our work indicates that neurosis is one of the four characteristics of our successful cases. The others are: aggressiveness at home, having no friends, and the child must be under thirteen years of age.

The opportunity we offer to each child to use environment in accordance with his particular needs is of immense importance. We believe that psychotherapy consists of removing the patient's resistance to the world, his self-encapsulation, as it were. Once this is done, living in a social environment is itself a therapeutic situation. As long as the patient isolates himself either through resistance, active aggression, or withdrawal, the world cannot get at him. He remains in a state of isolation and develops or continues with antisocial attitudes. When we make it possible for our clients to go out into their environment to a degree to which they are ready and in a manner suitable to them, we not only give them release and comfort, but their perception of the world as a hostile, destructive force to be feared or attacked changes. It is in this changed attitude that our therapy largely lies.

The therapeutic processes in individual treatment and group therapy parallel each other in many respects. Transference, catharsis, insight, relationship, attitude formation, authority, and limitations that are present in individual treatment have their counterparts in a therapy group. Group therapy, in fact, can be effective only when this similarity exists. The therapeutic process is the same whether it is in individual treatment or in the group. The difference is that the elements are derived largely from different sources and in different ways.

In some respects the group situation is more realistic to the young child. He is with other children, is active—which is a basic need of the young organism. He interacts with numerous facets of a realistic situation; he gains status, evolves interests, and relates to his contemporaries. Throughout, he tests this reality. He seeks to discover its nature and response. Will it hurt or reject him? Is it in any degree dangerous? Is it friendly and accepting? As he acts out his impulses and problems, the group reacts to him, and if he desires to be a part of the group, he curbs or modifies his behavior. As the withdrawn child gains strength and assurance, he tests himself against the group situation and the activities to gain further reassurance. He does this time and again, each time growing in strength, self-reliance, and self-acceptance.

The reality which we set for our clients extends beyond the group and its permissiveness. Eating in restaurants, trips, and excursions serve to take the children beyond the comforting confines and relations in the meeting room. Some children cannot face this challenge and stay away, but they gradually gain in power and take part in these extramural activities. Reality is further extended and each client is tested against it through the addition of new members, being assigned to a new group, changing of the therapist, and similar devices and strategies. Nurturing and feeding are also gradually reduced, materials become unavailable and their use restricted, food is no longer supplied, the therapist exerts mild pressure and constraint, and other methods are employed to dissolve dependence and aid the maturing process.

Such a group as described is one in which there is considerable *social mobility*. Our clients cannot fit into organized and stratified groups. They either cannot or are only too willing, as an escape, to submit to rules, regulations, group purposes and aims. Such groups of *social fixity* threaten some; others find their regimen and rules a comfort and escape through submission and ingratiation. To belong to a group of social fixity requires a certain amount of depersonalization, and many of our children are not capable of it. Others are depersonalized and need to build up confidence, self-assertiveness, and aggression. The value of a neutral environment from which each can draw according to his needs is obvious. Personal balance is achieved in a therapy group, however, not through habit formation or "learning," but rather by correcting intrapsychic disturbances, acquiring substitute mechanisms and sublimations.

We have stated that the first condition in our work is proper grouping. The second major factor is the personality of the group therapist. From what we have already said, it would seem that he is required to be all things to all children. Some may project upon him their hostilities toward parents and teachers; some become dependent upon him, some monopolize him, and others may seem indifferent. It would appear that the adult must meet the needs of all the children, which is, as can be readily seen, not a very simple matter. Should he attempt to do this actively, he would set up much confusion, emotional chaos, and hostility of the members toward one another. He can meet the requirements of the children by being a neutral person and as passive as one can be in a group. It is rather important that he does not activate a strong transference relation. Transference upon the adult is established to varying degrees by the clients themselves. This is almost inevitable, but what is important is that transferences be established toward fellow members, for it is because of their inability to do this that we accept children for group treatment. In this particular type of therapy, the focus of treatment is the relations among the members, and the adult should play a recessive role. This he can achieve by not obtruding himself, by not becoming the center of activity or the sole source of information, by abstaining from actions that stimulate and feed dependence.

Such neutrality on the part of an adult means to children that he is a kind, accepting, and approving person. Coupled with the facts that the therapist supplies and gives food, furnishes tools and materials, is helpful in case of need, and is kind and responsive, the adult emerges in the role of the all-sanctioning and comforting principle in life. In the child's mind this role is translated in terms of *unconditional love*. The child tests the genuineness of this love by exaggerated, aggressive, and irrational acts to see whether the therapist is really what he appears to be, and he must pass this test. He cannot become anxious, express disapproval, or display irritability by facial expression, muscular tension, or verbally. This requires a personality structure in the therapist capable of withstanding, without a feeling of discomfort, the turmoil, cruelty, and aggressiveness of the members toward each other. The fact that aggressiveness is accepted by an adult in the presence of others convinces the child he is being accepted and loved. Whether he intends it or not, the adult is a restraining agent by the very fact of his being an adult. When the child comes to us, he has already built up attitudes toward adults. To him, they have a definite prestige. He expects prohibition. Try as we may, we cannot entirely divest ourselves of the symbolic authoritarian role the child projects upon us. However, by accepting the child, and by not frustrating him actively, the therapist does not arouse resentment, aggression, or defiance toward himself. Restraint continues the child in his state of dependence, and the fact that he is thrown upon his own resources helps the maturing process, even though it may temporarily increase anxiety.

A child of prolonged infancy, if it is not charged with too intense emotions, needs restraint. The child who is loved but overindulged tends to persist in his infantile pattern. This may be manifested by annoying and interfering with others, by wheedling and whining, and dependence. The group therapist restrains and guides such a child even in the early period of treatment. However, even in these cases, restraint cannot take the form of disapproval or rejection. It must be given with a kindly mien, though firmly, with no emotion, and on a realistic basis. It should never take on the form of repression or nagging. Usually, infantile behavior continues in a group when there is more than one such immature child present, for they tend to reinforce each other, and reassignment of these clients into groups according to individual therapeutic needs have proved effective.

Control and setting of limitations by the worker is not confined to such children alone. At appropriate times in treatment, some limitations and denials are imposed upon all clients, but they are never arbitrary nor unkind. The timing of limitation and denial and their discriminative use with specific clients are of utmost importance. Bad use of these may undo many months and even years of treatment. When denial occurs before *frustration tolerance* is established in the members of the group, the consequent feeling of rejection only reinforces the child's conviction of the cruelty and unfairness of the adult world. It intensifies his hostility and defiance, activates retribution on his part, which may take subtle and indirect forms.

Rebuke and restraint if applied prematurely often bring on the defeat of the adult. Children have numerous ways in which they can defeat us. They can challenge or disobey, they build up patterns of passive resistance, they steal materials and tools, they incite the hostility of other children. Authority, therefore, must be used with caution and adapted to the total group and the individuals in it. It should be employed at stages of treatment when it can be effective. When this is not done, it may destroy the treatment situation. It must be kept in mind that attendance in groups is entirely voluntary, and when we fail to satisfy the children's cravings or hurt them, they drop out. This is another way in which they defeat us.

Since our project in group therapy was set up in 1934, there have been a large number of similar experiments in group treatment in different parts of the country. There is some disagreement on the part of other workers in this field as to the function of the therapist. We feel that there is unanimity in the basic concepts. The differences proceed from the fact that work was carried on in different settings, with different age groups, different types of workers, and probably different groups of children in regard to problems, age, and cultural backgrounds. Variation in any of these and other factors require adaptations of techniques. Since group therapy is situational therapy, any changes in the elements of the situation must of necessity require appropriate readjustments. We, too, have found it necessary to adapt our basic techniques to the treatment needs of different groups of clients.

An important fact must be recognized in group therapy which does not exist to the same degree in individual treatment. A number of sources of restraining authority besides the adult are present here. These arise from the group situation. Interest in a project, for example, restrains the child's impulses for immediate and easy results. Eating together makes it necessary to evolve some order at the table. Among the other restraining relations and situations are those which arise from the need to share and take turns with tools and materials from other children and the building superintendent.

In conclusion, a word of caution is perhaps necessary. Group therapy, in any of its forms, is no substitute for other types of psychotherapy. It is effective only with clients whose treatment needs are specifically met by it. It must be related to age, the nature of the difficulty, the readiness of the client to enter into a group relation, and numerous other factors. Under no circumstances must it be viewed as anything approaching universal application.

In our experience we have found that group therapy is entirely adequate in the treatment of some children, for some it is only of partial value, it is of no value to others, and may be injurious to clients whose problems and personalities are such that they are traumatized by permissiveness. It can be employed only in agencies where there is psychiatrically trained personnel and where psychiatric consultative service is available.

REFERENCES

1. W. I. Newstetter, M. L. Feldstein, and I. M. Newcomb, *Group Adjustment* (Cleveland, Ohio: School of Applied Science, Western Reserve University, 1938).
2. L. G. Lowrey, "Trends in Therapy," *Am. J. Orthopsychiat.*, IX, 4:697-699, 1939.
3. L. G. Lowrey, "Program for Meeting Psychiatric Need in the City," *Ment. Hyg.*, X:464-479, 1926.
4. S. R. Slavson, *An Introduction to Group Therapy* (New York: The Commonwealth Fund, 1943), p. 352.

20

SCIENTIFIC FOUNDATIONS
OF GROUP PSYCHOTHERAPY

J. L. Moreno

The late arrival of group psychiatry and group psychotherapy has a plausible explanation when we consider the development of modern psychiatry out of somatic medicine.[1] The premise of scientific medicine has been since its origin that the *locus of physical ailment is an individual organism.* Therefore treatment is applied to the locus of the ailment as designated by diagnosis. The physical disease with which an individual A is afflicted does not require the collateral treatment of A's wife, his children, and friends. If A suffers from an appendicitis and an appendectomy is indicated, the appendix only of A is removed; no one thinks of the removal of the appendix of A's wife and children too. When in budding psychiatry scientific methods began to be used, axioms gained from physical diagnosis and treatment were *automatically* applied to mental disorders as well. Extra-individual influence as animal magnetism and hypnotism was pushed aside as mythical superstition and folklore. In psychoanalysis—at the beginning of this century the most advanced development of psychological psychiatry—the idea of a specific individual organism as the locus of psychic ailment attained its most triumphant confirmation. The "group" was implicitly considered by Freud as an epiphenomenon of individual psychodynamics.[2] The implication was that if one hundred individuals of both sexes were psychoanalyzed, each by a different analyst with satisfactory results, and were to be put together into a group, a smooth social organization would result; the sexual, social, economic, political, and cultural relations evolving would offer no unsurmountable obstacle to them. The premise prevailed that there is no locus of ailment beyond the individual,

Reprinted from *Group Psychotherapy*, edited by J. L. Moreno, Beacon House, 1945, by permission.

242

that there is, for instance, no group situation which requires special diagnosis and treatment. The alternative, however, is that one hundred cured psychoanalysands *might* produce a societal bedlam together.

Although, during the first quarter of our century, there was occasional disapproval of this exclusive, individualistic point of view, it was more silent than vocal, coming from anthropologists and sociologists particularly. But they had nothing to offer in contrast with the specific and tangible demonstrations of psychoanalysis, except large generalities like culture, class, and societal hierarchy. The decisive turn came with the development of sociometric and psychodramatic methodology.* [3]

The change in locus of therapy which the latter initiated means literally a revolution in what was always considered appropriate medical practice. Husband and wife, mother and child, are treated as a combine, often facing one another and not separate (because separate from one another they may not have any tangible mental ailment). But that facing one another deprives them of that elusive thing which is commonly called "privacy." What remains "private" between husband and wife, mother and daughter, is the abode where some of the trouble between them may blossom, secrets, deceit, suspicion, and delusion. Therefore the loss of personal privacy means loss of face, and that is why people intimately bound up in a situation fear to see one another in the light of face to face analysis. (They prefer individual treatment.) It is obvious that once privacy is lifted (as a postulate of individual psyche) for one person involved in the situation, it is a matter of degree for how many persons the curtain should go up. In a psychodramatic session therefore, Mr. A, the husband, may permit that besides his wife, his partner in the sickness, the other man (her lover) is present, later his daughter and son, and some day perhaps, they would not object (in fact they would invite it) that other husbands and wives who have a similar problem sit in the audience and look on as their predicaments are enacted and learn from the latter how to treat or prevent their own. It is clear that the Hippocratic oath will have to be reformulated to protect a group of subjects involved in the same therapeutic situation. The stigma coming from unpleasant ailment and treatment is far harder to control if a group of persons is treated than if only one person is under treatment.

But the change of locus of therapy has other unpleasant consequences. It revolutionizes also *the agent of therapy*. The agent of therapy has usually been a single person, a doctor, a healer. Faith in him, rapport (Mesmer), transference (Freud) toward him, is usually considered as indispensable to the patient-physician relation. But sociometric methods have radically changed this situation. In a particular group a subject may be used

---

* Sociatry is applied sociometry. The group psychotherapies and the psychodramatic methods are subfields of sociatry, as the latter comprises also the application of sociometric knowledge to groups "at a distance," to intergroup relations, and to mankind as a total unit.

as an instrument to diagnose and as a therapeutic agent to treat the other subjects. The doctor and healer as the final source of mental therapeusis has fallen. Sociometric methods have demonstrated that therapeutic values (tele) are scattered throughout the membership of the group; one patient can treat the other. The role of the healer has changed from the owner and actor of therapy to its assigner and trustee.

But as long as the agent of psychotherapy was a particular, special individual, a doctor or a priest, besides being considered the source or the catalyzer of healing power—because of his personal magnetism, his skill as a hypnotist or as a psychoanalyst—the consequence was that he himself was also the *medium* of therapy, the stimulus from which all psychotherapeutic effect emanated, or at least, by which they were stimulated. It was always his actions, the elegance of his logic, the brilliancy of his lecture, the depth of his emotions, the power of his hypnosis, the lucidity of his analytic interpretation, in other words, he, the psychiatrist, was always the medium to which the subject responded and who in the last analysis determined the mental status which the patient had attained. It was, therefore, quite a revolutionary change, after disrobing the therapist of his uniqueness, showing for instance that in a group of one hundred individuals every individual participant *can* be made a therapeutic agent of one or the other in the group and even to the therapist himself, to go one step further and to disrobe all the group therapeutic agents themselves of being the media through which the therapeutic effects are attained. By means of a production on the stage a *third* element is introduced *besides* the healer and the patient-members of the group; it becomes the medium through which therapeutic measures are channelized. (This is the point where I went with psychodramatic methods beyond the methods I had used previously in group psychotherapy, even in its most systematic form— the group psychotherapies based on sociometric procedures and socioanalysis.) In psychodramatic methods the medium is to a degree separated from the agent. The medium may be as simple and amorphous as a still or moving light, a single sound repeated, or more complex, a puppet or a doll, a still or a motion picture, a dance or music production, finally reaching out to the most elaborated forms of psychodrama by means of a staff consisting of a director and auxiliary egos, calling to their command all the arts and all the means of production. The staff of egos on the stage are usually not patients themselves, but only the medium through which the treatment is directed. The psychiatrist as well as the audience of patients are often left outside of the medium. When the locus of therapy changed from the individual to the group, the group became the new subject (first step). When the group was broken up into its individual little therapists and they became the agents of therapy, the chief therapist became a part of the group (second step) and finally, the medium of therapy was separated from the healer as well as the group therapeutic agents (third step). Due to the transition from individual psychotherapy to group psychotherapy, group psychotherapy includes individual psychotherapy; due to the transition from group psychotherapy to psychodrama, psychodrama includes and envelops group psychotherapy as well as individual psychotherapy.

The three principles, subject, agent, and medium of therapy can be used as points of reference for constructing a table of polar categories of group psychotherapies. I have differentiated here eight pairs of categories: amorphous vs. structured, loco nascendi vs. secondary situations, causal vs. symptomatic, therapist vs. group centered, spontaneous vs. rehearsed, lectural vs. dramatic, conserved vs. creative, and face to face vs. from a distance. With these eight sets of pairs, a classification of every type of group psychotherapy can be made.

Table 20–1   Basic Categories of Group Psychotherapy

SUBJECT OF THERAPY

1. As to the *Constitution* of the Group

Amorphous	vs.	*Structured (organized) Group*
Without considering the organization of the group in the prescription of therapy.		Determining the dynamic organization of the group and prescribing therapy upon diagnosis.

2. As to *Locus* of Treatment

Treatment of Group in Loco Nascendi, In Situ	vs.	*Treatment Deferred to Secondary Situations*
Situational, for instance within the home itself, the workshop itself, etc.		Derivative, for instance in especially arranged situations, in clinics, etc.

3. As to *Aim* of Treatment

Causal	vs.	*Symptomatic*
Going back to the situations and individuals associated with the syndrome and including them *in vivo* in the treatment situation.		Treating each individual as a separate unit. Treatment may be deep, in the psychoanalytic sense, individually, but it may not be deep groupally.

AGENT OF THERAPY

1. As to *Source* or *Transfer* of Influence

Therapist-Centered	vs.	*Group-Centered Methods*
Either chief therapist alone or chief therapist aided by a few auxiliary therapists. Therapist treating every member of the group individually or together, but the patients themselves are not used systematically to help one another.		Every member of the group is a therapeutic agent to one or another member, one patient helping the other. The group is treated as an interactional whole.

2. As to *Form* of Influence

Spontaneous and Free	vs.	*Rehearsed and Prepared Form*
Freedom of experience and expression. Therapist or speaker (from inside the group) is extemporaneous, the audience unrestrained.		Suppressed experience and expression. Therapist memorizes lecture or rehearses production. The audience is prepared and governed by fixed rules.

MEDIUM OF THERAPY

1. As to *Mode* of Influence

Lecture or Verbal	vs.	*Dramatic or Action Methods*
Lectures, interviews, discussion, reading, reciting.		Dance, music, drama, motion pictures.

2. As to *Type* of Medium

Conserved, Mechanical, or Unspontaneous	vs.	*Creative Media*
Motion pictures, rehearsed doll drama, rehearsed dance step, conserved music, rehearsed drama.		Therapeutic motion pictures as preparatory steps for an actual group session, extemporaneous doll drama with the aid of auxiliary egos behind each doll, psychomusic, psychodrama, and sociodrama.

3. As to *Origin* of Medium

Face-to-Face	vs.	*From-a-Distance Presentations*
Any drama, lecture, discussion, etc.		Radio and television.

VALIDITY OF GROUP METHODS

All group methods have in common the need for a frame of reference which would declare their findings and applications either valid or invalid. One of my first efforts was therefore to construct instruments by means of which the structural constitution of groups could be determined. An instrument of this type was the sociometric test, and it was so constructed that it could easily become a model and a guide for the development of similar instruments. My idea was also that if an instrument is good, its findings and discoveries would be corroborated by any other instrument which has the same aim, that is, to study the structure resulting from the interaction of individuals in groups. After social groups of all types had been studied, formal and informal groups, home groups and work groups, and so forth, the question of the validity of group structure was tested by using first deviations from chance as a reference base, second by control studies of grouping and regrouping of individuals.

Deviation from Chance Experiments.[4] A population of 26 was taken as a convenient unit to use in comparison with a chance distribution of a group of 26 fictitious individuals, and three choices were made by each member. For our analysis any size of population, large or small, would have been satisfactory, but use of 26 persons happened to permit an unselected sampling of groups already tested. Without including the same group more than once, seven groups of 26 individuals were selected from among those which happened to have this size population. The test choices had been taken on the criterion of table-partners, and none of the choices could go outside the group, thus making comparison possible. Study of the findings of group configurations (resulting from the interacting individuals) in order to be compared with one another, were in need of some common reference base from which to measure the deviations. It appeared that the most logical ground for establishing such reference could be secured by ascertaining the characteristics of typical configurations produced by chance balloting for a similar size population with a like number of choices. It became possible to chart the respective sociograms (graphs of interactional relations) of each experiment, so that each fictitious person was seen in respect to all other fictitious persons in the same group; it was also possible to show the range in types of structures within each chance configuration of a group. The first questions to be answered read: What is the probable number of individuals who by mere chance selection would be picked out by their fellows, not at all, once, twice, three times, and so on. How many pairs are likely to occur, a pair being two individuals who choose one another. How many unreciprocated choices can be expected on a mere chance basis? The experimental chance findings followed closely the theoretical chance probabilities. The average number of pairs in the chance experiment was 4.3, in the theoretical analysis 4.68 (under the same condition of 3 choices within a population of 26 persons). The number of unreciprocated choices was in the chance experiments 69.4; the theoretical results showed 68.64 under the same conditions.

Among the many important findings the most instructive to the group psychotherapists were: (a) A comparison of the chance sociograms to the actual sociograms shows that the probability of mutual structures is 213 per cent greater in the actual configurations than in chance, and the number of unreciprocated structures is 35.8 per cent rarer actually than by chance; the more complex structures such as triangles, squares, and other closed patterns of which there were seven in the actual sociograms were lacking in the chance sociograms; (b) a greater concentration of many choices upon few individuals, and a weak concentration of few choices upon the majority of individuals, skewed the distribution of the sampling of actual individuals still further than took place in the chance experiments, and in a direction it need not necessarily take by chance. This feature of the distribution is called the *sociodynamic effect*. The actual frequency distribution compared with the chance distribution showed the quantity of isolates to be 250 per cent greater in the former. The quantity of overchosen individuals was 39 per cent greater while the volume of their choices was 73 per cent greater. Such statistical findings suggest that if the size of the population increases and the number of choice relations remain constant, the gap between the chance frequency distribution and the actual distribution would increase progressively. The sociodynamic effect has general validity. It is found in all social groupings whatever their kind, whether the criterion is search for mates, search for employment, or in sociocultural relations. The frequency distribution of choices shown by sociometric data is comparable to the frequency distribution of wealth in a capitalistic society. In this case also the extremes of distribution are accentuated. The exceedingly wealthy are few, the exceedingly poor are many. Economic and sociometric curves are both expressions of the same law, a law of sociodynamics.

Control Studies.[5] Two groups of individuals were compared. In the one, Group A, the placement to the cottage was made hit or miss, in the second, Group B, the placements were made on the basis of the feelings which the incoming individuals had for the cottage parent and for the other inhabitants of the cottage, and vice versa. Sociometric tests were then applied at intervals of eight weeks so that we could compare the structure of the control group A with the tested group B. Among other things it was found that the tested individuals undergo a quicker social evolution and integration into the group than the individuals who have been placed in a cottage hit or miss. At the end of a thirty-two-week period the control group showed four times as many isolated individuals as the tested group. The tested group B showed twice as many individuals forming pairs than the control group.

Indications and Contraindications of Group Psychotherapy. The indication of group psychotherapy or of one particular method in preference to another must be based on the sociodynamic changes of structure which can be determined by means of group tests of which two illustrations have been given above. Group psychotherapy has come of age and promises a vigorous development largely because group theory and group diagnosis have paved the way and have kept pace with the rapidly expanding needs for application.[6]

REFERENCES

1. G. Zilboorg and G. W. Henry, *A History of Medical Psychology* (New York: W. W. Norton & Co., 1941).
2. S. Freud, *Massenpsychologie and Ich-Analyse* (Leipzig: Internationaler Psychoanalytischer Verlag, 1921).
3. J. L. Moreno, *Das Stegreiftheater* (Berlin: Kiepenheuer, 1923); J. L. Moreno and E. Stagg Whitin, *Application of the Group Method to Classification* (New York: Beacon House, 1932); J. L. Moreno, *Who Shall Survive? A*

New Approach to the Problem of Human Interrelations (Washington, D.C.: Nervous and Mental Disease Publishing Co., 1934); "Interpersonal Therapy and the Psychopathology of Interpersonal Relations," *Sociometry*, I:9-76, 1937.

4. J. L. Moreno and Helen H. Jennings, "Sociometric Measurement of Social Configurations," *Sociometry*, Vol. I, Part II, 1938; U. Bronfenbrenner, *The Measurement of Sociometric Status, Structure and Development* (Sociometry Monographs No. 1; New York: Beacon House, 1945).

5. Helen H. Jennings, "Control Study of Sociometric Assignment," in *Sociometric Review* (New York: Beacon House, 1936).

6. J. L. Moreno (ed.), with a foreword by Winfred Overholser, *Group Psychotherapy* (New York: Beacon House, 1945).

21

PSYCHOANALYSIS AND GROUP PSYCHOTHERAPY

Nathan W. Ackerman

At the present time, the effort to shed light on the dynamics of group psychotherapy, through the application of psychoanalytic concepts, is fraught with complications. It is a task indispensable to progress, nevertheless, and in the end promises a substantial reward. The serious interest of psychoanalysts in group psychotherapy is distinctly on the increase. A number of them, myself included, have been groping toward a better understanding of the relevance of psychoanalytic principles for the dynamics of group treatment.

With the wide gaps of knowledge which prevail in this field, there is great room for prejudice in the approach of individual analysts to the issues of group therapy. My present views, highly tentative as they are, may reflect some amount of personal prejudice. For this reason, it may be useful to offer the background on which I have developed these views:

1. A primary orientation as a psychoanalytically trained psychiatrist.

2. Experience in the application of group psychotherapy to school-age children, adolescents, and adults.

3. Acquaintance with the literature on group psychotherapy.

4. A personal incentive toward the study of processes of social interaction, expressed in membership in two committees: The Committee on Social Issues of the American Psychoanalytic Association and the GAP Committee on Social Issues.

One episode out of the past will illustrate the particular slant with which I approached the problem of group psychotherapy. At a luncheon meeting of the American Orthopsychiatric Association, at which the plan for the American Group Therapy Association was launched, I timidly sug-

Reprinted from *Group Psychotherapy*, Vol. III, Nos. 2-3, edited by J. L. Moreno, Beacon House, 1949, pp. 204-215.

gested that a study of the processes of group therapy might provide a natural setting for the acquisition of sorely needed knowledge in a new science, social psychopathology. My remark was not then received with favor, but I still cling to that same prejudice. I believe careful study of the processes of group psychotherapy may yet give real substance to the new emerging science of social psychopathology.

I should like, first, to point concretely to some of the difficulties involved in applying psychoanalytic thinking to the problems of group treatment. Immediately, three types of phenomena and three kinds of knowledge are involved:

1. The psychodynamics of group behavior, including both the processes of group formation and the processes of group change.
2. The dynamic processes of emotional integration of an individual into a group.
3. The internal organization of individual personality.

In all three areas, we are handicapped by an insufficiency of knowledge, but the lack of knowledge is conspicuously great in categories 1 and 2; i.e. in the processes of integration of an individual into a group and in the dynamics of group formation and group change. In addition, there is the difficulty of correlating the intrapsychic functions of personality with those adaptive operations of personality which are involved in the integration of an individual into a group. Partly because of these handicaps, we are not yet able to set up an adequate conceptual frame for applying psychoanalytic principles to the processes of group treatment.

At the very outset, we are confronted by a thorny semantic problem. Conventional psychoanalytic terms and definitions have not yet achieved a satisfactory level of scientific clarity and precision. The term "psychoanalysis" itself has come to mean many different things. The more important usages of this term offer at least four distinct meanings:

1. A theory of personality.
2. A therapeutic technique.
3. A method of investigating the unconscious life of man.
4. A special point of view toward human nature and toward the problems of living.

In addition, each of these connotations of psychoanalysis has been continuously changing through a process of evolution, especially the psychoanalytic theory of personality and the psychoanalytic concepts of therapy.

It is now almost axiomatic that psychoanalysis, as a device for systematic exploration of unconscious mental life, does not by itself guarantee therapeutic change. In exceptional circumstances, it may even constitute a crucial danger to the therapeutic objective. Mental health is not achieved in a simple way: It is not achieved merely by increased awareness or release of unconscious urges. It means not only the elimination of specific disabilities of personality, but also the positive fulfillment of the potentialities of the individual in the context of prevailing patterns of social relations. It is reached through the establishment of an optimal balance between the individual's orientation to his deeper strivings and his orientation to the real requirements of his relations to other persons and to the group as a whole.

This immediately sets up a distinction between psychoanalysis as a means of study of the unconscious and as a therapy. This consideration has direct relevance for both the goals and processes of group psychotherapy.

Psychoanalysis, as a theory of personality, has added a wealth of insight into the nature of man's inner conflicts, but has not yet reached the status of a scientifically unified theory. As a biological psychology, psychoanalysis has done much to correct the deficiencies of the older academic theories of personality. Yet, this very advantage has introduced certain complications. Psychoanalysis stresses the individual's deeper relationship to himself and those operations of personality which are oriented to the task of gratifying basic biological needs. It emphasizes unconscious motivation, the individuality and the egocentricity of man, and the primary importance of the individual's relation to body function. It gives rise, however, to a definite complication; namely, the difficulty of integrating the concept of man as an individual and man as a social being.

From the first, Freud admitted the importance of the social determinants of behavior, with special reference to the conditioning influences of family life, but a measure of ambiguity has always characterized Freud's formulations of the interrelationship of the biological and social determinants of behavior. This is rather clearly reflected in Freud's own statement concerning individual and social psychology:

> A contrast between individual psychology and social or group psychology, which at first glance might seem to be full of significance, loses a great deal of its sharpness when it is examined more closely. It is true that individual psychology is concerned with the individual man, and explores the paths by which he seeks to find satisfaction for his instincts, but only rarely and under exceptional circumstances is individual psychology in a position to disregard the relations of this individual to others. In the individual mental life, someone else is invariably involved, as a model, as an object, as an opponent, and so from the very first, individual psychology is at the same time social psychology as well.[1]

Here we have an illustration of Freud's brilliantly penetrating wisdom and yet, at the same time, a fair sample of his tendency to somewhat beg the question as regards the precise relationship between the biological and the social determinants of behavior. While making his bow to the "social man," he tends to show a preferential interest in the "individual man." He sought to explain the social role of man and woman in terms of biologically determined instincts and the related unconscious drives; the social function of man was represented as a projection onto the social scene of his unconscious strivings and fantasies. The broader patterns of culture were similarly interpreted.

While sharply illuminating the role of family life in shaping the child's personality, he tended, nevertheless, to stereotype the roles of mother and father, failed adequately to take into account the cultural patterning of these roles, isolated the dynamics of family life from surrounding social institutions, and subordinated the feminine half of humanity. He failed to see the way in which child-rearing concepts were influenced by cultural as well as the developmental factors of neurosis.

But what has all this to do with group psychotherapy? Mainly this: In order to illuminate effectively the dynamics of group therapy, the conceptual frame for a theory of personality must be expanded in a way that satisfies two necessary conditions:

1. The operations of personality must be conceived in terms of a biosocial unit. The biological and social determinants of behavior cannot be dissociated. Out of the interaction between the organism and environment, a new unit of behavior emerges which is biosocial. The adaptive functions of personality must be so viewed as to take into account the continuous interplay between those processes that reflect the individual's relation to his inner (biological) being and those which reflect his orientation to social participation. It is necessary, furthermore, to find criteria for the dynamic relations between the adaptive expressions of personality in group action and the relatively more fixed internal structure of personality, as conditioned by developmental influences. In other words, man has an identity that is, at once, both individual and social.

2. The functions of personality must be defined within the context of a broader theory of social organization and social relations. The adaptive behavior of the individual must be viewed in relation to the characteristics of the group to which he belongs. Differences between individual and group behavior must be understood. The behavior of a group has certain unique characteristics of its own, and the adaptive processes of personality, both normal and pathological, need to be viewed within this wider frame.

Until we satisfy these requirements in the basic concepts of personality structure and function, it will be difficult to usefully transpose psychoanalytic principles to a group treatment setting.

In a group setting, the therapist cannot directly observe, nor does he have access to, the total potentialities of individual personality; instead, the therapist establishes emotional contact with the shifting adaptive phases of the personality in action, which are expressed through the role of the person in that social situation. The role of the individual in the group represents a particular form of integration of his emotional tendencies in a specific situation. The adaptive expressions of the person are limited and shaped in two ways: by the relatively fixed organization of the individual personality and by the requirements of a given situation, as this individual interprets them.

It must be emphasized, therefore, that the immediate therapeutic influence in a group is exercised not through what is called "total personality," but rather through those particular forms of emotional expression through which the patient displays his personality in the group—namely, through his role in the group. The continuity of group therapeutic experience is such, however, as to induce in the person a series of changes in adaptive role, and through these changes, the therapist may gradually achieve access to a variety of layers of the personality.

Thus, social interaction can be understood only if we broaden our conception of personality so as to consider the continuous interplay between the individual's relation to his biological make-up and the individual's orientation to social participation. Each individual has layers of emotional reactivity which are relatively fixed and others which are more pliable. Each individual is capable, within the limits set by his fixed intrapsychic structure, of modifying his adaptive form in diverse social situations; he can change his "social role." The identity of each individual holds both individual and social components. In a shift from one social situation to another, the dynamic equilibrium between the individual and social components of personal identity undergoes change.

In a recent paper, "Social Role and Total Personality," I endeavored to illuminate the relationship between the social functions of personality and individual personality. I suggested that the adaptive forms or roles of personality in different groups might be appraised by the application of the following criteria: the group-conditioned aim of the individual, his quality of apperception of surrounding interpersonal realities, the concept of self projected into the role (including personal values, ideals, standards, and so on), his techniques for control of the group environment, his pattern of conflict, the quality of anxiety engendered by this role, and the defenses mobilized against it.

It seems to me that some attempt to define the adaptive functions of the personality can be made in these terms, and this adaptive role can then be correlated with our knowledge of the fixed intrapsychic structure of this individual. In order to establish such correlation, more exact knowledge of ego functions is needed.

When we turn to a consideration of the relation of psychoanalytic therapeutic technique to the techniques of group treatment, it becomes imperative to contrast the different psychosocial potentialities of the two therapeutic situations. The two-person psychoanalytic relationship provides a unique experience in which the earlier patterns of child-parent relations are relived and their destructive elements removed. Group psychotherapy, involving three or more persons, however, has its dynamic base in the fact that the child's character is influenced not only by the mother, but all the interacting relationships within the family group, especially the relationship between the parents. These multiple interpersonal patterns, each affecting the other, also contribute to the distortion of personality.

The psychoanalytic method applies to a pair of persons, but the techniques are pointed almost exclusively to the experience of only one of these persons—the patient. In considerable part, the analytic relationship does not constitute a true social experience; it provides no model for society. It is a process of working-through of the patient's internal conflict with self, with the analyst acting as catalyzer of this process. External conflict with the analyst becomes translated back into terms of the patient's internal conflict with self. A further aspect of analytic therapy involves a degree of temporary shedding of the patient's inhibiting ego, of his rational control, a denuding of the social layers of the patient's identity, so as to accentuate the patient's awareness of inner conflicted emotion and biologically conditioned urges. Thus, the importance of outer reality, and reality as personified by the analyst, is temporarily diminished. Such an experience heightens the patient's deeper communication with his private self and his unconscious, but at some cost in terms of temporary subordination of social communication. As access to the deeper self is achieved, the reality elements of the patient's ego and the reality of the analyst are reasserted and play their part in reintegration of the patient's emotional life. In this sense, analysis is predominantly a therapy which moves from "inside outward."

The group situation is different. Interpersonal processes emerge in a group which either are not present in a two-person relationship, or at least not in an identical form. Contact between two persons provides the potentiality for a social relationship, but does not provide the foundations of a society. Only a group of three or more persons makes possible an organized social unit, with a set of dominant aims, ideas, emotions, values, and patterns of social relations. Here we have multiple interpersonal patterns, interacting continuously with each other. Some of these relationship patterns may be in harmony; others in conflict. They vie with each other for a position of dominant influence. The way in which the group forms, integrates, changes, and is affected by leadership, determines the channels along which emotion is released or restrained. Thus, in a group, a tangible social reality is always present. The patient's contact with this reality is immediate and inescapable. The therapeutic process moves back and forth between this social reality and the patient's inner emotional life. Here we have a basis for continuous impact between the patient's image of interpersonal relations and their actual nature, as perceived and interpreted in the group interaction.

In order to try to see the extent to which therapeutic mechanisms operate similarly or differently in the group and individual settings, it is useful to outline the partial processes of psychotherapy, in general:

1. The development of an emotional relationship with a dynamic "give-and-take" between patient and therapist.
2. Through this relationship, provision of emotional support for the patient.
3. Reality testing; modification of concept of self, and patterns of relation to others in the direction of more realistic perception.
4. Release of pent-up emotion.
5. Expression of conflict, both conscious and unconscious.
6. Change in patterns of resistance and defense against anxiety.
7. Diminution of guilt and anxiety.
8. Growth of new insight, and emergence of new and healthier patterns of adaptation.

All of these processes overlap, influence each other, and together they provide the dynamic basis for therapeutic change. A number of questions arise.

Is therapeutic change in the group and individual settings dependent on the same or a different set of processes? Are there some processes which are specific and unique for one or the other form of psychotherapy? Do some particular processes play a more important role in one form of treatment than in the other? Or, if the basic processes are in essence similar, are the separate elements of therapy integrated and balanced differently in the two situations? On these questions, I offer my present views humbly, tentatively, with keen awareness of the handicap of limited knowledge.

First, I would tend to doubt that the group therapy situation involves any unique processes. I do believe, however, that the different psychosocial potentialities of the group necessarily modify the pattern of the balance between the partial processes of therapy, intensifying some, lessening or inhibiting others. The therapeutic processes in a group tend to operate on an interpersonal level, rather different from that which prevails in psychoanalysis. The nature of group experience is such as seems to place a first emphasis on conflict with the environment, rather than with the self. In the group, conflict tends to be externalized, projected into the social scene. Through such projections are reflected the patterns of inner conflict with self. Externalization of conflict encourages some measure of "acting out" in the group relations. Expression of feeling in a group, therefore, is more than verbal, it extends to the sphere of social action and fosters a higher degree of motor discharge of tension. In individual psychoanalysis, the primary emphasis is in the opposite direction; namely, on conflict with self, and in harmony with this, the tendency to "act out" is discouraged. Through the conflict with self, one gets, in turn, the mirror reflections of conflict with the environment.

But there are other differences as well. The pattern of intensive exclusive dependence on one person is not so readily possible in a group as in psychoanalysis. Relationships in a group tend to be more influenced by reality. The irrationalities of transference are held in check. The multiple interpersonal relationships provide opportunity for displacement, division, and dilution of transference emotion. Magic expectations and omnipotence strivings are restricted.

In the group, the function of providing emotional support for the patient is divided. The therapist is not the sole source of security and gratification of emotional needs. The group, as a whole, shares this responsibility.

In the group, discharge of pent-up emotion takes place on a selective basis. Emotion which can be experienced in common with others is reinforced. Other types of emotion may be inhibited.

Free association, in the analytic sense, occurs on a more limited scale, if at all. In its stead, we have the spontaneous emotional interactions between members and with the therapist.

In the interaction between the person and the group environment, there is a two-way selective process. The individual takes out of the group what he needs. The group takes from each individual what its processes require. The individual combines his force with those tendencies in the group which will strengthen the effectiveness of his chosen role. Also, he may submit to being used by others in the interest of their self-assertion. This two-way selective process plays a part in the assertion of certain types of control, in releasing basic drives, and in dealing with conflict, guilt, and anxiety.

In the group setting, the therapist does not have immediate or direct access to the unconscious of the patient. In this respect, the analytic situation enjoys greater favor; here the access to unconscious conflict is more direct, and more systematic. In the group, conscious conflict is the first to appear. The working-through of such conflict and its reduction to concrete terms will often bring to light significant clues as to the nature of deeper conflict. Frequently, the manner in which conflict is externalized and "acted out" in group interaction, offers hints as to the content of unconscious conflict.

Some further comment may be in order here in relation to the therapeutic connotations of a patient's tendency to "act out" his impulses. In the analytic situation, "acting out" is conceived as harmful and is systematically discouraged. In a group setting, the urge to express conflict through "acting out" is, to some degree, natural. Group psychotherapy is intrinsically an "acting out," rather than a "thinking out," type of experience. Here, a patient deals with conflict by projecting it into a relationship; he lives it out with the other person. In this manner, inner conflict is translated into outer conflict with another person. It is this "acting out" in relationships which enhances the motor discharge of emotional tension. In this setting, the therapist can work with the irrational elements of conflict not in the form of fantasy but rather in those forms which are projected onto the social scene. The group therapist may then translate this back into the context of the patient's inner conflicts. Because of the selective nature of the group process, however, some kinds of unconscious conflict may remain totally inaccessible.

Patterns of resistance and defense against anxiety are dramatically transparent in the proceedings of a group. Resistance should not be regarded as pathological behavior; it can be defined as the natural mechanism of self-protection when a patient fears harm through exposure of himself in a close relationship. Anxiety, the defenses against anxiety, and patterns of resistance are a functional unit. By tracing out the resistance paths, and the types of defenses employed, one sees the way in which a patient attempts to escape his anxiety and conflict. By pursuing closely these paths of escape, one is led, step by step, to the actual content of the conflict.

Individual patterns of guilt can be modified to a variable extent by group treatment . . . some forms temporarily, others more permanently. The more superficial types of guilt are easily reached and relieved, especially if they represent a shared form of guilt. The technique of universalization is a device for mitigation of guilt through reassurance, but may not alleviate it at its source. A lasting relief of guilt in the more rigid, automatized types of reaction is more difficult in a group. In general, however, the impact between the impulse tendencies of the individual and the fluid standards and moral reactions of the group does offer a substantial basis for diminishing guilt feeling. Here, the standards of individual conscience, immature and inappropriate as they often are, are checked against the more balanced and realistic standards of the group.

The group situation provides a wide range of possibilities for the testing of reality. In this setting, social reality is not a fixed entity. Each member of the group, and each pattern of relationship, personifies a given form of interpretation of social reality. In this sense, social reality is fluid, relative, and is represented by multiple interacting concepts, rather than by a single fixed interpretation. As the group evolves, however, there is increasing unity and stability in these interpretations of reality. On this background, the patient tests out his fear of dangers from the real world, and his fear of his own impulses. In this setting, the clash between his impulses and the standards of this fluid form of social reality offers a chance to expand his emotional orientation to his own nature and the nature of society. Such increased understanding may develop with or without therapeutic interpretation. Patients often spontaneously offer their own interpretations. Sometimes these are uncanny in their accuracy, sometimes utterly inappropriate because of the patient's egocentricity and projections. It is the therapist's task to guide these emotional crosscurrents toward correct understanding. He may use the technique of interpretation sparingly and only when the emotional trends have become sufficiently ripened. Here we have a broad opportunity for growth of insight, modification of social standards and values, and the development of healthier patterns of social adaptation. Of particular importance in a group is a growth of confidence in dealing with people and a basic increase in self-esteem.

Some Differences between the Psychoanalytic Two-person Situation and the Group Therapeutic Situation

Psychoanalysis	Group Therapy
1. Two persons.	Three or more persons.
2. Couch technique.	Face-to-face contact.
3. Temporary subordination of reality.	Reality continuously asserted by group though reality takes fluid form.
Analyst reasserts reality according to patient's need.	Patient's impact with reality is immediate.
Analyst is observer; suppresses his own personality.	Group therapist is more real person, participant as well as observer.
Relationship is not social, except in later stages.	Group provides genuine social experience.
Social standards not imposed.	Group standards emerge, but remain flexible.
4. Exclusive dependence on therapist.	Dependent need is divided, not exclusively pointed to therapist.
Emergence of irrational attitudes and expectations.	Irrational attitudes and expectations appear, but checked by group pressures.
Magic omnipotent fantasy prominent. Irrational motivation may rise to dominant position.	Magic omnipotent fantasy is controlled.
	Irrational motivation not permitted dominant position.
5. Direct gratification of emotional need not given.	Group offers some direct gratification of emotional need.
6. Communication largely verbal; communication less real.	Communication less verbal; greater expression in social action and reaction.
Patient communicates deeply with self; also with therapist.	Higher degree of social communication.
Patient feels alone.	Patient belongs to group, shares emotional experience, feels less alone.
7. "Acting out" suppressed; little motor discharge of tension.	Higher degree of "acting out," and motor discharge of tension.
8. Access to unconscious conflict more systematic; greater continuity in "working through."	Access to unconscious conflict less systematic; lesser degree of continuity in "working through."
Emphasis on inner conflict with self; conflict with self mirrors conflict with environment.	Conflict is projected, externalized.
	Conflict with environment mirrors inner conflict.

Group Therapy	Psychoanalysis
Modification of specific internal disorders of personality more effective.	Modification of specific internal disorder of personality less effective.
9. Patterns of resistance and defense more uniform and specific.	Patterns of resistance and defense more variable.
10. Relief of guilt and anxiety more specific.	Relief of guilt and anxiety less specific.
11. Dynamic movement to large extent from "inside outwards."	Dynamic movement to large extent from "outside inwards."
12. Emotional change and insight more immediately related to intrapsychic conflict.	Emotional change and insight more immediately related to extrapsychic conflict.
Method more suitable for specific psychiatric symptoms; predominantly a therapy for disturbance in basic drives.	Method more suitable for change in character traits; predominantly an ego therapy.

REFERENCE

1. S. Freud, *Group Psychology and the Analysis of the Ego* (London: International Psychoanalytic Press, 1922).

- 22 -

DESCRIPTION OF A PROJECT
IN GROUP THERAPY

Dorothy W. Baruch

Since group therapy is becoming an increasingly important adjunct to individual therapy in a war and postwar period, and since techniques and procedures are still in a great state of flux, it is hoped that the present paper will hold some value even though it is an informal report rather than controlled research.

Twelve sessions of *therapeutic group discussion* which were held as part of a college course in techniques of therapy are described. The course also included a sampling of psychodrama and of creative writing used as a therapeutic tool. During the discussion sessions an attempt was made (1) to keep record briefly on what took place, (2) to analyze techniques of leadership, and (3) to tap the effects of the process through the expressed reactions of the group members.

Therapeutic group discussion might be likened to counseling with a group. The basic orientation of the therapist bears a major influence on the process, which accordingly becomes directive or nondirective, persuasive, suggestive, permissive, or what not.

Orientation in the present instance was to a type of group discussion characterized above all by permissiveness and acceptance.

Creation and maintainance of a climate where these qualities can function involves not only the therapist's—or group leader's—own attitudes but also the interacting attitudes of the group members. The therapeutic relationship is not on a one-to-one basis, but on a basis of manifold and shifting interrelationships. The resistance and guilt factors that need to be dealt with are not those of an individual counselee but of many. The all-important problem of maintaining acceptance involves not alone the therapist's feelings, but the feelings current among group members. As

Reprinted from *Journal of Consulting Psychology*, Vol. IX, No. 6, 1945, pp. 271-280.

discussion proceeds, subleaders rise in the group and the therapist's own attitude toward giving up leadership as well as the attitudes of group members toward having one another assume leadership—all enter in. The very complexity in these interrelationships is what makes the group process so subtle and the so-called leadership techniques so difficult both to analyze and to convey.

SUBJECTS

The present group was composed of twenty-three members, both men and women. Ages ranged from eighteen to forty-nine years, with a mean age of thirty-five ($\sigma = 6.9$). The members included a school administrator, a physician, a business secretary, a psychiatric social worker, an industrial counselor, an administrator and several group workers from the Los Angeles Youth Project,* and teachers from the nursery through high school. Education included a medical degree, three Masters', eleven Bachelors'. Eight people had not completed college. The majority were Protestant-Anglo-Whites, although there were five Jewish members, one Catholic, one Negro, and one Mexican. Sixteen were married, two were single, and five were separated or divorced. (See Table 1.) Eleven had attended a mental hygiene course given by the group leader.

PROCESS AND ANALYSIS OF TECHNIQUES

On the assumption that undergoing therapy themselves would best clarify and point up techniques for them, the group members spontaneously elected to have such an experience.

In the first two sessions, the therapist—or group leader—took a more active role than at any later time. She assumed major responsibility for establishing a warm friendly feeling in the group, for using first names, for seating members informally in circular arrangement. She saw to it that the process of therapy was briefly introduced and that her own nonadvisory role was defined. She brought out that the major function of the group members was to talk about matters that were troublesome, but that talking was not essential unless they felt like it. She stressed the fact that material would need to be kept in strictest confidence and defined some of the mechanics for carrying on group discussion, such as avoidance of asides, not stopping to raise hands, not waiting to be called on, and the like.

Some members felt that it would be difficult to discuss any real problems in a group. The leader accepted this initial resistance, nodded, and restated, simply: "You feel it will be difficult." Several concurred but went on to say that they would nonetheless like to try it out. In consequence,

* An interagency project focusing on the prevention of delinquency.

the leader asked that those who wished to do so cite some of their problems. Fifteen members presented problems which the leader then grouped
under larger, more collective headings—as marital problems, problems
with parents, and so on. The majority chose the latter to begin on.

As the various individuals talked and as it became clear to them that
the hostilities they felt toward their parents were common and acceptable,
they spontaneously brought up other items. Several were still bothered by
sibling rivalry or by feelings of having been rejected. Several were having
marital problems. Some were involved in the difficulties presented by con-
tinence and some by concern over extramarital affairs. Several felt that
their disappointments in marriage, such as lack of orgasm and difficulties
in understanding and accepting their partners, were directly tied up with
earlier attitudes. Important among these, they felt, were the conflicts that
had arisen from parental reactions to masturbation and bodily exploration.

After the twelfth session, leadership techniques were discussed and
analyzed by the group and were later summarized into a written schedule
by the leader. (See Listing of Techniques of Leadership in Group Discussion.)

Two members went over the running records made during the therapeutic sessions and separately categorized each leadership technique recorded. Out of the sixty-six paired judgments made in the assigning of
categories, there were sixty agreements, yielding an extremely high percentage of agreement—namely 91 per cent; and a difference of 9 per cent—
with a significantly small standard error of .01.

The records clearly indicated that major techniques had to do with
bringing resistances, embarrassment, guilt feelings, and other emotions into
sharper focus, to clarify them, to make collective meanings appear, and to
facilitate working them through. Many times the leader would do this
simply by restating feelings that had been expressed verbally or by putting
into words feelings that were indicated by nonverbal cues, as psychomotor
tensions, evasiveness, breaks, in discussion, and so on.*

The following excerpts from the seventh session illustrate this restatement technique.

One of the men (2M)† brought up that punishment received for having masturbated had made him feel cheap, unworthy, soiled. . . . The
leader accepted this, restating: "You felt that your body was cheap and unworthy; so the whole of you seemed cheap and unworthy." Others came in
with experiences that had affected them similarly. One (13F) had been
punished for playing under the bedclothes with her brother; another (3F)
had witnessed her parents having sex relations and had absorbed a recoil
attitude from her mother. The first (2M) said: "They put pepper on my

* This is similar to the restatement technique used by Rogers in individual counseling.
† M = male; F = female.

Table 22–1   *Face Data*

Total Enrolled	23
Age Range	18 to 49
Mean Age	35 ($\sigma = 6.9$)
Education	
High school graduate	1
High school and some college	6
College graduate	2
College and postgraduate	9
Master's degree	3
M.D.	1
Business School	1
Occupation	
Students	2
Teachers[1]	13
School Administrator	1
Group Workers (Youth Project)	2
Youth Project Administrator	1
Psychiatric Social Worker	1
Industrial Counselor	1
Secretary	1
Physician	1
Marital Status	
Single	2
Married	16
Separated	2
Divorced[2]	3
	—
	23
Religion	
Protestant	11
Catholic	1
Jewish	6
None[3]	5

[1] Teachers were from the following levels:

Nursery School	2
Elementary	8
Junior High	2
Senior High	1

[2] This face sheet information was collected at the middle of the term. At the end of the class two of the divorced members were married to each other.

[3] Three of the members listing themselves under "none" indicated backgrounds of religion, i.e. one baptized Protestant and converted to Judaism on marriage, one baptized Methodist, and one Congregational-Presbyterian. One member (Methodist) emphasized his deliberate withdrawal, at the age of fifteen, from the church where he had received complete indoctrination, in contrast to those whose withdrawal was due to "drifting," or to those who had "no religious background."

penis to keep me from masturbating. . . . Made me feel horrible and guilty. . . ." Another (20M) said, "Being good was being nonsexual. I had a feeling of being wicked. The devil had me by the tail because I enjoyed masturbation and necking"; and later, "Sex was one thing; you were another. Sex then couldn't be a part of any love relationship that you were involved in. . . . What chance for marriage?" The leader synthesized these various contributions, restating in terms of their collective meaning by saying, "Attitudes toward sex . . . were put in the dark, isolated without regard for the human relationships involved."

She continuously *put observed tensions into words*, thus: "It *is* hard to talk about these things. They're usually taboo. I'm wondering if you've felt, in consequence, that some of the group were nonacceptant?" Several were then able to come out with feelings of disapproval or of having been disapproved of.

Another of the important techniques was *to keep the focus on emotional content* either by pointing out frankly when the group began to intellectualize or by calling for concreting with such phrases as "Tell us what you mean" . . . "Can you give an example?" "Can you remember what you did and how you felt?"

Other techniques included *keeping the discussion dispersed* so that no one person monopolized it and *keeping it geared, also, to majority focus*, thus facilitating identification, acceptance, and increased ease in emotional release. Questions such as: "How do the rest of you feel about this?"—or, again, restating in such a way as to make a point collective— served to effect this end.

Important, too, appeared the *increasing passivity of the therapist*, her willingness to turn leadership functions over to group members, and her matter-of-fact acceptance of growth for its emotional value to the individual rather than in judgmental or moralistic terms.

Probably, the most important aspects of leadership, however, were the *permissiveness, acceptance*, and *empathy* that the therapist continuously expressed. In the words of one of the group members, "It was her warm and sincere interest in each one of us, and a kind of real affection, that made it possible to go on."

Listing of Techniques of Leadership in Therapeutic Group Discussion

I. *Sets up situation suitable for release*

1. Shows empathic, permissive attitude (sincere and warm interest in each individual).	Expresses warmth and empathy actively, though not necessarily verbally (i.e. does it through facial expressions, gestures, etc.).

2. Establishes informality.	Seats group in circular formation in not too large a circle; comfortable chairs where possible; no double row of chairs, but sitting on floor instead.	
	Refreshments beforehand with opportunity for exchange.	
	Asks group members to take on various responsibilities, as turns at bringing refreshments, setting up chairs, opening door, taking enrollment, fees, etc.	
	Uses first names.	
3. Introduces therapeutic process.	Concept that all people have troubles.	
	Value of release (what it does).	
	Value of talking as means of release.	
	Value of listening in a therapeutic group as another means of release until ready to talk.	
4. Defines relationships.	Brings up confidential nature of group therapy and the consequent necessity for each person to assume professional attitude toward material and to keep it inviolate. Calls on group for discussion and mutual agreement.	
a. Leader's role.	Major function to remain acceptant (nonadvisory, noncondemnatory, nonjudgmental).	
b. Group members' role.	Twofold:	
	(1) To gain release by talking of own troubles or by listening if not ready to talk.	
	(2) To help others gain release by remaining acceptant— not probing, questioning, or interpreting.	
5. Welcomes initial resistances to discussing personal problems in a group situation.	Restates any resistance that is expressed verbally.	"You feel it will be hard to voice your real feelings in public, as it were. . . ."
	Brings into open apparent resistances shown by psychomotor tensions.	"You look doubtful about something."

	If no resistance is voiced or shown, calls on group for expression of how they actually feel; or states that many people are at first concerned over the idea of discussing troubles before others.	"I'm wondering how you are feeling about telling about your troubles in front of others. . . ."
	Pauses for group expression and response.	"At first, it's often hard for people to believe it can be done. . . ."
	Shows by acceptant attitude that it is permissive to bring into group of this sort the negative feelings not ordinarily directly expressed.	
6. Introduces a few essential mechanics for carrying on discussion method.	Stresses free participation; not raising hands or waiting to be called on: "talk when feel like it," give-and-take idea.	
	No asides, whisperings, note-writing, etc. Desirability, instead, of bringing out into open whatever comes into mind.	
7. Helps group locate a common problem and to begin on it.	Calls on group members to name some of their troubles.	
	Places individually mentioned problems under larger categories so as to make them collective (as: problems with parents, husband-wife problems, etc.).	
	Asks group which type of problem appeals to most.	
	Calls on group to begin talking about experiences and feelings along line of problem selected.	"Imagine we're ready to start now on our troubles. . . . Perhaps A would like to go on with hers. . . ."

II. *Facilitates release*

1. Keeps discussion focused on emotional content vs. action content or theory.	Calls for *specifics* (i.e. for concrete experiences) and for feelings about these.	"Tell us what you mean. . . ."
		"Can you give an example?"
		"Remember what you did and how you felt?"
		"How did you feel when that happened?"

Points out frankly that group is theorizing or escaping into other peoples' problems vs. working through their own.

"There we go again talking in vague terms. . . ."

"We're not staying with ourselves and with how we feel. . . ."

2. Establishes and seeks to maintain mutual, interactive *acceptance* (i.e. both leader's acceptance of group members and their acceptance of each other).

   a. Clarifies what group expresses so that it becomes more understandable to all.

   *Restates feelings that have been expressed verbally.**

   "You felt very irked. . . ."

   "You felt antagonistic. . . ."

   b. Relates what various people express so that collective meanings and applicability appear.

   Puts into words feelings that have been expressed nonverbally (i.e. through psychomotor tensions, evasiveness, breaks in discussion, etc.).

   "Some of you are looking bothered. . . ."

   "It's hard to bring out things like this. . . ."

   "We're usually hesitant over talking about such things."

   c. Helps bring tensions and intergroup hostilities into the open so that they may be worked through.

   Pauses for group to let out these feelings.

   d. Helps bring discomfort, embarrassment, guilt feelings out so that they may be worked through.

   Occasional calls on group for how they are feeling.

   Again, restates etc.

   "I wonder how you are feeling now?"

3. Keeps discussion dispersed (i.e. so that no one person talks too long, especially at first, thus avoiding too fast exposure with too great guilt result-

   Turns point in question to group.

   "How do rest of you feel about this?"

* This section includes the major and most important techniques that the leader uses in group discussion. They come in over and over again as discussion advances.

ing and closing up on release or self-acceptance; also avoiding any one person becoming a target for criticism and rejection by others before they have learned to be sufficiently acceptant; reducing also the chances for shutting off release of more timid ones by more aggressive group members.

4. Keeps discussion geared to majority focus (thus facilitating identification, acceptance, and increased ease in emotional release).

Reiterating, when pertinent, the necessity for keeping together, for avoiding asides, etc.

Letting side lines run on if related to majority focus, but stopping them, if unrelated, by brief acknowledgment of sideline content and then restating what was under focus at point where majority focus was lost.

5. Occasionally brings in a relieving type of information.

III. *Facilitates self-direction*

1. Recognizes subleadership roles in group as these develop.

Is aware of fact that group members tend gradually to assume subleadership functions and that this is a sign of movement toward self-direction.

2. Is willing to relinquish own leadership role to subleaders.

Remains acceptant and nondefensive as this occurs (i.e. does not feel need to cling to any supposed prestige value in role).

At first, at least in some instances, shows recognition by reiterating what subleader says.

"As R says, we do seem to feel embarrassed. . . ."

Brings in fewer and fewer restatements or other techniques; relies more and more for these on the group members.

"As B just brought up, we're escaping again into generalizations. . . ."

3. Accepts reports of progress, of new ac-

Again, restates what members bring in, still remaining accept-

"It felt good to have done that. . . ."

tions, of help gained in the course, of new insights, and other types of forward movement, keeping emphasis still on emotions and on feeling values to the person himself.

ant rather than judgmental (i.e. does not, by voicing approval or gratification, put person in a position of having done this for leader; but, by simple acceptance, emphasizes that person has done this for himself, which in turn implies that having done it, he can continue to help himself grow).

Accepts growth for its emotional value to the person rather than in moralistic or judgmental terms.

"It made you feel stronger. . . ."

"You felt clearer and more free. . . ."

"Many of you feel that you could talk more readily because of having heard that others had similar problems. As a result now, your own problems feel less heavy."

GROUP MEMBERS' STATEMENTS AS TO EFFECTS OF THE THERAPEUTIC EXPERIENCE

At the end of the course, the group members were asked to write informal statements as to what they felt they had gotten, if anything, from the therapeutic experience. The necessity for honesty was stressed in view of the research purpose underlying the request. In addition, the group records were examined for statements made verbally during sessions. Thirteen of the twenty-three members turned in written statments while verbal statements of eighteen appeard in the records. Five failed to indicate reactions. (See Table 2.)

Among the outcomes was an increased understanding of self and gains in insight and in ability to face problems. (Mentioned by fourteen people.) As example, one person (13F) said, "I think part of my illness was caused by bottling up my hostility. It had to come out in some way so it came out through my body." Another said: "I began masturbation at three. Now I realize the relation of my guilt over this to my shyness. . . ." (18M)

A sense of increased ease and reduction in guilt, hostility, and in feelings of being different was cited by eleven people. "I haven't talked much" said one, "but I've gotten a lot of relief out of hearing feelings like my own expressed." (12F) Another: "I could remember hating my brothers but it was a guilty hate. Now I can face the fact that such feelings are normal. . . ." (15F) Another: "It makes me feel better to know that others don't have orgasm either. . . ." (13F)

Seven mentioned having acquired an increased understanding of other people. Three mentioned a reduction of conflict in family relations, and one, improvement in a speech handicap. Professional growth was mentioned by twelve. This included not only an extension of insights and understandings but a carry-over into improved practices with children and adults.

Table 22–2   Indications of Growth as Expressed by Group Members[1]

Easing of Personal Problems	No. of Cases	Gains in Personal Adjustment	No. of Cases	Professional Growth	No. of Cases
Sense of increased ease and reduction of guilt, hostility, and in feelings of being different	11	Increased understanding of self and gains in insight and ability to face and accept own problems	14	Understanding of the value of group therapy and clarification of techniques	11
Reduction of conflict in family relations	3	Increase in emotional capacity and expressiveness	5	Improved practices with children	3
Reduction in speech handicap	1	Increased understanding of other people and increased ability to accept them	7	Improved practices in working with adults	2
		Increased energy and better ability to direct it	2	Increased confidence in own work and in methods utilized	2

[1] This table is based on information from group members turned in on informal individual written reports and in oral statements made during group sessions and shown in the running record. Five members did not make either a written report or an oral statement (e.g. IF, 8F, 9F, 17F, and 21F.)

Seven mentioned an increase in emotional capacity and expressiveness. Said one, "I can feel more. I can express my emotions. Before I was a passive kind of person. . . ." (13F) Another, "I can feel things now. I never used to. . . . I never used to *feel*. . . ." (23F) Another: "The experience has helped me throw off a little of the restrictiveness in my emotional life and has allowed greater interplay of my personality with others, especially in the more intimate situations where restrictions and pressures exert a serious block." (3F)

This new acceptance of emotions in a culture which so restricts expressiveness that various neurotic patterns result was nicely illustrated by the freedom shown in some of the therapeutic writing done after the group discussion-sessions were over. One person wrote:

If I start to let the mad things through,
There's no telling where I'll stop.
There's the man whose car I pushed across the street just now
And got my grill bent in, for thanks;
And the folks who made me grow up
Burdened down with heavy guilt—

So a sense of fun was something new to learn.
There are lots of things, too, in between
Enough for several other poems. [17F]

Another said: "My mother's house is a mess . . . looks like a crazy house . . . good furniture . . . but dirty. Looks like a museum, disarranged and ugly . . . Now—I'm the same. B. [her husband] said, 'You're always trying to excuse yourself; I'm not going to help you rationalize any longer. . . .' This made me mad. . . . He went on . . . 'I give up! I never dreamed that I'd be glad to get back to a lousy job just to get away from this house. I never knew anyone who could ruin a weekend like you do.' I said, 'Well, if you'll just shut up, I'll get this work done.' My energy began to come up with my hate. . . . I started the dishes. God, I hate them! . . . [But]he seemed in a decent mood for the rest of the evening; and I ended up feeling pretty good myself!" (13F)

It was the subjective impression of the leader, supported by a similar impression of three members, that all but two people had received help, and a kind of "freeing," from the therapeutic experience in the group.

THE PSYCHOANALYSIS OF GROUPS

Alexander Wolf

The group therapy I am about to describe is psychoanalytic in character. The techniques, employed in a social setting, emphasize dream interpretation, free association, the analysis of resistance, transference, and countertransference. I am fully aware that, in expounding a theory and method of group analysis, I shall have to make out a case for its curative value. That I hope to do.

My active interest in group analysis began eleven years ago. Reluctant to turn away low income patients who could not afford sustained treatment and hopeful of finding a method that would meet such a contingency, I read widely in the available literature on group psychotherapy. Many obvious and disturbing questions immediately presented themselves. Would not the presence of others inhibit a patient's free association? Would the traditional transference relationship between analyst and patient be sacrificed if the analyst became one of a group? Suppose the group developed a tendency to destroy the analyst's authority? Might not a neurotic group violently attack one of its members, thus paralyzing his resources? How could multiple transference and countertransference be disposed of without their becoming hopelessly enmeshed? Could a conscientious analyst do justice to eight or ten patients in joint session, and would the consequent period of treatment be unduly protracted? These and other imponderables were equally bothersome and required careful consideration.

The writings of Drs. Paul Schilder and Louis Wender seemed particularly encouraging, however, and in 1938 I started an experimental group of four men and four women. So promptly and effectively were my uncertainties about group analysis dispelled that within one year I had telescoped most of my practice, and in 1940 I was working with five groups of eight to ten patients each.

Reprinted from the *American Journal of Psychotherapy*, Vol. III, No. 4, October 1949, 16-50; Vol. IV, No. 1, January 1950, pp. 525-558.

HOMOGENEOUS OR HETEROGENEOUS GROUPS

Four years of army experience facilitated the confirmation of numerous tentative theories and supplied answers to certain provocative questions. (Although service statistics showed that there was a high incidence of neurosis, the personnel turnover was so rapid that many of our experiments lacked finality.) We convinced ourselves, for example, that meeting patients in homogeneous groups was effective army procedure. Consequently, alcoholics, psychopaths, morons, and those suffering from common psychosomatic and psychoneurotic disturbances with similar underlying trends were regularly isolated for treatment.

The very presence of so many individuals with similar psychiatric disorders, a rare opportunity in civilian life where homogeneous groups are not so easily assembled, naturally prompted such a move. The resultant empathy, mutual understanding, and sympathy were exceptionally helpful factors. To be sure, the disadvantage of this psychic inbreeding was apparent: Patients had no opportunity to cope with individuals whose character structure differed markedly from their own. Specifically, since these army groups comprised men only, heterosexual problems were not adequately provoked, explored, and resolved.

Even more significant from the standpoint of group analysis was a finding which resulted from the carefully tabulated impressions of two army psychiatrists with whom I was associated. It was disclosed that, although we agreed on certain characteristics among a few designated patients, the three of us were listing patient idiosyncrasies that were different. Each physician was evoking specific responses to his particular personality. The inescapable conclusion was that the character structure of an examiner provokes disparate responses in the same patient. When an analysand leaves a therapist and comes to me for treatment, I always try to determine the nature of his former transference. Not infrequently he will have seen his previous physician as one parent, and he will see me as another. It seems to me that this puts some limitation on the depth and completeness of the therapeutic process in individual analysis where the therapist may not elicit multiple transferences. If treatment constitutes primarily the analysis of transference, is it not wiser to place the patient in a group setting in which he can project father, mother, and siblings as well? Does the analyst with a single patient have the skill to analyze or evoke all the transference responses by which the patient is victimized? In group analysis the early precipitation and recognition of these multiple transferences is greatly facilitated by the presence of numbers of provocative familial figures in the persons of the various members.

But these and other deductions from army experimentation, even when they appear unique, are not at present our chief concern. First of all, as private practitioners who are actively engaged in assembling groups, each of us must choose members from his own limited panel of patients. Although group formation has its particular difficulties and has opened up a formidable area of research, certain conventions are being tested and established.

At present I subscribe to the formation of heterogeneous groups. They reflect a microcosmic society and, of course, tend to reproduce that much-abused institution—the family, which, since it probably ushered in the patient's neurosis, is the logical agency for checking it. Despite the fact that, at first, many patients do not cope successfully with dissimilar character structures, the battle is best won where it was apparently lost.

Perhaps it is misleading to state bluntly that groups should be heterogeneous, for in reality they must be balanced. This means that concessions must be made to homogeneity. Neurotic patients, who make up the bulk of all groups, must not be promiscuously thrown together. It is wise, for example, to assemble patients of approximately the same age. Older patients, invested with parental cloaks, become targets of neurotic attack. A very young patient elicits transferences that overprotect and immobilize him. More often than not transferences evoked by wide disparity in age can be effectively resolved. On the other hand, the presence of both sexes is advisable to incite and sharpen projection: paternal, maternal, and sibling.

In private practice I have always combined men and women in the same group. I have no experience in the group treatment of boys and girls. While in the army I organized groups composed exclusively of men, only because no women were available, and it turned out that heteropsychosexual problems were resolved with greater difficulty. The presence of both sexes enables each participant to project more readily maternal, paternal, and various sibling relationships out of the past onto various people in the group whose sex corresponds with that of earlier vital protective associates. Occasionally, of course, a male patient will evoke a feminine transference and vice versa. There is some reticence at first about exposing oneself freely before members of the opposite sex, but such resistances quickly melt away. On a social level it is better to mix the sexes in a group, because the resolution of problems on the heterosexual gregarious plane is a catalytic agent in the cure of neurotic difficulty. The exclusion of either sex from a group limits the area of struggle in which the patient must learn to recondition himself. The inclusion of both sexes presents the patient with masculine and feminine facades which represent parental and sibling surrogates. They also offer him flesh and blood people with whom he acquires the ability to make a sound social adjustment at the deepest levels. Since the neurotic personality is in greater or lesser conflict with one—sometimes both—of the sexes, the inclusion of men and women in the group offers the patient a foil for the study of neurotically projected reactions and provides insight into the contrast between his responses to both the male and female.

It has been my experience that in forming groups certain readily identifiable types are best excluded: psychopaths, who are always dangerous and potentially group-disrupting; alcoholics, who, it appears, can be more effectively treated together; morons, who retard group progress and tax their associates and the analyst himself to a painful extent; stutterers, who like alcoholics, are most effectively worked with in groups of their own kind; hallucinating psychotics, and hypermanic patients. Any of these, however, can be organized into a group suffering from their common difficulty. Patients with neurotic character disorders, psychosomatic disturbances, psychoneuroses, and ambulatory psychotics can, in general, be included. Individuals in the same relative age group, with similar cultural and intellectual backgrounds, of approximately like intelligence do better together. This is not to say that borderline cases of any type are inadmissible. Particularly, it shouldn't proscribe ambulatory schizophrenics, who have labile access to the meaning of symbolic thinking. Schizoids are amazingly helpful as adjunct analysts of fantasies, dreams, and the latent meaning of behavior in the group. Having access to the unconscious material comprising the unreal world in which they live, they can often clarify material that baffles everyone else. Every group might profitably include one or two well-chosen schizoid personalities.

THE SIZE OF THE GROUP

The size of the group is important. It should number eight or ten. With fewer than eight members there is often not enough interpersonal provocation and activity. This will lead to lulls or dead spots in spontaneous interreaction and lessen the effectiveness of the group procedure. However, with more than ten it is difficult for both patient and analyst to keep up with what is going on. An overly large group is especially bad for the patient's morale. He is likely to feel threatened and "lost" in such a setting; what little "security" he has had in his relationship to the analyst would disappear. Too large a group might, then, immediately produce immobility. Four or five men and an equivalent number of women make up a practical working group. In my experience ninety-minute sessions, meeting three times weekly are most effective.

CLOSED OR CONTINUOUS GROUPS

Groups are self-perpetuating. Although there is infrequent transplanting of patients the group never disbands entirely. Patients join and leave groups by permission of their members as well as that of the analyst. However, I shall discuss these points later in more detail.

RESISTANCE TO JOINING A GROUP

The attitude of the prospective member is of considerably more importance than such generalizations on group formation. If he does not already know it, the analyst soon discovers that the average person views with prompt alarm the mere suggestion that he affiliate himself with eight or nine unknown neurotic patients. For the purposes of this discussion we can assume that candidates for group membership fall into three classes: the resistant (the majority), the enthusiastic, and the curious or open-minded. The latter commonly approach group analysis with the healthiest attitude. In preliminary individual treatment the therapist must study and gradually break down particular resistance to joining a group. The enthusiastic may be variously motivated: from honest need for social contact to exhibitionism, voyeurism, and a search for foils for neurotic destructiveness directed toward the group. Whatever the motive, it emerges and is analyzed in the group setting.

Patients who resist entry into a group should not be pushed too hard. Their premature introduction may precipitate such anxiety or resistance that after one or two meetings they fail to return. It is wiser to inquire into and analyze their opposition beforehand. In time the majority express a willingness to give the group method a trial. Usually in the first visit I propose to the patient that at a mutually agreeable time he will join a group for further analysis.

Specifically, among the most frequently encountered objections to group affiliation are the following:

Patients shrink from what they regard as a mortifying invasion of their privacy. The idea of baring their motives and acts to strangers is so completely alien that I imagine forcing them into a nudist camp might be less abhorrent. Suspicion that their revelations might be circulated by the indiscreet augment their fears.

Certain patients want exclusive neurotic possession of the therapist. Alone with him they can relive and realize the repressed affect originally directed toward early familial figures; they will not willingly agree to share him with others.

To some the word "group" unconsciously connotes the original family, and they refuse to subject themselves once again to its trying influence. Their difficulties started years ago in a nightmarish family, and it is the epitome of a social constellation from which they once escaped. Why return to it?

Those to whom a friendly glance or an unfriendly word is devastating, who are shaken by the slightest sign of criticism, coolness, or warmth, who shun the give-and-take of social living, resist group analysis. Why, they reason, should one sacrifice the gentle, detached, earnest, and expert consideration of a private doctor for the blundering crudities and rough handling one would probably get in a group?

Some patients are unconsciously afraid that they will have to relinquish a secretly cherished neurotic trend which the analyst will allow but the group would not tolerate. They cling to the illusion that the therapist will permit them to retain this gratifying obsessive design; they may even hope that the analyst will augment the obsession.

Others will protest at transfering from individual to group treatment because they "will get only one tenth the attention." Although member contributions may not be as professionally sound as those of the analyst, they are so intuitively significant and increasingly valid analytically, that in a sense treatment is really multiplied by ten.

Some patients project such painful or terrifying masks onto other people that they cannot easily enter group analysis. Such individuals require a relatively long period of individual preparation. And after entering a group they have to be desensitized in stages by permitting them to enter and leave the group at frequent intervals. Usually they are able to remain for longer periods of time following each successive absence.

And finally, there are some patients who experience intolerable pangs of anxiety at the freedom with which sexual material is discussed in the group. They too must be more thoroughly prepared in individual sessions by the therapist. He must gradually and persistently probe for the affect-laden unconscious conflict whose emergence they prohibit. This should be executed so delicately that anxiety is not created. After a while the succeeding increments of insight enable patients to attend group sessions with less alarm.

The analyst must do his best to allay these and other fears. He assures the prospective group member that, initially, he is under no obligation to reveal embarrassing facts and that his privacy will, in any event, be held strictly inviolate. Group patients, he is told, know each other by their first names only. They function under a rigorous injunction of anonymity and discretion. Patients are warned against gossip with the threat of discharge from the group. While such admonition early in treatment guards against exposure outside the group, as time goes on, mutual regard and respect for the members' privacy play a major role in preserving ethical secrecy. The exclusion of psychopaths is a further guarantee that confidences will not be betrayed. The patient is always advised that, in the therapist's eleven years of group analytic experience, no member has been dropped for disclosing intimate group affairs.

For the patient who prefers to have the analyst to himself the therapist may have to clarify, in stages, the infantile demand for the possession of the isolated parent or sibling in the person of the analyst; the transferred rivalry with other group members for his exclusive attention and the necessity, at last, of sharing with other members of this "new family" in the group a more satisfying mutual devotion and affection. For those to whom the group unconsciously represents the traumatic original family, the therapist tries to create a most permissive atmosphere. He interrupts any early possibility of cumulative interpersonal hostility and if a clash is imminent, he intervenes gently, asking for ventilating and cathartic material like dreams, fantasies, personal difficulties, and even biographical data. He emphasizes the fact that all the members are present because, for some time earlier in their lives, they were not allowd to express their feelings; that if the group plays a prohibitive role now, it will only underscore old traumatic influences; that we must try to permit particular irrationality and not play a prohibiting role. In this manner the therapist attempts to influence each patient toward becoming an ally of the liberating, creative, expansive, and social forces in every other member and also an enemy of the repressive, destructive, contracting, and antisocial trends.

For those who fear emotional contact the therapist may have to spend considerable time in prior individual analysis building up rapport and using this tentative affective closeness as a bridge to the group. Some patients are so afraid of the possibility of a positive or negative transference to the therapist, which painfully evokes for them repressed incestuous conflict, that they try to run eagerly into group sessions after just a few individual interviews. All of this is done in the hope of damming back what appears to them to be dangerous, emerging trends. Such members try to "hide out" in the group and attempt to use the group to resist the uncovering of affect.

With regard to the supposed expertness of the therapist and the clumsiness and misguidance of the group, patients cannot be underestimated for their intuitive perception and adjunct analytic facility. The analyst must use these qualities to common advantage. The members should be made increasingly aware of their considerable usefulness to one another. They are inclined to overestimate the parental authority in the person of the therapist and to underestimate their own production. The analyst continuously rewards each participant for spontaneous and intuitive speculation and points out how very often such prospecting leads to deep insight. Furthermore, he does not permit crude blundering which might distress others. He plays a moderating role. Gradually, as patients are rewarded with insight and respect for one another's feelings, mutual regard for what each has to offer develops.

Sometimes the benevolence of the therapist in individual treatment permits the patient to cling compulsively and for too long to a treasured neurotic pattern. The group has less of this tolerance for illness. It more vigorously demands and usually gets a more rapid healthy response. When it puts too much pressure on a patient to abandon old forms for new, before he is able to relinquish them, the analyst must use his position to intercede in the patient's interest.

When a patient requests a description of the group he is about to join, its members are portrayed for him, as he has in turn been anonymously introduced to them. It is explained that the association may be regarded as tentative by either party. Some patients gain solace from the assurance that they may leave the group if they become overanxious or unduly disturbed while undergoing treatment. From time to time patients do drop out temporarily after a clash of transference and countertransference, but normally a few private interviews will recondition them for a return.

THE FIRST STAGE OF TREATMENT: PRELIMINARY INDIVIDUAL ANALYSIS

Several stages of treatment are outlined in the following sections. Except for the first, these stages all coexist in the analysis of the group. Any member may be at one stage when the rest of the group will be at others. While a number may be going through the stages concomitantly, any one individual passes through the consecutive stages at his own pace.

Following the initial interview the patient is usually referred to a clinical psychologist for Rorschach, Goodenough, and Thematic Apperception Tests, occasionally the Bellevue-Wechsler. Before introducing him to a group it is best to interview him alone for a period of time. For some, all that is required is a single consultation. The majority need ten to thirty individual preliminary visits. In rare cases a recalcitrant patient may require as many as a hundred. In this preparatory phase the therapist explores present difficulties, biographical material, dreams, present, recurrent, and former nightmares, gets an impression of the patient's day-to-day activities, and strives to prepare him for group analysis by explaining something of its theory and practice. The patient is told, as early as possible, that he is being groomed for group analysis. His fears and doubts are studied. There is, of course, an occasional patient who never manages to transfer to a group because of his insurmountable resistance or because his psychopathy makes him unfit for group treatment.

This preliminary work is important in that it enables the therapist to obtain an initial impression of the diagnosis and character structure of the patient. He also gains insight into some of the unconscious conflicting trends and resistances. The physician uses this individual study period to make the transition to the group less anxious, to put the patient at ease with him, to enable him to understand a patient's initially bizarre responses in the group, to compare single and multiple transference reactions, and to exclude psychopaths from group analysis. Every patient is informed that, if he becomes too anxious, disturbed, or panicky in the group, he has the freedom to leave it for a while and to return to individual treatment for as long as may be necessary. In general, however, patients are discouraged from exercising this right and encouraged to resolve their difficulties in the group milieu. In most instances one or two individual analytic sessions are sufficient to unravel the problem and dispel anxiety, whereupon the patient returns to the group. It has rarely been necessary to keep a member away from his group for more than two weeks.

Patients who have had prior analysis elsewhere and are somewhat familiar with dream analysis, resistance, free association, and transference phenomena, usually can enter a group early. The point at which a patient will enter a group is determined by his diminishing resistance and anxiety about joining one and the availability of a suitable opening in a group. The degree of reluctance to enter a group is often a direct measure of the patient's resistance. A readiness to engage in group activity is conversely though not necessarily a frequent indicator of lesser neuroticism.

In the first or second visit the therapist should discuss fees for both group and individual analysis. In the group extreme flexibility is possible and can be determined by the patient's ability to pay. If the therapist knows he does not have to carry a patient to completion in individual analysis, even the fee in this preliminary work can be reduced. In his wish to be quite democratic the writer advised his first group, in 1938, that he required a given fee for the time extended them and suggested that they decide on the basis of their respective incomes and obligations what each should pay to make up the whole sum. A period of endless wrangling followed this suggestion, and the members were finally unable to agree upon a sum suitable for each. At last they approached the therapist and asked him to set the rate for each participant. When he did, the haggling and disagreement became even more intense. Out of this experience I took away the lesson that it is unwise to allow any one patient to know what another pays. There are areas enough for potential neurotic rivalry without introducing this one. Since then I have arranged privately with each member for a fee which he can manage to pay and asked him not to discuss these matters with other patients. It is understood by all that payments vary, but as long as specific sums are not mentioned, no one feels himself more or less favored than another.

As a rule, there is, in a group, a gradual absorption and harmonizing of interests. On rare occasions a group fails to assimilate a member. He may become so truculent and disruptive that the group will vote him out, a privilege which must always be allowed the membership. If this were not the case, group harmony and procedure might be shattered. Such a patient may be impossibly aggressive or dominating. He may be hypermanic or make excessive demands for recognition. He may command focal attention by masochistic or semisuicidal gestures which unbalance orderly consideration of the needs of each. A sadistic or psychopathic bent in one patient may tend to immobilize the larger body, hence forcing it to eliminate his pernicious influence. A person of this sort should return to private analysis for a period, to be reintroduced to his group, if it is willing.

If not, he may enter another group. I have had two patients who did not recover until they were assimilated by their third group. While it is true that rejection by a group is traumatic, it is at the same time also therapeutic. For the patient discovers the provocative trends in his personality which make him socially objectionable. He is then able to struggle at a new level of adjustment, in succeeding groups, to modify his personality in order to be accepted in the new milieu. If he should be discouraged and embittered at being put aside, the therapist should return him to individual treatment for a period long enough to reassure him and build up his morale. The therapist should work with him all the while to analyze those elements in his character which led to his being cast out. In this way a second rejection by the next group can be forestalled.

THE FIRST MEETINGS OF THE GROUP

When eight or ten patients have been prepared by individual analysis for entry into a group, the therapist schedules an opening meeting. They have all been asked to reveal only their first names, partly to preserve anonymity and partly to create an easy atmosphere of informality. Before the session begins they assemble in a waiting room, introduce themselves, and invariably converse. Spared inhibiting formalities, they almost always enter their first meeting chatting, more or less relaxed, and wondering what happens next. An occasional patient will deliberately come too late in order to avoid what he may envisage as an awkward or stuffy preliminary, but normally the group can be relied upon to break the ice adequately in its own way.

The therapist does what he can to prolong the informality. When the meeting opens, he seats his patients in a circle which he has joined himself and outlines procedure. No activity is urged upon anyone during the first two or three meetings. This enables the therapist to utilize this time to describe group analytic theory and technic. And it gives the patients a chance to relax in the knowledge that they will not immediately be called upon to participate. They also take this time to appraise one another secretly in sidelong glances. A third or fourth session may be spent in answering patients' questions with regard to details of procedure that are still unclear to them. The therapist assures them that, without permission, he will not expose a specific historical event disclosed to him in confidence during prior individual sessions. He insists, however, on his right to introduce, as often as necessary, the underlying psychodynamics which led to this particular historical event, so long as the psychic process is identifiable as resistance or transference.

In the exposition of the theory and practice of group analysis, the therapist would do well to sound a note of warning with regard to sudden infatuations and their potential involvements. Not that patients will all act out their incestuous wishes, but the record suggests that some of them indubitably will. The fact that the analyst knows that neither advice nor edict will rule out seductions should not prevent him from trying to keep group relations as uncomplicated as possible. The analyst neither forbids nor encourages sexual intimacy within the group. Were he categorically to deny sexual freedom to the group he would duplicate the parents' castrating role. If he gave his assent to it he would obscure transference phenomena which must be worked through before such a relationship is freed of destructive neurotic elements. Here, as elsewhere, he cautions against neurotic ties, sexual or otherwise, which obscure the full significance and realization of what should become a healthy relationship.

Each patient is warned that if he exposes mutual confidences heard within the group to outsiders, he will be dropped from treatment. Strict anonymity must be preserved in the unavoidable discussion that takes place between patients and friends and relatives. At first the therapist's warning and the fear of being dropped operate to prevent petty gossip. Later, with the development of general positive transferences, followed by genuine mutual regard, a wholesome *esprit de corps* and respect for the group's privacy preserve secrecy.

THE SECOND STAGE OF TREATMENT: RAPPORT THROUGH DREAMS AND FANTASIES

At the first session in which there is active participation, patients are requested to recount a recent dream, a recurrent dream, or an old nightmare. They are asked to free-associate around the dream content and finally to speculate about and interpret the dream—as a group. If a dream is not recalled, some peripheral aspect of their problems may be presented if they feel so inclined. In lieu of dreams the therapist encourages the group to present fantasies, reveries, and daydreams. He asks members to avoid censorship of fanciful speculation about one another's productions. In this fashion personalities inevitably begin to emerge. In succeeding visits the therapist concentrates on developing mutual rapport. He can accomplish this best by his own spirit of warmth and optimism; by not advocating too deep interpersonal or spontaneous interreaction of an aggressive or hostile nature prematurely; by a sympathetic, permissive attitude toward each patient's ventilating his frustrating problems, dreams, and aspirations.

The therapist will find that certain patients are catalytic agents, whose behavior stimulates the group in early meetings when natural reticence might keep it in check. It will be practical to include one or more such individuals in every group to insure its activity. The healthiest of these are patients who simply wish to do constructive work and get on with the process of mutual discovery and wholesome interrelatedness. Many others, however, are neurotically motivated in the way they spark the group. Nevertheless, the therapist can employ this activity to constructive ends. Concomitantly he can expose gradually for group study the neurotic character of the forces that impel them to participate. Among these helpful provocateurs are exhibitionistic persons, who do not hesitate, subtly or otherwise, to boast of their exceptional attributes and accomplishments, exposing themselves and arousing group responses in the process. Some elicit reactions by conscious or unconscious seductive objectives; by making covert allusions to their sexual prowess or libertinism. Others are so insecure, in such need of general approval, so fearful of the slightest criticism, that they repeatedly paint rosy self-portraits which elicit ever more penetrating group inquiry. Then there are chronically anxious patients who cannot endure a painful silent hiatus and feel, therefore, impelled to speak up in a quiet period. Even habitually detached individuals are conflictful with regard to being outsiders and in order to gain a feeling of belonging or to get their share of attention sometimes project themselves desperately into the group with an articulate now-or-never attitude. Still other types of catalytic agents are compulsive organizers, who are unable to tolerate any wasteful or chaotic waiting and make meticulous reports on themselves. Or, obedient to the therapist's request and under his protection, they follow his prescription and give detailed, relatively uncensored reactions. There is also a kind of compulsive sociability, superficial and dissembling as it is, which impels them nevertheless to grope formally for contact with the group. Even patients with somewhat psychopathic trends may provoke constructively participant group reactions. While such members may try anarchistically to exploit the group in order to express their irresponsibility, lack of discipline, and moral laxity, such behavior tends to evoke vivid responses and solidify group feeling in defense against it. Patients who chronically feel misused often carry their triggered fear into meetings at which they feel they must get their money's worth out of every session. They are driven to participate and project themselves into the work, anxious that not a moment be wasted. Hypomanics are obviously stimulant. And the schizoid facility with unconscious material has already been mentioned. The group analyst must be mindful of the latent catalytic potential resident in each patient, and endeavor to draw it out if it will serve some constructive purpose.

The astute analyst will look for or make opportunities to take advantage of such provocative trends to fashion an effective social unit of the group. Despite these maneuvers there are always several removed persons who are ill at ease, who look askance at group membership from the beginning, who sit tight-lipped until they are provoked into participation by some extraordinary act. One of the most successful ways of spearheading a drive on these isolated individuals is to urge them to tell a recent dream. This is an indirect approach which engages the unwary. A patient is less resistive to reporting dream material, of whose content he is unaware since it is "safely" obscured in symbolic forms. It is easier for him to tell what he believes may be less directly revealing than to admit publicly to his psychic impotence, his perverse sexual pleasures, or overt homosexuality. When reports of dreams are followed by reactive and interpretive comment, interreactive responses are inevitably forthcoming. By extension of this same process, the analyst invites accounts of fantasies and daydreams which are subjected to similar study.

All else failing to engage a patient, the therapist may ask for brief outlines of personal problems. This should come as a last resort, since it duplicates what has taken place in previous individual sessions and is commonly a resistive device employed to evade unconscious material. With notable exceptions most patients are prone to recite their current difficulties and case histories, and it is just this penchant that successful group treatment discourages. However, as an early meeting primer it may be justified.

Any of the above devices will contribute to the unending process of identifying emerging personalities. The therapist's permissive attitude toward the emergence of unconscious material infects the group. It becomes for each patient the new permissive family, whose tolerance and understanding fosters the essential development of generalized positive transference, group cohesion, solidarity, and morale. With the recessive role of the old, original family diminished, the enfranchised patient makes the exhilarating discovery that in joining a communal group he has, at the same time, added to his own freedom and stature.

Members are advised in prior individual sessions that group meetings will take place three times a week lasting one and one half hours per session. After a dozen or more sessions with the therapist have acquainted group members with methods and procedure, they supplement their three regular meetings with two or three weekly sessions at which he is not present. These alternate meetings are held at the homes of two or three patients who are centrally located and have no objection to their last names being known. After twelve to twenty-four meetings there is sufficient rapport to find such willing members. On occasion, sessions are organized outdoors or under similar acceptable auspices. Sponsored by various patients, they add materially to a friendly, sympathetic atmosphere in which uninhibited participation is vastly stimulated. Attitudes toward the therapist are ventilated at alternate sessions and subsequently brought into meetings at which he is present. These sessions precipitate the early emergence of transference attitudes toward the therapist, and thus shorten the duration of treatment. The unprohibitive atmosphere of meetings in the absence of the analyst stirs the deepest sort of reactions to him. These responses are introduced inadvertently or quite consciously at sessions the therapist attends.

Alternate meetings activate those who are reserved when the therapist is present. The shy become bolder, and the deviously aggressive exploit the opportunity to criticize. It is always illuminating to note the group's reactions when a member stays away. In his absence he gets an eloquent appraisal. When the absentee is the therapist, the otherwise guarded patient is often unreservedly outspoken. With this in mind, the therapist encourages fanciful speculation and ventilation about himself or any member absent from an alternate meeting. This too accelerates treatment by forcing more basic affect and transference attitudes into the open at an early date. During these meetings the patient expresses both rational and irrational attitudes toward the analyst. The majority of these estimates would certainly be blocked by the projected domination of the therapist in regular sessions.

There is no unanimous agreement on the analyst and his abilities at alternate meetings. Some think he is dull; others, domineering. He may represent the reincarnation of an old, repressive parental image, and the members may join forces to unseat him. The process of taking him to pieces is cathartic and liberating. The insight that follows from such an experience, which is brought into later regular sessions, proves to be invaluable. For self-destructive restraint in the presence of the therapist is a neurotic admission of the latter's overwhelming power. It is simultaneously a confession by the patient that the illusion of transference is a reality for him. On the other hand there are patients who stoutly defend the analyst, endowing him with exceptional capacities. As one would expect, however, he is invested with multiple qualities by all patients, reflecting the character structures of both parents.

How does the analyst know what has been said of him? Inevitably in later meetings, the group members always divulge such matters, whether consciously or not. The patients' reactions to these violations of implied confidence is one of anxiety followed by obvious relief when the doctor not only is not annoyed on hearing them, but rather welcomes critical and aggressive reactions to him. Later on he points out their transference character—in the main—and invites further development while he is present.

Let us examine one instance in which a young woman's hostility at an alternate session was encouraged and brought into a regular one. In the therapist's absence the group had discussed him. She felt he was too smug and self-complacent. Her forwardness in criticizing him led to the development of two camps. One was very critical; the other, overly defensive. Her leading the pack in depreciation of the analyst was accidentally exposed, but with unconscious intention, by another patient at a regular meeting in the therapist's presence. His persistent friendliness and warmth enabled her gradually to express fully enormous stores of resentment without fear of counterattack. The permissive atmosphere of an alternate meeting allowed for the eruption of wells of aggression which was then shunted into a regular session. There the analyst welcomed affect which she might otherwise have feared to express. By sponsoring her repressed animosity every facet of it emerged, so that it could be subjected to analytic study. The analyst knew from her dream material and previous individual treatment of her early erotic interest in a brother. He knew also of her having been sharply checked in this and other affective impulses by maternal authority for many years. He knew, he said, how hazed and rejected she must have felt under such discipline. Although he was more tolerant than her "hateful" mother, he suggested that he might similarly epitomize a kind of pressure which was infuriating to her. He proposed that she was transferring the bitterness which she felt earlier for her mother to him. While for some time she continued to make irrelevantly hostile comments about him, she eventually saw their repetitive and compulsive character and, finally, managed to erase the mother image from the face of the analyst. Countless similar neurotic attitudes toward the physician, which, if restricted to regular group sessions, might be submerged for weeks, are often first uncovered in the less inhibited atmosphere of alternate meetings.

These matters of procedure, although important, are all ancillary to a fundamental in the group analytic process: the interpretation of dreams, which continues through all stages of treatment. Dreams are continually discussed because they reveal essential unconscious data so reliably and with such demonstrative and liberating effect. The analyst asks for them in detail. He is particularly interested in dreams which involve other members of the group. Patients are requested to associate freely on one another's dreams in order to develop intuitive interplay at the deepest levels. Dreams including other patients occur with surprising frequency and arouse the keenest sort of attention. The whole group becomes engrossed in dream analysis with its attendant associations, catharsis, sense of liberation and mutuality, all of which contribute toward the group unity, which is so important in the first stages of treatment. Patients who have difficulty in remembering dreams are urged to give their fancies free play and to bring in uncensored reveries and daydreams about one another. These often prove to be as useful as dreams themselves. From the outset the analyst attempts to engage the patients in intuitive and imaginative comment on this unconscious material. It is always impressive how a group of untrained people, in an unprohibited setting, by spontaneous but somehow involuntary perceptive study of dreams, tend to exhaust their significant possibilities. Only occasionally does the therapist have to introduce a guiding hand.

Where the patients fall short of the mark, they study the analyst's interpretation of dreams. And by increments of cross association among group members about successive dream material, they become expert in translating it. Knotty symbolism or excessively vague latent content is sometimes left to the hands of the therapist. Even here he will sometimes be at a loss, and find himself obliged to a schizoid, intuitive, or otherwise discerning patient for the unraveling of certain aspects of a dream. The fact that the analyst fails at times where a patient succeeds has its therapeutic value. It is a corrective to a patient's predisposition to regard the therapist as an omniscient parent. It puts the patient on the level of an equal co-worker whose inner resourcefulness and creative powers are so highly regarded as to give him increasing self-assurance. The therapist tries not to leave dream analysis in the hands of a few experts. He encourages the less venturesome to take experimental steps in seeking for inner meanings. He urges them to engage their unexercised natural resources and attempts to stimulate initiative where there seems to be very little. In this way he also equalizes the work. To this end he contends that it does not matter that a reactive interpretation is far wide of the mark. It is important only that it be a spontaneous, unconsidered, and affective response. With these qualities it will throw light on the speaker's problems, though it may be of little direct use in clarifying the immediate issue. Through this reciprocal examination of their dreams patients develop insight into their mutual aberrations. This is a first step toward their disposal.

A patient's dreams are of paramount importance as a guide to the progress he is making. Neurotic conflict is continually reflected in them, and no patient should be allowed to leave his group permanently until his dreams certify to his increasing normality. For the restless or resistive member who would flee the group under the guise of an apparent recovery, it is always rewarding to ask for last night's dream. It can be used, if need be, to illustrate for the patient, just where his unconscious says he stands, and thus frequently forestall his premature escape from treatment. Conversely, for a dejected, despairing patient, the therapist can often find suggestions of healthy, unconscious struggle in a dream that will raise his hopes considerably and give him justification for continuing with renewed effort.

THE THIRD STAGE OF TREATMENT: INTERREACTION THROUGH INTERPERSONAL FREE ASSOCIATION

If good group rapport has developed out of the permissive atmosphere fostered by the expression of dreams, fantasies, and critical problems, the second stage of group analysis has been accomplished. The therapist can then lead the group into a following third phase of treatment: a period in which each patient free-associates about the next. In this stage of therapy the spontaneously interreactive process still makes good use of dreams and reveries. But more attention is given to this new procedure. It is controlled by limiting it to the expression of spontaneous, uncensored speculation about other members of the group. Moreover, to admit of wide group participation, a flexible time limit is usually imposed on each person associating.

Patients and therapist alike commonly refer to the procedure in which each member takes a turn at free-associating about the next as "going around." Out of this technic, which elicits the most electric kind of unpremeditated interreaction, a number of psychodynamic processes emerge. Patients are asked to be alert to these trends and to assist one another and the therapist in identifying them. In a sense they are asked to become adjunct analysts. This suggestion arouses their curiosity and alerts them for mutual examination. By making them active participants on a level with the therapist it provides them with reassuring status. It is suggested that, if a patient will say whatever comes into his head about another, he will intuitively penetrate a resistive facade and identify underlying attitudes. In the group we call this "ringing a bell," "hitting a target," "touché." Patients under examination are urged to admit freely to the striking of an inner target. This is partly to establish their basic identity and partly to reward the associator. Every neurotic so sadly underestimates his real potential that he needs to be told every time he puts his finger on something valid. Furthermore, he is usually so guarded about his spontaneity, so reservedly unspeculative and compulsively perfectionistic that rewards for unpremeditated accuracy having social value are of the utmost therapeutic benefit.

A patient is requested by the therapist to acknowledge the penetration of a facade if he feels something especially perceptive has been said of him. For the most part, he will admit to such penetration, and his affirmation is used immediately by all parties as a basis for further exploration. He may, however, resist insight or showing evidence of touché. In spite of his resistance, his unconscious will not usually be denied. And evidence of a bell's having been rung will present itself in a dream, a nightmare, a slip of the tongue, halting speech, a psychosomatic symptom, or some other irrational, affective constellation. With continuous piercing of the shell of resistance under the group's concerted, freely associated bombardment, the inner character structure and full identity of each patient gradually emerges. In fact both the patient under examination and the associator benefit. The member under scrutiny profits from the insight offered him. The speaker is applauded for his intuitive perception. Up to this point his resources have been minimized or crushed and his capacity to make a socially valuable contribution belittled by others and himself. Accordingly, with praise for his spontaneously productive accuracy, earlier feelings of inadequacy give way to a consciousness of his growing strength. The average patient is extremely wary of his unpremeditated reactions. He likes to review and polish his comments to make them unassailable. He strives for faultless performance in a compulsive fashion, because he feels so inadequate or because he dreads the expression of unrestrained affect which may invite counterattack or castration. An extremist in self-depreciation, he underrates whatever comes naturally. If called upon to speak impromptu, he may stammer and break down ignominiously. When he does talk, he is inclined to applaud other speakers, especially the therapist, whose pronouncements he accepts as ex cathedra. The pragmatic give-and-take of group intercourse is a healthy, demanding reality he resistively withstands. But the assaults made on his defenses by group associations and the rewards that follow his initial impulsive expression pave the way for his liberation from neurotic restraint.

The following is an illustration of how at an early meeting of a group, the naïve free association of one patient about another penetrated resistance and provoked a dream which elaborated deep, vital material. Patient B., a young woman, had been treated in individual analysis for three years by a therapist who had ignored her sexual problems. After she joined a group, J., a fellow member, commented in free association about her: "You're awfully tense and tight and ill at ease. You remind me of an overwound watch spring. I'm afraid you'll suddenly uncoil and snap at me. You seem so bound up, you remind me of an armed fortress with loaded cannon pouring over the parapets, ready to fire. I get the feeling you're unconsciously afraid of being raped." B. hotly resented this characterization, but at the following session she told of a dream which had been prompted by J.'s reactions. The setting of the dream was years earlier, and she was a little girl at home. Suddenly the sinister figure of her father was before her, and as she ran from him he tore off her dress. In stark terror, she leaned from a window, and there below her she recognized her previous therapist. She cried out to him for help, but nothing she did could attract his attention. On that frantic note the dream ended. The dream, instigated by J.'s intuition, had brought to the surface a significant, unconsciously obsessional fear of, and concomitant wish for, sexual aggression from the father. Her earlier analysis had left this underlying trend untouched and submerged. At this and succeeding sessions the deeper intricacies of her early erotic interest in and fear of her father were elaborated. It is interesting to note, however, that an untutored patient can uncover highly valuable repressed data which more expert hands sometimes fail to bring to the surface. Such an experience is eloquent testimony to the intuitive, adjunct analytic potential in every patient aroused in the course of "going around."

An inevitable by-product of the "going around" technic in free association is the penetration of facades to reveal each member's inner, conflictful trends thereby establishing his whole identity and character structure. Out of this procedure each patient's position becomes clearly delineated. He comes to know just where he stands in the eyes of his fellows and why. This does not proceed in any superficial way, but elicits reactions at the deepest levels. He learns which characteristics please the group and which disturb them. His discovery of just what his real status is in relation to others is reassuring, for down deep he is always apprehensive that he will be less welcome than he turns out, in fact, to be. He is given added security, because he discovers just what he is and develops a complete sense of self, an identity which affects others. He learns to modify this newly recognized self so that it functions with increasing harmony in the group.

An illustration of this group-imposed status and its consequences occurred recently in a group where a schizophrenic had been enrolled. Since we had discussed her before her appearance as a member, the group was not unprepared for her idiosyncrasies. But the members felt obliged to handle her delicately for fear of further traumatizing her. They withheld reactions that would have been expressed with any other neurotic patient. At her first meeting she lay on the floor instead of sitting in the circle with the rest of us, and as the session progressed, she ran a whole gamut of abnormal actions—all of which the group seemed indulgently to ignore. In later meetings she bickered persistently and irrationally with everyone, again with apparent tolerance from the group. One evening a man against whom she had railed with unusual bitterness voiced the pent-up anger of the group in a sharp retort which ended in a vigorous criticism of her. The effect was extraordinary. While she gave evidence of resentment of his censure, she admitted at the same time that his observations had a certain logic and validity. With surprising clarity and self-control she surveyed the group and replied to the irate member who had attacked her. "At last," she told him, "you are being honest with me. Now, thank God, I know where I stand in the group." By expressing his deeply felt affective response the man had finally come alive for her; he was no longer (as was the entire group) evasively protective. Her realistic response was so gratifying to the group that she was thereafter quickly absorbed as a full member toward whom each participant could fully react. This one man's explosion against her acted as a release for the other members. They no longer resented her, because she did not force them into overprotective, inhibited roles which denied them mutual freedom.

Unfettered expressions of feeling are one concomitant of the new permissive family that the group comes to represent for each patient. As members learn that it is safe both to give and accept spontaneous emotion, they realize that something formerly denied them in the old family has been added—tolerance. In this kind of atmosphere it becomes stimulating to plumb the causes of frustration and, communicating in a language that is dynamic, to liberate and develop resources temporarily stunted by earlier familial influence.

The naturally cautious therapist may legitimately ask: Is the average precariously balanced patient safe in the clumsy hands of schizoid and neurotically aggressive patients who may expose unconscious drives too swiftly or attack too cruelly the weak and defenseless? In the group's concerted attack on the neurotic character structure, will it not be too rapidly shattered, leaving the patient dangerously insecure and with such weak ego reserves that he may be forced into psychosis? It is certainly true that the atmosphere is sometimes charged and subject to the most explosive kind of interreaction. Will these intense situations become traumatic? The answer to this question is, indeed, reassuring. Nothing really inimical to the patient's interest ensues. If a member seems to be growing unduly anxious or overwhelmed, the analyst can return him to individual treatment for a short period. Patients are fortified against destructive attack by constant coaching from the therapist. They are cautioned to make the neat distinction between the valid and the neurotic in what is directed at them. When a member invests others with qualities they do not possess—when he projects—the therapist exposes his irrelevant and irrational distortions of reality as unreal. The patients themselves become adept at elaborating these enlightening differences between fact and fiction in every remark. Pained though a dissected member may feel, if the appraisal of him is unjust, he is usually so well fortified by well-disposed group opinion that his ego survives it substantially intact. As he progresses in treatment and learns to appreciate the neurotic character of aspects of ill-considered judgments of him, he develops an increasing immunity to them. If he had been wary of his own aggression, he learns to flail out where provocation invites it. But he educates himself best by extracting from neurotically tinged projection onto him that kernel of information which is useful to him as insight. The patient who is the target of free association learns why and in what ways he gladdens or irritates the group. He discovers his provocative role. He may have, up to now, always regarded himself as the victim of other people's aggression and cruelty or wondered why people fled him in distress. When they tell him face to face just how he provokes them, he develops acute insight into the way he evokes the environmental responses that in turn startle him. With an awareness of his provocative traits, both he and the group are impelled to search for the unconscious motives which arouse critical reactions in the others. Crass and unflattering as some judgment of him may be, it is always associated with an essential sympathy and friendliness from the majority of the group.

In the demonstration of a patient's provocative role the group is a natural and effective agent. In individual analysis the therapist is hardly so responsive as to clarify the patient's stimulating conduct with the same completeness as the group. The various members are each so sensitized by their particular neurotic constellations that they can more accurately discern and point up each participant's exciting peculiarities. Under individual treatment patients are impelled to review historical and present abuse at the hands of others. And the probing, sympathetic analyst is occasionally misled by the patient's complaints, unless he sees him in the animating current of the group. This has been proven to me many times after introducing a member to a group following a preliminary period of private treatment. In the social setting he often seems a quite different person.

The presence of others elicits so many diverse facets of his personality that he is barely recognizable. In this regard, it is instructive to introduce a new patient following the recovery and discharge of an old one. Almost everyone shows a new aspect of himself, hitherto unseen, in response to the character structure of the newcomer.

Let us briefly review the third stage of group analysis. In this period the therapist urges patients to regard themselves not merely as passive recipients of insight provided by the physician, but to become adjunct analysts by actively pursuing their uncensored speculation about one another. This approach encourages them to respect their unpremeditated fantasies, expands their resources, and gives them a feeling of reassurance. The technic consists primarily in asking each patient in turn to say whatever comes into his mind unchecked, concerning every other patient as well as the analyst. The group is encouraged to allow members the most fantastic kind of speculation. In the course of this free association directed toward each patient, all are called upon to look for what is said that penetrates the facade of each and reveals some deep, unconscious character trend in the personality. This gives the individual under examination a startling sense of self-understanding. To facilitate the process a given patient under scrutiny is expected to announce to the group the fact that inner psychic targets have been struck. Each member becomes less and less guarded in the technic of free association and develops a remarkable intuitive ability to discern underlying currents of affective psychic activity. While each is relatively resistive to discarding his own barricades against the emergence of inner trends, the uncontrolled fantasies of others pierce the hard shell of self-concealment with greater facility. Every participant acquires a core of insight and an identity for himself and the others which establishes his personality and position in the group. The groping of each speaker to identify the hidden character structure of his neighbor is a process that slowly outlines the basic personality by increments of ventured thrusts or flyers beneath the surface of the outer self. The character structure of each does not emerge clearly only through the addition of growing detail by each speculator. In the searching process every participant in turn subtly modifies the canvas, so that finally a realistic portrait is achieved.

THE FOURTH STAGE OF TREATMENT: THE ANALYSIS OF RESISTANCE

In the fourth period of group analysis, as patients continue to free-associate about one another, their resistances emerge with increasing clarity. In this stage these defenses are discovered, studied, delineated, and the forces that support them are examined. Finally, each member is offered increasing evidence of mutual regard and security, in an attempt to break down these defenses. Resistance manifests itself in the myriad forms encountered in individual analysis. But the group setting provides a special environment that lends itself to the elaboration of resistive forms peculiar to it.

For the patient "in love with" the therapist, transfer to the group is enlightening. She is soon as emotionally attached to another group member as she was to the analyst. Her "unfaithfulness," the rapidity and completeness with which she moves from one man to another, confronts her with the irrational and compulsive character of her behavior. The nature of her activity becomes obvious to her as transference. For the patient rigidly blocked in neurotic interest in the analyst, who insists she is truly in love with him and that she would be neurosis-free if only the therapist would return her genuine feeling, the group experience quickly dispels the illusion. There, if she does not transfer her affective claim to another patient, she is forced to examine her feelings more deeply in the face of similar resistance and transference on the part of other members. Their falsification of reality makes its impression upon her. In most cases, she is brought face to face with the "infidelity" that impels her to exchange the analyst for a patient and is obliged to plumb earlier emotional attachments. She then discovers the neurotic resistance implicit in every such episode.

Another manifestation of resistance is the compulsive missionary spirit. Here the provider persists in looking after group members in a supportive, parental way, using this device subtly to dominate and attack the other members and to repress more basic feeling. The group always resents this false charity and demands and evokes more spontaneous participation by rewarding the messianic for unguarded slips of feeling and by rejecting dogmatic helpfulness. This does not imply, of course, that warm and impulsive offers of assistance are rejected. The contrary is true. As long as supportiveness is not compulsive, but unpremeditatedly sympathetic, it is welcomed as a sign of good health. An interesting example of this kind of resistance is provided in the following case. In one group a professional teacher habitually preached to his fellow analysands until their hostility bordered on the explosive. Later he reported that during intercourse, sometimes an hour passed before his sexual partner had an orgasm. To him, the sexual act, like his compulsive stewardship in the group, was a gesture of generosity. The other patients encouraged him to be less providing and to strive to enjoy his wife's allure with more spontaneity and pleasure for himself. At the next session he reported an ejaculation within three minutes with a corresponding simultaneous orgasm from his partner. The group conjectured that his earlier largesse concealed unconscious hostility to which his wife had been responding with equal frigidity. They also suggested that his benevolent preachments and ostensible advice contained the same kind of irritating and unprovoked aggression. He was urged in this situation as well to abandon his compulsive role for one that was more spontaneous and acceptable. After some time he became aware that his specious charity was a form of resistance preventing the development of real feeling. Variants of this theme appear in the self-appointed do-gooder, in the overprotective, typical "mom" in the group. It is also eminently displayed in the "mother is always right" dogma.

Some patients "go blank" when asked to free-associate about others in the group. If they are blocked in this way, they are urged to compose fantasies about everyone in the group just before going to sleep at night. They are asked to "go around" the group in the safety of this isolation, and then to bring these speculations into regular meetings. Away from the inhibiting presence of other members, associative paralysis gives way to lively flights of fancy. The therapist asks such persons to visualize each member of the group, including the therapist, and to project them into the most imaginative and extravagant conduct he can. These inventive productions are then reproduced for the group, where they stimulate provocative discussion in the same way as dreams. By cultivating this technic assiduously, patients manage to break down this particular kind of resistance and react freely in the moment without the preparatory homework. However, all patients are requested to review for the group such dreamy thought which comes to them before going to sleep. For at this time much repressed and preconscious delayed reactions well into consciousness.

Voyeurism is resistance that is unique to group analysis. Some patients try to escape personal examination and engagement by taking grandstand seats which give them a gratifying view of what may be the equivalent of the primal scene or its lesser familial counterparts. They seem willing and even eager to allow others full interreaction, while they assign to themselves a tremulous watchfulness. Instead of engaging in the social intercourse of the group, they peer at it from a distance. But looking can be a sort of prelude to participation. The group tolerates no nonparticipants. It engages the voyeur by its welcoming self-exposure. It moves him by inviting and provoking him to become involved in the warm emotional life of the new family. His resistance begins to melt when the sideshow to which he was drawn by dubious surreptitious motives becomes a wholesome drama in which he is impelled to take a legitimate part. Projected aggression gives way to a recognition of reality, and he is prepared to act in concert with this unforbidding environment. In this fashion, voyeuristic resistance develops from an end in itself to a first step toward a normally complete relationship.

Hiding oneself behind the analysis of others is a common form of resistance in group analysis. The group may provide a convenient setting for the exercise of this specific kind of resistance. It is characterized by a concentration on the neurotic behavior of other patients and accompanied by an evasion of analysis directed toward oneself. Such a patient cleverly shifts attention from himself to the associator, in order to defend himself against disturbing examination. If he is adept in this technic, he will, when threatened by an observation that might become alarmingly penetrating, neatly parry the proffered insight. He manages to redirect the group's attention to any individual who dares to analyze him. He handles what is said of him, for example, by remarking that his critic had an interesting overtone in speech that he ought to examine. By endless devices he deflects what could add up to deeper self-understanding and immediately tackles his examiner. He parries every remark which to him is a dangerous thrust. Sometimes he produces brilliant, if compulsive, analyses in his own defense. Usually his technics are so able as not to be easily broken down under critical attack. However, the group gradually dissolves his resistance by expressing its gratitude for his incisiveness and by simultaneously demonstrating to him that behind his emphatic lecturing he makes himself inaccessible, in terror of humiliation, to the helping hands of the group. It is pointed out that fear of castration or its equivalent by the parental substitutes in the group is forcing him into this compulsive role. To the extent that the members understand the frantic insecurity that underlies his bravado, they extend a reassuring friendliness that enables him to relinquish his insistent critical study of others for self-examination. The maintenance of a compulsive complacency which regards the other patients as neurotic inferiors cannot withstand such an approach from the associated members. Their understanding enables them to become friendly enough to help him to give up his program of evasion.

The use of history as resistance deserves special comment. There is probably nothing in individual treatment more uselessly time-consuming and basically harmful to both patient and analyst than the practice of rehearsing the patient's past. Long irrelevant biographies, usually distorted by the narrator, can be a form of continual evasion. Even a recital of yesterday's events can assume this character. In its most unsatisfactory form the relationship between patient and doctor may be reduced to a day-by-day report of frustration which demands nonanalytic advice on ways of circumventing it. This insistence on guidance instead of therapeutically valuable interreaction is also used as resistance. The refusal to face the present with one's own reactive emotional and mental processes cannot withstand the impact of group stimulation. Talk of what happened in childhood and even accounts of last night's dream become vicarious and pallid when compared to the dynamic interpersonal outbursts pronounced by a suddenly articulate contact. Such dramatic provocation cannot be resisted by escape into the day before yesterday. Of course, I do not mean that we regard history as unimportant. On the contrary, it is of the utmost importance. History has the greatest significance when evoked and recalled by the discovery and analysis of resistance and transference in the moment of their occurrence—that is, when history has a bearing on the present which is meaningful to both the patient and the therapist. The present neurotic behavior is envisioned as a photograph of the *significant* past. Careful scrutiny of the immediate moment will recall pertinent traumatic events. Personal flashbacks may be vividly illuminating, and the exploration and understanding of the past in terms of its influence on the present is essential to the creation of a wholesome present and future. But allowing a patient to indulge these proclivities is encouraging him in resistive subterfuge, his attempt to escape the resolution of similar conflict in the present.

Some patients, perhaps a majority of them during the early stages of treatment, discuss sexual material with patent reluctance. This is a kind of diffidence I try to dispel at once. Slighting or repressing sexual data reproduces the prohibitive role of the original family. Unless the patient frees his own sexuality he cannot make an adequate recovery. Access to sexual material is obtained partly by intuitive free association in "going around," which is described above. Once the initial resistances are broken down in this process, there is usually little difficulty in getting patients to discuss this fundamental matter.

In the preliminary discussion of theory and technic I emphasize the intimate relation between abnormal social behavior and abnormal sexual behavior, pointing out their common psychodynamic substructure. Access to sexual material is obtained by illustrating how every variety of interpersonal conduct that appears in the group must have its sexual counterpart, perhaps as yet unseen. Since the average patient is wary, at first, of revealing his sexual predicament, and since he is hardly aware either of its extent or complexity, group members are urged, early in analysis, to examine the interplay of their personalities on the social level. Then I begin to suggest that for each of the character traits revealed by cross association there is a sexual analogue. Wherever an opportunity is presented to point out this relationship, I do so. My own ease in taking the parallel for granted, without criticism, tends to infect the group with a like tolerance for otherwise socially prohibited intimacy. I indicate that a manifestation of social impotence implies the existence of a corresponding sexual impotence; that they are both signs of a similar problem in the analysand's character structure. Similarly, for example, excessive attitudes of male supremacy suggest a corresponding compulsive sexual excess, organized to conceal deep-rooted castration anxiety. A statuesque poise on the social level is probably accompanied by some form of sexual frigidity. Thus, by schooling the group in the effort to uncover the usually concealed existence of these sexual correspondents of social forms, the members make numerous accurate guesses about hidden sexual data. Exposed in this fashion and by intuition, one after another uncovers the whole sexual material. In the light of this relationship, nuances in curious social conduct are clarified in turn. One exposure excites release in others, until in a surprisingly short time, the cautious lose their caution and proceed to unburden themselves of the most intimate detail. Melting resistance in this way yields a sharp and general increase in spontaneous group creativity.

A group of mine recently afforded an illustration of an instance in which psychic impotence was accompanied by social ineffectiveness. One of its preeminently male members, physically powerful and imposing, exhibited evidence of extreme shyness. His emotional reactions were, to say the least, deficient. References to plays, art, and literature both annoyed and embarrassed him, and when pressed for an explanation, he characterized them sweepingly as effeminate manifestations of weakness. He secretly regarded any display of feeling as "soft" and feared he might be seduced into affective response by any emotional stimulant. At an early age he had lost his domineering father and had been forced to go out on the streets to sell newspapers in order to support his mother, sisters, and himself. Attacked repeatedly by anti-Semitic hoodlums, he spent years toughening himself, until tenderness, sympathy, and by extension, any emotional symbol that did not connote struggle, were ruled out of his life. In group activity it was noted that he evaded those social responses which might betray any underlying emotional attitude. He was formally considerate, proper, and unreactive, except for a compulsive need to display his masculine excess. This latter consisted in exhibiting his masterful virility whenever possible, in missing no opportunity to engage in intellectual debate in which he excelled, and in a general supportiveness simulating strength which invited the dependence of other members on him, but which was unconsciously intended to dominate and exploit them. During various sessions, the group speculated about the sexual counterpart of his deficiency in feeling and gradually led him to a not-too-painful admission of his impotence. He was moved so deeply by the friendly reception accorded his confession of weakness that he burst into tears, the first crack in his resistive armor. With this disruption of neurotic defense against emotional expression he began dreaming, free-associating, and "going around" at deeper affective levels. This enabled the group, in time, to analyze his masculine conceit and striving for power as defenses against castration and passive homosexual submission. He was able to acquire insight into his compelling preoccupation with erotically tinged struggle between himself and other men that removed him from sexual engagements with women. He was able to trace his aggression toward men to his domineering father, and his later and repeated compulsive strivings with them as the ambivalent expression of submissive and aggressive conflict. He learned, too, how the loss of his father removed a masculine image with whom he needed to identify, leaving him with three feminine figures who played their part in further emasculating him, partly out of their playing a penile role and partly by providing him only with feminine example. This was added to by their own ambivalent eroticism with regard to him. To all this conflict he reacted with repression, attempting ever to surmount unconscious affective claims that would not be denied until he was both impotent and apparently unfeeling. But with the group's action, which inserted a wedge into his formerly impenetrable facade, he relaxed restraints successively, and steadily built up lively and cordial contact. With the return of feeling it became possible for him to relate to others with passionate intensity, to fall in love, and to consummate an erotic relationship with full potency.

One such confession has a catalytic effect in producing similar uninhibited discussion by others. With varying degrees of stubborn opposition, the members finally yield to the potentiating influence of self-revelation induced by the permissive aura pervading the group. Emboldened by avowals from all sides, each sees around him his counterpart in sexual discomfiture and exposes his particular variant of the sexual theme.

In the study of sexual and social counterparts the therapist must be careful not to generalize too broadly from one member to the next. A collective interpretation tends to obscure specific differences that vary with each patient. It helps him resist deeper and more refined interpretation. If the analyst probes every aspect of a member's reactions on the social level, he will be rewarded with rich and diversified allied sexual duplicates. The generalization that one can expect to find these correspondents should be utilized by the group to explore their every ramification. By playing insights back and forth, from the social and sexual planes in the procedure of "going around" in dream, fantasy, and unreserved speculation, the details appear. Social insight leads to sexual insight and vice versa. The emphasis on their interplay breaks resistance and swiftly leads to deep understanding. The patient's liberation in these two areas has a startling effect on his formerly inhibited resources. His spontaneity and creativeness expand freely, so that he finds himself effectively mastering reality in fields where he was once constrained.

Every variety of resistance that appears in the group cannot be covered in this paper. They are as manifold and distinct as are human beings themselves. Some resist by trying to hide in the group, whether by attempting to escape into group analysis from individual treatment, or by coming late and missing meetings. Some leave the room on various pretexts. Others cannot recall their dreams or fantasies. A few exploit their tears and other devious emotional or psychosomatic releases to evade more direct response. Some maintain a compulsive complacency among patients whom they regard as neurotically inferior, hence, not to be entrusted with important private matters. Their resistance takes the form of supercilious silence or contempt. Some try to overwhelm the group with endless outpourings of irrelevant talk that is neither self-revealing nor permissive of group emergence.

Sometimes alternate meetings are conducted in a picnic atmosphere at a beach, park, or summer or winter home of one of the participants.

Eating and drinking may reduce resistance by creating a casual and intimate atmosphere. But sometimes it is intended to stuff the mouths of prospective participants and thus block interreaction. The therapist persistently tries to alert the group to be on guard against any activity of a nonpsychoanalytic character which may interrupt the specific function of the group and act as resistance. Almost inevitably various members are drawn to one another and become friends. They tend to enjoy and share the same social functions. The therapist takes a neutral attitude toward these developments but always warns against the repression of transference attitudes in such relationships. The attempt on the part of some members to preserve a relationship at the expense of analyzing it must always be challenged by the therapist as resistance. While he may at times be perplexed by the variety of individual or concerted obstacles to the invasion of multiple unconscious reservoirs, he uses his own ingenuity and the group's involuntary, accidental, and intuitional reserves to penetrate them.

THE FIFTH STAGE OF TREATMENT: THE ANALYSIS OF TRANSFERENCE

Closely allied to resistance is the fifth and most important period in group analysis, the identification and resolution of transference. The projection of parental and sibling images onto other group members are phenomena requiring exhaustive study. The analysis of transference is the largest single area of group concentration. Under the therapist's leadership patients discover the extent to which they invest each other with early familial quality. In group treatment, where a member may not only project a significant historical figure onto the analyst but also may single out members of the group for the same purpose, the area for transference is appreciably extended.

Certain truisms about transference must be emphasized to the group. The therapist must explain that all human beings carry out of childhood a heritage of conditioned reflexes which impel them to endow the present with old forms; that we see others in terms of our own circumscribed experience; that investing others with attributes they do not possess is revelatory of distorted character structure in the investor; and that therapeutic progress is measured by the success with which a patient can revise these erroneous imputations and by the tolerance with which he can accept similar unwarranted and invalid appraisals directed against himself. Patients are alerted in their adjunct analytic role to recognize and point to transference reactions whenever they appear. The qualities of transference are described to them so that they can more readily become conscious of its nature. They are told that every transference reaction has the qualities of irrelevance, compulsion, repetition, irrationality and that these are accompanied by emotional disturbance and a sense of helplessness. The discovery and analysis of transference is the most important work of group analysis, since it repeatedly interferes with the patient's true estimate of reality. Transference prevents each member from being able to accept another by conferring traits on him which originally stood in the way of a full relationship to a member of his original family. Accordingly the group must be thoroughly schooled as to its derivation, qualities, and purpose. It is indicated that the transference response is unconscious and that as a result the patient making the investment will usually resist recognition of his projection; that transference is inappropriate to the situation at hand, since the patient is responding to a mask which exists in *his* mind, rather than to the objective actuality. It is noted that transference has the elements about it of illogic, unreasonableness, and absurdity; that these qualities aside, the patient inevitably persists in his untenable position with compulsive insistence and that he reproduces his irrelevant projection over and over. It is specified that the transferring patient experiences and usually exhibits some affective disturbance, such as mild anxiety, irritability, depression, fearfulness which may mount to the most unrestrained panic and terror. It may be erotism, infatuation, or romantic sentiment. It is associated with enormous feelings of helplessness which overwhelm rational considerations. Even though all its disarming and disadvantageous features are repeatedly demonstrated, the patient seems unable to control its imperative recurrence. It is revealed that the transference response is always excessive, well beyond that called for by the provoking circumstance and hence, overcomes and renders the member ineffectual. It tends simultaneously to startle, upset, and inhibit persons in the immediate environment by the enormity and suddenness of its appearance. Its unyielding quality makes it difficult to modify and it takes a fixed course of its own, which the patient and therapist seem for a long time unable to disturb or deflect. All of these characteristics have an immobilizing effect on the patient. Bound by these limiting restraints he cannot react with the freedom and plasticity demanded by diverse environmental stimuli. It is suggested that any transference reaction, in the moment, should be traced, if possible, by historical flashback to the earlier conditioning which determined the nature of the present response.

By example and illustrative demonstration from material at hand the therapist repeatedly verifies the singular features of transference outlined above. To this end he misses no opportunity to clarify any one patient's investment of another or the analyst. Whenever a reaction appears which has the characteristics of projection, he points out to the reactor the transference character of his response. With increasing clinical experience patients become expert in identifying one another's transference reactions. The extreme disparity of various investments confronts each member with the patently illusory nature of these responses. He learns to see his own particular masking of others with parental or sibling surrogate cloaks as equally irrational. It is emphasized that transference must be dealt with in the moment of its occurrence. Anything short of this is resistance.

In some respects the transference is so rigidly fixed in the character structure that the patient projects the same distortions regardless of the personalities around him. But there are penumbral variations in his reactions to every patient and to the physician that are a part of the transference. That aspect of investment which is so fixed as to be the same regardless of the personality on which it is projected is fairly readily discernible. Those nuances in the transference which vary depending on the nature of the provocative personality are less obvious. They require the vigilant attention of the therapist. But his close pursuit of these shadowy variants in transference relationships is most rewarding. It is the analysis of these trends, peripheral to the central transference, that makes group analysis an intensive process. While in individual analysis a patient may project onto the therapist at different times father, mother, or sibling, the analyst is less likely spontaneously to arouse these multiple investments than a group of people with variously stimulating character peculiarities. The central or thematic transference reaction, most generally elicited, appears as a reproduction of a relationship to a more significant parent with whom the patient was more ambivalently and affectively bound. Lesser peripheral or penumbral transferences, appearing with more subtlety and often altogether neglected in individual analysis, reproduce conflictful but less painfully traumatic relationships to the less significant parent and siblings. The multiplicity of ways in which a patient dresses up the other members accurately reanimates the old family, disclosing in the action both his history and the richly divergent facets of his personality.

In individual analysis it is often difficult for patient and physician to follow the projection onto the therapist of the roles played by a number of significant members of the family. The group provides all the familial actors and possibilities. Not only the number of patients but also the presence of men and women expose and more rapidly precipitate aspects of transference relationships to both male and female parental and sibling surrogates. The presence of patients of both sexes facilitates the appearance and resolution of early conflicting unconscious trends formerly elicited by father, mother, sister, and brother. The group recreates the family unit in which the patient can more freely reanimate the impelling and denying emotional demands whose contradictions he was once unable to solve. As he gradually becomes able to dispose of compulsive investments and discerns group members in fact, they become the social bridge to the establishment of normal communal relations.

A patient will not infrequently select several other participants who represent for him diverse aspects of the same parent on whom he projects the psychological heritage of the past. The choice of a particular patient or of the physician as a target for a specific aspect of the transference depends on the extent to which certain trends in the provocative personality most nearly resemble special characteristics of an earlier familial associate. The likeness may be near or remote. The approximation is in terms of sex, age, and primarily phases of character structure. The evocation of particular facets of transference by specific patients itself becomes a matter for study from the point of view of the provocateur's unique neurotic and healthy qualities that inspire revivals of outmoded forms in other members. For some patients it does not matter in the slightest what the age or sex of a given member is, with regard to eliciting a transference. They will project the mother image onto a man and the father image onto a woman. For them, as for most, the important element evoking a particular familial mantle is the behavior in the moment, or fragment of character structure in the provocateur rather than his gender.

I had the opportunity, some time ago, to alternate sessions with a female analyst, both of us conducting a meeting together once a week. My purpose in organizing the group this way was partly to teach and learn and partly to see the effect of introducing what might turn out to be maternal and paternal images in the persons of the two therapists. There was no uniform response to us. For some we evoked parental projection. Occasionally negative transference was directed by a patient toward me, if there was historically greater hostility toward the father, and toward the female analyst, if there was early resentment of the mother. But just as often it appeared that our parental roles were reversed by members. And perhaps just as frequently patients did not use us as father and mother surrogates at all, but utilized one another instead. This experience made it clear that there is no special advantage in introducing two analysts of opposite sexes. When a single therapist conducts group meetings for the whole duration of treatment, patients may choose some member of the group of a sex opposite to that of the physician as a representative of the missing parent. Sometimes if I am seen as a mother image, the patient may choose another male or female member as a father image. Occasionally a patient discovers two or three father and mother surrogates in the group and variously any number of sibling substitutes. Sometimes the analyst is not regarded as a parental equivalent but as a sibling or child, and parental proxies are chosen entirely from the patient membership. However, there are some few members who never seem to unsex others in projection. For them the presence of both sexes among the membership provides a target for the investment of heterosexual transference reactions which are elicited with more difficulty when patients are obliged to project them onto a parent or sibling deputy of the same sex. Thus a mixed group enables each patient to excite, evolve, study, and analyze projected relationships to meaningful figures of both sexes in his past.

An aspect of transference that receives repeated emphasis in the group is the analysis of such an action in the moment of its occurrence. It will not do to let a patient evade a consideration of his present irrational behavior by looking backward into history to seek the origin of peculiar conduct. It is a valuable exercise to search out critical causes. But the persistent probing into historical beginnings can become obsessional. It can enable a patient to neglect grappling with the forces that compel him even now to reconstruct the past against his better judgment. In individual analysis where the tendency exists to explore biography in excess, transference attitudes are not always revived with the startling vividness encountered in group analysis. This is true, in a measure, because in individual analysis the therapist probes, while in group analysis the patients react. Inquiry leads to insight, but interreaction has a boomeranglike, repercussive effect that stirs echoes of former times with resurgent clarity. In individual analysis a patient can unconsciously falsify his record by reanimating perjured likenesses of parental figures. No such distortion is possible in the group, if the therapist holds the patient to his projection in the moment of its occurrence. And while it is true, in individual analysis, that the therapist can likewise insist on interpreting transference responses to him as they appear, he is frequently so unprovocative and so commonly bent on searching, that the reactions to him are often minimal or else so subtly transferent that they are too obscure to be interpreted.

This does not mean that the therapist and the group neglect history altogether. They look upon biographical records as of central importance. But only insofar as they clarify transference. And only to the extent that they appear in significant bursts of recollection in association with the analysis of transference. By utilizing history in this way they eliminate long irrelevant excursions into biography which are largely resistive. There is a curious correlation between biography and transference. To the extent that history is studied outside the context of immediate transference it is relatively unrevealing and useless as therapy. To the extent that history is studied within the context of immediate transference it provides understanding and is useful as therapy. Furthermore, the recollection of valuable fragments of the past is enormously facilitated by free association around and examination of an acutely neurotic reaction in the moment of transference. And there is a rewarding interplay between history and transference, one elaborating the other until their close relation is established in detail. In spite of the therapist's emphasis on this procedure patients manage in early alternate meetings to ventilate many aspects of previous experience. As they come to see the misleading character of extensive biographical rambling, they abandon this form of resistance for the method prescribed. To the degree that the analyst is able early in treatment to effect such concentration on the analysis of transference, he shortens the duration of therapy. The handling of immediate projection stirs and highlights the salient repressed past. And it is this history alone suddenly welling into the present under the stimulus of transference that has illuminating value.

There is an element in the group setting that facilitates the analysis of transference: the confrontation of each member with his disparate projection on the same person. It is often baffling in individual treatment to try to convince a patient that his estimate of the physician is far from realistic but rather a reproduction of an unresolved conflictful attitude toward a parent. The neurotic person stubbornly insists that his feeling for and impression of the therapist are accurate. And while the analyst may grant their tangibility, he has great difficulty in persuading the patient that they are also an attempt to work through archaic familial constellations. His obstinacy melts more easily in a milieu where he is faced with divergent impressions of the same person projected by everyone present. He is forced to reexamine his perceptive faculties. He cannot maintain so readily his critical obstinacy that the therapist is brilliant, strong, and all-providing when another patient insists just as mulishly that the doctor is stupid, weak, and unreliable. He is obliged to reconsider his original investment of the therapist for possible misrepresentation. And in his reactions to other patients he is also forced to reinvestigate his projective devices.

There is another element in the group setting which is conducive to the fuller evocation of every transference possibility. And that is the variously provocative characteristics of the multiple personalities in the group. No matter how versatile a therapist is, he is still bound by the limitations of his character structure. This has an unstimulating effect on the patient as far as calling forth the multiple projective potentials in him are concerned. The disparate personalities in the group furnish a larger number of exciting agents whose particular differences elicit wider and more subtle facets of transference than is ever attainable by the therapist alone. If he is skillful, he may, by uncovering successively deeper levels of the patient's personality or by playing different roles, evoke less obvious and more many-sided penumbral transferences. But in general these shadings are lost. With little effort on his part but mere attention he can discern how naturally one patient animates another into revealing peripheral sides of neurotic investment that would otherwise be missed or extracted with great difficulty. This fact is underscored by the discharge of a recovered patient or the introduction of a new one. Under these circumstances the absence of an old or the insertion of a new infectious element stirs each member unconsciously to present a fresh side of his nature, projected or normal. This has the effect not only of enlarging the view of transference but of giving the patient an opportunity to test his developing healthy resources in ever-widening circles of society. Further striking evidence of the provocative effect of the group as compared with the therapist becomes manifest following the movement of a patient from individual to group analysis. From a comparatively static, single-sided individual he turns at once into an active, complex person with multiple facets that challenge investigation. The social correspondent of this observation is the varying behavior of any human being in accordance with the changing constitution or social setting of his environment.

Each patient's provocative role must be explored in terms of the healthy and neurotic responses he elicits. Members are asked to assist in discovering one another's inflammatory tactics. This becomes apparent gradually as eight or ten patients continually tell each one what he does to them in emotional terms. But how then can he distinguish what is truly provocative, originating in the provocateur, and what is neurotically derived from the reactor? In the interplay back and forth of mutual interreaction there are healthy and unhealthy forces at work between any two people. The therapist takes the lead, in the beginning, in demonstrating this. He shows that in every interpersonal encounter there is the possibility of developing vigorous and bilaterally rewarding affective interchange. He also points out how by pursuing neurotic investments in transference and countertransference, any two individuals may end up in attempts to dominate, control, exploit, or separate from one another. In order to intercept mutually destructive or detaching interplay he is continually alert to transference and countertransference possibilities. It is sometimes very difficult to discover the actual initiator of a neurotic circus movement. It is, however, most important to intercept and analyze the movement once it is under way and to establish the healthy and neurotic deportment of the players in mid-scene.

We have already seen how dreams may lead to insight, provoke elaborate free association, and cleave through resistance. But in the clarification of transference, dreams are also valuable therapeutic adjuncts. A member may, for example, project an associated woman patient in a dream in a dual role: both as a menacing figure and a lovable one as well. He may do this before free association or biographical acknowledgment has given us any indication of his mother's ambivalent attitude toward him. Interpretation of the dream enables him and the group to discover the castrating mother image with which he compulsively invests the woman. As he recognizes the transference features of his vision of her, and sees her, in fact, as a friendly associate, he is able to divest her of her threatening aspect and she becomes more lovable. As he progressively analyzes the compulsive character of his attachment to her, he dispels even this maternal hold and she becomes simply an engaging friend, stripped of mother-quality, but with an attractiveness of her own. In these instances, reality always proves much richer and rewarding to the patient than his illusion.

Perhaps the citation of a few examples of the transference process as it occurs in the group will be illuminating. In prior individual treatment H.P. evidenced erotic interest in me that was associated with some fear and anxiety, mixed unconscious feelings directed toward her father in childhood. These were never conscious or expressed. During an early group meeting I complimented G.S. on his brilliant intuitive appraisal of her. She felt, at once, that I was favoring him and reacted with jealousy and feelings that he was being more highly regarded by me for his intellectual talent. Immediately anxious, she challenged his statement and reacted with marked hostility toward both of us throughout the duration of the meeting. Despite her competition with him for my esteem, she felt that he would inevitably do better than she and that I would just as certainly always promote him because he was a man. The compulsive nature of her conduct together with its interesting sequel came out at our next session. H.P. told us that upon leaving the previous meeting she had gone automatically to a florist to order an elaborate bouquet for her mother. Suddenly confounded in the flower store, she stopped and tried to realize what she was doing. There was really no occasion for sending her mother a bouquet, for the latter was not ill, nor was it a holiday or an anniversary. Understanding followed directly. She knew then that in the group I had changed from a father to a mother image; G.S., the man I had complimented, had become a brother substitute with whom she had been in perpetual rivalry for her mother's attention. My praise of him elicited the projection of the mother image onto me. It also aroused a keen hostility toward him and especially toward me. The gift of flowers was to propitiate a mother who was annoyed by her conduct, to conceal her welling resentment, and to appease her conscience for coming so close to fully expressing her anger against her mother. Of striking interest was her abandonment of the father image in me, as soon as the group dynamics provided a situation in which I could reward a man who was at once invested with brother quality. Apparently she was able to recreate the father image in me as long as I was alone with her. As soon as the original family was reanimated by the group setting and more particularly by my approval of a man, a particular familial constellation was revived that necessitated a revision in her earlier investment on me. A high estimate of a man unconsciously recalled greater admiration of her brother and disapprobation for herself. Her mother was the prime agent in the construction of this historical configuration.

Later meetings brought out her mother's actual preference for H.P.'s brother because he was a boy, H.P.'s compulsive penis envy, her disregard for her feelings and excessive regard for excelling intellectuality, in the company of which she always felt doomed to come off second best, thus reproducing her relationship to mother and brother. By our constant attention to all the aspects of her shifting transferences to me and to G.S., we were at last able to help H.P. relinquish familial claims on her and to react to us in her own and our right.

In thirty preliminary sessions with me, J.R. and I got on famously. He was brilliant, serene, and exceptionally friendly. There was good rapport—

on both sides. We liked one another. He made rapid progress. There seemed to be no resistance. He interpreted a dream, and I would add an additional point. He accepted it, usually with a modification that seemed appropriate. There were no stumbling blocks. It all seemed too unneurotic. I proposed that he join a group, where certain areas of his personality might reveal themselves more adequately. It took the first group meeting to provoke the only indication of negative transference that I could discover. He was a changed man. Our harmonious relationship, his appreciation of what I had done for him, and his willingness to act upon my suggestions had all vanished. He challenged substantially everything I said, and his keen intuition, although extremely helpful in analyzing group personnel, was deliberately calculated to forestall and belittle my own contribution.

I noticed that, whereas in prior private sessions we had easy exchange, in the group he would hardly allow me to speak. He interrupted, he anticipated and predicted (often accurately enough) what I was about to say. I held my tongue for the time being. But very soon the group noticed his compulsive behavior and began discussing it. Then I called to his attention the contrast between his former complacent demeanor during individual analysis and his subsequent truculent attitude toward me in the group. He expressed surprise and embarrassment at having been guilty of such antisocial behavior. But even as he spoke, he was struck with a flash of historical insight. He recalled with what pontifical dignity and Victorian strictness his father held court at the dining table when J.R. was a child; how one had to tiptoe about the house when his father was napping on Sunday afternoons; how he was not allowed to speak unless spoken to in his father's presence. And he remembered other indignities extending to his not being allowed to enter the bathroom as a very little child when his mother was bathing—a privilege, however, that his father permitted himself. At subsequent meetings he explained how all his life he could talk freely and easily with one person just as he used to do with his mother. But in the presence of a group he felt driven to excel, to be the genius in the drawing room. In every social gathering he habitually recreated the family milieu and automatically strove to become its guiding intellect. The group suggested and J.R. acknowledged that he might now be playing an assumed paternal role in the new family. Then he remembered how as a child he had been almost irresistibly impelled to challenge his father in everything the latter did or said, but he had never quite dared to carry it off.

The reproduction of his relationship to his mother when alone with me and to his father and family when in the group became apparent to all of us and led to deeper insight into his Oedipal conflict, his attachment to his mother, his repressed rivalry with his father, and his compulsive replacement of the father in every regenerated family. Certainly, J.R.'s transfer to a group revived old family ghosts that could not have been so easily discovered or dispelled without reproducing the household unit.

There are at least three salient points involved in H.P.'s and J.R.'s stories. The first illustrates the sudden appearance of occasionally unforeseen bursts of transference toward the therapist or another member after a patient has been introduced to a group. The second throws light on the inevitable appearance of previously latent facets of personality, new and multiple transference in the recreation of the old family, so that movement into a group changes behavior. The third illustrates how significant incidents in early life are recalled by the flash-back method in relation to the analysis of immediate transference.

In difficult marital issues, the group method has proved effective. Through an unorthodox experiment which led to the treatment of husband and wife in individual analysis, with good results, I went even further beyond the realm of standard practice by organizing in 1940 a group of five married couples. The analysis of husband and wife in on-the-spot observation was most illuminating. I treated a man for some months and listened most sympathetically during this time to his embittered accounts of domestic strife. When a dream fragment appeared suggesting that he was not altogether the innocent in their relationship, I suggested a Rorschach for his wife and arranged for an interview with her. Later they joined a group together. It soon became apparent to us that he would, artfully and unconsciously, needle and humiliate her. He accomplished this with such subtlety that neither he nor she were, at the time, aware of it. This would go on for a week or so until she flared up and attacked him in return. For him this attack clinched his point. He appealed triumphantly to his fellow group members to support him in the contention that she was an impossibly aggressive woman. The group managed in time to demonstrate his provocative role to his satisfaction.

Marital differences are not always resolved so satisfactorily. Occasionally, when a couple seems to be hopelessly at odds in transference and countertransference, I start by treating them in separate groups. They are brought together in the same group when they are more aware of their projective technics. It is usually not too difficult to persuade couples to join the same group. When they do, each invests the other with historical familial qualities, and the happy resolution of their difficulties is determined by the effectiveness with which their mutual transferences can be dispelled. While real or fantasied philandering and cognate activities emerge with understandable reticence, they do gradually come up for discussion.

In the married couple group, each participant was sensitive to the difficulties peculiar to marital conflict. Members were able to crystallize quickly for one another the unconscious core of what was struggling to reach awareness. One couple that had managed successfully to cope with a problem would guide another to an equally gratifying solution of a similar impasse. Perhaps it should be added that, in the group composed of five married couples, two finally divorced each other, in their cases a wholesome dénouement. It is relevant to indicate that the therapeutic goal is not the preservation of a marital relationship at any cost. In this regard it is equally pertinent to remember that the current national divorce rate numbers one out of every three couples.

Let us summarize this section of group analytic work. Every member is asked to examine what investments he makes onto others and the physician. The patient is encouraged to observe his irrational, compulsive, repetitive, and disturbing reactions toward the other members of the group that have little or nothing to do with external reality factors or actual outer provocation. He finds himself relatively helpless at first in his attempt to discern the extent to which his perceptual faculties, warped by neurotic trends, prevent him from seeing people around him accurately. He recreates original familial figures in the persons of members of the group and reacts to them irrelevantly. He invests them with parental and sibling qualities which they do not possess. These projections appear freely in the practice of uncontrolled emotional interreaction and delineate the abnormal character structure. The various disparate emotional reactions of each member to the others and to the therapist force patients to study the extent to which they are impelled to misinterpret reality for neurotic ends by a rigid character structure. It is the study, modification, and resolution of these projected and inappropriate responses to familial surrogates in the group that constitute the main work of group psychoanalysis.

THE SIXTH AND FINAL STAGE OF TREATMENT: CONSCIOUS PERSONAL ACTION AND SOCIAL INTEGRATION

In this, the final stage of group analysis, the technic of spontaneous interreaction must be abandoned for conscious, methodical sifting and planning of verbalized responses in the best personal and social interests of the group. This is a period of intense struggle with one's own transference reactions, when they cannot be justified and conciliated; when insight without action cannot be tolerated; when character change must replace explaining and when group discipline demands personal reformation.

One test of readiness for discharge is a patient's ability to analyze and dispose of his own transference investments and his skill in not countertransfering to other patients who are disturbed by their projections onto him. A growing aptitude in detecting the component of irrelevant investment in another person's behavior enables him to avoid being drawn into countertransference. This is enhanced by rational resistance to impulsive reaction and the choice, instead, of responding to the real person behind the facade.

With time patients become more and more adept in spotting their own transferences. They contribute just as skillfully in the interpretation of the transference of others. To their cumulative satisfaction they become analysts themselves. Their interreactivity brings vital projection to the surface, material which is analyzed by them as illogical investment. Once having discovered and studied the nature of each patient's multiple transferences, all members struggle to reach beyond this illusory veneer and to identify the genuine person behind the neurotic "front." For it is this more substantial self, embryonic though it often is, that is the emerging, healthy, and likable side of a personality. As patients grope for this solid side of themselves, transferences atrophy from disuse, and the irrational motion of earlier meetings is gradually replaced by mutual friendliness and realistic regard.

At this point it is easy to see that all of the six stages that I have outlined blend one into the other. In the strictest sense there are really no stages at all. There are no sharp demarcations of time at which one begins and another ends. They may in some instances proceed simultaneously, each augmenting the other. One may think of them, rather, as levels of development in the course of reaching the point, called the sixth stage of group analysis, where constructive personality change is advocated and carried through. As I noted above, dream analysis and free association run like threads through all of the levels of progress and constantly serve as reference points in each patient's course. Yet the sequence I enumerate is valuable, because it allows for variations in movement, dependent on the quality of the analysand's neurotic state. If resistance and transference can, in the judgment of the therapist be analyzed in the second stage without jeopardizing the patient's progress, the analyst may choose to do so. It is wrong to think of these stages as closed for boxed-in technics employed in segments of time. Still, if the analyst ventures into "going around" prematurely in some groups, he may find intense resistances and hostile transferences and countertransferences developing that are hard to break. He may then be forced to return—as he should—to the second stage in which the emphasis is purely on personal dream and fantasy ventilation in a permissive atmosphere. He does this to recover that harmony which is necessary for adequate collective action. In a closed group the stages described are more easily identifiable. And the initial rapport so necessary for the newly admitted patient speaks for the wisdom of working with closed groups. However, I have almost always kept groups going continuously, discharging the recovered and introducing the sick, so that membership kept changing as the group went on. Apparently it is possible to do this, if the therapist is patient enough to wait for initial, generalized positive transference or rapport. Then, what resistances and negative transferences do appear later have less strength and intensity so that a newly introduced person is not traumatized by them. And he is rather impressed with the high level of group morale which soon includes and sweeps him along.

THE ROLE OF THE GROUP ANALYST

What, it is pertinent to ask, are the particular qualifications and functions of a successful group analyst? At present, since he is working with a technic that is relatively new, any answer will, of course, be tentative.

As Dr. S. H. Foulkes has recently pointed out, psychoanalysts are not *ipso facto* good group analysts, and, he goes on to say, it in no way impugns the former to emphasize that special attributes are required of the group analyst. He must first of all be a psychoanalyst. He must have adequate training, intuitive insight, a capacity for empathy, and an ability to dispose of countertransference attitudes. He must expect concerted efforts to deflate him. He must have the capacity to withstand neurotic attacks on him with composure. He must not be discouraged or thrown off balance by the intensity of interpersonal enmity which occasionally develops in early meetings. Such malevolent outbursts are largely projective in character, and his whole function as group leader is jeopardized if he fails to react to them with appropriate analysis. Even the most timid will assail him from their vantage point among the group, and destructive patients will test his tolerance of neurotic frustration and aggression to the utmost. In spite of the therapist's attempt to create a new, more benevolent and permissive family, the old one with all its rivalry, aggression, and dictatorship may assert itself and tax the new parent in the extreme.

He must patiently welcome the manifold variety of transferences with which he is invested and never be misled to accept them as real by inappropriate reaction. To be sure, the doctor is afforded the same group protection as his patients. If he is unreasonably attacked, some of them will come to his rescue and support him when the occasion seems to demand it. For, acting upon his injunction, they are continually engaged in reacting spontaneously to everyone present including the therapist. He, too, must expect both blame and praise according to their changing concepts of his desserts.

He must be strong enough to acknowledge his errors and secure enough to relinquish his leadership to the group or to a patient as the situation of the moment demands. It is distinctly no position for a practitioner who would evade the interpersonal give-and-take that is the very basis of group analysis. He must not approach the group with the missionary's urge to convert, with the supercilious spirit of the benevolent patron, or the oppressive dictatorship of the pedagogue. He cannot be pretentious, and any suggestion of pomposity will get short shrift from the group members, for he is a leader who at the same time must sit among his patients as an equal. The dual role is not an easy one. In short, his neurotic tendencies should be disposed of in his prior personal or group analysis.

The prime function of the group analyst is to guide his patients to full awareness and social integration. He can best accomplish this by avoiding conceited and compulsive leadership. He can more surely achieve such a goal by attentive regard to what group members can teach him. The therapist cannot alone know enough to provide adequate leadership. His nuclear, professional, and leading position does not by itself qualify him to provide his patients with the full insight they need.

His experience is not comprehensive enough to insure healthy social restoration. Therefore it is necessary that he supplement his clinical knowledge with that of the various group members. This means that he must constantly maintain an alert and intimate connection with the rich reservoirs of understanding which are potential in the group, catalytically interplaying their intuitive insight with his own. He must attend the least small voice as well as the loudest. It will not do for him to detach himself at his desk and hand down well-prepared instructions. While he seeks a solution to every neurotic problem, the proper answers cannot be found without vigilant regard to group experience which is continually testing his leadership. While he plans operations for the resolution of conflict, he cannot achieve his objectives without the help of the group. The patient members are an essential and final check on the extent to which communal aims are being fulfilled. The group's activity on a level with the therapist guarantees it a status equal to his, and finally enables it to dispose of him in the therapeutic process.

The group analyst's view of things is one-sided. He sees patients and their behavior from above. Accordingly, his impression of what is happening is limited by his paternalistic, relatively nonparticipant position. While he engages in group activity, the quality of his participation is different and modifies his perception of events. The group, on the other hand, appreciates interpersonal forces at work from another side. Its awareness is likewise limited by its position and function in the group. To accomplish that harmony which will lead to integrated group activity, the therapist and patients must interweave their complementary roles. Leadership which achieves this is therapeutic.

The successful analyst learns never to underestimate the significance of the contribution that can be made by the group to mutual insight and social integration. Patients sometimes show themselves to be closer to the unconscious truth than their physician. If he is wise, he consults them often and always supplements his experience with theirs. It may be said that neurotic conflict develops in the child out of contradictory influences imposed on him by his parents, who are both exploitative, dictatorial, selfish, and at the same time cooperative, democratic, and supportive of the child's developing resources. In the new, permissive family of the group, to the extent that the therapist is authoritarian and detached from the group, he duplicates the destructive role played by the original parents. In this way he can only reinforce the patients' difficulties and undermine their actual effectiveness. To the degree that he is continually attentive to the emerging intuitive potentials in the various members, he helps to create a new family unit of the group, in which each participant can realize increasingly gratifying levels of social adjustment.

The therapist must beware of unfeeling attitudes on his part in the group. Actually such an approach is evidence of his lack of specific attention to each member. There is danger in the group of thinking of it en masse rather than of each individual patient—his needs, his problems, his growth. Without special attention to each person the therapist may act at random, either commending them as a whole or disapproving of them *in toto*. Such insensitivity to particular individuals breeds dissatisfaction and bitterness. It leads to the formation of neurotic cliques of malcontents who may wreck the group. The therapist must be alert to individual differences, the falling behind of a given patient and his possible personal confusion. If not, a member here and there becomes increasingly disaffected and disgruntled and becomes a focal point of defection leading the group into disintegration.

The therapist who regards himself as the most active, critical thinker in the group and the patients as a relatively inert mass is likely to be led far astray. With such a misconception he tends to overestimate himself and look down on the group. He has the illusion that success or failure depends pretty much on him and that the group is lacking in creative, contributory power. He believes that his acuteness alone determines the successful outcome of treatment. Such a view condemns the group to passivity and excludes the membership from active social participation and organization essential to its recovery. It also reduces the group process to a series of dictated or accidental psychodynamics whose ebb and flow are determined by the prescriptions, needs, and fantasies of the "expert" therapist. The fact is that the group therapeutic process proceeds in accordance with definite laws, most of which are yet to be discovered. But while the development of the group moves on according to certain principles, the therapist and each patient are constantly modifying its progress. The therapist can play a most significant catalytic part in facilitating group movement by seeing further ahead than his patients. He can do this also by desiring and struggling to accomplish healthy group integration more vigorously than they. His effectiveness lies in his deep contact with each member, in his ability to integrate them, in his skill in foreseeing the historical course the group takes and in his confidence in the potential resources of the various members.

The course a group takes is primarily determined by the various character structures of the participant members, itself a product of their previous history. The personal qualities of the therapist only modify this course. This does not mean that the contributions the analyst can make should be ignored. Nor does it mean that group progress is exactly predetermined by the constitution of the patients in it. If this were so, it would make no difference whatsoever on the movement of the group, if one therapist were substituted for another. And the role of the group analyst would be a passive one in the face of the group's fatalistic course. But the influence of the therapist cannot be reduced to this kind of insignificance. He must possess skills which make him most capable of resolving intragroup conflict; of interpreting the problems presented by the group's previous history; of pointing up the new social needs created by the preceding development of the group's social relationships; of taking the initiative in satisfying these needs. He cannot stop or change the natural course of events. But his enormous influence lies in his giving conscious and free expression to this inevitable and unconscious course. Social relationships in the group have their inherent logic. Patients feel, think, and act in a given way and no other. Their mutual interpersonal reactions are determined by their prior history. But the therapist's attempts to combat this logic need not be fruitless. By observing the unconscious potentials for healthy movement in the group, he is able to influence them.

In this relatively new field of group analysis the therapist must be a person who is venturesome, for there are many new, experimental areas to explore. He should, therefore, avoid assuming dogmatic attitudes in the group's interest as well as his own. If he is opinionated he prevents the group's full emergence and contribution, which may enlighten him also. He must be capable of admitting his own mistakes openly, of examining the reasons for them, and of analyzing the conditions which gave rise to them in order to correct them. He must be able to show his own shortcomings, setting an example in this way to the others.

The group therapist who is psychoanalytically oriented cannot encourage an inspirational atmosphere which represses unconscious factors and creates unstable illusions of success which are bound to be short-lived. He promotes a spirit of deep, mutual examination and review of personal inadequacies and weaknesses. Such a procedure does not destroy the patient but merely attacks his neurotic character structure. Then he draws new strength from the group and rises to higher strata of personal and social coordination which makes unlikely a turning back to old and outmoded forms.

At times when the group falters, the analyst must remain firmly and consistently optimistic. He must take a vigorous stand against any one patient's exploitation of another. He must avoid in himself and discourage in the members the intellectual cliché that obscures the simple, richer, and more elemental meaning for which the whole group is groping. A calculated, scholastic approach leads to an evasion of affective contact indispensable for rehabilitation. Here, as elsewhere, he can turn to the group for the naïve phrase which is poetic, refreshing, and to the point in order to escape from the restricted language of professional associates. He must set an example in simplicity, honesty, and straightforwardness to encourage those patients who underestimate their large ability to make meaningful contributions. He will not always emphasize what is said, but rather how it is said. He will treat complicated questions without complexity. He should not strive for the elequent phrase. His thoughts must be clear and distinct; their intent plain. While he plays a leading role, he must always make the members feel he is one of them—not apart. He must not teach too much. If he should, he would find himself governing rather than liberating. In this regard it would pay him to lend an attentive ear to what is said of him in the group. There he will find his severest critics as well as his staunchest defenders. Regard for what they say will help him to continue his personal analysis. Again, he should not hesitate to show his feelings in the group. In doing this he sets an example of freedom and emotional contact that is infectious. If he hides affect, the group will respond in kind. His sadness or gaiety will strike healthy reactive chords in the others. But, if he is well, he will be realistically and steadily optimistic.

The analyst must be on guard against alliances in the group which conceal deeper, unrealized, and unspoken attitudes, which should be ventilated. Two patients, both fearful of criticism, may evolve a superficial and precarious neurotic amity, which undermines the therapeutic process. Their fradulent harmony is pure resistance and works to prevent the exposure of all the facets of character structure. Group progress cannot take place in an atmosphere of insincere and evasive peace and good will. It can move on if the therapist presses for mutual exertion and cross-exposure, which develops contradictory positions. Then, when intra- and interpersonal conflict is exposed, the group can proceed to overcome these seemingly irreconcilable attitudes. The neurotic character structure must sooner or later be attacked by the analyst, not coddled. Otherwise it fights for its existence and defends an outlived cause. At the same time the new and healthier personality is also struggling to emerge. The therapist must ally himself with the new and make himself the implacable enemy of the old and outmoded. He can do this best by openly and honestly exposing unconscious conflict and screened attitudes and encouraging the group to do likewise. In assailing the neurotic framework of the personality he must concentrate his attack on oppressive or prohibitive trends, on overprotective and exploitative tendencies, and most especially on ever-present male supremacist domination, whether it shows itself in men or women.

Conscious and unconscious overestimation of what is generally regarded as masculine plays a part in the evolution and resolution of every neurosis. The analyst must wage an incessant campaign against the obvious and insidious ways in which masculine excess is overvalued. To this end he takes every opportunity to establish the democratic and biologically complementary equality of the sexes. Whenever possible he exposes the devious and subtle ways in which the equivalents of masculinity are taken for granted as superior. He shows each member how, unconsciously, he has hardly progressed from the phallus-worship of his ancestors. Among male patients, the therapist indicates how this may manifest itself in compulsive pursuit of women to prove sexual prowess and to relieve castration anxiety. Among female patients he points out how male supremacy notions are reflected in what amounts to the same thing: the manifold varieties of penis envy. The analyst exposes the social counterparts of this overevaluation of the male sex organ as an incessant power drive that shows itself in diverse, antisocial efforts to establish individual dominance. He traces these sexual and social correspondents to their common cultural origin in an economy that prescribes personal and material security only at the expense of others. He challenges the psychopathic values demanded by such a social organization. In this way the analyst persists as the staunch enemy of male supremacy as it occurs in either sex. Members must be schooled to address each other not as men or women, but as individuals to whom sex is fortuitous and, given their therapeutic objective, secondary.

The therapist can foster harmonious accord if he takes pains to oppose psychopathic and neurotic alliances against healthy mutuality. He strengthens group unity by trying always to expose the destructive quality of such unwholesome compacts. He must, therefore, be alert to the fact that not all affinity in the group is necessarily salutary. The devils too may be in league. Often, under the pretext that "it is necessary to express hostility" —at times a true enough observation—they deviously, compulsively, and sadistically attack and provoke discord and regression among those patients who are progressing sufficiently to unite their efforts. He must join those forces in the group whose interests are not partisan, but generally and reciprocally emancipating. He stands firm against and thwarts clannishness and narrow self-interest. He must neutralize any attempt on the part of one patient to misuse another by exposing the act and analyzing its motivation. He must not allow appeasement of psychopathic tendencies which would dominate or manipulate members. Such concessions will inevitably bridle and delay the group's progressive evolution.

The analyst must constantly seek a theoretical base to keep pace with his practical work. A flexible theoretical background continually modified by concrete experience in the group gives patients and therapist alike the power of orientation, clarity of perspective, faith in the work, and confidence in ultimate recovery. But he must be equally strong in practical work. Study of theory and practice will enable him to see a long way ahead and thus anticipate successes and impasses in the group's best interests. Attention to the interplay of hypothesis and fact leads to the continuous elaboration and modification of each, establishing ever clearer insights into reality and corresponding changes in technic.

Every form of therapy is limited in what it can accomplish due to cultural restraints. While the analyst hopes to develop the patient and to help him realize his full possibilities, both he and the patient are partially blocked by a society which abuses our resources. Yet even within our present societal context, certain things can be achieved. The movement of a patient from individual to group analysis is a considerable step toward his socialization. It is a vital step away from our misleading glorification of individual freedom and spontaneity, which merely subjects each of us to a ruthless competition in which the majority get nowhere. To this unsound emphasis on detachment and individuality, which conceals the fact of actual cultural repression and vast inequity, the therapist offers genuine regard for each patient in the group, with a chance for all to liberate and coordinate unrealized reserves. That is, at least in the group context. Here too the therapist opposes any gesture which serves personal interests at the expense of group interests. He sees that no individual really gains anything at the cost of others; their loss is his loss and their gain is his gain.

Perhaps the most important function of the group analyst is to make clear in the terminal phases of treatment the relation between the individual patient's freedom to act as he pleases and the needs of the group of which he is a part. When awareness of his lack of free will presents itself to him as the impossibility of behaving in any way differently, and when, at the same time, his behavior is that most preferred by him, the social needs of the group become identified with his own freedom and his own freedom with that of the group. He is then bound only in the sense that he cannot disturb the identity between his personal freedom and group requirements. He discovers that these needs are not in opposition. He does not feel restrained or "controlled" by interpersonal demands. He finds his lack of "freedom" to be only apparent and actually unreal. His seeming restraint is a mere complementation of roles, a true social discipline, and a rich unfoldment of the democratic process. At that time he is able to relinquish his detached, masturbatory, and individually enterprising "freedom"—which amounted to nothing less than neurotic enslavement—for gregarious, heterosexual and communal relationships. The neurotic's compulsive insistence on "personal liberty" usually represents nothing more than his wish to exploit you, his desire to rob and master you. He is not free to do so, while you prevent him from accomplishing his purpose, or until he has overcome your resistance. When he can make no distinction between personally gratifying objectives and socially invigorating aims and can act upon them, he is well. In this higher form of group freedom he is liberated from his own neurotic restraints. His freer behavior becomes the expression of interpersonal needs. A simple example will clarify this notion. The neurotic patient may insist on his right to masturbate. It is only when he is alone that he feels free enough to enjoy an ecstatic orgasm. He is inhibited during coitus, when his penile skin feels anaesthetized. As he is liberated from unconscious prohibitions, he learns how to reach new heights of personal pleasure in mutually gratifying sexual intercourse, more pleasurable to him just to the extent that it likewise delights his partner. Rid of the neurotic illusion that contact involves "demands," he realizes himself in the only way he can—socially.

DESTRUCTIVE PATTERNS IN GROUP ANALYSIS

An unfavorable situation which may arise in a group is the development of intense generalized neurotic resistance, accompanied by hostile transference and countertransference, and the formation of allies in groups of two or three, leaving some individuals pretty well isolated except for a relatively warm relationship to the therapist. Sometimes even this association becomes strained, because the patient blames the therapist for having been exposed to such a trying, antagonistic environment. Such a group must be tackled vigorously by the analyst. Otherwise it may fall apart. Attendance may become low and demoralize those present. The therapist, while taking an analytic view of absenteeism, must threaten those who stay away with being dropped. He must study transferences that force aggressors into belligerent roles and point out their illusory character. He must be equally vigilant with regard to projective devices that impel the compulsively withdrawn to retreat further or to submit to the domination of other members. He must discover the causes for resistance to participation on deeper levels, pointing out explicitly the destructive character of particular defenses and encouraging free emotional ventilation. If the situation is unwholesome enough, he may for a while, suggest no "going around" in order to interrupt unanalyzed, aggressive attacks and propose a retreat to the second stage of treatment: the exclusive presentation of dreams and fantasies. A return to the airing of the personal, unconscious material which is interpreted with the help of the group is preparation for a new unity. All else failing, the analyst may be obliged to remove a patient here and there, one at a time, at varying intervals, introducing each retired member into a more cohesive group. Such a crisis can usually be avoided by not organizing a group with a majority of strongly sado-masochistic patients. Too many such members in the same milieu provide an unfavorable climate for the evolution of the fraternal good will that should be established early if the group is to proceed efficiently.

In my early experience with group analysis I felt a good deal of uncertainty as to the practicality of using free association and of trying to handle transference and countertransference reactions among numbers of patients. Might not a patient's resources be paralyzed by the "attacks" of others? Might his feelings of anxiety, exaggerated by mounting neurotic aggression in the group, force him into further withdrawal or irrelevant countersorties of his own? With a weak ego structure to start with, would he not beat a further psychic retreat in a setting that encourages free inter-personal, affective responses, some of which are bound to be charged with hostility? How easily might he tolerate an atmosphere in which sexual matters are freely discussed, without running for cover? However, repeated clinical experience reassured me. For a patient under inappropriate fire inevitably finds allies in the therapist and some other member or members of the group. Their support fortifies him against hurt and isolation. If a penetrating remark made in free association hits a target and makes him falter, the other members sustain him fraternally, until he can usefully tol-erate insight. If an acute observation is lost on him, because it is aggressively colored and he hears only the hostility, the therapist or patients dissect what is valid from what is neurotic attack. Then the group analyzes both his peculiar attention to ill will that compels him to lose sight of what may be useful to him in terms of further self-understanding (i.e. his counter-transference), and the character trend of the aggressor in terms of his pro-jection that impels him to design his comments in such a destructive way that it becomes difficult for others to extract what is very valuable from them and to accept them. This calls for analysis of the constructive and destructive content of the latter's comments. And it also involves study of his provocative role and transference devices. Attention to these details tends to dispel anxiety. The group finds that careful exploration of psy-chic recesses is ultimately less terrifying than shutting its eyes to them, so that the therapist's insistence on frankness is bound to be rewarding. Specters of the past vanish when the unconscious closet is thoroughly inspected.

Another occasionally troubling problem is the temptation of some patients to consummate intimate sexual relations. Sporadically, a couple will have intercourse within the first half dozen meetings. If the analyst forbids such intimacy, he duplicates the original parental proscription against incest. Besides, men and women who become so engaged do so compulsively and generally drift into physical familiarity whether the physician prohibits it or not. Then the therapist is faced with their sense of guilt, a tendency to hide aspects of the relationship, and a secret defiance that complicates and obscures the significance of the act. Furthermore, pa-tients who leap into bed with one another do so rather extensively with people outside the group. In the therapeutic setting the repetition of the sexual act has the advantage of subjecting compulsive promiscuity to exam-ination under the microscope. Whenever members reach out for one another in sexual release, the relationship is inevitably brought up for group discussion and analysis within a few sessions. But the therapist does not encourage sexual intercourse. He takes a neutral position. In the beginning of group treatment he presents the position I have outlined above and thus guards as best he can against playing the repressive role of original familial figures. If in spite of the points outlined by the analyst, patients still indulge in intercourse, the analyst and the group simply try to understand the full meaning of the act. Later on in the course of treatment when patients' embryonic, libidinous urgings emerge in healthier give-and-take, a more wholesome union can take place. Here certainly the therapist can be encouraging. For as long as affective yearnings are the expression of genuine affection or love, he must not match the original, castrating parent, but play a permissive if not promoting part. However, for the majority of patients tabus against incest are so strong and the family unit so sharply reanimated in the group, that excursions into sexual contact are forbidden to them by old and stringent incorporated disciplines.

What may be regarded by some therapists as a danger is the quick penetration of a facade and the sudden, premature presentation to a patient of deep, unconscious material by the intuitive association of another member. In over eleven years of clinical experience with the group analytic method no one has been driven into a psychosis by such precocious insight. I have always found that, if a patient is not ready to assimilate profound understanding, his resistance disposes of it. If a member seems on the verge of great anxiety or instability as a result of being exposed too precipitously to insight, he may be withdrawn temporarily into individual analysis for reassurance, repression, and ego strengthening until he is able to withstand intensive analysis.

The immediate investment of the group with terrifying, familial transference in the first or second group meeting is more difficult to handle. When it happens, a patient may run out of a session in terror, as if fleeing bogeymen. Trying to induce such a person to return to the group to face and analyze his illusory projections can turn out to be a formidable task. Such a member has probably been prematurely ushered into the company of other patients. The analyst must try to discern in advance his sensibility and prepare him better to cope with his compulsive distortions of reality. This may be accomplished by waiting for the development of more positive transference in prior individual treatment, followed in this case by more intensive preliminary study of his particular projective devices. Apparently such an individual straightway recreates his own ugly family in any small cluster of strangers, where original conflict is forced speedily and dreadfully near the surface, so that he takes flight hurriedly. A patient who behaves this way is commonly shy, withdrawn, and schizoid. He is fearful of a collection of people who may renounce etiquette and the superficial social forms that offer him some safety. He runs from the brutality he himself is repeatedly reincarnating. He is more comfortable in an outside world that assures him a precarious security as long as it remains conventional. He rarely shows up in a group, or if he does, his resistances finally give way to analysis, so that he constitutes no serious indictment of the group analytic technic.

Is there not an ever-present danger that the group, functioning as a re-created family, may become neurotic as a family per se? Without adroit management, or even with it, some groups undoubtedly might wind up this way. The therapist must watch for the elaboration of self-sufficient, in-bred, and incestuous trends that bind members together as neurotically as the original family. A recovering patient, for example, may be refused dis-charge from the group by a compulsively overprotective member who is parentally castrating. If a man and woman gravitate toward one another with erotic interest, they may be invested with father and mother roles, and other patients may react to them with detached respect, voyeuristic ag-gressive interest, or moralistic disapproval that corresponds to earlier am-bivalent curiosity with regard to intimacy between the parents. These investments are pretty easily dispelled by persistent analysis. Occasionally a member or two will exhibit some reluctance to permit a patient who has recovered to leave the group. They demonstrate the same kind of envy or jealousy earlier directed toward a sibling and feel the family group or paren-tal therapist is favoring the cured member with special regard which his performance does not deserve. The majority, however, generally welcome the improvement of any one and take pleasure in his progress. Transference which denies discharge to a patient who has recovered is also analyzable with little difficulty.

Then there is the patient whose love for the emotional climate of the group borders on the ecstatic. He revels in the luxury of what he considers an absolutely honest relationship. He is, *mirabile dictu*, in a family whose projections, having become at last analyzable and understandable, no longer alarm or hurt him. The danger in his case is that he runs from real life to the fabricated safety of an unreal laboratory. He finds the group warmer and saner than most associations on the outside. He must be in-structed how to carry the affective closeness he has consummated in the group to larger segments of society, beyond the confines of his fellow members. This, by the way, is a common objection to working in concert with other patients. How, it is asked, can one transpose the good-fellowship of the group to areas outside it? Group analysis lays no Polly-annish or grandiose claim to making the world a big happy family. Class differences are, of course, not touched by it. They should, in fact, be sharpened for each member, if the method is really scientific. But group analytic technic offers the patient a means of making conscious, trends that stand in the way of his vigorous affective contact with others, whether loving or hating. I say hating as well as loving, because there are some psychopathic influences still at work in our culture that are inaccessible to analysis. These must be destroyed before hatred can be dispensed with as socially unnecessary.

CONSTRUCTIVE PATTERNS IN GROUP ANALYSIS

A constructive use to which group analysis is put is the demonstration to each patient that he shares his problems with others. He loses the illusion of the uniqueness of his neurosis. How many times has the analyst working alone with a patient heard him inquire whether the therapist ever encountered such an unusual and complex case before. It is the discovery of common difficulties that leads to freer self-exposure. The group milieu is also a buffer against despair of recovery. If the patient falters or is set back, the improvement and recovery of others encourages him to go on. His fear that he will receive only a fraction of the attention available in individual treatment is dissipated by the actual experience, when he is transferred from private to group analysis. Here he finds himself scrutinized by the searching inquiry of people, whose analytic skill multiplies with successive visits. The group comes very quickly and accurately to the heart of a problem by progressive increments of cross association and intuition. The penetrating powers of the therapist are limited by his character structure. Alone with the patient the analyst evokes circumscribed responses in him determined by the physician's particular personality. For the rest the therapist must rely on his knowledge of unconscious forces and artificial and sometimes awkward devices to evoke all the unconscious facets of a patient's transference responses. The group makes this much easier. By providing a number of disparate character structures it spontaneously elicits in each member different aspects of himself. The divergent personalities provoke more varied sides of the individual that would perhaps otherwise remain unseen. Numbers of patients provide more agents to facilitate spontaneous interreaction and intuitive penetration of facades.

There are social rewards obtainable in a group that are not as accessible to a patient who chooses private analysis. The group appreciates proffered insight and acknowledges such favors with regard and affection. Besides, the patient who intuitively produces a bit of valuable information, hitherto unseen, learns to respect his inner reserves out of the esteem of others. This approval does not encourage compulsively brilliant performance which excludes affect. Rather it values unplanned, emotional responses that gratify all the members concerned. In this way a patient learns to appreciate his natural and uninhibited resources at the same time as he cultivates them along social lines. The group method also rewards the participant by making him feel increasingly helpful as an adjunct analyst, a function he cannot so easily play in individual treatment.

The group has a constructive effect in recreating the family—but with a new look. By cultivating a permissive atmosphere in which mutual tolerance and regard can flourish, the earlier prohibitive character of the original family is projected with less intensity and is more easily dispersed. Furthermore, the general acceptance and sense of belonging that follow make it possible to achieve similarly easy transition to correspondingly untroubled social relations beyond the confines of the group. The other patients, out of their numbers, provide more familial surrogates for transference evocation. Each member comes to a realization of the extent to which he recreates his own childhood family in every social setting and invests others with inappropriate familial substitute qualities. The number of participants also clarifies the variety and multiplicity of central and penumbral transferences. While in individual analysis the therapist tries to see clearly what perceptual distortions the patient makes of outer reality and what internal factors contribute to this social disfigurement, the analyst is often misled, because he does not see the patient in action. In group analysis the physician is interested primarily in what is happening at the moment so that the patient's unconscious warping of fact can be observed in motion. He can then be confronted with his projective technics and the inciting role he plays in precipitating the environmental disturbances he resents so much.

The group facilitates the emergence and acceptance of insight by confronting each member with his desparate investments of other patients and the therapist. In individual analysis it is most trying to persuade the patient to regard his endowing the physician with parental or sibling characteristics as a projective phenomenon rather than a true estimate of fact. When, however, he joins a group, he finds that each patient unconsciously warps his perception of the therapist and of the other patients as well. He begins to question the reality of his view of people in the group. As he studies his transferences, he becomes aware too of his provocative role. In individual analysis the therapist does not often react spontaneously to the patient. But the group always does—until the final stage of analysis. Each member tells him frankly what effect he produces, so that the character of his neurotic provocation and the part he plays in creating environmental responses becomes clear to him. Nowhere in individual analysis is there such a microscopic laboratory in which the patient can discover in action the interplay of unconscious forces. If occasional individual sessions are indicated, because insight has been imposed too quickly and the patient cannot easily handle his newly exposed conflicts, the therapist merely offers repressive support in a temporary return to individual treatment. If deep insight is tolerated, the analyst underlines that trend in the conflict which has a healthy social as well as personally gratifying objective.

The group has a curious explosive effect in the way it stirs the unconscious into activity. The analyst alone with a single patient appears to gain access to the repressed by probing analysis that is slower and more painstaking. The group, by its interreactive spontaneous free association, bursts the seams of resistance in a sort of chain reaction. It is as if the presentation of a nightmare to an assemblage had a socially agitating effect on unconscious energy, until now in check, that forces it into release. This animation in turn vitalizes others, and so on. It is startling to see one patient after another getting flashes of insight from the fantasies and dreams of successive free-associators. The stimulating power of each member's provocative inner self rakes up repressed trends all around him. Evidently there is so much closely shared unconscious material that the uninhibited imagery of one man stirs the deepest levels of another. The comments of the therapist are sometimes too interpretation-loaded and intellectual. This may remove him, if he is not careful, from an essential affective connection with the patient. No such dangers of emotional detachment can prevail in the group. Here the freely interreacting unconscious excitation of patient on patient is an endless source of provocation and passionate interconnection that furnishes material for analysis and good will. The effect of exposure to the naked, unconscious trends of other people cannot be resisted. "Going around" establishes a freely flowing generalized absence of restraint, so that resistances break down and deeply conflictful material is exposed. The awareness of another's buried impulses and contradictory strivings agitate the observer profoundly and force him to participate on his own deepest levels of emotional conflict. If, as rarely happens, the patient insists on not exposing some of these personal matters to the group, he discusses them with the physician in private.

Resistances seem to melt easily in the potentiating, catalytic atmosphere of mutual revelation in the group. The searching approach of the physician who hardly reveals himself makes the individual analytic relationship one-sided and has an inhibiting influence on the patient. And many of them complain of just this inequality. The necessity to expose oneself to another person without a corresponding disclosure by the therapist makes the patient self-conscious. He feels the difference in status to be unfair. His standing naked before a clothed examiner reinforces his sense of helplessness and inadequacy. He may become resentful or withdrawn and aggressively or deviously resist laying bare successively deeper levels of his personality. In the group each member is stimulated by the partial but always increasing self-revelation of another to expose more and more of himself. The discovery that the next man not only comes to no harm in showing himself but wins social approval besides, impels one to uncover as well. The general feeling of shared divestment in a benevolent atmosphere enables each to show himself more freely than is the case in individual analysis. This experience is confirmed by the psychic climate of a group after three or four months of operation. The casual observer entering a group at such a time, is invariably amazed at the high level of spontaneity and unmasking that takes place.

Every patient resists uncovering unconscious trends in himself. When the same tendencies are exposed in another person, he is better prepared to accept them in himself. Then, he has the further example from direct observation of how to cope with these same unconscious conflicts. More often he does not sit passively by, but works together with other members to disentangle and remove their common problems. Resistance that takes the form of irrelevant and evasive autobiography cannot be so easily exploited in the group. Freud himself alluded to his distrust of the self-told histories of neurotics. He felt that their reminiscences inserted inaccuracies intended to intercept disturbing, demonstrable relationships between significant early history and present symptoms. Even without the therapist's pushing for immediate responses and against elaborate background, the group climate is so electric that it produces on-the-spot reactions that contain the past. Another form of resistance that is by-passed in the group is the evasion of sexual material. This is managed by initial attention to the social counterparts of sexual trends, to which the members thereby gain indirect access. For attention to the characterological, interpersonal forms of behavior leads to speculation concerning corresponding sexual equivalents that are thus drawn into group discussion for analysis.

Still another constructive advantage offered by group formation is that it removes the patient from the danger of prolonged dependence on the therapist. In the isolation of private treatment the analyst tends to encourage the patient to pursue his deepest personal longings. Too often it turns out that these aspirations are extremely egocentric and that indulging them leads to detached, antisocial self-assertion. The gratification of his particular yearnings amounts to being allowed to exploit familial substitutes for neurotically satisfying ends. Humoring these impulses extensively is bound to bring the patient into provocative, neurotic conflict with his associates who will not tolerate such infantile actions. Accordingly, he is impelled to turn more and more to the permissive therapist as the only agent who allows him this immature privilege. In some instances such a positive transference develops out of the patient's discovery of an all-tolerant and loving parent in the physician that he can use the rapport to turn him toward more self-reliant and social contact. Too frequently, however, he misuses his dependency to prolong and entrench his childish pleasure in the analytic relationship. The group process permits of extensive reliance of one person on the next, but more quickly demands and gets an abandonment of prolonged, possessive, and parasitic attachment that excludes the possibility of mature kinship.

Perhaps one of the most valuable aspects of group analysis is that it facilitates the replacing of the ideal of a relationship to the single-parent analyst. Instead of offering the questionable shelter of a private relationship to one omniscient ego-ideal it presents the patient with a group with whose common aims he must align himself. Whereas the basis of a private relationship may well be evasive of social reality and tend to create an aura of isolation, the group acts in just the opposite way. Instead of enhancing the average patient's tendencies to neurotic individualism and his anarchic wish for a "free" mode of life, it poses the ultimate of group association which helps him to realize his full potential as a social being. This is an added bridge to the establishment of healthy social relationships outside of analysis. Rather than strengthening the entrepreneurial ideal— typified in the neurotic's mind by the notion of the omnipotent therapist —group analysis helps to destroy the false antithesis of the individual versus the mass by helping the patient to become aware that his fulfillment can only be realized in a social or interpersonal setting.

Certainly in noting the advantages of group analysis it must be pointed out that this method allows for a greater flexibility in fees and the reaching of more patients. It also allows the therapist to treat those who might otherwise be unable to afford the high cost of sustained individual psychoanalysis.

In conclusion, it seems to me that group analysis, even at its present state of development, is a natural outcome from the previous theory and practice of psychoanalysis. It enables the therapist who possesses an adequate understanding of the social character of man to unite this awareness with his methods of treatment of individuals who have been immobilized by the conflicts of our culture. It provides a means for the elimination of interpersonal dominance and exploitation among patients. It teaches them that appropriation of one another, the incorporation of our societal criterion, is immobilizing to all concerned. They learn, at least on this level, to throw off the binding sense that self-aggrandizement is the means to security and happiness. The patient socializes himself as best he can on the level of interpersonal relationships. Rid of our vapid cultural illusions which he had embodied, he is able better to attune himself with reality. By training each participant to be sensitive to the unconscious strivings in oneself as well as in others, group analysis provides a practice ground for deep rapport with others. This ability to establish an inner attunement provides group analysands with psychic antennae which are a social asset in the extent to which they help to establish a profound emotional closeness among themselves and subsequently with strangers outside the analytic circle. Group analysis is a balance between self-study and social study. Their dynamic interrelation reveals and promotes the whole man.

24

THE CASE FOR
DIDACTIC GROUP PSYCHOTHERAPY

J. W. Klapman

It is not to be expected that any new discipline or art, any new mode of therapy, should receive unqualified and universal approval and acceptance at the very outset. As a matter of fact, the method of group psychotherapy has gained quite wide acceptance and numerous adherents with rather astonishing rapidity. There is no cause for disappointment on that score. Nevertheless, a consideration of the resistance to its adoption here and there necessitates a recapitulation of its basic assumptions.

With some presumption it is here suggested that even the art of mental healing itself would appear to need some analysts and psychotherapy, for it is not wholly free of its own species of rationalizations. In a recent work on treatment in psychiatry the authors remind us that there is a body of scientifically well-founded therapies, such as hyperpyrexia, anticonvulsant chemotherapy, hydrotherapy, chemical sedation, and so on and on, more or less in contradistinction to the more nebulous and, by implication, less scientific psychotherapies. Among the scientific procedures are listed such methods as electroshock and insulin therapy. Now, any cursory perusal of the history and course of development of the shock therapies will easily reveal the chance character of their origins. But they are mediated through physical agencies; insulin in the one case and an electric current in the other, and the tendency to aquate the physical and tangible with the scientific dies very hard indeed.

But as psychotherapy it is to be noted that group treatment, being juxtaposed with the individual therapies, cannot avoid the implication of rivalry and competitiveness. Psychotherapy having long been considered as a certain relationship between two individuals with certain subtle interactions, has established itself as the framework and model of psychother-

Reprinted from *Diseases of the Nervous System*, Vol. XI, No. 2, February 1950, pp. 35-41.

apy more or less exclusively. When compared with actual prevalent conditions and needs it will be found deficient in a number of respects.

Even excluding the frankly psychotic individuals it is well known that many patients are not amenable to individual psychotherapy. When it comes to that *ne plus ultra* of psychotherapy, psychoanalysis, it is well known that the patients presenting themselves for its ministrations are already self-selected. Usually the subject has some smattering of knowledge of what the treatment will consist. He has no doubt deliberated some time over his decision. But even then the psychoanalyst may further exercise considerable selection, excluding major psychoses, those beyond an optimal age level, and those with more severe psychoneuroses, the so-called character neuroses. In other words, the candidate for psychoanalytic treatment must be of good intelligence, with psychopathology not too severe and still in *status nascendi,* and with deeper insights more or less ready to erupt into consciousness. And even in spite of all these favorable conditions failures with psychoanalysis are not infrequent.

Yet the total stratum of patients who would qualify for psychoanalytic treatment and similar therapies forms a very thin veneer over the vast numbers of individuals who are in dire need of psychotherapy. It would therefore seem like a bit of presumptuous nonsense and a plain breach of psychiatric obligation to insist that since these vast numbers cannot be reached by psychoanalysis or any similar individual therapy there is actually no treatment for them. The difficulty does not lie primarily with psychoanalysis per se, but rather in the failure to recognize that there are different levels of psychopathology and the failure to recognize the importance of calibrating techniques to conform with such varying levels. If, as Gardner Murphy[1] sees it, personality constitutes the individual plus his immediate environment, it must even appear reasonable that psychotherapy in some instances need not at all concern itself with what is inside the skin.

Now, because group psychotherapy assays to treat patients in groups the assumption is that the original impetus for its development was the scarcity of therapists and an attempt to economize on their time and thus reach larger numbers of patients; in other words, that it was originally devised as a kind of desperate expedient and makeshift. That is not entirely borne out by its brief history, because, as so often happens, its birth was as much a matter of chance as design. Its earlier pioneers such as Emerson[2] and Pratt[3] were not psychiatrists or psychotherapists and chanced upon this mode of therapy in the treatment of tubercular patients. Even Marsh[4] and Lazell[5] did not approach group therapy purely from the point of view of expedience; in the case of Lazell he was seeking a means of reaching regressed patients. That, incidentally and subsequently, especially during the recent war, its advantages in reaching numbers of patients was recognized, in nowise establishes its origin as a pure makeshift.

Misconceptions which arise from a poor perspective must inevitably lead to rivalries between schools of psychotherapy. This is especially true in the failure to realize that psychotherapy in itself is a kind of spectrum and that particular segments of the spectrum apply optimally to particular levels of psychopathology. Naturally, there is considerable overlapping, too. Such a statement looks to a time when specific indications and contraindications for psychotherapy based on a knowledge of psychopathology are so well worked out that a fairly exact prescription for the patient's therapy can be made. Such a point of view is not sufficiently appreciated even in certain authoritative circles, as witness the following quotation:[6]

> "Because so little is known about group therapy and because so many forms are employed, it is obvious that it is very difficult to assess and compare successes and failures. We have group therapies where the group is regulated by itself and the therapist acts as a catalyst. Other group therapies depend on leadership. Again others are actually nothing more than instructive lectures given to a group of people. It is interesting that all the group therapies which I am acquainted with even the most successful ones, can not compete with faith healing. . . . Group therapy should be the answer to many of the present day psychiatric difficulties, because a fairly large number of patients could be treated simultaneously. Therefore it is interesting that even though a good deal of experimentation has been done with it, it is still not very popular, most likely because no method has yet been found to compete successfully with the individual treatment procedures."

"Actually nothing more than instructive lectures," echoes a bias that has gained wide currency. As frequently happens, the pendulum swings back to a presumably outmoded method of treatment with a new conception and some new "twist." This has happened with hypnotherapy. This must happen, too, with the role of education. The question of education will have to be revaluated with regard to its place in mental health and mental ill health.

Time was when we naïvely assumed: "Only make the means of learning accessible to people; only multiply the printed word and education will become universal." We had not properly taken into account the factor of motivation. For, despite the present-day suffocating profusion of the printed word, despite the radio and other present-day means trumpeting their information and misinformation to the world, if the Gallup poll is any kind of reliable index there is surprisingly little education prevalent— often in unexpected quarters.

But education, in the sense of biological conditioning, is not the mere summation of facts and figures, although as part of the amalgam it constitutes, factual data can be extracted from it in considerable quantity. Neither is education a time interval spent in designated halls of learning, which interval is formally certified to by designated persons and institutions.

Education in its true and biological significance means the acquisition of a broad perspective of the surrounding world leading to adequate attitudes and beliefs. It imparts a sense of relationship of man to man and to the universe he inhabits. It encompasses mature judgment in the light of abiding values. It is one means by which that currently much bandied about desideratum, "emotional maturity," is acquired; also emotional stability, a stability which is not founded on insensitivity, but which, rather, is the fruit of a profound appreciation of the human scene, its significances, and connotations.

Have we swung so far in psychotherapy in our preoccupation with the manipulation of instinctual drives and affects as to lose sight of and generate a contempt for the role of conditioning and "education" in the maintenance of psychic homeostasis? Freud did not entirely lose sight of it when he voiced his hopes for the "future primacy of the intellect" in man's motives and behavior.

The contempt for pedagogy as an instrument of therapy is unwarranted on still other grounds. It is not difficult to demonstrate that what transpires in the class or the group of the skillful pedagogue is something more than mere exposition, and it should be recalled that it is often said of a professor or instructor, "He certainly knows his stuff, but he just can't teach." For it cannot be denied that what transpires in the class of the skillful pedagogue is a process akin to the transference of psychotherapy. The process of learning is not merely one of passive absorption, for its most powerful implement is motivation, and the most successful teacher consciously or unconsciously comes to employ it through the transference relationship.

The pedagogue is more concerned with the quantity and quality of the knowledge acquired by his students than the transference process per se; the group therapist quite deliberately attempts to enhance and manipulate the transference process though not entirely ignoring the therapeutic value which inheres in intellectual growth and perspective. That there is considerable overlapping of both disciplines cannot be considered discreditable to group psychotherapy.

It must be emphasized that group therapy is not merely an adjunct to individual psychotherapy. It does not appear sufficiently evident to many that it is the therapy of choice at certain levels of pathology. Mental and emotional disorders do not invariably arise at the deeper levels of psychopathology, nor do they always proceed primarily from maldisposition of instinctual energies. "A. Paranoiac" [7] has cited a number of interesting and amusing examples of personality disturbances originating from misapprehensions on the cognitive levels of psychic functioning. In the following case example it may be seen that that order of psychopathology can lead to dire consequences quite as much as the deeper instinctual disturbances.

Mr. A. was a little man in his sixties who had developed gastric symptoms, having suffered a sudden rupture of a peptic ulcer, and an emergency operation had barely saved his life. He was found to be the epitome of the henpecked husband. A more subdued and browbeaten male could hardly be imagined, and overshadowing the entire picture was the domineering, disciplinary Mrs. A. She was the second oldest in a sibship of seven sisters. Her father, a widower, arrived in this country with his bevy of daughters when Mrs. A. was in her early teens. She had practically no schooling, having adroitly outsmarted the truant officers. However, in the recurrent economic depressions of the last part of the nineteenth and the early part of the twentieth centuries there was considerable need for her scanty earnings. The father was a docile, ineffectual person, who, faced with the task of raising seven obstreperous daughters without the assistance of a wife, apparently threw up his hands in complete surrender and resignation. It is certain the girls quarrelled and bickered among themselves *ad nauseam*. In this setting and probably also by a variety of incidental and accidental circumstances, Mrs. A. may be seen to have adopted a life philosophy which may be paraphrased somewhat as follows: "If I have nothing to do with the 'other guy' he cannot harm me. I must look out for myself, and what the 'other guy' does and how he fares is no concern of mine. I want nothing to do or know of matters that do not touch me, and if I concern myself not with anything outside myself and know not what transpires about me no evil can assail me." Mrs. A. thus demonstrates that the state of pristine ignorance is sometimes an active process which has to be labored for to maintain pure and unsullied by alien information and "stuff." In fact, Mrs. A. sometimes boasted she did not think and cogitate or make plans as some misguided people are wont to do. Any question which implied the fulfillment of a personal obligation by her was apt to be countered with the staccato reminder to tend to one's own business. This philosophy, in any case, served Mrs. A. as an effective insulation, and her personality thus remained maximally insulated.

A personality cannot remain absolutely insulated in society, for other strong instinctual drives urge in a different direction. For example, marriage and a family, because of which "the other guy" comes to occupy a more preferential position than originally calculated. However, the insulated personality never concerns itself with such inconsistency, for the intellectual exercise necessary to its solution is alien to its nature; and thus, the insulated personality cannot realize that in having acted so contrary to the original intent the wall of personal insulation has been made slightly porous.

After their marriage Mr. and Mrs. A. established a small retail business in which they were quite successful. But Mr. A. soon found himself submerged under a barrage of orders, reprimands, browbeatings, belittlings, and every manner of conceivable insult from which he has never emerged. Even when his two daughters reached maturity he found no champion for his cause, for the three formed an iron-bound matriarchy and gynecocracy, and Mr. A. was more deeply submerged than ever.

Having been successful in the business by methods and management, which, though honorable enough, would not have earned any commendation from Better Business Bureaus, Mrs. A. arrogated all the credit to herself. Consciously or unconsciously, in her mind her close adherence to her philosophy, epitomized in that shining motto, "It pays to be ignorant," had been amply vindicated. It was not long before one arrived at the realization that Mr. A. was not the bearer of the original or most important psychopathology. The disease and pathological entity was constituted by the family as a unit, and the nidus of the disease process and source of infection was none other than Mrs. A.

When a slump came in the business Mrs. A. always had a convenient scapegoat. In no way could the lesser income be attributed to deficiencies in her management or poor economic conditions. Such a conception would have violated her self-image. The adversity was invariably ascribed to Mr. A.'s bungling and ineptitude. Be that as it may, the true reasons for any business *contretemps* were apparent to Mrs. A. Obviously Mr. A. as the "other guy" was helping himself to the contents of the cash register. For what purpose? To support a certain lady. Certainly! Some of the customers had informed her of seeing Mr. A. in that lady's hotel. From what was known of Mr. A. such an escapade was inconceivable, violating every tenet of sound psychological reasoning. And, furthermore, it was highly doubtful that the business in its palmiest days could have supported such a lady in the style to which she was accustomed. One could demur at this allegation only at the risk of indicting Mrs. A. as an outright liar.

Serving as a commentary on the dynamics of *folie a deux*, or *trois*, or *quatre* was the concurrence of opinion of Mrs. A. and her older daughter about Mr. A.'s playing the horses, another of his alleged depredations. Well, if the man found some pleasure and compensation in betting small sums why deny that to him? Small sums, nothing! Five and ten dollars a day and even twenty-five, and by way of proof the daughter and her mother deposed they had seen him at some distance sidling up to a newspaper stand and making a hurried transaction with the man. Seeing his wife and daughter approaching, Mr. A. had made a speedy getaway. They, wife and daughter, then went up to the newspaper man and told him that if he did not immediately return the money to them they would call the police. The man silently refunded two dollars. This certainly sounded like incontrovertible truth, but it was altogether inconsistent with the behavior of the self-effacing little Mr. A. The daughter, privately, was asked: "Were you there yourself at the time?" She hedged. After some further persistent questioning she finally admitted she was not present at the time, but that her mother had informed her of the incident of the two-dollar refund.

There were many other characteristics demonstrating Mrs. A.'s insularity, consequent immaturity, and paranoid reactions toward the "other guy." If, for example, Mrs. A. momentarily misplaced her diamond ring or other valuables, even her daughters, despite their well-nigh organic attachment to their mother, were not above suspicion (again, both the daughters' marital adjustment is another story). Many asocial characteristics and mannerisms in speech and deportment also resulted. When some acquaintance related some incident or event Mrs. A. frequently interrupted saying,

"No," then proceeded to relate the same occurrence giving precisely the same data, much as a child insists on holding the center of attention and at the same time, making light of the "other guy's" capacities and abilities.

In Mrs. A.'s case one may postulate theories about masculine protest, Oedipal situations, penis envy, and castration complexes. But it would not appear to the impartial observer that the psychopathology resides primarily within the skin. It lies primarily outside of the organism in the faulty interpersonal relationships, in the defective orientations, and in poor social conditioning. It lies predominently in the plan which Mrs. A. adopted early in life, which for her became a fixed set by which she has lived and which she has lived up to with singular devotion. In the goal of remaining as unaware as possible of the "other guy," of having no truck with him, and remaining as ignorant as possible she has achieved amazing if not praiseworthy success. This situation conforms far more closely to the Adlerian concept of the "life plan" or "life style" than to the concept of deeper instinctual or emotional disturbance. We are not yet fully accustomed to thinking in terms of suiting psychotherapeutic approach to the level of psychopathology predominantly involved, and in all situations we insist on the grand technique of individual psychotherapy exclusively. Even if Mrs. A. were treatable by psychoanalysis one wonders what would be the fate of the supernatant intellectual hiatus.

The educational role of group psychotherapy, then, may be one of the most important therapeutic functions, and from our point of view not lightly to be dismissed. It is possible to cite numerous examples in which a process of preparation must precede individual psychotherapy. What does observation of the usual psychiatric patient reveal? In one way or another, despite much initial resistance, he has finally mobilized enough courage to consult a psychiatrist. He sneaks into the doctor's office, if possible, by the byways and alleyways as if en route to a sorcerer's den. Finally, he finds himself closeted with a strange man who makes quite unusual requests of him. The patient has no idea what to expect. If he could concretize and verbalize his vague expectations they probably would be that the doctor will feel the bumps on his head, would administer a simple "twist of the wrist" to his spine or head; would try out some strange electrical gadget on his head, look deeply into his eyes and read his thoughts, or, at any rate, give him some strange nostrum or potion. When, instead of such procedures, the doctor tells him to go ahead and state what is in his thoughts and so much of the burden of treatment is thrown right back on his own shoulders, many of the patients are actually insulted, at least rendered highly uncomfortable. It is, at any rate, all very weird to the patient.

However, in group therapy, in the protection that the presence of his fellow patients provide he finds a much more natural setting. While he preserves a kind of anonymity he can at the same time hear and see that his own case is not so unique and that he has a great deal in common with the problems and difficulties of his fellow patients and classmates, and he is thus gradually brought out of his isolation and gradually induced to ventilate his own emotional problems. The class atmosphere is much more of a natural setting than the one in which he finds himself when closeted with a strange inquisitor. It has, indeed, far greater verisimilitude, for personality is to a very large extent the product of the social scene about us. Murphy[8] has put it this way:

> "But for the most vital purposes a cell must be understood as an aspect of the life of an organ and the organ as an aspect of the life of man. In the same way personality must be understood as an aspect of the social process; it cannot in most cases, be considered as a self-contained unit. Individually we balk at this fact, for it is very deflating; nevertheless we are reflections of a broad social process."

Obviously disorders which have their origin, at least in part, in social interrelationships are best treated in the setting from which they arose. As one of the direct benefits of group therapy we may see that at the very least it is a good preparation for intensive individual psychotherapy. This can be illustrated by the following case history example:

> B.C. was a young matron who had suffered a schizophrenic breakdown and had had one period of state hospital commitment. She was now out on conditional release. Required to return to the clinic for periodic checkup she is found exceedingly tense and uncomfortable. Asked about herself she gives a halting, very laconic summary of symptoms, and from there on any attempt to elicit biographical or psychological data meets with absolutely no success. Asked to talk about herself she is rendered extremely uncomfortable. "But what shall I say? I've told you everything." The best she can manage is to scrape up additional data about her symptoms, as if, as is usual in such cases, the individual believed the very accretion of such signs and symptoms, this continual piling of Ossa on Pelion, will of itself miraculously effect a cure. However, it was suggested that she attend group psychotherapy class. Two days later she attends such a session wherein the nature of mental illness, the injustice and groundlessness of the stigma are dealt with. The following day she is seen in individual interview. She now brings along notes she has made of her interim thoughts as she has been directed to do before but which she has not carried out until this interview. She now also relates many traumatizing incidents of her childhood. Another thing which greatly bothered her, she relates, was her resentment toward her husband and mother for having had her committed to a state hospital. "But," she hastens to add, "I wrote this down before I had been to the class. Now I don't feel that way any more."
>
> It is noteworthy that now she not only produces material more abundantly and freely, but her voice is louder and more steady, and her manner indicates greater self-assurance.

From the foregoing example it may be seen that not only may group therapy serve as a preparation for individual treatment but that it also acts as catalyst, speeding up and intensifying positive transference, helping to resolve negative attitudes and negative transference. That this should be so is not surprising in the light of what is already known of group behavior. Contrary to the critic of group therapy quoted earlier in this paper there is some scientific basis for this form of treatment, and to mention only a few such references we might cite Freud's *Group Psychology and the Analysis of the Ego,*[9] McDougall's *The Group Mind,*[10] Le Bon's *The Crowd,*[11] Redl's work [12] and so forth. One will find in these works some of the fundamental reasons why group dynamics are effective in treatment. While it is true the field is in great need of further experimental investigation, it would be a gross understatement that little or no psychological or scientific rationale is known for its employment at the present time.

As to the character of approach it is to be noted that there is a wide range of intensity of group therapy. The polarity of this range is marked by the repressive-inspirational at one end and the more or less analytical method at the other end. Marsh [13], who worked with groups as large as two hundred, apparently achieved a mild form of inspirational therapy, while Schilder[14] with groups of four to eight selected patients conducted intensive psychoanalytic group psychotherapy. As to method of implementation a division has already been made into analytic forms and didactic forms of group therapy. The distinction cannot be hard and fast, for much depends on content. The use which the therapist makes of his materials determines in large part how didactic or how analytical the treatment turns out to be.

Teaching or pedagogical methods are administered in a variety of ways. In many instances the therapist will depend on the patients bringing problems to the class for general discussion, therapist acting as leader and moderator and, where indicated, making appropriate interpretations. It may be remarked that such a regimen is successful when dealing with an unusually articulate group of patients who harbor strong resentments. In most other cases it devolves on the therapist to produce stimulus material to set the class into action. Such stimulus material is usually furnished by therapist's delivering a series of talks or lectures with subsidiary procedures combined in a variety of ways. Now, it would seem obvious that if the therapist delivers a series of lectures these should be reasonably well organized and planned. If the therapist has carefully planned this material and has designed it to be maximally stimulating to and provocative of patients' emotional responses and abreactions, it is patent he may as well commit them to writing. The fact is that many a treatise and textbook has had such an origin. An instructor gives a series of lectures which is well received and is for that reason induced to collect and edit them for publication. This is the case in group therapy employing the medium of a textbook.

The writer has used such a textbook and feels there are a number of advantages from its use. These advantages are:

(a) The textbook provides a systematic, planned, and logical sequence of material which serves to stimulate patients' associations, as well as serving the purposes of education and reeducation in the broadest sense.

(b) Instead of patients being passive auditors as they would be at lectures they become active participants when they read aloud from the book, recite, comment, and associate to the material.

(c) The textbook furnishes material which does not depend on therapist's forensic skill for effectiveness; which is always available and is especially useful in retaining continuity of purpose and method when a new therapist is required to take over.

(d) Although it would not seem possible to standardize the practice of group psychotherapy in all its phases, use of a textbook supplies the nearest approach to a standard and basis of comparison as between one class and another.

(e) The printed word carries some additional authority. Of course, the printed word is capable of great abuse. But in this case, employed in the interest of therapy, the stratagem is justifiable.

(f) Silences during class sessions have been noted by several group therapists. It is believed by Foulkes[15] that silence is not always an evidence of resistance. But whatever the silence of the group may connote it appears to be disconcerting. With the textbook always at hand to turn to, the therapist need have no concern about these arid interludes in the class sessions.

No grades are given and no constraint is exercised. While it is very desirable to absorb knowledge that is not the main desideratum. Nor is the quantity of material dealt with in any given session a great concern. If in the entire session only one little phrase of the book has been dealt with, which has led to copious comment or abundant associations; in which patients' attitudes and beliefs have been objectified and commented on liberally by the whole class, it is deemed a very worth-while session, indeed. At the end of each chapter is a list of review questions by which the preceding section is more or less recapitulated and summarized.

But the group therapy need not be confined to the textbook. As already indicated, the text performs the function of stimulus, calling forth patients' responses and reactions, often stimulating the production of deeper material and associated abreaction. But in addition to this central thread, this nucleus of the classwork, there are outside assignments for book reviews, and this in itself would constitute a form of bibliotherapy. Symposia and debates may be arranged and conducted. Written autobiographies may be called for. Even a well worked up case history of one of the class members may be discussed and commented upon by the whole class. This has been found very effective.

Results of group psychotherapy are not easy to assess. However, the clinical impression is not a totally unreliable guide. The factors which make for improvement in any given patient seem to be multiple and of some complexity. Many patients, invited to the class, appear once or twice and then drop out of sight; but, clinically, of those who attend regularly for any extended period of time, with only few exceptions, practically all show definite improvement. This observation is corroborated by psychological testing[16] which shows gains in personality organization in all patients with few exceptions. In one patient in the writer's group the improvement has been spectacular and dramatic.

To the skeptical inquisitor we can do no better by way of conclusion than again to quote from Murphy.[17]

> "It is quite likely (as in a dialectical moment) selfhood will be better understood when reference is made to the primordial non-self matrix from which it arises, and the synthesis, the capacity of human nature to function at self and non-self levels at the same time, to alternate when it so desires, may prove to be an enrichment of personality far greater than that which the cult of self-contained, self-defined individuality can grant."

REFERENCES

1. G. Murphy, *Personality* (New York: Harper & Bros., 1947).
2. W. R. P. Emerson, "The Hygienic and Dietetic Treatment of Delicate Children by the Class Method," *Boston M. and S. J.*, 164:326-328, 1910.
3. J. H. Pratt, "The Principles of Class Treatment and their Application to Various Chronic Diseases," *Hosp. Social Service*, 6:401, 1922.
4. L. C. Marsh, "Group Treatment of the Psychoses by the Psychological Equivalent of Revival," *Ment. Hyg.*, 15:328-349, 1931.
5. E. W. Lazell, "The Group Treatment of Dementia Praecox," *Psychoanalyt. Rev.*, 8:166-179, 1921.
6. P. H. Hoch, "Summary of Symposium Findings," in *Failures in Psychiatric Treatment* (New York: Grune and Stratton, 1948).
7. A. Paranoiac, "Paranoia from the Subjective Point of View," *Psychoanalyt. Rev.*, 13:200-209, 1926.
8. Murphy, *op. cit.*
9. S. Freud, *Group Psychology and the Analysis of the Ego* (London: International Psychoanalyt. Press, 1922).
10. W. McDougall, *The Group Mind* (New York: G. P. Putnam's Sons, 1920).
11. G. Le Bon, *The Crowd* (New York: Unwin, 1922).
12. F. Redl, "Group Emotion and Leadership," *Psychiat.* (White Foundation), 5:573-596, 1942.
13. Marsh, *op. cit.*
14. P. Schilder, "Results and Problems of Group Psychotherapy in Severe Neuroses," *Ment. Hyg.*, 23:87-98, 1939.
15. S. H. Foulkes, *Group Analytic Psychotherapy* (New York: Grune and Stratton, 1948).

16. J. W. Klapman and W. H. Lundin, "Objective Appraisal of Textbook-Mediated Group Psychotherapy with Psychotics," *Int. J. Group Psych.*, II:116-126, 1952.
17. Murphy, *op. cit.*

25

MECHANISMS OF GROUP PSYCHOTHERAPY: PROCESSES AND DYNAMICS

Raymond J. Corsini
Bina Rosenberg

Scientific progress in psychotherapy is dependent to a large extent on the ability of psychotherapists of different schools of thought to communicate. Lacking the universal language of mathematics which has enabled the rapid and orderly development of the natural sciences, social scientists may find that the medium of verbal communication sometimes actually forms a barrier to understanding and progress. The question of semantics and syntactics in psychotherapy is an important one and needs to be explored.

Group psychotherapy has expanded greatly in the past two decades and has already developed a considerable literature. But as may be expected, no differently from individual therapy, it has generated a number of special concepts couched sometimes in esoteric language. While diversity of language per se is not to be deplored, it does seem necessary to find means of effecting maximal communication between people exposed to different frames of reference. The question arises as to whether it is possible to come to semantic generalizations. This paper is devoted to an attempt along these lines.

THE PROBLEM

A central issue of psychotherapy is the nature of the dynamics that lead to successful therapy. What within the group therapeutic situation is of the essence?

A simple way to find the answer is to examine the literature. This is

Reprinted from the *Journal of Abnormal and Social Psychology*, Vol. 15, No. 3, November 1955, pp. 406-411.

perhaps the best way since it must be expected that those who have written on this subject, having gained their knowledge from clinical experience, should have at least partially valid opinions. However, the inquirer finds so much, stated so variously, often so convincingly, and mostly without reference to anyone else, that it is not to be wondered at that one often retires from the literature sadder but not wiser. This can be illustrated in miniature. Three articles are searched for the answer to the question of the dynamics of group therapy.

The first writer lists five dynamics: relationships, catharsis, insight, reality testing, and sublimation.[1] This list seems to make sense and the author's contention that these *are* the dynamics may assure the reader that the answer has been found. In the second article the reader finds five dynamics. This time they are transference, catharsis, abreaction, loss of isolation, and ego support.[2] The comparison is interesting. Only one dynamic, catharsis, is mentioned by both authorities, and between them they have listed nine mechanisms. Going to the third article, once again five mechanisms are listed: reassurance, reeducation, desensitization, catharsis, and transference.[3] The three writers each have contributed five mechanisms, of which only one, catharsis, is mentioned by all three; transference being mentioned by two. Each of the other ten mechanisms is mentioned by only one of the three experts.

How can this be explained? Have the authorities had different experiences and so found different mechanisms? Are there really 12 different mechanisms, and has each expert recognized only some of them? Or is it possible they are saying the same things in different ways? This problem, here illustrated in miniature, extends throughout the literature on psychotherapy. Had samples been taken from ten or from one hundred writers the list would have been longer and still more puzzling. What is needed is to find some way of arranging, classifying, and synthesizing these separate elements into an orderly and meaningful system. It is this that we have attempted to do.

THE METHOD

The procedures used were based on two assumptions. The first was that all writers on the question of the dynamic mechanisms of group psychotherapy are correct in their opinions, no matter how unusual or how unique their observations. The second assumption is that it is possible for the authors to make certain unifying classificatory judgments about concepts.

The procedures involved four steps:

Step 1. The literature on group psychotherapy was searched for expressions of dynamics. Data were sought in approximately 300 articles, amounting to about one-quarter of the entire literature on group therapy.

Step 2. More than 300 statements were abstracted from the literature and then examined critically to determine whether they could be considered dynamics rather than results, or something else. Eliminating doubtful items left 220 statements to be analyzed.

Step 3. All identical statements were combined. This resulted in 166 different mechanisms.

Step 4. The 166 statements were put on cards and examined to find combinatory hypotheses. For example, it was noted that some of the statements indicated that an often-occurring concept was one that involved a person doing something for another, being philanthropic or altruistic. All cards were then examined to locate statements such as "patient is a therapist to other patients," [4] "advice by patient," [5] "patients help each other." [6] All cards involving "altruism" were isolated to form a cluster. In this manner hypotheses were suggested and the remaining items searched and combined until a number of cards remained that could not be placed in any established category but yet did not seem to form other categories.

RESULTS

Ten classes of mechanisms were finally isolated by this procedure, nine of which could be assigned specific labels. A tenth group, consisting of items not otherwise assignable, was also formed. The nine chief mechanisms will now be defined. The actual statements will also be listed to show the diversity of opinions in this field and to permit further independent research on this problem.

Mechanisms

Acceptance. This statistically most frequent concept was taken to mean respect for and sympathy with the individual. Acceptance implies belongingness, a warm, friendly, comfortable feeling in the group.

Altruism. Closely related to acceptance, but in addition involving wanting to do something for others, is the mechanism of altruism. The essence of this mechanism is the desire to help others.

Universalization. This concept refers to the realization that one is not unique, that there are others like oneself with problems either identical with or very similar to one's own.

Intellectualization. This is a process of learning or acquiring knowledge in the group. Intellectualization leads to insight, which itself we considered not a mechanism, but a result of intellectualization.

Reality testing. This concept means that the group situation is one where real and important things happen; it is not only a temporary artificial environment. It assumes reality and in it the patient can test himself in a safe and unthreatening atmosphere.

Transference. This concept implies the existence of a strong emotional attachment either to the therapist, to separate members of the group, or to the group as a whole.

Interaction. Perhaps the most difficult of the mechanisms to understand and classify is the one which relates to relationships of unspecified nature within the group. What this process seems to amount to is that any interaction engaged in by a therapeutic group manages to have beneficial results.

Spectator therapy. Through this mechanism people gain from listening to and observing themselves and others.

Ventilation. As in individual therapy, one of the important mechanisms in the group is the release of feelings and the expression of ideas usually repressed in other nontherapeutic situations.

Miscellaneous. A number of statements remaining after classification are listed separately. It must be understood that the concepts in this set of statements need not be considered any less important or any less universal than others that have been either more frequent or easier to combine, Classification is not intended to be value-forming.

The Statements

Below are listed the original data from which the classifications were made. In many cases statements were compressed or reworded to get the essence of the authors' ideas. They are listed according to their classifications in order of statistical frequency, with bibliographic notations to the original articles.

Acceptance

    Group identification (23), (40), (58)
    Group status (25), (55)
    Esprit de corps (5), (33)
    Friendly environment (54)
    Communal feeling (7)
    Unification of the group (31)
    Group socialization (33)
    Loss of isolation (27)
    Emotional acceptance (63)
    Feeling of belonging (25), (31)
    Acceptance by the group (64)
    Cohesiveness (61)
    Identification with others (32), (62)
    Togetherness (16)
    Strength through belonging (6)
    Group is tolerant of the patient (52)
    Protection of the group (52)
    Ego support (27)
    Security of the group (52)
    Conviction of social approval (17)

Friendly relations between patients (28)
Permissivism (12)
"No longer feel alone" (33)
Security in a nonthreatening environment (6)
Supportive relations (54)
Therapist tolerant of patient (37)
Therapist is accepting of patient (37)
Loss of feeling of isolation (27)
Permissive environment (53)
Feeling of reassurance (25)
Group support (6)
Group cohesion (15)
Emotional support (4)

Universalization

Universalization (47), (5)
Patient recognizes his behavior has been duplicated by many of his mates (48)
Realization others have the same problems (28)
"People fighting what I am fighting" (26)
Realization others similarly affected (26)
Demonstrative universality of problems (51)
Recognize similar problems in others (13)
Illness not individualized (13)
Recognize other patients have same difficulty (60)
Resonance (36)
Realize others are in the same boat (41)
Realization of similar problems (34)
Knowledge of others with same problems (57)
Discovers he is not unique (55)

Reality testing

Testing reality (4), (35), (40), (45), (55), (56)
Working through (31), (33), (35)
Relive old family conflicts (60)
Put patient where he cannot fail (14)
Experience for personal interaction (53)
Recapitulation of family relationships (32)
Practice field for social relations (23)
Provides a testing forum (9)
Living out of ego frustrations (64)
Outlet for aggression (18)
Patient finds a setting where he can re-evaluate his concepts (8)
Test social reality (4)
Recreate family setting (49)
Surrogate family (64)
Reality of hostilities (33)
Revival of conflicts (51)

Defenses can be tested (25)
Field where one can relate self to others (54)
Catharsis-in-the-family (63)
Substitute family (55)
Appropriate targets for hostility (55)

Altruism

Encouragement (10), (66), (34)
Advice by patient (44)
Direction by patient (44)
Sense of being important in the lives of others (26)
Interpretation by patient (23)
Suggestion by patient (44)
Altruism (24)
Patient a therapist to other patients (21)
Patient sacrifices personal interest to group (39)
Patients help each other (44)
Reassurance by compassion (33)
Giving love (3)

Transference

Transference (5), (15), (16), (27), (31), (46), (49)
Transference to therapist (19), (20), (38), (40)
Transference to group (15), (20), (22), (32), (63)
Continued flow of emotional support (4)
Patient-to-patient transference (63)
Countertransference (31)
Attachment to therapist (58)
Identification to therapist (28)

Spectator Therapy

People patient can imitate (54)
Testimony of members (28)
Patient listens to himself objectively (19)
Passive participation (19)
Spectator therapy (42)
Example of others (44)

Interaction

Interaction (38), (49), (56)
Contagion (39), (61)
Relationship (55), (56)
Group interaction (34), (63)
Relationship to leader (46)
Relationship pattern (2)
Interaction atmosphere (67)
Contact with others (26)
Relationship of patient and therapist (34)

Experience for personal interaction (53)
Interstimulation (51)

Intellectualization

Interpretation (4), (19), (31), (55)
Intellectualization (19), (29)
Awareness of interpersonal relations (1)
Learning common thoughts of others (50)
Explanation (57)
Understanding defenses of others (1)
Understanding (18)
Intellectual comprehension (63)
Learning (61)
Reeducation (15)
Analysis of dreams (31)
Analysis of resistance (31)
Proper evaluation of symptoms (30)
Relearning (21)
Subject evaluates symptoms in others (48)

Ventilation

Catharsis (15), (21), (25), (27), (33), (35), (40), (43), (55), (56), (59), (63)
Abreaction (27), (62)
Ventilation of hostilities (9), (63)
Ventilation (33), (35)
Animosities abreact (20)
Verbalization of fantasy (40)
Emotional release (2)
Release of hostilities in a socially acceptable way (66)
Relief of guilt through confession (33)
Ventilation of guilt (11)
Release of hostilities (66)
Activity catharsis (56)
Ventilation of anxiety (21)
Attitude of verbal expressions (52)
Release of unconscious material (63)
Expression of unconscious tendencies (2)
Activate emotional release (4)
Release of repressed drives (4)
Releases emotional tension (55)

Miscellaneous

Sublimation (65), (66)
Spontaneity (43), (61)
Rivalry for improvement (28)
Suggestion (10)
Authority of the therapist (31)

Suggestibility of the group (28)
Heightening action (61)
Closure of tension systems (21)
Therapist's confidence in the patient (37)
Substitution (5)
Facing the traumatic past (6)
Inspired by others to greater effort (26)
Social coercion to think rationally (33)
Sharing mutual experiences (17)
Sharing (62)
Relief of isolation through sharing (51)
Reinforcement (61)
Integration of contradictory tendencies (6)
Shock (42)
Relaxation (61)
Desensitization (15)
Sharing difficulties (41)
Reassurance (15)
Rivalry (39)
Intensification (56)
Emotional infection (56)

DISCUSSION

The process of combining separate elements into general classes is known as taxonomy. Whether the reductions here effected are the most efficient possible, and whether others operating on other premises or even using the same procedures would have come to the same conclusions, is open to question and to further research. In any case, a rational beginning has been made in the combining of elements into general classes and in the providing of a series of relatively independent factors. This process can be utilized for more effective communication through the reduction of terms.

The nine classes found appear to reduce to three still more general factors. An *intellectual* factor consisting of universalization, intellectualization, and spectator therapy appears. Also, an *emotional* factor including acceptance, altruism, and transference evolves. And, there is an *actional* factor of reality testing, interaction, and ventilation.

From this arises the possibility of evaluating any method of group psychotherapy in terms of these three factors. For example, it seems that Klapman's textbook-mediated therapy and Dreikurs' group counseling have a high component of the intellectual factor; that Rogers' nondirective group counseling and Schilder's analytic group therapy have a relatively high degree of the emotional factor; and that Moreno's psychodrama and Slavson's activity group therapy have a large amount of the actional factor.

SUMMARY

Some 300 articles in the literature of group psychotherapy were examined to locate expressions referring to effecting dynamic processes of therapy. Some 200 items were obtained and reduced by inspection to nine general classes and a miscellaneous class. The nine general classes appear to reduce to three factors: an *intellectual* one, consisting of universalization, intellectualization, and spectator therapy; an *emotional* one, consisting of acceptance, altruism, and transference; and an *actional* factor, consisting of reality testing, interaction, and ventilation.

It is believed this reductionism can be useful in providing better communication between group therapists and can be the basis for further research in the basic components of group therapy.

REFERENCES

1. S. R. Slavson, "Advances in Group Psychotherapy," *Int. Congr. Ment. Health*, 24-26, 1948.
2. S. B. Hadden, "Dynamics of Group Psychotherapy," *Arch. Neurol. Psychiat.*, 65:125, 1944.
3. J. M. Cotton, "Group Psychotherapy: An Appraisal," in P. H. Hoch (ed.), *Failures in Psychiatric Treatment* (New York: Grune and Stratton, 1948), pp. 121-128.
4. J. M. Enneis, "The Dynamics of Group and Action Procedures in Therapy," *Group Psychother.*, 4:17-22, 1951.
5. H. Mullan, "Some Essentials of Group Psychotherapy," *Group Psychother.*, 5:68-69, 1952.
6. *Ibid.*

BIBLIOGRAPHY

1. Abrahams, J., "Preliminary Report of an Experience in the Group Therapy of Schizophrenics," *Am. J. Psychiat.*, 104:613-617, 1948.
2. Ackerman, N. W., "Group Therapy from the Viewpoint of a Psychiatrist," *Am. J. Orthopsychiat.*, 31:667-681, 1943.
3. ———, "Psychotherapy and Giving Love," *Psychiat.*, 7:129-137, 1944.
4. ———, "Some General Principles in the Use of Group Psychotherapy," in B. Glueck, ed., *Current Therapies of Personality Disorders* (New York: Grune & Stratton, 1946), pp. 275-280.
5. Altschuler, I. M., "One Year's Experience with Group Psychotherapy," *Ment. Hyg.*, 24:190-196, 1940.
6. Bettelheim, B., and Sylvester, Emmy, "Therapeutic Influence of the Group and the Individual," *Am. J. Orthopsychiat.*, 17:684-692, 1947.

7. Betz, K., "Gruppentraining und Bilderlefen," Z. *Psychother. Med. Psychol.*, 1:71-76, 1951.
8. Blackman, N., "Ward Therapy—A New Method of Group Psychotherapy," *Psychiat. Quart.*, 16:660-667, 1942.
9. ———, "Group Psychotherapy with Aphasics," *J. Nerv. Ment. Dis.*, 111: 154-163, 1950.
10. Buck, R. W., "The Class Method in the Treatment of Essential Hypertension," *Ann. Int. Med.*, 11:514-518, 1937.
11. Caplan, G., "Mental Hygiene Work with Expectant Mothers," *Ment. Hyg.*, 35:41, 50, 1951.
12. Coffey, H., Friedman, M., Leary, T., and Ossorio, A., "Social Implications of the Group Therapeutic Situation," *J. Soc. Issues*, 6:44-61, 1950.
13. Colthorp, R. W., "Group Psychotherapy in Patients Recovering from Psychoses," *Am. J. Psychiat.*, 104:414-417, 1947.
14. Cotton, J. M., "The Psychiatric Treatment Program at Welch Convalescent Hospital," *Res. Pub. Ass. Nerv. Ment. Dis.*, 25:316-321, 1946.
15. ———, "Group Psychotherapy: An Appraisal," in P. H. Hoch, ed., *Failures in Psychiatric Treatment* (New York: Grune & Stratton, 1948), pp. 121-128.
16. ———, "Group Structure and Group Psychotherapy," *Group Psychother.*, 3:216-217, 1951.
17. Curran, F. J., and Schilder, P., "A Constructive Approach to the Problems of Childhood and Adolescence," *J. Crim. Psychopath.*, 2:125-142, 305-320, 1940-1941.
18. Curran, F. J., "Group Therapy: Introductory Remarks," *Neuropsychiat.*, 2:43-47, 1952.
19. Dreikurs, R., "Technique and Dynamics of Multiple Psychotherapy," *Psychiat. Quart.*, 24:788-799, 1950.
20. Dreyfus-Moreau, J., "A Propos du Transfert en Psychotherapie Collective," *Rev. Franç. Psychoanal.*, 14:244-257, 1950.
21. Enneis, J. M., "The Dynamics of Group and Action Procedures in Therapy," *Group Psychother.*, 4:17-22, 1951.
22. Glatzer, H., "Transference in Group Therapy," *Am. J. Orthopsychiat.*, 22: 499-509, 1952.
23. Golden, M. M., "Some Mechanisms of Analytic Group Therapy," *Int. J. Group Psychother.*, 3:280-284, 1952.
24. Greenblatt, M., "Altruism in the Psychotherapeutic Relation," in P. A. Sorokin, ed., *Explorations in Altruistic Love and Behavior* (Boston: Beacon Press, 1950), pp. 188-193.
25. Grotjahn, M., "Experiences with Group Psychotherapy as a Method for the Treatment of Veterans," *Am. J. Psychiat.*, 103:637-643, 1947.
26. Hadden, S. B., "Group Psychotherapy: A Superior Method of Treating Larger Numbers of Neurotics," *Am. J. Psychiat.*, 101:68-72, 1944.
27. ———, "Dynamics of Group Psychotherapy," *Arch. Neurol. Psychiat.*, 65:125, 1951.
28. Harris, H. I., "Efficient Psychotherapy for the Large Outpatient Clinic," *New England J. Med.*, 221:1-15, 1939.

29. Johnston, M., "Experiment with Narcotic Addicts," *Am. J. Psychother.*, 5:24-31, 1951.
30. Jones, M., "Group Treatment with Particular Reference to Group Projective Methods," *Am. J. Psychiat.*, 101:293-299, 1944.
31. Kew, C. E., and Kew, C. J., "Group Psychotherapy in a Church Setting," *Pastoral Psychol.*, 1:36-39, 1950.
32. Klapman, J. W., "Group Treatment of the Mentally Ill," *Survey Mid-Monthly*, 82:80-81, 1946.
33. Kline, N. S., and Dreyfus, A., "Group Psychotherapy in a Veterans Administration Hospital," *Am. J. Psychiat.*, 104:618-622, 1948.
34. Konopka, G., "Group Work and Therapy," in C. E. Hendy, ed., *A Decade of Group Work* (New York: Association Press, 1948), pp. 39-44.
35. Krise, M., "Creative Dramatics and Group Psychotherapy," *J. Child Psychiat.*, 2:337-342, 1952.
36. Lebovici, S., Diatkine, R., and Kestenberg, E., "Applications of Psychoanalysis to Group Psychotherapy and Psychodramatic Therapy in France," *Group Psychother.*, 5:38-50, 1952.
37. Lipkin, S., "Notes on Group Psychotherapy," *J. Nerv. Ment. Dis.*, 107:459-479, 1948.
38. Lowrey, L. G., "Group Treatment for Mothers," *Am. J. Orthopsychiat.*, 14:589-592, 1944.
39. Marsh, L. C., "Group Therapy of the Psychoses by the Psychological Equivalent of the Revival," *Ment. Hyg.*, 15:328-349, 1931.
40. Mayers, A. N., "A Psychiatric Evaluation of Discussion Groups," *J. Nerv. Ment. Dis.*, 111:499-509, 1950.
41. Miller, H., and Baruch, D., "Psychological Dynamics in Allergic Patients as Shown in Group and Individual Psychotherapy," *J. Consult. Psychol.*, 12:111-115, 1948.
42. Moreno, J. L., "Psychodramatic Shock Therapy," *Sociometry*, 2:1-30, 1939.
43. Moreno, J. L., and Toeman, Z., "The Group Approach in Psychodrama," *Sociometry*, 5:191-194, 1942.
44. Mullan, H., "Some Essentials of Group Psychotherapy," *Group Psychother.*, 5:68-69, 1952.
45. Parrish, M., and Mitchell, J., "Psychodrama in Pontiac State Hospital," *Group Psychother.*, 4:80-84, 1951.
46. Pederson-Krag, G., "Unconscious Factors in Group Therapy," *Psychoanal. Quart.*, 15:180-189, 1946.
47. Pfeffer, A. Z., Friedland, P., and Wortis, S. B., "Group Psychotherapy with Alcoholics," *Quart. J. Stud. Alchol.*, 10:198-216, 1949.
48. Rome, H. P., "Group Psychotherapy," *Dis. Nerv. Syst.*, 6:237-241, 1945.
49. Scheidlinger, S., "Group Therapy: Its Place in Psychotherapy," *J. Soc. Casewk.*, 29:299-304, 1948.
50. Schilder, P., "Introductory Remarks on Groups," *J. Soc. Psychol.*, 12:83-100, 1940.
51. Shaskan, D. A., and Jolesch, M., "War and Group Psychotherapy," *Am. J. Orthopsychiat.*, 14:571-577, 1944.
52. Shaskan, D. A., "Development of Group Psychotherapy in a Military Setting," *Proc. Assoc. Research Nerv. Ment. Dis.*, 25:311-315, 1946.

53. Slavson, S. R., *An Introduction to Group Therapy* (New York: Commonwealth, Fund, 1943).

54. ———, "Differential Methods of Group Therapy in Relation to Age Levels," *Nerv. Child*, 4:196-210, 1945.

55. ———, "The Field and Objectives of Group Therapy," in B. Glueck, ed., *Current Therapies of Personality Disorders* (New York: Grune & Stratton, 1946), pp. 166-193.

56. ———, "Advances in Group Psychotherapy," *Int. Congr. Ment. Health*, 24-26, 1948.

57. Snowden, E. N., "Mass Psychotherapy," *Lancet*, 11:769-770, 1940.

58. Sternbach, O., "The Dynamics of Psychological Treatment in the Group," *J. Child Psychiat.*, 1:91-112, 1947.

59. Swenson, W. M., "Round Table Group Psychotherapy at St. Peters State Hospital," *Group Psychother.*, 4:63-65, 1953.

60. Teirich, H. R., "Was Ist Gruppenpsychotherapie?" *Psychother. Med. Psychol.*, 1:26-30, 1951.

61. Twitchell-Allen, D., and Stephens, F. M., "Some Theoretical and Practical Aspects of Group Psychotherapy," *Group Psychother.*, 4:9-16, 1951.

62. Wender, L., "The Dynamics of Group Psychotherapy and Its Applications," *J. Nerv. Ment. Dis.*, 84:54-60, 1936.

63. ———, "Group Psychotherapy Within the Psychiatric Hospital," in B. Glueck, ed., *Current Therapies of Personality Disorders* (New York: Grune & Stratton, 1946), pp. 46-58.

64. ———, "Current Trends in Group Psychotherapy," *Am. J. Psychother.*, 5:381-404, 1951.

65. Willner, G. P., "Preliminary Report of the Introduction of Group Psychotherapy on a Chronic Ward in a Mental Hospital," *Psychiat. Quart. Suppl.*, 26:86-92, 1952.

66. Wittenberg, R., "Psychiatric Concepts in Group Work," *Am. J. Orthopsychiat.*, 14:76-83, 1944.

67. Wolf, A., Locke, N., Rosenbaum, M., Hillpern, E. P., Goldfarb, W., Kadis, A. L., Obers, S. J., Milberg, I. L., and Abell, R. G., "The Psychoanalysis of Groups: The Analysts' Objections," *Int. J. Group Psychother.*, 2:221-231, 1952.

26

THE RELATIONSHIP OF GROUP THERAPY TO OTHER GROUP INFLUENCE ATTEMPTS

Saul Scheidlinger

One of the findings of the psychological sciences within the last two decades is the recognition that group life contains major motivational forces for change and growth. Attempts at influencing people through the use of such forces—for good or for evil—are as old as history. However, the planful, professional utilization of group psychology for promoting better human relationships or for purposes of therapy is a recent development.

All over the country attempts are being made to use small, face-to-face groups for advancing general mental-hygiene objectives. Besides educational settings, such work is being done with beneficial results in industry, in community or religious centers, and even in some government agencies. The term group therapy or group psychotherapy (I intend to use these interchangeably) has been applied by some people in such a way that it encompasses a broad range of approaches. There are those who include under this term all supportive, mental hygiene oriented work with groups. Others have seen it as "therapy of a group," a method of changing the character of the group as an entity, of modifying socially undesirable group goals and institutional patterns.

In this paper, group psychotherapy will be viewed in a narrower sense as a specific approach within the general field of psychotherapy. It refers to a psychological process wherein a trained practitioner utilizes the emotional interaction produced in small, especially planned groups to effect "repair" of personality malformation in *individuals* carefully selected for this purpose. In contrast to other professionally guided group influence attempts, group psychotherapy calls for a clinical setting with the availability of facilities for comprehensive diagnostic evaluations of the client's personality in its generic and dynamic, in its intrapsychic and external aspects.

Reprinted from *Mental Hygiene*, Vol. XXXIX, No. 3, July 1955, pp. 367-390.

The group as a unit constitutes a mere tool in promoting improvements in the individual patients who, generally speaking, accept the therapeutic purpose in order to obtain relief from suffering.

Group psychotherapy has undergone a rapid period of growth, especially during the past decade. It received particular impetus during World War II, when it proved itself of unquestionable value in the treatment of neuropsychiatric casualties. At the present time, group treatment of children and adolescents has achieved wide application in psychiatric clinics, in social agencies, and in some hospitals. Much of such work with children is patterned on Slavson's activity group therapy developed for clients between the ages of 8 and 14. This approach relies on the acting out of conflicts and of adaptive behavior patterns in a permissive group climate. The emphasis here is on experiencing, that is, on interacting with other children and an adult and on reacting to a specially designed physical setting—to simple tools, craft materials, games, and food. For children of preschool age, a modified form of activity group treatment has been evolved. Adolescents, on the other hand, were found to respond most favorably to discussion groups. Similarly, in group therapy with adults the major channel of communication flows through verbal interchanges among the group members and the therapist. Some such groups have one or more cotherapists, often of both sexes, who might also assume the role of observer or recorder.

There is, so far, no general agreement among therapists as to the criteria for the selection of patients for adult groups. Some stress the value of homogeneity of syndromes, while others prefer groups with heterogeneous personalities. Most practitioners avoid, as a rule, placing actively psychotic individuals with less disturbed ones.

As might be expected with such a new and energetcally growing field, the *practice* of group psychotherapy has been considerably in advance of its theoretical understanding and conceptual clarity. Insofar as group psychotherapy has in almost all instances been evolved from the broader field of psychotherapy, its concepts and techniques naturally reflect such a connection. There is, first of all, the earlier noted primary emphasis on curing mental ill health. Furthermore, in accordance with general clinical practice, even though a patient comes with isolated complaints, a comprehensive appraisal of the whole personality is involved. Closely linked with this kind of study is a planful but tentative decision regarding specific therapeutic aims and the methods and levels of treatment. While it might be advisable in one instance to work toward a thoroughgoing reorganization of personality, in another, modification of selected areas of conflict or of defensive patterns might be the more limited goal. In contemplating group treatment alone or in conjunction with other methods of help, its limitations for different types of patients, age groups, and even stages in treatment are all important considerations.

Within the last decade, almost every major "school" of individual therapy has begun to apply its methods and theories to the treatment of people in groups. Any analysis of the trends in this field is complicated not only by the considerable volume of written contributions, but also by the marked discrepancies in the frames of reference and standards of reporting, not infrequent even among the proponents of a similar ideological viewpoint. In the writings of the various practitioners with a psychoanalytic orientation, who, incidentally, appear to be in a majority at the present time, there appears a strong attempt to explain the therapeutic process in close relation to the psychoanalytic assumptions regarding personality development and malformation.

Despite the well-known theoretical differences with respect to the precise causes of personality pathology, a large majority of the practitioners with a psychoanalytic orientation would probably agree on certain generic, interrelated elements as characteristic of all psychotherapy. Among these elements are: (1) relationship, (2) emotional support, (3) catharsis, (4) reality testing, (5) insight, and (6) reorganization of defensive patterns. As I have noted elsewhere,[1] these same cardinal factors are believed to operate in group psychotherapy, albeit varying in quantity and quality, conditioned as they are by the existence of a complex group situation. For instance, the relationship patterns in a therapy group, such as positive or negative object choices, identifications, and transferences, assume a multipersonal character as they occur among the group members and between each member and the therapist. In this connection, there is much stress in the literature on the recreation of a family setting with the leader assuming the role of a parent figure and other group members representing the patient's siblings. The relationship of each patient to the therapist is believed to be a more impersonal one than in individual treatment as the transference is "diluted" (Slavson) by the shifting intragroup relationships. In addition, a permissive and accepting group climate, planfully fostered by the therapist—coupled with the stimulation accruing from the group interaction—breaks down many resistances, thus facilitating production of conscious and unconscious tendencies, of guilt, anxiety, and tensions. While some impulses can find direct expression in the group, others find acceptable outlets through sublimation. The constancy of the setting, as well as the sense of belonging and of being protected, tends to enhance the patient's concept of himself. Recognition that others have similar problems, that they are all "in the same boat," relieves painful feelings of isolation, stigma, and inadequacy. The reality inherent in the compresence of a number of people, each with his own needs and behavior patterns, offers numerous opportunities for trying out one's own attitudes and activities as part of the group experience. This is apt to further the individual's awareness of his own functioning, while the interpretations supplied by the therapist and the other members can promote insight into his unconscious motivations. Other well-known concepts of psychotherapy such as resistance or countertransference are also subject to special variations in group therapy because of the unique group dynamic elements at work.

The above formulations are necessarily highly generalized and are apt to vary with the settings of practice as well as with the preference and training of the therapist. Thus, in actual work with groups, some workers are apt to emphasize certain elements in the therapeutic process at the expense of others. There also are those who would focus exclusively on the momentary patterns and verbalizations in the group as exemplified in Powdermaker and Frank's so-called "situation analysis." [2] Others are primarily concerned with the genetic elements in each patient's past, while still others put exclusive emphasis on the unconscious currents of feeling *common* to all members. In general, therapists with a psychoanalytic background tend to assume a neutral, nondirective role, avoiding personal involvement in the stream of emotional interactions, and avoiding especially the promotion of specific values for conduct. On the other hand, therapists who rely on repressive-inspirational methods are apt to be more directive, utilizing persuasion and suggestion to achieve a high degree of group cohesiveness with marked dependence on the leader.

It should be noted that certain nonanalytic "schools" of therapy have also offered written contributions about group therapy. Among these is Burrow's "phyloanalysis," Levy's "relationship therapy," and Roger's "client-centered" therapy.

Since the last-named approach to groups appears to be utilized with some frequency under educational auspices it deserves consideration in this paper. In line with Roger's theory, it is assumed that the permissive climate of the therapeutic setting will offer the client an opportunity to explore himself and to change his perceptions. This is facilitated by the fact that every person has a basic urge to grow and to mature. Hobbs[3] expressed quite succinctly the differences between the so-called "group-centered psychotherapy" and the earlier noted analytic approaches to group therapy. First of all, the task of the "client-centered" therapist is seen as that of reconstructing the individual's perceptual field at the moment feelings are expressed and to communicate this understanding with skill and sensitivity. The techniques of treatment are listed as (a) acceptance of what is said by the client, (b) restatement of content, (c) clarification of feeling. Furthermore, "the concern with diagnosis is minimal, interpretation is not relied on as a therapeutic instrument, insight is not considered to be an essential change-agent in the process of learning, transference attitudes are handled just like all other affect-laden expressions. . . ."[4] In comparing group treatment to individual help, Hobbs stressed the additional emotional support derived from a situation where the client is accepted and understood not only by a therapist but also by a number of other group members. In this connection he advocated the exclusion of hostile or aggressive individuals from such treatment because of their threat to the supportive group climate. In a more recent contribution on the subject,[5] the role of the group therapist was stressed as also offering the group members a stable reference point because of the consistency of his behavior. It seems to me that in contrast to the analytic forms of group therapy where there is major emphasis on the uncovering and understanding of the conflicts which underlie problem behavior, the Rogerian approach is largely experiential and supportive in nature. It is also of interest that the client-centered group experience appears to be of limited duration, about twenty sessions in all, whereas in the other methods, sessions continue for much longer periods, rarely for less than a year with any given patient, depending on his needs and responsiveness.

I have shown in another context[6] how most theoretical writings on group psychotherapy tend to deal almost exclusively with individual patient behavior or with the therapeutic process. Consideration of the dynamic aspects of the group as a whole, which in all probability are basically the same for all face-to-face groups, has been largely neglected. Following Freudian hypotheses, I outlined a series of concepts pertaining to group psychological phenomena in small groups.[7] Group behavior can be viewed in the strictest sense of the word as the behavior of *individual* personalities in a special process of social and emotional interaction. Thus, every item of group behavior comprises two interrelated sets of factors: (a) individual personalities with their genetic and dynamic properties, some conscious and some unconscious, (b) group dynamic elements such as climate, structure, or code, constituting the product of the interactions within the group. These interactions can occur on conscious as well as unconscious levels. The nature of a group's functioning at any given point can be affected primarily by one or the other above set of factors; or as happens most frequently, by a mixture of both. In a broader sense, the network of interpersonal relations within a group can be depicted as an interplay of positive forces tending to strengthen group unity and of negative ones centrifugal in nature. Among the positive forces are identifications, libidinal object ties, and transferences. The opposing forces range from slight antipathies to hatred and aggression. They include identifications through fear, as well as negative transferences. The group's morale and often its very existence depend on a long-range predominance of the positive, unifying elements over the negative ones.

The Freudian assumptions about group psychology are admittedly hypothetical, incomplete, and at times unclear. They are geared primarily to unconscious emotional motivations and processes and thus require further broadening and refinement. There are a number of contributions from other fields of group study which deal with other equally important and broader aspects of group behavior; for instance, what psychoanalysts would consider as belonging to the sphere of conscious ego activity. Cartwright and Zander[8] have done a fine job in outlining the major, current approaches to the study of groups such as Cattell's concept of "group syntality," Bales' "interaction process analysis," Stogdill's views of organizational leadership. For the purposes of this discussion I would like to comment briefly on two such approaches which have had a direct impact on educational practice. The first of these is sociometry, introduced by Moreno, with its well-known sociometric test. Designed to elicit the structure of the interpersonal relations in groups, it constitutes a statement of a number of choices arranged in a preferential order by each individual group member with respect to certain specific criteria. The sociometric test offers us a most useful tool in gauging the momentary, conscious attitudes of individuals toward others, or their desire to be placed with certain people in a given situation. The sociometric data in itself, however, is not sufficient to explain the intensity of these attitudes or the underlying motivations. Also, it does not suggest the most effective way of guiding these relationships. There is also the question whether it always holds true that groupings based on free, spontaneous sociometric choices are *ipso facto* most desirable for the individuals or groups involved. Another psychological system which has contributed greatly to the study and work with groups is the "field theory" approach developed by Lewin and his followers. There are few, if any, educators who have not been involved in some way by the well-known Lewinian techniques of group problem solving, of "buzz sessions," of "feedback" or role playing. As a theoretical approach, field theory is very similar to Freudian psychoanalysis. Certain differences emerge insofar as Lewin's psychology places major emphasis on explaining individual or group behavior as a function of the *present* social field. This is apt to result in a neglect of the genetic factors and the individual differences in perceiving subjectively a current situation as related to previous experiences in the life history.

There is an urgent need for the further clarification of the dynamics of group behavior in group psychotherapy and in psychology generally. It is my firm belief that in this complex problem of "what makes groups tick," the collaboration of workers from all the above-noted orientations is essential. The joint participation of psychoanalysts, of group therapists, and of social psychologists, for instance, would make it possible to construct hypotheses and to devise research methods which would take into account the unique contributions of each of these fields. There could be regard for the frequently neglected "depth factors," the genetic and unconscious elements which are apt to be seen most clearly by a psychoanalyst. The group therapist could bring to bear his understanding of the therapeutic process, which is so different in a group from the interviewing

room. The psychologist could contribute his knowledge of the scientific requirements for research and of the existing concepts and methods in social psychology.

It is common knowledge that all small groups possess potential elements favorable to the influencing of member attitudes, values, or behavior. This is especially true of those groups which are geared to satisfy the
needs and interests of its members and where the climate promotes a
degree of permissiveness and a sense of security and protection. Every classroom teacher, social group worker, or industrial psychologist could probably offer many illustrations in which group processes have produced
desirable changes in individuals' behavior in the direction of healthy personality growth or of more democratic functioning. I would question, however, whether this circumstance would justify equating such influence attempts as group education, social group work, or group discussions in
industry, with group psychotherapy.

The confusion of group education or group work with group therapy
emerges in some of the writings in this field. For instance, in an article
addressed to teachers on the subject of group dynamics[9] the authors distinguished three separate teacher roles: the instructional one, that of a
democratic strategist, and of a therapist. This latter role of the therapist
referred to "group management to the end of helping all of the children
toward individual and social adjustment. This means a degree of permissiveness, the establishment of rapport with each child, and the conduct of
the work without the teacher's ego becoming involved. . . . In the therapist role, the teacher shares insights concerning human behavior, helps to
get at causes of conflict and to find methods of resolving it. Sometimes
the teacher serves this end by just being a friend, or he may provide, or
himself be, an example with whom the child can identify in the Freudian
sense." [10] I have stated before[11] that all of the functions and practices listed
above under the teacher's role of "therapist" actually are basic to good
group work, sound mental hygiene, and education. No useful purpose is
served by identifying these with psychotherapy, which is an approach distinct from education. There have been numerous reports in the literature
of instances where mental hygiene concepts and practices were applied
with success in a variety of educational settings. Among these is my own
past experience as a psychological consultant in a private school comprising children from nursery through high school age.[12] In this work, the
focus was on the positive aspects of mental hygiene—to foster the
healthy growth of individuals and their potentialities for leading personally satisfying and socially useful lives. Recognizing the potent role of
group experiences in personality development, a major aim of the school
was, accordingly, to create group situations which would be conducive not
only to academic achievement, or creative expression, but also to meaningful human relationships. There was frequent opportunity for children

and for staff to express their real feelings toward themselves or other people in free and permissive group discussions. The inevitable conflicts which arise in the course of group living were handled wherever possible on the spot by the teachers directly involved. Thus, a "mental hygiene" or sex discussion might take place in a science lab, on the playground, or in the English class during a reading of *Romeo and Juliet*. In such situations, the leader helped the group first, in understanding the nature of the problems at hand and then, in devising ways to solve them. Focus was placed on trying to understand and respect other people, their needs, and motives as well as one's own. Many of these discussions were replete with emotionally charged material. Despite this, they were held within the aims and level of education and mental hygiene. For it was our belief at the school that even a highly skilled group therapist would become a poor educator, and possibly in addition cause actual harm, were he to introduce psychotherapy with a group organized for purposes of education.

There are admittedly experiences in education where it is most difficult to maintain the role of teacher as distinct from that of a therapist. This occurs with some frequency in the supervision of practice or in the teaching of people in the related professions of psychiatry, social work, and psychology. I am reminded in this connection of a recent article by two psychiatrists well versed in therapeutic techniques who conducted group discussions with medical students learning psychiatry.[13] As might be expected, this undertaking was highly charged with emotions insofar as the actual contact with very sick patients, and the subject matter generally, reactivated many of the students' anxieties and personal problems. Nevertheless, the authors succeeded in maintaining the focus in their free and permissive group discussions on modifying the students' conscious attitudes toward psychiatric problems and on the ventilation of their feelings toward the patients and teachers so that better learning could occur.

There are a number of writers who have underscored the importance of differentiating between the aims of education and psychotherapy.[14] A group of psychologists who worked in a large city school system with the aim of enhancing mental hygiene practices concluded their recent report thusly: "Psychological efforts that fail to take full cognizance of the real educational rôle of the teacher cannot succeed. Mental hygiene's contribution is to help teachers become more effective teachers, not part-time therapists."[15]

I too would advocate that a clear distinction be maintained between group psychotherapy and the other mental hygiene based group approaches, such as group education or group work. The criteria for differentiation would evolve primarily around the specific aims of the practitioner for each group member and the particular group. The level of group interaction and the leader techniques would also need to be defined. Of least importance would be the kinds or degree of the client's disturbances because various group measures, among them social group work, can be utilized with considerable benefit with the sickest of patients. In contrast to group psychotherapy, with its focus on curing or alleviating diagnosed pathology in individuals through the conscious application of specific techniques in especially planned and balanced groups, the other group approaches, besides recognized goals for the group as a whole, focus on those aspects of the personality which are relatively untouched by the psychological conflicts. In these approaches there is emphasis on meeting people's needs for security, for belonging and companionship, the opportunity for the realization of individual capacities together with the development of a social consciousness. Speaking in general terms, these methods constitute a series of educational processes in the sense of enhancing the socialization of individuals and offering them emotional support, particularly at the points of inevitable developmental or reality conflicts. While on the one hand helping in the expression of feelings and impulses, they encourage at the same time the necessary control and redirection of those impulses which are not conducive to long-range personal and social usefulness. As I have noted earlier, all of the so-called group influence attempts can produce far-reaching therapeutic effects in individuals or in groups as entities, but this could nevertheless be different from therapy. For individuals can lose symptoms, have so-called spontaneous recoveries, or improve significantly in selected areas of functioning through any meaningful interpersonal experience.

Were we to accept the view of group therapy as expounded above, it would then follow that its direct application in educational institutions would be limited to its utilization as one of the treatment methods in the clinics attached to these institutions. Hinckley and Hermann's description of a group psychotherapy program at the students' Mental Hygiene Clinic of the University of Minnesota[16] would be a clear-cut example of such a setup. In a broader sense, however, despite its distinctive character, aims, and functions, group therapy has some elements in common with other professionally guided ways of helping people in groups. Some of its concepts and many of its techniques can therefore be present in all phases of group work in such institutions.[17] It might be of interest to note that a discussion of the similarities and differences between group therapy and other kinds of professional work with groups has been the subject of two interprofessional symposia.[18] Such discussions should go a long way toward clarifying the problems of theory and practice presented by the manifold and complex methods of influencing individuals in and through groups.

REFERENCES

1. S. Scheidlinger, "Group Psychotherapy," *Am. J. Orthopsychiat.*, 24:140-145, 1954.

2. F. B. Powdermaker and J. D. Frank, *Group Psychotherapy* (Cambridge, Mass.: Harvard University Press, 1953).

3. N. Hobbs, "Group-Centered Psychotherapy," in C. R. Rogers (ed.), *Client-Centered Therapy* (New York: Houghton Mifflin Co., 1951).

4. *Ibid.*

5. L. Gorlow *et al.*, *The Nature of Non-Directive Group Psychotherapy* (New York: Teachers College, Columbia University, 1952).

6. S. Scheidlinger, "Freudian Group Psychology and Group Psychotherapy," *Am. J. Orthopsychiat.*, 22:710-717, 1952.

7. S. Scheidlinger, *Psychoanalysis and Group Behavior* (New York: W. W. Norton & Co., 1952).

8. D. Cartwright and A. Zander, *Group Dynamics* (Evanston, Ill.: Row, Peterson & Co., 1953).

9. W. C. Trow *et al.*, "Psychology of Group Behavior: The Class as a Group," *J. Educ. Psychol.*, 41:322-338, 1950.

10. *Ibid.*

11. S. Scheidlinger, "Group Factors in Promoting School Children's Mental Health," *Am. J. Orthopsychiat.*, 22:394-404, 1952.

12. *Ibid.*

13. A. S. Votos and J. Glenn, "Group Techniques in Overcoming Medical Students' Resistance to Learning Psychiatry," *Int. J. Group Psychother.*, 3:293-301, 1953.

14. P. M. Symonds, "Education and Psychotherapy," *J. Educ. Psychol.*, 40:1-32, 1949; H. S. Maas, "Applying Group Therapy to Classroom Practice," *Ment. Hyg.*, 35:257, 1951.

15. M. L. Falick *et al.*, "Observations on the Psychological Education of Teachers in a School-Based Mental Hygiene Program," *Ment. Hyg.*, 38:374-386, 1954.

16. R. G. Hinckley and L. Hermann, *Group Treatment in Psychotherapy* (Minneapolis: University of Minnesota Press, 1951).

17. K. Herrold, "Applications of Group Principles to Education," *Int. J. Group Psychother.*, 4:177-182, 1954.

18. "Group Methods in Psychotherapy, Social Work, and Adult Education," *J. Soc. Issues*, Vol. 8, No. 2, 1952; "The Group in Education, Group Work and Psychotherapy," Round Table, in *Am. J. Orthopsychiat.*, 24:128-152, 1954.

27

THE CHALLENGE OF GROUP PSYCHOANALYSIS

Max Rosenbaum

(The first part of this article, relating to the resistances of patients, has been deleted.)

Up to now we have tried to describe the common types of reaction and resistance of patients who are asked to join a group. At this point it would be illuminating to discuss the reactions and resistances of psychoanalysts themselves. Many of the analyst's reactions are what we would recognize as resistance on the part of a patient.

During the fall and winter of 1951 this writer surveyed, via questionnaire, a group of thirty-nine practicing psychoanalysts as to their reactions to group analysis. Of the twenty-one analysts who replied to the questionnaire, all showed an awareness of the field. Six of the twenty-one had some experience with group therapy. The reactions of these six varied from enthusiastic acceptance, in the case of one analyst who had prolonged experience in private practice, to rejection of the method by another who had been in charge of some psychiatric services in the army. This "rejecting" analyst felt that group therapy was an unfeasible technique since it requires "an integrated and skilled therapist" who is able to "stand the manifest transferences or see them all. Since it is not possible to be such a therapist, it seems that those who do group therapy do not see all the problems involved." Between these two extreme reactions there was mild acceptance of the method as an adjunct process which was effective, but not as effective as individual analysis; and acceptance as an "interesting technique that is not a substitute for individual analysis. These are two completely different techniques."

The fifteen analysts who had never worked in the area of group ther-

Reprinted from *Psychoanalysis, Journal of Psychoanalytic Psychology*, Vol. I, No. 2, Fall 1952, pp. 50-58.

apy or group analysis were in the main favorable. Three were planning to acquire training in the method. This "no experience" group contained analysts who were strongly convinced that "the method is feasible," as well as analysts who felt that the "method is in the experimental stage but this should serve as a stimulant." There was a good deal of skepticism as to the depth of the method. There was question as to whether transferences could be explored and resolved in the group analytic situation. By some the group was accepted as a "more real situation" but suitable only for "carefully selected cases." One analyst commented that "since anything works in therapy . . . since life is therapeutic . . . group analysis may help in shot gun fashion. . . ."

It is worth noting at this point that the responses of the entire group of analysts surveyed are in the main favorable to the idea of group therapy. Yet there is a great discrepancy between the answers to the questionnaire and the actual clinical practice of even those analysts who are favorable to the concept of group psychoanalysis. These same analysts indicate considerable resistance to referring patients for group psychoanalysis. Is it possible that these analysts, in writing an answer to a questionnaire, must fulfill a self-concept of the permissive, accepting therapist? Do they actually fear the resolution of their own resistances toward the psychoanalysis of the individual in a group? This question will be discussed at length in a future paper.

It seems then that analysts object to group psychoanalysis because:

(1) They don't feel there is any "depth" to the method.

(2) They have questions regarding the technique and procedure of the method and consequent dangers to the patient who is exposed to the method.

(3) They don't feel there is a real substitute or equivalent for the individual analysis and the relationship which exists between analyst and analysand in such a method.

With regard to the objection as to the depth of group analysis there is the fear expressed that, in the group, transference relationships are diluted. It seems to be assumed that transference reactions can occur only toward the therapist and that patients therefore will have only short periods of time in a group framework where they can develop and work through transferences. But what of the multiple and shifting transferences that patients project upon one another? Are these transference reactions inaccessible to analysis? Experience has indicated that patients who are introduced into the group react in a manner never met in the individual analysis. The analyst is often seen as quite different—even in the first group session. With the support of the other group members the patient can feel much less anxiety about expressing hostile as well as loving fears. In the group the patient finally permits himself the expression of affective reactions, so long repressed for fear of the analyst.

A stimulating study by Drs. Powdermaker and Frank has indicated neglect of analytic methodology among psychiatrists conducting the groups studied. They state ". . . the doctor's uncertainty may cause him to confuse the group by being unpredictable in his attitudes and methods." It should be emphasized that the method of group analysis is the method of individual analysis. Group therapists who do not proceed analytically because of their anxieties cannot then conclude that the method lacks depth. Such criticism reminds us of the "mirror" concept of the analyst in early psychoanalytic history, which served as a convenient theory to absolve analysts of their shortcomings, since they could always blame the shortcomings on the patient. This same attitude is manifested when analytic methodology such as dreams, free association, transference, and countertransference are not used in group analysis and where, as a result, the therapist concludes "lack of depth."

The analyst who is reluctant to use analytic methodology in the group setting may have anxieties about his own individual responses and capacities, or he may have real anxieties about the ability of people to get together and to act in their own interest. There are group therapists who circumvent their anxieties by organizing groups with a common psychovisceral complaint, or nearly uniform character structure. This desire for homogeneity may be in reality a resistance of the analyst, who does not want to take advantage of the special opportunities the heterogeneous group offers. Or a therapist may reject group procedure because of his own unresolved overprotectiveness of his patients. Not unlike overprotective parents we find overprotective analysts who encourage dependency, out of a need to dominate patients. In a group, however, when the members combine both their neurotic and healthy rebellion, such an overdominating analyst will find very rough going indeed. Such analysts often conduct a group in a rigid lecture pattern and forbid any contact among patients outside of the regularly scheduled meetings.

It would seem that overconcern for patients can often mask the analyst's fear of patient insight regarding the analyst. One individual with whom this writer worked described a relationship with a psychiatrist whom he saw individually and then in a group. He saw this man for five years altogether and was assured that he was receiving analysis. While it is true that the method of analysis was used in some part, it is also true that the therapist sat behind a desk with the group seated in front of him, refused to permit the group to meet outside of regular sessions, and held a ruler in his hand "to emphasize my points." The reader can judge whether a helpful therapeutic relationship could exist in such a setting, although the therapist continues to be unaware of any shortcomings. The patient, after five years, finally recognized that, since his problem was fear of authority, he wasn't really going very far.

It is important to recognize that depth can often evoke countertransference on the part of the analyst, since he cannot escape careful scrutiny in the group: Depth works both ways. The analyst's own reactions are analyzed by group members who leave little or no time to think over or work through challenging situations. There is constant evaluation of the analyst's unconscious as the group makes him examine his reactions. Often the therapist rejects the group method because there is unconscious anxiety about exposing himself in the countertransference. His concern about depth often relates to self-concern.

Let us now survey some questions regarding the technique, procedures, and dangers of the group method. There are those who criticize the training of the group analyst as not being as thorough as that of the individual analyst. The answer is simple; the training must be even more thorough. The group analyst must have the training of the individual analyst plus knowledge and experience in the area of group functioning. Since group analysis is a relatively new method, the group analyst has, until the postwar period, been forced to search for adequate training. At present, however, there are constantly developing opportunities for study and training.

Some analysts feel the privacy of the individual analytic relationship is basic to analysis. But psychoanalysis is a two-way street. Discussions of method touch upon the therapist as well as the patient. Both analyst and analysand can hide in the "small get-together," where the perceptive patient can always be accused of projecting, since there are no checks on the analyst's judgment. Privacy in the individual relationship can be over-emphasized and may be questioned. The transference cure under such conditions is often an authoritarian cure, based on the patient's inference that the analyst is all-powerful. The patient may experience deep guilt and anxiety about questioning this all-powerfulness. In the group, on the contrary, the analyst may have a healthier relationship with the patient, strengthened and expressed in many ways. In a group the dependent personality soon expresses aggression when the longed-for parent-figure has relationships with other siblings and family figures, whereas aggression is rarely expressed by the dependent person in individual analysis until considerable time has passed, for fear of estranging the analyst-parent.

One of the analysts who answered our questionnaire, describing his work with group therapy in an army setting, was concerned about the ability of the analyst to recognize and withstand the many transference reactions that are directed at him in the group. He seems to have assumed that all transferences on the therapist are expressed at the same time. While such reactions are present and latent, it is only in the process of working through that they come to the surface. They rarely come to the surface at the same time. Even if a group of patients should all attack the analyst at once, it is possible to handle this temporary revolt, which is historically representative of rebellion against authority in the family. The therapist always finds several individuals in the group who will help explore the dynamics of the revolt. More usually, however, the patients express their hostility individually and the group forces them to compare their views of the therapist with the divergent feelings of the other members.

As in individual analysis, there are times when the analyst will fail to pick up a transference reaction in the group. But the pattern of reactions, as in individual analysis, comes through again and again. If the analyst is not perceptive enough, there are the patients who, as increasingly skillful adjunct analysts, will pick up the transference reactions. The group is active and moving. There is little opportunity for patient or analyst to escape into personal fantasies.

One often sees graphic illustrations of how the patient's transferences change constantly in the group. The patient who is constantly involved in a sexual contact and *loves* the analyst can see how *love* for the analyst is used by another or several other group members. The patient then works it through not only with the analyst but with all of the group members. The microcosm of life exists in the group. The transferences exist as they do in life—constantly shifting and variable. The analysis broadens from the first "unique" relationship with the analyst to a group relationship which is more helpful.

Many analysts show anxiety about the group structure because they feel that patients may move too quickly. They fear "acting out." Experience *has* indicated that most patients move more quickly in the group than in individual analysis. The presence of the stimulating group is vital for the patient. The analyst's authority and presence are diluted by the presence of other neurotics "in the same boat." Patients may minimize the reaction of another patient with the comment that "you're a neurotic and you're too sick to know what's going on . . ." but this does not minimize the effect when a fellow patient makes an analytic observation. Many problems do develop much more quickly within the group framework than in individual sessions. One analyst commented that such development was dangerous because the analysand ". . . might have a psychotic breakdown."

Yet in the combined clinical experience of the ten analysts who are members of the Workshop in Group Psychoanalysis there have been only three psychotic episodes reported by one analyst although a wide variety of personality problems have been handled. This analyst's patients had had psychotic episodes prior to his contact with them or their entrance into the group. The psychotic episodes which occurred while they were in group analysis were successfully handled in the group.

The reason why patients in the group are not endangered by "acting out" seems to lie in the fact that the group "goes with" the patient. The group leaves a session with the patient, who is thus still able to communicate with siblings in his "family"—siblings who often help him get through difficult periods—where the individual analyst would find it impossible to follow up. Group members have often noted that in individual sessions the patient leaves after the scheduled hour and "that's that. . . ." One of the limitations of the individual session is, indeed, that time schedules must be followed. While we can defend such a procedure on the basis of "reality"—a reality which the patient is asked to accept—it is undeniable that patients do sometimes leave analysts' offices under considerable stress and that many analytic hours terminate with the analysand depressed or overanxious.

Analysts who express concern over "acting out" in a group setting might well explore their own anxieties about patient behavior. "Acting out" takes place frequently enough. When it does, it is analyzed as part of the neurosis and resistance mechanisms. Patients also "act out" in individual analysis, but often do not discuss this with the analyst. Even experienced group therapists who do not want to use analytic methodology speak with anxiety about the combination of men and women in a group and the possibilities of sexual promiscuity. Are they not losing sight of the fact that the promiscuous patient has a problem which must be analyzed? Promiscuity does not result from group analysis. Patients who have been promiscuous will continue their pattern. But within the group framework these patients come to realize that such behavior should be analyzed and worked through. Let us not overlook the experiences of some patients who have met in group analysis, gone through neurotic love experiences, and analyzed these experiences. Nor those patients who have met within the group framework and developed healthy relationships.

Since patients get so much that is positive from the group and are sustained in moments of anxiety, some analysts object that the group reinforces the overdependent patient and encourages dependency generally. Experience indicates, however, that the group extends aid to those in need, but does not permit itself to be used by dependent patients. Patients recognize the distinction between a cooperative relationship which leads to growth and a relationship which is neurotically draining in nature. True, there are always some patients who permit themselves to be used, but this neurotic "missionary" type is exposed and analyzed. In one of my groups, one patient felt constantly driven to be a father figure. In every relationship he strove for this role, although he unconsciously rejected it. This compulsion was repeatedly analyzed as it occurred in the group, until ultimate clarification ensued.

Theodore Reik has aptly described psychoanalysis as a place where "dere's no hiding place." This apt observation certainly describes a group. Neither patients nor therapists can hide in the group setting. Therapist as well as patient shortcomings appear in the group, and the therapist is under constant scrutiny in the group. The therapist may overwork the phrase "it's your distortion" in the individual relationship. But can he really continue such comments when a group—albeit neurotic—with varying personality problems sees the problem that the analyst fails to see in himself? The analyst in the group often finds himself indebted to patients for sound insights. But there are analysts who can't accept such a relationship.

Martin Grotjahn, in a beautifully written exposition on analysis, has spoken of the competition that exists between the training analyst and the student analyst. Dr. Grotjahn notes the necessity of a secure training analyst. We may further note the extension of the same problem in a group where the analyst feels competitive with patients. Dr. Grotjahn in another article describes the group as a "gallery of mirrors"; certainly the insecure analyst has good reason to fear mirrors! The group always forces the analyst to evaluate his countertransferences. No one escapes scrutiny in the group, not even the analyst. The possibility that the analyst may escape into nonparticipation simply does not exist. A nonparticipating analyst, experience indicates, will only lead to group dissolution.

Analysts who fear the overactive group with consequent chaotic conditions may reflect upon their own analytic practice, which in many ways consists of an "all day" group. Patients often express anxiety in individual analysis as to whether the analyst can handle all the information that patients bring forth. The average individual analyst does manage, simply because he is not compelled to handle all his patients at the same time. But the situation is similar in a group. Group patients do not permit chaos to exist unless the analyst is unable or unwilling to interpret and handle this disorder. The group is bound by the common desire to get well. The autistic patient is brought out of his autism or is not accepted by the group. The psychopath is rejected. Nevertheless, even the patient who hallucinates in a group may be helped through his experience by the warmth and understanding of his "family."

One of my patients has said that "saying goodbye to a neurosis is like saying goodbye to an old friend. You don't know the new friend in advance. You are frightened by the effort needed to make new friends and are therefore reluctant to give up the old friend—neurosis. So very often you're afraid to cross the river and find out what's on the other side." The group offers the warmth and support to cross the river.

Basic to those who practice group psychoanalysis is the belief that the group process tends to maximize all healthy constructive elements in the individual. The individual may often seem so sick, and his resources so limited, that we forget that he does have some resources. In the group his healthy resources are reinforced manyfold through interaction. Group members do not confuse one another. Rather they see one another clear of all the psychological vocabulary that critics of psychoanalysis often rightly attack us for using. The group is the beginning area for communication. Analysts should take advantage of it.

Historically, new ideas are always met with doubt, and frequently with hostility and opposition. Group analysis faces skepticism and justly so. But analysts who have taken upon themselves the role of the questioner must also question their opposition to the practice of psychoanalysis in the group setting. If we as analysts do not question, who will?

BIBLIOGRAPHY

Alcoholics Anonymous (New York: World Publishing Co., 1939).

Freud, S., *Group Psychology and the Analysis of the Ego* (London: Hogarth Press, 1927).

Grotjahn, M., "The Process of Maturation in Group Psychotherapy and in Group Therapists." *Psychiat.*, Vol. 13, No. 1, February 1950.

————, "The Role of Identification in the Training of Psychiatrists." *Monthly Review of Psychiatry and Neurology*, Vol. 117, 1949.

Hobbs, N., "Group-Centered Psychotherapy," in C. R. Rogers, ed., *Client-Centered Psychotherapy* (Boston: Houghton Mifflin Co., 1951).

Klapman, J. W., "The Case for Didactic Group Psychotherapy." *Dis. Nerv. Sys.*, Vol. XI, No. 2, February 1950.

Powdermaker, Florence, and Frank, J. D., "Group Psychotherapy with Neurotics." *Am. J. Psychiat.*, December 1948.

Schilder, P., *Psychotherapy* (New York: W. W. Norton & Co., 1938).

Slavson, S., *Analytic Group Psychotherapy with Children, Adolescents, and Adults* (New York: Columbia University Press, 1950).

Wender, L., "The Dynamics of Group Psychotherapy and its Application." *J. Nerv. Ment. Dis.*, Vol. 84, No. 1, July 1936.

Wolf, A., "The Psychoanalysis of Groups." *Am. J. Psychother.*, Parts I and II, October 1949; January 1950.

Wolf, A., Locke, N., Rosenbaum, M., Hillpern, E., Goldfarb, W., Kadis, A., Obers, S., Willberg, I., and Abell, R., "The Psychoanalysis of Groups: The Analyst's Objections." *Int. J. Group Psychother.*, Vol. II, No. 3, July 1952.

The works cited here accompanied the original, longer, article.

28

PSYCHOANALYTIC APPLICATIONS TO LEVELS OF GROUP PSYCHOTHERAPY WITH ADULTS

Benjamin Kotkov

The practice of group psychotherapy, a review of the literature, and experimental work on goals[1] disclose three distinct levels of psychotherapeutic achievement in group psychotherapy: 1) social participation, based chiefly upon symptom identification; 2) increased confidence, based chiefly upon ego identification; 3) emotional insight, based chiefly upon modified superego identification.

The purpose of this presentation is to point out the similarity in dynamics for all psychotherapeutic echelons as well as to enumerate the special characteristics unique for each.

COMMONALITIES

There is a basic core applicable to all analytically oriented group psychotherapies regardless of nosological syndrome, age, intelligence, or presenting complaint, namely: reactions of patients to the group situation, psychotherapist's noninterventionalist's role, and use of patients as adjunct therapists.

Reaction of Patients. Anxieties are aroused in all patients in the very act of coming together in a group. Each patient becomes alert to an attack for fear of being victimized or appearing weak in some way. He may react against being afraid by aggressiveness and irritability. Another patient may reserve his thoughts. What if he should be compelled to speak? Would the other members of the group laugh at him? Would he appear

Reprinted from *Diseases of the Nervous System,* Vol. XIX, No. 9, September 1958, pp. 1-7.

physically disfigured or intellectually inferior? He fears rejection if he reveals too much of himself.

The mere presence of a psychotherapist evokes tense and hostile feelings. Relationships to a parental figure were those in which authority was imposed. The reactions of patients to authority were ones of ready rebellion, stubbornness, and strong temper. Hence the members of the group would tend to react to the psychotherapist as to a dominating parent. At such times, the patients in the group see the psychotherapist as an enemy who would push them into danger rather than a reassuring figure who would help them. Symbolic siblings project old, unconscious, competitive needs onto a misidentified parent with subsequent reality distortions and frustrations. The sicker the patient, the more do his fantasies infiltrate reality, and the more insidious do relationships become.

Psychotherapist's Noninterventionalist's Role. Group psychotherapy is stated simply as a way of working through emotional problems. The members of the group are then invited to talk about their thoughts, wishes, and feelings but are told that they need not feel compelled to speak. The group psychotherapist deliberately avoids stimulating additional anxiety, restrains accentuating the negative aspects of ambivalence, and guards against being goaded to reprisal by patients' provocations. The danger of mounting negative transference from members of the group is reduced by a minimum of untoward countertransference reactions from the psychotherapist and by inherent group interferences which detoxicate projections and dilute transferences. Demarest and Teicher[2] in an excellent paper on transference in group therapy missed their own countertransferences (by the use of active interrogation of their patients) with the result that undesirable transferences in their group were incited rather than diluted.

Patients As Adjunct Therapists. Every new group introduces a collection of unrelated and usually unknown people. The group psychotherapist could easily intensify the alienation of members from a potential group. In order to diminish initial feelings of rejection and dissociation, the patients are encouraged to take the lead. Patients need to be transformed from a collection of isolated individuals into an integrated functioning whole in order to effect favorable psychotherapeutic change. The group psychotherapist's basic task is to manipulate the power of the group, to discourage the patient's own efforts at internalization. "A group is extraordinarily credulous and open to influence; it has no critical faculty, and the improbable does not exist for it." [3] Patients have been used as adjunct therapists, more or less, in all types of group psychotherapies[4] and the entire nosological range.[5]

In the beginning of every psychotherapeutic group, the emotional reactions between the individual patients and the psychotherapist is paramount. As the group discovers a meaning and appropriateness to the sessions, interaction among the members of the group assume substantial proportions.

LEVELS

Echelon One: Social Participation

Participation group psychotherapy is employed primarily with schizophrenics. Many of these patients are nonverbalizers—a barrier which interferes with the development of relationships so necessary for conducting group psychotherapy. Often diversional therapies are used to prepare the patient for participation psychotherapy.[6]

Lazell,[7] Klapman,[8] and others have shown that the didactic approach is the method of choice in group psychotherapy with chronic schizophrenics. The crucial task here is to encourage the patient to graduate from an informational level to social participation. Chafetz,[9] Gray,[10] Gurri and Chasen,[11] and others, although sponsoring group psychotherapy with the chronically ill, maintained that its role is ancillary to ECT or lobotomy.

The psychotherapeutic goal in group psychotherapy with schizophrenics has remained unchanged since the turn of the century. It was then that Lazell[12] and Marsh[13] emphasized that the acme of psychotherapeutic achievement with this patient population is in social recovery. Grauer[14] and others remind psychotherapists of the "striking difference between a dilapidated schizophrenic in the chronic ward of a hospital and a socially recovered schizophrenic." Abrahams[15] and others have stated that although delusions do not disappear, they are decreased, patients talk and display more friendly behavior.

The analytically oriented approach is employed with carefully selected patients based upon their desire to be helped, degree of intactness, level of intelligence, and bids for socialization.[16] Nosologically, these patients may be acutely disturbed psychotics (nonchronic),[17] schizophrenics in remission,[18] incipient schizophrenics, and manic-depressives in a free interval period.[19] The psychotherapeutic goal is still socialization either in terms of leaving the hospital on a trial visit, promotion to better wards, and/or ground privileges. The psychotherapeutic technique is essentially that reported by Semrad[20] and his associates: no direct questioning, casual conversation, appropriate comment, handling of psychotic material by fellow patients.

Instead of relating through causes, schizophrenics relate through complaints.[21] One member identifies with another, not so much with people, as with symptoms and illnesses. Freud[22] stated that "identification by means of the symptom . . . has thus become a mark of coincidence between the two egos. . . ."

Gradually these patients are led into a group experience. They begin to formulate their attitudes in a less nebulous fashion. They plan with others and share some of their responsibilities. They develop latent capacities for participation and receive attention and recognition for their accomplishments. Participation serves as an opening wedge in the development of relationships.

Echelon Two: Increased Confidence

The literature is relatively sparse on techniques of short-term group psychotherapy.[23] During World War II, a number of such papers appeared [24] (and many others) under military auspices. With a few exceptions,[25] brief group psychotherapy in the armed services was principally didactic. Psychotherapeutic techniques were geared to goals which were either information-giving or frankly exploratory.

Applications of analytically oriented short-term group psychotherapy have been presented by the author in several publications.[26] The purpose here is to describe the distinguishing characteristics of the second distinct echelon of psychotherapeutic achievement in group psychotherapy. This level can only be reached by a nonpsychotic population. The ego is strong enough to collaborate in a psychotherapeutic movement towards newer, adaptive forms of relationships. In order to weld individuals into a group, certain of its needs have to be fulfilled. Patients' needs are met in terms of identifying themselves with other patients and thus acquiring inflated values, strength, and morale. A patient who voices a positive attitude toward treatment is an apt individual with whom another patient may identify.

To a certain extent, in every relationship to an object, a modified identification occurs. However, there are essential differences: Identification is a more intense and special type of relationship. It is a more intense experience in that the patient absorbs something from the group which he incorporates in himself. It is a special type of experience in that one might enjoy the company of guests but one might not wish to identify with them. "Identification," wrote De Saussure,[27] "may be produced by admiration, by affection, or by imitation. It always implies that the relation between subject and object with which he identifies is one of confidence." The symbiotic relation of members of the group to each other assists the individual in combating his isolation. Thus an individual who was isolated takes his place in the group.

Release Mutual Difficulties. Healing resides not only in the group's emotional relationship to the psychotherapist, and the emotional interplay of members of the group to each other, but also in a discussion of their mutual difficulties—only pertinent material becomes incorporated in their understanding. Initially, most patients present their complaints in physical terms. Others demand a cure "on the spot," while still others are unable to aerate. Resistance, in brief group psychotherapy, is undermined by permitting the group to say what it pleases without dispute.

The movement of the group is from a release of anxiety and hostile feelings against derivative figures to covert theoretical, philosophical, or stop-gap conversations reflecting similar feelings. A more personalized direction is obtained by the simple device of asking for their feelings on the current topic under discussion. A variety of reactions may ensue: much bickering, a shocked attitude, a creeping of understanding here and there, and finally a willingness to come to grips with personal material.

Very few patients in brief group psychotherapy—or group psychotherapy of an open, continuous type with goals fixed on the same modest level—have any real acceptance of the nature of their illness. It is a tremendous task for patients to be convinced that their symptoms are emotionally occasioned and that there is a relationship between a current conflict and its concomitant symptomatic manifestations.

Experience with many such groups shows that increased confidence results if identification can be augmented through loss of feelings of isolation and loss of fear of personal expression. However, improvement occurs in terms of ego identification alone, and patients leave the group oblivious to any understanding of their resistances. What is repressed and dissociated remains so. Insight into symptoms and their various manifestations are concealed. Patients are helped but not irrevocably.

Echelon Three: Emotional Insight

Group psychotherapy is a complicated process of emotional interactions involving many patients and a psychotherapist. It is precisely because group psychotherapy involves relationships that unresolved Oedipal components are easily projected upon one another, with transferred attributes and affect unconsciously distorting their perceptions of reality. Emotional insight relates to the clearance of projections in order to obtain proper assessments of reality. Hence, psychoanalytic concepts such as transference, resistance, and countertransference holds true for analytic group psychotherapy as it does for individual analysis. Current practice in analytic group psychotherapy presents the epistemology of treatment, works on resistances, focuses on the anxiety of the moment, and exercises countertransference precautions.

Presents Epistemology of Treatment. Most psychotherapists explain the role of transference to the group. It is pointed out that a person's knowledge is not always clear-cut, that there is an emotional recognition which is at odds with an intellectual grasp of reality. Patients are encouraged to detach their reason from their emotionally involved suffering self in order that they may understand the nature of their feelings and its derivation. Members of the group are led to feel that attitudes do exist which are in contradistinction to reality and to the consciously voiced opinion of the individual. It is usually emphasized that feelings of inadequacy are brought about after birth through relationships, that people who cannot accomplish their life tasks are handicapped by inhibitions in terms of their fears, rather than actual lack of endowment. The group feels helpless with regard to a number of pressing situations, and their old conflicts do not enable them to deal constructively with current affairs. Hence, members of the group are encouraged to talk about their feelings of inferiority and inadequacy, including the manner in which they may have acquired such concepts through family orientation, if they are to alleviate their disturbing obsessions.

Mullan[28] defined transference as "the human idiosyncrasy to distort the relationships that we have with others; giving others assumed roles reminiscent of someone in the past and present. Within these distorted relationships we find ourselves transferring attitudes and affects and seeking unwarranted gratifications."

Wolf[29] entered in lucid detail an illuminating discussion of the identification and resolution of transference. He stated in part:

> . . . the therapist verifies the singular features of transference. . . . To this end he misses no opportunity to clarify any one patient's investment of another or the analyst. Whenever a reaction appears which has the characteristics of projection, he points out to the reactor the transference character of his response. With increasing clinical experience patients become expert in identifying one another's transference reactions. The extreme disparity of various investments confronts each member with the patently illusory nature of these responses. He learns to see his own particular masking of others with parental or sibling surrogate cloaks as equally irrational.

Analytic group psychotherapists generally agree with Foulkes[30] that the group "demonstrates in action the meaning of a transference neurosis, its regressive nature, its oedipal significance, its compelling character, as a consequence of which the patient tends to demand the therapeutic reestablishment of a situation as close as possible to the original family constellation." Positive indications for the selection of patients for analytic groups were reported by Slavson.[31]

Centralizes Resistances. The clearance of resistances are essential to the promotion of emotional insight. Future immunity pivots about the successful overcoming of resistances. Redl[32] expressed the general opinion amongst practitioners of group psychotherapy when he stated of resistance that "diagnostically it reveals to us the real forces we fight, and therapeutically its removal is the only guarantee for lasting success." Spotnitz[33] indicated further that the five types of resistances present in individual psychoanalytic therapy are also encountered in analytic group psychotherapy.

> However, a special complication is the fact that each of these forms of resistance operates not only against the therapist in his efforts with each group member, but also against the group members in relation to each

other; and finally these individual resistances of the group members may unite to become a group resistance, such as group ego resistance, group superego resistance, group secondary gain resistance, and group id resistance. . . . First, it is desirable to call the attention of the group to the resistance. . . . Then the therapist may enlist the interest of the group sufficiently to attempt to understand the significance of the resistance, what caused it, how it developed and why it is being used.

Hence analytic group psychotherapists work on resistances rather than to place pressure on the recollections of experiences which are associated with strong and painful emotions. The members of the group cling tenaciously to their resistances in many ways. They attempt to control their insecurity either in silences or open hostility, in phobias or belligerences, control and avoidance of feelings, denial of emotions and anxiety. Details and ramifications of common forms of resistances are discussed by the author elsewhere.[34]

Anxiety of the Moment. At first, the anxiety of the moment relates from the group's suspicion as to what its members are going to accrue from the psychotherapist and his treatment. There is a stormy insistence for a prescription and a magical release, e.g., "I'm telling you what is wrong with me. What are you going to do about it?" And again, "You never know, you might get killed." The first statement expressed the marked dependency as well as the frustration of the gratification of needs. Beukenkamp[35] referred this to the "primacy of oral dependency." The second remark made by the patient is a projection of the patient's "unconscious wish to destroy the symbol of their dependency needs." Hence, "The associated murderous desires as well as the incestuous drive cause the facing of immaturity to be expressed similarly as a fear of self-destruction."

Pederson-Krag[36] portrayed other unconscious feelings which are likewise bivalvular:

> Members whose aberrations of feeling and conduct makes them feel like outcasts, now found that it was these very aberrations that drew the leader's attention and interest to them. . . . Oedipal anxiety is lessened by adding to the fantasy "My father loves me because of my hurts," the additional idea, "So he will not punish me because of my rivalry." Another feeling may be present: "My father loves me because of my hurts" is that the hurts have been accepted as castration. . . . Anxiety is lessened because the dreaded punishment has already been endured and need no longer be feared.

Later, the anxiety of members of the group are tied up with their own feelings of inadequacy and helplessness. One patient told the group: "I'm in a sad condition." He cited a nervous condition that he had five years previously. What circumstances are currently affecting this patient that makes him displace his present difficulties onto the past? Another patient stated that he was a "sissy" in his childhood. What gives the man the feeling that he is inadequate today? What is he troubled about in his dealings with his fellow man, on the job, in school, or at home? What troubles the patient to the extent that old feelings of inferiority are brought back from out of the past into the current situation?

Countertransference Precautions. The group psychotherapist has to exercise care that he does not disturb what is currently transpiring in the group, that he does not accelerate or maximize self-condemnations of the members of the group. Flescher[37] stated that the "term countertransference should include all emotions and attitudes in the therapist that, whether or not they are linked with his personality, influence his comprehension and his use of analytic psychotherapy." For "Anxieties connected with unresolved oedipal elements are mobilized very easily in the analytic situation because of the role of nongratification which automatically makes of the patient a forbidden (incestuous) object." Countertransferences are manifested in terms of "unresolved conflicts of the analyst," the "impact of patient's transference," and "suggestive influences running from patient to therapist."

Hadden,[38] Grotjahn,[39] and others felt that the group members were quick to detect countertransference and often attempted to convey appropriate cues to the group psychotherapist. Slavson[40] indicated that the psychotherapist may be biased either in the direction of approval or disapproval, and progress may be inhibited by the therapist's goals. Stein[41] warned against premature exposure of id impulses feared and repressed by the group. Kotkov[42] enumerated common forms of countertransference typical of student group psychotherapists, namely: anxiety, counterhostility, poor motivation, need to be omnipotent, and heterogeneous scotomata such as increasing the patient's sense of isolation, overevaluation of patient's ego strength, therapist projecting his own interests, and insufficient empathy. Powdermaker and Frank[43] conducted extensive studies for increasing the objectification of psychotherapeutic techniques. Loeser and Bry[44] re-presented the contention of many group psychotherapists that effective controls are exercised through the constant survey of one's role, intramural discussions, and tape recordings. One might also add the use of an observer. Loeser and Bry went on to state that groups are affected by defect in technique, acting out of therapist, identification with patient's difficulties, passivity as a defense aggression, omnipotence, pedagogy, libidinal interests, and narcissistic motives.

SUMMARY

For every group, regardless of depth of psychotherapy, the psychotherapist anticipates standard reactions of patients, exercises a noninterventionalist role, and invites the participants to become adjunct therapists. However, the characteristic defenses, the use of repression, the tempo and progress, and the standards of goals achievable will vary with the type of group. The group ego may be loose, rigid, or encouragingly flexible. Correspondingly, three psychotherapeutic levels are presented leading to social participation, increased confidence, and emotional insight.

REFERENCES

1. B. Kotkov, "Goals of Short Term Group Psychotherapy," *J. Nerv. Ment. Dis.*, 123:546-551, 1956.
2. E. W. Demarest and A. Teicher, "Transference in Group Psychotherapy," *Psychiat.*, 17:187, 1954.
3. S. Freud, *Group Psychology and the Analysis of the Ego* (London: Hogarth Press, 1948).
4. D. Baruch, "Description of a Project in Group Therapy," *J. Consult. Psychol.*, 9:271, 1945; H. Coffee, M. Freedman, T. Leary, and A. Ossorio, "A Technique of Group Therapy," *J. Soc. Issues*, 6:25, 1950; J. L. Moreno, *Who Shall Survive?* (New York: Beacon House, 1953); J. H. Pratt, *The Group Method in the Treatment of Psychosomatic Disorders*, Psychodrama Monograph No. 19 (New York: Beacon House, 1946); P. Schilder, *Psychotherapy* (rev. ed.; New York: W. W. Norton & Co., 1951); A. Wolf, "The Psychoanalysis of Groups," *Am. J. Psychother.*, 3:525, 1949; 4:16, 1950.
5. B. Kotkov, "Analytically Oriented Group Psychotherapy of Psychoneurotic Adults," *Psychoanal. Rev.*, 40:333, 1953; E. V. Semrad, "Psychotherapy of the Psychoses in a State Hospital," *Dis. Nerv. Syst.*, 9:105, 1948; S. R. Slavson, "Criteria for Selection and Rejection of Patients for Various Types of Group Psychotherapy," *Int. J. Group Psychother.*, 5:3, 1955.
6. L. Halle and J. F. Ross, "A Therapy Program for Schizophrenic Patients," *U.S. V.A. Dept. Med., Surg.*, Information Bulletin 1B 10-13, July 1951, pp. 3-8.
7. E. W. Lazell, "The Group Treatment of Dementia Praecox," *Psychoanal. Rev.*, 8:168, 1921.
8. J. W. Klapman, "Psychoanalytic or Didactic Group Psychotherapy," *Psychiat. Quart.*, 28:279, 1954.
9. W. E. Chafetz, "An Active Treatment Program for Chronically Ill Mental Patients," *J. Nerv. Ment. Dis.*, 119:428, 1954.
10. W. Gray, "Group Psychotherapy in a State Hospital," *J. Nerv. Ment. Dis.*, 108:485, 1948.
11. J. Gurri and M. Chasen, "Preliminary Survey of the Results of Group Treatment of Psychoses," *Dis. Nerv. Syst.*, 9:52, 1948.
12. Lazell, *op. cit.*
13. L. C. Marsh, "Group Treatment of Psychoses by Psychological Equivalent of the Revival," *Ment. Hyg.*, 15:328, 1931.
14. D. Grauer, "Problems in Psychotherapy with Schizophrenics," *Am. J. Psychother.*, 9:216, 1955.
15. J. Abrahams, "Preliminary Report of an Experience in the Group Psychotherapy of Schizophrenics," *Am. J. Psychiat.*, 104:613, 1948.

16. Marsh, *op. cit.*; Slavson, *op. cit.*; G. Willner, "Report on Further Developments in Group Psychotherapy on a Chronic Service of a Mental Hospital," *Psychiat. Quart. Supplem.*, 28:54, 1954.

17. F. Schnadt, "Technique and Goals in Group Psychotherapy with Schizophrenics," *Int. J. Group Psychother.*, 5:185, 1955.

18. *Ibid.*

19. Willner, *op. cit.*

20. Semrad, *op. cit.*

21. D. C. Wilson, "Group Psychotherapy and Manic Depressive Psychosis," *Am. J. Psychiat.*, 110:911, 1954.

22. Freud, *op. cit.*

23. Baruch, *op. cit.*; Coffee, Freedman, Leary, and Ossorio, *op. cit.*; Moreno, *op. cit.*; F. Redl, "Group Emotion and Leadership," *Psychiat.*, 5:573, 1942.

24. J. Abrahams and L. W. McCorkle, "Group Psychotherapy of an Army Rehabilitation Center," *Dis. Nerv. Syst.*, 8:30, 1947; J. R. Cavanagh and S. Gerstein, "Group Psychotherapy in a Naval Disciplinary Barracks," *Nav. Med. Bull.*, 49:645, 1949; J. J. Michaels and E. O. Milton, "Group Psychotherapy for Neuropsychiatric Patients Being Discharged from the Army," *Occup. Med.*, 1:60, 1946.

25. M. Grotjahn, "Experience with Group Psychotherapy as a Method of Treatment of Veterans," *Am. J. Psychiat.*, 103:637, 1947; C. N. Sarlin and M. A. Berezin, "Group Psychotherapy on a Modified Analytic Basis," *J. Nerv. Ment. Dis.*, 104:611, 1946.

26. B. Kotkov, "Experiences in Group Psychotherapy with the Obese," *Psychosomatic Med.*, 15:243, 1953; "Analytically Oriented Group Psychotherapy of Psychoneurotic Adults," *Psychoanal. Rev.*, 40:333, 1953; "Group Psychotherapy with Wayward Girls," *Dis. Nerv. Syst.*, 14:3, 1953; "The Group as a Training Device for a Girls' Training School Staff," *Int. J. Group Psychother.*, 4:193, 1954.

27. R. De Saussure, "Identification and Substitution," *Int. J. Psychoanal.*, 20:465, 1939.

28. H. Mullan, "Transference and Countertransference," *Int. J. Group Psychother.*, 5:169, 1955.

29. Wolf, *op. cit.*

30. S. H. Foulkes, "Group-analytic Observation as Indicator for Psycho-analytic Treatment," *Int. J. Psychoanal.*, 35:263, 1954.

31. Slavson, *op. cit.*

32. F. Redl, "Resistance in Therapy Groups," *Hum. Relat.*, 1:307, 1948.

33. H. Spotnitz, "A Psychoanalytic View of Resistance in Groups," *Int. J. Group Psychother.*, 2:3, 1952.

34. B. Kotkov, "Common Forms of Resistance in Group Psychotherapy," *Psychoanal. Rev.*, 44:88-96, 1957.

35. C. Beukenkamp, "The Nature of Orality as Revealed in Group Psychotherapy," *Int. J. Group Psychother.*, 5:339, 1955.

36. G. Pederson-Krag, "Unconscious Factors in Group Therapy," *Psychoanal. Quart.*, 15:180, 1946.

37. J. Flescher, "On Different Types of Countertransference," *Inter. J. Psychother.*, 3:357, 1953.

38. S. B. Hadden, "Countertransference in the Group Psychotherapist," *Int. J. Group Psychother.*, 3:417, 1953.
39. M. Grotjahn, "Special Aspects of Countertransference in Analytic Group Psychotherapy," *Int. J. Group Psychother.*, 3:407, 1953.
40. S. R. Slavson, *Analytic Group Psychotherapy* (New York: Columbia University Press, 1950).
41. A. Stein, "Resistance to Group Psychotherapy," *J. Hillside Hosp.*, 1:79, 1952.
42. B. Kotkov, "Vicissitudes of Student Group Psychotherapists," *Int. J. Group Psychother.*, 6:48, 1956.
43. Florence B. Powdermaker and J. D. Frank, *Group Psychotherapy* (Cambridge, Mass.: Harvard University Press, 1953).
44. L. H. Loeser and T. Bry, "The Position of the Group Therapist in Transference and Countertransference," *Int. J. Group Psychother.*, 3:389, 1953.

29

GROUP COUNSELING WITH PARENTS

Hanna Grunwald
Bernard Casella

It has often been our experience, in casework treatment of mothers who request help for their children's behavior problems, that although a change in attitude brings about improvement in the child, friction with their husbands comes to the surface. The friction appears to be intolerable for the mothers and jeopardizes the treatment gain. The mothers voiced their feelings about the problem by stressing their inability to explain to their husbands what had really brought about their change in attitude toward the child. When they were enabled through treatment to be more clearly directive with the child, the husbands accused them of being cruel. When they were more lenient, the husbands accused them of coddling the child. Mothers with better ego integration than those of the group with which we were concerned can be helped to overcome this problem. However, the mothers with whom we were working felt overwhelmed by the threat to the equilibrium of their marital relationship and longed desperately for a return to the former marital situation. We believe that the mother's gain in self-esteem resulting from casework treatment led to lessening of dependency on her husband, to which he had reacted with fear and anger.

The problem was aggravated when the child's rebellious behavior had been a source of unconscious satisfaction to the father. At times the father retaliated for being deprived of this satisfaction by pressuring another child whose behavior was a source of unconscious satisfaction to the mother. This in turn made the mother more anxious and led to a return of the children's problems.

This recurrent problem stimulated us to look for a new treatment method. We looked for a way out of it by trying to draw the father into a

Reprinted from *Child Welfare*, Vol. XXXVII, No. 1, January 1958, pp. 1-6.

meaningful contact. We were always aware of the importance of the father's role in the child's development and felt it unfortunate that, primarily due to technical reasons, we have to work more with the mother than with him. It is usually considered an achievement when we are able to see the father once or twice during the course of a one-year treatment of mother and child, since he may have long working hours which overlap with our office hours. We are also aware that the father's unavailability for treatment is due not only to technical reasons but also to the husband's strong feeling that any need for outside help with family problems reflects his own inadequacies. He may also feel that the responsibility for the children's rearing is mainly the mother's because he is so tied down realistically and emotionally with the obligation of wage earner. Basically, however, their defense against the deep-seated longing for dependency makes a help-seeking process too threatening to these fathers and therefore they avoid it.

We have been working in our agency for the last seven years with case-work-oriented counseling groups. Often this is the treatment method of choice. Many clients who would have been lost in an individual contact were helped in group treatment. In individual treatment the client often is overwhelmed by the fear of overdependency and uses various defenses to ward off this danger. In a group contact he feels protected against this danger. Energies that would have been needed for defensive purposes in individual contact are thus freed in the group and can be utilized for constructive purposes.[1]

We formed a parents' group in the belief that the benefits of group counseling would aid us in our attempt to help both mother and father. In three of these families the mothers had been seen for treatment either individually or in a group. They all had reported the problems in family living described earlier. We chose a fourth couple who had only recently come to our attention; however, we had sufficient evidence to assume that they had similar problems. The parents ranged in age from thirty-four to forty-one; the children's ages ranged from five to fourteen years. All of the couples had two children. The couples came from similar cultural and economic backgrounds. They were intelligent; some had superior intelligence. There was a conspicuous lack of spontaneity in their thinking. All members of the group had suffered from extreme emotional deprivations in early childhood. Severe rejection by their own inadequate parents led them to a constant search for ideal accepting parents, which they hoped to get by "behaving perfectly." This unrealistic goal, coupled with limited ability to form relationships reflected vividly that the behavior of these clients was determined largely by pre-Oedipal needs. Such clients require a more active and assertive role with regard to guidance and counseling.[2]

Because of this need for more active roles we felt that the presence in the group of a male and a female counselor would be an advantage, facilitating the application of major techniques (i.e. displacement) needed for the treatment of these clients. The presence of a father and a mother figure further enhanced the possibility of recreating a family situation. The fathers seemed to be especially encouraged by this arrangement. Since their wives had initiated the contact, they often were apprehensive that the treatment process would be "woman-dominated."

CHARACTERISTICS OF GROUP MEMBERS

The couples managed rather well on a surface level. The husbands were hard-working men. They had various white collar and semiprofessional positions. Because of their wish for security, they avoided competition, preferring instead sheltered work below their capacities. Their social life was restricted because of their concern to be "polite and friendly." The women were well groomed and meticulously dressed. They assumed the major responsibility for cohesiveness of the family and determined its cultural standards. They had a distinct quality of "going through the motions of living" caused by their wish to avoid conflict. Under great stress such a defense system cannot hold: Most members of the group had suffered from "nervous breakdown" for brief periods when under great stress. Some had previously benefited from brief psychiatric care. Two psychiatrists who had earlier treated two members of the group encouraged us to choose the counseling method rather than psychotherapy for their former patients.

The marriage of each couple was "an armed truce"; the partners had an unspoken agreement to be tolerant of each other's weaknesses. Occasional flare-ups reflected the unrest of the truce. The suspension of hostilities was especially threatened by the parents' differences about rearing the children. Some pressure was eased by leaving this responsibility to the mother. Both parents were terribly frightened whenever it seemed that the child's behavior would thwart their efforts to remain inconspicuous to the outside world. However, in many instances a child's behavior may have caused panic in one partner while satisfying unconscious needs of the other partner, which led to a complication of the marital conflict.

This need to conceal what was going on inside their homes was strong, and the mothers had come to the agency only because of great outer or inner pressure. The fathers fought longer against this involvement. Not having had the benefit of earlier treatment in the agency, they were at a disadvantage at first. Prior to the meetings, the male and female counselors each took the opportunity to see every father and mother individually. When they came to the first meeting the male counselor introduced the members to each other. Then he repeated what they had been told in the individual interviews: that we had invited them to participate in the group in the hope that they might be assisted through this to help their children in constructive ways. The members understood that they could discuss whatever they liked in the group. They were not obliged to talk when they preferred to remain silent. The requirement for keeping the names of the members confidential outside the group was especially stressed by the counselor.

He had barely ended this introduction when Mrs. Clare burst into an almost hysterical complaint: "Jack is still wetting the bed—it's terrible! What can I do?" This plea for help brought out from the members run-of-the-mill advice about controlling bed-wetting. This quickly resulted in a back-and-forth questioning about the ages of their children. They started telling one another about the problems of the children which had brought them to the agency: bed-wetting, restlessness at night, failure in school, shyness, inability to make friends. After several weeks group members frequently voiced their feelings of satisfaction when "right in the beginning" they came to see that the other members were "such likable people." They were pleased to find that the moral standards of the members were up to their own strict expectations. They quickly sensed that the other couples suffered from similar problems because "they are as sensitive as we." Of major benefit in group counseling is the help members derive from identification with each other. The members selected for the parents' group were quickly enabled to identify with each other because they were able to "like each other."

ISOLATION OF THESE PARENTS

The process of identification was enhanced by the fact that the members were victims of "social hunger." [3] They suffered from their isolation, which resulted from their fear that rejection by the outside world would constitute too much outrage to their sense of self. However, they were not isolated because of pronounced narcissistic make-up. Once the presence of protecting parental figures made them feel safe enough to communicate with other persons, they were quickly enabled to establish good rapport.

The members of the group were sensitive to each other's needs and it was gratifying for them that they were able to help each other.

When Mr. and Mrs. Alden complained about the "circus" at night in their home, the children running back and forth into the parent's bedroom, the Bateses and Clares helped them with support and understanding. Mr. Alden was angry that his wife was "too soft with the girls" when they did not stay in bed at night. The members in the group helped him to understand gradually that at least part of the difficulty stems from the fact that many children are afraid at night. They suggested that parents should help their children to cope with these fears. After more meetings, Mr. Alden was proud to report that he had read a story to the youngsters at their bedside. He also told them, "anyone can get afraid when it gets dark." He boasted, "They were like angels."

At times there were setbacks which were worked through by the members. A warm, positive climate developed in the meetings, in which there was a constant back-and-forth evaluation of daily problems. No topics were planned, the group process was unstructured, and associative material led to a nonsystematic flow of discussion.

A husband, feeling that his wife was under attack, might come to her rescue by holding her hand for a short time, or a wife may have looked at her husband with amazement and pride because he advised another member in a sure, patient, and intelligent manner.

> Mr. Clare said to Mr. Alden: "You get so mad at your wife's daily calls to her mother as if this takes something away from you, as if she spites you. Don't you see that she needs these calls to mother, that she is not yet quite grown up. . . ." Mr. Alden reported, after a number of meetings, that since he stopped nagging his wife about the calls by showing some "paternal concern" for her, she has let go of the daily calls. After the end of the group sessions Mrs. Alden told the counselors: "We had been married eight years when we came to the group. After some time in the group we had our honeymoon."

It was interesting that Mrs. Clare had started the discussion in the first meeting by complaining about Jack. In prior contact she had focused upon her strained relationship with her daughter whom she pushed forward, wanting her to be self-sufficient. In her husband's presence she immediately turned to discussion of the other child who was rejected by him.

WORKING THROUGH PROBLEMS

Gradually some focal theme became crystallized out of the group discussion. The members came to understand that they had equated human inadequacies with sin. They acted as if weaknesses might lead to a disastrous point of no return. They came gradually to see this concept as wrong when applied to the problems of other couples, but they took a longer time to understand that it was wrong as it applied to themselves. It was impressive to see how skilled each member became in unraveling the many rationales developed by the others in their attempt to ward off this new insight. In the beginning many members felt that they would prefer to be faced with the problem of another couple instead of types of problems they had to cope with in their own home. Gradually, however, they began to accept problem situations in their own homes. Towards the end of the group sessions they even came to feel that they preferred their own problems to those of the others.

The process of mutual help was intricately interwoven with assistance from the counselors. At times the members asked one or the other counselor a direct question which was always answered briefly. Questions on problems of feeding or weaning were usually addressed to the female counselor; those on educational problems and problems of contact with the community, to the male counselor. When a female member of the group was attacked by the male members—specifically by her husband, with resulting overwhelming anxiety—the male counselor came to her rescue. This technique was also used by the female counselor when one of the men was attacked. The rescue was usually given with the help of the method of universalization.

> Mr. Clare complained about Jack's "black hands" when coming to the table. "I won't tolerate it. My wife is too soft with him." "Oh you———," Mrs. Clare retorted. "No wonder he doesn't wash his hands! I have to remind you each week to take a bath." Mr. C. became white with rage, pounded his fists on the table, and stammered that he would not take this. He got up retreating to the door. The female worker in a quiet way stated that anyone would feel like running away when his weaknesses are suddenly and openly discussed—"we all would prefer to keep some habits to ourselves." Mr. Clare returned to his chair, the other members helping to reassure him. Mrs. Clare was still angry. She attacked him further and when he again threatened to leave, she insisted that "this is a place where to bring the dirty laundry—if not here, then where?"

In the next meeting the Clares reported that "After the storm last time we had a wonderful time." They also reported, with pride, some improvement in the boy. Treatment was enhanced because husband and wife cooperated in working throughout the week on newly gained understanding. Working together was a constructive experience as was the opportunity to report this to the group.

The couples found that since attending the meetings they were able to talk more readily with each other. Channels of communication which had been blocked for a long time were opened when they experienced that in the group such discussions were safe. The Bateses began to talk things over at home, even though Mr. Bates did not talk in the group sessions. However, he listened intently and even imitated some of the male counselor's mannerisms in greeting people, and later came to smoke the same kind of pipe. Mrs. Bates reported in a few of the meetings that during the last week her husband had spent some time reading to his son or playing ball with him. This revealed that Mr. Bates derived benefits from the group without verbal participation. The members of the group seemed to sense his need to remain silent. In individual counseling such a tendency might have blocked or even led to an interruption of treatment.

TRANSFERENCE IN THE GROUP

Group counseling differs from group therapy in that we do not interpret the transference that takes place both to the therapist and to the members of the group. However, just as in individual casework treatment, the counselors must understand the transference phenomena. In this parent group the transferences were subjected to a variety of modifications, different from that in groups of members of the same sex or of members of both sexes not belonging to the same family. The presence of a person important in the client's life, with whom he is in daily contact, reduces the intensity of some of the transference phenomena. The presence of the marital partner brings more reality of the living situation to treatment, which prevents the development of some aspects of the transference. Our group manifested fewer aspects of sibling rivalry and fewer attempts to gain special attention of the counselors. We believe that this was due to the fact that the partners' sympathies remained with each other rather than with individuals outside of their marriage.

At the same time other aspects of transference are more pronounced. The presence of a male and female counselor enhances the reproduction of the family scene which partially may account for this intensification. The presence of the partner and the other group members reduces the clients' fear of overdependency, thus allowing him to refrain from building up defenses against the transference. This may account for the fact that the members of the group faced the two counselors with less defensiveness than usually experienced either in individual counseling or in groups conducted by a male or female counselor alone. The fact that there was so much reality in the treatment situation lessened the chance of the establishment of a dependency relationship. This allowed the counselors to feel freer to nurture the members than is done in most other treatment processes. In turn, the clients' need for accepting parental figures was somewhat satisfied, which released energies for constructive purposes that heretofore had gone into the endless search for ideal parents. Their destructive hold on the children was therefore considerably lessened. We feel that we are not yet prepared to analyze completely this question of transference, after experience with only one group. However, these two trends of transference development were quite pronounced.

Another trend observed in this child-centered parents' group is similar to one often found in joint interviews with married couples. In interviews of this type, as in our group, we find that conflicts pertaining to the early childhood are less often recalled and that there is a lesser degree of hostility released against the partner and the child. However, the less the amount of hostility released, the greater is the impact upon reality testing. Hostility released against the partner or child in the presence of the partner is not accompanied by an ensuing overwhelming guilt when later seeing the partner, as might happen after an individual interview. Although this problem can be worked through with many clients it appears too difficult for the type of persons selected for our group. The availability of reality in this group also enhanced the utilization of the client's healthy ego strengths. Since regression occurred seldom, there was less manifestation of illness. This is desirable in counseling, in contrast to psychotherapy.

THE COUNSELORS' CONTRIBUTIONS

It was especially helpful that the parents could witness discussions of differences between the two counselors. Although both counselors have the same training, their responses often differed. The male counselor may have supported a parent who felt it was important to help a child to be weaned away from the parents, whereas the female counselor at this point may have stated that although it certainly is important to help the child to be independent, this can be very difficult. She remembered that she too had felt qualms, for instance, when it had become necessary to allow a child to cross the street alone for the first time. Such differences did not lead the counselors to change their attitudes toward each other. The members would witness that differences of opinion do not have to lead to conflicts.

Some therapy groups have a male and a female therapist, one of whom is a helper to the other. In our group the contributions of each counselor were equally valid. Differences stemmed from the distinction in sex and the individuality of human temperament. However, in basic professional social work training their understanding was similar. It was a new experience for both counselors to work together in the same interviewing situation and both approached this new task with the excitement of the untried. We had questioned, for instance, how we would discern which one should react to certain occurrences within the group. However, throughout the group sessions this did not prove a problem. The counselors took turns recording the interviews and found that discussing the material together was more stimulating in many ways than discussing it in consultation with someone who was not present during the meeting. The staff psychiatrist was available to the counselors on the same basis as in our individual casework.

The group started to meet in the fall once a week for an hour and a half. In addition to the group meeting, some members were seen individually when necessary. As in our work with individuals, children were seen when it seemed important for diagnostic clarification or for help with acute problems. We terminated the group at the time of the summer vacation period. The members of the group felt that they were helped through their group participation. Life at home became more enjoyable for them. They were especially pleased to report improvements of their children's behavior. Jack still has dirty hands at times but they no longer lead to stormy scenes at the dinner table. However he stopped wetting the bed and for the first time he even got interested in his school work. He no longer felt that his parents thought of him as a nuisance. They were enabled through treatment to communicate to him that they liked him and that they were proud of him—which in turn helped Jack to gain a better self-image. This enabled him to make better use of his potentials. The teacher was amazed that Jack no longer was a reading problem, although he had not received remedial reading help. The Clares' daughters learned to trust their parents more. The parents being less panicky about the children's fears helped the girls to lessen their fears. The Aldens and the Danes came to understand that although their children had improved they needed professional help for internalized problems and accepted referral for psychotherapy. They would have become panicky if we had referred them to a child guidance clinic prior to the group experience.

CONCLUSION

We felt that a child-centered parents group can be an important device in the treatment of specially selected clients. These parents, as mentioned above, were primarily motivated by pre-Oedipal needs. It seemed to us that they would not have had the strength to be amenable to psychotherapy, where they would have been helped to understand their own involvement in the child's symptom and the meaning a child's behavior has for them. Their good intellectual equipment would have enabled them to be active participants in a group educational project; however, their emotional limitations would have prevented them from applying the newly gained knowledge about child-rearing. We felt that these parents were best helped in changing their attitudes towards their children when they could become less panicky about the child's behavior. This kind of help is the proper domain of casework.

Individual casework often does not reach this type of client. We feel that group treatment filled this gap. In the group described the parents were able to raise their self-esteem through a positive identification with the counselors and the other group members. This, coupled with release of hostility, freed energies for bringing about change of attitudes towards the child, and in turn the child's behavior improved.

The emotional experience provided by the group was shared by both parents. This prevented a dangerous shift in the precarious family balance, which was essential to the parents and children for their emotional survival.

We are planning to work with more groups of this structure in the hope of widening our experience with this important new casework method.

REFERENCES

1. For an analysis of the modification of casework-oriented group techniques from methods used in individual contact see *Group Methods in Casework Agencies*, Welfare and Health Council of New York City, May 1955, Part I, p. 2; S. Sherman, "Group Counseling," *Casework Papers from 1955 NCSW* (New York: Family Service Assn. of America, 1955); Hanna Grunwald, "Group Counseling in a Casework Agency," *Int. J. Group Psychother.*, 4:183, 1954; 7:318-326, 1957.
2. S. L. Green, "Casework Diagnosis of Marital Problems," in V. Eisenstein (ed.), *Neurotic Interaction in Marriage* (New York: Basic Books, 1956), p. 241.
3. S. R. Slavson, *An Introduction to Group Therapy* (New York: The Commonwealth Fund, 1943), pp. 5, 85, 187, 200, 272.

30

MULTIPLE PSYCHOTHERAPY

Herman H. Spitz
Sheldon B. Kopp

The use of more than one therapist at one time in individual or group psychotherapy has been called by many names—multiple therapy,[1] co-therapy,[2] role-divided, three-cornered therapy,[3] three-cornered interviews,[4] joint interview,[5] cooperative psychotherapy,[6] and dual leadership.[7] In the literature, there is mention of the use of from two to as many as nine[8] and ten therapists[9] with a single patient; and mention of the introduction of guests (that is, interns and residents) who participate in discussions with patients in group therapy.[10] Furthermore, there are wide discrepancies, not only in the terminology applied and the number of therapists used, but more significantly, in the therapeutic methods employed when more than one therapist is in attendance.

The present evaluative review is undertaken, therefore, in an attempt to clarify the promising work done in this area and to relate meaningfully the various reports to date. It is hoped that by communicating this material to other workers in the field some further impetus may be given to the exploration of this potentially rich technique. For purposes of convenience, the term "multiple therapy" will be used throughout this article when reference is made to any joint psychotherapeutic approach.

HISTORICAL ROOTS

The beginnings of multiple therapy have two major sources: (a) as a discussion of the patient's problem in his presence and (b) as a teaching method.[11]

Reprinted from *The Psychiatric Quarterly Supplement*, Vol. 31, Part 2, 1957, pp. 295-331.

Discussion in the Patient's Presence

The early work of Alfred Adler and his co-workers at the Vienna Child Guidance Clinics is often cited as the starting point of multiple therapy. In 1930, those workers noted that: ". . . the appearance of the child before a large gathering . . . has a stimulating effect upon him . . . [because he is] surrounded with people who take a great interest in his fate and difficulties, without looking down upon him and without forcing this help upon him." [12] This is elaborated elsewhere[13] as follows: "It is advisable to say something good about the child to his parents or educator when he is within hearing distance. . . . He acquiesces in the consciousness of being appreciated . . ." Although these references may have stirred some interest in later therapists, they seem to the present reviewers to be of peripheral importance rather than a direct causal contribution.

A more structured handling of this sort appeared in 1947 when Hadden[14] permitted a group of interns and residents to attend sessions of didactic group therapy with neurotic patients. After a time, the students were asked to participate in group discussions and eventually to alternate as group leaders. Presenting and later discussing the cases of the patients present was found to give those under discussion "vicarious catharsis."

In the preceding two publications it is evident that there was no planned interplay between the therapists and the patients. The primary consideration was that the patient be present, thereby benefiting by hearing his problems discussed or by feeling appreciated. One finds more recent refinements of this technique in the work of Moreno,[15] who uses a "trained auxiliary ego" to play the part of the patient, or other important personages, in the patient's presence. Dreikurs and his co-workers[16] have one therapist use the patient's "private logic" to argue with another therapist, who interprets and evaluates while the patient "listens in." In conclusions drawn from a similar situation, Hayward [17] feels that the very intensity of the therapists' arguments impresses on the psychotic patient their desire to help him.

Use as a Teaching Method

Hadden[18] found that the direct employment of students in therapy sessions gives them a more intimate understanding of psychotherapy, while at the same time permitting continual supervision. In 1949, Whitaker[19] reported that for six years he had used multiple therapy to teach the general practitioner to handle some of the lesser emotional problems of patients. His findings were that the physician who had participated in such a course was less pessimistic in consequence about psychiatric patients and that his increased knowledge facilitated the patients' moving into more intensive psychotherapy. Whitaker, Warkentin, and Johnson[20] further report the didactic efficiency of this method in developing the capacities of the therapist.

Haigh and Kell,[21] in a more recent article, stress the fact that inexperienced students can learn only by participating and that multiple therapy reveals hidden difficulties and failings more readily than postsession supervision. Research possibilities inherent in the procedure are also pointed out.

Lott,[22] trained nonmedical psychotherapists (clinical psychologists) by this means. These psychologists employed nondirective methods with patients suffering from mild personality disorders; but, when problems arose, the psychiatrist conducted joint sessions, using a more direct approach.

Hill and Worden[23] report on the participation of senior physicians in the therapeutic endeavors of the junior staff. On weekly rounds the senior psychiatrist demonstrated techniques to the resident while helping and supporting the patient. However, in the cases reported there was little indication of three-way interaction. The senior member most often resorted to individual sessions, with the patients being seen by the resident.

Grotjahn,[24] who at times supervised his students as a participant observer, experimented with a few psychotic patients, whose doctors he supervised, and found that joining doctor and patient approximately once a week was very stimulating to the treatment situation. When he supervises or is consulted by group therapists, he joins the group, with little previous introduction or preparation—to get firsthand evidence of what is going on. Initially, he only observes, but later he takes over the conduct of the group, thus demonstrating to the therapist his constructive criticisms. This experience is analyzed and worked through in later meetings between supervisor and therapist.[25]

To several of the foregoing authors,[26] it soon became evident that although multiple therapy had been initiated as a teaching technique there were some unique therapeutic benefits to be derived by the patients from this approach.

TREATMENT-CENTERED MULTIPLE THERAPY

The present reviewers were able to isolate three major ways in which multiple therapy is used as a treatment technique, in contrast to its use in training or research. These are: (a) intervention multiple therapy, (b) alternating multiple therapy, and (c) full-term multiple therapy. Although all three methods are used when treating individual patients, the last method is most frequently used by group therapists.

Intervention Multiple Therapy

Intervention multiple therapy is multiple therapy used primarily to dissolve a therapeutic impasse. The consultant therapist enters an established therapeutic relationship and may leave before therapy is terminated.[27] There are times, however, when treatment is terminated only after multiple therapy sessions are completed.[28] Sometimes the second therapist may take over completely.[29]

Whitaker and his co-workers[30] describe the calling in of a consultant therapist when a therapeutic impasse is reached. In almost all cases, the patient and his original therapist band together to exclude the consultant and to deny the possibility of therapeutic failure. When this happens the consultant withdraws, having achieved his purpose of breaking the impasse.

Hayward [31] also has utilized multiple therapists to intervene in case of an impasse, particularly one created by transference and countertransference difficulties. He describes a hebephrenic patient who, after five multiple therapy sessions with nine doctors, was free of overt psychosis and able to leave the hospital. Hayward feels that multiple therapy allays the fears a single therapist might have in a dangerous situation and that the patient feels safety in numbers. Furthermore, it allows the patient to divide and direct toward different therapists intolerable mixtures of love and hate and increases the speed of treatment.

Dyrud and Rioch,[32] working mainly with psychotics, also find multiple therapy an excellent method for clarifying difficult transference and countertransference problems. The change of intensity of interaction between patient and original therapist following the introduction of multiple therapy is an important criterion of therapeutic improvement. As a side effect, the working relationship among staff members is found to improve.

Alternating Multiple Therapy

In this technique, multiple therapy is a predetermined, more or less fixed, consultive arrangement, with the consultant coming in for only a specified number of sessions. Here too, it may happen that the second therapist takes over.

This method was introduced by Dreikurs,[33] and later further elaborated by Dreikurs, Shulman, and Mosak.[34] It involved the first use of the term "multiple therapy." The process may be described as follows: The patient is first seen by the senior psychiatrist. In the second and third sessions, an associate attempts to determine the patient's "life style," which is then defined in the first joint interview (the fourth session). The conclusions of the joint session are then reviewed in the fifth session by the senior (active) therapist. From then on, following every two or three single interviews with the active therapist, there is a joint session in which the material brought up is reviewed. Although the active therapist may decide on the frequency of the joint interviews, they must occur at least once in five sessions. If a negative attitude toward the active therapist should develop, the second therapist may trade roles with him.

In contrast to other reports of multiple therapy, Dreikurs *et al.* find that emotional attachment to the therapist is not necessary for progress. Perhaps their particular use of the consultant therapist may account for the lack of development of intensive transference relationships and their feeling that two therapists hinder the development of countertransferences. They do, however, mention the necessity of evaluating any transferences which do occur. As the main values of their method, they hold that it enhances interpretations, shortens the reorientation period, and allows the patient to open up more readily without fear of abuse. The presence of two different therapists, each with his own personality and approach, allows the patient to modify his expectations about people and to see that one can be wrong without loss of stature. Thus introduction into group psychotherapy and ultimate termination of treatment are facilitated.

Full-Term Multiple Therapy

In Individual Therapy. In this method, multiple therapists operate in a fixed number throughout a treatment relationship.

Reeve,[35] using a social worker and a psychiatrist with a single patient in a joint interview, recognizes as one value of this technique the elimination of distortions of the patient's accounts. He also recognizes the requirements of complete acceptance by the staff because "our own anxieties and concerns were readily reflected in the responses of the patients."

Whitaker, Warkentin, and Johnson[36] initially used multiple therapy as a teaching method to develop the capacity of the therapist. Two therapists jointly conducted the entire course of individual therapy, while a separate psychiatrist assumed all administrative functions. These workers feel that "countertransference is the fundamental force in brief psychotherapy" but also stress the value to the therapists of sharing with each other their emotional experiences in the therapeutic interview. In another paper,[37] these same authors describe their work with 25 patients of all types, seen individually, in which a constant number of from two to ten therapists participated in from five to 30 interviews. As in their previous paper, Whitaker and his co-workers show considerable interest in the method as an aid to the professional growth of the therapists. They note that the intensity of the patient-therapist relationship is proportionate to that between therapists, or at least is limited by the latter. In their discussion of the advantages to the patient of this method, they include such factors as greater support and help, greater pressure permitted, and the fact that positive and negative attitudes toward different therapists give more incentive to work through these feelings at one time.

Bock, Lewis, and Tuck,[38] after working with five of nine ward cases in individual therapy, arrived at their "role-divided" method, which they then applied to their remaining four cases. They consider this method useful as a type of brief therapy.

In Group Therapy. For the most part, multiple therapists in group therapy operate in a more or less fixed number over an extended period. The second therapist may be a participant observer.[39]

In at least two instances, however, the length of treatment is comparatively short. Orange[40] used multiple therapy as a "modified" method of brief group psychotherapy with psychotics. Lundin and Aronov,[41] also working with psychotics, used two therapists for from 25 to 30 sessions with groups of 12 patients. They feel that reactions in the group reflect stability and instability in the home; and they find co-therapists better able than single therapists to evaluate the responses of the patients and of each other. In their groups, clarification of the patients' present attitudes was stressed. Two therapists offer a "broader dynamic area to which the group can react." Furthermore, they report, they could treat 12 patients rather than the usual six to eight treated by a single group therapist. They, too, underscore the need for good therapist-therapist relations so as not to reproduce traumatic family settings.

Demarest and Teicher[42] report group therapy with hospitalized schizophrenic men, using one man and one woman therapist and holding two one-and-a-half-hour sessions weekly for one and a half years. Stressing the use of working through transferences as a therapeutic tool, they point out the importance of the co-therapists' roles. They indicate the possible levels of transference to be patient-patient, patient-therapist, patient-group, therapist-group, and therapist-therapist, and consider the direction, depth, and intensity of these relationships. They further suggest that, because the therapist who is not crucially involved in an interplay at a given moment can be more objective, he can clarify what he observes.

In many instances a group's observer is drawn into the group interaction and treated much as a co-therapist. Joel and Shapiro[43] write of a co-therapist or "recorder" who summarized developments near the end of the group session, drawing much hostility which would have been directed toward the main therapist, and leaving the main therapist as a benevolent and nonthreatening authority figure. Powdermaker and Frank[44] also note that group therapy patients sometimes address comments to an observer instead of to the therapist and suggest that an observer may be used as an object of acceptance or hostility originally felt toward the doctor. Illing[45] delineates three types of multiple therapists: the co-therapist, the observer, and the visitor. He feels that—while the categories of co-therapist and observer have been fairly well defined and show some direction—the role of visitor is more nebulous. He points out the impact of the visitor on the group members and therapist and concludes that although the visitor's role differs from that of co-therapist or observer, all three have certain common generic transference elements.

Bach[46] suggests that a therapist who is carrying a group member in individual treatment sit in on the group sessions to avoid the negative effects of "parallel treatment" by keeping the focus group-centered.

Naturally there may be a number of variations in the use of multiple therapists. For instance, Linden's senile women patients[47] were seen three times a week over a two-year period by combined and alternating therapists. That is, the male doctor occasionally would leave the group and allow the nurse to take over, and vice versa. The occasional alternation of therapists tended to stimulate response and activity, keeping attention focused on the procedure.

DIFFERENT APPROACHES TO THE ROLE OF THERAPIST

Many of the papers reporting on multiple therapy place particular stress on the importance of the roles played by, or imposed upon, the therapists.

Roles in Individual Therapy

Bock[48] and his associates tried complete equality of therapists at first, but then felt that the resistances that developed stemmed from too much pressure from two authority figures. As a consequence one therapist became directive, controlling the discussion and increasing pressure. The second therapist became nondirective, giving support and reflecting feelings—thus enabling the patient to feel more secure and more at ease under pressure. This is an example of an attempt by therapists to impose their roles on the patients.

Reeve,[49] on the other hand, finds that patients impose roles upon their therapists. His seating arrangement approximated an equilateral triangle and allowed the patient to identify with one therapist and turn his back to show rejection by, or resentment toward, the other therapist. However, Reeve also felt that a man psychiatrist and a woman social worker more easily set up a parental situation.

Warkentin, Johnson, and Whitaker[50] are in agreement with Reeve that it is the patients who define the roles of the therapists. Their patients, they say, sensed differences in the personalities of the therapists and tried to play one off against the other. One therapist was defined as harsh and punitive, another as soft and giving.

Roles in Group Therapy

Demarest and Teicher[51] feel that, in group therapy as well, co-therapists of different sexes offer a more complete and realistic setting in which to learn new life-patterns. According to those authors, a man and woman therapist in group therapy allow the patient to relate to the figure of one sex alone, to one in the presence of the other, and to both together. Such a setting facilitates the acting out of a family group situation, sibling rivalry, mother-son and father-son relations, and heterosexual problems.

The therapists may consciously manipulate and reverse their roles and point out differences from real parental roles. Joel and Shapiro[52] agree that two therapists, particularly if they are of opposite sexes, more immediately revive the family situation.

Linden,[53] working with a group of 51 institutionalized senile female patients, felt the need to re-evaluate multiple group therapy as it relates to the chronologically aged. Male and female co-therapists provoked "hidden transferences into bolder expression," and the woman nurse in particular aroused a spirit of competition which carried over into habits of dress, personal hygiene, and feminine interest. The male and female therapists "may revive repressed ideals of comradeship in the disillusioned senile" and bring back a mixed social world. At a deeper level, the presence of the woman therapist in particular was felt to reconstitute a family pattern, by arousing Oedipal strivings and mother-dependent feelings, which then had to be carefully handled by facilitating identification and avoiding overprotection. Linden concludes that this type of group therapy adapts itself especially well to the treatment of these repressed, dependent, and affectively starved patients.

In a searching analysis, Lundin and Aronov[54] write that two authority figures help simulate a family setting especially well for schizophrenics, who, they consider, think symbolically. In group therapy, the group members may take on parental or sibling roles. In contrast to many other writers, these authors state that two therapists need not be of the opposite sexes to be given father or mother roles. Schizophrenics in particular respond to subtle psychological differences in the therapists. The more aggressive therapist is equated with the masculine role, the more protective with the feminine. The implication here is that the personality of the therapist not only determines the role he plays, but also the role given him by the patients, who will have a primary reaction to one of the two therapists. Once this reaction is fixed, the second therapist assumes in the patient's mind the secondary qualities associated with the less dominant parent.

Slavson[55] writes that, from the theoretical point of view, multiple therapists for nonpsychotic patients are undesirable, since transferences are diluted or confused. He goes on to remark that adolescent and adult patients who are otherwise suited for group treatment do not require the duplication of a setting similar to early childhood, and the presence of a male and female therapist may encourage abreaction rather than insight. He reports that—in an activity group of children about nine years old—the use of a man and woman therapist confused the children as to the roles of the two adults.

Although Illing[56] disagrees with Slavson's contention that co-therapists necessarily dilute transference; Solomon, Loeffler, and Frank[57] not only do not contest his statement, but rather feel that "diluted transference" may be a definite advantage in working with groups of psychotics, as they did. By the same token, they feel that "diluted counter-transference" in multiple therapy is another advantage of this method. These authors discuss rather extensively the problems of interpersonal relations between co-therapists. They point out the possible subtle manifestations of therapist-therapist conflict, as when the results of this conflict are displaced in the behavior and feeling of the therapist toward the patients. One suggestion they make is the construction of a directive-nondirective, active-passive rating scale. "The co-therapist method will produce optimal results when the personalities and orientation of the co-therapist are flexible enough to permit considerable variance along the active-passive, directive-nondirective continuae." They further suggest periodic discussions between co-therapists, preferably in the presence of a third person as moderator.

In a later paper, Loeffler and Weinstein[58] point out and summarize many of the advantages and special problems for patients, therapists, and students of multiple group therapy. They feel that, as compared with individual therapy, the co-therapist method improves the possibility of the patient's attainment of catharsis, reality testing, and insight.

GENERAL SUMMARY

Advantages and Disadvantages

It is significant that Loeffler and Weinstein[59] mention "special problems" rather than "disadvantages." With the exception of Slavson,[60] none of the papers reviewed really criticize the multiple-therapist method. Rather, there are warnings about possible pitfalls and mistakes, mainly revolving around the feelings of the therapists toward each other. Thus, one therapist may resent the intrusion of another or may compete unconsciously or feel threatened—with these difficulties subtly affecting the therapeutic process. This potential for disruption, however, is also mentioned as having equal possibilities for being turned, by postsession discussion, to the advantage of the therapists in terms of overcoming these difficulties and achieving professional and personal growth.

Almost all authors agree that multiple therapy is an excellent teaching method, since it lessens the initial threat for the student and gives him the advantage of participant-learning with continuing supervision, while at the same time offering some protection to the patient. There is some mention of its value as a research technique, but the present authors could not find anywhere any specific discussion of how the use of multiple therapists makes the material more amenable for research; and, indeed, there is only one indication of how one would use multiple therapy as a research tool at all. Haigh and Kell, writing on this method as a means of training and research, make use of recordings, and assert that ". . . in multiple therapy, the variable of client personality is held constant—both therapists are responding to the same client." [61] In other words, they maintain that here is a situation in which the patient is a constant and in which the reaction of two different therapists to this constant can be explored. They suggest that this is a means by which to test such differing techniques as deep interpretation and reflection of feelings. However, the present reviewers fail to see how it would be possible to separate just what factors the patient is reacting to, since the end product is a result of the interaction of the techniques and personalities of both therapists. Furthermore, both therapists are not reacting to the "same" patient, since each therapist sees him differently.

The advantages of this multiple-therapist method in individual therapy range from protracted assault on the delusional system of a single psychotic patient to intervention in case of an impasse and subsequent clarification of transference and countertransference problems. There is little doubt that one of the major advantages of this method in both group and individual therapy is the prevention of overinvolvement and the heightened objectivity and clarification given by a second therapist who is not, at the moment, involved in an interchange with a patient. The greater transference possibilities of two authority figures, sometimes of the opposite sex, is a frequently mentioned advantage, along with the important fact that, since all therapists have certain blind spots, two therapists lessen the area of these blind spots considerably and offer concomitantly a greater potential for awareness of the patients' particular personality problems.[62]

Some Comparisons of this Method with Individuals and with Groups

There are some differences noted immediately when multiple therapy is used with individuals and when it is used with groups. For one thing, when working with individual patients, there may be many more than two therapists; there may be as many as ten. In the group situations described, however, there are usually only two therapists, with perhaps a third as an observer. Furthermore, from the descriptions given, it appears that individual patients treated by multiple therapists are often much more acutely disturbed and out of contact than are those treated in groups. This is particularly notable in the case described by Hayward and his associates.[63] It has recently been contended that psychotics form extremely intense transference relationships. If so, this fact might make multiple therapy an ideal medium for these patients and their therapists in many cases, since the transference and countertransference relationships may be either "diluted" [64] or better clarified in the multiple-therapist method.[65] The possibility of directing such ambivalent feelings as love and hate toward different therapists may also account for some of the reported successes of this method with psychotics.

Other factors may also operate to the advantage of groups of psychotic patients, and Orange[66] mentions multiple therapy as one of the possible modifications employed when treating psychotic patients in brief group therapy. It is suggested elsewhere that the easy symbolization by psychotics in re-creating two authority figures into a family configuration is a relevant factor in their successful treatment.[67] However, the writers should mention here that, in their own experiences with groups of nonpsychotic sex offenders, two male therapists are often perceived and reacted to as mother and father figures; and these transferences are in no way "diluted," as maintained by Slavson.[68]

In therapy of an individual, the patient may find support in one of the therapists while being directly challenged by another, although one of the pitfalls mentioned by various writers is the danger of overwhelming and frightening the patient. For the therapist, too, there is the reassurance of having another therapist at hand while treating individual psychotics. In the group situation, on the other hand, the possibility of overwhelming patients is no longer of such danger, but the benefits of mutual support are perhaps much greater for the therapists. It seems probable that the addition of one more therapist to a group situation does not have the same impact as the addition of one more therapist in individual treatment, although it certainly must have meaning which is of equal importance to the patients. So very much is happening in a group at any single time that the benefits to the therapists of heightened observation and mutual support that are given by a second therapist must far outweigh the increased complexity provoked by his presence.

PROBLEMS AND IMPLICATIONS OF MULTIPLE THERAPY

One of the difficulties which plagues researchers investigating psychotherapy is the fact that the investigator affects what is investigated, an occurrence not unique to social science. This effect is especially marked when an observer or second therapist enters the therapeutic situation.[69] The only way to avoid this kind of situation would be to use a recorder or a one-way screen. However, a recorder misses the subtle nuances of therapy sessions, and although a one-way screen could conceivably eliminate many of these difficulties, such a setup is frequently not available.

Despite difficulties, it is felt that the opportunity for learning much more about transference and countertransference phenomena is inherent in the method of multiple therapy. At the moment, however, the subjective and qualitative elements must remain the primary subjects of investigation.

The present authors' experience in full-term multiple therapy may offer further understanding of the nature of the roles of the therapists. Although both therapists here are men, patients readily become involved in transference relationships, responding to either therapist with feelings originally directed toward parents and other important figures, regardless of the sex of the original object. Thus the family setting is easily reconstituted, though with each of the two therapists appearing at times to present the loved and hated aspects respectively of the same parent.

In the writers' opinion, these transference relationships are neither founded simply on the congruence of the given therapist's personality with that of the parent in question, nor on an arbitrary projection of traits onto the therapist. Rather, the actions and attitudes of the therapist set the limits and direction for transference reactions. That is, the patient's projected feelings are found to be the implying of meaning or intent—the selection of which is in keeping with the general structure, or is an actual instance, of the therapist's behavior or of his objectively typical attitude. Although everybody viewed the two therapists as being different in general demeanor, and as having consistently recognizable trends, the patient's interpretation and response depends on inherent selective possibilities.

This distinction will perhaps be clearer in specific terms. To begin with, there is a sharp contrast between the "global" characters of the two therapists; that is, one would be described as "aggressive" and the other as "passive" by most people. The two groups in which they conduct multiple therapy also differ in important ways. One group is more analytical, intellectualized, and verbal in its approach to problems, and its members are for the most part neurotic and schizoid individuals, with no prior institutionalization, no nonsexual offenses, and a superficial picture of social conformity. In contrast, the other group engages in much psychopathic acting out of problems within the group (to the extent of fistfights and open homosexual banter during treatment sessions) with most members having either been incarcerated in the past, having also committed nonsexual offenses, and/or having been alcoholics.

Although the therapists do not intentionally take different roles, each group interprets their actions differently. Specifically, the "analytic" group has characterized the "aggressive" therapist as the "hatchetman" who "always makes you uncomfortable by probing and making interpretations," while the "passive" therapist is seen as "a nicer guy," better able to "help you and give you some support." The "acting-out" group, on the other hand, sees the former as "a guy who talks up and gets something done" and the latter as "a deadhead." Of course, an alternative interpretation might be that each of the two therapists themselves reacts differently to each group. However, continual examination of countertransference problems and discussion of how the therapists see their own and each other's roles are conducted regularly in postsession conferences. This self-corrective aspect of multiple therapy sharply minimizes such countertransference patterns.

A clear instance of an individual patient's transference interpretations that were within the actual limits of the objective situation involved the introduction of an observer (a psychological intern). At first, there was no apparent reaction by the group. However, several sessions later, after much discussion of a patient's mother's lovers, this patient admitted seeing the observer as an "intruder." He became petulant and did not want to talk in the observer's presence unless the latter talked too, so that he could do battle with him. Thus the observer was intruding on the closed family circle of the group in a way that reawakened earlier resentments which would have been likely to be veiled for a longer time without this objective similarity of the entrance of a stranger invited by an important authority figure (first by the mother in the past and later by the therapist). The other side of the coin for this patient was seen when the temporary absence of the therapist called forth feelings originally directed toward the patient's own errant father. The patient then described the group as being "like sitting down to a family dinner with the father away."

Thus, the effects of the introduction of the second therapist appear to make clear the need to eliminate the concept of transference as an arbitrary attachment to the therapist of old feelings toward the parent. Multiple therapy also allows the therapists to realize more clearly the role that similarity of cognitive structures of the old and new situations plays in making for selection of fitting feelings. A further implication is that, having come to understand his own personality patterns, the therapist may learn to use them therapeutically, rather than simply attempt to eliminate their effects.

Still to be answered, is the question of whether the time given by more than one therapist is justified either by a shortened period of treatment or more successful results.

It is only within the last seven years that this new technique has received more than passing reference in the literature; and so the current survey reflects necessarily varied and as yet uncoordinated explorations. It is hoped that future papers will attempt more systematic investigations, from which may be gleaned the differing effects of various methods of multiple therapy with individuals and groups—neurotics, psychotics, and other types of patient.

REFERENCES

1. R. Dreikurs, "Techniques and Dynamics of Multiple Psychotherapy," *Psychiat. Quart.*, 24:788-799, 1950; R. Dreikurs, B. H. Shulman, and H. Mosak, "Patient-therapist Relationship in Multiple Psychotherapy: I. Its Advantages for the Therapist." *Psychiat. Quart.*, 26:219-227, 1952; J. E. Dyrud and M. J. Rioch, "Multiple Therapy in the Treatment Program of a Mental Hospital," *Psychiat.*, 16:21-26, 1953; G. Haigh and B. L. Kell, "Multiple Therapy as a Method for Training and Research in Psychotherapy," *J. Abnorm. and Soc. Psychol.*, 45:659-666, 1950; M. L.

Hayward, J. J. Peters, and J. E. Taylor, "Some Values of the Use of Multiple Therapists in the Treatment of Psychosis." *Psychiat. Quart.*, 26:244-249, 1952; J. Warkentin, N. L. Johnson, and C. A. Whitaker, "A Comparison of Individual and Multiple Psychotherapy," *Psychiat.*, 14:415-418, 1951.

2. Elinor W. Demarest and A. Teicher, "Transference in Group Therapy," *Psychiat.* 17:187-202, 1954; W. H. Lundin and B. M. Aronov, "The Use of Co-Therapists in Group Psychotherapy," *J. Consult. Psychol.*, 16:76-80, 1952; A. Solomon, F. J. Loeffler, and G. H. Frank, "An Analysis of Co-Therapist Interaction in Group Psychotherapy," *Int. J. Group Psychother.*, 3:171-180, 1953; C. A. Whitaker, "Teaching the Practicing Physician to Do Psychotherapy," *So. Med. J.*, 42:899-903, 1949.

3. J. C. Bock, D. J. Lewis, and J. Tuck, "Role-Divided Three-Cornered Therapy," *Psychiat.*, 17:277-282, 1954.

4. L. B. Hill and F. G. Worden, "Participant Teaching of Psychotherapy by Senior Physicians," *Psychiat. Quart.*, 26:228-243, 1952.

5. G. A. Reeve, "A Method of Co-ordinated Therapy," *Am. J. Orthopsychiat.*, 9:743-747, 1939.

6. G. M. Lott, "The Training of Non-Medical Cooperative Psychotherapists by Multiple Psychotherapy," *Am. J. Psychother.*, 6:440-447, 1952.

7. M. E. Linden, "The Significance of Dual Leadership in Gerontologic Group Psychotherapy: Studies in Gerontologic Human Relations III," *Int. J. Group Psychother.*, 4:262-273, 1954.

8. Hayward, Peters, and Taylor, *op. cit.*

9. Warkentin, Johnson, and Whitaker, *op. cit.*

10. S. B. Hadden, "The Utilization of a Therapy Group in Teaching Psychotherapy," *Am. J. Psychiat.*, 103:644-648, 1947.

11. C. A. Whitaker and T. P. Malone, *The Roots of Psychotherapy* (Garden City, N.Y.: Country Life Press, 1953).

12. A. Adler, *Guiding the Child* (New York: Greenberg, 1930), p. 23.

13. *Ibid.*, p. 158.

14. Hadden, *op. cit.*

15. J. L. Moreno (ed.) *Group Psychotherapy. A Symposium* (New York: Beacon House, 1954), p. 385.

16. R. Dreikurs, "Techniques and Dynamics of Multiple Psychotherapy," *Psychiat. Quart.*, 24:788-799, 1950; R. Dreikurs, B. H. Schulman, and H. Mosak, "Patient-therapist Relationship in Multiple Psychotherapy: II. Its Advantages for the Patient," *Psychiat. Quart.*, 26:590-596, 1952.

17. Hayward, Peters, and Taylor, *op. cit.*

18. Hadden, *op. cit.*

19. Whitaker, *op. cit.*

20. C. A. Whitaker, J. Warkentin, and N. L. Johnson, "A Philosophical Basis for Brief Psychotherapy," *Psychiat. Quart.*, 23:439-443, 1949.

21. Haigh and Kell, *op. cit.*

22. Lott, *op. cit.*

23. Hill and Worden, *op. cit.*

24. M. Grotjahn, "Special Problems in the Supervision of Group Psychotherapy," *Group Psychother.*, 3:309-315, 1951.

25. Grotjahn, "Problems and Techniques of Supervision," *Psychiat.*, 18:9-15, 1955.
26. C. A. Whitaker, "Teaching the Practicing Physician to Do Psychotherapy," *So. Med. J.*, 42:899-903, 1949; Hadden, *op. cit.*; C. A. Whitaker, J. Warkentin, and N. L. Johnson, *loc. cit.*; M. Grotjahn, *loc. cit.*
27. Hill and Worden, *op. cit.*; C. A. Whitaker, J. Warkentin, and N. L. Johnson, "The Psychotherapeutic Impasse," *Am. J. Orthopsychiat.*, 20:641-647, 1950.
28. Dyrud and Rioch, *op. cit.*; F. J. Loeffler and H. M. Weinstein, "The Co-Therapist Method: Special Problems and Advantages," *Group Psychother.*, 6:189-192, 1954.
29. Lott, *op. cit.*
30. C. A. Whitaker, J. Warkentin, and N. L. Johnson, "The Psychotherapeutic Impasse," *loc. cit.*
31. Hayward, Peters, and Taylor, *op. cit.*
32. Dyrud and Rioch, *op. cit.*
33. R. Dreikurs, "Techniques and Dynamics of Multiple Psychotherapy," *Psychiat. Quart.*, 24:788-799, 1950.
34. R. Dreikurs, B. Schulman, and H. Mosak, "Patient-Therapist Relationship in Multiple Psychotherapy: I. Its Advantages for the Therapist," *loc cit.*; "Patient-Therapist Relationship in Multiple Psychotherapy: II. Its Advantages for the Patient," *loc. cit.*
35. Reeve, *op. cit.*
36. C. A. Whitaker, J. Warkentin, and N. L. Johnson, *loc. cit.*
37. Warkentin, Johnson, and Whitaker, *op. cit.*
38. Bock, Lewis, and Tuck, *op. cit.*
39. H. T. Nash and A. R. Stone, "Collaboration of Therapist and Observer in Guiding Group Psychotherapy," *Group Psychother.*, 3:309-315, 1951.
40. A. J. Orange, "A Note on Brief Group Psychotherapy with Psychotic Patients," *Int. J. Group Psychother.*, 5:80-83, 1955.
41. Lundin and Aronov, *op. cit.*
42. Demarest and Teicher, *op. cit.*
43. W. Joel and D. Shapiro, "Some Principles and Procedures for Group Psychotherapy," *J. Psychol.*, 29:77-88, 1950.
44. Florence Powdermaker and J. Frank, *Group Psychotherapy* (Cambridge, Mass.: Harvard University Press, 1953), pp. 9-14.
45. H. A. Illing, "Transference Role of the Visitor in Group Psychotherapy," *Int. J. Group Psychother.*, 5:204-212, 1955.
46. G. R. Bach, *Intensive Group Psychotherapy* (New York: Ronald Press, 1954), pp. 60-64.
47. Linden, *op. cit.*
48. Bock, Lewis, and Tuck, *op. cit.*
49. Reeve, *op. cit.*
50. Warkentin, Johnson, and Whitaker, *op. cit.*
51. Demarest and Teicher, *op. cit.*
52. Joel and Shapiro, *op. cit.*
53. Linden, *op. cit.*

54. Lundin and Aronov, *op. cit.*
55. S. R. Slavson, *Analytic Group Psychotherapy* (New York: Columbia University Press, 1950), pp. 111-112.
56. Illing, *op. cit.*
57. Solomon, Loeffler, and Frank, *op. cit.*
58. Loeffler and Weinstein, *op. cit.*
59. *Ibid.*
60. Slavson, *op. cit.*
61. Haigh and Kell, *op. cit.*, p. 664.
62. C. A. Whitaker, J. Warkentin, and N. L. Johnson, "The Psychotherapeutic Impasse," *loc. cit.*
63. Hayward, Peters, and Taylor, *op. cit.*
64. Slavson, *op. cit.*
65. Solomon, Loeffler, and Frank, *op. cit.*
66. Orange, *op. cit.*
67. Lundin and Aronov, *op. cit.*
68. Slavson, *op. cit.*, pp. 111-112.
69. Joel and Shapiro, *op. cit.*; Powderman and Frank, *op. cit.*; Illing, *op. cit.*

31

HOMOGENEOUS VERSUS HETEROGENEOUS GROUPS

William Furst

This presentation represents the opinions of my former associates, Dr. Lewis H. Loeser, Mrs. Thea Bry, and myself, and is derived from the experimental work and experience we have gained in group therapy during military service and in private practice.

The problem of the homogeneous versus heterogeneous group has interested us from the onset of our work. In using these terms we are referring to diagnostic and psychodynamic criteria. Although the terms may equally well be applied to homogeneity of sex, age, color, religion, and so on, we have used and are now using this terminology only in reference to diagnosis and underlying psychopathology. A homogeneous group then, is one in which a reasonable similarity in psychodynamics and pathology is known to exist among the members of the group. All other similarities or differences, in this discussion, are set aside.

Our accent has been placed on research techniques and we have employed the method of parallel and control group to throw further light on certain basic questions. We have, for example, material based on intensive study of two homogeneous and two heterogeneous groups, otherwise similar in make-up and nature. Each group has been carefully selected; detailed observations of each session were recorded by an observer, and cases were reasonably well followed after treatment. We use an interview type of therapy, analytically oriented, and our patients are all private patients on a free basis who have voluntarily applied for treatment.

Only conclusions will be given here.

Observations on homogeneous groups of anxiety neurotics lead to the following conclusions:

Reprinted from *Topical Problems of Psychotherapy*, Vol. II, 1960, pp. 170-173.

(1) Group identification takes place quickly and transferences are rapidly formed.

(2) Insight develops rapidly.

(3) Psychodynamics are more rapidly laid bare.

(4) Duration of treatment is lessened.

(5) Attendance is more regular.

(6) Resistances and interactions of a destructive nature are lessened.

(7) Intramural groups or cliques are uncommon.

(8) Recovery from symptoms is more rapid.

On the negative side, in dealing with homogeneous groups, we note:

(1) Homogeneous groups are difficult to put together. Careful screening, and a large number of patients from which to select, are necessary.

(2) Because of the absence of interaction factors the level of therapy is relatively superficial.

(3) Despite removal of symptoms, character structure is relatively untouched.

(4) The opportunity for reality testing is lessened by the absence of interaction with heterogeneous personalities.

(5) The opportunity to develop multiple and shifting transferences in accordance to needs is lacking.

Our experience with heterogeneous groups would lead to the following observations. On the negative side we would conclude that:

(1) Recovery takes place more slowly. Anxiety neurotics, for example, in a homogeneous group become symptom-free faster than in a heterogeneous group.

(2) Problems of interaction and resulting tensions within the group become magnified. The problems of the therapist are multiplied.

(3) Group identification takes place slowly.

(4) Transference to the therapist is delayed.

(5) Insight is slow in developing. Common denominators are difficult to work out in the field of psychodynamics.

(6) Attendance is likely to be more irregular.

On the positive side there is evidence that:

(1) Heterogeneous groups by their very nature tend to take the therapist, whether or not he so desires, into deeper levels of therapy.

(2) Character structure as well as symptom formation are influenced by the process of therapy.

(3) Reality testing is more adequate and thorough.

(4) Intragroup transferences of a diverse and shifting nature can be formed readily in the heterogeneous group in accordance with individual needs.

(5) Heterogeneous groups are easy to assemble and screening need not be as thorough.

As a result of our observations, derived from actual comparison of homogeneous and heterogeneous groups, certain broad generalizations are justified. We are firmly convinced that both types of groups can be utilized in group therapy. However, the make-up of the group has an important bearing on the type and nature of therapy, and we submit the following conclusions for consideration:

(1) Heterogeneous groups are necessary for activity therapy, for inter-action therapy, and for group psychoanalysis. Homogeneous groups are not as suitable for these types of group therapy.

(2) Interview therapy, analytically oriented, can be carried out successfully with both homogeneous and heterogeneous groups.

The question of "level of therapy" is closely linked to the make-up of the group. It is difficult to do deep therapy with a homogeneous group. It is difficult not to do deep therapy with a heterogeneous group. Homogeneous groups do not put as much strain on the therapist and do not require the skill and experience on his part that heterogeneous groups require.

Homogeneous groups should then be chosen:

(a) When the interview type of therapy is utilized.
(b) When less profound and nonintensive therapy is indicated.
(c) When the therapist is not prepared or trained to handle deep levels of therapy.
(d) When the factor of time and expense are important.

Heterogeneous groups, on the other hand, are to be chosen:

(a) When deep levels of therapy are desired.
(b) When modification of character structure is necessary.
(c) When the training and experience of the therapist is adequate.
(d) When the time and expense are less important.

Glatzer has shown experimentally, by the creation of a heterogeneous group from two dissimilar homogeneous groups, that optimum treatment conditions and facilitation of the flow and handling of conflicting productions in the group were expedited.

Schwartz and Wolf have recently reported highly pertinent observations on heterogeneous and homogeneous groups as follows:

In Homogeneous Groups:

(1) There is created a limited and limiting form of therapy.
(2) There is bound to be more hostility in seeing oneself in others.
(3) There is a limit to any kind of intercommunication because the group analyzand starts with the assumption "I am like everybody else here," thus limiting comparisons and need to change.
(4) Interpretive interventions of the therapist always focus the group

analyzand on intrapsychic rather than interpsychic examination because of the sameness of all the members.

(5) There is a greater tendency in the homogeneous group to act out, to be more isolated from reality, from differences, and from the rest of the culture.

(6) A teaching or a form of social group may be more efficient if homogeneous.

In Heterogeneous Groups:

(1) There is opportunity to work through the problems of difference both with peers and authorities.

(2) Isolation is reduced by experiencing multiple reactivity possibilities.

(3) There is less mirror imaging and less identification.

(4) There are more transference and countertransference reactions, also more reality testing and working through.

(5) Superficially, at least, more interpersonal communication than intrapsychic preoccupation is encouraged.

(6) Eventually, intrapsychic communication is stimulated by virtue of comparison of individual with individual, because of differences.

(7) In the beginning, patients may act out more, but ultimately they will solve their problems.

(8) Differences do not have to come only from the authority figure, as in homogeneous groups, but many come from the peers.

In conclusion, one can make the following generalization:

Level of therapy and make-up of the group are factors which are closely correlated. Any discussion of one must involve the other factor. Neither homogeneous nor heterogeneous groups are best. They are to be used in accordance with the goals of the therapist.

32

CONCERNING THE SIZE
OF THERAPY GROUPS

Joseph J. Geller

The size of therapy groups is related to various techniques and depends upon their aims and goals. In general, the purpose of any psychotherapy is to bring about in the psychiatrically sick person more satisfactory and more effective relatedness to others. Group-psychotherapy techniques serve this purpose by adapting many of the principles of individual psychotherapy, as well as bringing into play two important aspects of group psychotherapy; namely, the effective utilization of group interaction for therapeutic ends and the employment of facilities to reach greater numbers of patients. Experience has shown that there are different sizes of groups that can be related to the different levels of therapeutic aims.

These levels of psychotherapy can be listed as: (1) those approaching the depth, breadth, and totality of psychoanalytic therapy; (2) the analysis and alleviation of the major presenting problems of a patient with these limited goals in view; (3) the use of repressive-inspirational techniques to strengthen the control exercised over symptoms; and (4) the use of group-orientation techniques. The various sizes of groups will be discussed in relation to these levels of therapy. As a general rule, it has been found that there is a correlation between the size of the group and the depth of therapy achieved: The depth of therapy decreases as the size of the group increases.

(1) In the first level of therapy mentioned, the psychoanalytic level requires the smallest size of groups. As few as three or four patients are included by some, while others have from six to ten patients in a group. The intensity of therapy, the need thoroughly to explore data presented by each of the patients, and the close attention given to an understanding of the many aspects of the interpersonal relations within the group, all require a fairly small group.

Reprinted from *The International Journal of Group Psychotherapy*, Vol. I, No. 2, June 1951, pp. 1-2.

(2) The next level is that in which efforts are directed toward handling one or more specific problem areas for a given patient. While psychodynamic concepts similar to those used in the foregoing level are here similarly employed, a more general approach to the treatment problem is used. As a consequence, slightly larger groups are permissible. From eight to fifteen patients is the size commonly allowed for a group of this nature. The essential difference between this level and the deeper one mentioned above is a quantitative, rather than qualitative one.

(3) Still larger groups are permissible in the repressive-inspirational approach to therapy. From thirty to fifty patients are brought together here. It is even possible, although not quite so effective for the individual patient, for such a group to work with one hundred or more people. For this type of therapy, the group is the vehicle par excellence for the development of mass-emotional phenomena which support and strengthen the individual's repressive abilities.

(4) The largest groups are found possible with the most superficial approach to psychotherapy: the guidance and orientation method. Here, theoretical and practical aspects of psychological functioning are presented to interested groups. Fifty or more patients in a group can conveniently be helped with this approach. The larger the size of the group, however, the less opportunity there is for individual discussion of points raised by the material presented.

We see, then, that therapy groups are roughly of four sizes: those under ten patients, eight to fifteen patients, thirty to fifty patients, and over fifty patients. These particular sizes are related to the nature and depth of the psychotherapy contemplated. It has been found that the more intensive and individually directed the therapy, the smaller the size of the group.

A subject related to sizes of groups that, for completeness, may briefly be considered here is that of the make-up of the professional component of the therapy group. As in individual psychotherapy, the usual arrangement consists of one professional person in the group as the therapist. Several modifications of this are made possible by the nature of the group structure. It is quite feasible to have a second professional person present to act as an "observer." This enables the therapist more effectively to validate his procedures and permits more adequate record keeping where this is desired. It is possible also to have the second professional person in the group act as an observer at times and at others change places with the therapist. Thus there is an "alternate therapist," both to maintain continuity of therapy in the absence of the original therapist, as well as to permit of more extensive transference phenomena than occur with a single therapist. Experiments have also been carried out with multiple therapists working simultaneously, from two to five persons being the usual number.

33

AN APPROACH TO THE SELECTION OF PATIENTS FOR GROUP PSYCHOTHERAPY

J. E. Neighbor
Margaret Beach
Donald T. Brown
David Kevin
John S. Visher

I

In the course of their experience in an outpatient mental hygiene clinic the authors of this paper have become convinced that group psychotherapy is the treatment of choice for a substantial percentage of patients whose problems are susceptible to clinic therapy of any type. By group psychotherapy we mean the process which takes place whenever people are gathered together for the consideration of personal emotional problems with the purpose of alleviating them, in the presence and with the aid of an individual skilled in both the understanding of the individual personality and the patterns of human interrelationships and group interactions.

In this paper certain criteria are discussed which have been found useful in identifying those individuals for whom this approach offers specific benefits as well as those who are unable to utilize it. In addition, the selection of patients from the standpoint of the requirements and limitations of the group itself is considered. These criteria are based on the authors' analysis of the unique characteristics of this form of therapeutic experience. A standard method for describing various kinds of therapy groups is proposed. It should be emphasized that problems of therapuetic technique have been excluded from consideration here except where they are directly pertinent to the selection of patients.

Reprinted from *Mental Hygiene*, Vol. 42, No. 1, April 1958, pp. 243-254.

The clinical setting is always an important factor in determining which of several possible therapeutic orientations is chosen. The authors are members of the staff of a state-supported mental hygiene clinic offering psychiatric diagnosis and individual and group therapy for adults and children. As the only such facility serving an urban and rural population of 1,500,000 we continually face a far greater demand for our services than our professional staff of seven full-time workers can possibly meet. Thus it has become our policy that all treatment offered be limited in intensity and duration.

In our attempt to offer psychotherapy to a maximum number of patients, the group approach was instituted experimentally in 1948, shortly after the opening of the clinic. Since that time group therapy has gradually become an increasingly important part of the clinic program. At present, under the direction of the group therapy consultant (J.E.N.), an average of six or seven therapeutic groups meet weekly, these comprising almost two thirds of the adult patients seen for extended treatment.

Members of the clinic staff concerned with this effort have met regularly to study the group process. In the course of these meetings it became apparent that certain empirically derived yet unverbalized clinical criteria were being applied in selecting, from among the applicants for therapeutic services, those who would be offered group psychotherapy. Further discussions resulted in a crystallization of these concepts in a more systematic manner, which made possible their more efficient application in the intake process. Subsequently we have become aware that other workers have arrived independently at somewhat similar conclusions. We refer especially to the papers of Freedman and Sweet,[1] Geller,[2] and to parts of the work of Bach.[3] Hulse[4] and Slavson,[5] while agreeing in part with our findings, are of course working under different circumstances and with different goals, which make direct comparisons difficult.

II

We are very much aware that criteria developed in this clinical setting might have validity only for our own or for nearly identical situations. In addition we have frequently encountered difficulty in making maximal use of the reports of some other authors who have failed to delineate specifically their particular settings and methods. We are therefore attempting to describe our therapeutic groups in a comprehensive and systematic manner with the primary purpose of providing adequate information about our own approach. We would also hope that a more general use of some such method of evaluation might reduce confusion in the literature and lead to more profitable communication among workers in the field.

Our description is a modification of a classification introduced by Dreikurs and Corsini in their review of twenty years of group therapy published in the February 1954 *American Journal of Psychiatry*.[6]

For purposes of clarity we have divided it into two sections, dealing first with administrative structure and then with internal group functions.

As can be seen, our program is under the auspices of a tax-supported outpatient general mental hygiene clinic. Fees are set individually on the basis of ability to pay and are identical with those charged for individual therapy. Our typical group is composed of 6 to 8 men and/or women usually between the ages of 20 and 40. They meet for one hour weekly for a 6-month period, following which they may be reassigned to another group or to individual treatment. The therapist may represent any of the three professional disciplines at the clinic, and there is usually a nonparticipant observer-recorder. Patients in group therapy are not seen individ-

Plate 33–1   *Administrative structure*

---

1. *In what clinical setting is therapy being done?*
Outpatient, tax-supported general mental hygiene clinic.*

2. *What fees are charged?*
Graduated depending on income; identical with fees for individual therapy.

3. *How many patients are usually assigned to each group?*
We may assign 10 to 12 patients initially, although the usual working group has 6 to 8 members.

4. *Are both sexes included in the groups?*
Some are exclusively male or female, others are mixed in sex.

5. *What is the average age range of the patients?*
Usually between 20 and 40 years.

6. *How long does each group therapy session last and how often does the group meet?*
Approximately one-hour sessions once weekly.

7. *For how many sessions does a group usually meet?*
24 sessions (a 6-month period) following which there may be reassignment to another group or to individual therapy.

8. *Which staff members act as therapists?*
Psychiatrists, psychiatric social workers, and clinical psychologists. (Staff members usually, rather than trainees.)

9. *How many therapists are assigned to each group?*
Usually one therapist and a nonparticipant observer.

10. *Do patients receive individual therapy concurrently with group?*
Only rarely, primarily in crisis situations.

11. *What diagnostic categories are represented among the group members?*
Usually a mixture of psychoneurotic, psychophysiologic, and personality disorders. Occasional ambulatory schizophrenic reactions.

---

* Answers refer to groups at the Berkeley State Mental Hygiene Clinic.

ually except in connection with specific crisis situations. Diagnostically our patients are usually classified among the psychoneurotic, psychophysiologic, or personality disorders with occasional ambulatory schizophrenic reactions. All diagnoses are usually represented in a given group.

As can be seen in Plate 2, we illustrate the functioning of our groups through the device of creating a series of continua upon each of which we assume a position relative to the theoretical extremes. We believe that patients in our groups achieve some modification of their defensive structure and certain insights into the origins of their current difficulties (I). In general, however, we do not expect basic personality changes.

Plate 33–2

I OPTIMUM GOALS OF THERAPY

IMPART INFORMATION	ALLOW CATHARSIS	REAPPRAISE REALITY	BUILD NEW DEFENSES	ATTAIN INSIGHT	CHANGE BASIC PERSONALITY
				*	

II ROLE OF THERAPIST

A. TYPE OF THERAPEUTIC ACTIVITY

CORRECTIVE, EDUCATIONAL	SUPPORTIVE, SUGGESTIVE	CLARIFICATIVE, INTERPRETIVE
	*	

B. AMOUNT OF THERAPEUTIC INTERVENTION

CONSTANT	FREQUENT	RARE
	*	

C. NATURE OF THERAPIST'S DIRECTION

CHOOSES TOPICS, LECTURES	CALLS ON PATIENTS	RESTATES CONTENT	QUESTIONS MEANING OF BEHAVIOR
		*	

III ROLE OF PATIENT

A. TYPE OF ACTIVITY ENCOURAGED

LISTENING	DISCUSSING	EMOTIONAL INVOLVEMENT
	*	

B. TYPE OF INTRAGROUP RELATIONSHIPS FOSTERED

THERAPIST–PATIENT. 100%	PATIENT 50% THERAPIST 50%	PATIENT–PATIENT 100%
	*	

IV CONTENT EMPHASIZED IN SESSIONS

MENTAL HYGIENE PRINCIPLES	PROBLEMS OF ADJUSTMENT	PERSONAL EMOTIONAL DIFFICULTIES	GROUP INTERACTIONS	FANTASIES, DREAMS
		*		

*REFERS TO THE POSITION ON THE CONTINUUM OCCUPIED BY OUR GROUPS.

The therapist in our groups tends to limit his therapeutic intervention to clarifying and interpreting the material produced by the patients. He rarely educates or reassures them. He remains relatively silent and allows the group considerable latitude in the selection of topics for discussion (II). He often raises questions which will call the groups attention to significant content or behavior.

The patient, on the other hand, is encouraged to become emotionally involved in the group process, with relationships among the group members being the primary focus (III).

The discussions usually deal with personal emotional difficulties and, secondly, with their expression in the group interaction (IV).

III

We feel that the group therapeutic process by its nature possesses certain unique characteristics which may influence both positively and negatively the selection of patients, and hence a consideration of these must be incorporated into the process of evaluation.

We believe that an essential point of difference between a therapeutic group and a purely social group results from the initial expectations of the members. Each individual comes with some anticipation that his symptoms will be relieved and with at least a minimal awareness of the contributory role of personal emotional problems. These factors plus the presence and activity of the therapist create a permissive atmosphere which encourages the free expression and acceptance of feelings. In contrast to the individual therapeutic situation there is less specific pressure on each member to reveal anxiety-provoking material. In some cases, competitiveness may stimulate early self-revelation; in general, however, individual psychological defenses are adequate to prevent premature and overly disturbing insight.

As the group continues to meet, relationships form among the members and with the group therapist similar to but lacking the intensity of the transference phenomena present in individual therapy. Particularly prominent are feelings analogous to those previously experienced in the sibling situation in childhood. The group also provides an ideal setting for the appearance of typical interpersonal defensive maneuvers which have an emotional rather than an intellectual impact. Denial of the existence of such behavior is more difficult under these conditions.

It is our opinion that individual members tend to utilize the group discussion according to their current level of psychological development. For example, some patients gain reassurance simply from learning that their problems are not unique; others become aware of their characteristic defensive patterns from observing their reactions to fellow group members.

Finally, the group serves some individuals by providing an opportunity to compare and contrast their own perceptions of reality with those of others.

IV

As a result of these considerations we have selected certain categories of patients who seem to respond to our therapeutic groups. One category includes those who gain primarily from the permissive atmosphere or relative lack of pressure in the therapy situation. These include individuals who are unable to use brief individual therapy because of inarticulateness and lack of social aptitudes but who can participate in group therapy even though nonverbally at first. To others who are quite fearful of intimate individual relationships, group treatment offers a way of safely experiencing the satisfactions and rewards of social and emotional interchanges.

Secondly, there are those patients who develop transference involvements which become unmanageable in a relatively brief individual therapeutic relationship. These reactions usually do not become so intense in group therapy. For example, exceptionally dependent character types whose problems often spring from severe deprivation in childhood are protected from regressing to an attitude of complete helplessness. Persons who become immobilized by guilt when they receive the undivided attention of a therapist are relieved of this pressure by group membership. Another type of patient, whose problem is his inability to express hostile feelings toward authority, gains courage from the support of others.

Group therapy is helpful for a third category of patients because it deals effectively with certain kinds of defenses which result in avoidance of awareness of emotions. We refer first to persons with predominately psychosomatic complaints, who often learn in the group that their feelings are connected with their symptoms. Individuals who deny feelings and maintain a psychologically naïve attitude often find this position difficult to sustain. The same is true of those who attempt to describe all experience in intellectual terms. Many such patients are able to benefit from brief individual therapy after an initial group experience.

Being faced with reality is particularly important for a final group of patients. Prominent among them are "acting-out characters" who constantly become involved in personal crises while denying their own involvement. This distortion is often clearly understood and challenged by other group members. On the other hand, psychotic patients who have partially reorganized their defensive structure seem to benefit from the opportunity to re-establish relationships with others in a protected yet realistic situation. This is also true of some patients who have worked through problems in individual interviews but who need the experience of applying their new insight in a supervised situation.

V

Just as there are certain categories of patients who seem particularly suited to group therapy, other individuals can be identified who are unable to tolerate the specific stresses created by the group process. First, there are patients with such intense social anxiety that they cannot even consider any kind of group participation. Moreover, in our particular groups the emotional tensions produced by the material discussed are such that patients with an imminent or active psychotic process are unable to carry the additional burden without further disintegration.

There are other individuals whose defenses, while identical with those of patients who respond favorably, are more rigidly maintained. For example, some persons with exclusively psychosomatic symptoms are threatened by even mild probing; also some extremely deprived patients are intolerably frustrated by failing to obtain the exclusive attention of the therapist. We are often unable to differentiate such patients at the time of their application. We frequently assign equivocal cases to groups for a therapeutic trial. For them, individual therapy on a once-a-week basis is ineffective in any case, and occasionally they surprise us by making effective use of the group process.

VI

Although the needs and defenses of the individual are considered first, we have found it equally necessary to evaluate certain factors arising from the requirements of the group itself in developing our criteria. The interaction of persons new and strange to each other results in the formation of a new type of social unit. Society offers no comparable experience. It is our impression that this unique social and psychological organization has certain needs which must be met by its members if it is to achieve its purpose.

An effective group must include some individuals who have an awareness of their anxiety and an ability to express it through a discussion of conflictual material. They stimulate the group's consideration of emotional problems. There also must be patients with a relatively high degree of perception and of sensitivity to the psychological problems and maneuvers of others. They are able to make interpretations which might be unacceptable if they came from the therapist. We believe it to be important also that there exist among group members a variety of social experiences, defensive structures and presenting problems. This provides an opportunity for contrast, comparison, and self-evaluation.

Occasionally we may assign patients to a therapeutic group who could equally well be offered individual therapy, because of their catalytic effect upon the group.

VII

In the same way that persons with the characteristics mentioned above have proved indispensable for group progress, there are others whose behavior inhibits it. If they appear too deviant from the group norm, they should be excluded—even though they might gain personally from the group experience—to avoid a possible disruption of the group. Thus certain patients use incessant irrelevant and uninsightful talk as a defensive device. They monopolize group time and energy in this way, preventing constructive exploration of their own or others' problems. Others persist in attempts to engage the therapist in competition or to obtain his exclusive attention, ignoring the needs and rights of the rest of the group. In these circumstances the frustration of other group members often causes intolerable antagonism and guilt, which results either in isolation of the offender or in flights from the group.

The anxiety of another type of patient leads him to make a defensive attack upon other group members, the therapist, the therapeutic method, or even the basic concept of treatment. Such intense attacks, occurring as they usually do in the opening sessions, destroy the confidence of other group members in the enterprise upon which they are embarking. Other patients have a self-destructive urge to reveal socially unacceptable symptoms in their initial contacts with the group. This means that patients must be excluded who are frankly delusional, who openly display bizarre ideation, or who would be indiscreet in discussing deviant sexual behavior. The above manifestations of pathology are very frightening to the majority of our group members.

We prefer to exclude patients who display tendencies toward overt suicidal, homicidal, or infanticidal acts. Our groups are unable to deal with such traumatic material yet are prevented by its emergence from dealing with other less dramatic but nevertheless important problems.

Plate 33–3   *Summary of indications and contraindications for group therapy*

PATIENT NEEDS

Our therapeutic groups are *indicated* for patients:

Aided by group support to express hostility to authority figures.	Needing to participate, even though nonverbally.
Needing supportive social experience.	Needing protection from too intense transference feelings.
Whose emotional unawareness is reduced by group interaction.	Benefiting from group protection against regressive trends.

Aided by group's pointing out and interpreting acting out.	Reacting with extreme guilt to individual attention.
Made too anxious by one-to-one therapeutic relationship.	Needing protected, though realistic, interpersonal experience.

Our therapeutic groups are *contraindicated* for patients:

Chronically experiencing intolerable frustration in sharing a therapist.	Unable to consider participation in groups because of intense anxiety thus aroused.
For whom material discussed could accelerate psychotic processes.	

GROUP NEEDS

Our therapeutic groups are *strengthened* by patients:

With awareness of anxiety and ability to verbalize.	With a variety of defensive structures, social experiences, and presenting problems.
With perception of others' problems and defensive maneuvers.	

Our therapeutic groups are *weakened* by patients:

Appearing so deviant as to be disintegrative to the group.	Whose anxiety leads to destructive self-revelation in opening sessions.
Whose exaggerated defensive reactions disrupt essential group exploration.	Likely to perform overt suicidal, homicidal, or infanticidal acts.
Whose anxiety is manifested by intense attacks in opening sessions.	

DISCUSSION

It should be re-emphasized that the foregoing considerations have been developed within a specific clinical setting with its own characteristic structure, function, and limitations. Because of this it is recognized that conclusions drawn from this experience need not have universal validity. We hope, however, that therapists in somewhat similar situations may be able to use these criteria or to modify them to suit their particular needs. We are convinced that among the applicants to a general mental hygiene clinic some will be unsuitable for any type of outpatient therapy while others will be specifically amenable to the group approach.

A question may be raised as to the difficulty of predicting the complex types of behavior which have been described above, on the basis of a limited evaluation period. It has been our impression that, given a skilled interviewer who has had experience as a group therapist, sufficient data may be accumulated in an initial interview to permit a reasonably accurate estimate of how the applicant will react to the group meetings. Our interviewers make such judgments on the basis of information about how the patient has related to his immediate environment, both past and present, as well as his behavior in the interview and his response to tentative suggestions or interpretations made with the specific purpose of testing his defensive structure. Often, information from collateral sources (family members, referring agencies, and so on) can add to the total picture. At times we may place the applicant under emotional stress to determine his characteristic ways of reacting or his ability to respond in a constructive manner. In borderline cases, psychological testing may provide additional clues. All the information available is evaluated at an intake conference, the participants in which are for the most part themselves active in both group and individual therapy. This tends to eliminate any undue positive or negative bias of the individual interviewer.

Despite all these measures, it is at times unclear whether or not a given patient can make use of our therapeutic groups. Usually there are both positive and negative indications and some balance must be struck. As previously noted, in such equivocal cases, especially where the patient seems clearly unsuitable for individual therapy of relatively limited intensity and duration, we will often assign him to a group for a therapeutic trial.

We have not attempted to cover completely the question of balancing various types of patients for optimum group functioning, although we believe that this matter is of as great importance as that of the initial selection. Nor have we considered in this paper the effect upon selection of the anxieties and therapeutic skills of the group leader. It goes without saying that a skilled and experienced therapist can deal adequately with potentially more difficult group constellations.

Increasingly, community mental hygiene clinics are finding it difficult to offer individual psychotherapy to the ever-growing numbers of applicants for psychiatric treatment. Since we feel that group psychotherapy is the treatment of choice for a large proportion of these individuals, we believe it essential that there be continued study of the group process and the elaboration and perfection of criteria for its use.

SUMMARY

In this paper the hypothesis is advanced that certain types of outpatients are most successfully treated by group psychotherapy. The authors speak from a background of seven years of cumulative experience in an outpatient mental hygiene clinic. They discuss the structure within which they operate and its influence on the type of group psychotherapy offered. A standard method of classification of the therapeutic group is suggested. Dynamic considerations which contribute to patients' ability to utilize the group approach as well as personality characteristics which appear to contraindicate group therapy are discussed. Finally, the needs of the group itself as a special therapeutic medium are explored for their effect on the selection of patients.

REFERENCES

1. M. Freedman and B. Sweet, "Some Specific Features of Group Psychotherapy and Their Implications for Selection of Patients," *Int. J. Group Psychother.*, 4:359, 1954.
2. J. Geller, "Group Psychotherapy in a Community Psychiatric Clinic," *Int. J. Group Psychother.*, 4:103, 1954.
3. G. R. Bach, *Intensive Group Psychotherapy* (New York: Ronald Publications, 1954).
4. W. Hulse, "Dynamics and Techniques of Group Psychotherapy in Private Practice," *Int. J. Group Psychother.*, 4:65, 1954.
5. S. R. Slavson, "Criteria for Selection and Rejection of Patients for Various Types of Group Psychotherapy," *Int. J. Group Psychother.*, 5:3, 1955.
6. R. Dreikurs and R. Corsini, "Twenty Years of Group Psychotherapy. Purpose, Methods, and Mechanisms," *Am. J. Psychiat.*, 110:567, 1954.

NONVERBAL COMMUNICATIONS IN GROUP PSYCHOTHERAPY

Milton Miles Berger

INTRODUCTION

Improvement of the processes of communication with and to one-self and others is one of the goals of all psychotherapies, whether the therapist is consciously aware of this or not. To bring man closer to the whole reality of himself and others involves expanding his awareness of and capacity to utilize channels of communication which are potentially available to all men.

Definition: Nonverbal communications are all those manifest and latent messages, other than verbal, which reach ourselves and others about ourselves and others and the time-space continuum of the world we live in. These messages may be perceived through any of our bodily senses such as seeing, hearing, smelling, tasting, touching and through thinking, feeling, dreaming, intuiting as well as extrasensory and other ways still unknown but in process. Expression, transmission, perception, and evaluation are aspects of the communication process. That which is communicated by its absence is often at least as significant if not more significant than that communicated by its presence.

In this paper my use of the term "group psychotherapy" refers to group-psychoanalytic psychotherapy which utilizes free associations, dreams, fantasies, transference-countertransference reactions, verbal and nonverbal communications, and focuses upon bringing that which is unconscious into awareness wherever this is considered therapeutic. Experiencing without awareness may also be in the direction of health. There is an analysis of individual and group processes involved in the interactions and transactions which occur, and our goal is growth and increased use of

Reprinted in slightly condensed form from *The International Journal of Group Psychotherapy*, Vol. VIII, No. 2, April 1958, pp. 161-178.

available constructive forces as well as development of creative potentials in each individual in the group in his strivings toward self-fulfillment. Believing we cannot survive in a completely individualistic society, there is an experiential emphasis on relatedness, on moving toward and being with others as well as self. In the spirit of Rabbi Hillel, we attempt to learn through adventuring in experiencing the implications of "If I am not for myself who will be? If I am only for myself what am I?" while we are being and becoming.

My purpose in this introductory paper is to spell out in greater detail than I have found in the literature pertaining to group psychotherapeutic processes the values for patients and therapist in greater interest in and utilization of NVC.*

Intriguing patients into greater interest in their multiple simultaneously experienced and expressed NVC, intrapsychically and interpersonally, is a process which parallels the interest of the therapist in NVC. Increase of therapeutic interest in and utilization of NVC can help reduce the number of failures in therapy and of interminable analyses. Emphasis upon NVC decreases overfocus on words, intellectual insights, and understanding of psychodynamics which do not sufficiently stimulate and motivate patients toward being, toward self-realization, toward that dynamically knowing self which inherently implies accepting self with and without understanding.

The group-psychoanalytic setting affords an unparalleled opportunity to group members to become familiar with NVC in themselves and to learn that some NVC are primarily expressive and others are primarily communicative. A single nonverbal communication may serve for expression and communication, e.g., squirming in one's chair may serve to discharge and thus relieve heightened neuromuscular tension and at the same time communicate to the patient or others that he is involved in a tension-increasing experience. The therapist and the group may feel it is in this person's interest for him to experience involvement in anxiety, conflict, or discomfort as he is a person always driven to seek escape from tension-increasing, painful aspects of life. They may therefore continue to focus on the content of the moment; or if they feel he has had about all he can tolerate at this specific time, they may "turn the heat off," change the subject, or move away from directly focusing on this person to someone else in the group.

Group members learn through experiencing in the group situation that how a person is really being rather than what he is saying or doing is of prime significance in their attitudes toward him and themselves when they are with that person or persons. They learn that NVC play the most significant communications role in all their relationships.

---

* NVC is used in this paper to mean *nonverbal communications*.

NVC are processes which may be expressions of pure fact and/or may be symbolic expressions. A man who scratches his arm where he feels his arm itching tells us the pure fact that he is scratching and also informs us symbolically that he is itchy, which may be a reflection of inner itchiness, irritability, turmoil, anger, or unrest, and that he is scratching to seek relief.

SYMBOLS IN DREAMS AND IN NVC

Knowledge of the attributes and values of dream symbols helps us to understand and to utilize more fully the expressive and symbolic aspects of nonverbal communications in our therapeutic work. Familiarity with the dynamics of coming to what is manifest and what is latent in dreams helps us effectively to experience, integrate, and interpret what is manifest and what is latent in NVC.

CHARACTER STRUCTURE IN NVC

NVC, being an aspect of one's total self functioning, are used in the service of healthy and unhealthy character-structure trends and express the compulsive neurotic trends overtly and covertly. The resigned, detached individual [1] with marked alienation from self and people, described by H. Leopold [2] as "emotional illiterates," that is, those who do not adequately know the language of feelings, attempt consistently to deny or hide from verbal or nonverbal awareness and expression of feelings. The moment the group or therapist comments on nonverbal signs that such persons have been reached or touched emotionally by some interaction process, they reflexly activate all their defenses aimed at controlling and squelching and manipulating feelings. Faced with incontrovertible evidence that they have been "caught," experienced by such patients as if in a criminal act, feeling feelings, especially tender sentiments, which to them means weakness, such a patient may react with face-flushing embarrassment of reddening suffusion of his eyes. He may attempt to divert attention from what is going on by provoking laughter at his own expense or by expressing hostility toward the therapist.

The expansive group patient may indicate his drive for power, recognition, and prestige in his aggressive, lordly, [3] or spirited gait, a chip-on-the-shoulder attitude, and an air of inconsideration and callous disdain for the rights, weaknesses, and communications of others. His character pattern may be indicated by his frequent looks of disapproval and disagreement; by an air of excessive independency and self-sufficiency, and not too well-concealed facial attitudes of arrogance and snobbery evidenced in whom he attends to and addresses, forms a clique with, and how he functions particularly during, before, and after group coffee klatches and alternate sessions when he attempts to control and master others in numerous ways.

The self-effacing patient reveals himself as a "schnook" in multiple ways. His or her colorlessness in attire, indrawn, constricted body without backbone indicating a body image of weakness and inadequacy; his dependency mannerisms as if constantly seeking a handout of help and approval and affection; the telltale, sickening, repeated, covering-up smile which marks him as "a nice guy" who is compliant, sweet, and everybody's friend—these are some of the clues to this appeasing person who is driven to seek peace and love at any cost.

I shall now describe in greater detail some of the major areas of NVC interest, namely, resistance, silence, body language, transference-countertransference, group atmosphere, the therapist's NVC, acting out, prejudice, art, growth and constructiveness, and some miscellaneous observations. The focus is on multiple simultaneous processes occurring in unison in which the various cues and codes for understanding the communications are perceived in the light of the whole context of each individual in the group and of the group itself.

RESISTANCE

NVC of resistance in the group[4] are expressed to us in the occurrence of the following:

(a) silences; absences from regular or alternate sessions; physically absenting oneself from a session during a session ostensibly to go to the toilet, to leave early because of a previously arranged appointment, to go out for a glass of water, for cigarettes, or to cry in privacy; spiritually absenting oneself during a session by daydreaming or "listening without listening"; lateness;

(b) body language, expressed with the body as object or in motion, or gestures, as with a tight, defiant face, a clenched fist and held-in body or sitting with one's chair back from the group circle;

(c) acting out, e.g., the patient who comes into the group and stretches out on the floor to provoke the therapist and group;

(d) the sudden appearance of signs of fatigue, sleepiness, yawning, or looking blank; or restlessness and looking at one's watch;

(e) a return to former modes of gait, dress, and manners to indicate superior status[5] and to decrease relatedness with peers and therapist.

SILENCE

Therapies and therapists who overemphasize the importance of the intellect and verbalizing tend to regard silences as evidence primarily of resistance to the analytic process. Silence does not invariably mean resistance. Patients in a group who have rarely said a word for many months and sometimes even a year or two have made measurable progress. A patient who verbalized nothing for fifty group sessions spoke up one day, stating, "I'm getting married tomorrow. I want to thank all of you. You've helped me a great deal.*

Contrary to the notion held by some beginning therapists, silence in a group does not mean that "nothing is going on." There is silence which communicates togetherness and cooperation, silence which is questioning, silence which is appraising and asks, "Are you aware of me? Are you with me?"

We must differentiate between silence as a definite expression of or way of communicating something and silent expressions and communications which may concomitantly be occurring in or not in harmony with the verbal expressions of an individual patient or of the group.

The attitude of the therapist in regard to silences and what is non-verbally communicated during silences and/or silently through gestures and bodily expressions will determine through imitation or contagion the attitude of the group members about these processes.

Silence of a group patient or of the therapist may indicate decreasing tension, an increasing sense of belonging, an increasing capacity to sit in and with feelings and fantasies and thoughts of all types with less judg-mentalism, increasing awareness of self-limits and the rights, pressures, and tensions of others, and may promote integrative processes.

Some silences are purposive in the direction of resistance. They are in the service of blocking or retarding the growth of the individual and the group. Such general or selective silences may be vindictive, and a patient functioning this way may sit with a smug, arrogant demeanor of face and body. Fear of judgment, criticism, condemnation, or retribution with their accompanying increase of anxiety, pain, and discomfort may also provoke silence.

BODY LANGUAGE

Body language encompasses the body as object and in motion. Non-verbal communications are expressed through total appearance, clothes, body mass, height, and configuration; smells, skin reactions, specific features, and deformities; movements and gestures in gait; walking, standing and sitting postures; head, facial, trunk, arm, hand, finger, leg, foot, and other movements; facial and eye expressions with major emphasis on looks and looking, smiles, laughs, yawns, and tears; respiratory movements, rhythm, depth, and sighs, intestinal gurglings, muscle fibrillations, tics, and

* Personal Communication from A. E. Moll, Montreal, Canada.

attitude toward own sex and body image. Vocal intonations are included by some as NVC and are most revealing of the inner truth.

These and other internal body reactions which may be intuitive and unconscious in their connecting linkages occur in one moment to communicate to us and influence us in our relations to self and others. Particularly significant are the eyes, referred to popularly as the "windows of the soul." The eyes, face and hands perform a major portion of our NVC through the various nonverbal pictures they create.

Probably visual perception and expression through looks make the eyes the most significant nonverbal communications agency. They express unintentionally as well as intentionally what is going on intrapsychically and interpersonally and communicate nonverbally what a person may be unable to state verbally or may not want to or may be unaware of wanting to verbalize. The eye and face expressions can inform us of the following feelings* going on in another person in relationship to himself: confusion, guilt, frustration, anxiety, fear, terror, anger, hate, jealousy, envy, self-satisfaction, self-esteem, self-love, inner peace, agreement, pensiveness, wholeness or self-possession, self-sufficiency, depression, anguish, grief, sadness, enjoying, light-heartedness, rigidity, brittleness, tenuousness, shadowiness, featherlikeness, or emptiness.

And in relationship to others, the eyes can inform us of the following states of being: questioning, provoking, surprised, confused, frustrating, demanding, seducing, piercing, killing, terrorizing, crushing, accusing, grasping, pleading, helplessness, burdened, vulnerable, dependent, independent, tortured, anguished, panicky, fearful, anxious, desperate, absent-withdrawn, blank-vacant, distant-far away, close-togetherness, understanding, communion, loving, appreciating, grateful, abeyance, waiting, watching, innocence, sophistication, knowing, affirming, agreeing, seeking affirmation, differing, denying, suspicious, interested, disinterested, embarrassed, or guilty.

The lids and eyes[6] may be open in the usual interested conversational manner indicating interest and togetherness or closed in the usual manner as in sleeping, resting, free associating, relaxing, or simulating sleep. A patient may appear open-eyed as in surprise, astonishment, amazement, disbelief, a startle reaction, being terror-stricken, angry, or enraged. Droopy lids occur in states of fatigue, tiredness, low blood sugar, not listening, simulating disinterest, active withdrawal, boredom, feeling guilty and therefore finding it difficult to look fully or directly at others, or may indicate a former or present nerve injury or illness such as Bell's palsy. Squinting may serve to reduce peripheral vision and concentrate actual visual perception on a specific person, position, or process. A patient may screw his eyes tight to look more clearly into his own present feelings or past rec-

---

* It is impossible to create a complete list.

ollections and feelings. Eyes squeezed tightly occur in states of forcibly wanting to blind self, to not see, to shut out, to resist perception of something or someone. Unmoving fixed lids occur as with a stare as in a condition of spiritually absenting oneself while physically present, in states of catatonia, seeing without seeing, and in autohypnosis.

Smiles may attest to such states of being as enjoying, feeling good, nostalgia, reminiscence, experiencing pleasure, or humor; irony, as with a sardonic smile; sadness, as with tears and sorrow in one's eyes; contempt, arrogance, or smugness; a covering up of shame, embarrassment, guilt, feeling silly, stupid, or caught; an expression of unexpressed rage especially when accompanied by gritted teeth; smirking, mocking, and ridiculing; expressing resigned, sadistic, vindictive, or masochistic satisfaction. A smile may represent "an arrangement of the face rather than an expression of the heart," according to Jean Stafford, the short-story writer.

Some other miscellaneous body language communications are: (a) chin stroking, which is commonly associated with a reflective state but may also have a sensuous value with the firmness of one's chin serving as a symbolic substitute for one's erect penis or it may stimulate peripheral awareness of one's own solidity; (b) the thumb clasped in the clenched fist which is more common in girl children making a fist than in boy children. In adult patients this may be a security mechanism occurring as it does involuntarily when certain patients are in an increased anxiety-tension state though unaware of this. To some who do this the sensations aroused may give one a feeling of holding onto self as in (a) above, or it may simulate the oral sensations of sucking on a nipple. This thumb-clasp may occur more often in those who do not light up a cigarette to relieve increasing anxiety in the group-interpersonal situation; (c) finger tapping may serve not only as a common sign of nervousness but may, as with one of my patients, be a way of Morse-tapping to oneself certain unedited messages which thus move from unawareness to awareness. The context of their occurrence became a clue to their meaning and associating to the tapped word or phrases became a fertile source for repressed material; (d) doodling with finger or foot in repeated patterns such as a circle, triangle, X, Y, !, or other figures can be a direct clue to "the heart of the matter" if attention is brought to it by the therapist; (e) the patient who repeatedly takes off one shoe and not the other may be expressing his conflict about openly plunging into a significant aspect of his personality.

TRANSFERENCE AND COUNTERTRANSFERENCE

Transference and countertransference reactions are frequently activated and manifested by NVC in the group. This has an evolutionary genetic background in infancy and childhood where many of the child's learning and growth experiences have been for the most part in response to nonverbal pictorial communications from the parents and siblings, especially during the prolonged period when the processes of imitation and modification of undisciplined biological and reactive behavior in response to parental facial expressions are in the foreground.

The marked frequency of looking at the therapist or other authoritative transference figures for facial evidences of approval or disapproval in the group is seen to diminish as such patients feel strengthened by group support and learn through the corrective educational and reeducational experience of the group with its working through and reduction of transference distortions and projections the feeling of acceptance and belonging more or less unconditionally, which is so important in the development of inner security.

The therapist's silence is sometimes considered as evidence of his support of one patient in the group who is attacking or belittling another patient. Either the victim of the attack or other group members may feel hostility toward the therapist for not openly coming to the defense of the target person. This is usually a transference reaction with the demand for a protective verbal response from the therapist as none came from the patient's father. Such patients may be unable to recognize or experience the nonverbal expression of compassion, empathy, or support by the therapist unless it is also verbalized.

The therapist's countertransference reactions may be involved in a situation such as the aforementioned where his silence is in fact related to his countertransference. His nonverbal expressions of favoritism and approval may also be on a countertransference basis.

GROUP ATMOSPHERE

Group atmosphere is a changing process and according to Flowerman[7] "you may notice group atmosphere less by its presence than its change." Group atmosphere is influenced markedly by contagion and there may be one or more atmospheric currents present simultaneously. R. Bross[8] refers to one of her groups as "a congenial group of disturbed people."

Nonverbally, group atmosphere is governed and communicated by such matters as the manner and presence of the current peer group leaders in the pregroup waiting room; the manner of the therapist as he calls the group in; the degree of aliveness and eagerness of the group to be with the therapist or conversely the sluggishness, deadness, reticence of the group to come in; the degree of current competitiveness and sibling rivalry manifested in the movement toward seats, toward the most comfortable seat, the seat nearest the door, the seat nearest or furthest from or opposite to the therapist; the presence or absence of specific group members or an "observer."

THE THERAPIST'S NONVERBAL COMMUNICATIONS

The therapist is the single most influential person in the therapeutic group structure. How and what he is being as well as saying and doing profoundly affect the group as a whole and the individual members of the group.

Through numerous nonverbal means he communicates his attitude toward himself, toward his patients, toward his family, professional associates, and the community at large. The notion of anonymity maintained by some therapists is a myth and the need to attempt to remain unknown to the patient, to remain uninvolved with him may impede and retard the therapeutic progress of the patient. This does not refute the concept that the therapist should not place the burden of his problems on the patient, but implies that the sooner the patient does get to know and feel the therapist as a human being, as an authority who can be loving, giving, rejecting, and accepting, the sooner will he give up magical expectations of the therapist as an omnipotent figure and accept the reality limitations of the therapeutic relationship.

The selection of patients for the group informs the patients as to the therapist's preferences. Is it a group of all women? All men? Younger people? Older people? Mixed ages? Does the fact of the group being homogeneous reflect that that is how the therapist prefers life and people to be? Does it say he is afraid of contrasts and differences and that the price of nonconforming to the values or attitudes of the group majority will bring on disapproval from the therapist? Will there be room to develop and express one's own unique potentials even though they differ from others?

How the therapist furnishes his room for group psychotherapy, whether the chairs are of different types, or all the chairs are exactly alike including the therapist's chair may indicate to patients a feeling for a democratic attitude if this is borne out in other ways. Patients will sense that their therapist is being driven to prove to his patients how democratic he is when his other actions and functioning belie this. Is the office clinical and sterile? Or does it impart a lived-in "let's feel at home here" attitude?

Does the therapist indicate favoritism by the attention and approval he pays verbally as well as nonverbally to one or more group members? Which one is so rewarded? The most intelligent? The prettiest female? The most sexually free group member? The one who pays the most? The one who affirms the therapist most frequently? The one who has the best command of psychoanalytic jargon? Is the therapist aware of his nonverbal cues which indicate interest, support, or approval? Is the group predominantly leader-centered or peer-centered? This development is attributable to the therapist and is evidenced by whether the members more frequently address their communications directly to the therapist or to peers.

Is the therapist really able to trust the constructive potentials of the group? This may be manifested by whether he forbids the group to meet without him for fear of deleterious acting out or whether he encourages pre-, post-, or alternate group meetings, which allow for growth and cohesiveness without his presence, which allow for socialization interaction including some acting out, and allow for release of tension and for airing of repressed experiences which a patient is not yet ready to reveal to the therapist for fear of criticism or censure.

The kind of person the therapist is may be communicated by his attitudes concerning smoking, eating, and sharing of candy, gum, coffee, and so on, by group members and the extent of his own participation in these kinds of shared experiences. Does he ever provide coffee for group members? Food-sharing experiences reach patients and therapists on deep primitive nonintellectual levels and may have profound and long-reaching therapeutic impact. They may be evidence of acting out, of transference and countertransference reactions by the therapist. They may be a form of interaction which implicitly expresses togetherness, trust, and deep communion between the mutually accepting patients and therapists who no longer fear one another. "Breaking bread together" has most significant implications.

The therapist's head-nodding, bodily positions, state of health and physical being, whether he is fresh, clean-shaven, and relaxed or tired, irritable, and unshaven influence the group markedly. They may be afraid to express hostility and have to pussyfoot for fear of guilt or retribution when the therapist seems overtired or irritable.

ACTING OUT

I do not believe that acting out is always a form of resistance. Acting out always implies a transference phenomenon is taking place. It is important to not glibly or too quickly label all acting or behavior other than nonverbal functioning as acting out. If the behavior or action is not based on an unresolved transference, then it is acting or reacting to be experienced and examined in the light of its constructiveness and destructiveness for self and others.

PREJUDICE

Group psychotherapy diminishes irrational prejudices of all types.[9] In the therapeutic group there are revealed prejudices based not only on the more usual differences of race, nationality, color, and religion, but also on sex, intelligence, education, body cleanliness and odors, body build, physiognomy, deformities, manner of dress, age, values, attitudes, cultural background, degree of aggressivity or passivity, dependence or independence, hostility of friendliness, and constructiveness or destructiveness predominant during group meetings with and without the therapist.

The prejudices are revealed nonverbally by looks of superiority, smugness, arrogance, and looking down on others with contempt as well as looking through and ignoring certain group members; by avoidance of sitting next to certain individuals or chancing any bodily contact with that person, or by inattentiveness; by formation of a clique with other group members having similar prejudices.

ART

The use of art forms and processes in psychotherapeutic groups has been increasing as it has been recognized that this is a valuable nonverbal tool for expression and communication. This is especially so for more disturbed persons and others who have stronger inhibitions against verbal communications of inner experiences. The capacity to express contrast may be an index of ego strength.

The bringing into the group of one's artistic creation whether a painting or a poem may be experienced as a gift to the therapist or group or may indicate increasing trust in others; decrease in fear of criticism or needs to be perfect; a desire to bring out what has been taboo as an expression of increasing feeling of self; or a patient may feel his back against the wall and be driven to force himself at least to open up in this way.

NONVERBAL COMMUNICATIONS OF GROWTH AND MORE CONSTRUCTIVENESS

In the group there is less of the initial need to impress, less sibling rivalry, less resistance in all forms, especially absences and collusive resistive silences or excessive verbosity aimed to confuse rather than to clarify, less turning to the therapist for direction and approval, and more of a capacity to go along with what comes up and out and with what is. There is more spontaneous interaction, greater mutuality and respect for others as well as less distrust and hostility.

In individual patients in the group there is a greater capacity to listen with greater ease, to wait in abeyance, to sit in silence, to empathize and identify nonverbally, not to conform where they were formerly driven to conform, and to conform where such patients were formerly driven to defy. There is less looking to the therapist for approval. A formerly alienated patient who can now get up to go to the toilet without embarrassment during the group session indicates his increasing acceptance of his biological being.

CONCLUSION

The story is told in a cartoon of a boy of 5 reading to his younger brother, age 3, and saying, "What are words for? Why, words are for people who can't read pictures!"

The exact manner and timing for the more active utilization of non-verbal communications in the group-psychotherapeutic process is something which calls for the greatest skill and trust in intuitive feelings which the therapist may possess. It is an aspect of therapeutic technique which cannot be more than implied in this paper. The main goal of this paper has been to focus greater interest in NVC. A secondary goal has been to suggest means of interpreting and using the myriad forms of NVC in the hope that this will reduce some of the pain and time involved in the psychotherapeutic experience as it is currently known and make for better therapy.

REFERENCES

1. K. Horney, *Neurosis and Human Growth* (New York: W. W. Norton & Co., 1950).
2. H. Leopold, Lecture to Association for Group Psychoanalysis, October 1956.
3. W. Reich, "Character Analysis," in *An Aristocratic Character* (London: Vision Press and Peter Nevill, Ltd., 1950).
4. S. R. Slavson, "A Contribution to a Systematic Theory of Group Psychotherapy," *Int. J. Group Psychother.*, 4:3-29, 1954.
5. H. Mullan, "Status Denial in Group Psychoanalysis," *J. Nerv. & Ment. Dis.*, 122:345-352, 1955.
6. M. Riemer, "Abnormalities of the Gaze," *Psychiat. Quart.*, 29:659-672, 1955.
7. S. Flowerman, "Group Atmosphere." Lecture to candidates in training with the Association for Group Psychoanalysis, November 1956.
8. R. Bross, Lecture to Association for Group Psychoanalysis, December 1956.
9. G. W. Allport, *The Nature of Prejudice* (Boston: Beacon Press, 1954).

BIBLIOGRAPHY

D. Barbara, "The Value of Non-Verbal Communication in Personality Understanding," in *Your Speech Reveals Your Personality* (Springfield, Ill.: Charles C Thomas, 1958).
C. Beukenkamp, "Further Developments of the Transference Life Concept in Therapeutic Groups," *J. Hillside Hosp.*, 5:441-448, 1956.
M. Buber, *Between Man and Man* (Boston: Beacon Press, 1955).
C. Darwin, *The Expression of the Emotions in Man and Animals* (New York: Appleton Press, 1872).

S. Freud, A *General Introduction to Psychoanalysis* (New York: Boni and Liveright, 1920).

E. Fromm, *The Forgotten Language* (New York: Rinehart, 1951).

T. Hora, Lecture to Association for Group Psychoanalysis, March 1957.

K. Horney, "On Feeling Abused," *Am. J. Psychoanal.*, 11:5-12, 1951.

A. M. Johnson and S. A. Szurek, "Etiology of Antisocial Behavior in Delinquents and Psychopaths," *J. Am. Med. Assn.*, 154:814-817, 1954.

H. Kelman, "Life History as Therapy; Part III: The Symbolizing Process," *Am. J. Psychoanal.*, 16:145-173, 1956.

M. Proust, "The Guermantes Way," in *Remembrance of Things Past* (New York: Random House, 1934).

J. Ruesch and W. Kees, *Non-Verbal Communication: Notes on the Visual Perception of Human Relations* (Berkeley: University of California Press, 1956).

H. A. Witkin, H. B. Lewis, *et al.*, *Personality Through Perception* (New York: Harper & Brothers, 1954).

R. L. Woods, *The World of Dreams* (New York: Random House, 1947).

- 35 -

COORDINATED MEETINGS
IN GROUP PSYCHOTHERAPY

Asya L. Kadis

Wolf's introduction of the alternate meeting[1] and later publications on the theory and practice of this procedure[2] have stirred up a lively controversy in the profession. In this paper are condensed several papers on the subject of alternate and other coordinated meetings.[3]

WHAT ARE COORDINATED MEETINGS?

It has been the practice of a number of group psychotherapists to ask members of each group to hold regularly scheduled meetings on their own. In these coordinated meetings, held one or more times weekly, patients are encouraged to continue the group analytic process as in regular meetings when the therapist is present.

In the protective atmosphere of regular sessions it is difficult if not impossible for many patients to resolve their strong transference resistance toward the authority figure, whereas in coordinated meetings they can transfer their displeasure, aggression, hostility, or feelings of love to a substitute parental figure in the group.

The three principal types of coordinated meetings are identified here as alternate, pre-, and postmeetings. Alternate meetings[4] usually take place in rotation at the homes of group members. Refreshments are sometimes served, or everyone may go out later for coffee or a meal, continuing the discussion meanwhile. Although the therapist's office may be used for convenience, a freer atmosphere is likely to prevail elsewhere. The alternate meeting, which represents the ideal integration of the peer and parental group, is perhaps the most desirable form of coordinated meeting.

From *The American Journal of Psychotherapy*, Vol. X, No. 2, April 1956, pp. 275-291. This article was rewritten and based on two articles including the one cited.

Premeetings, held in the therapist's office immediately before regular group sessions, serve as a warming-up process. Closest within the therapist's orbit, they often pave the way for post- and alternate sessions, particularly in institutional settings. In instances where group ego is unlikely to develop, or where the therapist has to be a constant agent of control, the premeeting may be considered an end in itself. This is especially true of hospitals, clinics, and schools, where the group is confined to an authority setup. Patients who mistrust their ability to handle their own anger or positive feelings toward fellow members, or those who fear the group's hostility, find reassurance in the therapist's proximity. His momentarily expected appearance, as well as the time limitation, imposes greater control over premeetings than is sensed in either of the other coordinated sessions.

Postmeetings,[5] the so-called cradle of alternate meetings, are also of three types: scheduled meetings held in the therapist's office in his absence,[6] scheduled meetings held elsewhere, e.g., at members' homes, and spontaneous meetings[7] at a restaurant or other eating place. Even when the members meet in the therapist's office, they feel less confined and anxious than in premeetings where he will soon appear. The postsession is thus characterized by a release in tension and assumes an intermediate position.

Subgroups, spontaneous social gatherings of two or more members,[8] should be strongly discouraged. Such meetings, which are conducive to acting out transference resistances, are bound to come to the therapist's attention. He may take this opportunity to bring up the subject of coordinated meetings, explaining that the emotions engendered among members must be analyzed by the whole group at regular sessions.[9]

The child reaches out to establish himself with his peer group at the same time that he seeks protection at home. He experiences anxiety and hurt—an inevitable part of growing up—as he shuttles back and forth between these two worlds. The consequences are similar when patients alternate between regular sessions with the parental figure and coordinated meetings where they are on their own. The ensuing struggle makes for greater separateness and more profound personal involvement, a basic aim of mature human development.

INITIATION OF COORDINATED MEETINGS

Any new group requires considerable preparatory experience before post- and alternate meetings can be launched. They should be suggested only when the members have developed inner controls and a group ego, including a sense of group belonging, and are able to handle outbursts with some effectiveness.

When group members who have been together for several weeks or months begin to express a desire to increase the intensity of their analytic work, the therapist may say, "You seem to have many things to discuss and not enough time. Why don't you meet regularly once or twice a week and work without me?" Haphazardly arranged meetings are undoubtedly already taking place, and the therapist's expressed interest serves to include them within the total therapeutic framework.

It goes without saying that some patients are reluctant to participate in coordinated meetings. But like a timid diver who finally decides to plunge into icy waters, they experience a certain exhilaration once they have left the pier. Despite feeling safer with a parental figure, they usually welcome the opportunity to explore feelings they have kept firmly locked in their inner recesses. They may restrain feelings of warmth, anger, or rebellion when the therapist is present, simply because of their distorted views of the parental figure. At coordinated meetings, patients begin to shed some of their restraints and defenses; they find it easier to attack a lesser authority than to attack The Authority.

Frequently patients reluctantly agree to participate in coordinated meetings then fail to attend regularly or act out in various ways. The therapist must understand and analyze the fears and rationalizations underlying this behavior.

The criteria of readiness are both subjective and objective. The therapist senses the development of group cohesion and *esprit de corps*. If he is thoroughly comfortable and at ease in the group he is likely to know when the bonds between group members are sufficiently strong for them to carry on for a few hours a week on their own. The therapist's hunches about readiness appear to have objective counterparts: Members tend toward overt manifestations of hostility and also toward feelings of greater warmth; they react to hostile outbursts with less upset and disturbance. In a cohesive group there emerges a system of checks and balances in which the outburst of one member seems to be handled by the reassurance of another. In short, the group has developed ego strength of its own.

THE THERAPIST AU COURANT

Once coordinated meetings are under way they must be integrated into the therapeutic framework. How does the therapist become aware of what takes place in his absence? Communication between sessions is possible without the members' recounting all events that transpire—a type of behavior reminiscent of tattling to the teacher or parent. The desired attitude is for members to bring up their spontaneous reactions to happenings at the last session, whether a regular or a coordinated one, without feeling obligated to relate all the specific events and disclosures.

Therapists frequently open a regular session by saying, "Have there been any after-reactions to your last meeting without me?" Various responses to the same event enable him to understand the interactions. Of course, he may be kept in the dark for some time, especially when the group is in a phase of resistance to him. If this is the case he may say frankly, "Why leave me out of things?" or "I feel hurt at being left out." Such a remark usually brings forth strong positive or negative feelings toward him which had been concealed by resistances. My impression is that little important material is withheld. One of eight or nine group members will bring up his reactions because of overwhelming personal anxiety or fear that the group will lose its equilibrium.

MATERIAL VIEWED IN TOTAL THERAPEUTIC CONTEXT

The characteristic properties of coordinated meetings must be described in terms of the total therapeutic context, not as isolated happenings. In contrasting and comparing patterns of behavior at regular and coordinated meetings, it is apparent that the latter represent a phase of testing, exploring, and consolidating, wherein the patient learns to separate himself from parental dependency in its various forms. Four aspects of the struggle for separateness may be described as exploration, vacillation, acting out, and incorporation. Although simultaneously observed in the course of therapy, they will be discussed separately for the sake of clarity.

Let us first briefly consider the characteristics most commonly shared by persons seeking psychotherapy and the conditions commonly considered essential to their achievement of a fuller measure of well-being. The core feeling of most patients, regardless of the professed complaint, is one of helplessness, loneliness, and mistrust of their own judgment. It arises from a distorted conception of themselves which, by elaboration, leads to distortion of other human relationships. It is assumed that such difficulties in the patient's interpersonal relationships reflect in some degree certain failures in emotional growth. Most therapeutic endeavors are directed toward correcting the personality deficiencies arising from these failures.

THEORETICAL CONCEPTS

Coordinated meetings provide a climate of testing and exploring in which the patient learns to consolidate discriminations between past and present relationships (working through) and is thereby enabled to function without leaning heavily on parental figures. Such meetings represent a mediating bridge which permits peer-group members to use their affective resources independently.

In the historical family setting there is constant interaction between the peer group, the bridge to the external world, and the family group. The child's way of relating to his peers is determined by his status at home, and the treatment he is accorded by his peers is reflected in his reactions to the home situation. Again we find a similar interaction between coordinated and regular sessions. Without special encouragement from the therapist, patients relay their experiences in and reactions to coordinated meetings; conversely, they wait until they are alone with their peers to vent their strong negative and positive feelings or to "act behind the therapist's back."

The above-mentioned therapeutic properties require a particular type of social organization as well as group cohesion and participatory leadership—salient characteristics of coordinated meetings. French [10] has demonstrated that group cohesion is closely related to the members' tolerance for aggression and frustration.

It has been found that individuals tend to shift perceptions of relatively innocuous stimulus material more readily under group-centered leadership than under an authority figure.[11] Furthermore, the changes are either strongly toward or away from group norms. In coordinated meetings, where the stimulus material is highly personal and very powerful, the likelihood of shifts in perception is even greater. Studies by Preston and Heintz[12] show that an important factor in bringing about such shifts is the constantly changing leadership. Also, participatory leadership is proportional to the meaningfulness, personal stimulation, and enjoyment of the over-all group experience. It seems especially desirable to create a group climate fostering group solidarity, participatory leadership, and facile shifting of roles.

Patients interacting in both coordinated meetings and regular sessions exhibit strikingly different behavior in the two social climates, especially early in therapy, and these discrepancies—present since childhood—become a major objective index of their distorted relationships.

THE ASPECT OF EXPLORATION

During adolescent development and neurotic struggles, the individual invariably wishes to conceal an important part of his world from parental scrutiny but will often "open up" to trusted peers.

In coordinated meetings, patients feel free to explore and experience feelings they have previously kept locked in a chamber of secrecy. Those who feel that a show of affection will be punished by a "parent" also may choose these meetings to express their positive feelings. Because of the emphasis in our culture on asexual relationships in the home, patients think they must maintain a similar attitude during regular sessions. Despite the permissive atmosphere that generally prevails there, they regard the therapist as a forbidding parental figure from whom they must withhold sexual and other strong feelings. It is of course true that apparently warm and sexual gestures at coordinated meetings are frequently motivated by concealed hostility, stemming from the patient's desire to act behind the therapist's back and express himself despite presumed parental disapproval. But even these pseudowarm reactions have a positive element for in this way some patients may for the first time experience positive affect.

Patients who are shy and withdrawn at regular sessions may exhibit aggressive and boisterous behavior at coordinated meetings. This is especially true of those with passive dependent traits, who seize this opportunity to explore the assertive feelings they have previously denied.

Discrepancies in behavior at coordinated and regular sessions are found to be more pronounced early in therapy. If patients do not exhibit these differences, combined treatment—individual and group—for a considerable period of time may be valuable, regardless of the clinical diagnosis.[13] Group members come to respond in the same way at all types of sessions as they learn to share parents freely with their peers—an essential part of ego building.

One factor underlying affective exploration at coordinated meetings is a lessening of restraint and defenses in the absence of a titular figure. At times the explosive potential becomes frightening to certain members who seek out the therapist at a regular session to protect them from their own impending explosion. Others dare to explode only in the presence of the therapist who represents a safety valve at the moment, depending on the specific transference phase.

THE ASPECT OF VACILLATION

Joining a coordinated meeting can be likened to the first loosening of family ties. Both the therapist-parent and the group-member-child may at first resist the change. The patient clings to parental shelter and the therapist wishes to protect his children by keeping them under his wing.

The therapist often minimizes his patients' importance to him, despite his intellectual awareness of countertransference factors. His protective clinging manifests itself in subtle rationalizations.[14] The main argument against coordinated meetings is rooted in fear of the parent's losing his children. The charge that patients meeting on their own will become an unruly mob is partly based on the therapist's feeling that they can function effectively only under his surveillance. Similarly, the debate over whether socialization after group meetings should be permitted or forbidden has the ring of benevolent authority. Socialization is inevitable, for children feel that they must break away from home. One of the functions of therapy is to examine each patient's techniques for escaping so that the break can be made in as wholesome a way as possible.

Various rationalizations are offered by patients who resist entering coordinated meetings. An attitude of contempt may alternate with one of professed self-sufficiency. "I can analyze things as well as any of those people. It'll be just a waste of time" or "What's the use of meeting with a bunch of nuts like that?" An examination of such statements reveals the patient's fear of exposing himself or assuming a burden of responsibility he is as yet unwilling or unable to take on. There is also a fear of being exposed to the "wolf pack" of hostility or of expressing or responding to warm feelings.

Refusal of a member to participate must be understood, analyzed, and coped with by the therapist. A resistance, which can be analyzed, is always involved. Whenever a member consistently stays away from coordinated meetings, the other group members become resentful. Failure to attend is usually analyzed and resolved. However, if the group cannot handle the problem the therapist should schedule an appointment with the defecting member to help resolve his negative transference. If he still refuses to return it may be advisable to switch him to another group, an alternative that is preferable to having him stop therapy completely.

In this phase of vacillation some patients with a little encouragement will leave the safe parental orbit to accept the fearful though exciting challenge of being on their own. The therapist may tend to overprotect them by delaying their participation in coordinated meetings where the fluctuating climate fosters independence.[15]

THE ASPECT OF ACTING OUT

Coordinated meetings are not only relatively free of "parental" restraint but directly stimulate freer behavior. Physical proximity, the informal seating arrangement, the likelihood that four-letter words will be used, the socializing over cokes or coffee—all these factors contribute to a more relaxed atmosphere than is usual in regular sessions. Although lowering of defenses may foster acting out, therapeutic use of such behavior may well result in over-all gains.[16] While sexual and aggressive acting out at coordinated meetings is negligible, shouting, tantrums and cursing, and regressive behavior such as stuttering are fairly common.

Acting out in a therapy group and in an individual therapy setting must be evaluated and analyzed differently. Acting out has two essential components: the motor discharge and awareness of the transference context. When there is a considerable time lapse between the two, acting out is truly blind and repetitive. But when the transference nature of a patient's behavior is pointed out immediately after the motor act, he begins to acquire control over his previously blind behavior. Perception of the transference image takes precedence over the motor act, and the patient can act upon his genuine feelings.

The following factors, briefly outlined, facilitate acting out in response to feelings: (1) immediate therapeutic scrutiny of the affective outburst—the concept of simultaneity. The sooner the association is established, the more readily the patient perceives the meaning of his behavior and the sooner the group can analyze it. Also, the group in coordinated meetings tends to challenge the purely defensive aspect of sexual or aggressive outbursts; (2) sharing of the emotional reaction by the entire group. The patient, faced with multiple and varied responses to his acting out, is more likely to alter his perceptions; (3) motor behavior clues. Evidence seems to support the view that in our culture, where the heavy burden of defenses is carried by verbalization, motor behavior breaks through them very effectively. Important working-through components emerge when a patient is immediately confronted with his motor behavior during an outburst.

While the group may stimulate acting out, it may also inhibit such behavior. For example, members often frown on two patients in the group who are especially affectionate toward each other, feeling that the group's unity is thereby threatened. Impending sexual or aggressive acting out is usually strongly opposed, especially if the involved persons tend to act out compulsively and repetitively. On the other hand, sporadic emotional outbursts by a previously silent and "mousey" member usually have a highly salutory effect.

Acting out in coordinated meetings raises the question of the therapist's responsibility. How, indeed, can he be answerable for his patients' safety and well-being when he is not present? Actually, a therapist is responsible for his patients whether he sees them one hour or five hours a week. He cannot possibly survey all their life activities. The best he can do is to select the best possible group for both regular and coordinated sessions[17] and be available when patients express their need for him. Clearly psychotic patients, psychopathic, epileptic, and cardiac patients are not suitable candidates for coordinated meetings.[18]

Besides controlling and preventing certain kinds of acting out, group members always immediately notify the therapist of impending danger which they feel unable to cope with. When one realizes that a patient in acute distress will not see the therapist for four or five days, this protection is not slight. From the outset, group members must be given a certain degree of trust and responsibility. As they grow in therapy the leader gradually surrenders his responsibility until they can fully assume it. The minimal danger inherent in coordinated meetings seems to be overbalanced by genuine advantages which help loosen defenses, overcome exclusive dependency ties, and bring to the surface hitherto repressed affect.

THE ASPECT OF INCORPORATION

Ego building goes forward when patients have an opportunity to assume authority and autonomy and when they learn how to give and withhold affective experiences. The management of giving and withholding is significantly modified according to whether or not the therapist is present.

The patient, only too willing to lean on the therapist and attribute to him any therapeutic gains, tends to say, "My analyst feels . . ." One of the goals of psychotherapy is to effect a transition to "The group feels . . ." and finally to "I feel . . ." His achievement of this objective may be facilitated by working through problems in the intermittent absence of the therapist, whose psychological presence is undeniably felt. Affective experiences, analysis of transference and resistance, and the development of a sense of authority lead to autonomous action.

Patients who compulsively withhold, require considerable support from the group before they can share personal happenings with the therapist as well as their peers. Patients' experiences in the two milieus help them to acquire the means of giving and withholding. In one case, a young woman allayed her anxiety by confessing, although she was not required to share everything with the therapist. To withhold secrets from a parent and still feel accepted appears to be part of a wholesome and trusting child-parent relationship. If a patient feels obligated to share everything with the thera- pist at all times, he may develop guilt feelings about consciously or unconsciously withholding material. In fact, the tendency to tell all in great detail may be a form of resistance. After imparting all his antisocial thoughts and actions the patient may feel no further responsibility for them, thereby removing the anxiety implicit in tolerating his own tension —anxiety which is necessary for working through.

In individual analysis the therapist usually controls the timing of material and decides whether the patient is ready for certain interpretations. In group psychotherapy the timing is largely controlled by the members; it becomes less important simply because it is not instigated by the therapist. There is a common feeling that poor timing, both in introducing subject matter and in interpretation, may precipitate a crisis and thus constitute a hazard particularly in meetings without the therapist. In setting up coordinated meetings the therapist is not telling his patients to sink or swim, but is trusting them to confront the unknown. In effect he is saying, "Your feelings are not as dark and you are not as helpless as you think. The group has enough positive resources to handle most crises that may arise. When you run up against something you can't handle, you can call on me." Although the therapist must always have enough time for individual sessions, it is my observation that the less anxious he is the fewer crises will loom up requiring his help.

Participation in concerted group action enables the patient to assume a responsible role himself at a critical time when some member needs support or threatens the unity of the group. He may also request help, in return for help given. The interchange of help, protection, encouragement, and support is a most important element in ego-building activity.

Patients who in all their relationships tend to shield themselves by nonparticipation or withdrawal usually behave in the same way at peer-group meetings. They try to create authority figures of their own so they can resume their dependency pattern. Prominent members accept the authority role for a while but reject it as they progress in therapy. Thus, the less effectual members are thrown on their own again, and this very fact mobilizes their resources.

SELF-ASSESSMENT REQUIRED

Many *avant-garde* leaders in the specialty are convinced of the value of coordinated meetings, while other psychotherapists are either unwilling to try them or have, for various reasons, given them up after a trial. Surely the therapist's personality, value system, and philosophy of psychotherapy and of society as a whole have influenced his strong stand on this controversy.

It has been charged that group regulatory defenses will not permit patients to maintain group structure and boundaries. However, my experience indicates that the therapist's control is only indirect; in practice the group acts as his agent. As we well know the gang acts either positively or negatively and often endorses much stricter disciplinary measures than does the authority. And each member's earnest wish to identify with the therapist makes the group carry out his wishes. Group control is thus exerted mainly by the members—out of their positive identification and transference—not by the therapist.

Built-in group control provides a theoretical and empirical foundation for the generalization that acting out becomes less frequent once coordinated meetings are under way, and when it occurs its impact is less damaging than in situations outside the therapeutic framework. A system of checks and balances helps to control it. But just as children in a family act out their parents' delinquent or antisocial wishes, patients in the group may respond to the therapist's unconscious wishes.

And what of us therapists? While seemingly priding ourselves on non-interference, may we not unconsciously—like some parents—wish to acquire more and more knowledge of how our children behave? Most of the vital material from coordinated sessions comes to us in time, either directly or indirectly. Do we then probe closely because we unconsciously desire to take a greater part in their experiential worlds? It is an oversimplification to label a therapist permissive or controlling according to whether or not he decides to launch coordinated meetings.

Group therapists may be classified under three familiar parental types: (1) Responding to his patients' quest for an ideal parent, he also provides a favorable therapeutic climate (see all, hear all, know all), ideal siblings, and understanding playmates. He strives to be the wise omniscient parent who is constantly concerned with his children's whereabouts and welfare. (2) He attempts to free himself of his patients' dependency demands by adopting a laisser-faire, *laisser-aller* attitude. He unconsciously desires freedom for himself and also wants to close his ears to the children's constant clamoring for attention and satisfaction. (3) He initiates coordinated meetings to increase his control of the patients' lives by receiving additional information about them from other group members.

Before deciding to start coordinated meetings, each therapist must carefully analyze his conscious and unconscious attitudes. He should be wary of this departure if he believes that: (1) his own authority is all-important; (2) group structure, with himself as focus, is immutable; (3) any acting out is destructive; (4) complete control at all times is desirable.

He should try to decide whether he can tolerate—without undue disturbance—a considerable amount of aggression and regression, a conflict between the group's value system and his own, temporary exclusion, or direct challenge by the group. Once started, coordinated meetings should be carried through. Offering and then taking them away would serve to reinforce the patients' early experiences with interfering and punitive parental figures.

The controversy over coordinated meetings did not spring up overnight, nor will it be resolved quickly. The answers to many puzzling questions await further investigation and research. What are the essential differences in patient behavior at coordinated and regular sessions, and what are the origins and consequences of such variations? Can we define and measure the particular contribution made by the therapist, other members, and the group as a whole to each patient's progress? What is the contribution of coordinated meetings as a special variable? Finally, what are the significant therapeutic experiences in any kind of psychotherapy for individual patients and for the group as a whole? Can patient, group, therapy, and therapist variables be described reliably?

If therapists as well as observers and co-therapists continue to pool their clinical experiences and improve research techniques we may find at least partial answers to such questions. In any event self-searching and keen observation should help each of us assess the value of coordinated meetings in the entire group therapy context.

REFERENCES

1. A. Wolf, "The Psychoanalysis of Groups," *Am. J. Psychother.*, Vol. III, No. 4, October 1949; Vol. IV, No. 1, January 1950. [Also reprinted as Chapter 23 in the present volume.]
2. A. L. Kadis, "The Alternate Meeting in Group Psychotherapy," *Am. J. Psychother.*, Vol. X, No. 2, April 1956.

3. Kadis, *ibid.*; "The Role of Coordinated Group Meetings in Group Psychotherapy," *Acta Psychother.*, Vol. 7, 1959; "Alternate Meetings," *Topic Probl. Psychother.*, Vol. 2, 1960.

4. Wolf, *op. cit.*; Kadis, "The Alternate Meeting in Group Psychotherapy," *loc. cit.*

5. G. R. Bach, *Intensive Group Psychotherapy* (New York: Ronald Press, 1954), pp. 107-108.

6. Wolf, *op. cit.*

7. Kadis, "The Alternate Meeting in Group Psychotherapy," *loc. cit.*

8. Bach, *op. cit.*

9. A. Wolf et al., "Sexual Acting Out in the Psychoanalysis of Groups," *Int. J. Group Psychother.*, Vol. IV, No. 4, October 1954.

10. J. R. French, Jr., "The Disruption and Cohesion of Groups," in D. Cartwright and A. Zander (eds.), *Group Dynamics* (White Plains, N.Y.: Row, Peterson & Co., 1953), pp. 121-134.

11. E. W. Bovard, Jr., "Group Structure and Perception," in D. Cartwright and A. Zander (eds.), *Group Dynamics* (White Plains, N.Y.: Row, Peterson & Co., 1953), pp. 177-189.

12. M. G. Preston and R. K. Heintz, "Effects of Participatory Versus Supervisory Leadership on Group Judgment," in D. Cartwright and A. Zander (eds.), *Group Dynamics* (White Plains, N.Y.: Row, Peterson & Co., 1953), pp. 573-584.

13. E. Fried, "The Effects of Combined Therapy on the Productivity of Patients," *Int. J. Group Psychother.*, Vol. IV, 1954; W. C. Hulse, "Transference, Catharsis, Insight and Reality Testing During Concomitant Individual and Group Psychotherapy," *Int. J. Group Psychother.*, Vol. V, 1955; E. Fried, "Combined Group and Individual Therapy with Passive-Narcissistic Patients," *Int. J. Group Psychother.*, Vol. V, 1955.

14. A. Wolf et al., "The Psychoanalysis of Groups: The Analyst's Objections," *Int. J. Group Psychother.*, Vol. II, July 1952; H. Mullan, "Transference and Countertransference: New Horizons," *Int. J. Group Psychother.*, Vol. V, April 1955.

15. E. Fried, "Ego Functions and Techniques of Ego Strengthening," *Am. J. Psychother.*, Vol. IX, 1955.

16. A. Wolf et al., "Sexual Acting Out in the Psychoanalysis of Groups," *loc. cit.*

17. C. Beukenkamp, "An Indication for Group Psychotherapy," *J. Hillside Hosp.*, Vol. IV, April 1955; S. R. Slavson, "Criteria for Selection and Rejection of Patients for Various Types of Group Psychotherapy," *Int. J. Group Psychother.*, Vol. V, 1955.

18. H. S. Leopold, "Who Should Be Excluded from Group Psychotherapy?" Presented at the Second Meeting of the Eastern Group Psychotherapy Society, May 27, 1955.

Part 4

APPLICATIONS TO PARTICULAR DIAGNOSTIC ENTITIES

THIS SECTION CONTAINS PAPERS WHICH RELATE specifically to particular settings in which group psychotherapy has proven to be effective. Each of the settings described is important to the student of group functioning, particularly to the sociologist. Recent research on the hospital as a community has indicated that group therapy cannot be seen in isolation in an institutional setting. Frank engages this point at the very outset of his paper on group therapy in a mental hospital, since he notes that group therapy in state hospitals may awaken in patients a sense of belongingness in a hospital community through increasing their participation in a therapeutic program. He is concerned about the hospital culture in this regard. Among contemporary group therapists Frank stands out as one of those who is strongly aware of the importance of group dynamics. This probably is related to his original background in the field of social psychology and his early association with Kurt Lewin, as well as his sympathy to Sullivan's interpersonal theory as a theoretical base for psychotherapy. His point of difference from those psychoanalytically trained group therapists who are more rooted in a Freudian approach to human behavior appears in his recognition of the socializing drives of individuals and his belief in group cohesiveness and the importance of membership in a group.

Freudian theory, which emphasizes identification with the leader, appears to deny much of the cohesiveness that can stem from the group members' relationships with one another and their discovery that they have a common ground in their difficulty in living. Frank's belief in group membership is echoed in the following paper by Foulkes, who describes some of his early experiences with group psychotherapy in military service. The importance of the group as an experience is also attested to by Standish and Semrad in their work with psychotics. It is interesting that this paper was part of a symposium organized by a group of social workers. The symposium emphasized the group dynamic aspects of group psychotherapy. The remaining papers in this section indicate the variety of individuals with

451

whom and settings in which group psychotherapy can be utilized effectively.

A very important paper in our opinion is the one by Mathew Ross, who describes treatment of the aged within a group setting. With the increase of the aged in our population, this treatment approach becomes ever more significant and timely.

36

GROUP THERAPY
IN THE MENTAL HOSPITAL

Jerome D. Frank

In the past decade the use of group therapy in mental hospitals has grown by leaps and bounds. Groups are conducted by aides, nurses, the clergy, social workers, occupational and recreational therapists, as well as by psychiatrists. The kinds of groups are as varied as the group leaders. They range in size from a handful of patients to the population of an entire building, and the forms they take are legion. There are discussion groups, social clubs, round-table groups, psychodramatic groups, administrative groups, and occupational and recreational groups, to mention some of the most common.

This extensive development of group methods reflects in part an increased interest in the psychotherapy of the hospitalized mentally ill, coupled with a need to stretch limited personnel as far as possible. It also seems to express a general cultural phenomenon in that it is paralleled by a similar trend in our society.

Our competitive, urbanized, highly mobile culture has drastically reduced opportunities for intimate, nondefensive relationships with others, such as might have characterized the large family of a previous era engaged in running a family farm or business. Each of us meets many more persons in a day than our grandparents did, but these contacts are apt to be superficial and often tainted by some degree of self-seeking. Thus, despite much socializing, we may feel inwardly isolated. The multiplication of small face-to-face groups engaged in a cooperative activity may be viewed as an effort to reintroduce a kind of relationship which restores a sense of belongingness to some of our lonely citizens.

The spread of group therapies in state hospitals may express a similar socially induced need, namely that of awakening in patients a sense of be-

Reprinted from Monograph Series No. 1, December 1955, pp. 1-17, American Psychiatric Association, Mental Hospital Service.

longingness to the hospital community through increasing their participation in the therapeutic program.

This function of group therapies can be understood, however, only in terms of their effects on the group members. So before considering them from the standpoint of their place in the hospital culture, it seems best to discuss some of their psychotherapeutic aspects. To do this intelligibly it is necessary as a preliminary to review some points about psychotherapy in general.

From the standpoint of psychotherapy the functional psychoses are seen as maladaptive processes resulting from disturbance in normal growth and maturation. These disturbances arise from conditions, especially in the formative years, which do not afford suitable opportunities for growth or create chronically anxiety-producing situations with which the inadequately equipped child must deal. As a result of these unfortunate early occurrences, the patient experiences conflicting urges and feelings which he cannot effectively resolve; for example, feeling utterly dependent on a parent whom he at the same time fears. These conflicts and his futile efforts to deal with them lead to habitually distorted ways of perceiving himself and others, resulting in inappropriate responses to current interpersonal situations. That is, he carries over his childhood conflicts into his adult life.

Psychopathological manifestations are seen in part as direct expressions of the emotions involved in these conflicts (such as fear, anger, shame, guilt, anxiety) and in part as bungling efforts to resolve the conflicts in such a way as to preserve self-esteem and to alleviate the unpleasant emotions.

To avoid possible misunderstanding, it should be made clear that this formulation does not imply that such failures in emotional functioning need be wholly psychogenic in origin or that they cannot be benefited by physical or chemical means. The inability of a patient to resolve his emotional conflicts may well be related to disturbances in physiological and biochemical processes. Psychotherapy, however, focuses on the role of life experiences in leading to the patient's failure to adapt. It may be added, that, just as interventions at the physiological level can improve the person's psychic functioning, so improvement in psychic functioning may result in amelioration of organic disturbances.

The crux of the problem from the standpoint of psychotherapy is that mental patients seem unable to profit by experience. Instead they continually repeat the same maladaptive patterns, and each new experience of failure or frustration, instead of leading them to modify their behavior, seems to reinforce the neurotic or psychotic pattern. Perhaps the major reason why psychiatric patients fail to learn by new experience is that they are too demoralized. Their self-esteem is so damaged by their repeated failures that they lack the courage to try new responses but instead cling to their habitual ones which, however self-defeating, are comfortably familiar and often yield pseudo solutions to their problems.

The object of psychotherapy is to supply new interpersonal influences which help the patient resolve his conflicts, develop a more accurate picture of himself in relation to others, and so become able to behave more fittingly toward them. As the patient begins to experience some successes in his dealings with others, this reinforces the new ways of behaving; and so, if all goes well, the maladaptive patterns are progressively weakened and the more successful ones strengthened. Thus his potentialities for further emotional growth are progressively mobilized. At first glance the means by which psychotherapy tries to produce these fortunate results seem to be legion, but all varieties of psychotherapy share three aims. The first is to strengthen the patient's self-respect so that he gains the courage to seek better ways of dealing with his conflicts. The second is to help the patient to maintain a level of tension or distress sufficient to keep him working toward better solutions, but not so great as to force him back into his maladaptive patterns. With some patients the problem is to increase tension, to stir up inappropriate responses so that the patient becomes more clearly aware of them and is more strongly motivated to correct them. With others, the task is to keep the patient's tension within manageable bounds. In individual therapy with outpatients the desiratum is usually to raise the level of tension; in group therapy, especially with hospitalized patients, it is to keep tension within bounds. This is primarily because a group, with its potentialities for emotional contagion, multiple transference reactions, clashes of differing viewpoints and so on, presents more opportunities for emotional stimulation than a two-person relationship.

The third aim of all forms of psychotherapy is to supply some guides or models to the patient as he struggles to modify his attitudes, in an atmosphere which encourages him to experiment, provides him with accurate information as to how well he is doing, and minimizes the penalties for failing. All this may be summed up in the phrase "reality testing." This aspect of therapy is more apparent in group methods than in the individual form because of the multiplicity of models afforded each patient by the other group members, the greater freedom with which advice and guidance are offered, and the greater nearness of the therapy group to "real life" situations.

In furtherance of the aims of increasing the patient's self-respect, maintaining an optimal level of tension, and encouraging reality testing, all forms of psychotherapy offer the patient a certain kind of relationship and present him with some sort of task. The common factor in all psychotherapeutic relationships, whether group or individual, seems to be that the patient feels that he is taken seriously by a person in whom he has confidence, and will continue to be taken seriously no matter what weaknesses and faults he may reveal. This permits him to gain self-confidence by finding himself acceptable to a person he respects—to shine by reflected glory. Group therapy, in addition to offering patients this relationship with the therapist, introduces a new dimension of it which may be termed "group belongingness," to be discussed below.

All therapies involve a task in which patient and therapist engage collaboratively. It is with respect to this that therapies differ most. The task provides the medium by which patient and therapist (or patient and patient in a group) relate to each other. The task is also linked to the patient's self-respect in that the more successfully he carries it out, whether it be to free associate or to beat a drum in a rhythm band, the more he is rewarded by the approval of other participants. The nature of the task also affects the amount of tension felt by the patient. The more poorly a situation is defined, that is, the more ambiguous it is, the greater the anxiety it produces.[1] Hence, if it is desired to increase tension, the definition of the task is ambiguous; if it is desired to diminish tension, a task is chosen which is within the patient's grasp and it is clearly defined. Thus it is that classical psychoanalysis and nondirective therapy in which the task set the patient is only vaguely defined, seem most useful for patients who are not too sick, while therapeutic social clubs and psychodrama, which structure the task for the patient quite elaborately, have found their chief applicability in the treatment of psychotics.

The usual task set by both individual and group psychotherapy is to help the patient to become aware of and correctly label his present feelings and behavior and to re-evaluate his past experiences in the light of his current attitudes and goals. In short, it is to increase the patient's self-understanding or insight. This task is based on a sound rationale. To the extent that a patient understands himself better, he is more able to modify his behavior constructively. Without this clearer vision, his renewed efforts to solve his conflicts under the stimulus of psychotherapy will tend to run along habitual patterns, and he will end up more discouraged than before, having again experienced a failure. Increased self-understanding heightens the patient's self-confidence in various ways. Identifying the motives behind a response carries the implication that it is caused by the patient, rather than by circumstances beyond his control. Therefore he has the power to change it. Conversely, finding the explanation for a present faulty attitude in the patient's past experience shifts responsibility from him to figures in his background with concomitant reduction of guilt. The mere act of naming an attitude or a feeling reduces the anxiety connected with the unknown. Furthermore, a labeled feeling is automatically a shared one, and the patient gains reassurance by finding that the therapist and other group members, knowing the dreadful secret, are not upset by it.

Finally, to the extent that the therapist and other patients accept the task of aiding the patient's self-understanding they must continually try to understand him better. This helps them to maintain a consistent interest in the patient which in turn increases the patient's feeling that he is taken seriously and thereby increases his self-confidence.

The task of fostering insight is so admirably suited to producing beneficial changes in so many patients that it is easy to regard it as the only "real" form of psychotherapy and to view all other approaches as merely palliative. It does have one drawback, however, which is that it is beyond the reach of many patients who need psychotherapy most. Insight therapy is the treatment of choice for many psychotics. But quite a few already have too much insight in the sense that they cannot cope with the urges and feelings of which they are aware. Focusing on the feelings of such patients often increases their anxiety to a degree which impedes therapy. Other psychotics are largely incapable of verbalizing their feelings, and when faced with this task by the therapist become more discouraged, frustrated, and angry. The accumulating experience with therapeutic groups has made clear that there are other possible therapeutic tasks which can produce beneficial change of attitude. Even primitive group activities such as rhythm bands may succeed in mobilizing a spark of self-confidence in very regressed patients and in encouraging them to reach out a little toward others. A more complex task, suited to patients in better contact, is posed by the didactic group of Klapman.[2] Here the therapist takes the major responsibility for how the group functions by presenting material to it and guiding the discussion. He can easily control the level of difficulty of the task so as to keep it within the members' abilities, and the use of neutral material stimulates interaction at the intellectual level and dampens emotional interplays which the patients are not ready to handle.

A similar type of task is offered patients by therapeutic social clubs,[3] whose major aim is to strengthen their social skills as a means of combating their isolation and heightening their self-confidence. These groups are organized on parliamentary lines, elect their own officers, and plan their own activities, the therapist functioning as an advisor only.

Rhythm bands, didactic groups, and social clubs aim to strengthen the ability of patients to function socially and to reduce their emotional tensions by channelizing them into rigorously structured activities. A more flexible approach is afforded by the methods of psychodrama.[4] At one extreme, psychodramatic scenes can be used to train patients to handle the ordinary situations of daily life; at the other, to mobilize intense and regressive emotional responses. All have in common that the director exercises control over what transpires, aiming to foster spontaneity in the actors and to minimize the likelihood of emotional experiences too intense for the patient to deal with constructively.

The task of a therapeutic group is an important means of fostering a sense of belongingness among the members. It does this by giving them a common focus which encourages them to relate to each other and supplying a vehicle for them to do so.

Members' sense of belongingness to a group, more simply termed group cohesiveness, plays an analagous role in therapy groups to the relation between therapist and patient in individual treatment. That is, it supports the self-esteem of the members and so increases their tolerance for unpleasant emotions and their ability to function as free and responsible persons. The intensity of emotional interplay which members of a group can stand without excessive anxiety is largely a function of the cohesiveness of the group. Since emotions supply the motive power for change of attitude[5] fostering of group cohesiveness is a major goal in group therapy. As it is particularly hard to achieve with psychotics, it requires some discussion.

All humans possess disjunctive and socializing drives. A philosopher has made an apt comparison of human beings to hedgehogs in winter. The hedgehogs try to cuddle together to keep warm, but run into each others' spines and are forced to draw apart. Finally, they find the proper distance which will afford maximum warmth and minimum discomfort. Just so, each of us seems finally to discover that distance from others at which he can function with the most gratification and least uneasiness. Mental patients have particular difficulty in entering into close, satisfying relations with their fellow man. This is evident in their group behavior, much of which can be understood as the resultant of a conflict between disjunctive and cohesive forces. The most disjunctive end of the scale may be represented by a patient who spent entire group meetings standing with his back to the group and his fingers in his ears, shouting out the window. Even this man, it may be surmised, felt some pull toward the group or he would not have resorted to such extreme measures to shut the others out. A slightly higher degree of cohesiveness, though still minimal, is shown by what has been termed asyndetic communication.[6] By this is meant that a patient hears only enough of what another says to use it as a take-off point for his own fantasies. This phenomenon is not entirely unknown in other group meetings, including those of professional societies.

Perhaps the first reliable sign of group cohesiveness in hospital groups is common griping. From the standpoint of group dynamics, this may be viewed as an attempt of the members to move closer together by directing disjunctive feelings away from each other to targets outside the group. Many other phenomena, especially in early group meetings, can be profitably viewed as attempts to strike a balance between cohesive and disjunctive forces. An example is the search for superficial similarities, whereby at the same time efforts to become more intimately acquainted are forestalled. The conflict between attraction and repulsion is also expressed in the "peer court" in which patients advise and criticize each other, implying both interest and disapproval,[7] in competition for various roles, such as the doctor's assistant,[8] or the sickest, and even in explosions of open hostility. Antagonisms often are a sign that members of the group have come close enough emotionally to get under each other's skins, to return to the metaphor of the hedgehog.

Some of the disjunctive forces underlying these behaviors are easily identified in schizophrenics, though every human probably experiences similar stirrings to some degree under certain circumstances. At the top of the list may be put their deep distrust of themselves and others, leading them to approach each new potential relationship with the expectancy that it will be painful, if not disastrous. This is often expressed in early group meetings as suspiciousness of the motives of the group leader, who is especially suspect because he is in a position of power and because he says he is trying to be helpful. At the close of the first session of a group, for example, a patient buttonholed the observer and with the air of one who invites a great confidence asked to be told the "real" reason for holding these meetings. In another group, one of the patients asked the doctor why she came to the group. When she replied, "To help you solve your problems," this announcement was met by jeering laughter from a number of patients, one of whom stated it was the funniest joke he had heard in a long, long time. In another group, a patient said, "All doctors are insincere. Doctors are trying to learn things about foreign relationships. What trusts are they trying to break?" When the doctor attempted to reassure this patient of his sincerity, the patient immediately demanded a pass from him. When the doctor explained that he did not have the authority, the speaker shouted angrily that he "didn't like people crossing me up." [9]

Another disjunctive force in early group meetings is the fear of the stranger, probably innate in all gregarious animals including humans. A stranger is an ambiguous figure, an unknown quantity, hence he arouses anxiety. In therapy groups, whose task includes self-revelation, the anxiety caused by the presence of strangers is heightened by the knowledge that one is expected to expose one's weaknesses to them.[10] Yet another disruptive force in therapy groups is the mutual contempt of the mentally ill, a reflection of their self-contempt. To the extent that a patient feels stigmatized by having to undergo psychiatric treatment, this feeling is heightened by having to admit it publicly, as it were, especially to a group of people he feels to be equally unworthy.

Fortunately, in addition to disjunctive forces, there is in every human a force, however twisted in its expression, which leads him to seek satisfaction from intimate contact with his fellows. All forms of therapy must ultimately rely on this. In therapy groups this basic drive is strengthened by certain factors. First among these is the dependence of each patient on the therapist. The expectancy of help from the group leader is probably the only cohesive force that the latter can rely on initially. According to Freudian theory,[11] identification with the leader remains a route toward identification with other members throughout the group's life. Another cohesive factor is the existence of a shared task or goal, already mentioned as essential to the therapeutic process. Focus on the task, besides supplying a common point of reference for everyone, diverts members from concentrating on the differences which keep them apart. The development of group cohesiveness is encouraged by the presence in the members of the group of a shared background of experience, including that of suffering from a mental illness. Patients' discovery that they have symptoms or problems in common draws them together. "Misery loves company" expresses a sound psychological truth. Some patients derive self-respect from finding that others are worse off than they are, and this may motivate them to keep attending.

As a group continues other cohesive forces emerge, such as the development of a body of shared experiences and each member's sense of being taken seriously by the others, growing out of the group interactions. A particularly effective binding force is a spirit of mutual helpfulness,[12] which is of slow and uncertain growth but may occasionally be achieved. With luck, all these influences, and others not mentioned, add up to produce a feeling in each member that he belongs to an in-group, that he is participating in a special and rewarding kind of experience which is not shared by everyone. The therapeutic impact of any group on its members is at least partly a function of the extent to which this sense of group belongingness is achieved.

It is true that a mere aggregation of patients has some therapeutic potentialities. Each may gain sufficient support from his individual relationship with the therapist to derive some therapeutic benefit despite tensions created by the presence of the others. Moreover, such a situation is useful diagnostically in that it tends to elicit from each patient his characteristic interpersonal ways of dealing with his anxieties, affording valuable clues to an observant therapist. The special values of group therapy, however, are in large part dependent on some feeling of cohesiveness among the group members, and the therapist should consciously work to foster its development. In order to do so successfully he must first of all have a realistic appraisal of the potentialities and limitations of group treatment. A therapist who starts a group reluctantly or lacking faith in its therapeutic possibilities is handicapped in his efforts to create a cohesive atmosphere. The same holds for the overenthusiastic therapist who expects miracles. He is bound to be disillusioned, and the resulting discouragement will infect the members of his group.

With respect to group composition, a basis for cohesiveness is provided by including in the same group patients who are undergoing a common experience in the hospital. Thus patients may be selected from the same administrative unit, since they have the same physical environment and the same treatment personnel. This also facilitates transfer of administrative responsibilities to the group, which will be considered presently. A shared experience which seems to supply a good basis for forming a group is insulin therapy. Patients after coming out of insulin coma are unusually accessible to the influence of other persons. The group approach seems an excellent way of capitalizing on this.[13]

The experience of being admitted to a mental hospital forms another useful basis for organizing groups. Intake groups are useful in their ability to convey quickly to patients information they should know about the hospital regimen. They also give the patients a chance to express feelings of anger, anxiety, and humiliation or other reactions to being hospitalized. Thus they admit the patient at once into a treatment relationship.

Similarly, groups may be based on the shared experience of being about to leave the hospital. Such "exit groups" have been found useful for patients who, because of prolonged hospitalization, have lost the confidence to face the outer world. This anticipatory anxiety may be effectively combated by opportunities to rehearse their behavior in situations they expect to face. The psychodramatic approach seems especially helpful for this purpose. Therapeutic social clubs are also useful in easing the transition from the hospital to civilian life, as they focus on developing and strengthening social skills. They also supply patients with a continuity of relationship in that they join a club while in the hospital and continue in it after they leave. This continuity is strengthened by the fact that relatives of patients often attend these groups while the patients are still in the hospital.

Though the presence of a shared experience in the hospital is one basis for organizing a group, further selection may have to be exercised to avoid including in the same group patients who are unlikely to be able to interact in any useful way. This is especially important if a type of group therapy is contemplated which fosters direct emotional interactions. Here clinical diagnosis is of some, but limited, aid. The same group should not contain patients who are too far apart with respect to degree or type of illness, for example belligerent paranoids and regressed hebephrenics. On the other hand, a group should not necessarily consist exclusively of patients with the same clinical picture. It depends on the nature of the condition. Alcoholics do well together, but—to take an extreme example—mute catatonics do not.

More important than diagnostic categories in guiding composition are the ways in which characteristics of the patients in a given group can be expected to interact. Thus one excessively aggressive patient in a group of timid ones may create an unworkable situation, but several may foster useful interaction. They hold each other in check, and encourage the timid ones by their example or by seeking allies among them in their battles with each other. Similar considerations apply to the personal characteristics of patients in relation to the therapist. For example, certain therapists seem to enjoy aggressive patients and can do well with them, while others may have to struggle so hard to control urges to counterattack that they cannot be therapeutically effective. A motherly woman therapist may do better with a group of dependent patients than a younger male colleague.[14]

Even before the first group meeting, its cohesiveness will have been influenced by how the therapist offered the group to the participants. Since the patients' reliance on him for help is the chief unifying force in initial meetings, it is important that his approach to the patients inspire confidence in him. This is done by presenting group therapy to the patient in terms that he can understand, discussing his misgivings with him, and then simply prescribing it as one would any other form of treatment, with the understanding that the patient may reopen the question after trying a few meetings, should he wish to do so. Unless the patient is so ill as to be unable to assume any initiative at all, he should probably not be compelled to attend a group, because this damages his self-esteem. On the other hand, it is perhaps worse to leave the decision entirely in the patient's lap. This amounts to abdicating one's therapeutic responsibilities. The patient may interpret it to mean that the therapist does not have much faith in the treatment. Also, seeming to let the patient decide may confuse him because he knows that the staff has the power to compel his attendance if they wish. Thus a therapist's take-it-or-leave-it attitude may diminish the patient's confidence in him and so weaken one of the main cohesive forces in the group.

In conducting the group, the therapist can foster cohesiveness by deliberately making himself the focal point and by keeping the group's task clearly before it. Even in a free discussion group he should be definitely in charge, facilitating communication between patients and encouraging those types of interaction which seem to him to hold most promise. He should define his role clearly to combat the ambiguity with which he is certain to be initially perceived, and thereby lessen the patients' anxiety. The group's task should be one within the members' capacity, and the therapist should try to avoid letting the members experience failure. In this connection it must be kept in mind that psychotic patients often resort to irrelevant activities, and the therapist's disapproval of these may further demoralize them. He should set the task and guide the group by example more than precept, permitting the group to follow him by identifying with him rather than by taking orders from him. In this way he may be able to avoid becoming the target of disruptive resentments as an authority figure, while encouraging the group's sense of responsible participation in what goes on.

The development of a sense of belongingness to a therapy group facilitates patient participation in an over-all hospital program organized along democratic lines. Democracy means many things to many people. A British Peer defined a democratic society as one in which every man considers himself to be the equal of his betters. A democratic society, as this term is used here, is one in which each person is treated as an end and not as a means to somebody else's ends. This implies that the process of decision making about matters concerning the welfare of the society and its members is actively shared by all of them, each to the extent commensurate with his capacities. The successful functioning of such a society depends on free, undistorted communication within and between all its levels, coupled with a feeling of reciprocal responsibility between the group and its members. A democratic society in this sense fosters in each member a feeling of freedom based on respect for himself and his compeers. To the extent that therapy groups develop these qualities, they foster the development of a democratic hospital society and prepare patients to function as responsible members of it.

The goal of patient participation does not mean that all patients should join in making all decisions, but rather that each has an opportunity to participate to the extent that his condition allows. Democracy can be overdone. Those aspects of state-hospital life which have been severely criticized as antitherapeutic, such as conformity, utter simplicity or routine, and relief from all responsibility, may be helpful to certain patients at some stages of their illness. By keeping the ambiguity of the situation at a minimum they help to reduce anxiety. Under such an organization patients are not apt to be set tasks beyond their ability so that they are not faced with the threat of failure, and this may permit restitutive forces to begin to operate. It is not rare for patients to show prompt improvement on transfer from a private hospital to a state institution, suggesting that active therapeutic efforts may have impeded the recovery process of such patients by setting them tasks they could not manage. However, it seems true that for most chronic patients a highly simplified hospital program offers little help. If a patient after a few months has not been able to mobilize his healing processes under this regime, its continuance is self-defeating, since he progressively loses his incentive to get well as he becomes more and more remote from his usual activities and relationships.

To return to therapy groups, membership in them heightens patients' sense of freedom in that it enables them to enter into interactions and activities which were previously unavailable. Since these activities require cooperation, controls exerted by a successful group on its members are felt by them as enhancing rather than diminishing their freedom. Members' sense of group identification leads each to experience guides imposed by the group not as external forces but as coming from within themselves. Thus the parliamentary rules of a successful therapeutic social club are experienced by members not as restrictions on their freedom of activity but as means of progressing toward shared goals.

In this connection, since patients identify more easily with each other than with a staff member, controls exerted by other group members are more apt to be internalized than those imposed by the staff.

Just as a successful group both enhances and constructively limits the freedom of its members, so it heightens each member's sense of responsibility but makes the burden easier to bear by sharing it. Group cohesiveness implies a greater awareness in each member of the problems of the others and therefore some assumption of responsibility for their welfare. But since the group shares these responsibilities they do not fall with crushing force on any one patient. Baker and Jones point out, for example, that a patient group which dealt with patients who broke hospital rules was often more lenient to the offender than he was to himself.[15]

Group activities foster communication between patient and patient, patients and staff, and among staff members themselves, in this way facilitating the growth of democratic attitudes at all levels. The development of a sense of freedom and responsibility in members of a group is concomitant with improvement of communication between them. All groups foster communication between their members. Even at the level of a rhythm band members must learn to respond a little to each other in order to keep in time. Groups with a common task, such as discussing a book or organizing a party, stimulate mutual communication, because the successful carrying out of the task depends on this. In discussion groups the major task is to improve communication, and the extent to which this is achieved is a measure of the group's success.

Parenthetically, increased communication between schizophrenic patients may not be an unmixed blessing. These patients are extraordinarily easily upset by close emotional contact, and their initial reaction to a group experience may be an increase in behavioral disturbance. In a study at Perry Point Veterans Hospital it was found that the introduction of group therapy was accompanied by an increase in combative and destructive behavior on the ward as compared with a control ward not receiving group therapy. These and other signs of disturbance, however, fell off more sharply in the group therapy than in the control ward with the passage of time. More importantly, they were accompanied by evidence of improvement at a deeper level, such as a drop in night-time sedation to about half the previous level and a striking decline in urinary incontinence, which was probably a sign of increased self-respect.[16]

Concomitant with improving communication among patients, group therapy facilitates communication between patients and staff and within the staff. In fact, this must occur if the group therapy program is to succeed, for a democratic atmosphere cannot be successfully maintained in one part of an organization if the rest of it is run along authoritarian lines. Some of the disturbances in patients just referred to may have been caused by the stress of having to shift between a democratic therapy group and an authoritarian ward. Similarly, a staff accustomed to an authoritarian structure regularly fears that the introduction of group therapy will lead patients to gang up on them. Thus group discussions among staff members should ideally precede and accompany group therapy with patients. In this way their misgivings can be met, and they can experience something of what patients feel in group therapy. Conscious or unconscious efforts by the staff to sabotage the program are forestalled, and attitudes of cooperation are fostered.

Group therapy increases the urge of patients to communicate with the staff, because they look to it for verification of their enhanced feeling of freedom and responsibility. Communication between patients and staff is enhanced by the well-known fact that patients can more easily express their real feelings, especially hostile ones, to an authority figure in a group than when they are closeted with him face to face. The therapist is literally a terrifying figure to many schizophrenics. This was vividly illustrated by two in different groups, both of whom were ambulatory, who were also being seen in individual treatment and who would never sit next to the therapist in a group meeting. They always saw to it that another patient was interposed. Both finally confessed in the group that they were afraid the therapist would strike them. Neither had been able even to hint at this in individual sessions. Thus the group facilitates expression of feelings to the therapist simply by its geographical arrangement. In addition, the public nature of the occasion diminishes the patient's fear of retaliation, such as might occur in private where others would not be aware of it. Patients are further encouraged to speak up when they sense that they are spokesmen for other group members.

Sometimes a group may communicate too successfully with the staff in the sense that the group leader identifies too closely with the patients. Patton[17] reports this experience with residents starting groups. The young doctors tended temporarily to identify with the patients and echo their complaints against the hospital administration. After a difficult period the end result, here as elsewhere, was that the doctors recovered their objectivity while achieving a better understanding of their patients. In another hospital in which the doctors saw in the group the same patients that they were treating individually, it was noted that they began to see them more as whole human beings and less as examples of psychopathology. The doctors became more aware of the patients' integrative powers and ego strengths, and began to speak about them in everyday language instead of psychiatric jargon.[18]

An example of how the group improves communication between patient and staff was shown by a group of adolescents at the Henry Phipps Psychiatric Clinic. This group was started because the adolescents were creating minor disturbances on the ward—teasing the nurses and finding various ways of irritating their doctors. In early group meetings their attitude toward the therapist, a staff physician, was markedly reserved. In the course of discussing how to accumulate some athletic equipment in which the leader participated, the group gradually came to see him as one of themselves. This was neatly shown when the group advised him how to best approach "them"—the other staff members—to facilitate getting the equipment. Incidentally, the behavior of these boys on the ward improved remarkably after the group was started.

Improved communication between patients and staff inevitably stimulates improved communication among staff members—and not only by posing a threat to their authority. Groups arouse emotions in their leaders and present them with challenging new experiences to share with their colleagues. A group therapy program also increases the number of staff members on whom patients impinge. Typically the patient's individual therapist, if he has one, is not the same as his group therapist, so that each patient automatically is involved with at least two staff members. As patient groups participate in administrative responsibilities, problems arise which can only be solved by a meeting of the staff members involved.

The most direct way of using patient groups to increase the democratization of a hospital is by giving them limited administrative responsibilities. In accordance with the principle of suiting the difficulty of the task to the capacity of the patient, the degree of responsibility entrusted to these groups depends on how sick the patients in them are. For example, Cruvant [19] describes administrative groups of patients on a maximum-security ward. These groups are run along parliamentary lines and elect their own officers, but follow an agenda prepared in advance. Their activity is limited to discussing administrative problems of the ward, not of individual patients, and communicating these to the leader who is the administrator of the ward. Cruvant comments that in this way he may unearth conditions of which he might otherwise be totally unaware and which he can readily correct. Competent attendants appreciate the group. Less competent ones often improve in response to group-developed social attitudes, and the others can be easily identified in a way not otherwise possible.

Wender and Stein [20] describe groups of less ill patients in a private hospital which assume responsibility for organizing their own activities. In addition, members are encouraged to make suggestions concerning the over-all hospital program, but the final decision about these is made by the director of the hospital. Wender and Stein note that the patients in such groups tend to lose their originally indifferent attitude about the hospital: "They had begun to think of the hospital as something in which they had a share, and they tried to make it something of which they could be proud." A further extension of administrative responsibility is illustrated by the round-table groups of McCann. [21] These groups are self-selected; that is, patients elect new members to the round table as vacancies occur. Their administrative responsibility extends to making recommendations for parole or discharge of patients which are taken seriously by the administrator. Thus the round-table group assumes a high degree of responsibility for the conduct and welfare of its members.

This discussion may be concluded by reference to a recurrent phenomenon which well illustrates how therapeutic groups foster the growth of freedom, communication, and responsibility. The first activity of almost every therapeutic group is patient griping about aspects of the hospital such as food, passes, and cleanliness of the ward. Griping, as already mentioned, is one means of facilitating group cohesiveness by diverting hostile feelings to targets outside of the group. It also means that patients feel freer in that they can talk about matters which they were unable to bring up in other settings. Griping also implies a willingness to communicate more openly with the staff and perhaps some increase in self-respect in the sense that the complainer must have a trace of hope that his complaint will be received seriously or he would keep silent. In initial group meetings patients imply that the responsibility for doing something about the complaints rests solely with the staff, and inexperienced leaders share this view. In this way the attitudes of both reflect the dominant hospital culture. The patients express it by their demands that the leader do something, the leader by pointing out that he is not the administrator or in other ways trying to evade having to act. A properly oriented leader, however, strives to shift the discussion from the complaints to what the individuals or the group can do about them. This is easiest, of course, with respect to the discharge of a patient since when a patient leaves depends ultimately on himself. A skillful leader can divert a barrage of demands for discharge into a discussion of what one does in order to achieve discharge. Similarly, complaints about aspects of the hospital can be referred back to the group for suggestions as to what is best done. In this way along with freedom and increased communication there is gradually built up in the group a sense of individual and group responsibility which is a powerful therapeutic agent for the members and increases their participation in the functioning of the hospital.

In summary, group therapy programs can benefit hospitalized patients in two ways: through direct influence on the patients themselves and by facilitating beneficial changes in the hospital organization. With respect to their effects on patients, two potential advantages of group over individual therapy have been stressed. First, groups offer a wide range of therapeutic tasks which can be tailored to the needs of different types of patients. Secondly, through fostering a sense of belongingness they strengthen patients' feelings of freedom and of responsibility for themselves and each other. These inevitably lead to improved communication throughout the social structure of the hospital. Thus from the standpoint of the hospital, therapy groups are both expressions of the democratically oriented therapeutic community and necessary means toward this end.

REFERENCES

1. E. S. Bordin, "Ambiguity as a Therapeutic Variable," *J. Consult. Psychol.*, 19:9, 1955.
2. J. W. Klapman, "Group Psychotherapy in Institutions," *Group Psychother.*, 4:181, 1951.
3. D. A. S. Blair, "The Therapeutic Social Club," *Ment. Hyg.*, 39:54, 1955.
4. J. L. Moreno, "Group Psychotherapy, Theory and Practice," *Group Psychother.*," 3:142, 1950.

5. J. C. Whitehorn, "Physiological Changes in Emotional States," *Research Publication, Association Nervous and Mental Disease*, 19:256, 1939.

6. W. F. Hill, "A Six Phase Theory of Group Development," mimeographed.

7. G. R. Bach, *Intensive Group Psychotherapy* (New York: Ronald Press, 1954), p. 245.

8. J. D. Frank *et al.*, "Behavioral Patterns in Early Meetings of Therapeutic Groups," *Am. J. Psychiat.*, 108:771, 1952.

9. Florence Powdermaker and J. D. Frank, *Group Psychotherapy: Studies in Methodology of Research and Therapy* (Cambridge, Mass.: Harvard University Press, 1953).

10. J. Mann, "Some Theoretic Concepts of the Group Process," *Int. J. Group Psychother.*, 5:235, 1955.

11. S. Scheidlinger, *Psychoanalysis and Group Behavior, A Study in Freudian Group Psychology* (New York: W. W. Norton & Co., 1952).

12. W. McCann and A. A. Almada, "Round-table Psychotherapy: A Technique in Group Psychotherapy," *J. Consult. Psychol.*, 14:421, 1950.

13. M. H. Hyroop, "Simultaneous Group and Insulin Therapy," *Int. J. Group Psychother.*, 2:67, 1952; R. D. Scott, "The Psychology of Insulin Coma," *Brit. J. Med. Psychol.*, 23:15, 1950.

14. Powdermaker and Frank, *op. cit.*

15. A. A. Baker, M. Jones, J. Merry, and B. A. Pomyrn, "A Community Method of Psychotherapy," *Brit. J. Med. Psychol.*, 26:222, 1953.

16. J. D. Frank, "Group Therapy with Schizophrenics," in E. B. Brody and F. C. Redlich (eds.), *Psychotherapy with Schizophrenics* (New York: International Universities Press, 1952).

17. J. D. Patton, "The Group as a Training Device and Treatment Method in a Private Psychiatric Hospital," *Int. J. Group Psychother.*, 4:419, 1954.

18. J. Miller, S. Kwalwasser, and A. Stein, "Observations Concerning the Use of Group Psychotherapy in a Voluntary Mental Hospital: Effects of Group Psychotherapy on the Training of Residents," *Int. J. Group Psychother.*, 4:86, 1954.

19. B. A. Cruvant, "The Function of the 'Administrative Group' in a Mental Hospital Group Therapy Program," *Am. J. Psychiat.*, 110:342, 1953.

20. L. Wender and A. Stein, "The Utilization of Group Psychotherapy in the Social Integration of Patients: An Extension of the Method to Self-governing Patient Groups," *Int. J. Group Psychother.*, 3:210, 1953.

21. McCann and Almada, *op. cit.*

37

GROUP ANALYSIS IN
A MILITARY NEUROSIS CENTER

S. H. Foulkes

Apart from the two extremes in which very strong predisposition or violent precipitating causes have brought about a breakdown, most psychiatric casualties in the army are the result of conditions to which their units have been subjected. Good or bad handling by the army as a whole, and more especially by the unit and subunit, decides how many men will sooner or later cease to function happily or at least adequately.

Once the soldier has become a casualty he loses contact with his comrades, officers, unit, and job. All sorts of problems in connection with his home, civilian affairs, and his future, hitherto submerged, raise their heads afresh. Having escaped from hell once, many a soldier is not keen to return to it; and after a comparative rest from army life and discipline he is afraid of facing them again. In the individual soldier the disturbance follows old ingrained patterns on symbolical lines: Old traumas are revived; regression to old fixation levels of libido and ego development and to old modes of defense takes place. But if we allow ourselves to be fascinated by this individual view of behavior we may not see the wood for the trees.

In all our patients there is evidence that their interpersonal relationships have been disturbed. A soldier who enters the hospital is a failure in three respects: (1) He has failed in his competence to perform his duties as a soldier and as a citizen of a community at war; (2) he represents a failure of the preventive mental hygiene of his unit and the therapeutic efforts of the psychiatric services so far; and (3) he is a failure in his own eyes. His belief in himself is shattered; he is isolated, out of contact and context with his fellows, disoriented to his present, and ill at ease over his allegiances and their conflicting claims. Deemed unfit to perform any useful function many neurotic soldiers miss the salutary participation in a con-

Reprinted from *The Lancet*, Vol. I, 1946, pp. 303-310.

certed effort, even though they are glad to escape from it. Their mind is disturbed, their body refuses to function, sometimes the body-image shows signs of disruption. A host of complaints grows on this ground on top of a general state of apathy, hopelessness, and unwillingness. Many soldiers put it thus: "I am fed up," "I am browned off."

What can be done at this stage? How can treatment be directed? A man who has been mentally wounded needs time and conditions in which his wounds can heal and all possible assistance to encourage and expedite this process. He may need sedation, abreaction, suggestion and hypnosis, or short-cut analysis, with or without the help of drugs. He benefits from understanding and sympathy and may respond to some extent to encouragement, "pep" talks, and the like. All these methods and many more are potent tools in the right case at the right time and in the right context; but they cannot have any lasting effect unless the basic problem has been faced; and sometimes they may merely gloss over the salient problem.

AIM OF TREATMENT

Having in mind that the patient's stay in hospital is on an average 6-8 weeks, we cannot reasonably expect to alter the basic reaction pattern, nor can we undo completely the effects of the patient's experiences. But we can aim at restoring his self-confidence and his ability to do useful work and at improving his tolerance for the strains of army life. The soldier's attitude must be corrected, and we must restore his ability to take interest in work and people, to become absorbed into the group and its task, and thus to be open to the wholesome influence of the group on him.

In all the individual methods mentioned above, even in those where obedient activity is demanded, the patient is essentially passive, yet he can be active in such a reorientation at every step from the moment he enters the hospital. In this way self-confidence and sense of value can best be restored, orientation and outlook revised, and adjustment toward others and the army improved. The soldier can then accept more willingly his obligation to further service. To create activity and spontaneity is half the battle; and if this battle is won the healing process will largely look after itself.

The hospital should thus become not only the locus but also the primary medium for this therapeutic process, a new frame of reference in which a better social attitude can be developed. By his actions and reactions in his present unit, in his present world, in the hospital, we shall know him.

METHOD OF TREATMENT

It has been found possible within the framework of a military hospital so to arrange treatment that the emphasis throughout is on the *social* aspects of treatment and on the *spontaneity* of the group activities. Patients run ward meetings as far as possible by themselves, with the psychiatrist mainly in the role of observer. They select their own committee to represent the ward. These ward committees assemble once a week as a kind of parliament, when they debate the different complaints, proposals, and so on to help formulate hospital policy. Patients run their own hospital club. Their selected activities bring them into contact and cooperation with other patients. Inside this setting their changing behavior can be observed and their situation manipulated in cooperation with the psychiatrist so as to have the maximal therapeutic effect on their condition. Preferably they should look on themselves as sharing in a common job of work, a so-called group project, so that they have a common aim.

Inside this framework they are taking part in group therapeutic sessions, the meaning and scope of which acquire a new significance. For this group therapy certain principles were developed from earlier experiences.[1] Essentially this experiment, carried out in civilian practice in 1941 and 1942, consisted in the free application of psychoanalytic principles to the treatment of groups, combined with intensive individual psychotherapy. It had been found possible to discuss and even analyze a wealth of material inside a group based on the free associations of these patients. This not only stimulated the individual patient but also intensified the therapeutic effect considerably. Moreover, the group situation, itself a potent therapeutic agent, brought into play a number of factors—such as exchange of information, the realization of similar difficulties in others, and the double role of the patient in understanding others while benefiting from their understanding— which were peculiar to the group and had their own therapeutic effects. In this way group treatment showed itself to be of specific value apart from the economy in time.

This experience was used in the outpatient department of a clinic where group treatment replaced individual treatment almost entirely, and results were much better. The patients attended these group meetings weekly for various periods, but essentially the period of attendance was indefinite. In a military hospital time is limited and as a rule is not sufficient to work through the deeper levels which this form of group psychotherapy tends to activate and lay bare. Further, most of the staff are not trained and experienced psychoanalysts and can therefore rarely embark on psychoanalysis. Nevertheless any knowledge and experience of psychoanalysis which the prospective group therapist possesses will be of good use to him. It will enable him better to understand and handle the reactions of the group. He will be less surprised by their transference reactions, negative or positive, or their resistances. He will be better able to bear anxieties and tensions and less taken aback by the varied claims which a group thrusts on him.

While it was necessary to accept further considerable modifications, it was nevertheless found possible and useful to maintain the fundamental position. Such a group now consists of 7-9 people who assemble in an informal way in the psychiatrist's consulting room, in the ward, or out of doors. The session varies in length between a minimum of an hour and a maximum of 2 hours. If the group meets more than once a week an hour is adequate; but for weekly sessions 1½ hours seems more appropriate. The psychiatrist combines the role of a conductor and observer with that of a member of the group. The patients in a group are told that they should bring forward anything they wish and that they need not stick to any one point brought up but should continue to express anything which comes to their mind. They are sometimes given some initial explanations of how this helps their condition, but in general they are left to discover it all by themselves.

The therapist may have to be more active and talk more in the initial stage than later on. His function is to put people at their ease, encourage them to talk and exchange information and opinions, and help them to formulate and interpret their views, in which he acts as a kind of host and mediator. His primary aim is to get the group going as a whole, to provoke their interest, and generally to invite all-round participation before he attempts to delve deeper with any individual member. Even at this stage of initiation he may find it useful to keep up a reserve, to resist the temptations of helping too readily and of feeling under an obligation to entertain and interest the group actively on his own part. The sooner he refuses, gently, persistently, and without being provocative, to accept the position of a leader, the better he will succeed in throwing the onus of responsibility back on the group and helping their own spontaneous activity to emerge. In such a way the group learns to accept responsibility for everything happening within it or brought before it.

It is essential that the therapist's approach should be spontaneous and in accordance with the reality situation of the group and their mood at the current moment. It would therefore be more misleading than enlightening to try to give a standardized description of his technique. This can only be acquired in living contact with such groups. It would need a textbook to describe technique problems adequately and illustrate them with living examples. Topics brought forth in the group comprise the whole range of human experience; but every group will bring forth the most relevant of them and state their salient problems at any time, if only they are allowed sufficient liberty and spontaneity to do so.

The following is an example of a typical well-conducted group session. It happened in one of the groups conducted by Captain George Day, R.A.M.C., who kindly put his record at my disposal.

> Eight ex-prisoners of war, hitherto only on nodding acquaintance, are assembled in the psychiatrist's consulting room. Cigarettes are lit, and there is an expectant pause. Silence. Then a corporal asks, "Can you explain, Sir, why I cry so easily at anything sentimental at the pictures nowadays? I used not to be like that." The psychiatrist does not answer directly but asks if other members have experienced the same change. There is a small

murmur of agreement from four men, one of whom adds that nowadays he cannot stand music, although he used to love it. There are murmurs of agreement from others. The group is beginning to stir with mutual interest. The psychiatrist asks, "What other changes have you noticed in your-selves?" A sergeant volunteers that he finds his family getting on his nerves; he has to rush out of the sitting-room to avoid explosions of anger. Another man recalls that he slinks away upstairs when company arrives.

By now the members of the group are talking freely to each other; the psychiatrist has little to do but observe and show his interest. They become bolder. One confesses to an irresistible tendency to nag at his wife and snub his child; further, that he feels a savage satisfaction in doing it. Whereupon another slaps his thigh with a heartfelt, "By God, you're right. I do the same, but I never thought I'd admit it in public."

In this way, with growing confidence and lessening self-consciousness, the group compares notes not only of symptoms but also of ideals and ethical codes. There are, of course, irrelevancies, reminiscences, leg-pulls, and laughter. Most are talking freely. The psychiatrist unobtrusively con-ducts the group like an orchestra, drawing out the quieter voices, giving cues to the shy and hesitant, and preventing the extrovert from swamping the rest with his solos.

"We were so completely cut off from the world," reflects a corporal. A withdrawn private, who up to now has said nothing, suddenly blurts out, "We are still cut off." Coming from him, this remark raises a good-natured laugh, and he colors up; but one of the more thoughtful patients at once supports him and proceeds fumblingly to explain how. It is as if the P.O.W. had been caged not only behind barbed wire but also behind a wall he had built to protect himself from the realities of prison life. This concept is accepted with thoughtful nods. . . . "Well, how is this barrier to be broken down?" They turn expectantly to the psychiatrist, who asks them what else they think they have been doing for the past hour, and judges this to be the right moment to end the session.

RESULTS ACHIEVED

By thus receding into the background the therapist can best observe the dynamics of the group and the interpersonal relations between its mem-bers besides fulfilling his real role of steering the group delicately toward a therapeutic end. One of the great advantages of such an approach is that the group is brought up against its own difficulties, resistances, and opposition; it rarely fails to realize that these are self-manufactured, and, under rising pressure of tension, it cannot in the long run avoid tackling them.

A group may clearly show to a psychopathic member that, whereas he is accepted by the group, his behavior is not acceptable. In this respect, therefore, treatment is not only in a group but also of and through a group. Resistances have sometimes to be taken up and directed, brought to the fore, and made the main topic for a while or even for a whole session. This applies in particular when difficulties are bound up with the person of the therapist through transference. In dealing with this situation he must set an example to the group in abiding by the same rules as any other member. He must be frank, honest, and true to the situation.

The yoke of the army falls heavily on all. When the psychiatrist has a fellow feeling for those suffering under rough justice—the disappointed and the misunderstood—he must be honest and show it. He cannot successfully simulate a tolerance he does not feel nor dissemble his shocked feelings when his own particular code is outraged. On the whole, the group is confronted with its own difficulties and obliged to deal with them itself.

Individual interviews arising out of the group session in turn gain greatly in value and purpose and are the more appreciated. They are valuable to supplement the group and sometimes necessary to deal with very personal problems. At the same time they are used to adjust the patient better to his particular group, and he can be encouraged to bring forth his points in the group session. This helps to eliminate unnecessary barriers which separate the patient not only from the particular group but also from the community at large and hold him to his neurosis.

A group session of this type is not didactic (as are some other forms of group therapy), nor is it primarily used for the direct treatment of symptoms by way of persuasion, reassurance, and so on. It adheres to the principle of centering the group on itself, weaning it from its desire to be led, and even leaving it to find its own aim and purpose. Under these conditions a set of newly created forces spring to life. The group presents itself as a new object for observation and treatment—a new organism as it were, distinct from the individuals composing it. The therapist must appreciate and master these group dynamics and use them as levers to influence the individuals composing the group. If he can penetrate the surface and take the unconscious dynamics into account as well as bring them to light and into active interplay, he is a group analyst.

The advantages of group treatment are manifold. They fall into three categories:

(1) *Practical.* Economy of time, occasion to obtain and impart all sorts of information, and so on. This need not be elaborated.

(2) *Clinical.* By observing people in a quasi-real life situation it is possible to get to know them much better than in the artificial setting of the individual psychiatric interview. One can see what the patient's symptoms and complaints mean in reality, how they affect his behavior, and how he is setting out to overcome his difficulties. Unexpected light is thrown on the patient's attitude, morale, cooperation, and powers of resilience and compensation. In this way the group situation helps to bring out finer psychodiagnostic points. Once some experience has been gained, it is possible, and sometimes even preferable, to see new patients together in a group before

seeing them individually and thus to allow the first individual handling to arise from observations made in the group.

(3) *Therapeutic*. The group approach appears to intensify and shorten therapy considerably; but, apart from this, there appear to be intrinsic factors operating in group treatment that are lacking in individual treatment. Thus group treatment is probably the only means of treating social difficulties directly on the spot, difficulties which are basically important for behavior and its disturbances. Another important point is the self-treating nature of the group. It is difficult to assess the therapeutic effects exactly at this stage on an "objective"—e.g., statistical—basis, because there are so many variables, and in our own field of observation these variables change so rapidly. Comparison between group therapy and the equivalent individual treatment, both under civilian and under military conditions, leaves no doubt in my mind about its manifold therapeutic aspects. Full theoretical explanations must await further more systematic research.

THERAPEUTIC FACTORS

Group treatment shares with individual treatment several therapeutic factors. Apart from those we have previously singled out, the following are peculiar to the group:[2]

(1) The group situation is a social situation and socializing agency.

(2) A composite of factors which we termed "mirror reaction."

(3) The activation of the "collective unconscious."

(4) The "exchange factor."

(5) The function of the group symbolizes the community as a whole, as a powerful forum. The individual sees himself in a new light by consent or disapproval, the boundaries of the ego are under revision. The same is true for the superego, which represents in the last resort the restrictions imposed by the community on the individual as imparted by parental authority and incorporated into the mind. By its rejection, or tolerance, or approval, the group seems to be able not only to revise but also to modify this formation efficiently. Its effect can therefore be said to be a genuine reconditioning of the structure of ego and superego.

(6) A peculiar transformation and modification of the individual transference situation (intragroup transference). The group absorbs a good deal of what in individual treatment becomes focused on the therapist himself. This is a very useful feature, especially when there is no time to work out the individual transference situation fully. The improved social adaptation can be carried over much more easily from one particular therapeutic group to any other and in the last resort refers to the community as a whole.

TRAINING THE GROUP THERAPIST

In a short time medical officers of comparatively little psychiatric experience have been able to learn to handle groups, in the way here described, efficiently and successfully. Some of them had a very good natural feeling for group therapy and therefore could improve their technique spontaneously in the light of their own experience once they had exposed themselves to the dynamics of the group. It appears, however, that management and technique can, to an increasing extent, be taught. For such purposes a weekly seminary conducted as a type of group has proved a favorable means of mutual instruction. The successful conduct of group therapy here outlined makes considerable demands on the therapist's patience, balance, and judgment, and also depends somewhat on his personal skill. But it seems to be more interesting from a scientific point of view than any other form of group therapy. It is also largely self-regulatory, and the beginner is not likely to overreach himself.

It has been possible to train for group work in other fields a number of nonmedical unit officers. They appear to have derived stimulation and benefit from the group sessions which they could observe and in which they could take part. It is not too much to hope that these experiments in free group therapy will prove of increasing value for positive mental hygiene besides psychiatric practice in general.

REFERENCES

1 S. H. Foulkes and E. Lewis, "Group Analysis: A Study in the Treatment of Groups on Psycho-Analytic Lines," *Brit. J. Psychol.*, 20:175-184, 1944.
2. *Ibid.*

38

GROUP PSYCHOTHERAPY WITH PSYCHOTICS

Christopher T. Standish
Elvin V. Semrad

A general review of group psychotherapy with psychotic patients was done by Drs. James Mann and Elvin Semrad of our staff in 1947 in a paper entitled "Notes on the Use of Group Therapy in Psychoses." [1] This present paper for the greater part is an elaboration of their earlier paper bringing up to date our collective experience in group psychotherapy at the Boston State Hospital.

Group techniques were first used with psychotic patients by Dr. E. W. Lazell at St. Elizabeth Hospital in 1919. Until recently, in contrast to other modes of psychiatric treatment, group psychotherapy in psychoses has remained a relatively unexplored sphere of endeavor. Important contributions in this field have been made however by Moreno, Schilder, Blackman and Klapman, in addition to Lazell. Gifford and Mackenzie have reviewed the literature in 1947.[2]

The principal types of group psychotherapy as applied to the psychoses may be classified according to the method of approach. Opposite extremes are seen in the repressive-inspirational and the analytic or investigative methods. Between these two extremes lies a third approach which may be appropriately designated as didactic.

The repressive-inspirational technique exploits the strong collective transference to the leader and the force of suggestion exerted over the group. Evangelists and political demagogues attest to the effectiveness of this method with normal groups of people. The investigative technique on the other hand in general makes use of productions and interplay in the group while the therapist maintains a neutral role. In the didactic method, emphasis is placed upon some form of lecturing to the patients. The therapist is a teacher and mental mechanisms are interpreted in order to impart conscious intellectual insight.

Reprinted from the *Journal of Psychiatric Social Work*, Vol. 20, 1951, pp. 143-150.

Group therapy was begun at the Boston State Hospital in June, 1946 [3] in an effort to define the role of group therapy in the treatment of the psychoses. The discussion that follows covers some of the problems of organization and technique with an estimate of our observations and results growing out of our experience in the active use of group therapy with psychotic patients.

The organization of a group of psychotic patients for the purpose of instituting group therapy is accompanied by many misgivings and anxieties. We could not help but notice in our own project a marked reluctance to begin and often to continue group therapy. In seminar discussions before and during our project we found it helpful to acknowledge honestly our own fears, indecision, and ignorance of the situation. The exchange of such feelings among members of the staff served as a source of security and allayed anxieties preventing progress in conducting group therapy. These seminars were expanded to include not only staff psychiatrists, but, in addition, social workers, clinical psychologists, and experienced psychiatric nurses now working with psychotic patients in groups. It is our feeling that one of the chief obstacles to group psychotherapy lies in the therapists themselves, assuming that the patient in his desire for health constantly seeks our assistance, albeit in a manner evoking uneasiness in those who try to help him.

Having overcome our initial reluctance to begin group therapy, further problems arose in the course of treatment. These too were aired in seminar discussion, and as a result further observations and experiences were better understood and formulated.

Diagnosis does not seem to be of great importance in terms of choice of patients for group therapy. In the early stages of our work, it was generally felt that the inclusion of a manic patient would be certain to stimulate conversation in the group. Similarly, articulate paranoids were found to be equally helpful. We no longer regard these as necessary preliminary selective measures, since the need for a flow of conversation in the group, we feel, is in large part an expression of the need of the therapist. As the therapist proceeds, the nature of group dynamics is apparently such that sooner or later most of the members of the group will participate verbally while all participate on a nonverbal level.

The location of the meeting place is of some importance. The meeting place in our experience should be free from distraction and sufficiently attractive so as to afford an atmosphere of importance to this special type of treatment. The therapeutic setting should be one that the patient feels has been selected for a special type of helping situation.

Seating arrangement of the group members is not prescribed so that each patient is free to select his own seat. As members come to know each other, they will sit near those whom they like. Invariably one or more patients will vie for a seat near the therapist. On the other hand a patient will sometimes indicate his hostility and remoteness from the group by sitting far away from it or even turning his back to it. After a number of sessions, seating arrangement tends to become static.

In determining the frequency of meetings, we considered the following points: How many meetings best serve the interests of the group? How much can the group take? And how much can the therapist take? In our experience two or three meetings weekly have worked out to good advantage. Meetings last usually about one hour. Meetings of this duration permit arrival at a subject of common appeal and interest, as well as time for discussion, without undue fatigue on the part of either the therapist or the patients from the emotional tensions that go with the discussions.

Attendance in our groups is not compulsory although we do use social pressure to enforce attendance. All therapists respect the patients' wishes by leaving open invitations to all recalcitrants. Reiterance of this invitation by the therapist between sessions and by nurses and attendants before each session reduces the problem of absenteeism. In some cases pressure is exerted by members of the group on the absentees.

We have found it desirable to limit the group to a maximum of fifteen patients. In a larger group it is very difficult for the therapist to keep track of what is going on in the group. Many of us feel that even smaller groups of about ten or eleven are preferable as the therapy progresses. Addition or subtraction of members seems in the long run to make little difference to the progress of the group. In our Reception Services rotating groups have been successfully conducted.

All of our therapists introduce the first meeting with a brief orientation as to the purpose of the meetings. Patients are asked to express their opinions freely and are assured that they can speak of anything they care to. It is suggested that in this way the patients may be able to help each other. With further experience we introduce a meeting with a contract of sorts in which we more specifically define the objectives of the group meetings and what the therapist expects of the members as well as some definition of his own role in the group. In general, no restrictions are placed on behavior.

Our technique can be described as "Participation in Casual Conversation" with appropriate comments being made at opportune times. The therapist's role we term as that of a catalyst in which he attempts to arouse action and reaction on a feeling level.

The term catalyst was borrowed from the field of chemistry and was chosen by us to emphasize that a catalyst keeps a reaction going. The implication for therapy is that the therapist facilitates interaction between patients but takes care not to use the situation to act out his own personal conflicts or problems.

In this respect we feel it better to avoid a lecturing or all-questioning role, thus not becoming established as forbidding or authoritative figures. Rather we try to insinuate ourselves as members of the group. We feel that the therapist should be discouraged from impressing on the group what an intelligent person he really is or how much he really knows about emotional problems.

It has been our experience that a therapist's sincere interest in the patient as a person and an appreciation of the patient's dilemma is a great asset in therapy. Patients seem to sense very keenly when the therapist, by his attitudes and comments, shows a lack of interest. It also seems helpful if the therapist is honest with patients particularly with regard to his own feelings and actions towards them. It is quite a comfort to patients when the therapist can objectively discuss his own responses in the treatment situation. In this way he can indicate that he also is human and subject to much the same feelings as his patients. Indicating respect through attempting to understand the patients' feelings and difficulties is also of help in the therapeutic situation. We have our own special way of saying this; that is, "the therapist must provide an atmosphere of 'all-rightness'!"

In treatment we make use of ordinary everyday conversation in preparing the patient for investigation of more intimate material regarding personal conflicts and problems; what we have called participation in casual conversation with appropriate comments at opportune times. We are not exclusively preoccupied with the content of what is said by patients, thus focusing attention on feelings which lie behind what is said or done at the moment. We might say that we are more concerned with what the patient means rather than what he says.

We talk with our patients on any topic whatsoever, no matter how trivial or inconsequential the conversation may appear to be. Such apparently trivial conversation is an excellent entree into the emotional life of the patient and may often reveal a good deal about his sentiments and attitudes. We have also noticed that just as much feeling can be linked with superficial conversation as with so-called "deeper productions."

We use the term "appropriate comment" mainly in an attempt to define the role of the therapist with respect to the interpretation of material brought forth by the patients. In general we do little in the way of interpretation in the sense of relating present conflicts and interpersonal issues to those of infancy and childhood. Rather we attempt to understand what the patient is trying to convey to us in terms of what he feels. The appropriate comment may be a query, approbation, mild disagreement, or any sort of remark which helps to stimulate the flow of conversation and the emergence and recognition of these underlying feelings. Ideally the appropriate comment should indicate the "all-rightness" of the feelings expressed by the patient. It should also show that the therapist has some appreciation and understanding of the preoccupations of the patient which are hinted at in the material brought forth. The appropriate comment is more effective in our experience when use is made of the patient's own words.

The therapist has further opportunity to indicate his understanding when questioned about psychotic symptoms such as delusions and hallucinations. Such questions are usually phrased so as to create an issue over the validity or truth of the experiences. We prefer that the group answer questions of this sort. However we may often comment from a premise which runs roughly as follows—that hallucinations, for example, are not only valid but also very vivid personal experiences and that it is of interest to both the therapist and the patients to figure out what possibly could have given rise to them, for they are without doubt unusual and naturally clamor for explanation. This diverts discussion from the validity of the experiences to a more profitable area; namely, what everyday experiences and feelings past and present are associated with these psychotic symptoms.

The therapist has the opportunity to indicate his understanding of questions in which the patients ask about themselves, but in disguise, as it were. It seems helpful to answer such questions as much as possible in terms of the patient's own needs rather than the therapist going into any details of his own personal life. Patients of course do show a personal interest in the therapist. Personal opinions and preferences are frequently asked of him. Such questions seem better answered in a brief and straightforward fashion.

Our patients seem to be much more sensitive to the therapist's inadvertent or unconscious behavior than to his conscious attitudes. A warm smile, the twist of a lip, the tone of one's voice, a quick adjustment of one's clothing, a glance at one's watch, and so forth, are much more accurate indicators of the therapist's actual interest and understanding than anything he might say to his patients. The therapist indicates interest, boredom, anxiety, or frustration mainly through his own inadvertent responses or nonverbal cues. This may easily affect the material which the patients bring forth. In this way the sentiments and prejudices of the therapist have their effect on the therapeutic process.

We usually find it unnecessary to actively restrict or prohibit patients in their overt behavior. It seems to us however that the therapist sets limits to the patient's behavior by his own inadvertent responses and may even in the same way invite patients to go too far. Occasionally it is necessary to interfere actively.

The setting of limits may possibly have a more subtle meaning for the patient than is at first apparent when attention is focused on the mere prohibition of antisocial behavior. A patient may for example feel quite ineffectual in his everyday experience when other people behave aggressively towards him. By being aggressive towards the therapist, he is forcing the therapist to give a practical demonstration of how such situations can be handled more effectively. Instead of seeing "how far he can go" with the therapist, the patient may rather be challenging the therapist to show him how he can learn to handle these disturbing situations in a more grown-up way. The setting of limits may thus have potentialities for emotional growth of the patient.

Our experience indicates that group therapy with psychotic patients goes through recognizable stages. The first stage is one of testing out the situation and is characterized chiefly by hostility in as many forms as the patient has at his command. The conversations deal quite exclusively with the hospital and the representatives of the hospital (rarely direct attacks on the therapist) and the special situation the hospital produces. Agreement in this sphere fosters a good deal of group unity which permits the advent of the second stage.

In the second stage there is fairly free expression of anxiety-laden psychotic material. Hallucinations and delusions are most frequently disclosed and such repeated disclosures are finally met by attempts of the various members to explain such phenomena. It must be said in this regard that some of the most astute observations are made by the patients.

Gradually the material discussed takes on a more personal tinge in relation to feelings about the self and feelings about others. Thus the third stage is entered as the patients begin to introspect, mutually criticize, and work through some of their emotional problems.

A fourth or closing phase of the group is not yet entirely clear. However it is observed that patients who show the most improvement gradually begin to speak about their future plans and become more concerned about their situation outside the hospital, the persons in that external situation, and the problems that the total situation of leaving the hospital and returning to the community presents.

Recently in a paper by Drs. Rosen and Chasen,[4] attention was focused more closely on individual group sessions in an effort to clarify some of the ways in which psychotic patients resist frank discussion and easy interaction in a group setting, as well as the issues lying behind such resistances. Those who published this study felt that it could not be categorically stated that overcoming particular difficulties would bring about good results. Rather the immediate goal is to help what might be called a "poor" group to change in the direction of a "good" group.

A "poor" group we feel is one with much disorganization and chaos and great indirectness of language. Many evidences of regression and persistent lack of change over a period of months fall into the same category. A "good" group on the other hand is a group in which there is a general feeling of cohesion or working together with attentiveness on the part of individual members and participation and interaction of at least a few of the members. Fairly clear language with some direct verbal expression of feeling, some attempts to deal with present and past problems, and absence of a persistent and unrelieved block also indicate a "good" group.

We have observed many manifestations which serve as resistance to straightforward discussion. It is our impression that perhaps they arise out of the current situation between the patients and the therapist. Some of these indicators of anxiety and resistance follow.

First, hostile acts in general may indicate anxiety and resistance. These acts range from the most obvious and overt to the most subtle. References in speech to violence and destruction are frequent. Hostile imitations of the therapist occur as well as hints about evil or authoritative persons. Patients may aggressively take over in the group or become excessively passive or inhibited.

Accentuated defenses are seen, both neurotic and psychotic, including the more typical symptoms of schizophrenia. To these, we would add evidence of specific regression both in speech and behavior.

Finally, we would mention persistent and unrelieved block with freer discussion outside the group, formation of cliques, and more obvious signs of group disintegration. Some of the latter would include patients aimlessly wandering about the room, much hubbub and murmuring, and various expressions of desire to quit or leave. As therapy goes on there may appear direct verbal expression of feelings of emptiness, of worthlessness, and even of being dead. Expression of emotions like fear and hostility usually leads into or accompanies the issues which are currently disturbing the patients. These feelings are frequently expressed to another member of the group before being directed at the leader.

It would seem that nearly everything we see happening in the group or to the patients is meaningful for the immediate situation among the patients, and in particular between the patients and the therapist, since these phenomena are seen arising out of or being accentuated in any given group session.

It should also be mentioned that sometimes a useful clue that something is wrong in the group is the therapist's awareness of his own discomfort. He may sense that the patients are making him feel tense or hostile in some way or are forcing him into unintended activity. As a result he may be didactic, overtalkative, or make premature comments arising from his own associations instead of clarifying from patients' associations.

In a general sort of way the issues lying behind the various resistances shown in therapy seem to concern ideas of physical danger, rejection, and feelings of being attracted to the therapist. Usually the patients have to deal with problems concerning their relationship with the therapist and the hospital before they feel free to discuss the prototypes of these problems in their prehospital and earlier life.

There is no doubt that the therapist is at times actually rejecting to the patients. This may be rather subtle, as when the therapist is excessively interested in some special attribute or talent of the patient, thus frequently through implication rejecting the rest of his personality. Also in the category of rejection is treating the patients like children, as for example, bringing in unannounced guests, acting in a dogmatic or patronizing manner, sleepiness, not consulting the patients about changes in schedule, broken promises, lateness, and missed meetings.

Some problems are inherent in the group situation itself. Jealousy over the many patients sharing the therapist's attention and the reluctance of patients to expose their private problems before a crowd are to be expected. More difficult to detect are resistances growing out of conscious or unconscious preferences by the therapist of patients who are most intelligent or who verbalize better than others. It is difficult for the therapist to remain objective in such circumstances and to discuss the patients reactions as problems of the patient even if they are provoked by real attitudes in the therapist.

The resistances are handled by clarifying their manifestations and investigating the feelings and issues lying behind them. We usually assume that the resistance grows out of some issue that has currently arisen between the patients and the therapist. When the therapist arrives at some appreciation of what is causing the patients' concern, the issue can be discussed honestly and realistically. The therapist need not feel that resistances are caused by his own mistakes; they are inevitable during the course of therapy. An observer is frequently useful in clarifying causes of resistances which may be in the therapist's blind spots, since many of the issues are precipitated through the therapist's unconscious behavior. The more the therapist can tolerate severely irritating attitudes and promote interaction, the more secure, accepted, and understood the patients will feel.

We are aware that in spite of much recent work on psychotherapy of chronic psychotic patients the idea is still rather widely held that psychotics are living in their own world and do not respond to cues in the immediate environment. The great preponderance of our experience contradicts this view.

It might be of interest at this point to comment on some observations made in comparing normal groups with psychotic groups. Resistances in psychotics though more easily recognized as such are exceedingly tenacious. Resistances can be much more subtle in normal groups, but at the same time we see a stronger desire to investigate, a much shorter period of testing, and a more rapid emergence of tender feelings. We have noticed that normal persons work much more effectively as a group in helping and trying to clarify for one another and in trying to apply what they learn. Psychotics on the other hand have a marked tendency to monopolize the therapist. The tendency for normal groups to use a show of excessive positive feeling for the group experience as a resistance is rarely seen in psychotic groups and then only on an individual level.

Although therapeutic results must be reckoned in long-term changes, general benefits to the patients are fairly specific. The group situation provides the patient with a safe permissive tool of relating himself once more to others. It encourages the expression of suppressed hostility, mobilizes unconscious tensions, and permits their release. It further provides a setting in which the patient can learn more about how he operates as a person in his dealings with others and possibly acquire more effective ways of dealing with other people.

The self-imposed isolation of the patient may relent as the opportunity is offered him to compare himself with others who also have severe conflicts over problems of everyday living. He is provided with a setting in which he may acquire a better perspective on his own problems and feelings.

Group therapy facilitates the task of caring for patients. Patients become more cooperative and less resistive with attendants, less abusive and assaultive on the wards. Many of those who are incontinent show better control of excretory functions. Others are less destructive of clothing and property, and the majority show greater neatness in dress and appearance.

In addition to these benefits to the patients, group therapy contributes to the general therapeutic atmosphere of a large state hospital in that it is possible to have more patients under treatment. The feeling that something is being done for the patients permeates the allied personnel, who often show subtle but definite improvement in their attitude toward the patients.

The therapist shares too in the benefits of group therapy. It contributes to his growth by affording the observation of patients in a new light. The group functions as a miniature of society in many ways and reveals much about how patients handle themselves with others. In addition, the therapist becomes aware of the effect he has on the group as a person while he also learns his limitations. Certainly the therapist will become more keenly aware of the nonverbal cues through which human beings so often convey their most intimate feelings to one another.

The effectiveness of group therapy in terms of statistical results is much more difficult to evaluate, though we have attempted such an evaluation of our group therapy program which was begun in June, 1946. This was done with a total of 165 patients who had been or were currently in group therapy in April of 1947 when an initial survey was made by Dr. Gurri and Chasen[5] of our staff. It was decided at the time to keep these patients in group therapy as long as they remained in the hospital and to periodically evaluate benefits to these patients.

A total of 165 patients were treated, originally in 12 separate groups. Of this number 52 per cent were schizophrenic disorders, 28 per cent affective disorders, and the remainder other types including psychopathic personalities, alcoholic psychoses, organic psychoses of different kinds, and so forth. The age range of these patients was from 14 to 84 years. The average age was about 35 years and the average hospital stay about three years. Of the 165, slightly less than one third were acute patients, the remainder chronic. Four-fifths of the patients were females. This disparity was due only to the fact that most of the participating staff members were on female services.

In April, 1947, our survey showed that results with acute patients were, as would be expected, much better than results with chronic patients. Of the acute patients, 51 per cent had been released on trial visit as compared to 27 per cent of the chronic patients. An additional 25 per cent of the acute patients showed noticeable improvement as compared to an additional 37 per cent of the chronic patients.

Three years later in January, 1950, a survey by Dr. Gurri showed that 65 per cent of the acute patients were now on visit as compared to 34 per cent of the chronic patients. In other words, in the intervening three years additional patients, both acute and chronic, were released on visit. The increase in patients on visit in this period was 14 per cent in the acute and 7 per cent in the chronic patients. The proportion of patients showing progressive improvement over the three-year period was slightly lower than the percentage of patients who had showed initial improvement in April, 1947.

BIBLIOGRAPHY

Chasen, M., Finlayson, M., MacKenzie, J. M., "Further Follow-up of Results of Group Therapy in Psychoses." Read at Massachusetts Society for Residents in Psychiatry, May 1948.

Fidler, J., Jr. and Standish, C., "Observations Noted During Course of Group Treatment of Psychoses." *Dis. Nerv. Sys.*, Vol. IX, No. 1, January 1948.

Gifford, S. and MacKenzie, J., "A Review of Literature on Group Treatment of Psychoses." *Dis. Nerv. Syst.*, Vol. IX, No. 1, January 1948.

Gurri, J., Personal communication re follow-up of patients in group therapy, January 1950.

Gurri, J. and Chasen, M., "Preliminary Survey of Results of Group Therapy of Psychotics." *Dis. Nerv. Syst.*, Vol. IX, No. 2, 1948.

Mann, J. and Mann, H., "The Organization and Technique of Group Treatment of Psychoses." *Dis. Nerv. Syst.*, Vol. IX, No. 2, February 1948.

Mann, J. and Semrad, E. V., "Notes on the Use of Group Therapy in Psychoses." *J. Soc. Casework*, May 1948, pp. 176-181.

Rosen, I. M. and Chasen, M., "Study of Resistance and its Manifestations in Therapeutic Groups of Chronic Psychotic Patients." *Psychiat.*, Vol. 12, No. 3, August 1949.

Semrad, E. V., "An Analytically Oriented Group Therapy Program in Boston State Hospital." Read before the American Psychoanalytic Association, mid-winter meeting, December 16, 1947.

Standish, C. T., Mann, J. and Rosen, I. M., "Further Observations on Organization and Technic of Group Therapy in Psychoses." *Dis. Nerv. Syst.*, Vol. X, No. 12, December 1949.

39

A REVIEW OF SOME RECENT GROUP PSYCHOTHERAPY METHODS FOR ELDERLY PSYCHIATRIC PATIENTS

Mathew Ross

According to the U.S. Bureau of the Census estimates, by 1975 there will be 21,000,000 persons in the United States who are 65 years of age and older. Since 1900, while the total population of the United States has doubled and the number of persons from 45 to 64 years old has tripled, the number of persons aged 65 years and more has quadrupled. Because of this indicated growth of population at older age levels, interest in the methods to secure, maintain, and restore their health has quickened. This report, highlighting some representative efforts relative to the psychiatric problems of elderly persons, may serve as a review of current efforts and a guidepost for future efforts.

In the United States, the number of persons living beyond the age of 65 in 1950 was nearly double that in 1900. For the practice of medicine this statistic had numerous implications, one of which was the increasing number of emotionally disturbed elderly patients seen by the physician in his daily practice. Now many journals, texts, films, and symposia attest to the increasing attention these emotional problems of older-age patients receive, since progress in clinical psychiatry and geriatrics has mitigated the therapeutic nihilism which heretofore vitiated the attack upon the emotional ills of the elderly.

Reprinted from the A.M.A. *Archives of General Psychiatry*, Vol. I, December 1959, pp. 578-592. Originally published under the title "A Review of Some Recent Group Treatment Methods for Elderly Psychiatric Patients."

THE PSYCHOLOGY OF AGING

Successful management of the psychiatric ailments of the elderly must be predicated upon knowledge of the "normal" mental health of this period of life.

An attentive physician who listens to any elderly person may hear a tale of an individual's struggle for survival in the face of a whole long series of partial amputations of capacities. How this decline in adaptive powers limits the range of operation of the homeostatic processes has been variously described.

Meerloo[1] has noted:

> The onset of involution and decline differs widely in many persons. We may suppose that much of it depends not only on the somatic body instrument and the decline of homeostatic capacities, but also on underlying compulsions and lifelong frustrations. In some people the process of what might be called psychosclerosis may start early in life. Others are able to develop new capacities in very old age.

In psychobiologic terms, Gitelson[2] sketched this picture:

> With advancing age not only is the person confronted with the experience of failing personal powers but the involution of the vegetative organs deprives him of the balancing compensations which the infant finds in his vegetative functions. Finally, while the helpless child may be coddled and protected by his mother pending his maturation and self-sufficiency, the helpless grandfather may meet with short shrift. The old man's memory may be full of past glories and his heart empty of hope. It is this overlapping of the waning powers of the maturity and the increasing helplessness of the second childhood that is the basis for the psychological picture with which old age presents us.

Heredity and constitution in part mold the senescent's psychologic picture, as they do at any age. Kallman[3] states:

> On the basis of our twin observations it is no longer questionable that heredity and constitution play a basic role in determining the variable ability to maintain a state of physical and mental health until and through the period of senescence.

Elsewhere,[4] I have detailed some psychologic changes in the elderly person whose boundaries and equipment are being constantly and unceasingly restricted and depleted by the aging process. The dulling of recent memory and the increase of the conservative mental outlook are apparent, as are the exaggeration of lifelong character traits, prejudices, biases, and opinions. Attenuated interest in the new, and reminiscent indulgence in the good old days have supplanted the young person's inclination to form new associations and ways. Accuracy and speed of thought are diminished. Self-assertiveness, and even domineering attitudes, attempt to compensate for feelings of inadequacy and insecurity. Often, death, in taking its toll of family and friends, undermines the delusion of invulnerability to which we all cling and leaves a sense of growing isolation and loneliness in its stead. Mild depression may ensue. Slights are often, because of increased sensitivity, perceived in paranoid fashion.

Postmortem examination evidence deprives us of those tempting explanations which would attribute these phenomena to physiologic and pathologic changes in the central nervous system. It is not always possible to establish one-to-one relationships between mental symptoms and structural damage.[5] Although Alpers[6] has demonstrated that there is but a 30 per cent to 40 per cent correlation between the presence of retinal arteriosclerosis and cerebral arteriosclerosis, the presence of the former continues to result in the diagnosis of the latter with concomitant prognosis. Indeed, in a fairly well-balanced person very considerable cerebral damage is withstood, while in those less well emotionally balanced minimal cerebral pathology may produce a frank psychosis. The cerebral pathology seems to be a "final straw" that utterly disrupts the homeostatic mechanism of the person already emotionally overburdened.

Concomitant to aging are some special predisposing factors which tax the homeostatic capacities. For the mother, as a result of the loss of children who grow up and leave home, there may be lessened self-esteem resulting from lessened opportunity for service to her children, with an accompanying loss of purpose in life. The retirement of the male all too frequently is perceived by him as an indication that "he's through," especially when his retirement is proclaimed in a ritualistic ceremony complete with banquet, speaker, and gifts conveying a sense of graduation to a living death. A lengthy marriage is conducive to a symbiotic relationship in which the death of one may soon be followed by that of the survivor without much apparent correlation to the second member's state of health. Other potential disruptive forces are the excessive survival of parents which may burden the aging patient. On the other hand, where there has been an overly prolonged and exaggerated child-parent relationship, the inevitable loss of parents may produce a stressful situation.

As in psychiatry for other age groups, a variety of approaches has been employed for the elderly: intra- and extramural; psychotherapeutic, pharmacologic, and physical therapies on an individual and group basis, separately and in combination. In this report those therapies emphasizing the pharmacologic and physical aspects of treatment will not be detailed; rather, those emphasizing the intra- and extramural applications of individual and group psychotherapeutic practices will be reported.

THE MENTAL HOSPITAL AND GROUP THERAPY

Therapeutic efforts with groups of elderly patients in mental hospitals have ranged from tea parties to actual gerontologic group therapy. It is readily apparent that many psychiatrists are achieving encouraging results working at these varying levels with the geriatric patients under their care. Some examples of these efforts, arranged roughly in order of increasing complexity, follow.

One ward psychiatrist [7] approached his ward "as a total social situation with a constantly dynamic interplay involving all the personnel and patients." Observation and study revealed that there were four groupings of patients on the ward, which, "although loosely structured, had definite dynamic interaction." One group, the senile group, occupied the same seats each day. Its members did not communicate verbally, and each of the individuals seemed to have an isolated life, wherein anything but routine behavior was regarded as an unwelcome change. They considered music and dancing frivolous. Even though the senile patients were capable of doing only the simplest tasks, the initial psychiatric objective was to encourage these patients to do as much as possible for themselves. The aide was attentive to the individual patient's personal hygiene, and most of her time was devoted to this. Encouragement to empty ashtrays, water flowers, sweep floors, and help care for one another was given. Nothing more specific was attempted at first. Later, a simple form of group meeting was organized, patterned somewhat after a tea party, with the aide acting as mother. Milk and cookies were served. The degree of brightness manifested was surprising. At bingo parties, the next phase, their ability to play was remarkable. No longer was this group in any way an eyesore. The most obvious change was the improvement in personal hygiene and general appearance. The earlier tendency toward general deterioration decreased. Lichtenberg recognized:[8]

> It is quite clear that the content of the psychotic patient was not in any way directly affected by the program. However, there was an improvement in the general level despite psychotic content or affect.

This method of initiating group therapy at Central Islip State Hospital, Central Islip N.Y., has been described by Corcoran:[9]

> We have found the following arrangement to be satisfactory. We start with a musical program—folk songs printed in large letters visible to the entire class, are placed on a rack, each sheet carrying about 14 lines, and easily turned. If the leader wishes to repeat a page, she so directs with a pointer. Another member of the group plays the music for each song. Most of the songs become familiar to the class and are known to all the leaders. If the patients are unable to sing, they hum. This feature alternates

with individual singing. Individual patients not able to sing in English will sing their native folk songs in their own tongue. Folk dancing, jigs and recitations alternate in this part of the program. Refreshments are then served, consisting of coffee, doughnuts, cookies, soft drinks, etc. This entire procedure creates a pleasing and stimulating effect, and the therapist-aide circulating among the group is watchful of the reactions of each patient. The group becomes more cheerful, accessible, and enters into conversation more easily, at which time the psychotherapist takes over the class. The Gray Ladies and Canteen Workers of the American Red Cross play an important part in assisting at these sessions.

At Verdun Protestant Hospital,[10] in Montreal, 17 senile psychotic patients between 70 and 80 years of age, who had been hospitalized from 1 to 13 years, met twice every week in group psychotherapy. The group was convened by the ward nurse and was told that they were going to meet with the ward doctor. Upon arrival, the physician explained the purpose of the meeting, namely, to give the group members a chance to discuss their problems with him. The greatest response was produced by indicating to the patients that there would be a concrete gain from talking. After about 20 minutes, the keenness and interest of the therapist and the group produced by the stimulus of meeting together began to lag; so tea was served at this time. Interest revived and carried through the remaining time. In contrast to other groups, these participants were mainly concerned with going home, and only by persistent exercise of an interviewing technique could the discussion be guided toward these topics of prominent interest to the group: physical complaints, the good old days, socioeconomic concerns, loneliness, wishful fantasies, and rejection. Specific therapeutic obstacles were short attention span, amnesia, and persistence of ideas. Adjunctive therapy consisted of nicotinic acid, occupational therapy, and music. Improved patient morale, cleanliness, and general behavior were noted. A by-product of the experiment was an increased cooperation on the part of relatives.

In a 20-month period at the Osawatomie State Hospital, in Kansas,[11] a total of 28 patients, meeting in groups of 4 men and 4 women, averaging 70 years of age, were treated once a week by group psychotherapy for periods of two to six months. Group therapy was undertaken in a combination with somatic and milieu therapy. Noisy, aggressive, and very restless patients were given chlorpromazine or reserpine. For those manifesting impaired memory and disorientation, sodium glutamate or pentylenetetrazol (Metrazol) was prescribed. Depressed patients received electric shock therapy. All group members were encouraged to participate in occupational therapy and recreational activities. At the group meetings the patients were encouraged to help themselves to fruit juice and cigarettes and to talk informally about their problems. After introducing the members to one another, the therapist told them that the meetings were for them to become friends, to learn about one another's problems, and to help one another. They were encouraged to criticize the hospital's food, methods, organization, and staff, including the therapist, whose attitude was a passive one of merely listening to what the patient had to say and who interfered only when the patient was shy, silent, or needed encouragement. Considered an understanding brother, the therapist often answered questions of general interest to the group. Among the topics favored by Wolff's patients were religion, past life, paradise, life after death, and heavenly reward expectations.

Twelve patients, nearly one half the total group, of 28, treated in this fashion by Wolff [12] were sufficiently improved to be discharged from the hospital to their families or to nursing homes. The improvement was manifested by increased self-esteem, decreased hostility and delusions, and improved socialization. While they still showed signs of chronic brain syndrome (defective memory for recent events), they were better oriented, in better contact, and more interested in their surroundings or ward activities; had a more optimistic outlook on life; dressed more carefully; were friendly and cooperative with other people, and had lost some of their psychosomatic complaints. The greatest obstacle to improvement in these geriatric patients was their ambivalence about leaving the hospital. Family cooperation was required to handle this problem.

A series of papers by Linden [13] presented a considerable body of data on gerontologic group psychotherapy. He emphasized resocialization of the individual and recognized a greater need for promoting tranquility, a potential for happiness, and a return of some degree of self-sufficiency, rather than for producing deep insights in a group whose years are numbered. At the State Hospital in Norristown, Pa., a group of 51 women whose average age was over 70 met for more than two years, twice a week, for one-hour periods. Each group therapy session was attended by a majority of those enrolled. A period of indoctrination was followed by an effort to encourage free association, uninhibited public expression, and mutual interpretation. At the onset the limited success gave the group a discouragingly quiet aspect. The members waited dependently and helplessly for the lectures from the doctor. A rotation method of calling on as many members as possible and questioning them about biographical items proved more stimulating, yielded fewer embarrassing silent periods, and kept the group alert. Much later an educational element was introduced by members volunteering brief presentations of subjects of group and seasonal interests. There seemed to be no real group formation, and the conversations that occurred were stereotyped complaints between individual patients and the therapist about the food, alleged mistreatment by hospital personnel, and going home. Linden said that "a pall of gloom charged with slight expectancy hung over the group and was punctuated by stifled laughter in response to an occasional witticism."

For about six months the leader patiently persevered, keeping up a nearly steady stream of informal talks on a variety of topics, and questioning, coercing, and chiding patients into talking about themselves. The total effort seemed futile, and the temptation to give up the group as an unsuccessful experiment was very strong. The first noticeable effect of group therapy was a pronounced change in the atmosphere of the ward. A morale factor was emerging as the atmosphere of pessimism, inactivity, stagnation, and futility began to diminish. In a few months ward visitors detected and commented on the change. A crucial turning point occurred, however, when the physician leader, called to the telephone from the session, left the group under the guidance of a nurse, and on his return noticed the group was in spirited discussion with the nurse. This was not always the case, to be sure, for when the nurse conducted almost the entire session the lively spirits at the beginning of the hour waned, and the return of the male therapist was greeted with some exuberance. Once the nurse was introduced as coleader, true group identity and conventional psychotherapy ensued in the seventh and eighth months. Discussions on the items of feminine interest—clothing, cosmetics, personal hygiene, living arrangements, the cattiness of women, jealousy, the nature of men, and the like, which up to the eighth month were offered only to the female therapist—now in the eighth and ninth months were increasingly directed to the male therapist. The reverse also occurred. Interest in the group became keen and strong. Affectional ties sprang up. Hitherto neglected recreations, occupational therapy, the library, card games, and movies received increased attention. Parties, picnics, dances, and group singing were often discussed, planned, and even financed during group sessions. After about the 12th month of therapy the subjective personality of the building had changed completely, and with it its reputation.

Only after the nurse was introduced as the coleader and occupied an authority-sharing position did a group *esprit de corps* or identity develop. Linden[14] reviewed the group development and presented the following analysis:

> During the early period the helplessness and dependency of the bewildered aged women forced the physician-therapist to become the dominant personality in the group. Consequently, he was the recipient of all the individual attitudes. He assumed the role of the strongly authoritative, but protective, parental figure toward whom appeals for succor and support were directed. Submerged in the pathetically pleading atmosphere was a sycophantic transference which went unrecognized because of its heavy disguise. The introduction of the nurse co-leader presented a multifaceted factor, one of its early effects apparently being a reawakening of oedipal strivings. Since the male therapist's mere presence stimulated rivalries at this juncture, the female co-leader served to intensify them. She was also an object of emulation. The patients reestablished feminine identifications

and progressively returned to adult-like sexuality. This occurred in more than half the patients as revealed by their dress, jokes, and dreams. The commonality of affect gave the group solidification and identity. Thus a simultaneous morale factor developed which became the agency through which affect, externalization and lateralization could be realized.

The elements characteristic of senility, of vacillating amnesia, capricious disorientation, and variable confusion which may have presented an insurmountable obstacle to therapy were partially overcome by two factors: the spacing and frequency of the sessions, and dual leadership. The first gave the group a predictable, routinized, serial continuity generating a rhythmic expectation in the participants. This allowed them to find other realities as well as space-time guideposts. Dual leadership reinforced the first factor in the following way. The importance of the male therapist waxed and waned with his appearance and withdrawal during his visits to the ward and group sessions. The nurse, on the other hand, was a benevolent authority on the ward. She remained with the patients so that she continued to serve as the supportive and therapeutic factor during the intervals between group sessions.

The initially faint transferences are provoked and stimulated to bolder expression by the elements of wholesome competitiveness and rivalry generated by appropriate therapists. Dual leadership accomplishes for the senile group what individual leadership cannot because it is (1) an affect activator, (2) a social reality exemplifying the roles of the sexes, (3) a structured opportunity for appropriate object choice, and (4) a synthesized form of cultural authority and thereby represents pictorially and dynamically many familiar social forces.[15]

Of the 51 group therapy patients, 23 left the hospital for their own homes, county homes, or placements, or were ready to leave after an average of 54 hours of group therapy, whereas of the 279 patients in the same building who were not group therapy patients, 37 left or were able to leave the hospital.

These examples indicate, as does the one of the Columbus Receiving Hospital,[16] described in the section on "The Day Hospital," the broad spectrum of use and type of group therapy in the management of the elderly psychiatric patient.

HOME FOR THE AGED

Although mental hospitals logically should be looked upon as places where active treatment prepares the patient to return home, in actual practice this is not the case. All too often, mental hospitals have become domiciles for terminal custodial care, for which they may not have been well designed or staffed. Increased interest in the provision of more complete services, including psychiatric, in homes for aged persons has been an outgrowth of these circumstances.

Goldfarb[17] has described one such home, where the goal has been to maintain aged persons within its walls in active relationship to the general community, with a maximum of freedom, comfort, dignity, and, where possible, some productivity. The transfer of cases to mental hospitals dropped sharply when the amount of psychiatric aid available increased, as psychiatric techniques improved, and as the staff acquired more psychiatric understanding. Patients who heretofore had been considered intolerable, unmanageable, or risky were handled without locked doors or barred windows and with relatively little augmentation of nursing and medical care.

Most of these persons who came to the attention of the psychiatrist are also otherwise chronically ill. This nonpsychiatric disease process usually plays a part in determining the psychologic and emotional attitudes displayed, and, conversely, psychologic attitudes probably influence the progress, severity, or symptomatology of the illness. Because physical illness is common and fears about it are also common, good nursing and medical care are the foundation for psychiatric care. Indeed, sound sensible medical practices themselves have psychotherapeutic influence. On the other hand, medical care without psychiatric understanding is often inadequate. The psychiatrist who treats the aged should possess, and be prepared to use, reasonable general medical skill in cooperation with the general medical staff.

The need for psychiatric care, in addition to specific and supportive measures, is probably not being met even to the degree possible because many psychiatrists, when confronted by chronic illness in older persons, feel a degree of uneasiness which produces a nihilistic approach. True, the extent and severity of the physical ills, when compounded by social and economic problems, are as discouraging as is the impressive amount of psychopathology which emerges under these circumstances of diminished personal and material resources. Goldfarb feels that the very helplessness of the aged, dependent, chronically ill person impelled to seek assistance weakens possible therapeutic measures, which need not be time-consuming, and which consist mainly of reassurance and support in brief, evenly spaced interviews, wherein the physician demonstrates an interest in and ministers to the patient. The patient feels safer because medical skill has been placed at his disposal and he has gained and held a powerful ally. A great deal can be accomplished toward relieving mental suffering, improving social behavior, and relieving symptoms of emotional overaction by means of 10- to 15-minute interviews once or twice a week, or even by "catch-as-catch-can sessions here or there on the ward or in the corridor." Flexibility in handling the aged sick is paramount. Detailed case material illustrating this approach will appear in the section on "Individual Psychotherapy."

THE DAY HOSPITAL

In April, 1946, at the Allan Memorial Institute of Psychiatry, in Montreal, an experimental form of hospitalization was initiated.[18] To this hospital, called the day hospital, patients came at 9:00 in the morning, remained throughout the daylight hours, receiving the appropriate forms of treatment, and returned to their homes at four o'clock in the afternoon. All types of psychiatric patients were admitted, the only criterion being that they should be well enough to stay home overnight. From this modest beginning a number of variations have been developed in various parts of the world. The following two examples illustrate the use of the day hospital in the management of the elderly psychiatric patient.

In the geriatric unit of the Cowley Road Hospital, Oxford, England, is a day hospital for patients of all types where no distinctions are made for psychiatric, as opposed to other forms of medical, illness. Resources for immediate admission or readmission to an active medical unit, along with physical treatments for psychotic patients, are available. The Oxford day hospital, housed in the occupational therapy department of the geriatric unit, is under the immediate control of the occupational therapist. Once in the day hospital, the patient is given a program of activities consistent with his abilities and disabilities, and there is considerable individual variation. The social workers do much of their work in quiet interviews in the occupational therapy department, rather than by formal interview in an office. Cozin[19] presents a case protocol to exemplify what can be accomplished in such a unit.

> A widow of 63 . . . was referred from a mental hospital for continued care in the day hospital. Following the sudden death of her husband, whom she appears to have dominated throughout married life, in 1951 she sustained a personality collapse displaying mental symptoms of paranoia and confusion. Incontinence of urine . . . has recurred at times of emotional stress, disappearing again as the situation improved. . . . Relatives to whom part of the house had been sublet were unable to remain more than several months because of her untidy, unpredictable habits, occasionally urinary incontinence and strange food habits. Her relatives pointed out that she had always been moody, interfering, selfish and easy to take offense or to suspect selfish motives in others. She would retire to bed for several days when thwarted. Repeated clinical observations revealed . . . a strange lack of interest over gross self-neglect; her reported delusional episodes caused her relatives and doctor much concern.
>
> The diagnosis of a space-occupying lesion in the left frontal region . . . was confirmed in part by electroencephalography a year ago. . . . Three months later a transient epileptiform fit and several attacks of fainting and vomiting appeared to supply additional confirmation. Neurological investigation, however, has been more inclined to regard the symptom

complex as due to hypertensive encephalopathy (blood pressure 215/120 Hg).

Since attending the day hospital each afternoon, considerable improvement has been noted by the occupational therapist. In spite of now living alone, urinary incontinence has entirely ceased. She dresses neatly, no longer neglects herself, and does her own shopping. The occupational therapist has reported a steady increase in sociability, and notes that she takes an interest in other patients' work and that she is beginning to initiate conversation with others. She is very helpful to other patients and volunteers to make tea and wash up. She attended regularly and punctually each afternoon, and was a very good, although somewhat automatic, worker.

Thus a bereaved, lonely patient with a difficult personality, intellectual deterioration, hypertension, and a possible space-occupying lesion in the left frontal cortex, nevertheless demonstrated considerable improvement in personality and managed to live alone supported by the relatively small hospital services provided by the day hospital. Her ability to cope with the admittedly difficult situation was increased by the interest of the occupational therapist and the social worker in her.

The day hospital unit at the Receiving Hospital in Columbus, Ohio,[20] which is set up as a psychiatric, but not exclusively geriatric, unit has a daily routine as follows: The patients gather at eight o'clock in the morning as an informal group and over coffee discuss their experiences since the previous day. A psychiatrically trained nurse is present at this get-together and tends to lead in the discussion. From this meeting are gleaned many points leading to an understanding of the individual patient. The hour from 9:15 A.M. is spent in occupational therapy. From 10:15 to 11 A.M., the patients are seen by their individual therapists if this is requested by the patient. It is also at this time that various physical procedures are carried out four times a week. At 11 A.M. the men and women gather in groups according to sex for group psychotherapy, led by one of the psychiatrists. After lunch there is a rest period, during which the patients may read available pamphlets on mental hygiene or a book of their own choosing, or lounge and talk among themselves. Three afternoons a week, after the 2:00 to 3:00 P.M. recreational therapy led by a nurse or an occupational therapist, there is mixed-sex group psychotherapy. At 4:30 P.M. the unit closes, and the patients return to their respective homes. Practical talks are given by the dietetic and social service departments once a week. Individual therapy is made available only upon request of the patient. To round out the program once a week, the relatives of the patient meet as a group with the social worker.

A case history is descriptive of the approach in the unit.

A rather large, aggressive, 62 year old, successful, white, professional businessman . . . was admitted to a closed unit of the hospital [with] a severe, incapacitating tic which consisted of a marked jerking of the entire upper half of his body with an accompanying expiratory grunt. [When] this symptom was brought under control, he was transferred to the Day Unit, [where] he was aggressive and frequently hostile, pushing himself to the head of the line in front of the women patients in the cafeteria, cheating at cards and being generally vociferous during the recreation period. The patient group was cold and rejecting of this behavior and finally effective in helping to produce a change in it. The attitude of the staff was to be firm but non-interfering except when it seemed necessary to maintain some order. Eventually, as he changed, he became leader of the group and was accepted by all the patients. He related well in formal group psychotherapy sessions, and his changed behavior paralleled his developing a better relationship with his individual therapist, which led to his working through previously unexpressed material. Here was an aggressive, compulsive man of retirement age who was finding it difficult to give up gracefully [and who] on the unit had a corrective living experience, gained some understanding of his problem, and so was able to make a satisfactory readjustment to his changed life circumstances. This patient was in treatment 13 weeks and follow-ups reveal that he is continuing to adjust well in a mildly compulsive way.[21]

INDIVIDUAL PSYCHOTHERAPY

"The age of the neurosis is more important than the age of the patient." So said Karl Abraham[22] in 1919, writing on the applicability of psychoanalytic treatment to patients of advanced age.

Since the fallacy of attributing all emotional disorders of persons living 65 years and more to organic cerebral changes, for which nothing could be done, has become more widely apparent, many psychiatrists have attempted various individual psychotherapies with favorable outcome.

Diagnostic classifications and groupings have been proposed as a first step in planning the psychotherapeutic effort.[23] Attention has been called to the value of individualization of treatment in the aging period. Various psychotherapies have been utilized.

Goldfarb[24] has written extensively of his experiences with the aged, from which he has developed a form of brief therapy for those behavior disorders with interrelated psychologic and somatic elements which he has based upon an adaptational frame of reference utilizing the rationale whereby the behavior disorders of the aged were viewed as maladaptive efforts, arising from a sense of helplessness and fear, to gain pleasure and satisfaction by dominance of parent-surrogates. The assumption was made that the senescent's behavior was "goal-directed, motivated problem-solving," albeit inefficiently, with poor psychologic and emotional tools, which emphasize their loss of resources. These persons utilize a dependency pattern, which Goldfarb felt became a therapeutic resource when the patient was assisted toward the illusion that he had achieved success in manipulating, controlling, dominating, or directing persons around him. The therapeutic transaction was one wherein the patient was permitted to indulge in the illusion of a victorious struggle with the powerful parent-surrogate therapist. The struggle was purely an illusion on the part of the patient, a distortion of reality, wherein the therapist accepted the role of feared and resented parent and permitted himself to be won over in a manner which seemed to the patient's best interests. The promotion of the illusion that the therapist was mastered and that his power was available to the patient was a source of pleasure for the patient whose healthy, affectionate attitudes were so poorly developed or whose sense of worthlessness and disbelief that he could be loved was so great that the only bond between people he could envision was one of power. In these patients the provision and assurance of love and care was not enough; the significant feature in their improvement was the illusion that they had earned, won, or wrested such care and love from someone. When the behavior of the therapist conveyed to the patient that an emotional bond had been formed with him, the patient reacted as though dominance over a powerful figure had been achieved. Whether this domination of the therapist was obtained by superficial submission and compliance or by a behavioral expression of anger on the part of the patient, it meant two things to him: (1) that the powerful person's services were available on call and (2) that the patient himself had proved his great powers by his victory. The experiences in this treatment method led Goldfarb to conclude that, while "the psychiatrist may believe himself acting as a friendly advisor, counselor, or supportive figure, the success of treatment actually rests on the patient's secret and somewhat contemptuous conviction that he has tricked and overpowered the doctor. This conviction he masks from himself as well as from the doctor. Unless the doctor is endowed with a magic mantle of power, such a victory is hollow, meaningless, and therapeutically valueless."

Here is an example of the approach used by Goldfarb and Sheps.[25]

> Mr. T., 80 years of age, a native of Germany, who never married, had been a lifelong seclusive misanthrope, and a chronic alcoholic. He was considered a misfit in the family and left home when 18 years old because of a scandal involving a young woman. He came to the United States in 1890 by himself and worked in various restaurants and hotels. . . . In 1943, he underwent a prostatectomy, and in 1946, at the age of 74, he entered the Home for Aged and Infirm Hebrews. For three years he made a choleric marginal social adjustment. In 1949 cerebral thrombosis caused right hemiparesis which confined him to the infirmary. There he became a serious problem because of explosive angry outbursts with threatening and assaultive behavior, set off by the doctors' and nurses' attention to his severe conjunctivitis. He was relatively immobile, and sulkily refused to

make efforts which could help the staff determine the true extent of his disability. He was referred for psychiatric help and therapy was instituted in 1951.

In the first two very brief sessions he was questioned about his angry behavior in such a way as to moderately reinforce his preconception of the therapist as an injunctive, prohibiting, and threatening parent. In the third interview he angrily denounced the therapist and the Home staff for implying that he was mentally ill. He went into a lengthy diatribe about how his eyes had been spoiled by an incompetent doctor before he came to the Home and how the trouble was being perpetuated by the incompetent Home physicians who prevented him access to better ones. His hemiparesis he attributed to a trifling insult which the physicians aggravated by neglect and inept therapy; for example, the rehabilitation procedures which he violently opposed. In the session he was encouraged to vent his anger on the medical and nursing staff and especially toward the therapist who appeared suitably distressed, cautiously self-defensive, and semiapologetic without ever admitting that the patient was actually correct.

At the end of ten minutes it was tactfully agreed he could leave the interview. He left with an air of righteous indignation triumphant. For the next few days he was relatively silent and cheerful, there were no angry outbursts, his attitude was that of one who has bearded the lion in his den and emerged victorious; he was contemptuous of the harmful potentialities of those about him and submitted to their ministrations without protest. Needless to say a further opportunity for him to vent his anger and emerge triumphant was offered in another five-minute interview about a week later.

In the fourth interview, two weeks after the first, there was a change in his attitude. He seemed to feel safe with the "defeated" therapist who seemed none the worse for wear. He spoke angrily of the staff and his plight, but as though to an ally. He came to this session, for the first time, in street clothes which he had demonstrated he could help put on himself. The therapist listened sympathetically, suggested the patient could probably do a great deal despite the opposition he felt existed, and offered to have a medication added, which was done. Following this, in a series of interviews for "backsliding" on the part of the patient, there was, according to the needs of the patient, a shifting of role-playing between that of the strong parent who can be vanquished and that of the strong parental ally. After eight interviews over four months there was some improvement sustained for eighteen months. The patient altered his status from one of angry immobility to relatively peaceful but limited ambulation.

To recapitulate briefly: This man whose lifelong feelings of helplessness were reinforced by hemiplegia and the concomitant effects of brain injury handled the anxiety this generated by an angry show of force. This was ineffective in overcoming his fear and in fact increased his retaliation fear. In this setting he was depressed, immobile, and had explosions of anger. The therapist stepped in to provide him with an illusion of omnipotence through triumph over a powerful, threatening physician. Some omnipotent feelings could only be short-lived but were later replaced by acceptance of the "defeated" therapist as a powerful parental ally. Safely entrenched with him, the patient's helplessness decreased, his anxiety diminished, and reparative rage was unnecessary so that there was simultaneous improvement in behavior and decrease of his suffering. His dependence on the therapist was assumed, without incident, by the social worker, whom the patient identified with the therapist. When she "abandoned" him for a vacation, he subsided into depressed and sullen immobility and then reacted with episodes of assaultive rage of such violence as to require transfer to a psychiatric hospital before opportunity for further therapy.

A modified psychoanalytic approach to the senescent has been developed by Wayne.[26] In essence, after sufficient historical material has been obtained to permit the construction of a genetic, psychodynamic formulation and a basis for understanding transference, a goal limitation is decided upon. Although an understanding of the patient's characteristic way of handling situations is sought, structural character changes are not necessarily the therapeutic objective. Where there is a crucial current problem, this is employed as the main stream in therapy, and the patient's interest and hope are thereby maintained. While it follows that many personality problems are not entirely worked through, this often is not indicated in the aged. The therapist must make an active effort to create a consistently warm, empathic climate while he plays a relatively active role in directing therapy. The vis-à-vis position is used so that the patient can see the therapist "reacting" with positive emotional rapport, which reduces anxiety and minimizes dependence. The patient must be given a readily perceivable part in solving his own problems rather than being allowed to fall into a dependent-passive attitude. Some time must be devoted to realistic discussions of the cultural attitudes toward the elderly, the immediate living problems, and the physiology of aging. The duration and frequency of therapy must be judged individually. Scheduling is flexible, and the plan is to decrease sessions progressively until therapy is terminated.

An extensive case report of Wayne's approach has already appeared.[27] The following is another less detailed example.[28]

> Mr. D. may have reached the compulsory retirement age set for university professors. After 30 years of efficient service he is superannuated, though he still may be a capable and efficient teacher. He feels depressed, agitated and unworthy. He believes his wife no longer loves or understands him, and after many years of satsifactory marriage there is talk of separation and divorce. The children become emotionally involved and take sides. A personal emotional problem has developed into a family imbroglio. With this situation as the focal point of interest in psychotherapy, it becomes possible for the patient to begin to understand his competitiveness towards other instructors and even towards his wife and children—feelings which were never a problem under circumstances more favorable to him. In therapy he can be shown that, in his current "depre-

ciated" state, he feels a sense of dependence on his wife which his masculine pride makes it necessary for him to hide. He can become aware of present feelings of impotence, which differ in no essential way from similar feelings earlier in life but which occur this time within a different framework and with another kind of catalyst. His intense anger towards every frustrating agency can be minutely examined and shown to be the source of feelings of guilt, depression and unworthiness.

In one's approach to the individual psychotherapy, it is well to be mindful of the following representative comments:

> Too many physicians, nurses, and social workers have in the past allowed their sense of frustration at not being able to understand the aged to be projected as resentment against old people. Those of us who have worked with the aged know how challenging and stimulating this work can be, what wonderful patients old people are, how appreciative they are of small attentions, and what marvelous results modern medicine and surgery, as well as psychiatry, can achieve even in the highest age bracket.[29]

> Direct psychotherapy of older people is not so hopeless a task as was once thought. While the disturbances involving specific neurotic and psychotic manifestations require the intervention of the specialist in psychiatry, a large number of the emotional problems presented by these patients can be dealt with satisfactorily by the medical men.

> I find my work with the aged most instructive. The handling of their neurotic illnesses is fundamentally similar to the treatment of such neuroses in younger persons.[30]

> Psychoanalytic psychotherapy can definitely help the final task of self-acceptance.[31]

> Active psychotherapy is possible and can be successful in more than 50% of senile cases, even when shock therapy has been applied unsuccessfully.

> The treatment of neuropsychiatric disorders of the aged must be a community project in which neuropsychiatrists, internists, and social service workers must contribute materially to the maintenance and preservation of the physical and mental health of this group.[32]

> The therapeutic approach in the treatment of the aged is now as wide in its orientation as is the treatment of younger patients. The emphasis is directed to the prevention and the early therapy of psychiatric conditions as well as to the treatment of those disorders which have progressed to the point where the patients require hospitalization.[33]

> Though Sigmund Freud was pessimistic about psychoanalytic therapy with the elderly, it has proven recently to be quite successful.[34]

Meerloo's[35] method of analytic psychotherapy is exemplified by the following protocol:

> A 72-year-old bachelor [had] a syndrome of agitated melancholia after a gallbladder operation, the first disease in his life. He cannot sleep any more and he cannot stop crying. The slightest noise disturbs him. All

the steam-pipes of the central heating system are plotting against him. He begins to worry about his food, that it seems to contain poison. He cannot concentrate any longer on reading and he becomes impotent.

This man was sent to me for pyschotherapy after electro-shock treatment had made him more agitated, and institutional treatment seemed to be indicated. During his first interview, this highly intelligent man showed himself very *hostile* toward every form of medical treatment. All he wanted was to obtain sleeping drugs, which he did not get from me. He accused the surgeon and the shock-therapist of having caused his predicament. In the beginning he resented my questioning, because up to now nobody had bothered to question him about himself. During his whole life, our patient had been a stingy, compulsive man, financially responsible for his family in which mental and physical diseases were prevalent. He often had nightmares. Last night's dream, however, was a typical sex dream of women lying in his arms. In relating the dream he started to laugh for the first time, and readily admitted that he resented his physical illness and his weakness very much. He admitted that he used the surgeon as a convenient scapegoat.

We started an analytically oriented form of psychotherapy of two sessions a week. The payment roused the greatest resistance. He wanted to pay me only by sending some of his rich friends to me.

All in all, we saw each other 19 times in the course of 2½ months; then, grumbling about the final payment but much improved, he left me. Now, 3 years later, he is still in good shape. He reports to me from time to time.

During the period of therapy which started with a rather good interpersonal rapport, the nightly anxiety disappeared after the third session. The same thing happened in regard to the steam-pipe hallucinations which he began to explain not as a plot against him but as a result of his own over-sensitivity. He produced dreams at every session, which he started to interpret himself without intervention. So uppermost were they in his mind that some dreams pictured direct childhood memories; special anxieties made their appearance: anxiety about taxes, about food, about losing affection. Other anxieties involved the fear of blackmailing women, or of being eaten by a dog. There were repeated nightmares and feelings of suffocation.

In a later period his basic fear of nearing death came more clearly to the foreground. There was fear of sleeping-drugs—fear that they would not work too well or would kill him. His suitcase was stolen, as a magic defense against the last trip to nowhere. Let me report one dream precisely: "I was in the railroad station buying a ticket. There was not much time. The clerk stood on the same side as I stood, and gave me some change. I put it with the ticket in my side pocket. Will I find the ticket? Will I be able to catch the train? The loudspeaker voice called the passengers to track 999."

In an orthodox analysis, the attention would be directed more to specific symbolism. In this case I limited myself to letting the patient understand the general patterns. Track 999 was for him the last station of departure. He spontaneously interpreted the other part of the dream as his unwillingness to go. The clerk was the analyst selling him the certainty of an eventual trip he did not want to take.

In later dreams the girls forgave him his impotence. And in the last dreams he let other people jump out of the window. In the meantime he had been able to go back to work.

As far as his own anxiety feelings were concerned, he had made his own pact with death, and let other people go before him. Our transference relation was always, as he felt it, on a teacher-student basis. He, by producing unconscious material, was instructing me. After his cure he stuck to that notion and kept on sending me clippings from time to time.

The importance of this case lies in the therapist's role: indeed, he did play the part of a student. This role-taking freed the patient from his anxiety and hallucinatory distortions of reality. This situation was in contrast to what he felt had been an authoritarian intrusion by the surgeon and shock therapist into his illusion of longevity. As a matter of fact, this patient was a real teacher. He shared his own insight regarding the fallacies of old age. He was a sharp and witty observer and part of his experience has been used in this paper.

TRANSFERENCE AND COUNTERTRANSFERENCE

There are some technical points to consider in the psychotherapy of the elderly, which for purposes of exposition may be divided into transference and countertransference factors.

Linden,[36] in his extensive discussion of his concept of the transference in gerontologic group psychotherapy, has stated that there are three forms of actual transference in the aged: (1) neurotic transference, which is personality specific; (2) recession transference, which occurs concomitantly with physiologic regression; and (3) sociologic transference, which refers to feelings the aged as a quasiminority group have toward an outside culture that rejects them and the manner they transfer these counterattitudes to any culture representative. Linden believes that the transference attitudes of the aged are determined by restitutive phenomena, which, in turn, are determined by mechanisms utilized to manage masochism, recessive feelings, and counterreactions to the elder-discarding trends of our culture. Using clinical material, he describes 11 types and 7 subtypes of transference, along with speculations regarding their psychodynamics.

When older people who feel themselves lost in a hostile world are given time and shown patience by a therapist, a strong transference often results. The transference in therapy with the aged differs from that with children and younger adults because the therapist often is considerably younger than the patient and may represent for the patient not a parental figure but one of the patient's children, or frequently a combination of parental and filial images. There is no therapeutic indication to resolve the transference, according to Meerloo,[37] who has found that "even when the patients themselves ask for the dismissal signal of being called 'cured' it is better to let them come back from time to time, so that they may feel that contact is not lost." The same strategy is to be followed with patients seen in private practice.

On the other hand, Grotjahn[38] has stated:

> The most favorable transference situation in analytic treatment of the elderly is one which I call the "Reversed Oedipus Constellation." In my opinion it is necessary to allow the development of such transference situation, to experience it fully, to utilize it, to interpret it, and finally to dissolve it again and integrate the entire experience. It is possible, however, that the experience of this transference neurosis has to be much stronger and much more intensive than in the psychoanalysis of neurotics of younger age. This may constitute a principal difference between the psychoanalysis of a psychoneurosis and of an old age psychosis. Differently expressed, it could be considered an essential difference between working through and living through.
>
> The patient is allowed to see in the therapist the younger person. He may later accept in his therapist the representative of the younger generation and perhaps of the future. It was once the task of the son to work out his conscious and unconscious relations to his parents. It is now time for the father to go once more through his unconscious relation to another man in reversed order. In relation to the therapist, he has once more the chance and task to analyze in the transference relationship the Oedipus complex, but this time in reverse. The father should not submit to the son, nor should he kill him like the father of Oedipus tried to do. The father should realize that his life may be continued in his son.

Therapy with the elderly, as with any age group, involves the personality of the therapist and countertransference reactions. A young therapist may feel self-conscious and apologetic, while an old therapist may feel superior and exemplary. A thorough awareness of one's attitudes toward his parents, and even his grandparents, will assist the therapist in eschewing the complications which arise when the unconscious identifications, hostilities, guilts, and dominations of the therapist intrude and confuse the therapy. For example, the therapist may become anxious when the symbols of old age, typified by loneliness, helplessness, feebleness, and economic distress, arouse his deep-rooted, archaic castration anxieties and fears through an unconscious identification. When the therapist's narcissism is hurt by the irreversibility of some factors in his elderly patient's situation, he may react, out of a sense of frustration, with harshness, impatience, or even hostility, which, in their turn, may induce further complicating reactions in therapist and patient.

It has been suggested:[39]

> The therapist does not need to idealize his elderly patients. This would be unrealistic and is a defensive compensation against underlying

hostility. Such a therapist may offer himself as a submissive child looking up to his patients as parental images. He expects them to be strong, powerful parental figures which they neither are nor should be. A therapeutic attitude based on such unconscious expectations does not help the confused, insecure old person who looks for the stronger, younger, healthier person with whom he can identify and who may satisfy some dependency needs.

Many different variations of countertransference difficulties may be observed. A therapist who wishes to be older than he is may hide unresolved sexual conflicts behind such a wish. He hopes in an unrealistic way that the old persons will live beyond sin and sex, like little angels. Such a therapist may not be tolerant and realistic enough to understand his elderly patients in one of their most important sources of conflict, guilt and depression.

Most therapists are agreed that if there ever is a time when sexual information and advice are needed, it is when people reach old age, because the sexual feelings of the elderly create a confusion which is often compounded when countertransference denies sexual gratification to the old. The therapist has to work these feelings through with his elder patients, who are often so frightened and ashamed to reveal them that enforced abstinence and increased guilt predispose to an intensified depression. Meerloo[40] comments:

> The study of sexual problems in the old-aged has only just begun. Superficially it appears as if there were less demand in this age group. However, in deeper analysis we find that under an apparently tranquil surface there may lie a sleeping volcano full of underground turmoil.

The good son-therapist should not feel guilty for being younger. An almost paternal attitude may be developed, if necessary; but above all the therapist must be secure enough to deal with the older patient's hostility and with his efforts to make the younger man feel guilty and defensive for being younger. Ideally, the therapist who has resolved his unconscious feelings of guilt and ambivalence toward his own parents will not be overbearing, patronizing, idealizing, or avenging, but will be able to "offer himself quietly and calmly in order to repeat and analyze the reversed Oedipus situation as a therapeutic experience." [41]

SUMMARY

This review of the management of elderly psychiatric patients by primarily psychotherapeutic methods indicates that any aura of therapeutic nihilism in regard to this increasing patient population is unjustified.

REFERENCES

1. J. A. Meerloo, "Transference and Resistance in Geriatric Psychotherapy," *Psychoanal. Rev.*, 42:72-82, 1955.
2. M. Gitelson, "The Emotional Problems of Elderly People," *Geriatrics*, 3:135-150, 1948.
3. F. J. Kallman and G. Sander, "Twin Studies on enescence," *Am. J. Psychiat.*, 106:29-36, 1949.
4. M. Ross, "Some Psychiatric Aspects of Senescence: A Review of the Literature," *Psychiat. Quart.*, 28:93-112, 1954; "Current Treatment of the Emotional Problems of Elderly People," *Geriatrics*, 12:603-606, 1957.
5. M. Ross, "Current Treatment of the Emotional Problems of Elderly People," *loc. cit.*; D. Rothschild and M. L. Sharp, "Origins of Senile Psychosis," *Dis. Nerv. Syst.*, 2:49, 1941, D. Rothschild, "Neuropathologic Changes in Arteriosclerotic Psychoses and Their Psychiatric Significance," *Arch. Neurol. & Psychiat.*, 48:417-436, 1942.
6. B. J. Alpers, F. M. Forster, and P. A. Herbert, "Retinal, Cerebral, and Systematic Arteriosclerosis: Histopathologic Study," *Arch. Neurol. & Psychiat.*, 60:440-456, 1948.
7. J. D. Lichtenberg, "A Study of the Changing Role of the Psychiatrist in the State Hospital," *Psychiat. Quart.*, 28:428-441, 1954.
8. *Ibid.*
9. J. J. Geller, "Proposed Plan for Institutionalized Group Psychotherapy," *Psychiat. Quart., Suppl.* 24, pp. 270-277, 1950; discussion by D. Corcoran, p. 275.
10. A. Silver, "Group Psychotherapy with Senile Psychotic Patients," *Geriatrics*, 5:147-150, 1950.
11. K. Wolff, "Group Psychotherapy with Geriatric Patients in a Mental Hospital," *J. Am. Geriatrics Soc.*, 5:13-19, 1957.
12. *Ibid.*
13. M. E. Linden, "Group Psychotherapy with Institutionalized Senile Women: II. Study in Gerontologic Human Relations," *Int. J. Group Psychother.*, 13:150-170, 1953; "The Significance of Dual Leadership in Gerontologic Group Psychotherapy: III. Studies in Gerontologic Human Relations," *Int. J. Group Psychother.*, 4:262-273, 1954; "Transference in Gerontologic Group Psychotherapy: IV. Studies in Gerontologic Human Relations," *Int. J. Group Psychother.*, 5:61-79, 1955; "Geriatrics," in S. R. Slavson (ed.), *The Field of Group Psychotherapy* (New York: International Universities Press, 1956), pp. 129-151.
14. Linden, "The Significance of Dual Leadership in Gerontologic Group Psychotherapy: III. Studies in Gerontologic Human Relations," *loc. cit.*
15. *Ibid.*
16. P. C. Rond, "The Day Hospital Unit—Milieu Therapy, Its Place in the Treatment of the Mentally Ill," *Ohio Med. J.*, 49:1093-1096, 1953.
17. A. I. Goldfarb, "Psychotherapy of Aged Persons: I. The Orientation of Staff in a Home for the Aged," *Ment. Hyg.*, 37:76-83, 1953; A. I. Goldfarb and H. Turner, "Psychotherapy of Aged Persons: II. Utilization and Ef-

fectiveness of 'Brief' Therapy," *Am. J. Psychiat.*, 109:916-921, 1953; A. I. Goldfarb, "Recommendations for Psychiatric Care in a Home for the Aged," *J. Gerontol.*, 8:343-347, 1953; A. I. Goldfarb and J. Sheps, "Psychotherapy of the Aged: III. Brief Therapy of Interrelated Psychological and Somatic Disorders," *Psychosom. Med.*, 16:209-219, 1954; A. I. Goldfarb, "Psychotherapy of Aged Persons: IV. One Aspect of the Psychodynamics of the Therapeutic Situation with Aged Patients," *Psychoanalyt. Rev.*, 42:180-187, 1955; "Psychiatric Problems of Old Age," *New York J. Med.*, 55:494-501, 1955; "The Rationale for Psychotherapy with Older Persons," *Am. J. M. Sc.*, 232:181-185, 1956; "Psychotherapy of the Aged: The Use and Value of an Adaptational Frame of Reference," *Psychoanalyt. Rev.*, 43:68-81, 1956; "Contributions of Psychiatry to the Institutional Care of Aged and Chronically Ill Persons," *J. Chron. Dis.*, 6:483-496, 1957.

18. D. E. Cameron, "The Day Hospital: An Experimental Form of Hospitalization for Psychiatric Patients," *Mod. Hosp.*, 69:60-62, 1947.

19. L. Z. Cozin, "The Day Hospital," *Lancet*, 2:204-205, 1953; "The Place of the Day Hospital in the Geriatric Unit," *Practitioner*, 172:552-559, 1954; "The Place of the Day Hospital in the Geriatric Unit," *Int. J. Soc. Psychiat.*, 1:33-41, 1955.

20. Rond, *op. cit.*

21. *Ibid.*

22. K. Abraham, "The Applicability of Psychoanalytic Treatment to Patients at an Advanced Age," in *Selected Papers*, trans. D. Bryan and A. Strachey (London: Hogarth Press, 1948), pp. 312-317.

23. F. J. Braceland and J. Donnelly, "Early Detection of Emotional Disorders of Old Age," *J. Oklahoma M. A.*, 47:33-37, 1954; J. Donnelly, "Psychiatric Therapy in the Geriatric Patient," *J. Am. Geriatrics Soc.*, 2:655,661, 1954; V. Norris and F. Post, "Treatment of Elderly Psychiatric Patients: Use of a Diagnostic Classification," *Brit. M. J.*, 1:675-679, 1954; F. Post, "Mental Disorders in Old Age: Differential Diagnosis and Management," *M. Press*, 238:177-180, 1957.

24. See note 17.

25. A. I. Goldfarb and J. Sheps, "Psychotherapy of the Aged: III. Brief Therapy of Interrelated Psychological and Somatic Disorders," *loc. cit.*

26. G. J. Wayne, "Psychotherapy in Senescence," *Am. West. Med. & Surg.*, 6:88-91, 1952; "Modified Psychoanalytic Therapy in Senescence," *Psychoanalyt. Rev.*, 40:99-116, 1953.

27. Wayne, "Modified Psychoanalytic Therapy in Senescence," *loc. cit.*

28. Wayne, "Psychotherapy in Senescence," *loc. cit.*

29. F. D. Zeman, "Constructive Programs for the Mental Health of the Elderly," *Ment. Hyg.*, 35:221-234, 1951.

30. Wayne, "Modified Psychoanalytic Therapy in Senescence," *loc. cit.*

31. M. Grotjahn, "Analytic Psychotherapy with the Elderly," *Psychoanalyt. Rev.*, 42:419-427, 1955.

32. Meerloo, *op. cit.*

33. I. J. Sands, "The Neuropsychiatric Disorders of the Aged," *New York J. Med.*, 51:2370-2375, 1951.

34. Donnelly, *op. cit.*

35. Grotjahn, *op. cit.*
36. Meerloo, *op. cit.*; "Psychotherapy with Elderly People," *Geriatrics*, 10:583-587, 1955.
37. Linden, "Tranference in Gerontologic Group Psychotherapy: IV. Studies in Gerontologic Human Relations," *loc. cit.*
38. Meerloo, "Transference and Resistance in Geriatric Psychotherapy," *loc. cit.*
39. Grotjahn, *op. cit.*
40. Meerloo, "Transference and Resistance in Geriatric Psychotherapy," *loc. cit.*
41. Grotjahn, *op. cit.*

GROUP THERAPY OF ALCOHOLICS
WITH CONCURRENT GROUP MEETINGS
OF THEIR WIVES

Lester H. Gliedman
David Rosenthal
Jerome D. Frank
Helen T. Nash

The question of what can be done for the alcoholic has recently received increasing and well-deserved attention. The extent of alcoholism and the personal, familial, and community effects of this disease need no elaboration. The therapeutic challenge is a great one and only a beginning has been made toward meeting it. One of the more frequently employed ways of dealing with this illness has been by means of group therapy. The popularity of this form of treatment reflects not only the rising application of the group approach to many types of emotional illness but also the success of Alcoholics Anonymous. Not only has this lay organization transformed the outlook for many alcoholics from one of despair to one of hope, but it has demonstrated the therapeutic value of the group in their recovery.

To study the value of the group in a psychiatric setting, an exploratory project in this type of treatment of alcoholics has been in progress in the Outpatient Department of the Henry Phipps Psychiatric Clinic of the Johns Hopkins Hospital for the past 18 months. This project was limited to married male alcoholics whose wives would participate in concurrent but separately conducted discussion meetings.

Previous experience in the treatment of alcoholism had led us to believe that inclusion of the family in the recovery process of these patients

Reprinted from the *Quarterly Journal of Studies on Alcohol*, Vol. 17, No. 4, December 1956, pp. 655-670.

would be desirable. Where antisocial actions constitute the major part of the presenting picture of an illness, these are often directed against a specific target, i.e. a particular person, object, group, or relationship, because of an underlying emotional disturbance. In married alcoholics, the actions center on drinking behavior and the target is most often the wife. Therefore, both the alcoholic and his wife were included in this attempt to gain better understanding of the underlying emotional disturbance as well as the relationship between the alcoholic and the person who is most frequently the object and the stimulus of the drinking behavior.

Two other considerations prompted the decision to involve both the patients and their wives. (*a*) It was thought that this might attract couples with high motivation for therapy in both partners and that the wife's acceptance of some responsibility for the treatment would enhance the patient's motivation and help sustain him through a course of therapy. (*b*) It was felt that systematically obtained information from both partners might provide a check on the validity of information received from each.

The general plan was first to describe the patients and their marriages by several measures and next, after thus spelling out the task confronting therapy, to estimate how effectively this was met by group treatment.

PROCEDURE

Considerable difficulty was experienced in obtaining patients for this study. Of 45 couples contacted, only nine accepted treatment and appeared for processing. This points to a frequently made observation that alcoholic patients are often not motivated to accept psychiatrically or medically sponsored treatment, even when a departure from traditional approaches is offered. At any rate, the patients in the present study constitute a highly selected sample and the results must be considered in this light.

Each of the nine patients who kept appointments for treatment had some current, compelling reason for doing so—such as pressure from the wife, threatened loss of job, marked deterioration of financial status, or varying combinations of these. Though these circumstances may be thought of as forms of coercion, they at least pointed to the fact that these patients were accessible to external influence.

The Evaluation Process

The nine patients and their wives were evaluated before and after treatment by four measures: a drinking checklist, a symptom checklist, an adjective checklist, and a social ineffectiveness scale. Patients and wives were interviewed separately.

The drinking checklist consists of 29 items describing characteristics of pathological drinking which can be rated in terms of 4 degrees of severity, and was derived in part from Seliger[1] and in part from Jellinek.[2] Each patient and his wife separately completed this form as it pertained to the patient's current drinking.

The symptom checklist is a modification of the Cornell Index[3] and consists of 33 distressing symptoms of a psychological nature which are rated on a 4-point scale of severity. These symptoms can be grouped into several subscales: anxiety; depression; irritability; obsession-compulsion phobia; and paranoid-schizoid traits. Each patient and his wife rated the patient's symptoms on the basis of how the patient currently felt.

The adjective checklist, specially designed for this investigation, is made up of 52 adjectives that have been commonly applied to alcoholics. Five judges were able to divide these into two groups. One group implies something good, complimentary, rewarding, or satisfying. The other group implies something bad, critical, unrewarding, or dissatisfying. For example, adjectives such as mature, close, trusting, would fall in the former category, while bragging, nagging, and deceitful would be classified in the latter. Each patient was requested to select those adjectives which described him when sober and when intoxicated. He was asked also to describe his wife with these adjectives as she appeared to him when he was sober and when he was intoxicated. Each wife was requested to describe herself with these adjectives when her husband, the patient, was sober, and again when he was intoxicated. Likewise, she was asked to select those adjectives which she thought described her husband when he was sober and when he was intoxicated. By means of the adjectives selected, and the group in which they fell, it was possible to characterize the satisfaction or dissatisfaction associated with sobriety and intoxication, and the satisfaction or dissatisfaction associated with the marriage when the patient was sober or intoxicated.

The social ineffectiveness scale is made up of 15 categories of interpersonal ineffectiveness which were operationally defined and rated on a 5-point scale of severity, based on the inappropriateness and frequency of these behaviors as they occurred in relation to the various significant persons in the patient's current life. The categories are: overly independent; superficially social; extrapunitive; officious; impulsive; hyperreactive; overly systematic; overly dependent; withdrawn; intrapunitive; irresponsible; overcautious; constrained; unsystematic; sexually maladjusted. The rating of social ineffectiveness and its rationale are discussed by Parloff, Kelman, and Frank.[4] Husband and wife were rated on this scale following a structured psychiatric interview of each. This interview emphasized present as opposed to past interpersonal functioning.

As a result of these procedures, it was possible to estimate each patient's current drinking severity, psychological discomfort, interpersonal ineffectiveness, and satisfaction or dissatisfaction derived from sobriety and intoxication. For each wife, it was possible to estimate her present interpersonal ineffectiveness and her satisfaction or dissatisfaction when the patient was sober and intoxicated. For each couple, it was possible to describe the current satisfaction or dissatisfaction of the marriage when drinking occurred and when it did not. Since each of these measures was completed and scored before and after group therapy, the effects of treatment on each could be examined not only clinically but statistically as well.

Preparation for Therapy

Following completion of the initial evaluative procedures each patient and wife were oriented with regard to the forthcoming group sessions. The routine aspects of the program were stressed, such as frequency and duration of meetings; length of treatment; place; billing; procedure for cancellation of visits; absences; the fact that meetings would be recorded and the reasons for this; the purpose of the observer who would be present; and the confidentiality of the proceedings. All of the participants were informed that they need talk about themselves only as they saw fit, but that it would be through the medium of their experiences, especially current ones, that they could be helped and possibly help others. The patients were told that medications were available and would be employed as necessary, that is, to help them when they needed help. The role of the therapist, as both a member and leader of the group and as a resource person, was outlined. The parallels between the projected group sessions and their life situations were emphasized so that the rationale for group therapy would be more apparent. The patients were informed that their wives were to be involved in concurrent but separate discussion sessions to broaden the base for recovery by insuring that both marital partners would better understand the nature of the patient's alcoholism and have a share in its amelioration. This was also made explicit to the wives.

In addition, the patients and their wives were told that alcoholism was a disease in which the goal of treatment was total abstinence; that though the aim is to help the patient stop drinking, the term "illness" implies a certain progression of events which the patient may not be able at all times to control, any more than a person even with a well-regulated chronic disease can avoid periodic exacerbation; that there is little or no place for such things as condemnation and threats in the treatment of any sickness, medical or psychological; and that though it was preferable for the patients to attend the treatment sessions while sober, it was expected that this would not always be possible and, therefore, they should plan to be present regardless of condition. This last policy was adopted because it was strongly felt that sick patients should not be turned away at a time when their need for treatment was greatest. All were informed that individual therapy sessions were available if needed. The essence of the above information was mimeographed on sheets which were given to each patient and his wife and was repeated again in the early group sessions.

The last part of the interview was devoted to determining what were the most convenient times for the meetings. From this, two 1½-hour sessions per week were arranged for the patients and one weekly session for the wives. The particular nights and hours scheduled were those which the participants themselves selected, even though the administrative problems raised by this were considerable. It was planned to see the patients twice as often as their wives because of Greenbaum's[5] finding that group therapy with alcoholics was more effective at twice weekly than at weekly intervals and to differentiate between the programs for the patients and the wives. To categorize the participation of the wives as treatment and as identical with that of the patients seemed unwarranted and at the same time likely to increase the possibility of the wives being uncooperative. To help distinguish between the two programs, it was planned that the wives would have a nonphysician female leader.

Description of Therapy

The therapeutic orientation was analytic in a limited sense, stressing the need to keep anxiety with its known disastrous results from overwhelming these patients. Use was made of methods of controlling such tension in therapy as have been reported by Bordin.[6] To this end, the sessions were somewhat structured, although no prearranged topics were employed as discussion guides. The structuring developed out of the ongoing activity in each meeting. Direct requests by the patient for information and advice were more frequently satisfied than is usual in analytically oriented group psychotherapy. Interpersonal transactions of one patient with another were analyzed only rarely, while those described by a patient as going on between himself and persons outside the group, including his wife, usually were. This permitted the discussion of important psychological issues in a less anxiety-arousing context. Medication was used when the patients described situations which required it. The drugs employed were reserpine, dexedrine, mephenesin, antihistamines, and vitamins. These were used more frequently early in treatment and served as a further means of controlling tension in the patients and enabling them to stay in the treatment program.

As therapy progressed, the group therapist became impressed by these patients' preoccupation with the temporal present. They seemed especially insulated from their own past experiences and peculiarly unable to project into the future. They appeared to operate more in the "here and now" than other groups of patients. Because of this, a deliberate attempt was made to bring the past into the present by having patients review their previous alcoholic outbursts in detail, with the hope that this might function as a deterrent to current drinking. Likewise, attempts were made to rehearse for the future and to cultivate planfulness by discussion of impending life problems. An account of the temporal orientation in alcoholics has been presented elsewhere by Gliedman.[7]

An additional observation in the group therapy sessions was the hypersensitivity of the patients to depressive feelings and the rapidity with which they experienced them. Specifically, in the group interplay, one or more of the members involved, usually the relatively inactive ones who were less in the therapist's attention, silently recoiled from the proceedings. As time passed, it was apparent that these patients were feeling depressed, let down, inadequate, and hurt following such engagements. This came to our attention by the return of such members to subsequent meetings in an intoxicated state or through their reports of intoxication after these meetings. It was therefore necessary, in the later sessions, to take steps to support the less active participants in the meetings, and especially the silent ones, by rephrasing the matter being discussed to include the possibility of viewpoints other than those of the active participants, or by controlling monopolizers of the meetings. In short, the therapist intervened more frequently and was more supportive than with other patients.

The wives group functioned more like the usual analytically oriented therapy group. Though they were highly defensive and found a common rallying topic in criticism of their husbands, still much of the discussion tended to be about themselves. Such intimate topics as sexual frigidity were profitably discussed, and helpful interpersonal exchanges with other group members occurred. In contrast to the preoccupation of the patients with the temporal present, the wives were concerned with the future and the past. If they felt attacked, they did not react by silence and depressiveness, as their husbands tended to do, but instead retaliated actively and often overcommitted themselves in the expression of their attitudes. Therefore, an important consideration of the group leader was to keep the wives from such overcommitment by rephrasing their expressed points of view in such a way that a subsequent modification of attitude would not be construed as a loss of face. Frequent interventions of this sort were required. The marital relationship was discussed often, the wives usually maintaining that even when their husbands were sober the marriages were lacking in important aspects. Although initially the discussion sessions were not viewed by the wives as treatment, they tended to use the meetings not only to participate in the recovery of the husbands but as therapy for their own problems. This was an outgrowth of their inability to reconcile their constant criticism of their husbands with the many years they had endured the unhappy state of affairs.

A total of 32 sessions was planned for the patients and 16 for the wives. When these were completed, the program was stopped and each couple was studied again.

RESULTS

A total of 9 couples was processed initially. The patients' attendance ranged from 4 to 26 meetings; 4 attended 20 or more sessions. Two patients dropped out of treatment and their final processing was not possible. The attendance of the wives ranged from 1 to 15 meetings; 4 attended 12 or more sessions. One wife dropped out of the program and was not available for re-evaluation. Complete data are therefore available on 9 couples initially but only on 7 finally.

General Description of Subjects

All the patients tended to recognize alcoholism as their main problem. Table 1 itemizes some relevant characteristics of the nine patients and their wives prior to treatment. It makes clear that this is a seriously ill group of patients, currently ambulatory and employed, for whom heavy drinking had become, in a sense, a way of life. In recent years the drinking was becoming worse. They came to treatment only under duress, largely at the insistence of their wives. The wives appeared better organized than their husbands, had slightly more education, and were the main force

Table 40–1   General Characteristics of Nine Patients and Their Wives Prior to Treatment

	Patients	Wives
Age, years, average	41	40
Age range, years	27-54	27-54
Education level, grade	10	12
Duration of alcoholism, years		
16-20	4	—
10-15	2	—
5-9	2	—
3-4	1	—
Course of alcoholism during previous year		
Improving	0	—
Worsening	6	—
Fluctuating	3	—
Stationary	0	—
Previous hospitalization for mental complications of alcoholism	3	—
Previous hospitalization for physical complications of alcoholism	3	—
Reported physical complications of alcoholism	6	—
Arrests for intoxication	6	—
History of alcoholism in antecedents	6	1
Disturbing childhood experiences	6	0
History of other emotional illness	0	1
Previous psychotherapy	2	1
Previous Alcoholics Anonymous membership	4	—
Currently employed	7	6
Active desire to enter combined treatment program	0	7
Active pressure from wife to enter treatment program	5	—

holding the families together. Almost all of them held full-time or part-time jobs to insure a dependable source of income.

Table 2 lists some characteristics of the patients' marriages. In most instances the initiative for the marriage rested with the woman, who usually had desired marriage for reasons other than the man's attractiveness. The women seemed to have been aware of their prospective husbands' excessive drinking so that the marriages tended to be incidents in a drinking career that already had started. The course of the marriages was stormy and the patients' alcoholism became increasingly worse. Currently the marriages were battlegrounds, and the family life was so organized that everything tended to be viewed as having or not having an effect on the patients' drinking.

Table 40–2   General Characteristics of Marriages of the Nine Couples Prior to Treatment

Duration, years, average (and range)	14(1-35)
Excessive drinking of patients before marriage	7
Ulterior motivation of wives for marriage	6
Previous marriages of wives	3
Previous marriages of patients	0
Childless marriages	3
Sexual maladjustment	8
Separations during present marriages	9
Currently reported "happy" marriages	0
Total organization of family about alcoholism	9
Nondrinking (totally abstinent) wives	6

Initial Description of Patients on Scales

The seriousness of the patients' drinking was reflected on the drinking checklist. The wives' ratings agreed with those of the patients, except that the wives rated the patients as significantly more violent when intoxicated than the patients scored themselves ($P < .05$).

Though the patients did not appear so clinically, the symptom checklist revealed high scores in the areas indicative of depressiveness and irritability. The wives agreed with these findings but saw the patients as even more irritable than the patients saw themselves ($P < .05$) and also rated them as higher in the paranoid-schizoid spectrum of symptoms ($P < .05$) than the patients scored themselves.

Interpersonally, as indicated on the social ineffectiveness scale, the patients were rated as very ineffective. The wives also scored high on this scale but less than the patients in every instance. The wives consistently rated the patients as more ineffective than the interviews with the patients alone indicated. A translation of this scale into clinical terms reveals that the patients socialized in a very limited, impersonal fashion. They related to people in a stereotyped, shallow, cliché-ridden manner, with a paucity of the shared, deeper feelings, and often knew no way of participating in closer interpersonal relationships without alcohol. They were impulsive and labile, frequently finding themselves propelled into situations beyond their depth. In such states, they either overreacted or did not react at all. They were unreliable and unpredictable, excessive drinking being only one aspect of this trait. They were dependent and, at the same time, fought against those on whom they depended. Ambivalence characterized much of their behavior. Their sexual life was quite unsatisfactory.

The wives were highly opinionated, forceful, openly critical of their husbands, and given to manipulations of one sort or another presumably to control their husbands' drinking and to stabilize the family life. Though they were capable of closer interpersonal relationships, their husbands' drinking had narrowed this activity. There was a high degree of sexual frigidity which was acknowledged without great difficulty. They used sex as a bargaining weapon for the husbands' maintenance of sobriety. Nevertheless, they had good work records and ran their homes in an orderly, responsible manner. Where there were children, the wives reacted to the patients more as if they were uncontrollable offspring than marital partners. It is emphasized that this was the presenting picture at the start of treatment, when the patients' alcoholism had created such a crisis as to obscure most of the more positive aspects of the functioning of each marital partner.

In spite of the rather dismal picture reflected by the ineffectiveness scale, the adjectives selected by the patients to describe themselves in the sober and intoxicated states revealed that they received much more satisfaction from sobriety than from intoxication. Only two patients indicated the reverse. The wives, however, in contrast to their outspoken, positive characteristics as evaluated on the ineffectiveness scale, revealed ambivalence toward themselves on the adjective checklist both when their husbands were drinking and when they were sober. This ambivalence was greater, however, when the patient was intoxicated.

Seven of the patients described their wives with adjectives which implied that they were satisfied with their marital state when sober. This is just the opposite of the implications that might be drawn from the adjectives selected by the wives to describe the patients when sober. Six of the wives viewed their marital state as unsatisfactory. However, during the patients' intoxication each partner was markedly dissatisfied with the other, except one wife who described her husband in the intoxicated state in such a way as to imply that she was receiving some satisfactions from his drinking.

Description of the Patients Following Treatment

Because of the drop-outs, only seven couples could be evaluated after treatment. The two patients who discontinued treatment seemed to do so because of events in group therapy. One was a silent member; the other was repeatedly involved with a more active, more psychologically sophisticated patient but in such a manner as to be placed in a relatively inactive, passive role. Both might have remained in therapy had earlier cognizance been taken of the implications of their behavior on their status in the group. One, after a session in which he suffered what in retrospect was not just an exchange of views but an interpersonal defeat, though it did not seem so at the time, kept returning to the group meetings in an intoxicated state. Then, while drunk, he would reply to the patient with whom he was involved in the prior meeting. He finally left, presumably after obtaining a job which precluded his attendance. His wife, who continued to attend the wives' discussion sessions until their completion, reported that he was furious following his encounters in the group with this patient, but continued in treatment at her insistence for a total of ten sessions. According to her, he then stopped drinking and obtained a job so that he could announce this to the group as his reason for quitting and thereby show up the other patient whose alcoholism was unchecked. She stated that he remained sober and working until two months later, when she was re-evaluated, after which he resumed drinking excessively. The second drop-out was never actively involved in the group but obviously was reacting to it. Treating him as one would a silent patient in a neurotic group probably was important in his termination of treatment. Instead, attempts should have been made to elicit his participation, at least by acknowledging that though he was silent his unexpressed and possibly different feelings and attitudes were just as worthy of consideration as those of the more vocal group members.

The seven couples who could be evaluated before and after treatment showed several changes in each of the measures employed. On the drinking checklist, five of the seven patients improved. Two were totally abstinent, two reduced the frequency of their drinking by half or more, and one only slightly. One pretreatment monthy liquor bill of approximately $350 was decreased to $40. In general, the drinking expenditure of each patient was decreased and represented a realiable index of improvement. Though the wives generally acknowledged the patients' improved status with regard to less drinking and less expenditure for liquor, if a patient did any drinking at all she tended to rate the effects of this drinking at the time of final evaluation just as she did prior to treatment. The difference between the patients' pre- and post-treatment scores on the drinking checklist bordered on a level of acceptable statistical significance $(P > .05 < .10)$. The difference between the preliminary and final scores of the wives' ratings was not statistically significant.

The symptom checklist scores showed moderate decreases in five of the seven patients. Two of the patients who showed improvement in their drinking behavior showed a small increase in psychological symptoms after treatment. On the subscales of this checklist, however, the patients as a group showed statistically significant decreases in depressiveness $(P < .05)$ and irritability $(P < .01)$. The wives agreed with this and also reported a statistically significant reduction in the patients' paranoid-schizoid symptoms $(P < .05)$.

Other than the changes in drinking, there were only slight modifications in social ineffectiveness. Interpersonally, the patients and their wives continued to operate in a manner not much different from that which prevailed before the onset of the group program. More than half of the couples, however, showed improvement in sexual adjustment. More than half of the wives showed slight increases in intrapunitiveness—a reflection of the fact that they eventually came to see themselves as sharing to some degree the responsibility for the patients' excessive drinking.

Statistically significant changes on the adjective checklist revealed that sobriety became more satisfying to the patients $(P < .02)$ than it was before treatment. The wives, however, tended to describe themselves in an ambivalent fashion, just as they did initially. In addition, the patients under the condition "sober" described their wives with significantly more of the satisfying adjectives than initially $(P < .01)$ and the wives described the patients similarly $(P < .05)$. This suggests an improved outlook with regard to marital status.

The above changes are not statistically related to the duration or intensity of the patients' alcoholism. They do bear a significant relationship to the initial descriptions of the patient when intoxicated. Those patients who did not improve or improved only slightly were the ones whose adjective checklist descriptions under the condition "intoxicated" showed the most disagreement with their wives' description of them under the same condition. The greater discrepancies resulted primarily from patients having selected adjectives denoting satisfaction to describe themselves during intoxication, while the wives selected the opposite. To a lesser degree, a minority of the wives initially selected some adjectives denoting satisfaction with their hunbands in the intoxicated state, while the patients selected the opposite adjectives in so describing themselves. Had both the patients and their wives selected adjectives indicative of satisfaction derived from the patients' intoxication, it is unlikely that they would have entered into treatment.

DISCUSSION

The four measures employed defined the challenge facing group therapy. They indicated that this was a chronic and severely alcoholic population, with marked symptoms of depressiveness and irritability; severe interpersonal ineffectiveness characterized by extreme, ambivalent behavior;

and much marital dissatisfaction. What did the group form of treatment have to offer?

The changes which took place fall into a certain hierarchy that is suggestive of the value of group therapy in this illness. The greatest changes were in the areas of marital milieu (satisfaction of patient and wife with each other) and personal morale (satisfaction with self). The next largest change was recorded in psychological symptoms, especially in irritability and depressiveness. Fewer, though important, changes took place in drinking behavior, and the least change occurred in social ineffectiveness. If the first three of these are accepted as components of what is known as self-esteem, it seems clear that the major contribution of the group program was in this area. It emphasized that despite the patients' facade to the contrary, this particular group of alcoholics was characterized by troubles in this area. As a group, they tended to be demoralized prior to therapy, most clearly demonstrated by those symptoms indicating depressiveness which were characteristic of all the patients. This is to be distinguished from the syndrome of depression. These patients are not clinically depressed. However, their tolerance for the feelings of depressiveness appears to be low. They seem to be highly sensitive to the experiences of defeat, failure, and inadequacy for which their psychological make-up, especially their propensity to live as if there were no yesterday or tomorrow, predisposes them. Such feelings are less likely to be cushioned by the knowledge of having effectively dealt with them in the past or by the expectations of having another opportunity in the future to manage better the events responsible for them. The depressiveness of the hang-over state may well represent these feelings in pure culture.

In any event, it is tempting to speculate that the need to cope with depressiveness, lowered morale, or feelings of damaged self-esteem in general, is one of the more important motivations for excessive drinking. It is with regard to these feelings that the group seems to make its special contribution in the treatment of alcoholism. The group can accomplish this for several reasons. Firstly, it provides a controlled milieu in which alcoholics may use one of their major interpersonal resources, superficial sociability, without having it threatened; or they can try to improve this technique of relating and to experiment with other techniques. The opportunity to socialize in a manner for which they are equipped is valuable in itself. It enables them to continue having esteem-enhancing experiences similar to those achieved in the past, yet at the same time they are made aware that these are not the maximum of which they are capable.

Secondly, in a group the patients can take treatment at their own pace. They can participate psychologically as desired or withdraw psychologically if needed while still being physically present. Again, this has the effect of decreasing the threatening aspects of treatment.

Thirdly, an all-alcoholic group fosters mutual identification and support, which ordinarily is difficult for these patients to achieve. Usually, they are so preoccupied with their own crises that they are insulated from many available healthful influences. In a group, they can be encouraged more readily or even pulled up by the bootstraps of a fellow alcoholic's successes.

Fourthly, the alcoholic's preoccupation with the temporal present is more readily modified in the group situation. The "here and now" orientation of a member may be expanded by the presence of other patients who share this orientation but not quite to the same degree. In a group, therefore, more can take place that falls within the optimal communication range of these patients while still affording the opportunity of a different and potentially healthier experience.

Finally, the group tends to dilute the transference reactions so that the strong, often esteem-damaging, drink-precipitating feelings for which these patients are notorious are more comfortably controlled and more likely to be faced. In other words, the group maximizes the conditions for the more optimal functioning of alcoholics in a treatment situation, while minimizing the occasions for realization of their worst potentialities. This enhances morale or self-esteem by creating a nonthreatening, supportive, socially rewarding, flexible, yet challenging atmosphere which is within the patient's range of capabilities, so that a desired goal, sobriety, is perceived as attainable.

The involvement of the wives added a very special value to this program. The patients and their wives were both implicated materially in the pathological drinking. In fact, the wives constituted the major pressure which forced the patients into treatment. It was almost as if the patients as a group had the pathological sign, while the wives experienced the suffering. Considered in this way, the family unit was the patient and properly the focus of the therapeutic effort.

There seemed to be other advantages in having concurrent groups for the patients and their wives. The procedure had the effect of emphasizing the marriage and other related psychological factors which play an important role in alcoholism, without requiring special therapeutic tactics to accomplish this. For immature individuals such as these couples, setting the proper therapeutic task, especially in a more or less automatic, nonverbal manner, was a major accomplishment. It enabled them to know what was expected and served as a constant frame of reference within which the therapy proceeded. The fact that the two groups did not meet together provided the needed privacy for consideration of the very conflict-laden marital situation. Again, with both members of the couple in the program, coming into treatment was less likely to be construed as an admission of guilt or to be used as a weapon than if only one of the pair were involved.

The use of the adjective checklist as a means of describing the marital status and observing the changes which occur in it proved quite fruitful. In the future it may be used to fit other situations where the family rather than one of its members is the treatment unit. It also seems potentially valuable as a means of penetrating the obscuring features of the alcoholic crises and estimating the healthful motivation some of the patients may have. In the present study, it revealed that sobriety was satisfying enough for several of the patients to want more of it, while intoxication was sufficiently dissatisfying to act as an important spur to change.

Not only this, but satisfactions obtained during intoxication were related to lack of improvement. These satisfactions from intoxication could be experienced either by the patient or by his wife. This finding corroborates a frequently expressed opinion that when either partner has a stake in the patient's drinking, the prognosis is less favorable. The value of the adjective checklist arises precisely from the fact that this information is not readily available when alcoholics are first seen. On the surface, alcoholics may look very much alike. In addition, they tend to elicit hostile reactions from those trying to help them because the nature of drunkenness is such that it usually is responded to as something offensive or immoral. Regardless of the reasons for this, the effect is to hide not only many of the healthier characteristics of these patients but the unhealthier ones as well. The checklist is an attempt to gain a better evaluation of these patients in spite of their pathological drinking and in spite of the prevailing attitudes on intoxication. It is in process of further exploration as a means of estimating motivation, but the small number of patients and the need for follow-up studies make additional generalization unwarranted at present.

The present investigation also serves to highlight another finding. Each of the patients entered treatment unwillingly. Traditionally, this has been considered antitherapeutic. Yet the changes obtained in this limited study would seem to indicate otherwise. It may be that the adverse effects are dissipated if the source of the pressure to enter therapy is also included in the treatment program. Implicit in the participation of the wives may be their tacit recognition of their own need to change. This may not only lessen many of the esteem-damaging implications perceived by the patients as associated with coming into treatment, but may also represent a constructive, hopeful attitude on the part of both.

SUMMARY

Nine married male alcoholics took part in a group therapy program that included parallel but separate group discussion meetings of their wives. The preparation for therapy and the nature of the specific group treatment offered have been described. The patients' initial status and their progress were described by four scales. These scales highlighted their deficient self-esteem, unsatisfactory marital state, depressiveness, and irritability. The group therapy program fostered healthful changes in these areas in addition to amelioration of the drinking behavior. The advantages of the group approach in the treatment of alcoholism and the values derived from concurrent group sessions of the patients' wives have been discussed. The need to interpret these findings on the basis of the essentially self-selected, unique population which made up this study cannot be too strongly emphasized.

REFERENCES

1. R. V. Seliger, *How to Help an Alcoholic* (Columbus, Ohio: School and College Service, 1951).
2. E. M. Jellinek, "Phases of Alcohol Addiction," *Quart. J. Stud. Alc.*, 13:673-684, 1952.
3. Cornell Index Manual, New York; Psychological Corporation; 1948.
4. M. B. Parloff, H. C. Kelman and J. D. Frank, "Comfort, Effectiveness and Self-awareness as Criteria of Improvement in Psychotherapy," *Am. J. Psychiat.*, 111:343-352, 1954.
5. H. Greenbaum, "Group Psychotherapy with Alcoholics in Conjunction with Antabuse Therapy," *Int. J. Group Psychother.*, 4:30-41, 1954.
6. E. S. Bordin, "Ambiguity, as a Therapeutic Variable," *J. Cons. Psychol.*, 19:9-15, 1955.
7. L. H. Gliedman, "Temporal Orientation and Chronic Alcoholism," *Maryland Rev. Alcsm.*, 2:1-2, 1955.

41

AN EXPERIMENTAL STUDY OF DIRECTIVE GROUP THERAPY WITH DEFECTIVE DELINQUENTS

Robert Snyder

Lee Sechrest

During recent years a great deal of effort has been expended in attempts to determine the limits of effectiveness of group psychotherapy. With many types of patients the results of investigations have justified a rather sanguine outlook, although it must be said that in a number of cases the lack of proper experimental controls has tended to vitiate the otherwise hopeful results. However, if any two groups of patients have been cause for pessimism, it has been the mental defectives and the delinquent or criminal population. Very few studies report favorable results of group psychotherapy with either defective or delinquent samples. It must be admitted then that the probability of success with a population of patients who are both defective and delinquent would seem to be quite small. Indeed, the seemingly low probability of success with such groups may in part acount for the paucity of work which has been done on defective delinquent patients. Of two available studies, one[1] reports some success; the other[2] does not.

It will be the thesis of this paper that a part of the failure to produce therapeutic progress with defective and/or delinquent patients has resulted from the applications of group therapeutic procedures inappropriate to the patients in question. A survey of the literature revealed that many of the group therapists who have attempted to work with defective patients have believed at the end of their experiences that it will be necessary to modify both nondirective and analytic techniques in the direction of greater

Reprinted from the *American Journal of Mental Deficiency*, Vol. 63, No. 7, July 1959, pp. 117-123.

direction and guidance from the therapist. Vail,[3] who offered no direction to his defective patients, reports an unsuccessful experiment and considers a failure to depart from traditional nondirective techniques the cause. Cotzin[4] and Wilcox[5] both discovered that if therapeutic progress was to be made, they would have to reorient their thinking toward increased leadership on the part of the therapist. Geller,[6] who found the theoretical basis for his therapy in Freudian concepts, stated that a modification of techniques was necessary with his defective females. In the same vein Ringleheim and Polatsek[7] tried therapy using analytic, nondirective, and counseling techniques and found that an unmodified version of each produced no significant results. Only one research effort with defectives, that of Yonge and O'Connor,[8] reports success using an unmodified nondirective approach. The research of Yonge and O'Connor, an experimental success, is one of two studies published relative to defective delinquents specifically. The other study, by Mann,[9] was essentially unproductive of therapeutic success.

The present research is a basic endeavor to determine whether or not group therapy is a feasible treatment technique for use with institutionalized defective delinquents. In order to assess more thoroughly the effects of therapy the design of the study provides for both a control, or no-treatment, group and a "placebo" group.

The investigators, taking cognizance of the suggestions of other researchers, assume that if group therapy with defective delinquents is to be effective, it must be directive in nature. The therapy techniques employed in this investigation were intended to be verbal, structured, and at times didactic, thereby making this research one of the first therapy studies with mental retardates whose initial emphasis was a departure from traditional, nondirective techniques.

CHARACTERISTICS OF THE SAMPLE

The defective delinquent is defined variously by different state and institutional agencies. The following criteria must be met before an individual can be committed to Huntingdon as a defective delinquent:

> a. Chronically delinquent male
> b. IQ below the dull normal category
> c. Potential capability of profiting from a rehabilitative program aimed at the development of habits of industry and obedience. (Idiots and psychotics are thereby excluded.)

The above gross characteristics describe both the population of defective delinquents at Huntingdon and the research sample.

In addition to the limitations imposed by the characteristics of the inmate population several other requirements were imposed for inclusion in this investigation. First, an attempt was made to obtain inmates in the IQ range of 50-79. Although none of the Ss had an IQ over 79, there were six Ss with tested IQ's below 50 who were selected on the basis of probable higher ability as indicated by Stanford Achievement Test scores or obviously higher functioning. Furthermore, inmates were excluded for the following reasons: "organicity," "honor" inmate, having an individual therapist, having previous group experience, having a definite time limit on his sentence, and having spent less than one year or more than ten years in the institution.

PROCEDURE

The method of investigation was to constitute three homogenous groups: one to receive group therapy, one to meet on the same schedule as the therapy group and to function as a "placebo" group, and one to serve as a no-treatment control group. The therapy and placebo groups each met once weekly for one hour sessions over a 13-week period. To increase homogeneity and reduce group size, the therapy and placebo groups were divided into Negro and Caucasian units. Therefore, there were actually two therapy and two placebo groups of nine members each. The no-treatment group consisted of nine Negro and nine Caucasian members.

There were two methods by which results of the group therapy were measured. Both methods involved the use of standard institutional procedures, and the eventual outcome was entirely dependent upon the decisions of reporting officers. None of the officers had any knowledge of the research or of the assignment of the inmates to any of the groups. Thus, experimenter bias was precluded, and the results were concrete and relevant to the situation in which the therapy took place.

Behavioral violations at the institution result in the supervising officer submitting a written, formal report (a "check") to a behavior court which decides upon the disciplinary measure. Any violation is given serious consideration and, hence, is a matter of weighty significance to an inmate who must "earn" his way out of the institution. Obviously, then, there was a clear-cut approach to assessment of overt behavior, viz., the number of "checks" written during any given period.

A "housing report," filled out by the officer in charge of each ward, was the other source of information. These reports are completed every four months on every inmate and are concerned with a description of the inmate as to conduct and personal characteristics. Constructed in the form of a checklist, the housing report has 31 items under "conduct characteristics" and 36 items under "personal characteristics." These 67 items can be readily dichotomized as favorable or unfavorable, e.g., note the following sample items: "polite," "quarrelsome," "respectful," "insolent in manner," "clean and neat of person," "feelings easily hurt." The housing reports were scored separately for positive and negative comments. Housing reports were available for Ss both prior to and following the period of experimental treatment. The same officers filled out the checklists for all Ss, and all Ss remained on the same unit throughout the experiment, except as they were removed for disciplinary reasons.

From an initial group of 123 inmates 54 were selected for inclusion in the research. Ss were matched on the number of negative comments on their last housing reports prior to the beginning of therapy and assigned randomly to the three conditions, thus forming three groups of 18 Ss each.

Table 41–1   Mean IQs, Ages, and Literacy Levels of the Three Groups

	IQ	Age	Literacy Level (Grades)
Therapy	62	19	2.8
Placebo	60	22	2.7
No-treatment	60	20	2.5

Table 1 presents data on the IQs and literacy levels and ages of the three groups which indicates that they were reasonably well matched on these variables.

Due to unreplaceable drop-outs, the therapy group's final number was 16, the placebo group numbered 16, and the no-treatment group 13. It was on these surviving Ss that the final evaluations of the housing reports were made. The measurement of the incidence of behavioral violations involved 16 in each group—the number who completed at least four weeks of the investigation. (One of the reasons for a drop-out was a behavioral violation and subsequent disciplinary measure involving transfer of the inmate to a rigid security ward where further transgressions were all but impossible.)

DESCRIPTION OF THE THERAPY

The role of the therapist was that of a guiding, manipulating leader who interacted minimally but did not hesitate to structure and organize when necessary. At times the therapist instructed in a truly didactic fashion, but at such times, upon completion of his educationally aimed discussion, he stimulated retort. Each of the sessions began with a predetermined topic selected on the basis of its concrete applicability to the lives of the inmates. The insertion of a more valuable topic by one of the inmates was not only tolerated but encouraged. Examples of topics discussed are: Why have discipline reports? Why do we need jails? Is it possible to love another boy?

The therapy Ss were instructed in the mechanics of group therapy, informed that their goal was to improve their individual adjustment to the institution's program, and told that at times one could benefit from discussion with one's buddies. The therapy Ss were also told that they were selected because they showed adjustment potential superior to that of the general inmate body. In that the penal environment tends to be restricting, authoritarian, and frustrating, the inmates were encouraged to give free vent to their aggressions and hostilities. As is typical of such groups, the initial sessions were largely given over to testing limits and villification of authorities. However, acting out was not allowed to dominate the sessions endlessly, and the therapist attempted to keep the Ss to the therapeutic topics.

The sessions were planned, the role of the therapist was directive, the climate permissive, and the material concrete.

The members of the placebo group were told that they had been especially selected for participation in a "study" and that it might prove helpful for them to attend the meetings. They were told that attendance at the meetings was desired but not mandatory. Further, they were assured that while at the meetings they could talk about whatever they liked. An attempt was made to give them the feeling that someone was interested in them and that they were involved in something different from the typical institution routine. Also an attempt was made to *permit* them to talk about the same things which were discussed in the therapy groups.

It should be recognized that the placebo group as devised in this investigation might not constitute a true placebo effect.* The placebo group was not told that the primary purpose of their participation was improvement of their adjustment, and the orientation of the "treatment" was not consistently in that direction. Thus the effects found in this study may not be entirely due to therapy itself. Some effect may have accrued from the "suggestion" that improvement would be expected. The present findings do indicate, however, that a therapeutically oriented program is superior to the attention which often is given through inclusion of persons in some "special" program.

HYPOTHESES

It was hypothesized that following therapy the experimental group members would show significant improvement over members of the placebo and no-treatment groups in their institutional adjustment, as represented by a reduction in the number of negative comments on their housing reports and in increase in the number of favorable comments. Housing reports were available both pre- and post-therapy, and the significance of the change among the groups was determined by analysis of covariance, rejection of the null hypothesis being at the .05 level.

* The authors are indebted to Dr. Donald T. Campbell for making this point.

Table 41–2   The Differences Among the Groups in Number of Negative Comments: Test of Significance of the Discrepancies in the Errors of Estimate

Source of Variability	SS	df	V	F	P
Total errors of estimate	1194.37	43			
Errors of estimate from combined within-sample regression	1184.91	41	30.75		
Discrepancies in the errors of estimate	9.46	2	4.73	.15	> .05

It was hypothesized that the therapy groups would show improvement in their institutional adjustment by receiving fewer reports for serious conduct violations than members of the placebo and no-treatment groups. The significance of the difference was tested by means of the X^2 test for k independent samples, rejection of the null hypothesis being at the .05 level.

RESULTS

There was a significant difference at the .05 level between the experimental, placebo, and control groups in the number of positive comments on the housing reports at the conclusion of 13 weeks of group therapy. There was, however, no significant difference among the groups in the number of negative comments. (See Tables 2 and 3.)

Table 41–3   The Differences Among the Groups in Number of Positive Comments: Test of Significance of the Discrepancies in the Errors of Estimate

Source of Variability	SS	df	V	F	P
Total errors of estimate	905.86	43			
Errors of estimate from combined within-sample regression	467.88	41	11.41		
Discrepancies in the errors of estimate	437.98	2	218.99	19.19	< .05

The adjusted means for the three groups show the direction of improvement. The adjusted mean for the no-treatment group shows an addition of .78 favorable comments per individual. The adjusted mean for the placebo group shows an addition of 1.40 favorable comments per individual, and the therapy group shows a gain of 3.38 favorable comments per inmate. The housing reports for those inmates receiving therapy were clearly superior.

The evaluation of the differences among the groups in terms of the number of appearances of group members before the behavior court yielded a nearly significant difference. The X^2 test revealed differences among the group significant at less than the .10 level (see Table 4). The experimental therapy group had only two members disciplined, the placebo group six, and the control group eight.

Two and one half months after therapy had ended, the investigators totaled the number of "checks" which had then been earned by the Ss since the beginning of therapy. It was felt that such a follow-up was important in view of the initially short term of investigation. At that time the therapy group was maintaining its superior conformity, having received only three checks. In contrast, the placebo group had received six checks and the no-treatment subjects had received ten.*

Table 41–4   The Differences in Number of Behavioral Court Appearances of the Group Members: The X^2 Test of Significance

Group	Number Disciplined	Number Not Disciplined
Therapy	2 (E = 5.32)	14 (E = 10.68)
Placebo	6 (E = 5.32)	10 (E = 10.68)
No-treatment	8 (E = 5.32)	8 (E = 10.68)
$X^2 = 5.25$	df = 2	p < .10 > .05

The follow-up was definitely confirmatory of the findings at the conclusion of therapy. There seemed to be no differences between Negro and Caucasian Ss, and the data for both therapy and both placebo groups have been combined.

DISCUSSION

In terms of behavior court appearances, the most observable aspect of the behavior of the inmates, we can conclude that group therapy improved at least the immediate institutional adjustment of the inmates. We may also conclude that the changes were of a fairly general nature since the therapy Ss also received a significant increase in the number of positive comments on their housing reports. It is somewhat contradictory to note that there was not a corresponding reduction in the number of unfavorable comments after therapy, but it is the opinion of the investigators that some tendency of the officers to pigeonhole inmates at least partially accounts for the discrepancy. That is, when an inmate is seen as a "bad actor," he continues to be viewed in that way. Although an officer

* There obviously were considerably fewer behavioral checks given during the 2½ months following therapy than during the therapy period itself. The explanation for this lies in the fact that a behavioral check rather effectively eliminated a "bad actor" by resulting in his segregation in a rigidly administered ward in which bad behavior was all but precluded. Thus there was attrition in the sample from which behavioral checks might be expected over a period of months.

may recognize some improvement in attitude and note it by adding favorable comments, he will be reluctant to give up any initially unfavorable impressions.

It is gratifying to find any positive therapeutic benefits for a group which is so patently a problem as the chronically delinquent defective person. However, it is doubly gratifying to find benefits which are immediately relevant to the total treatment program of the institution and which are independent of the biases of both therapist and patient. Aside from statistical evidence for the efficacy of group therapy, the observations of the therapist indicate that the therapy group members became more free in relations with the clinical staff, sought guidance more readily, and disseminated information gained in therapy sessions to other inmates.

During the course of the investigation the placebo group members gave ample evidence that they seriously felt their goallessness. Although they were not retained under threat, and relations were amiable between the therapist and the Ss, at times the continuation of the group was doubtful. Overt resistance was readily observable at every session of the placebo groups. The placebo groups, although valuable in assessing the effects of group therapy, probably received little benefit from weekly meetings which lacked structure or goals. An examination of the data shows superiority of the placebo groups over the no-treatment group at the conclusion of their meetings, which may reflect the vague benefits which accrue from merely being included in a special program.

The results of this research run counter to the opinions of most therapists who claim that therapy with defectives is contraindicated. This study specifically identifies group therapy as a desirable adjuvant to the treatment program for institutionalized defective delinquents. It is strongly believed that in addition to careful selection and larger numbers of subjects, and more functional measures, the results of this research are attributable to a definite departure from standard group therapy procedures in the direction of decidedly directive, didactic approach.

SUMMARY

This research presents the results of an investigation of the application of group therapy procedures to institutionalized, chronically delinquent defective males. Departing from most procedures which have been followed in the past the therapy was directive and didactic in nature. Two therapy groups, two placebo groups, and one no-treatment group were followed over a 13-week period.

At the end of 13 weeks of treatment the inmates receiving therapy were superior to both placebo and no-treatment Ss in their institutional adjustment as represented by significantly more positive comments on routine housing reports and fewer appearances in behavior courts for more serious violations.

The writers believe that the results are attributable to the more structured, directive nature of therapy and to the nature of the measurements, which were definitely and closely related to the institutional program as a whole.

REFERENCES

1. K. Yonge and N. O'Connor, "Measurable Effects of Group Psychotherapy with Defective Delinquents," *J. Ment. Sci.*, 100:944-952, 1954.
2. A. Mann, "Group Therapy Irradiation," *J. Crim. Law, Criminol. & Pol. Sci.*, 46:50-67, 1955.
3. D. Vail, "An Unsuccessful Experiment in Group Therapy," *Am. J. Ment. Def.*, 60:144-151, 1955.
4. M. Cotzin, "Group Psychotherapy with Mentally Deficient Problem Boys," *Am. J. Ment. Def.*, 53:268-283, 1948.
5. G. Wilcox, "Changes in Adjustment of Institutionalized Female Defectives Following Group Psychotherapy." Unpublished doctoral dissertation, Pennsylvania State University, 1956.
6. M. Geller, "Group Therapy with Girls Institutionalized for Mental Deficiency." Unpublished doctoral dissertation, New York University Publication No. 6265, 1956.
7. D. Ringleheim and I. Polatsek, "Group Psychotherapy with a Mentally Deficient Group, A Preliminary Study," *Am. J. Ment. Def.*, 60:157-162, 1957.
8. Yonge and O'Connor, *op. cit.*
9. Mann, *op. cit.*

42

GROUP THERAPY
WITH RETARDED READERS

Bernard Fisher

The importance of the problem of the retarded reader is indicated by the large time allotment that is assigned to remedial reading in the elementary school, the wealth of teaching devices that have originated in relation to it, and the numerous investigations that have been made in this field. Authorities are in agreement that most other school subjects are affected by reading ability. "These are admitted facts and are examples of an increasing number of findings that emphasize the value of establishing good reading habits."[1]

Failures in reading are frequent and many pupils never acquire adequate reading skills. Gates states: "Despite the quantity of experimental data, the wealth of ingenious teaching devices, the range of interesting children's reading material and the large amount of school time available for teaching reading, a surprisingly large number of pupils still experience difficulty in acquiring satisfactory reading skills."[2]

In one study it was found that reading was "the most frequent cause of school failure."[3] Schonell[4] found that the amount of reading failure in ten different primary classes averaged 22.6 per cent. Betts[5] estimated that approximately ten per cent of American school children require special assistance because of reading disabilities. These estimates of the number of children troubled by reading failures indicates the magnitude of the problem.

The varied approaches recommended for the remediation of reading disabilities are usually related to the authorities' beliefs concerning the cause of the disability. These causes may be grouped under the general categories of physical, psychological, educational, emotional, and social, or a combination of causes. Gann[6] reviewed a large number of representa-

Reprinted from the *Journal of Educational Psychology*, Vol. 44, No. 6, October 1953, pp. 354-360.

tive investigations and points of view that stress particular functions or group of functions that produce reading difficulty. She concludes: "Though the review presents points of view bearing a positive relationship to reading difficulty, numerous studies can be located in the literature negating these findings." She concludes: "The conclusiveness of the various approaches already existing cannot be established."

Despite this variety of inconclusive evidence, remedial reading teachers who use different approaches based upon the findings of the authority or authorities with whom they are acquainted usually achieve some degree of success. It has recently been suggested [7] that in addition to the improvement of reading techniques for the correction of reading disabilities, the psychotherapeutic relationship of the teacher, tutor, or clinician was a major factor in the correction of the reading disability. This suggests the possibility that all of the remedial methods may have had in common a psychotherapeutic relationship that arises when one person attempts to help another.

In support of this hypothesis, Axline briefly noted the varied attacks that had been made upon the reading problem. "[The varied attacks] gave the same results: successful in many cases, useless in others. These varied methods have one characteristic in common: the motivation of the teacher." [8] She described an experience with thirty-seven second-graders who were poor readers or nonreaders and whose teacher tried to help them by using a nondirective therapeutic approach. She employed art materials, free dramatics, puppet plays, music, creative writing, and so on.

Axline concluded by stating: "This study indicates that a nondirective approach might be helpful in solving certain 'reading problems.' It indicates that it would be worth while to set up research projects to test this hypothesis further: that non-directive therapeutic procedures applied to children with reading problems are effective not only in bringing about a better personal adjustment but also in building up a readiness to read." [9]

Bills described a study in which he worked with a class of third-graders who had previously been classified as slow learners. He concluded that: "(1) Significant changes in reading ability occurred as a result of the play therapy experience, (2) personal changes may occur in non-directive play therapy in as little as six individual and three group play therapy sessions, and (3) there appears to be no common personality maladjustment present in [his] group of retarded readers." [10]

An earlier investigation into the relationship between the improvement in emotional adjustment and the improvement in reading is Redmount's[11] "before" and "after" study of a resident six-week summer clinic for twenty-three children with reading difficulties. Reading tests showed that 48 per cent improved and 12 per cent seemed to regress. Rorschach tests indicated that 39 per cent showed personality improvement, with 26 per cent adversely affected.

Many articles have called attention to the relationship between personality and the reading process. Strachey[12] from the psychoanalytic point of view, stated that reading represents a sublimation of oral tendencies, especially those of a sadistic and destructive nature. He feels that skill in reading breaks down when these oral drives are unstable or completely repressed and sublimated. Klein[13] suggested that for those children whose neurotic conflicts are largely concerned with trying to keep aggressive drives repressed, sublimated expression of reading may not be permissible to ego and superego. A recent investigation by Vorhaus[14] tends to support these early hypotheses. Blanchard[15] described two groups of individuals who display reading disabilities: (1) the nonneurotic who develops emotional conflicts largely out of inability to read, (2) the neurotic whose emotional conflicts and difficulties in personality have preceded the reading difficulties which have arisen from these early maladjustments. Hardwick[16] stated that many reading cases show evidence of timidity and inferiority. Bennett[17] noted lack of persistence and attention, preference for solitary and inactive life, fears, indecisions, loneliness, and crying spells among the retarded readers. Gates[18] pointed out that children with reading difficulties lack persistence, do not concentrate well, show marked sensitivity, are withdrawn, daydream, and show a lack of aggressiveness, necessary for effective adaptation in learning to read. Tulchin[19] came to the conclusion that undesirable behavior patterns or personality maladjustment may be traced to reading disability. Witty and Kopel[20] found that fully 50 per cent of seriously retarded readers are characterized by fears and anxieties which require a program of re-education aimed at the re-establishment of self-confidence and the removal of anxieties.

Evidence like the above caused this investigator to hypothesize that if reading disabilities are in large part caused and effected by emotional adjustment, then psychotherapeutic steps would help to remove the disability. To test this hypothesis the following study was conducted.

DESIGN

The subjects were twelve residents of the Children's Village, an institution for delinquent boys. These twelve were part of a larger group which was receiving special remedial reading instruction. The subjects were all designated as having a reading disability on the basis of their past school history, case record, and psychological test results. As is indicated in Table 1 they ranged in age from ten years, five months to twelve years, nine months. Their initial reading abilities, as designated by reading age, ranged from six years, seven months to eight years, ten months. They were all more than three years retarded in reading, had the same regular classroom teacher, and received remedial reading instruction for three hours each week from the same remedial teacher.

Table 42–1   *Test Data for Experimental Groups*

	IQ	Age	Initial Reading Age	Final Reading Age	Gain in Months
Therapy Group					
A	90	11-1	6-7	7-11	16
B	97	12-0	7-5	8-1.5	8.5
C	92	12-2	7-6	9-0.5	18.5
D	85	11-7	7-9.5	8-3.5	6.0
E	92	11-8	8-0	8-7.5	7.5
F	96	11-9	8-7.5	9-8	12.5
Mean	92	11-8	7-8	8-7	11.5
Nontherapy Group					
AA	82	10-5	7-1.5	7-10.5	9.0
BB	97	12-9	6-11	7-8	9.0
CC	86	12-4	7-6	8-10.5	16.5
DD	88	11-11	8-5	9-6.5	13.5
EE	93	12-1	8-7.5	8-9.5	2.0
FF	107	11-11	8-10	8-9.5	—.5
Mean	92.1	12-3	7-11	8-7	8.25

All the subjects were initially tested with the Wechsler Intelligence Scale for Children and the Gates Advanced Primary Reading Tests. They were then divided into two groups by the paired comparison method and were matched for age, IQ, and initial reading ability. While both groups received remedial reading instruction, one group was arbitrarily chosen to participate in nondirective or group-centered therapy meetings which followed the principles established by Rogers,[21] Hobbs,[22] and others and were conducted by the author.

The subjects met as a group once each week for one hour. The therapist started the meetings with an initial structuring of the situation. The subjects were told that the opportunity to speak freely about their feelings, attitudes, and past and present experiences is usually helpful in making a better adjustment to their present situation and eventually to their homes. They were told that they were free to discuss any topic without restraints or value judgments imposed upon them by the therapist. The therapist's role was to reflect and clarify to the group the ideas, feelings, and behavior that occurred in the group meetings.

The group meetings and the remedial reading program were continued for six months. The twelve subjects were then retested with an alternate form of the Gates Advanced Primary Reading Tests. The "before" and "after" reading test results plus other pertinent data are presented in Table 1. The final reading results indicate that the group which received group psychotherapy in addition to remedial reading instruction showed the greater improvement in reading. The nontherapy group showed a range of improvement in reading from —.5 to 16.5 months for a mean gain of 8.25 months. The group that received group psychotherapy ranged in reading improvement from 6.0 to 18.5 months for a mean gain of 11.5 months. This latter group gained 3.25 months or 39.4 per cent more than did the nontherapy group.

SUMMARY AND CONCLUSION

Many approaches are presently being used to correct reading disabilities. Many of these approaches seem as often to be successful as unsuccessful. The present study hypothesized that it is the improvement in emotional adjustment that occurs because of the psychotherapeutic relationship between the reading clinician and the disabled reader which is the common factor in most of the remedial reading techniques which are in use. To test this hypothesis, one of two matched groups of retarded readers participated in a program of group psychotherapy in addition to the regular remedial program. This group showed a 39.4 per cent greater improvement in reading than did the control group. It is therefore concluded that with the subjects studied the psychotherapeutic relationship was an important factor in the correction of reading disabilities.

REFERENCES

1. A. I. Gates, *The Improvement of Reading* (New York: The Macmillan Co., 1947).
2. *Ibid.*
3. W. P. Percival, A *Study of the Courses and Subjects of School Failures.* Doctoral dissertation, Teachers College, Columbia University, New York, 1926.
4. F. J. Schonell, *Backwardness in the Basic Subjects* (Edinburgh: Oliver & Boyd Ltd., 1942).
5. E. A. Betts, "Teacher Analysis of Reading Disabilities, *Elem. Eng. Rev.,* Vol. XI, 1934.
6. E. Gann, *Reading Difficulty and Personality Organization* (New York: Kings Crown Press, 1945).
7. G. Arthur, *Tutoring as Therapy* (New York: The Commonwealth Fund, 1946); V. M. Axline, "Non-directive Therapy for Poor Readers," *J. Consult. Psychol.*, 2:61-69, 1947; R. E. Bills, "Non-directive Play Therapy with Retarded Readers," *J. Consult. Psychol.*, 2:140-149, 1950; B. Fisher, "A Psychologist's Evaluation of Teachers' Reports and Suggestions for Their Improvement," *Educ. Admin. and Superv.*, 38:175-179, 1952.
8. Axline, *op. cit.*
9. *Ibid.*
10. Bills, *op. cit.*

11. R. S. Redmount, "Description and Evaluation of a Corrective Program for Reading Disabilities," *J. Educ. Psychol.*, Vol. 39, 1948.
12. J. Strachey, "Some Unconscious Factors in Reading," *Int. J. Psychoanal.*, Vol. XI, 1930.
13. M. Klein, "A Contribution to the Theory of Intellectual Inhibition," *Int. J. Psychoanal.*, Vol. XII, 1931.
14. P. G. Vorhaus, "Non-reading as an Expression of Resistance," *Rorschach Research Exchange*, 10:60-69, 1946.
15. P. J. Blanchard, "Psychoanalytic Contributions to the Problem of Reading Disabilities," in *The Psychoanalytic Study of the Child*, Vol. II (New York: International Universities Press, 1946).
16. R. S. Hardwick, "Types of Reading Disability," *Childhood Education*, 8:425, 1932.
17. C. C. Bennett, *An Inquiry into the Genesis of Poor Readers*, Teachers College Contributions to Education, Number 755 (New York: Bureau of Publications, Teachers College, Columbia University, 1935).
18. A. I. Gates, "Failures in Reading and Social Maladjustment," *J. of Natl. Educ. Assoc.*, Vol. 25, 1936.
19. S. H. Tulchin, "Emotional Factors in Reading Disabilities in School Children," *J. Educ. Psychol.*, 26:444, 1935.
20. P. Witty and D. Kopel, *Reading and the Educative Process* (Boston: Ginn and Company, 1939), p. 231.
21. C. R. Rogers, *Counseling and Psychotherapy* (Boston: Houghton Mifflin Company, 1942).
22. N. Hobbs, "Group Centered Psychotherapy," in C. R. Rogers (ed.), *Client Centered Therapy* (Boston: Houghton Mifflin Company, 1951).

Part 5

TRAINING

THE PAPERS THAT ARE INCLUDED IN THIS SECTION indicate the development of training concepts in group psychotherapy. Perhaps one of the more interesting things about the papers that follow is that principles of social psychology and group dynamics in the training of individuals as group therapists are not suggested. Although Warkentin, in his paper on group therapy, recognizes the importance of continual group experience for the therapist in order for him to recognize his "ordinariness as a person," there is no comment about any principles of group composition which may aid the therapist in his work. The recognition of the values that are embodied in the training of group therapists are pointed to by Beukenkamp. This is not discussed in any great detail but can be found amplified from the perspective of the philosopher in Part 6, New Trends in Group Psychotherapy. (See Friedman's paper.)

The last paper in this section consists of the findings of Aaron Stein in his survey of practices in the field of group psychotherapy. Again, there is no acknowledgment of the importance of the contributions of social psychology to the training of the group psychotherapist. For example, Stein does not report any group psychotherapists as being aware of the distinctive difference between the closed dyadic group experience that exists between therapist and patient in individual psychotherapy and the more open group experience in group psychotherapy.

43

THE UTILIZATION
OF A THERAPY GROUP
IN TEACHING PSYCHOTHERAPY

Samuel B. Hadden

The amount of teaching time allotted to psychiatry in most medical schools is not sufficient to give the student more than a sketchy appreciation of the nature of mental illness, its symptomatology and classification. The average internship does not include much training in the management of mental illness, and as a result most physicians enter the practice of medicine incapable of rendering adequate psychiatric service to their patients. Major psychotic disturbances are referred to psychiatric centers, but the neuroses, not fully understood, are often mismanaged.

Students and physicians ought to be better acquainted with psychotherapeutic procedures; at least they should be more familiar with the results obtained by psychotherapeutic techniques so that they may treat patients more satisfactorily, or refer them for early specialized treatment, rather than continue the mismanagement so common today. There is little doubt that psychiatric teaching has improved greatly in the last ten years, but newer methods must be tried in order to use the allotted time more efficiently. The utilization of a therapy group in a teaching program offers this promise.

Shortly after we began the use of the group method in the treatment of psychoneurotic patients at the Presbyterian and Philadelphia General Hospitals, interns attended as guests, and they were very much pleased with the understanding of psychopathology and psychotherapeutic methods which they acquired. Some attended regularly and indicated that the sessions had proved an excellent way of learning the fundamentals of psychotherapy. In an early communication on the group method [1] I stated:

Reprinted from the *American Journal of Psychiatry*, Vol. 103, No. 5, March 1947, pp. 644-648.

"Although the group clinic has not been a part of the formal instruction in psychiatry of any class of students, the interns, residents and others who attended have been enthusiastic about its possibilities. At this time when there is need for the rapid training of psychiatrists in the management of the neuroses, the group method ought to be considered in such a program." Additional experience has strongly confirmed this belief.

From the beginning those interested in psychiatry who came to the sessions were very enthusiastic despite the fact that they simply sat in on the sessions as observers, had no contact with patients and little opportunity to discuss what they observed. About three years ago we were requested by Dr. Gammon, director of the department of neurology, to take over the treatment of psychoneurotic patients in the neurological outpatient department of the Hospital of the University of Pennsylvania. Here students were assigned to observe, and many were stimulated to greater interest. When the neurological outpatient service assumed responsibility for the treatment of discharged service men with neuroses, a special clinic was organized for their treatment on a group basis. Student volunteers were requested, and seniors were assigned to take histories of the men referred. This first group functioned during their senior year, and students attended the group sessions regularly. All reported favorably on their experiences.

With the reopening of the fall term in September, 1944, volunteer senior students began to attend the clinic. They took histories, conducted follow-up interviews, attended the group sessions, and participated in discussions on the mechanisms of the therapy sessions. With few exceptions the volunteers were regular in attendance and their interest was most gratifying.

Each patient referred to the clinic was assigned to a student who took his history, did the indicated examinations, and arranged conferences with his patient each week before or after the period devoted to group discussion. The students participating were mainly seniors in the army or navy medical program and were accepted by the recently discharged neurotic veterans for what they were—sincere, earnest students soon to become a part of army or navy medicine.

Patients enrolled in the clinic were either discharged veterans or men rejected for military service because of neuroses. They were referred by the Veterans' Bureau, the Red Cross, and other agencies. New patients were accepted at any session. Meetings were held once a week and lasted from one hour to an hour and a half. Before the discussion period each week I tried to see as many patients and students as possible and discuss specific problems or answer questions. Because I had no teaching assistants it was impossible to give as much supervision as was desirable, and I could not become personally acquainted with the problems of every patient or lend much assistance to the students in the handling of their patients. Despite the lack of adequate supervision the students acquired some knowledge of dynamics and acceptable psychotherapeutic procedures, and the patients improved.

At each weekly meeting, after the students had spent twenty to forty minutes with their assigned patients, the student-physicians and patients assembled and a group session was held. The patients were encouraged to do most of the talking, but the students were directed to participate and to ask questions and make comments when the discussion lagged or when they saw an opportunity to direct attention to the specific problems or needs of a patient under their care.

In the early sessions we presented fundamental psychodynamic principles in simple language and helped the patient and student to understand how disturbance of body function may be produced by emotion.[1] At later meetings mental mechanisms such as repression, sublimation, rationalization, projection, introjection, and regression were plainly described and were illustrated by common examples to draw the patient into the discussion and have him indicate his awareness of the working of these mechanisms in himself. It was a surprise to students and physicians alike to discover how readily patients recognized and spoke of their own use of rationalization, projection, and similar mechanisms.

After patients acquired a reasonable appreciation of simple psychodynamics, brief histories were presented for discussion. These cases were selected to show the role of rejection, overprotection, and other experiences in the production of neurotic traits. We have found this very valuable because it is an effective method of vicarious catharsis and patients identify themselves with the experiences of the persons under discussion. As various features of the cases were analyzed by the group, insight into the workings of their own minds as well as that of the person whose case was discussed was effectively obtained. During such presentations patients divulged their problems and life histories very freely and rapidly acquired an objective attitude toward themselves and their difficulties.

The effectiveness of the therapy sessions was heightened for the patients by the presence of the students. Patients in attendance understood that the sessions were part of the training of the students, consequently comments made by the therapist or students were accepted by the patients as being authentic. During the first year of our experimental use of the group, students were selected in turn to direct at least one session. This gave them valuable experience in presenting their views, but as they were not sufficiently advanced to guide the discussion into proper channels the practice was discontinued in the last year.

It is not the purpose of this paper to present the dynamics of group therapy but to indicate its usefulness as a means of teaching students. By attendance at therapy sessions students have had the opportunity of observing the development of a patient's history as well as the explanation of his symptoms. They have watched the uncovering of repressed experiences, with resulting abreaction during the discussions. They have also had the opportunity of dealing with patients as they began to understand their acquisition of neurotic patterns of behavior and gradually recognize their visceral symptoms as emotionally determined. During discussion of patients' difficulties students have been able to observe rationalization, projection, and other mechanisms utilized by patients in attempts to protect themselves in the discussion before the group. They have seen how patients were assisted to recognize their use of these mechanisms in such a way that no additional psychic trauma was effected. In the group they have watched feelings of resentment and flagrant hostilities manifested by patients and have observed the handling of these situations by the therapist with the aid of the group. Discussion of the situations after the termination of the sessions has helped students to understand what they have witnessed. They have acquired an appreciation of methods used in dealing with the patients during the therapeutic process. The acquisition of insight by patients has been demonstrated to the group, first in its intellectual aspects, and frequently full emotional insight has been observed in patients under their care.

The benefits to students in attendance have been considerable. Before participation in the group sessions few of the students had any appreciation of what could be accomplished for neurotic complaints, and to have them realize that such symptoms as pain, cardiac palpitation, nausea, vomiting, syncope, giddiness, uncontrollable anger, and irritability could be improved by psychotherapeutic manipulations was a revelation to many. The attitude of hopelessness in dealing with neurotic symptoms has been dissipated. Most of the students are now able to understand that neurotic symptoms are real and not imaginary. It was interesting to observe the students as they interviewed their patients and felt it necessary to give them some kind of medicine, even though it be a placebo. However, since no medication was administered to any of the patients, students have come to know that these crutches are seldom of value in dealing with the neurotic.

One of the most beneficial effects to these volunteer students has been the awakening of a real interest in psychiatry. Several have admitted that prior to their experience with the group they had little regard for psychiatry, but have since decided that it is a hopeful as well as an interesting branch of medicine. About one third of those who attended sessions during the two-year operation of the veterans' clinic have decided upon psychiatry as their specialty, and many have already begun their career in army or navy psychiatry.

Comments of some of the students are of interest. One of the most frequent remarks was that this was the first opportunity they had had to work with the neurotic patient on such an intimate and prolonged basis.

These students have emphasized the fact that although they heard much about "treating the patient as an individual," they had no practice in doing so and no occasion to observe the handling of patients' emotional problems. Several expressed the feeling that after they had handled a patient in the group they felt it was as much an improvement in teaching the treatment of neuroses as going to the patient's bedside was an improvement in the teaching of clinical medicine. It was common for students to express surprise at the ease with which the neurotic patient was helped to accept his illness as an understandable entity, and how this understanding created hope in the patient. Many were surprised when I asserted that the symptoms of the neurotic were real, and some entered into lengthy disagreement with the viewpoint as to how pain could possibly be established by neurotic mechanisms unless on an imaginary basis. It was an interesting experience for me to observe the skepticism with which many of the students regarded any assurance of improvement in these patients. They were all so thoroughly impressed with the organic side of medicine that it was difficult for them to accept functional disturbance on any basis other than a conscious or near-conscious level. Several expressed amazement that such symptoms as tachycardia, breathlessness, epigastric pain, and digestive disturbance could be influenced by psychotherapy. Many were disturbed when their patients were not given some kind of prescription for their symptoms, and some were surprised when patients returned after they had not been given any medication. As the course ended most of them were enthusiastic, and some were quite critical of the great emphasis placed on the psychoses and of the failure to recognize and handle neurotics properly in other departments.

It may be illuminating to quote from a few of the students' reports. One stated that as he proceeded through medical school he felt the "art of medicine was a thing of the past." He had developed such an intense reliance upon "scientific methods" that he was considerably prejudiced, and it was as "a very skeptical senior" that he "volunteered to attend the Tuesday evening sessions." Of the first session he reported:

> I left the class with a realization that something must be done about the one-sided view I held. My first encounter was with a veteran who had served three years overseas. He seemed acutely ill mentally, and I was completely at a loss as to what course to follow, so I urged him to keep talking. I kept trying to remember what we had been told in our third year—"permit the patient to talk and ask leading questions to direct the conversation along the path you desire."

The student permitted the patient to talk, and suddenly he realized "the patient had apparent confidence in me, despite the fact he knew I was a student doctor" and he, the patient, was anxious to be helped. This experience was unique to the student-doctor because he somehow had a fixed idea that neurotics *liked to stay sick.* Incidentally, this particular patient had a very intense anxiety neurosis with many visceral components, and the student expressed further amazement that marked improvement of these symptoms was eventually effected without medication.

Another student wrote:

> At the end of our lecture courses I had a rough idea of what a neurosis was, but not much more than that. I had the impression that the psychoses, rather than the neuroses, made up the bulk of psychiatric practice.

To this student it was surprising to observe patients—such as he had seen in medical dispensary—with common complaints on a neurotic basis, resistant to all medication, respond to psychotherapeutic measures in the group.

One of the first physicians in regular attendance at the group sessions was an intern at the Philadelphia General Hospital. He had attended regularly during his senior year in medical school and continued attendance as an intern. He is now an army captain doing psychiatric work, and recently wrote me that up until his senior year in medical school—when he first attended the group sessions—he had no appreciation of any curative procedures for the psychoneurotic disturbances. He stated: "As you know, the treatment of the 'neurotic' individual in medical dispensaries was to give them a pat on the back and a bottle of elixir of phenobarbital." He further remarked:

> Observing a group of patients over a period of several sessions impressed upon me far more of the psychodynamics than I had been able to grasp anywhere else—despite the fact that my interest had always been in psychiatry. . . . Some of my most vivid recollections of group psychotherapy have to do with the hate, fear, explosive antagonism, guilt and sorrow that would unfold like a drama during an evening's session. Having witnessed the handling of these reactions has helped me infinitely in coping with similar situations that I am now meeting.

Other students have commented as follows:

> The group experience teaches in the same way that clinics and ward work teach in medicine. It provides practical experience by dealing with and handling patients—something books and lectures cannot provide. I have learned to believe that every person who is sick has some degree of psychoneurotic overlay, and that handling this is an important factor in speeding recovery.

Another in reporting his experience said: "It caused me to revolt against the physician who damns the neurotic and prescribes bromides."

In presenting suggestions for improvement of the group method of instruction every student favored its expansion and recommended:

1. Additional instruction which should include more guidance of the student's individual session with his patient.

2. Better training in history taking prior to participation in the group procedure.

3. Holding of sessions more often than once a week.

4. More discussion and instruction after each group session, that students may receive a clearer explanation of the subtleties of the comments made by patients.

All the opinions of students were obtained shortly before or after their graduation, and all were secured after the termination of their contact with the group.

In addition to the remarks of these undergraduate students, naval officers in attendance have been very enthusiastic in their comments about the value of the course as a method of instructing them in handling psychoneurotic problems in the services. These men attended for rather brief periods and, as those who have had experience with group therapy realize, in order to understand its effectiveness it is usually necessary to attend many sessions to observe the group interaction and appreciate its benefits to the patients.

Although this experience with the group as a teaching medium has been rather brief, and the views expressed by the students must be evaluated in the light of their lack of experience and their immaturity, I personally believe that the method is valuable for teaching sound psychotherapeutic procedures to students and physicians, and for making them more proficient in the handling of psychosomatic disorders. For a long time there has been rather general agreement that it is very difficult to teach students psychotherapeutic methods because of the intimate patient-physician relationship which is disturbed by the presence of another individual. In the group method the student can see and observe all of the potent psychodynamic mechanisms employed to effect improvement in the emotionally disturbed. Rapport and transference can be satisfactorily established, and every psychotherapeutic measure seems to be increased in effect in an active group. I have gained much from the group discussions and have learned how to handle individual patients far better after noting behavior in a group.

In discussing with students in attendance the benefits they derived from participation in the group project, it surprised me to learn that many of them stated they had received invaluable assistance in effecting a better personal adjustment in their own lives. Many reported that they had become aware of the genesis of undesirable personal characteristics which they possessed and were able to direct curative measures. Several were enthusiastic about this phase of the project and believed it was the only experience through which they had personally benefited in their whole medical school course. When we realize the harmful effect of personality maladjustment in the physician, we can fully appreciate the value of this group training to the medical student.

In conclusion, I believe that group sessions, with adequate supervision, can be used to teach psychotherapy just as satisfactorily as clinical medicine is taught. It gives students the opportunity to interview, examine and discuss cases with their chiefs, and then observe the technique and result. They become participants in a dynamic psychotherapeutic relationship. Group therapy permits the gaining of experience under supervision, and makes the training of therapists shorter and more effective. It gives to all students a better understanding of the value of psychotherapeutic mechanisms, and for many it develops insight into some of their own personality difficulties and gives remedial assistance.

REFERENCE

1. S. B. Hadden, "Group Psychotherapy: A Superior Method of Treating Larger Numbers of Neurotic Patients," Am. J. Psychiat., 101:68-7, July 1944; "Treatment of the neuroses by class technic." Annals Int. Med., 16:33-37, January 1942.

44

TRAINING IN GROUP PSYCHOTHERAPY:
A SYMPOSIUM

Cornelius Beukenkamp
Milton M. Berger

SOME OF THE VALUES INVOLVED IN TRAINING GROUP PSYCHOTHERAPISTS: C. BEUKENKAMP

When faced with the responsibility of teaching, it is of more than mere academic value to ask oneself, "Why am I teaching?"

It is well known that to teach is to learn; to learn is to grow. However, in the case of psychotherapy, other factors are involved. Here learning is not always synonymous with growing. In fact, there is a knowing-knowing which is opposed to emotional knowing. The difference may be, at times, hard to convey in words.

The holistic emotional understanding of the human being, that Andros Angyal so capably reveals in his book, *Foundations for a Science of Personality*,[1] theoretically supports the belief that for teachers the teaching experience may mean the formation of a healthier ego structure.

In teaching group psychotherapy, the teacher soon appreciates the impossibility of separating the purely academic process from the growth process, for all those involved. And if he is alert, the teacher realizes that although the academic process remains in the foreground, he finds himself in an essentially therapeutic environment. In the past, the formation of this therapeutic climate has been largely attributed to the needs of the student. However, my own feeling is that the needs of the teacher are as great in this development as those of the student.

Unfortunately, sometimes the teacher's inability to grow via the role of a student or patient results in the premature attempt at gaining status by being a teacher. It seems that such an individual may find this a less

Reprinted from the *American Journal of Psychotherapy*, Vol. XII, No. 3, July 1958, pp. 3-13.

ego-alien approach to his growth needs. Associated with this difficulty, it is not uncommon to see teachers identify with their specific theories, ideas, and beliefs as though they were actual parts of their own ego structure. Consequently, the student who can accept the teacher's concepts is "liked" and considered to be in a state of positive transference, whereas the student who disagrees is in the eyes of the teacher in a state of rebellion and is often treated as though he were a threat to the teacher's ego.

If these assumptions be true, it would logically follow that in the case of teaching social sciences, the format of the small group (eight to ten), with its attitude of mutuality, might resolve the impasse between teacher and student. Many professionals involved in the fields of both treating and teaching have found these difficulties with "relating" and the subject has been covered from many angles, but the author who comes to mind with respect to group psychotherapy, is Samuel Hadden.[2] For example, he believes that the optimum approach for medical students to understand human dynamics and clinical psychiatry is through the use of the semididactic and semitherapeutic small group.

The resistances the small group workshop or seminar experiences on the surface appear to include differences in theoretical concepts; actually, they are often the result of the members' concern about their individuality in the group. Conceivably, this may be best resolved when the aim is not the demand to adjust to the group per se but, rather, the growth of the individual as he encounters the multiple facets of human psychology. It is quite possible that the group might further aid the development of the individual's security. The difficulty with which the group and the teacher are confronted lies in creating enough security for a given individual to enhance his growth and development within a group, rather than leave him continuously anxious lest he lose his individuality by being part of a group.

As in groups that are formed with the objective of therapy (and not of training or education), the area of new experiential behavior comes into focus. It is during the terminal phase of the group's existence that this is to be found. The hoped for psychologic result in either group is the emergence of a behavior in the members which the writer has termed a "beyond-transference behavior."[3] When applied to the academic group, this would refer to the fact that all members openly feel like "students" at the end of their experience, and that the earlier gap between teacher and student has disappeared.

In therapy groups, patients and therapists have expressed analogous feelings as attitudes they have gained by their peer-type of interpersonal orientation.

Certainly, the subject of this symposium cannot be discussed without acknowledging that when the peer-level orientation has reached its fruition, a broader appreciation of human psychology has occurred. There appears less stress upon mechanistic approaches and less ardent need to discover the why's and the unknowns of the case at the expense of appreciating human behavior on a broader basis. The understanding of the multiple human psychology the individual encounters in the group may be the indication that a harmonious integration of the academic and the emotional-growth components has been attained.

REFERENCES

1. A. Angyal, *Foundations for a Science of Personality* (The Commonwealth Fund, New York, 1941).
2. S. Hadden, "The Utilization of a Therapy Group in Teaching Psychotherapy," *Am. J. Psychiat.*, Vol. 103, No. 5, March 1947.
3. C. Beukenkamp, "Beyond Transference Behavior," *Am. J. Psychiat.*, Vol. X, No. 3, July 1956. [Chapter 49 of the present volume.]

PROBLEMS OF ANXIETY IN GROUP PSYCHOTHERAPY TRAINEES: M. BERGER

Trainees who are not anxious must be sick. Anxiety is a coin of the realm we are all familiar with. It can be experienced and utilized constructively or destructively in the group therapy trainee as well as in his patients. The supervisor's identification with the trainee helps to bring anxiety areas into focus at the supervisory session.

The anxiety of the beginner in group therapy is due to: (a) his own general anxiety as a person; (b) his resistance to the group psychotherapeutic experience. Knowledge and recognition of the factors which contribute to the therapist's anxiety may help in the development of more competent therapists. Some of these factors are:

1. His "heritage" and goal as a therapist which lead him to feel obliged to cure his patients. In recent years, understanding of what is curative in individual and group psychotherapy has increased, but this understanding is still an open matter. What has become increasingly clear is that the compulsive urge to "cure" may be a reflection of the therapist's neurotic need to be omnipotent; or it may be due to his compulsive helpfulness and thus may retard the curative process. A conscious, active need to cure may prove to be a block to therapeutic progress when the patient feels coerced by the therapist's pressure to change him. The patient's overreactions to coercion are stimulated, and these may lead to overt and covert attempts to maintain his neurotic status quo, not to be "pushed around" by the authorities. This is an experience the patient has known all his life. The patient may stall and his counterreactions may lead to even greater anxiety in the therapist. The therapist may then push still harder and thus additional confusion arises.

2. His failure to be aware of himself as an active participant as well as observer in the group therapeutic process and interaction and of his own transference and countertransference reactions. His attempt to deny how he is in reality and to cover up slips of his tongue. His own unreresolved neurosis and character structure may allow him to treat certain types of patients successfully but not others. He may, for example, have difficulty with overly dependent or dominating patients.

3. The therapist's demand for verbal participation and his own increasing anxiety during periods of silence in the group. The trainee usually considers silence as resistance. Because of his lack of appreciation for the nuances and types of nonverbal communication between group members and between the members and himself, the trainee may conclude that "nothing is going on." He is the victim of cultural and therapeutic overemphasis on acting and verbalizing. Silence in groups can be a very active process. As the therapist learns to be more aware of and to live with his aloneness, his silence, his own nonverbal communications, and comes to know silence as having, at times, the deep spiritual significance of togetherness, he will perhaps give up not only the notion of "nothing is going on" but be concerned more with what and how the group members, including himself, really are and less with what they are saying.

4. The trainee's need to maintain the reins of leadership or, conversely, his difficulty in asserting his leadership may keep him anxious. An analogy is that of the horseman who is afraid to hold the reins too loosely and to give the horse his head, yet demands that his ride be a smooth one. The horse is too busy challenging the leadership to give a smooth ride. In the group, the extremely authoritative leader will find that his leadership is often challenged by the group, which is trying to grow and to develop its own leadership potential. If there is constant overt compliance, there will be covert rebellion and resistance. On the other hand, if the therapist is unable to assert his own leadership functions, he will be too anxious to make the tentative, intuitive conjectures and interpretations or to ask the provocative questions which can lead to deeper exploration, interaction, and change.

5. The trainee's need to impress the group members with his skill and competence as a therapist frequently leads him to overfocus on manifestations of psychopathology. At times, this is accompanied by a neglect of what is healthy and constructive in the individual group members and in the group as a whole. This may lead to increasing feelings of self-hate, depression, emptiness, anxiety, and resistance in the group members. Their increasing anxiety (as they feel that their neurotic crutches are taken away with little else to replace them) then disquiets the therapist by a feed-back mechanism.

The need to lead and to impress also induces the therapist to talk too much, especially in the early sessions. He may be inclined to lecture and thus create a classroom situation in his group. This attitude, while it may be helpful symptomatically, tends to retard the interaction necessary for therapy. Verbalization by the group members of what is experienced in the interaction may also be curtailed because of fear lest they be considered stupid or wrong or lest they provoke the therapist's disapproval.

6. The group, because of its very structure and nature, is more sensitive than an individual to the personality of the therapist. Because of the mutually supportive nature of the group, patients may express more openly what they directly or intuitively perceive about the therapist and, especially, what is neurotic in him. This may increase his anxiety markedly. He may be driven to deny or to be vindictive, which is even more destructive to the group.

7. The lack of knowledge by the therapist of the dynamics of individuals in groups and of groups themselves may lead to anxiety. This can only be decreased through experience and training and knowledge accrued from experience.

8. The group therapist may manifest his own resistance to the group psychotherapeutic experience by such matters as: (a) his selection of a personal analyst who does not practice group psychotherapy and (b) his attempt to find numerous reasons for delay in starting a group and for coming to his assigned or selected group therapy supervisor. The therapist's own resistance helps to perpetuate his anxiety, and this must be brought to his attention in order to explore and undermine the reasons for this resistance and thus to decrease the anxiety associated with it. The resistive therapist finds himself in the ambiguous position of encouraging his patients to participate in an experience of which he himself is fearful.

This leads to two conclusions in supervision: First, it is impossible for a group therapy supervisor to supervise a group therapy trainee without becoming involved in the therapy of the trainee. Second, the experience of being a patient in a psychotherapeutic group is to be highly recommended to those who intend to practice group psychotherapy as an art as well as a science.

45

THE TRAINING OF
THE GROUP PSYCHOTHERAPIST

Aaron Stein

INTRODUCTION: SOME DEFINITIONS

It might be well to begin with some statement explaining what group psychotherapy is. If we know what group psychotherapy is, we might begin to have some idea of the kind of training the group psychotherapist needs.

A working definition of group psychotherapy indicating the important elements involved might be given as follows: Group psychotherapy is the utilization by a therapist of a group and a group method in performing psychotherapy, with psychotherapy defined as a type of treatment of mental and emotional illness which is based primarily on verbal (and non-verbal) communication (through the establishment of a relationship) with the therapist. Combining the two definitions, one could then say: Group psychotherapy is a method of treating mental and emotional illness in which the therapist fosters the establishment of relationships (to the therapist and between the patients) in the group, and by encouraging the development of interaction among the patients in the group (both in relation to each other and the therapist), he facilitates verbal (and non-verbal) communication in the group.

This definition of group psychotherapy refers to the treatment of mental and emotional illness and indicates that the presence of such illness has been established or diagnosed. It also states that the treatment involves a relationship with a therapist and that through this relationship, interaction and spontaneous verbal expression of the factors entering into the mental and emotional illness occurs in the group. Defining it in this way differentiates group psychotherapy from other group psychotherapeu-

Presented as a lecture at the Fourth Annual Institute of the American Group Psychotherapy Association, New York City, January 27, 1960.

tic methods, such as group counseling and guidance, and from various other group activities that are therapeutic, such as social activities, artistic activities, and occupational activities performed in groups.

MATERIAL OBTAINED FROM PERSONAL EXPERIENCE IN TRAINING GROUP PSYCHOTHERAPISTS

The writer's own experience in training group psychotherapists has comprised three distinct activities connected with training three different groups of students. The first group consisted of psychologists and social workers connected with a social agency. The second was composed of psychiatric residents in a voluntary mental hospital. The third group was composed of graduate psychiatrists in the psychiatric outpatient department of a general hospital.

The training of the psychologists and social workers will be described first. This occurred in connection with the writer serving as consultant in group psychotherapy to a private social agency that had set up a group psychotherapy project* for the treatment of young adolescents, both male and female, ranging in age from 12 to 15, who had been referred because of delinquent behavior. They were treated with combined activity and interview group psychotherapy by the social workers and psychologists belonging to the project. The work in supervising and training these group psychotherapists began in 1954 and is continuing.

The instruction in group psychotherapy with this group was accomplished in two ways: (1) through supervision of the group psychotherapy and (2) through regular meetings of a workshop or case study seminar. In the supervisory sessions, the group therapists met on a regular basis, once a week, with experienced group psychotherapists, and every phase of their work with the group was gone into.

In addition, once a month a seminar or workshop was held which all of the group psychotherapists and their supervisors attended. At these seminars the work was divided into two parts. In the first part, one of the group therapists read a session from his group with the entire group participating in a discussion concerning the material from this group session. The second part of the seminar usually was devoted to a general discussion of group psychotherapy according to questions and problems brought up by the group therapists. However, this discussion sooner or later centered around the group psychotherapists' anxiety and countertransference difficulties (although these were not labeled as such) in relation to their role as a therapist. The point that needed to be clarified most often was to give them a clear idea of their function as a group therapist.

Several characteristics of this group should be mentioned. First, they

* The Group Psychotherapy Project of the Girls' Service League, New York, N.Y.

were all relatively young and with one or two exceptions had not had too much experience in their respective fields. Because of their lack of knowledge and experience in dealing with various types of psychiatric patients, many of them became quite anxious if some of the adolescents showed possible psychotic symptoms or when they showed such symptoms as a moderately severe depression. The second point was their lack of experience in individual psychotherapy. While many of them had been exposed to much didactic and theoretical material concerning the psychodynamics of interpersonal relationships and of psychotherapy, their lack of actual experience in the one-to-one relationship in individual psychotherapy handicapped them greatly and often prevented them from seeing what was going on in the group.

The third and most important difficulty that was encountered was getting them to use the group and the group method in performing the group psychotherapy. Only their experience in doing group psychotherapy and their having repeatedly pointed out to them in their supervision and seminars the way in which a group could be used enabled them finally to understand what was meant by using the group method in performing group psychotherapy.

Next, the experience obtained in the training of the psychiatric residents in a voluntary mental hospital will be described.* The psychiatric residents were first- and second-year residents in psychiatry receiving their psychiatric training at this hospital, some with no previous psychiatric experience.

Briefly, the training of the residents in group psychotherapy was as follows: The first-year residents were given a series of about twelve didactic lectures in which the basic points concerning group psychotherapy were covered. Following this they attended a weekly or biweekly continuous case seminar or workshop, in which a second-year resident reported his experience in selecting and preparing patients for a group, in setting up the group, and in doing the group psychotherapy. The material from the group sessions was followed at these meetings for the rest of the year so that the residents could follow a group from its inception well into the group psychotherapy.

In addition, each first-year resident who wished to do so (this was not *required*) could act as a recorder-observer for a second-year resident who was conducting a group. The recorder-observer was instructed not to participate in the group sessions. He took notes, and later, he and the group therapist went over the notes for each session with a supervisor who was skilled in group psychotherapy. This was a particularly valuable and most instructive experience for the first-year residents.

* The Hillside Hospital, Glen Oaks, N.Y., a voluntary mental hospital of some 280 beds with an approved three-year psychiatric residency training program.

In the second year, the resident began to do group psychotherapy by himself under the supervision of an experienced group psychotherapist and had as a recorder-observer a new first-year resident. The second-year residents were not required to attend the didactic lectures or the continuous case seminars that were given to the first-year residents, but most of them chose to do so and contributed greatly to the variety and spontaneity of the discussions.

In the third year it is planned to have the third-year residents, who will have had one year of experience in group psychotherapy with inpatients, do group psychotherapy in the outpatient department, again with weekly supervision from an experienced group psychotherapist. At the end of the three-year period those residents that participated in the group psychotherapy program will have had three years of experience, with the first year as a recorder-observer, the second year as a group therapist with inpatients, and the third year as a group therapist with outpatients.

Now to point out some of the difficulties that were encountered in this type of training program. Two of them are exactly like the difficulties that were encountered with the psychologists and social workers and are related entirely to lack of experience and knowledge of the residents. This manifested itself, especially in the first-year residents, in anxiety and in all kinds of countertransference attitudes which they clearly demonstrated in their questions and discussions in the continuous case seminars. Similar difficulties were noted also in relation to their lack of experience in individual psychotherapy.

However, at Hillside, the residents receive intensive training in clinical psychiatry and in individual psychotherapy. Because of this, they were in a much better position when it came to beginning to do group psychotherapy than the psychologists and social workers mentioned previously. The results were clearly evident. The residents in their second year with one year of training in individual psychotherapy and with intensive training in clinical psychiatry as well were much less anxious, much more knowledgeable, and consequently more adept and more secure in their approach to group psychotherapy.

However, the psychiatric residents, just as with the psychologists and social workers, had a great deal of difficulty at first in understanding the concept of using a group and a group method in performing group psychotherapy. In some ways this difficulty was aggravated by the emphasis that they had received on the utilization of individual psychotherapy in their first year. The idea of letting the patients in the group express and interact and work out the problems that were brought up was quite difficult for the residents to grasp. They would deal with the individual patients in the group instead of the group as a whole and would let themselves be drawn into participating in the group when the group would best have functioned on its own.

This was helped to some extent by having the first-year residents attend as a recorder-observer in the group psychotherapy led by a second-year resident and then attend the supervisory session with the group leader. By the time the resident in his second year began to do group psychotherapy, he had some idea of how to use the group and the group method in performing group psychotherapy. However, it was chiefly their own experience in performing group psychotherapy in the second year (and now in the third year) which was most effective in helping them understand how to use the group and the group method properly in doing group psychotherapy.

One more point might be mentioned. At one time it was proposed that the residents participate as patients in a psychotherapeutic group, one composed of residents themselves. This was opposed by the senior medical staff because it was felt the residents had enough anxiety and other difficulties to cope with, including, especially, marked tendencies to identify with the patients in the hospital. It was thought that it might lead to further complications in an already complicated situation if residents were put into a psychotherapeutic group as patients. Also, in the discussions and in the continuous case seminars, no attempt was made (and this was adhered to deliberately) to do any therapy for the very obvious difficulties that the residents showed. All discussions were centered upon the work at hand, and whatever therapeutic effects there were (and there were many) were arrived at in this indirect fashion, not as a result of direct therapeutic management.

Now to come to the third group—the graduate psychiatrists who were trained in group psychotherapy. These were members of the attending staff of the Psychiatric Outpatient Department of a large general hospital in New York City.* All of them had completed their psychiatric residencies and their psychiatric training. The work with the group was begun in 1955 and is continuing. In the beginning all of the men involved were somewhat older men, all of whom had been analyzed and some of whom had had analytic training. All had had many years experience with individual psychotherapy of a psychoanalytically oriented type. They had joined the staff of this particular clinic at the hospital upon learning that it was going to become a Group Psychotherapy Clinic and thereby showed their interest in learning group psychotherapy. This was then a relatively experienced group of mature psychiatrists, psychoanalytically oriented, who at this stage in their work undertook training in group psychotherapy.

Since none of them had any previous training or experience in group psychotherapy, a training program was begun with a series of about 12 didactic lectures in which the basic elements of group psychotherapy were covered. Because they were experienced individual psychotherapists, they

* The Mount Sinai Hospital, New York, N.Y.

were permitted upon completion of these basic lectures to begin to select patients for a group, to prepare them, and then to begin to do group psychotherapy.

The instruction with respect to performing group psychotherapy then proceeded in two ways. First, each one of the psychiatrists met once a week with the chief of the clinic (the writer) to receive individual instruction and supervision in such matters as the selection of patients, structuring of the group, preparation of the patients, the first session, the various phases of group psychotherapy, and so on. Concurrently with this individual supervision, a continuous case seminar was held where all the members of the clinic, the chief of the service, and various other people, including some experienced group psychotherapists, participated. Here one of the men presented material from his group and then various aspects and problems relating to the material were discussed. During the first year of the clinic, when most of the men in the clinic were new, one group was followed straight through. In addition, once a month, one of the other therapists would present material from his group so that each one had the opportunity to present. The discussions were quite active and spontaneous, and many points relating to techniques, dynamics, and so on, were raised and thoroughly discussed.

In the following years, the training program has varied a little bit. Several new members have joined the clinic staff, including some younger men who had completed their training in psychiatry but whose experience was not as extensive as those previously mentioned. For these newcomers, the didactic lectures and the individual instruction and supervision were continued. For the more experienced men, weekly conferences or workshops were held, covering a large variety of topics relating to the technique and dynamics of group psychotherapy. There has been a continuing effort to understand the functioning of the group with the idea of establishing valid criteria for using group psychotherapy as a selective form of treatment.

As would be expected because of their initial interest, this group was quite enthusiastic about the work. A very interesting result of this was that all of them, after a year or two of experience at the clinic, set up psychotherapeutic groups in their private practice.

Now to point out some of the difficulties involved. First, all of these experienced psychiatrists and psychotherapists showed anxiety, of course, when they first began to do group psychotherapy. However, their anxiety was not as much related to lack of knowledge and experience as had been true with two previous groups of trainees that were mentioned. Instead, it was the experience of being exposed to the group in a fashion so different from what goes on in individual therapy that was anxiety-provoking to all of them.

Second, their previous concentration on individual psychotherapy of a psychoanalytic type made it difficult for them to work freely at first in this new psychotherapeutic technique. They tended to carry the attitudes and ideas they had accumulated in their individual psychotherapy experience into their work as group psychotherapists. Very frequently it was found that they were all treating the patients in the group as individuals and not utilizing the group and the group method in performing group psychotherapy, the same difficulty that was encountered in training the less experienced psychologists and social workers and psychiatric residents.

Again this difficulty in using the group and the group method in performing group psychotherapy was overcome by their performing group psychotherapy by themselves under adequate supervision. However, it must be said that the resistance of this experienced group to utilizing the group and the group method in performing group psychotherapy was more persistent and more difficult to deal with in certain ways than that encountered with the fresher and younger and less experienced trainees previously mentioned.

Before completing the description of the training experience with the graduate psychiatrists two points might be mentioned. The training program at first did not include having the younger group psychotherapists act as a recorder-observer for the more experienced group therapists. However, in the future, particularly as younger men come for training, it is planned to institute as part of their training their participation as a recorder-observer in group psychotherapy conducted by more experienced group psychotherapists.

The second point to be mentioned about this group is that here again there was no attempt to include as part of their training participation as a patient in a psychotherapeutic group. The reasons were somewhat similar to those previously stated for the psychiatric residents—the orientation of the senior medical staff and a definite feeling on the part of all concerned that such a participation as a patient in a psychotherapeutic group was not an essential part of training for group psychotherapy.

REVIEW OF THE LITERATURE ON THE TRAINING OF THE GROUP PSYCHOTHERAPIST

Several writers (Wolf et al.,[1] Scheidlinger,[2] Knopka,[3] Kugelmass and Schossberger,[4] and Hulse[5]) indicate in a general fashion the type of training a group psychotherapist should have. The view of Slavson,[6] that only experienced psychotherapists with adequate knowledge of basic psychopathology should undertake group psychotherapy since it is much more difficult than individual psychotherapy, summarizes the feeling of this group.

Detailed accounts of methods of training group psychotherapists are described in the next three articles. The first of these is Boenheim's account[7] of the three-year training program in group psychotherapy at the Columbus State Hospital in Columbus, Ohio. In the *first year*, the trainees (1) receive lectures in general psychopathology, (2) do individual psychotherapy under individual supervision, and (3) hear lectures on group psychotherapy. During the *second year*, they begin to participate in group psychotherapy, first as a visitor and later as a recorder-observer in a group led by an experienced group psychotherapist. They also begin to participate in a "dynamic doctors' group" which is devoted to discussing their problems with patients but which is conducted in such a fashion that it is somewhat of a group psychotherapeutic experience. In the *third year*, the residents work as a cotherapists with a more experienced group therapist and then begin to do group psychotherapy themselves. They participate also "in regular group meetings of group leaders."

Ross[8] and his co-workers describe how training in group psychotherapy was integrated with psychiatric training in the three-year psychiatric residency program at the University of Cincinnati. In the *first year*, the residents receive lectures on and review the basic literature in group psychotherapy. They also attend a weekly "Patient-Care Conference" with other ward personnel and present their individual psychotherapy cases to a group of residents under leadership of an experienced therapist for supervision and discussion. In these conferences it was felt the first-year resident learned something of group dynamics and had "the personal experience in being part of and working in a group." In the *second year*, the residents begin to participate in group psychotherapy either as observers through a one-way screen or as a recorder-observer in a group run by an experienced group psychotherapist. They attend and participate in a group supervisory session at which material from the group psychotherapy sessions is presented. In the *third year*, the resident forms a group and begins to do group psychotherapy with a junior resident as an observer. His work is supervised in the group supervisory sessions.

The most carefully thought-out and detailed plan for training of the group psychotherapist is given by Mullan[9] in the second part of a symposium on "Training in Group Psychotherapy." He states that group psychotherapy training should be available only to those who have already (1) acquired competence in individual psychotherapy, including two supervisory control periods (of individual patients) of 50 hours each; (2) attended graduate courses in psychiatry, psychology, and psychoanalysis; (3) undergone a personal, individual psychoanalysis.

Mullan feels "The Graduate Training Program for the Group Psychotherapist" should consist of: (1) a one-year required course in the fundamentals of small-group functioning and group psychotherapy, including elective courses centering about the application of group psychotherapy to special age groups, special conditions, special settings, and so on; (2) participation in small continuous workshops of from seven to ten members, with the experience level of any workshop being constant. They should be moderately unstructured but not to such a degree as to verge upon becoming therapeutic. Mullan feels this is an excellent form for training group psychotherapists because the workshop experience embodies many of the characteristics of the therapy group, and workshop members actually experience to a degree the dynamics and conceptions to be found in group psychotherapy; (3) experience of personal group psychotherapy. The trainee should be selected for a group according to his psychological needs and should be placed in a group of patients and *not* in a group made up of his colleagues or other professionals. He should continue as a patient in such a psychotherapeutic group until he has completed his treatment; (4) supervision on a weekly basis for a period of at least 50 sessions when the student starts to conduct a therapy group.

The next group of reports deal with a specific aspect of training—the supervision of the trainee in the performance of group psychotherapy. Geller[10] accomplished this by means of "unstructured" supervisory seminars with excellent results. Grotjahn,[11] as soon as he had established a good relationship with the student, entered the students' groups as an interested observer. Papenek[12] also stressed the need for establishing a good relationship between the supervisor and the student. Spotnitz[13] used a group psychotherapeutic technique to help group psychotherapists learn how to deal with their resistance to the impact of intensive emotional reactions from severely disturbed patients in groups.

Up to this point, the literature reviewed has dealt more or less directly with training in group psychotherapy. There are a number of reports which deal with the use of group psychotherapy and group psychotherapeutic techniques in teaching and training in psychiatry, social work, psychology, and related fields as well as for training in group psychotherapy. Hadden[14] has reviewed this literature and divided it into two main techniques. The first, to which Hadden and his co-workers[15] are among the chief contributors, consists in having the student attend group sessions as an observer-recorder or as an "auxiliary therapist." As already noted, Ross[16] and Boenheim[17] utilized this technique in training for group psychotherapy, and the present writer, in association with Miller[18] and Wender,[19] has also reported on the use of this method in teaching group psychotherapy and psychotherapy to psychiatric residents. Kowert[20] also used this approach in teaching group psychotherapy. Lorand [21] found it most helpful to use psychotherapeutic techniques in teaching and in supervising psychiatric residents in individual psychotherapy. The use of psychodrama and its techniques in demonstration and training with student psychotherapists and with Red Cross workers has been reported by Moreno,[22] Merchant,[23] Hagen and Kenworthy,[24] and Winder and Stieper.[25]

In the second of the techniques mentioned by Hadden, the students

—either in an actual psychotherapeutic group or in a group in which group psychotherapeutic techniques are used—through an examination of their own behavior and reactions in the group, learn not only group psychotherapy but psychiatry, psychotherapy, and other related matters as well. In reports already noted, Geller,[26] Kugelmass and Schossberger,[27] and Ross[28] utilized this technique in teaching group psychotherapy. Patton[29] used this method for teaching and training in psychiatry, psychotherapy, and group psychotherapy. Votos and Glenn[30] used a similar method in overcoming medical students' resistance to learning psychiatry with very good results. The efficacy of this method in the training of medical students in psychiatry was independently confirmed in two reports by Ganzarain and his co-workers.[31]

Similar experiences with the effectiveness of the use of group psychotherapy or group psychotherapeutic techniques in teaching by using the students' own reactions in the group as material are reported by several others. Kotkov[32] and Brawnthel [33] found the method very useful in the training of social workers and others in special situations. Geller,[34] Semrad and his co-workers,[35] Glenn,[36] Rhoads and Dlin[37] utilized this type of technique in training psychiatric hospital personnel such as social workers, psychologists, nurses, and aides. Berman[38] also used this approach with psychology students and educators, and Laughlin[39] utilized it to train executives in handling personnel problems.

The use of a group psychotherapeutic technique in teaching indicates that treatment to a greater or lesser degree is being carried on at the same time. There is a group of workers who emphasize that the therapeutic effects obtained in using group psychotherapeutic techniques in teaching are the most important factors in helping students to learn. Not only are resistance and defensive inhibitions (true blocks to learning) lessened but increased awareness of their own reactions enables the students to see and understand what is occurring in patients. The work and the views of Whitaker and Warkentin, Sutherland and Warson (as cited by Hadden[40]), Glenn,[41] Ganzarain,[42] and Beukenkamp[43] are along these lines.

Obviously, a logical development of such views would lead to the conclusion that a group psychotherapeutic experience is a necessary part of the training of the group psychotherapist, and several authors have stated this. In reports previously noted, Boenheim's "dynamic doctors group" [44] is essentially a psychotherapeutic group composed of psychiatric residents. In this he is following the lead of Balint,[45] who used group psychotherapy in teaching general practitioners and social workers psychotherapy. Wolf [46] and Berger[47] feel that a group psychotherapeutic experience in a "therapeutic group of professionally trained persons" is an essential part of the training of a group psychotherapist in order that he may "directly experience the process of group psychoanalysis as a patient." The clearest and most emphatic statement to this effect is the one already cited by Mullan,[48] who differs from Wolf in feeling that the group psychotherapist trainee should be placed in a group of patients who are not trainees.

PRESENT-DAY VIEWS CONCERNING THE TRAINING OF THE GROUP PSYCHOTHERAPIST

In addition to reviewing the literature, it was thought it would be of interest to obtain the current views of workers with experience in the training of group psychotherapists. The method used was to submit a questionnaire to a number of such experienced workers. The questionnaire used was arbitrarily divided into five headings to facilitate the collection of the data. This was submitted to 54 members of the AGPA who are recognized authorities in group psychotherapy and all of whom have been, and for the most part still are, active for many years in the training of group psychotherapists. The professional background of these 54 members is as follows: 32 psychiatrists, 10 psychologists, 9 social workers, and 3 educators. Since all of them have been active for many years in the training of group psychotherapists their combined experience is an extensive one. In addition the group is quite representative, including all of the "schools" of psychology and a variety of institutions and settings—hospitals, clinics, social agencies, and private practice. Up to the time of the writing of this paper replies had been received from 30, or over 50 per cent, of those to whom the questionnaire had been submitted with half or more of the the psychiatric group replying and a little less than half responding in the nonpsychiatric group. The data obtained in this fashion can best be summarized under the headings used in the questionnaire, as follows:*

1. Clinical Psychiatric Training of the Group Psychotherapist

(The question: "How much knowledge and experience or background do you feel a group psychotherapist should have in clinical psychiatry, psychopathology, or other related fields?")

All felt that a thorough knowledge of the dynamics and psychopathology of mental and emotional illness was essential as well as experience with

---

* The author wishes to acknowledge gratefully the valuable assistance of those who replied to the questionnaire. Many spent a great deal of time and effort on the replies, and by their thoughts and comments contributed in no small measure to the findings in the paper. The names of those who replied are: K. A. Adler, M.D.; N. Beckenstein, M.D.; B. J. Becker, M.D.; I. L. Berger, M.D.; M. M. Berger, M.D.; W. Briehl, M.D.; H. E. Durkin, Ph.D.; G. H. Fenchel, Ph.D.; J. D. Frank, M.D.; E. Fried, Ph.D.; M. Grotjahn, M.D.; H. Grunwald; J. Krasner, Ph.D.; M. Linden, M.D.; A. A. Lippman, M.D.; L. H. Loeser, M.D.; I. M. Marcus, M.D.; H. Mullan, M.D.; J. Munzer, M.D.; H. Papenek, M.D.; M. Rosenbaum, Ph.D.; W. D. Ross, M.D.; S. Scheildlinger, Ph.D.; D. A. Shaskan, M.D.; S. R. Slavson; E. Somerfield, M.D.; C. T. Standish, M.D.; E. Varon; C. A. Whitaker, M.D.; A. Wolf, M.D.; I. Ziferstein, M.D.

a wide variety of various psychiatric conditions and syndromes. The time required for such basic training was most often estimated to be three years —the same as that required for completion of a residency in psychiatry.

2. *Individual Psychotherapy Training of the Group Psychotherapist (Other than Analytic Training)*

(The question: "How much training and/or experience do you feel a group psychotherapist should have in individual psychotherapy other than analysis? Do you feel he should have such experience before beginning his group psychotherapy training?")

All agreed that a thorough grounding and considerable experience in individual psychotherapy was essential for the group psychotherapist. Most workers felt that at least some experience, adequately supervised, in individual psychotherapy should be acquired before beginning training in group psychotherapy. Estimates of the time required for such training in individual psychotherapy varied from one year to five years, with two or three years mentioned most frequently. Several workers, anticipating question three, felt that the training in individual psychotherapy should be as intensive as that required in a psychoanalytic institute.

3. *Analytic Experience of the Group Psychotherapist*

(The question: "Do you feel a group psychotherapist would benefit from or should he have a personal analysis? In addition, how desirable or necessary is it for the group psychotherapist to have training and/or experience in the analytic treatment of patients?")

Several workers did not feel a personal analysis was absolutely necessary for the group psychotherapist, but all agreed that it was highly desirable for anyone going into group psychotherapy and essential for those who contemplated doing analytically oriented group psychotherapy, since it helped the therapist deal with his own neurotic difficulties and become aware of areas that could lead to troublesome countertransference difficulties. As regards analytic training as well as a personal analysis, some observers did not feel it was absolutely necessary, although all agreed it would be helpful to the potential group psychotherapist. On the other hand several people stated that a personal analysis and analytic training should be required of all trainees in group psychotherapy.

4. *Training in Group Psychotherapy*

(The question: "It has been suggested that training in group psychotherapy consists of the following:

    a. Didactic lectures and/or courses.
    b. Demonstration or continuous case seminars.
    c. Performing group psychotherapy under supervision.

From your own experience, does the above type of training program seem adequate? Other than participation in a psychotherapeutic group, do you feel any other elements should be included in a group psychotherapy training program? How long should such a training program take: one year? two years? or more?")

In regard to this question, the replies were more diversified but on the whole showed a great deal of agreement. *All* of the respondents felt that doing group psychotherapy under supervision (part "c" of the question) was the most valuable and necessary part of the training program and two felt that this was the only important part of the training program. Most other workers felt that a combination of the three parts of the training program—didactic courses, a case seminar, and performing group psychotherapy under supervision—was the most useful type of training program.

An additional part of the training which almost all workers felt was a necessary and valuable one was for the trainee to spend some time—at least six months to one year—as an observer (or an observer-recorder) in a group run by a more experienced group psychotherapist. Several felt that the trainee should act as a cotherapist as well as an observer.

Another important part of the training program which most people felt was particularly useful was workshop participation. This seems to be a way of doing supervision in a group, and some workers feel that this is the most effective way to do supervision.

As regards the time required for training in group psychotherapy, the estimates in the replies varied from one to three years. Most people agreed that the trainee should not begin to do group psychotherapy until he had had at least six months to one year of instruction of some sort in doing group psychotherapy. All agreed that the beginning group psychotherapist should be supervised adequately for at least a period of one year—and preferably two years—before he should begin to do group psychotherapy on his own.

5. Participation in a Psychotherapeutic Group as Part of Training in Group Psychotherapy

(The question: "It has been suggested that part of the training in group psychotherapy should consist of participation as a patient in a psychotherapeutic group. Do you feel such participation is a necessary or desirable part of training in group psychotherapy? Why would it be necessary or desirable? From your own experience, how do trainees react to such participation? Is it your opinion that such participation is *not* a necessary or desirable part of training in group psychotherapy? On what is this opinion based?")

The responses to this question fell into three categories: (1) those who felt it was a necessary part of the training of the group psychotherapists, (2) those who felt it was not necessary but that it might be desirable, and (3) those who felt it was neither necessary nor desirable.

In the first group, those who felt participation in a psychotherapeutic group was an essential part of the training of the group psychotherapist emphasized that the group psychotherapist needs the experience of being a patient in a group. This helps him understand how the patients feel in group psychotherapy, and it also helps the potential group therapist to appreciate the differences between the way a patient functions in a group compared with in individual therapy. Also, many felt that the psychotherapeutic group experience was most valuable in helping the trainee to work out tension difficulties in his relationships to groups and especially to peers and to authority figures. As regards the reaction of the trainee to participation in a psychotherapeutic group, those who felt it was necessary stated that they had not encountered any unfavorable or untoward reaction on the part of the trainees. The trainee showed the same type of resistance to the treatment as would any other patient.

Ten observers felt that participation in a psychotherapeutic group was not absolutely necessary for the trainee but was a desirable part of his training. It may be of some significance that only one of these had had a personal experience of this type, while many of the first group had participated as patients in a psychotherapeutic group. Several of the second group had been leaders of groups in which psychiatrists and other professionals had participated, and they received the impression that this had been a helpful experience. Three commented that they had noted that the trainee tended initially to take over the views of and to imitate the technique and mannerisms of their group therapist, indicating possible unresolved transference problems, and one raised the question of the countertransference of the group therapist toward a trainee whom the group therapist had treated in a group and whether or not this would influence the senior therapist's evaluation of the trainee's ability as a group psychotherapist.

Coming now to those observers who felt the trainees' participation in a psychotherapeutic group was neither necessary nor desirable, two were emphatic in indicating this, especially for an analyzed group therapist. One did not believe that a trainee would be free to reveal himself sufficiently clearly to obtain real benefit from the experience as a patient in a psychotherapeutic group when this was part of his training, while others felt it was not a necessary part of the training of the group psychotherapist and that it imposed an unnecessary burden upon him.

SUMMARY AND CONCLUSIONS

Material concerning the training of the group psychotherapist has been presented from three sources: (1) the writer's personal experience with three different groups of trainees of varying background and experience; (2) the experience of others, again with students of varying background and experience, as presented in the literature; and (3) the views of 30 experienced group psychotherapists working in different settings and with students of various types. The somewhat surprising and rather reassuring finding is that the experience of all concerned leads to a more or less complete agreement (with the exception of one or two points) on what is essential in the basic training of the group psychotherapist.

Now, to summarize these points:

(1) The group psychotherapist should have acquired a *thorough* knowledge of basic clinical psychiatry, psychopathology, and dynamics and should have had a *well-rounded experience* with a wide variety of psychiatric cases. Some feel that such training should extend for three years and should be the equivalent of what is required in a three-year psychiatric residency training. Many believe that this basic psychiatric experience should be acquired before beginning group psychotherapy training.

(2) The group psychotherapist should have had a *well-supervised and adequate experience* in individual psychotherapy, and preferably, this should precede his group psychotherapy by at least one year.

(3) A personal analysis is considered essential by most observers so that personal areas of conflicts should not lead to blind spots in the therapist and also to help him become aware of the nature of emotional reactions. Analytic training or its equivalent with regard to the dynamics and technique of individual analytic psychotherapy was felt to be highly desirable (or even absolutely necessary by some) for the group psychotherapy trainee.

(4) The most useful parts of the training in group psychotherapy itself (in order of decreasing importance) were considered to be as follows: First, performing group psychotherapy under *adequate* supervision (individual or group) for a period of one to two years is unanimously considered to be the essential part of training in group psychotherapy. Second, participation in a group as an observer, observer-recorder, and/or as a cotherapist all agreed gave the trainee a firsthand view of group psychotherapy that was most helpful, particularly if it preceded by six months or a year the trainee's doing group psychotherapy himself. Third, participation, under an experienced leader, in a workshop or seminar with others of the same level of experience for discussion of problems related to doing group psychotherapy was considered by all to be a helpful experience in training. Continuous case seminars and didactic lectures were also considered useful in training by most workers, but to a lesser degree than the first three experiences already mentioned.

Another comment may be appropriate at this point. The method of training in group psychotherapy, as Hulse[49] pointed out, has been influenced by the methods of training in individual psychotherapy, and the stages of development of the training in group psychotherapy in some ways parallel those of individual psychotherapy, as for example, the finding that performing group psychotherapy under supervision is the essential part of training. However, the nature of group psychotherapy permits an additional dimension to training which is not possible in individual psychotherapy training. This refers to the fact that the trainee can observe and even participate in the group psychotherapy by acting as an observer, an observer-recorder, or a cotherapist in a group led by a more experienced group psychotherapist. Such observation and participation is obviously impossible in individual psychotherapy without profoundly affecting the basic one-to-one relationship.

As already noted, this feature of group psychotherapy has been used by many to demonstrate and to teach group psychotherapy in general. A further application in teaching and training in many fields was the use of group psychotherapeutic principles and techniques with groups of students. The combination of the two techniques—actual demonstration plus the therapeutic effects of group participation—has been widely utilized.

This leads us back to the last point in the summary of the material on training in group psychotherapy as follows:

(5) Participation by the group psychotherapist trainee as a patient in a psychotherapeutic group is considered necessary or desirable by many observers in helping the trainee further work out personal problems, especially those connected with difficulties in relation to peers and authority figures. It was also felt that such personal participation in a group as a patient gives the trainee a first hand knowledge of group psychotherapy. On the other hand, others felt that such an experience was neither necessary nor desirable and raised some question as to its effectiveness.

No clear-cut data is available concerning the question of the trainee's participation as a patient in a psychotherapeutic group. While many workers who have had the experience regard it as valuable, there have not been any reports in the literature describing such an experience or such a group in any detail. In discussing this with some students who participated in such an experience, this writer's impression was that it was quite disturbing to some and not nearly as valuable as others have indicated.

However, the whole question needs to be further evaluated. Slavson* raises an important point when he questions how effective such a therapeutic experience can be when it is undertaken in connection with training. The same question can be raised about the so-called individual "training analysis." It is a very common experience for analysts who have completed their "training analysis" to find it necessary some years later to undergo an additional analysis. In part, this may be, as Freud [50] pointed out, in relation to needs engendered by doing analysis, but some of the

* Personal communication.

need may stem from the fact that the original training analysis could not be as therapeutically effective as an analysis conducted under different circumstances.

Some other important points that need further clarification and evaluation are those related to the concepts of "group" and "a group method of performing psychotherapy." These questions have been the source of much discussion in recent years and this has been reflected in the literature. Undoubtedly, some of the difficulties involved in clarifying certain undecided points concerning training in group psychotherapy stem from the still unsettled issues as to what a "group" is and what constitutes "a group method of performing psychotherapy."

However, sufficient experience has accumulated by now, as the material cited here demonstrates, to indicate the unmistakable need for certain kinds of knowledge, experience, and skills in the group psychotherapist. These were pointed out in the introduction after a working definition of group psychotherapy had been given. Stated briefly again these are: The group psychotherapist needs to know something of mental and emotional illness and its treatment, especially the type of treatment that utilizes a group and a group method to facilitate communication in the group, both verbal and nonverbal, through the establishment of relationships and interaction to the therapist and between the patients. Adequate training for the group psychotherapist should fulfill these needs.

REFERENCES

1. A. Wolf, N. Locke, M. Rosenbaum, E. Hillpern, W. Goldfarb, A. Kadis, S. Obers, I. Milberg, and R. Abell, "The Psychoanalysis of Groups: The Analyst's Objections," *Int. J. Group Psychother.*, 2:221-231, 1952.
2. S. Scheidlinger, "Social Group Work and Group Psychotherapy," *Social Work*, 36-42, July 1956.
3. G. Knopka, "Knowledge and Skill in the Group Therapist," *Am. J. Orthopsychiat.*, 19:56-60, 1949.
4. S. Kugelmass and J. Schossberger, "Problems of Initial Training for Group Psychotherapy in Israel," *Int. J. Group Psychother.*, 8:179-184, 1958.
5. W. C. Hulse, "Training for Group Psychotherapy in the U.S.A. and Abroad," *Int. J. Group Psychother.*, 8:257-264, 1958.
6. S. R. Slavson, "Qualification and Training of Group Therapists," *Ment. Hyg.*, 31:386-396, 1947.
7. C. Boenheim, "Clinical Experience with Group Psychotherapy," Lecture given at Third Annual Institute, American Group Psychotherapy Association, New York, N.Y., January 1959.
8. W. D. Ross, *et. al.*, "Integrating Training in Group Psychotherapy with Psychiatric Residency Training," *Int. J. Group Psychother.*, 8:323-328, 1958.
9. H. Mullan in C. Beukenkamp, H. Mullan, H. Papanek, F. Tate, and M.

Berger, "Training in Group Psychotherapy: A Symposium," *Am. J. Psychother.*, 12:493-507, 1958.

10. J. J. Geller, "An Experience in Group Psychotherapy as a Teaching Device," *Group Psychother.*, 7:130-138, 1954.

11. M. Grotjahn, "Special Problems of Supervision in Group Psychotherapy," *Group Psychother.*, 3:309-315, 1951; "Problems and Techniques of Supervision," *Psychiat.*, 5:9-15, 1955.

12. H. Papanek in Beukenkamp, Mullan, Papanek, Tate, and Berger, *op. cit.* (See note 9.)

13. H. Spotnitz, "Resistance Reinforcement in Affect Training of Analytic Group Psychotherapists," *Int. J. Group Psychother.*, 8:395-402, 1958.

14. S. B. Hadden, "Training," in S. R. Slavson (ed.), *The Fields of Group Psychotherapy* (New York: International Universities Press, 1956), pp. 302-316.

15. S. B. Hadden, "The Utilization of a Therapy Group in Teaching Psychotherapy," *Am. J. Psychiat.*, 103:644-648, 1947; W. L. Peltz, E. H. Steel, S. B. Hadden, M. L. Schwab, and F. Nichols, "Group Therapeutic Experience as a Method of Teaching Psychiatry to Medical Students," *Int. J. Group Psychother.*, 5:270-279, 1955.

16. Ross *et al.*, *op. cit.*

17. Boenheim, *op. cit.*

18. J. S. A. Miller, S. Kwalwasser, and A. Stein, "Observations Concerning the Use of Group Psychotherapy in a Voluntary Hospital," *Int. J. Group Psychother.*, 4:86-94, 1954.

19. L. Wender and A. Stein, "The Utilization of Group Psychotherapy in Teaching Psychotherapy," *Int. J. Group Psychother.*, 3:326-329, 1953.

20. E. H. Kowert, "A Demonstration of the 'Laboratory Method' in the Investigation and Teaching of Group Psychotherapy," *J. Clin. Psychopath.*, 3:426-436, 1943.

21. S. Lorand, "The Teaching of Psychotherapeutic Techniques to Residents in Psychiatry," *Acta Psychotherap., Psychosom. et Orthopaegog.*, Supplement, 1954, pp. 218-224.

22. J. L. Moreno, "A Frame of Reference for Testing the Social Investigation," *Sociometry*, 3:4, 1940.

23. K. C. Merchant, "The Place of Psychodrama in the Training of the Clinician," *Psychol. Bull.*, 37:748, 1951.

24. M. Hagan and M. Kenworthy, "The Use of Psychodrama as a Training Device for Professional Groups Working in the Field of Human Relations," *Group Psychother.*, 4:1, 1951.

25. A. Winder and D. R. Stieper, "A Prepracticum Seminar in Group Psychotherapy," *Int. J. Group Psychother.*, 6:410-417, 1956.

26. J. J. Geller, *op. cit.*; "Supervision in a Hospital Group Psychotherapy Program," *Int. J. Group Psychother.*, 8:313-322, 1958.

27. Kugelmass and Schossberger, *op. cit.*

28. Ross, *op. cit.*

29. J. D. Patton, "The Group as a Training Device and Treatment Method in a Private Psychiatric Hospital," *Int. J. Group Psychother.*, 4:419-428, 1954.

30. A. Votos and J. Glenn, "Group Techniques in Overcoming Medical Stu-

dents' Resistance to Learning Psychiatry," *Int. J. Group Psychother.*, 3:293, 1953.

31. R. Ganzarain *et al.*, "Group Psychotherapy in the Psychiatric Training of Medical Students," *Int. J. Group Psychother.*, 8:137-153, 1958; "Study of the Effectiveness of Group Psychotherapy in the Training of Medical Students," *Int. J. Group Psychother.*, 9:475-487, 1959.

32. B. Kotkov, "The Group as a Training Device for a Girls' Training School," *Int. J. Group Psychother.*, 4:193-198, 1954.

33. H. Brawnthel, "A Casework Training Course as a Group Therapeutic Experience," *Int. J. Group Psychother.*, 2:239-244, 1952.

34. J. J. Geller, "Supervision in a Hospital Group Psychotherapy Program," *loc. cit.*

35. E. V. Semrad, and J. Arsenian, "The Use of Group Processes in Teaching Group Dynamics," *Am. J. Psychiat.*, 108:358-363, 1951; E. V. Semrad, J. Arsenian, and C. Standish, "Experiences with Small Groups in Teaching Group Psychology," *Group Psychother.*, 10:191, 1957.

36. J. Glenn, "Values of Group Discussions with Psychiatric Aides in a Mental Hospital," *Int. J. Group Psychother.*, 1:254-263, 1951.

37. J. M. Rhoads and B. M. Dlin, *Problems of Group Psychotherapy with Nurses*. Paper read at the Tenth Annual Meeting, American Group Psychotherapy Association, New York, 1954.

38. L. Berman, "A Group Psychotherapeutic Technique for Training in Clinical Psychology," *Am. J. Orthopsychiat.*, 23:322-327, 1953; "Mental Hygiene for Educators: Report on an Experiment Using a Combined Seminar and Group Psychotherapy Approach," *Psychoanal. Rev.*, 40:319-332, 1953.

39. H. P. Laughlin, "A Group Approach to Management Improvement," *Int. J. Group Psychother.*, 4:165-171, 1954.

40. S. B. Hadden, "Training," *loc. cit.*

41. Glenn, *op. cit.*

42. R. Ganzarain *et al.*, *op. cit.*

43. Beukenkamp *et al.*, *op. cit.* (See note 9.)

44. Boenheim, *op. cit.*

45. E. Balint and M. Balint, "Dynamics of Training in Groups for Psychotherapy," *Brit. J. Med. Psychol.*, 28:135-143, 1955; M. Balint, "Training General Practitioners in Psychotherapy," *Brit. Med. J.*, 1:115-120, 1954.

46. Wolf, *et al.*, *op. cit.* (See note 1.)

47. M. Berger in Beukenkamp *et al.*, *op. cit.* (See note 9.)

48. *Ibid.*

49. Hulse, *op. cit.*

50. S. Freud, "Analysis Terminable and Interminable," in *Collected Papers*, Vol. V (London: Hogarth Press, 1950), pp. 316-357.

AN EXPERIENCE IN TEACHING PSYCHOTHERAPY BY MEANS OF GROUP THERAPY

John Warkentin

In a school setting, the psychotherapist is definitely a hybrid creature. His function is not clearly that of a physician, who heals sick patients with the single purpose of making them healthy. Neither is he a traditional teacher, who helps the student acquire information and certain standardized skills. The therapist in a school combines some functions of both the teacher and the physician. The proper mixture of these functions is difficult to determine.

This paper reports an experiment which was intended to clarify the extent to which it is possible for a teacher to contribute to the emotional growth of students. The teacher cannot avoid contributing to the affective learning of students. His very position before a class makes the teacher a recapitulation of other parental figures, whose attitudes are inadvertently learned by students; yet the social responsibility for such affective learning may not always be consciously acknowledged by the teacher. Students are even more likely to be quite unaware of the unacknowledged therapeutic parent-child relationship. All concerned will readily deal openly with intellectual needs, but often remain silent regarding evident emotional needs. In the present experiment this was changed to place conscious emphasis on feelings, attitudes, and motivation. The purpose was to determine the value of directly therapeutic approach by the teacher.

This experiment was conducted twice, once for two years with grade school teachers, and then for eight years with medical students. In both cases our effort was to help groups go through a growing experience which would make the members free to use their own person therapeutically.

Reprinted from *Progressive Education*, May, 1955, pp. 79-82.

Group psychotherapy was begun with some of the same attitudes as those which prevail in a teacher's college, where classroom procedures are acted out by the teachers in training. At times there was a competitive element similar to that of the mock trials held in a law school. As opportunity arose, we discussed openly the need for an emotional experience, such as might be expected of theological students before they enter the ministry. The quality of any such "corrective emotional experiences" undertaken with student groups was always modified by the fact that nobody present acknowledged a need for treatment. When pathology was discussed by a group member, this was not taken as evidence of illness, but rather as "growing pains." This emphasis decreased the shame and fear, and increased the expectation of achieving greater stature as a whole person.

GRADE SCHOOL TEACHERS

The experiment with teachers was done in a grade school with 800 pupils. The principal agreed to have a psychotherapist be at the school from 3 to 4 P.M. every Wednesday, to talk with the teachers about personality problems in children and adults. Attendance was voluntary, but most of the teachers consistently came to every meeting. The principal usually attended, but he exercised no authority.

At first the therapist did all the talking, giving some lectures on psychodynamics, psychosexual development, and interpersonal relationships. From the first he explained that he was talking to get the group acquainted with his thinking and feeling, and that he would stop lecturing as soon as more discussion developed. After about three months, very little lecturing was necessary.

At first the group discussions dealt with problem children, with the teachers asking the therapist what to do about them. The therapist never gave advice in so many words, but commented on the attitude of the teacher as she described the problem child. The therapist also offered guesses as to how the teacher might cause problem behavior in her children. Some teachers were extremely hesitant to acknowledge feelings of resentment or even revenge concerning difficult pupils. The "anesthesia" of group participation and support gradually helped some of these rigid teachers to be more spontaneous in giving expression to their emotions. By the end of the first year the therapist did much less leading, and was often a participant in discussions between the teachers. The issues considered branched out from problem children to such other subjects as relationships to parents, relationships between teachers, and functions of the principal. In one respect the therapist remained alert to his responsibility as leader, and this was to prevent the development of excessive anxiety. For example, when one teacher spoke of unusual sexual feeling, the therapist suggested that the group seemed large for this, and that some members present might be uncomfortable if such material were discussed. In a similar manner the therapist tried to protect teachers who were not well liked against too much aggression from the rest of the group. This also occurred in terms of the principal, who was repeatedly criticized.

During the second year, the group took over much of the therapeutic function. The original leader remained an active participant, expressing his own feelings as he had opportunity, or helping to clarify the expressions in the group. Sometimes he even discussed the psychodynamics operating at the time to assist with conscious insight. The leader never quite became an ordinary member of the group. As occasion arose, he pointed out the wisdom of not giving direct advice, or the danger of gossiping about therapeutic confidences, the value of silence in answer to some questions, and the use of fantasy in developing feeling relationships.

After two years, the results were gratifying, particularly the increased enthusiasm of the teachers for their work with children and each other. A kindergarten teacher spoke of being happier with visits by parents. She had felt free for the first time to have mothers stay all day with their children when they started school in the fall. Another teacher spoke of feeling "less trapped" by her pupils. Several referred to having discovered the principal as a person, and that this had enriched their teaching eperience. There were also negative comments, such as that the therapist had failed to do enough factual teaching. Several teachers spoke of not attending regularly because they did not like him, or doubted his sincerity, or considered him too impractical. However, most comments were positive. Several teachers felt themselves to have grown as people in both their professional and private living.

An additional outcome was a special treatment procedure initiated by the teachers for problem children. This pertained only to pupils who were conspicuous in the classroom because of unusual shyness, asocial behavior, or other evidences of marked emotional disturbance. Some teachers had asked the therapist to take the most difficult children for individual treatment, but he had refused. He explained that he was there to help the teachers meet their problems, not to remove them. As a result, the teacher with a behavior problem would ask another teacher to have lunch with the problem child a number of times, so that the "strange" teacher became the therapist. In this way the therapeutic function was isolated from the teaching function. This isolation helped to intensify the therapeutic relationship in these special cases. Transcripts of some of these interviews were written out, and later presented to the group for comment. In this way the school did not export its emotional problems, but worked through them within its own framework. The teachers continued this kind of work for some years after the end of our experiment. The success of this program was taken as further indication of the emotional growth of the teachers participating.

MEDICAL STUDENTS

Our grade school work served as preliminary experience for a more pretentious effort in teaching psychotherapy to medical students. This was undertaken in a medical school which had no previous active department of psychiatry. It was arranged that each student would get 300 hours of work in psychiatry during his four years. About one-fourth of this time was devoted to group psychotherapy.

During the first three months in the fall, the entire freshman class met every Monday at 9 A.M. for an hour of introductory lecture on interpersonal relationships. In December the class was divided into groups of 12 to 15 students, with a staff member assigned to meet with each group for an hour every week through the rest of the freshman and sophomore years. The instructor introduced himself as offering no direct teaching, but willing to share his knowledge and feelings with the group. He explained that the students would not be graded. Attendance was voluntary, but whenever somebody was absent repeatedly, the others usually took this up with him.

The initial response of medical students to this division into groups and to the free discussion varied from outright hostility to tentative acceptance. Each year some of the freshmen objected that they did not want to discuss personal problems in public. Some even asked sarcastically whether the instructor (group leader, therapist) considered them all to be mentally sick. The instructor would then explain that the extent to which members of the group became "patients" was not predetermined, but each would get out of the group as much or as little as he wanted. He also indicated that the group itself had complete control over how it functioned. In the earlier sessions, students expressed various fears, such as of becoming too upset or that members of the group would gossip if intimate material was revealed. They stated that it would be easier to see the instructor alone. They complained that a student could not expect much help from his colleagues since they "were all in the same boat," and that the instructor should be more directive in getting the group started. Some of this early discussion was met by the instructor with complete silence, some with further questions or with explanations. The instructor spoke quite freely about his own life, of experiences with previous groups, and sometimes about private patients in such a way that they could not be identified. The students were told that all the instructors had been psychotherapeutic patients, and questions regarding that experience were answered as openly as seemed appropriate.

By the end of the freshman year, most of the groups had gone through some rather warm exchanges of feeling, including open expressions of hostility toward the instructor and authority generally. Other issues discussed were complaints about various courses in the school, attitudes toward academic achievement, questions regarding sex and marriage, and the difficulties in being free with each other in the group. In contrast to the work with teachers, the instructor did not try to control the anxiety level in these medical student groups. Consequently there were disturbing occasions of much anger or affection, as members of a group overcame the usual barriers between them.

When the group met as sophomores after the summer vacation, there was usually a strengthening of group feeling. The basis for this increment is not clear, but it was as if the interval of three months had served to integrate the group experiences of the freshman year. Much of the interpersonal irritation had disappeared, and the group was more ready to spend the second year working, each member to get help for himself, or to offer help to his colleagues in the group. During the weekly hour of the sophomore year it was not uncommon for some student to announce that he needed some help. At such times the other members of the group withheld their own therapeutic need in order to function as multiple therapists to the man who had made himself a "patient." It was a measure of the therapeutic capacity of the group that such a patient often toook up fundamental problems, such as self-esteem, identification, fears of self-destruction, and moral values. It was rare for the same student to be a patient in two consecutive weekly sessions. On occasion the group offered to help some member, by pointing out his lack of adjustment in some area, or his lack of growth. This was often done with such gentleness and intuitive skill that it amazed the instructor. A characteristic experience toward the end of the sophomore year, and therefore the end of the group, was the need of the students to discover inadequacies in the instructor, and to be able to help him grow. Another aspect was an increasing freedom to express positive feelings, and a desire for some kind of social meeting with wives and girl friends at a party. This was usually held in the home of the instructor.

In the eight years of this program, it has been the opinion of the staff that about 75% of the medical students profited personally and professionally, and were positively oriented toward the whole area of psychotherapy. In their later work with patients, students repeatedly referred to their group experiences to provide a basis for evaluating difficult relationships. A minority of the students showed little or no benefit, but even some of these men later were found to be utilizing their psychotherapeutic teaching in practice. The staff received many grateful remarks from men who felt that the group therapy sessions had been a major integrating factor in their education. A third year student said, "I used to think I'd start living after I got through school; now I want to learn to live before I get through." One man came to the surprising realization that his honesty was primarily a fear of getting caught if he were dishonest, and he was seeking a sense of personal integrity within himself. Another had expected to be successfully married if he once got his M.D., but decided that presentation of this degree to a girl would be a rather inconsequential aspect of building a satisfying marriage.

Certain sociological factors were worth noting, since psychotherapy is somewhat "off center" from the conventional focus of an educational setting. This was of particular concern in the medical school, where the faculty raised questions. There were comments that group therapy might be anti-educational, since it emphasizes motivation and feeling, rather than logic and factual learning. Some of the faculty thought that the medical students were becoming too uninhibited in their critical evaluation of medical teaching. A few parents also came to the Dean to complain about the new thinking their sons were learning in the group meetings. The staff took these comments seriously, and discussed them in the groups.

DISCUSSION

The experiment described leads to the conclusion that a psychotherapist can perform a significant function in an educational program. By force of tradition, the American school places a heavy emphasis on learning facts and reporting these accurately in tests. When the student has achieved a standard level of intellectual and mechanical skill, he is rewarded with a degree. The teacher's responsibility for the student's emotional growth is minimized. For 12 to 20 years of his early life the curriculum impresses on the student the overwhelming importance of performing successfully in competition with others. There is little open encouragement of affective growth. Perhaps our culture is now producing the psychotherapist as a counteremphasis, to acknowledge that meditation, love, fear, and dreams also constitute a legitimate area of systematic growth. *Progressive Education* is to be congratulated on devoting an entire issue to exploring the affective factors in education.

In the preliminary work with teachers, the therapist was primarily helping the group to permit themselves to consider their feelings about their work and themselves. There was a loosening of rigid teaching attitudes. Teachers were helped to take their feelings seriously as related to children, co-workers, and parents. The developing respect in the teacher for herself as a person then in turn resulted in more concern for the emotional development of her pupils. However, the changes seen in the teachers were not of a deep personality re-integration. The therapist had simply helped the teacher to use more adequately and with less fear some capacities already present.

With the medical student groups, the therapist functioned with less hesitancy. His manner encouraged "explosions" of feeling as these developed. He often gave his own free-associations, even though these might disturb the group. The result was a much more tumultuous experience than had occurred with the teachers. However, the group repeatedly had the experience of coming through interpersonal conflict to a new affection and respect for each other. In the case of some students, the therapist also saw signs of rather profound intrapersonal growth. The final outcome was judged to be the emergence of capacities which seemed new to the student.

In both parts of this experiment, the therapist felt considerable surprise that such work was possible within conventional school hours. This preliminary success leads to many other questions regarding the affective dimension in education. For example, the relationship between the work of the therapist, as described above, and that of the regular teacher who feels responsible to present more than her subject matter, remains largely undefined. What has been possible to demonstrate is that interaction in a group offers an approach to emotional growth in a school setting.

SUMMARY

Group psychotherapy with grade school teachers and medical students, conducted one hour per week for two school years, was possible with very satisfactory results. The response of the groups was positive and encouraging. In both experiments, follow-up contacts made two and three years later indicated that growth which was encouraged by the group sessions was continuing. It was found that a prerequisite for teaching psychotherapy in this way was a relatively permissive atmosphere. Given such a setting, group therapy was found to be a powerful method of developing the therapeutic capacity of teachers and students.

ADDITIONAL AUTHOR'S NOTE (1961)

Since the publication of the paper, the group with whom I am associated in the practice of psychotherapy has continued to work together. We have become convinced that the teaching of treatment by means of group experience is a valuable adjunct in the education of the "psychotherapist" at all levels, from the relatively untrained status of the grade school teacher to the fully accredited psychotherapist with many years experience. It seems to me now that the tendency toward the "hardening of the categories" (in Esther Menaker's phrase) is likely to be inevitable for the full-time psychotherapist, unless he is repeatedly challenged both professionally and personally in group experiences with colleagues. Such training for the experienced therapist by means of an on-going group experience was well described by Dr. Carl Whitaker. He points out that the resistances to further growth found in the mature therapist are likely to be so great that only group psychotherapy in some form can bring enough pressure on him to once again learn humbly about human nature. After the therapist has graduated from his own personal therapy, he is likely to find few experiences that can regress him enough to make further growth possible. Patients so effectively assign status to us in our function as therapists that we very much need the group experience with colleagues in which we are accepted as ordinary people with much room to learn and to grow.

Part 6

NEW TRENDS IN GROUP PSYCHOTHERAPY

IN THIS SECTION WE HAVE INCLUDED PAPERS which deal with current conflicts as well as provocative themes in contemporary group psychotherapy. The first paper, by Mullan, has created considerable controversy. What he has set forth in this paper is the denial of the leader function as patients usually perceive the leader within the therapy group. Essentially, he has rejected the concept that the leader of a psychotherapy group need be "frozen" into a particular social role. In this sense, his paper is oriented toward denying the psychiatric culture which stresses pathology in human behavior. He has stressed the importance of the group as an *experience* for each group member. The paper is oriented toward denying the doctor-therapist as the miracle-magic helper in the group setting and notes the importance of encouraging the patient to become more and more aware of his self-worth and healing potential for himself and others. Whether this pattern of active denial of the doctor status is just talk felt by the patient as a particular idiosyncrasy of the physician (who knows full well that he is the physician) or whether this talk is helpful in the patient's denial of the rituals that motivate him in much of his life may be answered by the reader of this paper. It is possible that there are no answers. Mullan's effort to emphasize the group as a living experience does not mean that the element of leadership has to be denied as well. Advocacy of group treatment through denial of therapist roles in essence is oriented toward the promotion of the quality of parity with patients which in turn lessens the expectations and dependency of patient. However, this orientation toward group therapy may result in the therapist's giving up his role of leadership. The question is whether the therapist ever really gives up his role of leadership by denying that he is the doctor or the leader. If we were to assume that every therapist who leads a group is patient as well, we would have to conclude that the skilled therapist who denies his "doctor" status would still be perceived by his fellow patients as the most astute and least sick patient because of the elements of training and self-awareness that he brings to the group experience. It is possible that out of his enthusiasm for the

587

promotion of the group experience, Mullan has gone too far in attempting to deny the fact that, however phrased, the leader who forms the group *remains* essentially the leader. It is unfortunate that Mullan's paper does not cover those studies in the field of social psychology which have emphasized leaderless groups where groups move toward certain goals without formal delineation of a leader. It is possible that even in these so-called leaderless groups one or more superior individuals take on the responsibility for group organization or the assignment of specific activities to each individual who is a member of the group. Bion has found in his work that a group deprived of a leader will search for one.

The paper by Friedman relates the values that are to be found in the positive existentialism of Martin Buber. They have particular relevance to workers in the field of group psychotherapy, since Buber's concern is with the authenticity of human experience. Buber emphasizes the importance of the meeting between individuals as they grow toward fuller awareness of their responsibilities toward one another and to the community and life relationships. This paper has been included because it points to the importance for all group therapists of organizing and exploring a philosophical basis for the work that they are engaged in. The impersonalization that so often characterizes psychoanalytic treatment is rejected by many contemporary therapists and the importance of the here and now experience is emphasized. This has been noted earlier and is stressed again in the paper by Beukenkamp called "Beyond Transference Behavior."

These papers (Mullan, Beukenkamp, Friedman) essentially deny the somewhat inflexible orientation of those psychoanalysts who view the group experience primarily within the familial framework. The group therapist's awareness of his subjective involvement as well as his conceptualization of the group therapy experience as essentially interpersonal appears to be more and more stressed in contemporary psychotherapy. Many therapists who practice individual psychotherapy exclusively criticize this emphasis on the importance of the here and now orientation, which is certainly apparent when individuals are in a therapy group. The here and now orientation has been criticized as being so reality oriented that it denies the intrapsychic mechanisms of the individual patient. The answer of many contemporary psychotherapists who support experiential or existential psychotherapy which embodies a here and now approach is that their therapeutic approach constantly brings to the attention of the patient his belonging to the human community and his responsibilities in all life relationships and that his intrapsychic functioning is repeatedly reflected and demonstrated in his interaction with others.

One paper that we have included in this section has particular relevance because of the increasing use of tranquillizers and various types of psychotropic drugs. Sandison, in this paper, cites some of the analytic philosophers, such as Carl Jung, in terms of what our physical approach to psychiatric treatment can mean for the specific patient. Sandison points out the significance of group membership for the efficacy of the drug used for a particular patient as well as the importance of the therapist's enthusiasm for the particular drug that is being used. While none of his observations have specific relevance to group composition as such, they are an interesting sidelight on the effect of group membership in its relationship to the physiological approach to psychiatric disturbance. The circle comes round again. Even the biochemical approach to psychiatric disorder acknowledges the influence of the group.

Bell, in the last paper in this section, summarizes recent work in the field of family group therapy. He approaches the family from a transactional point of view and tries to reconcile small group theory, from social psychology, with psychotherapy of the family. He proposes a definition of the family in terms of social psychological theories. This is quite dissimilar from a psychoanalytic approach.

47

STATUS DENIAL IN
GROUP PSYCHOANALYSIS

Hugh Mullan

The rapidly growing use of the group method of psychotherapy is attended with many unanswered questions. Many of these questions pertain directly to the results of the group method while others encompass generally the interpersonal dynamics which allow for personality change in group members. This paper is offered in the hope that it can throw some light upon the central dynamic involved, particularly as it is experienced by the therapist. It may be too that this dynamic operates, to some degree at least, in all psychotherapeutic endeavors. Six adult, heterogeneous, mixed, and continuous groups have been observed and interacted with for a period of five years in both private and outpatient clinic practice.

THE DISTINGUISHING FEATURE OF PSYCHOANALYTIC GROUPS

We perceive a primary structural difference in the psychoanalytic group which identifies it, separates it from other "group" therapies, and radically removes it from the category "group" in our culture. This structural difference is the deep interrelatedness of persons who become, as the group analytic process proceeds, less and less encumbered with statuses and roles. (Status is defined as state, condition, or relationship and any relative position or rank either biologically or culturally determined. Status is static and is always accompanied by its dynamic aspect, role. Role is behavior related to characterization and functions.)

Psychoanalytic groups are composed of individuals whose initial behavior within the group is governed by certain culturally ascribed statuses. These statuses, upon which each individual relies so heavily, define his

Reprinted from *The Journal of Nervous and Mental Diseases*, Vol. 122, No. 4, October 1955, pp. 345-352.

state, condition, relative position, and relationships to the other members and to the therapist.[1]

These statuses too describe certain rights, privileges, and duties that each individual feels he must exercise in the group. And as these rights, privileges, and duties are put into effect, roles are assumed, behavior emerges, and group interaction occurs.

At this early moment in this process, the "psychoanalytic" group is merely a microcosm of society. It has the characteristics, including "advantages" and "disadvantages," of all social groups. It is relatively "nontherapeutic" in its functioning. It is mostly structured around certain statuses and certain role dynamisms which are affixed to these statuses. For the psychotherapeutic potential of the group to evolve, we believe that ascribed statuses and their accompanying roles must be denied.

This denial is quite general. It includes those statuses partially determined by biological [2] and physical factors, as well as those achieved through intellectual competence or social position. They are challenged and gradually minimized.

With this gradual denial of statuses, role behavior lessens in the psychoanalytic group, and a more fundamental relationship arises. Therapist and patient become *being and being*; leader and led become *being and being*; male and female become *being and being*; the younger and the older become *being and being*; the infirm and the study become *being and being*; the neurotic and the healthy become *being and being*.

THE IMPORTANCE OF STATUS DENIAL

It is hoped in group psychoanalysis (as it is in all psychotherapeutic ventures) that the prescribed behavior (thinking, feeling, acting, intuiting, and dreaming) of those who come for assistance will be undone and that a new behavior will arise.

I think it is significant to realize that all ascribed statuses are assigned to persons regardless of their innate differences, talents, or longings. And insofar as individuals are adjusted to these statuses and play the roles designated, culture is transmitted without change, and society functions smoothly. This represents a sacrifice upon the part of the individual, a sacrifice which we can no longer in the therapy group allow him to make. We canot permit him to be only his status and his status-directed behavior, for we know that he is much more.

When statuses and roles are rigidly maintained within the analytic group, we observe the tendency to overevaluate commitments demanded by culture. After all, we must realize that it is our culture, albeit, unhealthy elements within it and its faulty transmissions, that makes it mandatory that we have therapy groups.

Group members attempt to bring into the group the same environment which made them ill. Thus, the members at the start see the group as a classroom, as a religious meeting, or as a workshop in better living, and later on, the original family, and so on. These preconceived and conceptualized authority-submissive occurrences are gradually disproved, and in the process the members (and therapist) become anxious. A new group member often gets very upset when the therapist is roughly and openly attacked by another member. His behavior always having been conditioned by an authority in the past, other than himself, his need will be to have this continued. He usually rigorously defends the therapist or counterattacks the "unruly" one. Or, he may deny the experience totally or partially by deceiving himself. The most common self-deception practiced is a rationalized belief that what he is observing is merely technique. He thinks that neither the attacking member nor the therapist really *means* his behavior. The interaction between the two, as he observes it, has an ulterior motive determined by their particular statuses, and it is only a means to an end. If these status-maintaining devices fail, the new member may have to leave the group.

The therapist, in his deep emotional involvement with the individuals in the group, is primarily interested in allowing new behaviors to emerge. Statuses, particularly if fixed, controlling as they do the reciprocal interplay between persons, prevent the emergence of new behavior. Thus, in a group, as is almost always the case, if a person identifies himself as patient, he is denying his therapist-part or potential.[3] And because of this, behavior which is related to his *being therapist* does not emerge. And, alas, the therapist who does not undermine the status "patient" in the group establishes himself as "therapist" or "doctor" and mistakenly implies through this adherence to status that he alone needs no help and no direction.

Our culture sanctions conscious activity to a much greater degree than unconscious activity. It follows from this that culturally determined behavior many times is deficient in integrated subjective determinants. It is my conviction that much role action based upon status relegates the unconscious potential of an individual to second place. Fantasies, dreams, intuitions, and anxieties are kept in abeyance in making a choice or stating a preference. But even more striking, our culture decries that when unconscious activities, i.e. fantasy making or intuiting, are in the ascendancy, this is a manifestation of a psychic disorder. We feel that this is not so. Psychic illness is probably dependent upon the undue repression and faulty utilization of this portion of our beings—known as the unconscious.

The creative urge, deep within all humans, is not in harmony with the status quo. In order to create (and self-creation in the sense that Erich Fromm[4] uses it is all-important), one must overstep one's bonds. Creation occurs in conflict. One cannot remain complacent while challenging the gods.

The task of status reduction within the analytic group cannot be entered upon lightly. It is of crucial importance as it alters in a most thera-peutically significant manner the group milieu. First, through this happen-ing, the group becomes more truly cohesive. Individuals *belong* because they see themselves and others *sub species aeternitatis*. The matrix of our relatedness within the group is what we *are* and not what we are supposed to be or might become.

Secondly, we have found that empathic relatedness is directly propor-tional to the degree of status reduction. Thus, when a group member com-mitted suicide and I was filled with sorrow, self-questioning, and doubts, my status of therapist or leader was extinguished. I suggested an extra group meeting following this tragic occurrence. During this meeting the "pa-tients" became my "therapist"—we were aware of this, and I thanked them for their help and did not charge them. It was during this period that empathy was greatest—that a bond emerged which brought us together and through this crisis. Deep empathic relatedness can only occur in status-free relationships when there is minimal role activity on the part of both therapist and members.

THE METHOD OF STATUS DENIAL IN GROUPS

We feel that much of the beginning group psychoanalyst's activity might be devoted to the means of status denial. This is crucial because these measures insure his development of empathy, as indicated in the previous section, as well as his evolvement as a *therapist*.

If we clearly see the reciprocal nature of status, that therapist and pa-tient are at fixed positions of opposite polarity, our procedure in status de-nial becomes somewhat clarified. We need only to alter our status (the therapist's) in order to alter the patients'.

The therapist's subjective investigation of his need for status and fixed role then becomes both meaningful and decisive. It is meaningful for upon this investigation depends his depth of empathy and decisive because without this investigation his over-all therapeutic effectiveness is limited.

The group psychoanalyst is therapist because he can jettison more easily and more completely the many statuses ascribed to him by his cul-ture and by the group members than can the other group members. This is his *leadership*. His commitments to culture are minimal whereas the oth-ers are maximal. He welcomes the unconscious determinants of his and their behavior whereas the others reject or are skeptical of them.

To put this more absolutely, the therapist may not allow himself any measure of self-imposed omniscience or omnipotence. And still more diffi-cult to achieve is the requirement of not allowing himself any significance stemming from either transferred or projected godlike attributes. These in-junctions are clear enough. However, the very nature of the group, its orig-inal conception and fabrication, and its continuing operation, all under the aegis of the therapist, make these injunctions very difficult ones, to say the least! [5]

Some believe that it is *too* difficult, and they are critical of the group therapist and his method. They point out, and perhaps rightly so, that some therapists use the group method because of their need to be the *leader* with all that this implies.

It seems to me that the superior intellectual status of the therapist, supported by the transferred and projected attitudes and actions of the group members, becomes the most formidable obstruction to status denial within the group.

If this be so, a fundamental step that the group psychoanalyst must make is to question the significance of his intellectual competence. This is achieved by allowing himself fully to experience in the group and at the same time to have his interpretative activities dependent upon feelings and intuitions as well as his intellect. The group analyst does not *know* how to live better than the members although in fact he may be living better than they are.

Recently a colleague permitted me to enter one of his psychoanalytic groups. We attempted from the start to keep my status obscure so that I would not know how to behave. Our attempt was only partly successful. I was introduced as Dr. Mullan, and immediately the others established a status and a role for me to enact. They said, "He is here to observe"; "He is not one of us"; "He is another therapist"; "He is in competition with Max." This, however, did not prevent me from having feeling reactions. I got extremely angry at another group member, blurted out that his simple smile annoyed me, and yelled at him for his inattention in always being late. This display of feeling was very upsetting to everyone. "If he is a therapist and well trained, how can he react so?" "Doesn't he *know* better?" "How can he treat unless he is better controlled?" "Can't he intellectualize his feelings rather than express them?" and so on and on. I found that I could do either one of two things. First, I could experience myself and my anxieties, let go with my feelings, and thereby become close and connected with the group. Or, second, I could intellectualize and conceptualize, either expressing my observations or not. In this latter situation I was unfeeling, remote, and at a distance from the others. Also, in this latter instance, I was relatively free from an awareness of anxiety.

From this experience, from an experience in a leaderless therapy group, and from my experience with continuous heterogeneous groups in my private practice, I have begun to realize that it is only through a longitudinal (life-span) emotional intertwining with the individual that status and role finally disappear. The therapist must have emotion for the individual at each moment in his development, and a cross-sectional knowing of him at the present moment does not suffice.

The therapist, in this deep (life-span) relationship, must be able within himself to match qualitatively, if not quantitatively, every symptom, "trouble," conflict, fear, anxiety, perversion, emotion, defense, resistance, and so on, expressed and felt by those around him. He must be truly accepting of this, his patient role, as he is of his therapist role. He is therapist because he can better accept being patient than the other members.[6]

As the therapist's intellectual and conceptualizing function is minimized, anxieties are felt, feelings, fantasies, and intuitions prevail. Interpretative activity then becomes a total biological function in which all of the metabolisms play a part.

We have a distrust for organization and order in any form in the group. It bespeaks of compulsiveness on the part of the therapist and an unfounded reverence for conscious activity over the thought-to-be chaotic unconscious.

INCLUSIVENESS: A FACTOR IN NONREJECTION

If, as I have indicated, status adherence is detrimental to group psychoanalytical experiencing, statuses which designate certain behaviors may not be used to determine admission or participate in the group. This is so for statuses both biologically and culturally ascribed. Thus, the placement of an unmarried virginal woman with a grandfather is possible as is the placement of a physician (psychiatrist) with an unemployed stenographer.

Recently I was approached by a group of doctors who had begun their psychiatric training, i.e. resident training. They came to me en masse and wished to be treated en masse. This posed many difficulties, all of which were used by them as resistance—that is, resistance to further and closer group experiencing. They could not reveal themselves as openly as they might have because of the competitive nature of their work and their extragroup relationships. Part of this road block, however, was overcome upon the introduction of women, none of whom were physicians.

Status derived from social position cannot be acknowledged in group formation. To allow the social position of a prospective group member to control his group entrance (or to determine the group into which he might be placed) is to admit that the therapist has unresolved problems in this area.

It follows from this that therapy groups may be and perhaps should be basically inclusive and not exclusive. From a purely technical standpoint, this is advocated because the resultant behavior, both individual and interpersonal, becomes molar rather than molecular. We are certain that the segment of behavior that we observe and react to within the inclusive group is more revealing of personality than the behavior observed and reacted to in the more traditional one-to-one therapeutic relationship.

Our tendency toward greater inclusiveness limits to a minimum psychological testing of a person prior to his admission to a group. Rather than this, we relate ourselves to a new individual in the hope that immediately or in the near future he will be ready for the group experience. To routinely or spasmodically test individuals is to demand tacitly a certain status of them. In doing this we imply that all of what he is is not acceptable to us, and we indicate that we are concerned mostly with adaptation and not creative unfolding.

Groups which are heterogeneous, mixed (male and female), and continuous follow our policy of great inclusiveness. The therapist who uses these stratagems fits into the natural order and is unrejecting. This therapist resembles the accepting parent. This is the parent who after conceiving the child accepts him regardless of sex, physical or mental facility, and regardless of the presence or absence of inherited talent. Inclusiveness in the selection of members for analytic group participation closely approximates this ideal.*

The policy of great inclusiveness in the fabrication of a therapy group is only reasonable if two further conditions are espoused by the therapist. First, the therapist must prevent any procedure from becoming ritualized. Each session and each moment of each session are entirely different and cannot be blunted by a fixed procedure of any sort. Second, the therapist must prevent the group or the individual from behavior which is goal-directed. Behavior which is slanted toward some future accomplishment denies the all important immediate experiencing.

THE VALIDITY OF GROUP EXPERIENCING

From my experiences, I believe, as I am certain most psychotherapists do, that the validity of the therapeutic venture rests unequivocally upon the results attained from this venture. Thus validity is mostly related to the "ends" and much less directly related to the "means." And, most important, validity is rigidly attached to our theoretical frame of reference, to our value system, and to the cultural concept of what is normal.

When one concerns himself with the validity of a therapy he is in a "status-fixed" state, for he is defining conditions that exist before and after therapy. And he is designating who is sick and who is well. This fact

---

* This philosophy of inclusiveness has its counterpart historically and presently in the United States. "For how did it happen, after all, that that people which confessed the most heterogeneous racial stocks, the most varied soils and climates, the most diverse and contrasting economic interests, the most variegated religious pattern achieved a stable and enduring national character with an ease that confounded not only the expectations of her critics but history and experience as well?" (See H. S. Commager, The Gottesman Lecture, University of Uppsala, Sweden.)

must be remembered when we consider the value of group experiencing in the next section.

The results of group psychoanalysis in which status denial is central are numerous and individual for each member. Thus far my results, although fragmentary, warrant its continued use and experimentation, and perhaps even to make the skeptical slightly less so.

Highlighting the signs of its effectiveness as a therapy is changed and changing behavior of the members and therapist. This changed and changing behavior is the resultant of two factors which I believe indicate that deep and lasting personality alteration is occurring. First, defensive and alienating behavior is lessened and second, wishing, wanting, desiring for the *self* emerge with increased ability for making responsible decisions. These two decisive happenings stated with such facility and composure are not achieved easily. It is only after long, arduous hours of mutual expending of ourselves in nonstatus interrelatedness and nonrole action that changes do occur. And as with all true therapies that change the basic personality, anxiety and despair[7] are often prominent and frightening features of my group endeavors.

To describe more fully these changes which do occur, individuals move from self-interest behavior to self-disinterest behaviors (or to group interest behaviors). These expressions are confusing and need elaboration.

Self-interest behavior is egocentric, having to do with one's preference for his pregroup (experience) personality, especially its neurotic components. Self-interest behavior advances one's own interests while ignoring those of the group. It is possessive behavior, exploiting the other for one's benefit. It is activity so prejudiced in one's behalf that all risk is removed, thus allowing the individual to maintain all of his rigidities which many times approach a moribund *status quo*.

This self-interest behavior seems to be required by culture or by the individual's concept of what is required by his culture. However, it is due to *faulty transmission* of the culture by parents and significant adults in the past and by most extragroup contacts in the present. It is not that the culture is completely or even partially at fault (although undoubtedly it is, in some respects), but rather it is the manner or *means* of transmissal of the culture which is the key to our problem.

Self-disinterest activity is in reality group interest behavior and is for the good of the whole group *including oneself*. It is not sacrificial, and it is not based upon feelings of loyalty to the group nor any compliance to group mores. Its main characteristics are spontaneity and willingness to risk with an absence of possessiveness and prejudice. It is behavior which is truly experimental with no preconceived idea of gain or even of result.

In every instance it seems to me that self-disinterest behavior is synonymous with group interest behavior. This behavior is the behavior of the *real self*.[8]

Within therapy groups untrusting distance is very gradually replaced by a personal closeness and an intimate connectedness. In ways quite peculiar, each individual reveals more and more of himself. This is only in part an intellectual process. More important, it is an emotional and somatic revelation. It is as though the truth about one's existence (or what he perceives his existence to be) may be revealed with emotional and body participation for the first time.

Each individual transmits to all the others his own particular culture and his reaction to it. As time goes on, this transmission of these experiences—both past and present—becomes less inhibited and is for the purpose of the mutual (group) experience. Directly correlated with this we note that there is less and still less expediency in an individual's behavior as the group process unfolds. (This is in contrast to their parents who transmitted their [the parents'] experiences, but with a large degree of personal expediency.)

Group members find that they no longer have to deny their *beings* in order to minimize, limit, or control the response of others. Acceptance is two ways—the doer does and the responder responds, both in more total fashion.

The group has indicated to me a most certain equivalence—to be helped is synonymous with helping. One does not occur without the other. Help does not come from neatly conceptualizing the other's behavior, but rather it comes from a deep response which changes one, perhaps ever so slightly, and in turn the changed one will cause changes in the other's behavior. Although this is an oversimplification of the therapeutic transaction, it is, I believe, the fundamental of personality change within groups. It remains for us to investigate carefully and elaborate upon this most intimate happening if we are better to understand the "curative process" in groups.

Intrapsychic and psychosomatic disturbances flare up and gradually lessen within the group. In all instances of *real* change as contrasted with mere shifting, there is the essential internal affect-symbol alteration. This alteration is in the quantity and quality of the affects attached to all images, such as mother, father, significant person, past experiences, and so on.

THE VALUE OF GROUP EXPERIENCING

The value of the therapeutic venture is entirely different and separate from its validity. The value stems *not at all* from the results but rather from the momentary hour-to-hour, day-to-day happenings. The value for the group members and therapist alike who continue to relate over long periods of time must come, it seems to me, at each second of emotional contact. Thus value is a function of *the means*. It is not directly related to *the ends*. And most important, value is rigidly attached to our need, as human beings, for satisfaction regardless of our theoretical frame of reference, our value system, or the cultural conceptions of what is normal.

When one is concerned with value, he is in a "status-free" state, for he is primarily, if not totally, experiencing the moment at hand, and conditions existing before and after are not present in his consciousness. He cannot, nor does he try to, differentiate sickness from wellness. This is in contradistinction to validity of therapy.

I have been questioned repeatedly by my family, friends, and colleagues as to why the group experience is so important for me. Even though at times I become fatigued and desire a vacation, I do not feel that I want to leave the group. (Since my groups are continuous, they remain for the most part intact. There are, of course, departures and new admissions, but at this time and for the past two years, I have formed no new groups.) I would like to suggest that although the group is extremely important to all members at particular times, it is most meaningful to the therapist all of the time. If this is not so, the therapist might wonder *what he is doing in the group.* Shouldn't he be elsewhere? Or what might he do to make the group experience more valuable for *himself?*

Aside from the material (making a living) needs which are met quite satisfactorily in group psychoanalytic practice, there are other needs, much more essential, which are achieved by the therapist (and members) in the group. These needs are certainly fulfilled outside of the therapy group in all relationships but, I believe, to a much lesser extent because within the analytic group there are less status restrictions to symbolic experiencing. Thus the therapist as well as the members has the opportunity for a more complete relationship.

Psychoanalysis differs from most other psychotherapies in that one individual in the transaction is expected and encouraged to form a fantastic relationship with the other individual, the therapist. The patient's experience then is an experience in fantasy, i.e. a symbolic experience. What I suggest, as do others,[9] is to make this unilateral fantastic relationship bilateral. It is not enough for the therapist to enter the fantasy relationship silently and passively, but he must be its instigator and its promoter.

In the group it is more difficult for the therapist to maintain symbolic relationships. But insofar as he is able, certain intense satisfactions accrue which are directly related to his being human.*

---

* The importance of symbolization to the human being has been described by many. I would refer the reader to Ernst Cassirer (see E. Cassirer, *An Essay on Man* [Garden City: Doubleday, 1953]) and Bernard Berenson (see B. Berenson, *Aesthetics and History* [Garden City: Doubleday, 1954]). Berenson states, ". . . Art is not actual life it is true but is ideated life and perhaps as important. What distinguishes us from the other mammalia is precisely the capacity for this ideated life. . . ." However, my idea about the importance of symbolization most closely approaches those of Susanne Langer. ". . . This basic need which certainly is obvious only in man is the need of

First of all, the therapist and members all become material for certain sensuous and perceptual satisfactions.[10] This satisfaction, not unlike the artist's when he contemplates his materials and perceives certain forms and movements, is inherent in the group and in the group's being together. This value is enhanced when one is contemplative, disinterested,* and unattached. The mood for this appreciation is one of cosmic indifference or of impersonal sympathy with all of mankind whose common destiny we share. When achieving this value, our interpretative activity should be minimal.

Secondly is the satisfaction which is derived from observing the relatedness possibilities of individuals who differ vastly culturally and in their culturally determined behaviors. This satisfaction grows as members become more individual and yet relate more openly and more closely to the others. Once again this value is enhanced when one is contemplative, disinterested, and unattached. The mood too is one of cosmic indifference or of impersonal sympathy, as mentioned above. And again our interpretative activity should be minimal.

And thirdly is the intense and continual satisfaction of self-discovery. The psychoanalytic group in which therapist and members are bereft of status and rely heavily upon mutual symbolic fantasies gives the therapist the best opportunity to come face to face with himself. Some central questions for which he seeks answers are, "What am I doing here? What needs are being fulfilled and by whom? Whom do I prefer and what behavior do they possess which pleases me? Who am I with or without their behavior?"

This satisfaction comes only when one is emotionally intertwined longitudinally (life-spanwise) with all the members. There is no contemplation, no separateness, no distance—only deep interest, feeling, and attachments. At this time the interpretative activity should be maximal.

One's feelings and intuitions must play the predominant part in all interpretative descriptions. Interpretations then are meaningful for members and therapist alike. The authenticity of an interpretation is assured when there is a resultant change in the behavior of both therapist and member, or member and member. From this it can be seen that valid behavior-changing interpretations can originate in either therapist or patient. Thus, therapist is patient and patient is therapist. And the status therapist and patient are both meaningless.

The mood for the therapist's achieving this satisfaction is just the op-

---

symbolization. The symbol making function is one of man's primary activities like eating, looking or moving about. It is a fundamental process of the mind and goes on all of the time. . . ." (See S. K. Langer, *Philosophy in a New Key* [New York: New American Library of World Literature, 1948].)

* Disinterest may be defined as not serving to advance one's own private interest and of no personal concern. Disinterest, too, includes two additional conceptions: nonpossessiveness and unprejudiced activity.

posite of the cosmic indifferent attitude. It is a deep human concern and awareness, and in this mood interpretative activity is most valid.

All individuals upon entering a psychoanalytic group, conditioned as they are by their culture, confuse validity with value. They all have preconceived notions as to the purpose of the projected group experience. These purposes are individual and tenaciously clung to. Even when an individual is confronted with five or six reasons for group participation which differ from his, he still clings to his purpose for being with us.

The common denominator of all of these purposes for being in the group is that they are goal-directed. Individuals want to get something from the group experience which will modify their adjustment to others, make life situations easier, or make them feel better by reducing some bothersome symptoms, and so on. In short, as individuals begin in group psychoanalysis, they are prone to use the group experience *only* as a means toward some preconceived, self-interested end. The group for them at this moment has mostly an extrinsic worth. This extrinsic worth is similar to the (therapist's) validity of the therapy as I have explained.

As status is denied and as ritual and goal-directed activity are scrutinized, the value of the group as a living experience comes to the fore. We find ourselves in the group not because the group conveys or is likely to convey some meaning about life but *because it is our life*.

Members become anxious when they ask the question, "If I am not a patient, why am I here?" particularly when there is no answer to this question but an *intense longing to be here*. Another question packed with status and role connotations is "If you are not 'doctor' why do I pay you?" I answer this depending upon the momentary emotional interrelatedness within the group. "You pay me to remain 'patient.' You pay me to keep me 'doctor.' Today you pay the 'doctor'; perhaps tomorrow you will pay *me*," and so on.

Gradually the intrinsic value of the group is discovered, and all of the behaviors within the group have momentary meaning and essentiality. In the *being* and *being* relationship members discover a closeness never achieved before even in the biological family. The group then becomes substitutive for desired and needed relationships outside of the group.

We have questioned why individuals remain in groups, particularly analytic groups, when status is denied. Certainly the conception of positive transference is helpful in explaining the need to attend, particularly at first. But after statuses have been undermined, transferences are difficult to maintain and still an individual continues in the group. I feel that the intrinsic value of the group experience has been established, and until he finds similar value in his extra (therapy) group relationships, he necessarily will have to remain in his group.

We might wonder too about *our* need to remain in the group. I believe it is closely allied to our need to be psychotherapists. My own need for the group is contained in the validity and value of the group experience.

CONCLUSION

An important constituent of group psychoanalysis is an understanding of the significance of status denial. The undermining of status is a function of the therapist. He must be aware of his own status needs before he can gradually lessen status and role activities within the group. Empathy, the core of psychotherapy, only occurs in status-free transactions.

It is believed that a group psychoanalytic orientation which is slanted toward obtaining mutual value (therapist and members) will open new vistas, ask new questions, and will bring the "here and now" into much clearer focus.

REFERENCES

1. R. Linton, *The Cultural Background of Personality* (New York: Appleton-Century-Crofts, 1945).
2. A. Wolf, R. Bross, S. Flowerman, J. S. Greene, A. L. Kadis, H. Leopold, N. Locke, I. Milberg, H. Mullan, S. J. Obers, and M. Rosenbaum, "Sexual Acting Out in the Psychoanalysis of Groups," *Int. J. Group Psychother.,* 4:369-380, 1954.
3. C. A. Whitaker and T. P. Malone, *The Roots of Psychotherapy* (New York: The Blakiston Co., 1953).
4. E. Fromm, *Man For Himself* (New York: Rinehart & Co., 1947).
5. H. Mullan, "Counter-Transference in Groups," *Am. J. Psychother.,* 7:680-688, 1953.
6. Whitaker and Malone, *op. cit.*
7. S. Kierkegaard, *Fear and Trembling and The Sickness Unto Death* (Garden City: Doubleday, 1954).
8. K. Horney, *Neurosis and Human Growth* (New York: W. W. Norton & Co., 1942).
9. J. N. Rosen, *Direct Analysis: Selected Papers* (New York: Grune and Stratton, 1953); M. A. Sechehaye, *Symbolic Realization* (New York: International Universities Press, 1951); Whitaker and Malone, *op. cit.*
10. H. Mead, *An Introduction to Aesthetics* (New York: Ronald Press, 1952).

48

DIALOGUE AND THE "ESSENTIAL WE"

The Bases of Values in the Philosophy of Martin Buber

Maurice Friedman

The bases of values in Martin Buber's thought are his philosophy of dialogue and his philosophical anthropology, or the study of the problem of man. On this twofold foundation he establishes such basic value categories as the distinction between "I-Thou" and "I-It" relationships and that between "dialogue" and "monologue," the responsibility of the whole person to meet and respond to what addresses him in the "lived concrete," the primacy of the dialogical over the psychological, confirmation and "imagining the real," genuine speech and the "essential We," the distinction between "existential guilt" and neurotic guilt-feelings. These categories can help illuminate the value problems that arise in group psychotherapy and that are central to the goal and direction of such therapy.

"I-THOU" AND "I-IT"

Martin Buber's philosophy of dialogue is best known through its classic presentation in his little book *I and Thou*. In this book Buber makes his now famous distinction between the two relationships or basic attitudes that constitute human existence: the "I-Thou" and the "I-It." What distinguishes these relationships is not the object of the relation, but the nature of the relationship itself and the difference between the "I" that enters into the one relationship and the "I" that enters into the other. The "I-Thou" relation is direct, mutual, present. In it the other person is related to in his uniqueness and for himself, and not in terms of his relations to other things. In an "I-Thou" relation my partner reveals himself

Reprinted from *The American Journal of Psychoanalysis*, Vol. XX, No. 1, 1960, pp. 26-34.

to me directly, as just the person he is. I do not seek for his meaning by enregistering him in one or another general category. In the "I-It" relationship, on the other hand, the other is my object and not my partner. I observe him and use him; I establish his relation to this or that general category. I know him with the same detachment that I know any object, or I see him purely in emotional terms, but, in either case, not as a really independent person standing over against me. Hence this relationship is never really direct or mutual or truly present. In the "I-Thou" relation emotion and reason, intuition and sensation are included in the wholeness of the person responding to what he meets. The "I" of the "I-It" relationship, in contrast, is always partial, and it is just as much "I-it" if it is emotional as if it is rational, if it is subjective as if it is objective.

Both "I-Thou" and "I-It" are necessary for human existence. "I-it" again and again provides the base for ordered civilization, for technical accomplishment, for scientific advance. Yet "I-It" is not sufficient for human existence even on the barest terms. Without the "I-Thou" relation, the biological human individual would not become a person, a self, an "I" at all. He begins with the "I-Thou" in his relation to his mother and family and only later develops the separating relationship of "I-It." As long as the "I-Thou" and the "I-It" remain in healthy alternation, ever new material from the realms of the physical, the biological, the psychological, and the social is brought into the "I-Thou" relation and given new, present meaning. When "I-It" becomes predominant and prevents the return to the Thou, however, man loses authentic existence and ultimately falls into pathological self-contradiction. Thus, Buber's "I-Thou" philosophy is both descriptive *and* normative, fact and value. The normative comes in in the difference between mere existence and authentic existence, between being human at all and being more fully human, between holding the fragments of the self together sufficiently to get by and bringing the conflicting parts of oneself into an active unity, between having partial, disparate relations with others and having fuller, more responsible ones.

THE LIFE OF DIALOGUE

In *Between Man and Man,* Buber expresses his basic distinction in terms of the contrast between "dialogue" and "monologue." Dialogue may be silent and monologue spoken. What really matters in genuine dialogue is my acceptance of the "otherness" of the other person, my willingness to listen to him and respond to his address. In monologue, in contrast, I only allow the other to exist as a content of my experience. Not only do I see him primarily in terms of his social class, his color, his religion, his IQ, or character neurosis, I do not even leave myself open to him as a person at all.

Values as a living human reality only exist in the "life of dialogue," in the direct, reciprocal relation between man and man, for in it alone are we able to know and respond to the other in his uniqueness. It is only when I "really have to do" with the other that I can really be responsible to him. "The idea of responsibility is to be brought back from the province of specialized ethics, of an 'ought' that swings free in the air, into that of lived life. Genuine responsibility exists only where there is real responding." [1] Responsibility, to Buber, means the response of the whole person to what addresses him in the "lived concrete"—his full concrete situation. No abstract code is valid in advance of particular situations. None has universal validity, because value does not exist in the universal at all, but in the particular, the concrete, the "interhuman." This does not mean that moral codes are of no use if they are recognized as what they are—abstractions, generalizations, rules of thumb that may be helpful in pointing us back to the concrete values that men have discovered in real meeting. But they cannot take the place of our discovering for ourselves, each time anew, what is the right direction in a particular situation. The movement of values, therefore, is from the concrete situation and the deep-seated attitudes which one brings to that situation to the response and decision that produce the moral action.

> No responsible person remains a stranger to norms. But the command inherent in a genuine norm never becomes a maxim and the fulfillment of it never a habit. Any command that a great character takes to himself in the course of his development . . . remains latent in a basic layer of his substance until it reveals itself to him in a concrete way . . . whenever a situation arises which demands of him a solution of which till then he had perhaps no idea.[2]

The "ought" which arises in the concrete situation is not the pure "I-Thou," but what Buber calls the *quantum satis*—the sufficient amount of what one can do in that hour and in that situation. Just because real values arise in the concrete situation and in terms of the particular person confronted with that situation, the "ought" must include and be based on the real concrete person and all the limitations and resources that he brings with him into the situation.

But this can never be done by advance assessment, no matter how thorough one's knowledge of oneself or another, for, except in general terms and over-all predictions, one's resources are only known in the situation itself. One's potentialities do not simply inhere in one as a part of one's make-up, but are called out of one in response to what meets and demands one in this hour.

> What is possible in a certain hour and what is impossible cannot be adequately ascertained by any foreknowledge. . . . One must start at any given time from the nature of the situation in so far as it is at all recognizable. But one does not learn the measure and limit of what is attainable

in a desired direction otherwise than through going in this direction. The forces of the soul allow themselves to be measured only through one's using them. . . .[3]

PHILOSOPHICAL ANTHROPOLOGY

Buber's philosophy of dialogue has found its most thoroughgoing philosophical base in the philosophical anthropology which Buber has developed in his later years. Philosophical anthropology is concerned with the uniqueness of man, what makes man a problem to himself.

In "What Is Man?" Buber establishes the focus of the problem of man in the "interhuman," the "sphere of the between." Man, essentially, is neither a self-sufficient, primarily isolated individual, such as Freud saw man, nor an organic collectivity. The fundamental fact of human existence is man with man, the genuine dialogue between man and man. The psychological, the psychic stream of happenings within each man, is only the accompaniment of the dialogical. It is not itself the reality and goal of human existence. "All real living is meeting." Individuation is not the goal, only the indispensable way to the goal. This point is absolutely central to Buber's thought and it cannot be emphasized too strongly. Many psychotherapists and psychologists, such as Erich Fromm and Carl Rogers, who today recognize the essential importance of mutual relations between men still see these relations largely as the function of the individual's becoming and the means to that end. As long as dialogue is entered *merely* as a means to the end of health, maturity, integration, self-expression, creativity, "peace of mind," "positive thinking," and richness of experience, it will not even produce those things, for it will no longer be true dialogue and will afford no real meeting with the other.

DISTANCE AND RELATION

Through contrasting man with the rest of nature, Buber derives a twofold principle of human life consisting of two basic movements: "the primal setting at a distance" and "entering into relation." The first movement is the presupposition for the second, for we can only enter into relation with being that has been set at a distance from us and, thereby, become an independent opposite. Only man can perform this act of setting at a distance because only man has a "world" (*Welt*)—an unbroken continuum which includes not only all that he and other men know and experience, but all that is knowable now and in the future—while an animal only has an environment or realm (*Unwelt*). "Only the view of what is over against me in the world in its full presence, with which I have set myself, present in my whole person, in relation—only this view gives me the world truly as whole and one."

Distance given, man is able to enter into relation with other beings ("I-Thou") or to enlarge, develop, accentuate, and shape the distance itself, turning what is over against him into his object ("I-It"). An animal cannot see its companions apart from their common life, nor ascribe to the enemy any existence beyond his hostility. Man sets man at a distance and makes him independent. He is, therefore, able to enter into relation, in his own individual status, with those like himself.

CONFIRMATION AND "IMAGINING THE REAL"

The basis of man's life with man is . . . the wish of every man to be confirmed as what he is, even as what he can become, by men; and the innate capacity in man to confirm his fellow men in this way. . . . Actual humanity exists only where this capacity unfolds.[4]

This mutual confirmation of men is most fully realized in what Buber calls "making present," an event which happens partially wherever men come together, but in its essential structure only rarely. Making the other present means to "imagine the real," to imagine quite concretely what another man is wishing, feeling, perceiving, and thinking. The particular pain I inflict on another surges up in myself until, paradoxically, we are embraced in a common situation. It is through this making present that we grasp another as a self, an event which is only complete when he knows himself made present by me. This knowledge induces the process of his inmost self-becoming, "for the inmost growth of the self is not accomplished, as people like to suppose today, in man's relation to himself." An animal does not need confirmation because it is unquestionably what it is. A man needs confirmation because he exists as a self, at once separate and in relation, with unique potentialities that can only be realized if he is confirmed in his uniqueness.[5]

Buber describes "imagining the real" as a "bold swinging" into the life of "the particular real person who confronts me, whom I can attempt to make present to myself just in this way, and not otherwise, in his wholeness, unity, and uniqueness." [6] "Imagining the real" is crucial for genuine ethical responsibility, in which one's response is not to subjective interest or to an objective moral code, but to the person one meets. It is also essential for friendship and love, in which each member of the relationship is made present by the other in his concrete wholeness and uniqueness. But imagining the real is also essential for all the helping relationships—pastor and congregant, teacher and student, therapist and patient. If we overlook the real "otherness" of the other person, we shall not be able to help him, for we shall see him in our own image or in terms of our ready-made categories and not as he really is in his concrete uniqueness. But if we allow him to be different and still accept and confirm him, then we shall have helped him realize himself as he could not without us.

"HEALING THROUGH MEETING" AND ONE-SIDED "INCLUSION"

In friendship and love, "inclusion," or experiencing the other side, is mutual. In the helping relationships, however, it is necessarily one-sided. The patient cannot equally well experience the relationship from the side of the therapist or the pupil from the side of the teacher without destroying or fundamentally altering the relationship. This does not mean that the therapist, for example, is reduced to treating his patient as an object, an It. The one-sided inclusion of therapy is still an "I-Thou" relation founded on mutuality, trust, and partnership in a common situation, and it is only in this relation that real therapy can take place. If "all real living is meeting," all true healing also takes place through meeting. If the psychotherapist is satisfied to "analyze" the patient, "i.e. to bring to light unknown factors from his microcosm, and to set to some conscious work in life the energies which have been transformed by such an emergence, then he may be successful in some repair work. At best he may help a soul which is diffused and poor in structure to collect and order itself to some extent. But the real matter, the regeneration of an atrophied personal center, will not be achieved. This can only be done by one who grasps the buried latent unity of the suffering soul with the great glance of the doctor: and this can only be attained in the person-to-person attitude of a partner, not by the consideration and examination of an object." [7] But a common situation does not mean one which each enters from the same or even a similar position. In psychotherapy the difference in position is not only that of personal stance, but of role and function, a difference determined by the very difference of purpose which led each to enter the relationship. If the goal is a common one—the healing of the patient—the relationship to that goal differs radically as between therapist and patient, and the healing that takes place depends as much upon the recognition of that difference as upon the mutuality of meeting and trust.

> . . . the specific "healing" relation would come to an end the moment the patient thought of, and succeeded in practising "inclusion" and experiencing the event from the doctor's pole as well. Healing, like educating, is only possible to the one who lives over against the other, and yet is detached. [8]

This excludes neither Erich Fromm's conviction that the therapist at the same time heals himself in some measure through his own response to the patient, nor Carl Rogers' feeling of the equal worth and value of the client (which leads Rogers, mistakenly in my opinion, to stress the full mutuality of the client-therapist relationship), nor Trigant Burrow's and Hans Syz's emphasis on an "inclusive therapy" in which, particularly in group therapy, the therapist aids the patients by allowing them to see some of the social and personal distortions in himself.[9] But it does preclude accepting the therapist's *feeling* of mutuality as equivalent to the actual existence of full mutuality in the situation *between* therapist and patient. The scientific impersonalism that characterized the orthodox conception of the psychoanalyst is rightly rejected by many present-day therapists. But this should not lead us to a sentimental blurring of the essential distinction between therapy and other, less structured types of "I-Thou" relations. In the latter, as Buber puts it, there are "no normative limitations of mutuality," but in the former the very nature of the relationship makes full mutuality impossible.

THE ESSENTIAL WE

The relation between man and man takes place not only in the "I-Thou" relation of direct meeting, but also in the "We" of community. As the "primitive Thou" precedes the consciousness of individual separateness, whereas the "essential Thou" follows and grows out of this consciousness, so the "primitive We" precedes true individuality and independence, whereas the "essential We" only comes about when independent people have come together in essential relation and directness. The essential We includes the Thou potentially, for "only men who are capable of truly saying *Thou* to one another can truly say *We* with one another." This We is not of secondary or merely instrumental importance; it is basic to existence, and as such it is itself a prime source of value. "One should follow the common," Buber quotes Heracleitus, i.e., join with others in building a common world of speech and a common order of being.

> Man has always had his experiences as I, his experiences with others and with himself; but it is as We, ever again as We, that he has constructed and developed a world out of his experiences.

Thus amid the changes of world image, "the human cosmos is preserved, guarded by its moulder, the human speech-with-meaning, the common logos." [10]

The importance for group psychotherapy of Buber's concept of the common world as built by the common speech-with-meaning can hardly be overestimated. Speech, from this point of view, is no mere function or tool, but is itself of the stuff of reality, able to create or destroy it. "Man has always thought his thoughts as I . . . but as We he has ever raised them into being itself, in just that mode of existence that I call 'the between.'" Speech may be falsehood and conventionality, but it is also the great pledge of truth. Whether he takes refuge in individualism or collectivism, the man who flees answering for the genuineness of his existence is marked by the fact that he can no longer really listen to the voice of another. The other is now only his object that he observes. Only if real listening as well as real talking takes place will the full possibility of healing be present in group psychotherapy, for only thus, and not through any mere *feeling* of group unity, will the full potentiality of the group as a group be realized. "He who existentially knows no Thou will never succeed in knowing a We." [11] One *should* follow the common, and that means that lived speech, "speech-with-meaning," is itself a value. Values are not just the content, the building blocks of speech. They exist, in the realest sense, in the "between," in the dialogue between man and man.

It is not only the fate of groups that depends upon the common "speech-with-meaning." If man does not recover the genuineness of existence as We, he may cease to exist at all.

> In our age, in which the true meaning of every word is encompassed by delusion and falsehood and the original intention of the human glance is stifled by tenacious mistrust, it is of decisive importance to find again the genuineness of speech and existence as We. . . . Man will not persist in existence if he does not learn anew to persist in it as a genuine We.[12]

GUILT AND GUILT-FEELINGS

The centrality of man's existence as We is basic to Buber's distinction between "groundless" neurotic guilt—a subjective feeling within a person, usually unconscious and repressed—and "existential guilt"—an ontic, interhuman reality in which the person dwells in the truest sense of the term. The analyst must see the illness of the patient as an illness of his relations with the world. "A soul is never sick alone," writes Buber, "but always through a betweenness, a situation between it and another existing being." True guilt does not reside in the human person but in his failure to respond to the legitimate claim and address of the world. Similarly, the repression of guilt and the neuroses which result from this repression are not merely psychological phenomena but events between men.[13] Existential guilt is "guilt that a person has taken on himself as a person and in a personal situation," an objective dialogical guilt that transcends the realm of inner feelings and of the self's relation to itself. Existential guilt is the corollary of the answerability and responsibility of the self in the concrete dialogical situation. It is failure to respond and, by the same token, failure to authenticate one's existence. "Existential guilt occurs when someone injures an order of the human world whose foundations he knows and recognizes as those of his own existence and of all common human existence." [14] This "order of the human world" is not an objective absolute existing apart from man: it is the interhuman itself, the genuine We, the common logos and cosmos. What it means to injure this common order is known to every man who has experienced real guilt, but also to every group therapist who has had to discover the direction his group must take for real therapy, and in so doing, like Alexander Wolf, distinguish between constructive and destructive group trends and constellations.[15] The therapist may lead the man who suffers from existential guilt to the place where he himself can walk the road of illuminating that guilt, persevering in his identification of himself as the person who took on that guilt, and, in so far as his situation makes possible, restoring "the order of being injured by him through the relation of an active devotion to the world." [16] "In a decisive hour, together with the patient entrusted to him and trusting in him," the therapist "has left the closed room of psychological treatment in which the analyst rules by means of his systematic and methodological superiority and has stepped forth with him into the air of the world where self is exposed to self. There, in the closed room where one probed and treated the isolated psyche according to the inclination of the self-encapsulated patient, the patient was referred to ever-deeper levels of his inwardness as to his proper world; here outside, in the immediacy of one human standing over against another, the encapsulation must and can be broken through, and a transformed, healed relationship must and can be opened to the person who is sick in his relations to otherness—to the world of the other which he cannot remove into his soul." [17]

REFERENCES

1. M. Buber, "Dialogue," in *Between Man and Man*, trans. Ronald Gregor Smith (Boston: Beacon Paperback, 1955), p. 16.
2. M. Buber, "The Education of Character," *op. cit.*, p. 114.
3. M. Buber, *Pointing the Way: Collected Essays*, ed. and trans. Maurice S. Friedman (New York: Harper & Bros.; London: Routledge & Kegan Paul; 1957), p. 206.
4. M. Buber, "Distance and Relation," trans. Ronald Gregor Smith, *Psychiat.*, Vol. XX, No. 2, May 1957, p. 102.
5. *Ibid.*, p. 104.
6. M. Buber, "Elements of the Interhuman," trans. Ronald Gregor Smith, *Psychiat.*, Vol. XX, No. 2, May 1957, p. 110.
7. M. Buber, *I and Thou*, trans. Ronald Gregor Smith (New York: Charles Scribner's Sons, 1958), 2nd revised edition with new postscript by author, p. 132 ff.
8. *Ibid.*, p. 133.
9. Erich Fromm's statement is from a personal conversation I had with him in which he indicated his full acceptance of the principle of "healing through meeting." That of Rogers is from a dialogue I moderated between him and Martin Buber at the University of Michigan in March 1957, the transcript of which has been privately circulated by Dr. Rogers but not printed. In this dialogue the difference between the two men becomes apparent, not only in this point, but in Rogers' belief that man is basically good, Buber's that he is polar, with his strongest capability of good being coupled with his strongest potentiality of evil; Rogers' emphasis on unqualified acceptance

as opposed to Buber's emphasis on a confirmation which, while it accepts the other as a person, may also wrestle with him against himself; Rogers' emphasis on subjective becoming and dialogue as a means to that becoming, Buber's emphasis on dialogue with the becoming of the self only an aspect of dialogue rather than its goal. Buber could not accept Rogers' statement that he treats neurotics, schizophrenics, and paranoiacs the same and that he has full mutuality with them as a description of the situation but only of Rogers' feeling about the situation. For a description of the approach of Burrow and Syz, *cf.* Hans Syz, "An Experiment in Inclusive Psychotherapy," *Exp. Psychopathol.*, 1957, pp. 129-169.

10. M. Buber, "What is Common to All," trans. Maurice S. Friedman, *The Review of Metaphysics*, Vol. XI, No. 3, March 1958, p. 377.
11. *Ibid.*, p. 378.
12. *Cf.* 10 above, p. 378.
13. *Cf.* 3 above, p. 95 ff.
14. M. Buber, "Guilt and Guilt Feelings," trans. Maurice S. Friedman, *Psychiat.*, Vol. XX, No. 2, May 1957, p. 117.
15. Alexander Wolf, "The Psychoanalysis of Groups," *Am. J. Psychother.*, Vol. III, No. 4, October 1949, Vol. IV, No. 1, January 1950. [Also reprinted as Chapter 23 in the present volume.]
16. *Cf.* 14 above, p. 22.
17. *Cf.* 3 above, p. 96 ff.

49

BEYOND
TRANSFERENCE BEHAVIOR

Cornelius Beukenkamp

The term transference, introduced by psychoanalysis, refers to the behavior of the patient toward the therapist. It is the reproduction of the repressed and forgotten experiences of early childhood. This reproduction not only takes the form of the reactions but also appears in the dreams. Freud limited the term to displacements occurring during the therapeutic psychoanalysis. Jung held that the patient must find a relationship to a living present object in his strivings for adaptation.

Generally, therapists see transference as coming from any of the various segments of the psychic structure. For example, there is superego transference, ego transference, ego-ideal transference, and id transference.

Usually, when the patient no longer shows evidence of transference behavior, this then, is felt to be a manifestation of the resolvement in a beneficial manner.

This paper does not find any disagreement with these long established tenets. However, when attending clinical meetings, how often do we not hear wide differences in interpretations concerning the same segment of behavior. In fact, many erudite discussions have ended without any understanding being reached.

And later on with reflection, we have seen that the other interpretations given carried considerable validation as well. This experience, along with a decade of group psychotherapy experience, brought about the following thoughts: Perhaps human behavior cannot be divided so arbitrarily by placing it upon a single dimensional plane. Further, since the usual therapy setting includes only one plane, the interpretations by the therapist must be obviously unidimensional in their orientation. When others hear clinical material by report, they may render valid interpretations which ap-

Reprinted from the *American Journal of Psychotherapy*, Vol. X, No. 3, July 1956, pp. 467-470.

pear in conflict with those presented since the observer may be speaking from a different plane. In the past, these differences were always attributed to the different theoretical formulations held by each. This no doubt does play an important part. Nonetheless, it might be, simply as suggested, a different vantage point from which to observe the multiplicity of levels involved. For, if we return to the basic concept of transference-behavior, we realize that it is predicated upon an understanding of a projectional system of recall. The patient in such a setting is the donor. It is he who decides what we shall see or listen to. It is he and not ourselves who permits us to see into which of his levels the type of inadequacy he cares to have revealed. And, when I speak of levels, I mean not psychosexual levels but levels of interaction. Levels of interaction refer to the concept of multidimensional behavior.[1] This concept sees three levels in operation. The first, is that of the child-parent configuration (Primary Polarity); the second, the sibling-to-sibling and family member to society feelings (Secondary Polarity); and finally, a self-limited and prepropagational, antioriginal familial directed enterprise closely resembling normal adolescence, labeled Tertiary Polarity.[2]

This then, may be a cogent reason why so many observers disagree when attempting to understand a patient's behavior in therapy. That is, the interpretations given may appear to be in conflict only because they are speaking from one of these dimensions and thus fail to take in a most vital realization that man is not, in his normal life, a single psychic dimensional organism. He is born into a group, develops as a part of the group, his adjustment is to the group, and even in his death his departure is felt as a loss to his group. So then, is it not obvious that when we are attempting to evaluate human behavior one must think in a multidimensional way bearing in mind that the family configuration with its ramifications is the prototype of social structure.

If then, we are not outflanked by the patient's need to control his environment and ourselves, as a part of it, he has the possibility of then engaging in multiple interactions. This is essential if ever he is to leave behind him his symbiotic level of behavior. Not to do so may be the etiology of the formation of the iatrogenetic neurosis or "transference neurosis."

These considerations are based upon seeing therapy conceptualized as an interpersonal process—one in which the ego emphasis should be on growth and repair. The growth and repair is designed to give the ego strength so that it can separate itself in its symbiotic struggle—free itself from the cravings of its orality and of equal import, cease in its excessive identifications. This kind of therapy should, therefore, attempt with proper timing to become an experiential occurrence. If this occurs, within multiple meaningful relationships approximating normal family life, the ego will then engage in behavior, after repair, which may be called "beyond-transference behavior."

It is not necessary or even at times advisable to place every patient into a group therapy program; nor is it wise for every therapist to do so in order to practice multidimensional therapy. We state these values for we feel that not every patient is suited in terms of his psychopathology; and not every therapist's personality, from a talent-interest viewpoint, is predisposed for such undertakings.

The therapist using individual treatment is undoubtedly familiar with the shiftings of identities projected upon him [multiphasic behavior[3]]. He, the individual therapist, can use these shifting identities of the one-to-one relationship in such a way that multidimensional therapy becomes possible. For example, if he emphasizes the patient's expressed interest in the mentioned third parties and drives away from the circumscribed and overly introspective concern of the patient's ego, so common in this setting, he can then create a specialized form of group configuration. This type of special creative pursuit by the therapist will aid his patient in releasing him from his parasitic dependencies, excessive orality, and resistant symbiotic identifications.

Naturally, those using combined therapy (individual and group) have this above-mentioned opportunity structured before them.

This multidimensional therapeutic approach is further enhanced if the therapist uses an objective appraisal of his subjective involvement with his patients. By this is meant an active participation with those present in the therapy setting, as if he was observing not the patient alone, but instead, himself together with his patient in action.

Suggestions offered to aid therapists both to reach and understand "beyond-transference behavior" are as follows: Strive to have the reliving process of therapy approximate as closely as possible human multiple psychology. This you can do by taking into consideration that the single human being is normally found in a multiple human setting. In other words, emphasize "the other people" in his life when he, the patient, refers to them in his communications. This will bring about not only the desirable clinical results already mentioned but reveal the two types of "beyond-transference behavior." First, that which is new experiential behavior within a given single configuration or polarity, i.e. behavior not based upon a reliving process. Second, that behavior which is not based upon recall and possesses the emotion present in the family feelings or the feelings of belonging to a multiple human structure.

REFERENCES

1. C. Beukenkamp, "The Multidimensional Orientation in Analytic Group Therapy," Am. J. Psychother., IX:477-483, 1955.

2. C. Beukenkamp, "Further Developments of the Transference Life Concept in Therapeutic Groups," *Hillside Hosp. J.*, V:441-448, 1956.
3. C. Beukenkamp, "The Multidimensional Orientation in Analytic Group Therapy," *loc. cit.*

50

THE ROLE OF PSYCHOTROPIC DRUGS IN GROUP THERAPY

R. A. *Sandison*

The purpose of this paper is to examine those aspects of the drug treatment of mental disorder which relate to the human environment or group in which the patient finds himself. Although great claims are made for modern drug therapy, a distinction must be drawn between the specific effects of drugs and the effects of the environment itself. Psychotropic drugs are not specific in a particular disease, although they may modify specific symptoms. Two special cases are selected for an examination of the effects of the environment on drug action—deep insulin treatment and lysergic acid diethylamide. The psychological phenomena induced by deep insulin differ according to whether treatment is given individually or to a group of patients; and the psychological significance of insulin treatment lies in the ability of the treatment situation to help the patient to become a full member of the group. Similarly the group influences relating to LSD treatment are examined.

It is concluded that the attitude of social groups to psychotropic drugs is determined by the real or apparent effects these drugs have on superego function. This appears to have some relationship to the so-called placebo phenomenon.

The fact that clinical trials tend to lead to results unduly favorable to the drugs tested is noted and some suggestions are made as to how these trials can be improved.

Physiological treatment is booming; the past year [1956] has seen a glut of conferences and papers on chlorpromazine, the rauwolfia alkaloids, and the newer drugs intended to relieve neurotic and psychotic symptoms. World-wide publicity has stimulated public interest and demand, while the

Reprinted from the *Bulletin of the World Health Organization*, Vol. 21, 1959, pp. 505-515.

indiscriminate use of the drugs for the common neuroses, conduct disorders, reactive states and depressive states, where they are least effective, has led to official protests and countermeasures.

Thus Wortis[1] summarizes the situation created by the inventiveness of chemists in the field of psychiatric treatment, concluding:

> The new drug treatments have practically abolished lobotomies and greatly diminished the need for both electro-shock and insulin, although E.S.T. remains almost specific therapy for depressions.

MODE OF ACTION OF DRUGS AND THE PLACEBO RESPONSE

Ancient chemical methods of treatment were directed towards the expelling of real or suspected causal agents of disease from the body. Out of sympathetic magic and the empirical use of galenicals homeopathic medicine arose. Findlay[2] dates the commencement of modern chemotherapeutics from the discovery of arsphenamine by Ehrlich and Hata in 1910. The great advances in this field did not occur until the introduction of prontosil rubrum by Domagk in 1935, rapidly to be followed by sulfonamides, antibiotics, and other specifics. Drug therapies can now therefore be classified as follows:

1. Specific remedies, e.g., penicillin.
2. Remedies which modify disease or control symptoms, e.g., anticonvulsants in epilepsy, insulin in diabetes mellitus.
3. Remedies which modify symptoms, e.g., insulin in schizophrenia, tranquillizers.
4. Remedies which may modify symptoms but are not of proven value.

One notices as one descends the list (*a*) that the remedies become more numerous, (*b*) that their action is less susceptible to proof by clinical trial, and (*c*) that their action is more susceptible to group, cultural, and other environmental influences. Presumably penicillin will cure pneumonia, provided the causal organism is sensitive, equally well in any country or culture in the world, whereas not only is proof lacking concerning the efficacy of most drugs used in psychiatric practice but their beneficial effect varies from one country to another and even between different wards in the same hospital. The position is further complicated by the fact that we do not know how ataractics work. Are they specifics like penicillin, are they modifiers, or do they partially replace metabolic deficits? Nor are psychiatrists clear as to what they are looking for in the search for new drugs. North American opinion appears to favor the old medieval idea of a drug to counteract an alleged toxin (i.e. the search for a hallucinogenic substance circulating in schizophrenics and research into anti-hallucinogens). Others are content with drugs which modify behavior. While so little is known even as to which of the psychoses are functional and which are organic, physiological treatment must remain empirical and therefore subject to wide fluctuations in its results in different syndromes in different places.

HISTORICAL

The remarkable development of drug therapy during recent years appears to mark the climax of many years' development of physical treatments in psychiatry, which have arisen not perhaps so much out of conviction or proof that mental disorder is organic in nature but as a reaction after a century of moral, philosophical, and psychological treatment. It is also an inevitable by-product of a materialistic and scientific age. Drug treatment in psychiatry revives the whole question of the nature of mental disorders and of group and community attitudes towards all those substances which interfere with central nervous activity. Right down the ages man has looked with mixed fear and fascination upon natural products which can change his mental outlook. Alcohol, one of the oldest, has become partially accepted and has gained an uneasy and, in some countries, a highly taxed place in society.

Of all the natural products which soothe, excite, or change the psyche, the hallucinogens form one of the most interesting and exciting groups. Rejected by Anglo-Saxons, our knowledge of them has come only recently with the medical uses of mescaline and lysergic acid. Wasson[3] has extensively investigated the social use of hallucinogenic toadstools in many cultures and has decided that

> East Indo-European people is by cultural inheritance either "mycophobe" or "mycophile." . . . The great Russians, we find, are mighty mycophiles, as are also the Catalans, who possess a mushroom vocabulary of more than 200 names. The ancient Greeks, Celts and Scandinavians were mycophobes, as are the Anglo-Saxons. There was another phenomenon that arrested our attention: wild mushrooms from very earliest times were steeped in what the anthropologists call "mana," a supernatural aura.

From Wasson we learn that "Among the [American] Indians, their use is hedged about with restrictions of many kinds. Unlike ordinary edible mushrooms, these are never sold in the market place and no Indian dares to eat them frivolously, for excitement. The Indians themselves speak of their use as 'muy delicado,' that is 'perilous.'" These empirical observations of Wasson have now been confirmed by the extraction and synthesis of psilocybin by recent experimental work, which makes it almost certain that psilocybin is hallucinogenic (see Hoffman *et al.*[4] and papers by A. Cerletti and by A. Hoffman presented at the meeting of the Collegium Internationale Neuro-Psycho Pharmacologicum held in Rome in September 1958).

These observations fit in with our knowledge of the use of powerful drugs, amulets, or charms in many societies until recently. Such was the power attributed to the remedy that responsibility for its use was divided amongst the group who gathered round the afflicted person. In some countries the group is also employed to ward off the evil god held responsible for the disease (*cf.* Pettigrew[5]). The secrets of the apothecaries and others were closely guarded, and there was frequent rivalry between the medical man and the priest as to who had the more effective remedy. In the years before homeopathy was practiced the principle of treatment was, according to Culpeper,[6] "All diseases are cured by their contraries, but all parts of the body maintained by their likes." Thus the more serious diseases were held to be curable only by remedies of an obscure nature which were expensive and difficult to prepare and which had to be administered by a person of undoubted authority supported by the utterances of the group with which he himself was identified, e.g., by the prayers or incantations of the people. The Anglo-Saxons do not appear to have recognized group influences so greatly as more primitive peoples in relation to drug taking. According to Wasson the American Indians eating the hallucinogenic mushrooms do so in a group and do not themselves expect a curative effect; they only ask a question and expect a prophetic answer. Thus they frequently take the mushrooms for advice when someone is ill. This ritual has something in common with the Chinese casting of hexagrams mentioned in the *I Ching*, in that the particular time at which the experiment is carried out is important, a group of people must be present, and a definite question must be asked. As to how the answer is given, it is clear that the primitives believe that the gods speak to them through the mushroom. We might say in the language of contemporary psychology that the archetypes are raised into consciousness as hallucinations or ideas which can be communicated to others. Wasson reproduces a Mexican drawing of the sixteenth century in which there are three mushrooms on one side, a man eating them in the center, and a god behind him, who is speaking through the mushroom. This, in passing, is exactly what one feels about the action of LSD (lysergic acid diethylamide)—that it compels the unconscious to speak and that the archetypes appear in consciousness in the form of images, thoughts, feelings, and sensations which are strange and unusual but which are nevertheless part of the subject concerned.

It is likely that in ancient times the use of drugs was attended by a group, and that the individuals taking part had to expend some effort, mental or physical or both, if the value of the substance was to be realized. Dale[7] points out that the curative value of drugs in the sixteenth to eighteenth centuries was proportionate to their rarity, value, or difficulty of preparation, and this must be an indication of the psychological power inherent in the preparations. One can therefore see the necessity for the group being present, dissolving the magical power of the drug lest it should prove too dangerous for the patient. In ancient legends the more effective drugs were also dangerous to life. Now these same drugs or their modern equivalents have become debased, sold in vast quantities over the counters of chemists' shops, or worse, dispensed for next to nothing on the doctor's prescription, demanding from the patient no effort for their collection or preparation and no contribution from him on either a psychic or social level while under their influence.

It might therefore be helpful at the present time to write down a little of what we know about the effects of drugs in relation to the group influences which surround the patient. The drugs which we are about to consider are called psychotropic, those which alter the state of mind of the patient. They might therefore be supposed to carry great "mana" value and we should expect their action to be unusually susceptible to group influences.

PSYCHOTROPIC DRUGS AND THE ENVIRONMENT

It is well known that the action of certain drugs which modify central nervous activity varies according to the mood of the individual at the time and according to the environment. For example, the state of mind induced by alcohol in the solitary and secret drinker is usually different from that observed when alcohol is taken socially. It is not certain whether this difference is related only to the temperament of the individual, but one suspects that the environment also plays its part. Environmental conditions under which psychotropic drugs are given have hitherto largely been a question of expediency. For example, insulin coma treatment is usually administered to patients in a group, whereas LSD is almost invariably given to a patient who is confined to a single room. Little attention, until recently, has been paid to the different conditions under which tranquillizers are administered.

In the field of neuropharmacology evidence is being collected concerning the existence of neurohumoral transmitters within the central nervous system, and it is being suggested that the brain stem and midbrain reticular arousal systems are peculiarly susceptible to external stimuli conveyed through receptor mechanisms. Experimental evidence is accumulating which suggests that those drugs which act on the brain stem and midbrain structures with their associated nuclei may be modified by sensory impressions.* There is already much clinical evidence to support this. We know that LSD phenomena can be modified by the extent to which the

* Elkes, J. Address to the Section of Psychiatry, Birmingham Medical Institute, 1957.

patient concentrates on his environment. For example, if a patient is asked to read an interesting book following a dose of LSD the psychic manifestations of the drug can be entirely inhibited. Concentration on manual tasks or irrelevant conversation with another person can also inhibit them. On the other hand, the presence of another person who reminds the patient of a psychological situation can intensify the reaction. This intensification is best seen in the case of paranoid patients. The author has found that the production of repetitive and irritating noises close to the room in which such a patient is having LSD can arouse him to a great intensity of fury and hostility. In one case a faint whistling noise from some nearby machinery brought back wartime experiences. Excitation of the sense of smell has been found to be a powerful stimulator of emotionally charged memories.

Bannerjee,[8] most of whose work has been done in Calcutta, believes that the efficacy of the Rauwolfia alkaloids is much enhanced by group therapy of an active kind carried out when a patient is taking the drug. He believes that Rauwolfia has a specific effect on paranoid and confused mental states. One method of demonstrating this is to devise group games in which patients are compelled to make some positive contact with each other; to work as teams and to trust each other. He reports not only that the patients undergoing Rauwolfia treatment lose their suspicions when these methods are applied but that the degree of cooperation is much greater in those groups receiving the Rauwolfia alkaloids.

DEEP INSULIN TREATMENT: INFLUENCE OF THE GROUP

For several reasons deep insulin treatment may be taken as a model for examining the role of psychotropic drugs in group therapy. The treatment has been widely practiced for over twenty years. The patients are almost invariably treated in a group under conditions which are favorable to a study of the psychological factors at work both in the patients individually and in the group as a whole. Although it is generally held that insulin is a purely physical method of treatment, there are some who say that the good results achieved by insulin are attributable only to the individual attention and resocializing effects resulting from the patients living in a small group and being looked after by a relatively large number of staff. The truth, however, would appear to lie midway between these, since close study of an insulin group reveals that the patients are capable of producing a great deal of significant psychological material. Few observers appear to have noticed this. Close questioning of the patients reveals, however, that they do have the most interesting fantasies, which at first concern only themselves but which subsequently concern the rest of the insulin group, and if this latter occurs it is invariably associated with clinical improvement. One of the best examples of this, in my experience, concerns a young girl who at the beginning of the insulin treatment had a childish fantasy during recovery that she was playing with a ball. Within a few days the fantasy extended to the doctor and she had an idea on waking that she was playing tennis with him. Finally all the patients were drawn into this game, the patient thinking that she was throwing the ball round to each one in turn. This coincided with clinical improvement. The critical psychological phase for a patient undergoing deep insulin treatment is during the period of recovery from the coma, and one not infrequently finds patients who are afraid of dying during this period and who experience a great struggle to come to consciousness again. There are other patients who object to being brought out of the coma, preferring to remain out of touch with the realities of life, and this is usually associated with a bad prognosis. Many patients describe the insulin experience as unpleasant, like dying. One of my patients cried out loudly and screamed against death, but at the end of the struggle she saw an urgent need to live and a great impulse came over her to eat, and she stuffed quantities of food into her mouth almost to the point of choking. Another patient on waking from coma every day would think she was dead; this went on for weeks without any change, and the patient said "Now I take it for granted that I am dead." Another patient thought she had had a serious operation during treatment; that she was dead and the process of restoration to life was too hard to go through. The interest of these death experiences lies in the fact that they are not entirely individual, for sooner or later the patient becomes concerned about the other members of the group. I had one patient who insisted on being brought round from coma before any of the other patients because she felt that she could then watch over them and assist in their recovery. Another patient was convinced that I was giving insulin to the other patients to make them die and on one occasion actually tried to prevent me from giving the injection. Another patient in the course of a group meeting expressed much the same idea, saying "Why do you put them in a coma? You must be hurting them." There are psychological reasons for believing that the overcoming of the death experience and of the state of regression induced by insulin are factors of great importance in the patient's recovery. It is well known that both animals and human beings under the influence of danger tend to congregate into groups and that this has the effect of diminishing the individual fear of death. There is therefore every reason to believe that the gathering of patients undergoing insulin threatment into a group is a most desirable thing.

Another type of experience frequently observed amongst those undergoing insulin treatment may be described as the experience of initiation or rebirth. This phenomenon has been well described by Scott.[9] Initiation ceremonies amongst primitive peoples are carried out with the support of the whole group, and they are presided over by the senior members of the community. A study of primitive initiation ceremonies shows that their chief object is to mark the physical and psychological passage from one way of life to another. In the Arapesh society, where the girls as well as boys go through an initiation ceremony, there is no change in the way of life of the girls before and after the ceremony. They have already been betrothed to their husbands at the age of seven or eight, and usually for four years or so have lived in their husbands' households, assisting the women with their tasks. The true psychological significance of the initiation is, therefore, seen best in the case of the girl in that she is initiated into the being of another woman. In Greek mythology the figures of Pallas Athene, Artemis, and Persephone give us some idea of the threefold nature of woman as an ideal image.[10] Jung remarks that this image in the man is the anima in its various forms, but in the woman it is the superordinate personality, the one which she has to experience and come to terms with before she can consider herself initiated into the completeness of womanhood. Among the women of western Europe this process of psychological immaturity is common and is seen in neurotics, particularly hysterics, and also in schizophrenics. Among the schizophrenics those who are married with children of their own are psychologically undeveloped and are still children at heart. This is demonstrated by the fact that schizophrenia, particularly in the female, is likely to follow a love affair or to occur shortly after marriage or childbirth.

One example can be given of the need for the group. A female patient, 28 years of age, married and with a child, had a schizophrenic breakdown in which she thought she was being hypnotized. She was confused, aggressive, and restless. As she was so disturbed insulin treatment was carried out in a single room. She became progressively more regressed, incontinent, and degraded. She later explained that she believed there were three dragons on one arm and three on the other which were trying to make her completely insane. Her remedy was to retreat into infancy so that she became childish and incontinent, and she actually believed herself to be taking refuge in the womb. As soon as she was transferred to the insulin room she started to recover. She had a fantasy that on recovery from treatment the bedclothes became like a tunnel and that she was born over the end of the bed. We could not help being impressed by this change after the patient was removed from the isolation of the single room.

Jung, analyzing the different forms of rebirth, considers that the rebirth or transmutation experiences of groups sharing a common experience are a form of identification with a group and that this is something entirely different from experiencing the rebirth in oneself. These insulin experiences seem to be both; there is evidence that the transmutation experience is personal and that the group is required both for its completion and its performance.

Another female patient, after 34 comas, had an idea that those undergoing insulin treatment could not endure legal marriage and that they either had to experience natural unions or else remain virgins. This patient, herself married, felt after the next coma that she was no longer married; that the group and her husband were mutually exclusive. She said it was like being married to the group instead of to him. In the 36th coma this notion was developed, and she feared that the treatment had turned her into a harlot. We have, therefore, in this experience the chief feature of the initiation rites—namely, the subjection to those in authority, the pain and discomfort of the treatment, the segregation in hospital, the emergence into the group, and the acceptance of the patient when he is better as a more adult and balanced individual. One may conclude that these results can be obtained only through giving the drug, in this case insulin, to the patients as a group. The phenomena can quite easily be demonstrated and worked out by anybody who cares to look for them, and it seems unfortunate that studies on the effects of insulin treatment have not included any commentary on these important psychological factors. Whether insulin is the only method of bringing out these phenomena remains to be seen. Leyton[11] has recently reported on the treatment results in two identical groups, one of which received distilled water injections and the other insulin. The results in the two groups were similar. Furthermore, she adds in a personal communication, some of the patients in the placebo group thought they had been in coma after the injections.

LYSERGIC ACID DIETHYLAMIDE AND GROUP THERAPY

This raises the whole question of the circumstances under which lysergic acid diethylamide (LSD) should be given. For a considerable period the author met a number of patients undergoing LSD treatment as a group, when they were not under the influence of the drug. In the case of these LSD patients the basic material was much the same as that obtained from neurotic groups not having LSD. Men and women were mixed, and they were roughly within the 20 to 40-year age group. Patients from several different therapists formed the group, including the group leader's own patients. It must be noted that in a community where some of its members are taking LSD there is an immediate tendency for the subjects to get together and to discuss its effects. This has been noticed many times among volunteer groups, who immediately form themselves into a kind of club among whom the sole topic of conversation is LSD. This was immediately noticed among the patients in the hospital. All the male inpatients were in a ward of about 30, most of whom were recent cases, neurotic and early psychotic cases being mingled. The woman inpatients were in a ward of about the same size, but in their case the majority of the patients were psychoneurotic with only occasional cases of early or convalescent psychoses. Some patients were being treated as outpatients and these either came in for the day or stayed in hospital for one or two days of each week. These patients also joined the group. It was noticed quite soon after we started giving LSD to patients that this tendency for them to get together and discuss their experience was strongly present. Furthermore, we found that patients having treatment on a particular day often liked to have another patient with them who had received treatment on a different day. Nevertheless there grew up a great deal of rumor and mythology concerning the treatment, particularly among those about to receive it or in the early stages of treatment. Several of the patients thought that it was a necessary part of the treatment that they should show uninhibited behavior such as screaming, breaking windows, tearing up clothes, and so on. This atmosphere of rumor was the chief reason for forming the group, on the grounds that knowledge is the best dispeller of fear and anxiety. Important differences were observed between this group and the group to whom no drugs were being given. The patients in the LSD group were not only bound by the common experience of neurosis, which to many patients is something they would prefer to be without, but they were bound by the much more whole and telling experience of LSD. Such patients are subject to fear and rumor, and because of the intensive nature of the treatment there is a greater sense of urgency and a greater drive towards endeavoring to solve psychological problems.

In the early stages of the experiment it was necessary for the therapist to take a more active role than usual as the one who could explain the treatment. The author came to the conclusion that the techniques which were used were only partially successful in solving the problems presented by this kind of group. For example, if one included one's own patients in the group the others regarded them as specially privileged and on occasion openly accused them of inventing material. Discussions on transference were exceedingly difficult; those patients belonging to other therapists started maintaining that transference problems did not exist and expressed great surprise that any of the therapist's patients could have other than purely professional feelings for him. When these patients were removed from the group transference difficulties continued to arise, the patients being inclined to compare one therapist unfavorably with another; this was good in its way, but it must be remembered that the techniques of giving LSD were still in their early stages and the therapist was always in a difficult position where he felt that the methods of a colleague ran contrary to his own ideas. It was concluded that the best solution was for the therapist to see only his own patients, but this was not entirely satisfactory as it was felt that much of the point of group therapy was thereby lost. The patients tended to take a less serious view of the group sessions and to withhold more intimate information on the grounds that this could better be discussed in private. The biggest problem, however, was the development of a group neurosis which revealed a marked psychological inflation in the patients. They tended to become highly introspective and spent more and more time trying to work out problems which were insoluble. It is true that all these difficulties provided important material for the therapist and naturally they were discussed with the group. It does seem that this combined individual and group therapy can go on only for a few weeks at a time, and it is best to break up the group every eight or ten weeks and start again three or four weeks later. This fact has led the author to the idea that LSD treatment should be carried out after the fashion of school terms and holidays as they are normally thought of in England, with three holidays a year of from four to eight weeks' duration. Some of the patients never became absorbed into the group, and these were usually those with rigid, obsessional personalities who produced little material during the LSD sessions. These patients usually felt on the fringe of the group, but they derived a certain amount of help from other members.

One should now consider the benefits to be derived from this method of group therapy. Although it has been held that a group of patients taking tranquillizers would have their aggressive feelings damped down to such an extent that the object of group therapy and the bringing out of latent aggression would be frustrated, in this group the reverse holds good. In fact, the problem is to know how to deal with the breaking down of the resistance against aggression which occurs during LSD treatment. In some patients it is noticeable that their aggressive drive is put to use. For example, one patient in the course of treatment gave up a routine job and started his own business, although it was interesting to observe that his chief problem—namely, the lack of sexual ability—was unchanged. This conversion of aggression into other channels yet missing its main object is one of the great problems of LSD treatment, and when carried a stage further aggression becomes converted into anxiety, bodily symptoms, often of a severe nature, depression, and suicidal impulses. In my view this material can be satisfactorily dealt with in the group, and some patients who might have been forced to give up LSD treatment were undoubtedly helped to continue.

FUTURE RESEARCH ON INSULIN AND LSD GROUPS

One might appropriately here put forward a few suggestions about the future study of insulin and LSD groups, for both treatments require much basic research. Insulin treatment has been practiced for 21 years in many countries; a great many reports have been published concerning the results, and long-term follow-up studies have also been carried out. The most these studies tell us is that a definite percentage of schizophrenic patients are improved as a result of the treatment and that in all probability the remissions obtained are superior, both in their quality and in the length of time they can be sustained, to other known methods of treatment. Although evidence has been collected that the long-term use of the phenothiazine drugs may be a close rival to insulin treatment, nevertheless there is no definite evidence that the *immediate* recovery rate with insulin treatment is superior to other accepted methods, including such methods as occupational group and individual therapy. It is of the utmost importance that further studies on insulin should pay attention to the group aspects of the treatment. Quite apart from the urgent need to study comparable groups of patients receiving insulin and other forms of treatment, there is a great need to divide the insulin patients themselves into two groups. In one group the insulin should be given purely as a physical method, and in the other the psychological material should be studied and discussed with the patients at group therapy sessions. Similarly with LSD there is a great need to study the precise effects of group influence on the treatment, and here a rather similar program should be carried out. Research into LSD groups should be directed towards making studies on the behavior of patients. Too little is known about the type of reaction to LSD in relation to the personality of the patient. The influence of others on the inhibition or reinforcement of the LSD experience also needs investigation. All the material requires classification and analysis before we can come to understand the best way to use this and allied drugs. Only then should we be in a position to carry out controlled clinical trials which will accord or deny LSD a place in the psychiatric armory.

ATARACTICS AND GROUP THERAPY

The next question concerns the role of the tranquillizing drugs in group therapy, and here we must confess that much less is known and that there is great scope for further experiment. The attitude of the general public, patients, and staff towards the taking of what they usually refer to as drugs must first be considered. Certainly in England there are deeprooted prejudices against long-continued drug taking unless it can be clearly shown, as, for example, in the insulin treatment of diabetes, that the drug taking is essential to life. Even among epileptics, who know quite well that the anticonvulsion drugs will stop the fits, there is a tendency to discontinue the tablets. This is not just laziness on the part of the patient. We can see evidence of the emotional content of people's attitude towards drugs when we consider tobacco and alcohol, the evil effects of both of which are frequently exaggerated. Some drugs of addiction have

particularly severe sanctions applied to their use. The same kind of prejudices are involved when patients are advised to take drugs for the treatment of mental and neurotic disorders. The very term "tranquillizer,"

Table 50-1   Psychological Effects of, and Social Attitudes towards, Certain
Drugs

Drug	Psychic Action	Social Attitude
Alcohol	Diminishes superego control; ego becomes expansive and disinhibited.	Varies from condemnation to acceptance.
Barbiturates	Diminishes superego control; tranquillizes ego in small doses; may increase unconscious contents.	Widespread addiction; limited condemnation.
Minor tranquillizers (e.g., meprobamate)	Tranquillizes ego; may diminish superego control.	Widespread addiction; limited condemnation.
Major tranquillizers	Reduces flow of unconscious contents; may improve superego control.	Widespread acceptance.
Hallucinogens	Increases flow of unconscious material; ultimate strengthening of superego control.	Limited acceptance; general anxiety and religious criticism more usual.
Morphine group	Increases flow of unconscious material; permanent damage to superego if long continued.	Almost universal condemnation.

conveying freedom from anxiety, leads, in people's imagination, to the
idea that those taking tranquillizers will have a diminished sense of moral
responsibility. It has even been stated that sexual perverts taking these
drugs will be able to continue their perversions without feeling guilty
about them. It is probable that the word "tranquillizer" is a misnomer,
but so far a more satisfactory term has not been introduced. Lastly, it is
not surprising that many patients object to taking drugs over a long period
and frequently tell their doctor that they have tried to leave off the tablets. One occasionally meets patients who say that the tablets made them
feel worse. Others fear that tolerance and addiction may develop. Chlorpromazine, in particular, is inclined to cause feelings of anxiety in patients
with active sympathetic systems, yet the fact remains that sedative drugs
of various kinds are consumed by Western communities in enormous
quantities, and the impact of this drug taking on groups of various kinds
is by no means clear.

It may be interesting to try to tabulate the psychological effects of
some drugs and to correlate social attitudes towards them; this is done in
the table above.

Thus the attitude of social groups to psychotropic drugs is determined
by the real or apparent effects these drugs have on the superego func-

tion. People are less concerned by the effect of the drug on unconscious activity unless this leads to psychosis or suicide, both of which possibilities lead to therapists fearing to use LSD and which are occurrences the frequency of which has been exaggerated.

Among hospital groups one begins to get an idea of the factors involved. I have tried the experiment of taking ten patients in a ward of thirty patients and putting them all on one of the phenothiazine drugs and observing them closely both as individuals and as a group. The first thing to notice when these groups are started in various parts of the hospital is that the response to treatment appears to depend to some extent on the attitudes of the nursing staff. Some nursing staff are very enthusiastic about drug treatment. Others, more prejudiced against the use of drugs, will regard such groups as just another whim on the part of the doctor, and there is no doubt that these patients do not do so well. Therefore one immediately has a situation in which both directly and unconsciously the patients are influenced by the environment. The psychological forces which bind the LSD group together are largely absent, but one finds that in those cases where the nursing staff are enthusiastic the patients on the treatment gain a sense of importance, and in such wards requests are received from other patients to be allowed to take the drug. These matters are of the greatest importance and should be discussed with the patients as a group, and these group discussions require to be continued after the patient has left the hospital. If drugs are to be given with any benefit to schizophrenics they should be continued for a long time, perhaps for years. Long-term drug therapy occasionally meets with resistance from relatives and from the general practitioner, and it may be not only that the treatment should be discussed with the patients as a group but that groups of general practitioners and other interested people should get together to consider the relationship of drug therapy to mental disorder. About two years ago we had a large group of patients taking a phenothiazine compound known as NP 207. This substance was superior to any known drug in the phenothiazine group, but unfortunately its use had to be discontinued owing to the development of eye changes in some patients receiving large doses. We were therefore forced to change over to chlorpromazine for some of the patients who were unable to discontinue taking drugs altogether. Many of these patients showed marked symptoms of anxiety and some for a time even had pseudo manifestations of their original psychosis. Although these cases were dealt with individually, they could probably have been dealt with better and more expeditiously by getting them together as a group and discussing the meaning of the symptoms and of their anxieties. Thus one would appear to be coming to the stage where patients undergoing long-term drug therapy should be seen in groups, but again the kind of material one must expect to obtain must differ from that in groups not receiving any other form of treatment. It is possible that the phenothiazine drugs diminish dream and fantasy material. The first changes to be observed when phenothiazines are given to schizophrenics are reduction of thought disorder and hallucinations, and it is only later that the affective state of the patient undergoes improvement. The function of group therapy should therefore be directed towards improving the affective life of the patient—a role for which it is particularly suited. This no doubt accounts for the more rapid rate of improvement among those patients undergoing group and occupational therapy.

Foulds[12] has reviewed recent drug trials on both sides of the Atlantic and has drawn attention to the misleading results to be obtained from clinical impressions. Uncontrolled studies are of little, if any, value and may lead to clinically ineffective substances being given to psychotic patients for whom there are more efficient remedies.

The clinical results obtained with new drugs diminish as time goes on, and there is no really satisfactory explanation of this unless we accept the psychological power which new remedies subtly exert over the judgment of the investigators. How else can we account for the world-wide enthusiasm which was accorded to cortisone in the treatment of rheumatic disease when it was introduced ten years ago, while later clinical trials show it to be no better than aspirin? Sakel's early work with deep insulin treatment gave a recovery rate in schizophrenia of 80 per cent, a figure never since approached, while recent studies[13] have suggested that the results may be no better than those obtained with amylobarbitone. Not only are we in the dark concerning the usefulness of many psychiatric treatments which are introduced as "specific" for certain syndromes, but even the most elaborately designed clinical trials have frequently failed to distinguish between remedies which offer an advance on their predecessors and those which do not. Baker and Thorpe[14] review the literature in which inert tablets and active substances, when compared, had the same action. They report an experiment in which the inert tablets led to a favorable response not observed with the so-called active drug. The authors attribute this, in part, to the fact that the placebo was sugar-coated. "Thus in terms of total experience, our control group received several small sweets daily from the nurses while the other group received a bitter pill." A number of suggestions follow as to how these environmental influences can best be estimated or limited.

Suggestions

1. Most clinical trials lead to results unduly favorable to the drugs being tested for three main reasons.

(a) The spontaneous improvement rate of a similar group of patients is not estimated accurately. *Remedy:* controlled trials, "double blind" procedure and so on, but even these trials may favor drug action.

(b) The methods of measuring improvement are inadequate and are susceptible to conscious or unconscious bias on the part of the observer. *Remedy:* better rating scales and improved design of trial (Rashkis).[15]

(c) The trial is influenced by the "placebo" response. *Remedy:* Research is still required but the following suggestions are put forward. First, the pressure from drug manufacturers on clinicians to carry out *rapid* clinical trials should be resisted at all costs. The patients should be on placebos for weeks or months before the drug is introduced. Before a controlled clinical trial is carried out the staff should learn how to use the drug and get some idea what can be expected of it. The editors of medical journals should insist that authors have used the drug for at least a year before their paper is accepted for publication. Secondly, the first few clinical trials at any one hospital must be regarded with suspicion because of the placebo response. Thirdly, group meetings must be held in wards where clinical trials are going on, and the attitude of the staff and patients towards the trial must be ascertained. All the uncertainties and errors in clinical trials at mental hospitals or outpatient clinics lie within the emotional lives of the staff, and the operating factors should be clearly stated. The size, training, and personality of the staff must be assessed, the daily lives of the patients studied, the frequency of parole and leave, and so on, compared. How these factors can be assessed is difficult to say, and whether anyone would accept the loading of the results according to the group situation in the ward is doubtful. Nevertheless, until more objective studies of the social factors surrounding a clinical trial are published alongside the clinical results, data will be lacking on the real efficacy of the drugs, and psychiatry will continue to be bewildered by an alarming confusion of new drugs.

2. The most favorable results of clinical trials are obtained in backward hospitals or in wards where little effort has been made to resocialize the patients. In some mental hospitals (e.g., Warlingham Park, England) nearly all the social benefits achieved elsewhere by ataractics have been produced by group therapy, and the advocates of the open-door system and rehabilitation claim that drugs are unnecessary (Rees).[16] The more severe critics of intramural socializing programs state that the patients have become in a way more institutionalized because the hospital has come to depend on them for its social structure and for much of its labor for carrying out routine tasks in the hospital. Many feel that paid employees should carry out the work of the hospital and that the doctor-patient relationship should be directed towards healing the mind. When as much as possible has been done in hospital the patient should be returned to the community where, if necessary, treatment can be continued. In other words, what is done inside some hospitals by rehabilitation and occupational therapy should be done outside the hospital by the community assisted by social workers and psychiatrists.

One must conclude from these observations that the occupational program for the ward must be static for a drug trial to be of any value. So often the patients who improve are given more stimulating forms of occupation. This tendency must either be resisted or reliably assessed.

Only by attention to all these factors and possibly many others, can Wortis' claim made at the beginning of this paper that "new drug treatments have practically abolished lobotomies and greatly diminished the need for both electro-shock and insulin . . ." be reliably measured.

REFERENCES

1. J. Wortis, "Physiological Treatment," *Am. J. Psychiat.*, 113:611-615, 1957.
2. G. M. Findlay, *Recent Advances in Chemotherapy*, Vol. 1 (London: Churchill, 1950).
3. G. Wasson, *Life*, June 10, 1957, p. 45.
4. A. Hoffman, R. Heim, A. Brack, and H. Kobel, "Psilocybin ein psychotroper Wirkstoff aus dem mexikanischen Rauschpilz," *Experientia* (Basel), 14: 107-109, 1958.
5. T. J. Pettigrew, *On Superstitions Connected with the History and Practice of Medicine and Surgery* (London: Churchill, 1844).
6. N. Culpeper, *The Physician's Library* (London: 1653).
7. H. Dale, "Medicinal Treatment: Its Aims and Results," *Brit. Med. J.*, 2:423-433, 1957.
8. S. Banerjee, *Psycho-Therapy*, Vol. 1, No. 3, p. 2, 1957.
9. R. D. Scott, "The Psychology of Insulin Coma Treatment," *Brit. Med. J.*, 23:15-44, 1950.
10. C. G. Jung, "Verschiedenen Aspekte der Wiedergeburt," in *Eranos Year Book* (Zurich: Rhein Verlag, 1940); C. Kerényi and C. G. Jung, *Introduction to a Science of Mythology* (London: Routledge and Kegan Paul, 1951).
11. S. Leyton, "Glucose and Insulin in Schizophrenia," *Lancet*, 1:1253-1254, 1958.
12. G. A. Foulds, "Clinical Research in Psychiatry," *J. Ment. Sci.*, 104:259-265, 1958.
13. B. Ackner, A. Harris, and A. J. Oldham, "Insulin Treatment of Schizophrenics," *Lancet*, 1:607-611, 1957.
14. A. A. Baker and J. G. Thorpe, "Placebo Response," *Arch. Neurol. Psychiat.*, 78:57, 1957.
15. H. A. Rashkis and I. R. Smarr, "Drug and Milieu Effects with Chronic Schizophrenics," *Arch. Neurol. Psychiat.*, 77:89-94, 1957.
16. T. P. Rees, "Back to Moral Treatment and Community Care," *J. Ment. Sci.*, 103:303-313, 1956.

RECENT ADVANCES IN FAMILY GROUP THERAPY

John Elderkin Bell

When I first spoke in Scotland on family group therapy in 1955, it might have been said that the therapy had progressed through much of a first developmental phase, the advancement of the idea and somewhat random pioneering exploration. Experience in working with whole families had allayed my initial anxieties lest I precipitate a damaging emotional crisis, and had modified a somewhat unfavorable attitude to parents developed in the traditional child guidance setting. It had also proved that the patterns established in the first five years of life are often less resistant to change than had been thought. It demonstrated the therapeutic value of factors not previously much considered, such as freedom in communication and active group participation within the family. It had also proved that behavior of children and adults is more responsive to current social influences than many personality theories would indicate.

It had been demonstrated that many disturbances among older children and adolescents could be alleviated by therapeutic efforts that consistently involved both the parents and all children over nine years of age. The sequence through which family therapy progresses had been defined, permitting refinements in technique. The role of the therapist was becoming more deliberate. Sufficient control over the treatment had been attained to suggest that family therapy was feasible, economical and widely applicable (21).*

By this time others had also initiated new approaches to dealing with the family for both research and therapeutic purposes. Primarily these investigators (Dreikurs (37-39); Adelaide Johnson (64); Ackerman (1-13,

Reprinted from *Journal of Child Psychology and Psychiatry*, 1962, pp. 1-15. Pergamon Press.

* All numbers in parentheses refer to the bibliography at the end of this article.

19); Bowen and his group (23-26, 29, 42)) applied observations of various family members to the understanding of disturbed individuals, and permitted extension of theories about personality development and pathology in individuals. For example, Brodey (29), a spokesman for the last group which had experimented with hospitalization of total families of which one member was schizophrenic, detailed how the narcissism of parents led to their dealing with their schizophrenic child as an externalized projection of their own ungratified needs, preventing them from facing realistically and helpfully the child's own unmet needs. As a consequence the child reacted with schizophrenic responses.

A CRITICISM

Theories such as these, extending systems developed to explain pathological processes within individuals, may prove less efficient for understanding family processes than those which start from a social psychological orientation. We have to ask whether or not the narcissism of the parent of a schizophrenic or of any disturbed child is different in quantity or quality from that of the normal parent. If so, there should be some method of defining the distinctions and determining the extent of the narcissism. It is doubtful, however, that this can be accomplished. Social group theory would suggest that we are dealing here with a phenomenon that is virtually universal rather than distinctive for these types of family.

One might propose that all individuals in their social relations, whether parents, children, friends, are constantly engaged in a balancing act, juggling the self-wishes against the imposed demands from other individuals. Out of this elemental action in the social group emerges the variety of roles possible within the group. As a consequence, the child and parents will function in certain ways, which will differ from parent to parent and from child to child. Each will attempt to induce the others to accomplish what he is unable to accomplish himself. Each will interpret the needs of others in the light of his own ungratified needs. These simply represent two among many mechanisms through which social interaction is accomplished, and which are not necessarily pathological.

AN EXTENDED PERSPECTIVE

The point of view on family process to be developed here has been anticipated in the publications of Spiegel and Norman Bell (95-99). They follow the philosophic position of Dewey and approach the family from a transactional point of view. They postulate that the events involving the family occur within a total system of interdependent sub-systems, any one of which—for example, the individual, the family, the community, the value system—may become temporarily a focus of observation. The "world" being observed must include the observer and his observing. Within the field encompassing the interconnected sub-systems, a component system, such as the individual, can be isolated and studied as an entity. But this is an heuristic device that will involve some distortion or sacrifice of precision and predictability.

With others, they composed a multi-disciplinary team to develop the relationships among three levels of systematic concept formation, namely, the intrapsychic, the interpersonal relations in the family, and the culture. In the first, they used the theory of psychodynamics from psychoanalysis; in the second, the concepts of social role and role-conflict resolution; in the third, culture-value orientations.

They especially emphasized the cultural and social role aspects of family differences, in marked contrast to the individual-orientated perspective of some of the therapists mentioned above. They dealt with such phenomena as the presence of an emotionally disturbed child in families from Irish, Italian or early American families. In such families they reported acceleration of attempts to assimilate new cultural values. Undue rapidity of these efforts resulted in intrapsychic conflict in the parents, which intruded into the social relations between the parents and the children, leading to selection of a child as a scapegoat to accomplish a pathological stabilization of the parents' role-conflicts. Here is a demonstration of differences of explanation that emerge from different foci of observation. The definition of "family" determines the theory that will eventuate.

THREE DEFINITIONS OF FAMILY

Basically three definitions of the family have been reflected in theory and practice:

(1) The first is based on the family as seen through the eyes of a child, or as reconstructed by an adult patient. The family appears as a beneficent or a malicious influence, determining alternately the growth of healthy and pathological personality reactions. In the major writings upon which our clinical practice of psychotherapy with both children and adults was founded, the basic idea of the family turned around an individual seen genetically in polar relationship with other family members, particularly the parents. To the observer, the members of the family interacting with the individual were given form primarily by the manner in which they appeared to this individual. Any amplification of the picture provided by therapeutic interviews with a mother, or occasionally a father, or a home visit, still did not modify the orientation toward the child, but simply expanded the information available for understanding him and his reports and fantasies about his family.

(2) The second definition uses a sociological approach. This leads to theories concerning communication in the family, group attitudes and

ideals, family group decisions, and family group activities. This point of view de-emphasizes the individual and focuses on the interactive aspects of the family; this is the direction of some theories relating to family group therapy, and will be explored in detail later.

(3) Thirdly, we observe the cultural approach, emphasizing the family as an institution in both its nuclear and extended aspects; this leads especially to theories concerning the culture and the community as a source of values, norms, standards of behavior, roles, generalizations about fathers, mothers, children, the style of the family, and sociocultural factors in the development of pathological conditions.

These three modes of defining the family are not necessarily compatible in the present stage of theoretical development. Eventually we may be able to arrive at a single theory which will deal simultaneously with the phenomena of family behavior as seen from these three perspectives. For the moment it may be more productive to isolate the relationships within these three modes of observation and to organize our theories accordingly.

FAMILY GROUP THEORY

Family group theory represents an application of small group theory from social psychology to the natural group of the family. The therapy which led to the development of the theory and which is also, in its later stages, an outgrowth of theory, is an effort to apply knowledge of the operation of small groups to the production of change in the family unit. The aim is to answer a series of questions.

The Family as a Group

The first question concerns the nature of the family as a group. To understand the processes in family therapy, it is necessary to attend to three social units:

(1) The first is the single collective unit composed of the parents and children. This unit is founded on and developed from the organic base of a biological relationship. This is a given. Even an artificial, or adoptive, family is modeled on the biological family. This unit is commonly referred to as the nuclear family. Family group therapy consists normally of treatment of this collective group as a unit.

(2) Secondly, we must recognize that within the single collective unit of the family, there are a series of subgroups, not static in composition, but forming, expanding, contracting, dissolving. These subgroupings help to explain the dynamic processes in family life. Whereas the collective unit of the family has identity as a concept and as a structured entity, the subgroups within it are characterized more by their functional aims and action than by any defined structure as social units. These subgroups may be discerned when we observe two individuals in a family teaming up together

for some mutual purpose that excludes the rest of the family members. Such teams are constantly being formed, dissolved, or expanded, as when a team opens its group to include one or more additional members. In reverse, a larger subgroup may shove a member out and close ranks against him. The process of family life may be described, then, as a sequence of emerging subgroupings within the collective unitary nuclear group. The unitary group may be regarded as an assumed system of subgroups which may be separately identified at any point in time. In point of fact, despite the physical contiguity of its members, the family may seldom appear as a single group, particularly when observed over a span of time. While not forgetting that the overall family is a group with recognizable boundaries, one is usually made aware of the subunits.

(3) Thirdly, as will be amplified later, it seems valuable to acknowledge that the group therapy situation involves a third group, composed of the family members plus the therapist. In regarding the family as a collective unit, we consider it in isolation from the observer. Similarly, when we identify subgroupings within the unit, we deduce structure and describe behavior as though they existed apart from the social process of observation. The resultant over-simplifications are partially corrected through focusing on the total social group in the therapy situation, which, of course, in its dynamic progress involves subgroupings comparable to those in 2 above. In contrast to the first two natural groupings, the total therapy group is constructed, encouraging us to apply extensive published findings about such groups (compare reference 60).

Processes of Group Formation

Having identified the above three social units, we encounter a second question: how may we define the processes of group formation in the family? As with all human relationships, we may think of those in the family as beginning when the aims of an individual confront those of others in his situation. "Aims" is used here as a general term encompassing the meanings of the words "instinct," "drive," "motive" and "goal." Two consequences may follow:

(1) First, when the individual's aims are complementary to those of others, he receives their support for his goal-seeking activity. Action then ensues.

(2) Secondly, when the individual's aims are non-congruent with those of others, an ambiguous situation is created which the respective individuals, singly or in small groups, seek appropriate ways of resolving. There is an oscillation of action and reaction, moving individuals together and apart. These actions I have called *transitive actions*, for want of a better overall term to cover all the specific transitive verbs such as "love" and "hate" that describe the process. I have avoided terminology sometimes used for this purpose, such as "interaction," "inter-relationships,"

because it carries too much emphasis on the subject and the object, and too little on the process between them. Under conditions which we cannot fully specify, these processes eventuate in the resolution of the conflict by the use of either new or habitual patterns of behavior.

Applied specifically to the family, we may define the processes of group formation as *action processes leading to the accommodation of complementary or conflicting demands of individuals who are contiguous by reason of specific biological relationships or of selection after the pattern of these relationships.*

Such action processes are observed within the manifold relationship possibles in the various combinations of family members. The processes may be further specified in terms of their *purposes*, that is in terms of their motivational origins; the *media* in which they are couched, whether verbal or nonverbal, i.e., as processes of communication; and the *mechanisms* observed as the family members maneuver in the attempt to reconcile their conflicting aims through such action processes as decision, evaluation, and revision. They may be further described by the *form* of the structure of interrelationships observed at any point of time, especially by specification of such polarities as dominance-submission, independence-dependence, leading-following, or through such mutual correspondences as loving, hating and fearing.

Some common-sense observations about the family permit us to elaborate our understanding of these action processes. Normally the family goes through a longer and more varied history of group action than any other small group in our society. It is distinguished from other groups by some particular characteristics of its relational possibilities.

For one thing, it is composed of individuals at different age-levels, developing at different maturational rates, and with disparate age-valuations. The psychological characteristics of particular ages produce dissimilar requirements for change and possibilities for action. At particular periods, new processes of interaction are demanded with great speed. For instance, parents of a first-born child are often amazed at the rapidity with which they have to revise their ways of handling him in view of the sudden and dramatic shifts in behavior that take place overnight. A pattern is no sooner established than the child's maturation requires a new schedule or a new method of handling. This, it seems to me, is part of what is implied in the statement that "children keep you young." Their maturation requires flexible reactions from their parents.

No maturational process is more telling in its effects than the growth of language. As the development of language progresses from communication with the simple signs available to the young child to the complicated symbolic language of the adult, new possibilities for action and demands for changes in family relations continually emerge. We shall see how inability or failure to accommodate to such demands may be related to the breakdown of the family and the precipitation of psycho-pathological behavior.

Other agents (of a dynamic and changing nature) which help to define the action potentialities of the family group are found in the biological or genetic make-up of the individuals; yet others are found in the community and cultural pressures on the individuals and the group. We are not overlooking the importance of these when we concentrate on the family as a social group, but rather simplifying our own analysis of the nature of the family. We acknowledge the need to revise our points of view to take into account these other components of family interaction.

As stated in our definition, the action process of the family leads to mutual accommodation, which consolidates complementary aims and reconciles the conflicting demands of individuals, thus leading to the structuring of the formerly ambiguous and inchoate operational field (forming of groups). This process includes action within the whole unit or between subgroups of the larger unit. The group units are being revised constantly as other action steps are needed. Thus we describe the forming, remaking and dissolving of the family group(s).

Health and Pathology in the Family

Next we must consider the question of health and pathology in the family. We are speaking here of social health and illness, especially the latter, which may subsume a broad range of social problems shown in one or more family members. We recognize that health and pathology are value-judgments applied to the behavior of the family group or individual members by those inside or outside the family. In dynamic terms, the judgment that behavior is pathological is a demand for change in present behavior, whether or not this is possible. Health, in similar terms, represents behavior which is socially supportable and sanctioned within the family group, outside it, or both. Behavior may be called healthy or pathological as though it were clearly one or the other, which is never actually the case, since the judgment is always related to the personal standards of the judge, none of which occur universally.

To speak of the healthy and efficient family implies then some broad concurrence on the characteristics of such a family. Among those that might secure such broad agreement are the following:

(a) It shows, by the mutual satisfaction of its members and by action in concert, that complementary aims exist and are supporting the functions and structure of the group as a group.

(b) It has available multiple methods for accommodating the mutually incompatible demands of its individual members. It demonstrates from day to day a variety of patterns by which it faces and handles the conflicts between individuals and factions within it.

(c) It has means of repeatedly evaluating the consequences of its achievements of accommodation.

(d) It chooses to operate flexibly, so that new methods of accommodation may be discovered and taken up when radical shifts are required.

In contrast, we believe that the family that produces a disturbed individual has not been able yet to achieve the above action patterns.

THE SYMPTOM AS COMMUNICATION

In attempting to explain the development of pathological behavior from the family group point of view, we have found it necessary to differentiate the conditions within which acute symptoms are developed and those within which chronicity is produced. It would appear that when symptoms develop suddenly, we have especially an effort on the part of an individual to bring about a change within the family group. In this light, the acute symptom may be regarded as a sign about a person's needs, his desires and anticipation for the other, and his resulting goals. Thus, among other concepts the symptom may be thought of as an attempted communication expressed in such a manner and intensity as to effect disturbance in the group. Often signs learned in early life are used because of their simplicity, even though they may have lost their historical sign-value and be now less efficient in most situations than more complicated symbolic language. The use of a more primitive sign language suggests the breakdown of more complex communication, and ineffectiveness in more mature language. This inadequacy may be the result of defects in the symbols formerly available, as when the symbols are too ambiguous, when their meaning to speaker and listener is not equivalent, when the intended recipient is not attending, when, having heard, he fails to respond or mobilizes powerful counter-communications in protest against what he hears.

In practice, the acute symptom is commonly expressive and/or motoric rather than verbal, in accordance with the observation that nonverbal communication generally takes precedence over verbal communication in the family. In a group with such a long history of development, where the earlier nonverbal language was a required form of communication, a brief gesture often speaks a whole paragraph. Analysis of the communication system in the family leads to the following observations:

(1) Frequently the nonverbal is the preferred language, especially when there are young children, but also with older children and adults.

(2) For the most part, the verbal and nonverbal are interchangeable as modes of communication; this is a basis for family group therapy, where the nonverbal must for a great part be translated into the verbal.

(3) Sometimes the nonverbal represents a breakdown of the verbal method of communication. The latter may then be restored only when there is especial support and sanction for expressing content verbally.

(4) Sometimes the nonverbal represents that which has not attained consciousness and cannot therefore be expressed verbally. Support may lead to the development of insight, awareness of the meaning of the behavior, and the ability ultimately to verbalize; but expression cannot be attained until insight is present.

(5) Sometimes the nonverbal and the verbal are mutually contradictory or inconsistent.

(6) Sometimes nonverbal language tends to be used for private communication within the family group in preference to the more public verbal communication. Particular words and verbal expressions may also develop a private symbolic value within the family and be used in intimate ways, even though the outward form is public.

Returning to consideration of the acute symptom, if the crisis it represents is not resolved, then the symptom processes are incorporated into the patterns of family action, and groups are formed on the basis of the existence of the symptom action; such groups may include or exclude the individual with the symptom. The symptom then is perpetuated as a role, partly developed, partly assigned. Such a role may retain to a certain extent some of its communicative purpose, but it tends to lose this aim as it is reinforced by the pressures of the family group and thus becomes habitual. Here we have, then, the development of chronicity. An illustration may help to clarify this. In one family, a small boy had been traumatized when his mother forced him out of the family car and told him to walk a short distance home because he had been misbehaving; his acute response was the development of car-sickness. Had this been effective in telling his parents of his anxiety that he might be ejected from the car, the symptom would have accomplished its communicative purpose. Instead, the family reorganized its life around the car-sickness, avoiding occasions for the boy to ride in the car, but also insuring, in effect, that the car-sickness would persist when riding was necessary. In family therapy, when the family could recognize and attend to the communicative intent in the car-sickness, they heard his memory of the early trauma, and about the anxiety that had persisted for the ensuing eight years.

The chronic symptom becomes a way of interrelating—a mode of action—and attains the usefulness of the familiar as the family works out its purposes. It is perpetuated because it has become integrated into an established web of family interactions and its persistence is necessary to the continuation of this structure. Within this pattern the value of the symptom to the respective family members may vary; it would not serve the same purposes for the patient who carried the symptom as for any other. Though each may use it in his own way, the family significance is primarily its functional necessity to a stabilized mode of interaction. No one may consciously wish it to persist, although an unconscious need for the pathology may be demonstrated by the emergence of symptomatic behavior in one or more other family members when the patient begins to improve. The symptomatic mode of action seems to be forced on another family member in order to preserve the overall pattern of the family process.

CONCOMITANTS OF CHRONICITY

When chronic symptomatology is deeply entrenched in the behavior patterns of an individual, we may often observe one or more associated conditions or situations in the family.

(1) There may be a limitation or reduction in the range of methods of accommodation to conflicts between the family members, for instance, progressive limiting of the action patterns permitted in the family. Patterns of behavior become stereotyped; the manners of relating become fixed and unresponsive to modifying influences. The stereotypes may be represented in the rigid structuring of subgroups within the family; in the constriction of the expressed goals toward which individuals, subgroups, and the family as a whole direct themselves; and in the inflexibility of their choice of action patterns.

(2) There is a diminution of symbolic communication and an increase in the use of simple signs. Thus the messages which can be transmitted are impoverished quantitatively and qualitatively. There is also reduced reception of messages through failures in listening, hearing, and in the visual perception of gestures and facial expressions.

A particular form of impoverished communication, the contradictory or ambiguous message, has been described especially by Jackson, Bateson, Haley, Weakland, et al. Reporting on their research on family communication in schizophrenia (16-18, 56, 104, 105) they discriminate two levels in the exchange of messages that leads to the defining of relationships. The first is the simple message conveyed by the words. The second is the qualification of the message conveyed by the mode of speech and the accompanying motoric elements—movement, gesture, facial expression and tone of voice. Sometimes the qualifications are congruent with the message; in other instances they are incongruent.

The authors trace the schizophrenic problem in part to a particular form of contradictory communication which they call "double-bind"; this is defined as a situation in which one member of the family imposes mutually inconsistent requirements on another, thus preventing movement in any direction. This complete stifling of decision or action forces the individual out of direct communication and into incongruent responses.

(3) There is a breakdown in the evaluation process through which individuals attain and revise their perceptions of others, their awareness of their own methods of responding to others, and their aims, both personal and mutual. Consequently, they act in such a way as to perpetuate the pathological behavior and as though it were impossible to revise. Verbally

they may protest their distress at the behavior of the sick family member, while at the same time perpetuating, without insight, the conditions that result in the pathology.

(4) The family values "change" insufficiently or excessively. Change is an aim of families in varying degrees. This difference is reflected in the extent of the development of family lore which provides traditional patterns of interaction. For a family to be effective as a group, a balance seems to be necessary between the aim of preserving tradition and achievement of change. If the clinging to old ways is too strong, as in immigrant groups, the family will face disruption, both because of the conflict in values with the culture and the internal rigidity of the family; if, on the other hand, change is overvalued, advantage cannot be taken of the economy of stable patterns.

FAMILY THERAPY AS A MECHANISM FOR CHANGE

Let us now consider some points of view about how family group therapy produces change in face of such pathology. We do not know if the processes are fundamentally different when the symptoms are acute and have produced a crisis in the family, or when they are chronic and integrated into the family interaction. We suggest that, in the latter case, some crisis must be precipitated, perhaps by the pressure of community reaction, or perhaps by some change in the state of the person who has been carrying a pathological role in the family.

The initiation of change through family therapy begins with the referral, which is itself a request for change, but characteristically for change in an *individual*. The first problem in family therapy is to translate this request for change in the individual into one for change in the *family* where it may be assumed change is needed. Such an assumption would not be foreign to the thinking of family members in most instances. The therapist supports this point of view when he insists on seeing the family as a group rather than as a series of individuals in isolation.

When the motivation for family change is established, the therapist forms a group with the family in which he attempts to play a planned, controlled, and communicated role. He establishes with each individual a subgroup, each of which demonstrates to the whole some new possibilities of action for each of the family members. As an outsider, he calls into play actions embodying patterns that the individual uses in his public life beyond the family. These patterns have been potentially available to use within the family, but have been crowded out or never permitted among the customary stereotyped actions there. The therapist must insure the participation of all the members of the family. Since this will be primarily on a verbal level, there are certain requirements as to age, ability to conceptualize abstractly, knowledge of language, that require a particular level of maturity. Also, there must have been enough extra-family life to initiate patterns of behavior beyond those used in the family. It has been found that nine years of age is about the lower limit for the average child to participate according to the method I have developed. It may be feasible, however, by using other modes of communication, to work with family groups that include younger children.

In order to promote participation, the therapist must develop and maintain the clearest possible definition and presentation of his own functions. As with all groups that are constructed, there is an initial stage of common exploration of the respective roles of individuals and the sanctioned modes of communication. The speed with which this may be accomplished depends on the therapist's clarity about his own role, and his ability to communicate to the other members of the conference the ways in which he will and will not take part. Thus, the orientation of the parents and the children is especially important.

Equally important are:

(1) The therapist's clear awareness of the formal responsibilities he will undertake;

(2) His defining of the manner in which he will accomplish them;

(3) The relationship between what he says and what he communicates nonverbally; this determines the extent to which he can make his role explicit. The less ambiguity there is in the role of the therapist, the more rapidly the group will structure itself into a functioning conference.

When the therapist has established working relationships with each individual participant in the family, the members begin to perceive the new possibilities of action which are being revealed to them and to incorporate them experimentally into their joint action. Normally this begins in two-person subgroups in the family (parent-child, husband-wife, etc.). These two-person subgroups are consequently enlarged, combined, grouped and regrouped toward inclusion of as many family members as is optimal for the action to be accomplished.

The therapist's overall activity may be described, then, as an effort to promote social interaction through communication within the family unit, permitting it thereby to experience, appraise, define, and reorder its relational processes. The therapist builds social action on the basis of his own methods of participation. He conducts relationships—now with one, now with two, now with all—in the presence of the others. He disrupts unsatisfactory patterns of relationship as he permits individuals to reaffirm old intentions that have been frustrated. He calls up new intentions. He encourages the family to clarify its goals, to choose more appropriate group goals for the whole family and more suitable personal goals for use in life outside the family's direct involvement. He demonstrates, through the ways individuals relate to him, that within the family there may be:

(a) increased fluidity in communication;

(b) greater flexibility in roles and functions; and

(c) greater discipline in the choice and forms of relationships.

He promotes thereby new evaluations within the family of the potentialities and skills of the individual members. He encourages reassessments of the past, of the responsibility for earlier difficulties, of the meaning of symptomatic behavior, and of the family climate within which it grew. He prevents any family members from evading the implications of their relationships with him and others. He demonstrates forms of relationship that can be transferred to other interactions in the family. This leads the family to the conviction that change is possible and desirable and may bring about a greater measure of behavior that the family would interpret as positive.

Family group therapy is, then, a treatment method which depends on the presence and control of the therapist. He uses his own personal and social skills to help the family attain what it has shown itself unable to reach before, the ability to live for its own total welfare, for the welfare of each of its family members, and ultimately for the betterment of the community.

SUMMARY

The history of the development of family group therapy, and of other recent studies of the family, has been reviewed briefly. Various definitions of *family* were discovered, and a proposal was advanced to define family in terms of social psychological theories of small group behavior. From the perspective of such a definition, formulations were attempted relative to the development of the family group, its stability, its action processes, its health and its pathology. In light of these conceptions, a brief analysis was undertaken of the processes involved in family group therapy as a mechanism for the promotion of change.

BIBLIOGRAPHY

1. Ackerman, N. W. (1951) Group Dynamics 1. "Social role" and total personality. *Amer. J. Orthopsychiat.* 21:1-17.
2. Ackerman, N. W. (1954) Interpersonal disturbances in the family: Some unsolved problems in psychotherapy. *Psychiatry* 17:359-368.
3. Ackerman, N. W. (1956) Psychoanalytic principles in a mental health clinic for the pre-school child and his family. *Psychiatry* 19:63-76.
4. Ackerman, N. W. (1957) A changing conception of personality: a personal viewpoint. *Amer. J. Psychoanal.* 17:78-86.
5. Ackerman, N. W. (1957) An orientation to psychiatric research on the family. *Marriage Fam. Living* 19:68-74.
6. Ackerman, N. W. (1958) *Psychodynamics of family life.* Basic Books, New York.

7. Ackerman, N. W. (1958) Toward an integrative therapy of the family. *Amer. J. Psychiat.* 114:727-733.

8. Ackerman, N. W., and Behrens, M. L. (1955) Child and family psychopathy: problems of correlation. In *Psychopathology of childhood*. Hoch, P. H., and Zubin, J. (Eds.), Grune and Stratton, New York, pp. 177-196.

9. Ackerman, N. W., and Behrens, M. L. (1956) A study of family diagnosis. *Amer. J. Orthopsychiat.* 26:66-78.

10. Ackerman, N. W., and Behrens, M. L. (1956) The family group and family therapy: the practical application of family diagnosis. *Int. J. Sociometry* 1:52-54.

11. Ackerman, N. W., and Behrens, M. L. (1957) The family group and family therapy. Part II. The practical application of family diagnosis. *Int. J. Sociometry* 1:82-95.

12. Ackerman, N. W., and Neubauer, P. B. (1948) Failures in the psychotherapy of children. In Hoch, P. H. (Ed.), *Failures in psychiatric treatment*. Grune and Stratton, New York.

13. Ackerman, N. W., and Sobel, R. (1952) Family diagnosis: an approach to the study of the preschool child. *Amer. J. Orthopsychiat.* 20:744-752.

14. Alanen, Y. (1958) The mother of schizophrenic patients. *Acta psychiat. neurol. scand.* 33:Suppl. 124.

15. Barrabee, P. (1957) The family as the unit of treatment in mental health therapy. *Marriage Fam. Living* 19:182-186.

16. Bateson, G. (1958) *Cultural problems posed by a study of schizophrenic process*. Presented at the American Psychiatric Association, Conference on Schizophrenia, Honolulu.

17. Bateson, G. (1958) *The group dynamics of schizophrenia*. Presented at the Institute on Chronic Schizophrenia and Hospital Treatment Programs, Osawatomie State Hospital, Osawatomie.

18. Bateson, G., Jackson, D. D., Haley, J., and Weakland, J. (1956) Toward a theory of schizophrenia. *Behav. Sci.* 1:251-264.

19. Behrens, M. L., and Ackerman, N. W. (1956) The home visit as an aid in family diagnosis and therapy. *Soc. Casewk.* 37:11-19.

20. Bell, J. E. (1953) Family group therapy as a treatment method. *Amer. Psychologist* 8:515 (T). Also privately published.

21. Bell, J. E. (1961) Family group therapy: a new method of treatment for older children, adolescents, and their parents. *Publ. Hlth. Monogr.* 64.

22. Beatman, F. (1957) Family interaction: its significance for diagnosis and treatment. *Soc. Casewk.* 38:111-118.

23. Bowen, M. (1960) A family concept of schizophrenia. In Jackson, D. D. (Ed.), *The etiology of schizophrenia*. Basic Books, New York.

24. Bowen, M. (1957) *Family participation in schizophrenia*. Presented at the annual meeting of the American Psychiatric Association, Chicago, May 15.

25. Bowen, M., Dysinger, R. H., and Basamania, B. (1959) Role of the father in families with a schizophrenic patient. *Amer. J. Psychiat.* 115:1017-1021.

26. Bowen, M., Dysinger, R. H., Brodey, W. M., and Basamania, B. (1957)

Study and treatment of five hospitalized family groups each with a psychotic member. Read in the sessions on Current Familial Studies at the annual meeting of the American Orthopsychiatric Association, Chicago, March 8.

27. Bowlby, J. (1949) The study and reduction of group tensions in the family. *Human Relations* 2:123-128.

28. Brady, J. P. (1958) Language in schizophrenia: review of several approaches to the problem. *Amer. J. Psychiat.* 12:473-487.

29. Brodey, W. M., and Hayden, M. (1957) Intrateam reactions: their relation to the conflicts of the family in treatment. *Amer. J. Orthopsychiat.* 27:349-355.

30. Burgum, M. (1942) The father gets worse: a child guidance problem. *Amer. J. Orthopsychiat.* 12:474-485.

31. Chance, E. (1959) *Families in treatment.* Basic Books, New York.

32. Clausen, J. A., and Yarrow, M. R. (1955) Mental illness and the family. *J. soc. Issues* 11:3-5.

33. Clausen, J. A., Yarrow, M. R., Deasy, L. C., and Schwartz, C. G. (1955) The impact of mental illness: research formulation. *J. soc. Issues*, 11:6-11.

34. Cleveland, E. J., and Longaker, W. D. (1957) Neurotic patterns in the family. In Leighton, A. H., Clausen, J. A., and Wilson, R. N. (Eds.), *Explorations in social psychiatry.* Basic Books, New York.

35. Deutsch, M. (1958) A research approach to family diagnosis and treatment. *Marriage Fam. Living* 20:140-145.

36. Dicks, H. V. (1955) The predicament of the family in the modern world. *Lancet* 1:295-297.

37. Dreikurs, R. (1949) Counseling for family adjustment. *Individual Psychol. Bull.* 7:119-137.

38. Dreikurs, R. (1949) Psychotherapy through child guidance. *Nervous Child* 8:311-328.

39. Dreikurs, R. (1951) Family group therapy in the Chicago Community Child Guidance Center. *Ment. Hyg.* 35:291-301.

40. Dublin, T. D., and Fraenkel, M. (1949) Preventive medical services for the family. In *The family as the unit of health.* Milbank Memorial Fund, New York.

41. Dunn, H. L. (1956) Public health begins in the family. *Pub. Health Rep.* 71:1002-1010.

42. Dysinger, R. H. (1957) The "action dialogue" in an intense relationship: A study of a schizophrenic girl and her mother. Presented at the annual meeting of the American Psychiatric Association, Chicago, May 15.

43. Fibush, E. (1957) The evaluation of marital interaction in the treatment of one partner. *Soc. Casewk.* 38:303-307.

44. Fisher, S., and Mendell, D. (1956) The communication of neurotic patterns over two and three generations. *Psychiatry* 19:41-46.

45. Fleck, S. *et al.* (1957) The intrafamilial environment of the schizophrenic patient. II. Interaction between hospital staff and families. *Psychiatry* 20:343-350.

46. Fleck, S., Freedman, D. X., Cornelison, A., Terry, D., and Lidz, T.: *Intra-*

familial environment of the schizophrenic patient—V. The understanding of symptomatology through the study of family interaction. Read at the annual meeting of the American Psychiatric Association, May, 1957.

47. Foote, N., and Cottrell, L. S. (1955) *Identity and interpersonal competence: New directions in family research.* Univ. Chicago Press, Chicago.

48. Foster, R. (1956) A point of view on marriage counseling. *J. couns. Psychol.* 3:212-215.

49. Galdston, I. (1958) The American family in crisis. *Ment. Hyg.* 42:229-236.

50. Gerard, D. L., and Seigel, J. (1950) The family background of schizophrenia. *Psychiat. Quart.* 24:47-73.

51. Glasmann, R., Lipton, H., and Dunstan, P. L. (1959) Group discussions with a hospitalized schizophrenic and his family. *Int. J. group Psychother.* 9:204-212.

52. Goolishian, H. A. (Univ. Texas, Medical Branch, Galveston). Personal communication.

53. Green, R. (1948) Treatment of parent-child relationships. *Amer. J. Orthopsychiat.* 18:442-446.

54. Griffiths, W. (1954) Changing family health patterns: A review of recent research. *J. Home Econ.* 46:13-16.

55. Groves, E., and Groves, C. (1946) *Dynamic mental hygiene: With special emphasis on family counseling.* Stackpole, Harrisburg, Pa.

56. Haley, J. (1959) Control in psychoanalytic psychotherapy. *Progr. Psychotherapy* 4:48-65.

57. Hall, B. H., and Wheeler, W. (1957) The patient and his relatives: initial joint interview. *Social Work* 2:75-80.

58. Hallowitz, D., *et al.* (1957) The treatment process with both parents together. *Amer. J. Orthopsychiat.* 27:587-607.

59. Halpert, H. P. (1958) Activities of the National Institute of Mental Health which affect American families. *Marriage Fam. Living* 20:261-269.

60. Hearn, G. (1957) The process of group development. *Autonomous Groups Bull.* 13:1-7.

61. Henry, J. (1951) Family structure and the transmission of neurotic behavior. *Amer. J. Orthopsychiat.* 21:800-818.

62. Henry, J., and Warson, S. (1951) Family structure and psychic development. *Amer. J. Orthopsychiat.* 21:59-73.

63. Jackson, D. D. (1951) The question of family homeostasis. *Psychoanal. Quart.* 31:79-90.

64. Johnson, A. M., and Szurek, S. A. (1952) The genesis of antisocial acting out in children and adults. *Psychoanal. Quart.* 21:323-343.

65. Kluckhohn, F. R. (1958) Variations in the basic values of family systems. *Soc. Casewk.* 39:63-72.

66. Koos, E. L. (1946) *Families in trouble.* King's Crown Press, New York.

67. Lewin, K. (1947) Group discussion and social change. In Newcomb, T. M., and Hartley, E. L. (Eds.), *Readings in social psychology.* Holt, New York, pp. 330-334.

68. Lidz, T. (1958) Schizophrenia and the family. *Psychiatry* 21:21-27.

69. Lidz, T., Cornelison, A. R., Fleck, S., and Terry, D. (1957) The intra-

familial environment of schizophrenic patients. I. The father. *Psychiatry* 20:329-342.

70. Lidz, T., Cornelison, A. R., Fleck, S., and Terry, D. (1957) The intra-familial environment of schizophrenic patients. II. Marital schism and marital skew. *Amer. J. Psychiat.* 114:241-248.

71. Lidz, R. W., and Lidz, T. (1949) The family environment of schizophrenic patients. *Amer. J. Psychiat.* 106:332-345.

72. Lidz, T., Parker, B., and Cornelison, A. (1956) The role of the father in the family environment of the schizophrenic patient. *Amer. J. Psychiat.* 113:126-132.

73. Liebman, S. (Ed.). (1959) *Emotional forces in the family*. Lippincott, New York.

74. Lippmann, H. (1954) Emotional factors in family breakdown. *Amer. J. Orthopsychiat.* 24:445-453.

75. Mangus, A. (1957) Integration of theory, research, and family counselling practice. *Marriage Fam. Living* 19:81-88.

76. McKnight, W. K. (1948) Care of patient's family in a private mental hospital. *Ment. Health Bull.*, Penna. Dept. Welfare, 25:6.

77. Midelfort, C. (1957) *The family in psychotherapy*. McGraw-Hill, New York.

78. Milbank Memorial Fund. (1949) *The family as the unit of health*. Milbank Memorial Fund, New York.

79. Mitchell, C. (1956) The place of counseling in a family agency. *J. Jewish Communal Service* 32:356-367.

80. Mittelmann, B. (1948) The concurrent analysis of married couples. *Psychoanal. Quart.* 17:182-197.

81. Mittelmann, B. (1952) Simultaneous treatment of both parents and their child. In Bychowski, G., and Despert, J. L. (Eds.), *Specialized techniques in psychotherapy*. Basic Books, New York.

82. Mudd, E. (1951) *The practice of marriage counselling*. Association, New York.

83. Mudd, E. *et al.* (Ed.) (1958) *Marriage counselling*. Association, New York.

84. Parsons, T., Bales, R. F., *et al.* (1955) *Family socialization and interaction process*. The Free Press, Glencoe, Ill.

85. Pollak, O. (1956) *Integrating sociological and psychoanalytic concepts: An exploration in child psychotherapy*. Russell Sage Foundation, New York.

86. Reichard, S., and Tillman, G. (1950) Patterns of parent-child relationships in schizophrenia. *Psychiatry* 13:247-257.

87. Richardson, H. B. (1945) *Patients have families*. The Commonwealth Fund, New York.

88. Ruesch, J. (1953) Synopsis of the theory of human communication. *Psychiatry* 16:215-243.

89. Ruesch, J. (1954) Psychiatry and the challenge of communication. *Psychiatry* 17:1-18.

90. Ruesch, J. (1955) Non-verbal language and therapy. *Psychiatry* 18:323-330.

91. Ruesch, J. (1957) *Disturbed communication.* Norton, New York.
92. Ruesch, J., and Bateson, G. (1951) *Communication—the social matrix of psychiatry.* Norton, New York.
93. Ryckoff, I. M., Day, J., and Wynne, L. C. (1958) *The maintenance of stereotyped roles in the families of schizophrenics.* Read at the American Psychiatric Association Meetings, San Francisco, May.
94. Schwartz, C. G. (1957) Perspectives on deviance: Wives' definitions of their husbands' mental illness. *Psychiatry* 20:275-291.
95. Spiegel, J. P. (1954) New perspectives in the study of the family. *Marriage Fam. Living* 16:4-12.
96. Spiegel, J. P. (1956) A model for relationships among systems. In Grinker, R. R. (Ed.), *Toward a unified theory of human behavior.* Basic Books, New York.
97. Spiegel, J. P. (1957) Interpersonal influences within the family. In *Group Processes, 3rd Conf.* Macy Foundation.
98. Spiegel, J. P. (1957) The resolution of the role conflict within the family. *Psychiatry* 20:1-16.
99. Spiegel, J. P., and Kluckhohn, F. R. (1954) Integration and conflict in family behavior. *Group for the Advancement of Psychiatry.* Report No. 27. Topeka, Kansas.
100. Stroup, A., and Glasser, P. (1959) The orientation and focus of marriage counseling. *Marriage Fam. Living* 21:20-24.
101. Szurek, S. *et al.* (1942) Collaborative psychiatric therapy of parent-child problems. *Amer. J. Orthopsychiat.* 12:511-516.
102. Tietze, T. (1949) A study of the mothers of schizophrenic patients. *Psychiatry* 12:55-65.
103. Van Amerongen, S. (1954) Initial psychiatric family studies. *Amer. J. Orthopsychiat.* 24:73-83.
104. Weakland, J. H. (1960) The "double-bind" hypothesis of schizophrenia and three-party interaction. In Jackson, D. D. (Ed.), *The etiology of schizophrenia.* Basic Books, New York.
105. Weakland, J. H., and Jackson, D. D. (1958) Patient and therapist observations on the circumstances of a schizophrenic episode. *Arch. Neurol. Psychiat.* 79:554-574.
106. Wertheim, E. S. (1958) Family casework in the interest of children. *Soc. Casewk.* 39:2-3.
107. Wertheim, E. S. (1959) A joint interview technique with mother and child. *Children* 6:23-29.
108. Wynne, I. D., Ryckoff, I. M., Day, J., and Hirsh, S. E. (1958) Pseudo-mutuality in the family relations of schizophrenics. *Psychiatry* 21:205-220.

AN EXHORTATION

GROUP PROCESS ANALYSIS: PAST IS PROLOGUE

Eugene L. Hartley

Just as the publication of the volume of *Readings in Social Psychology*, prepared for the committee on the teaching of social psychology of the Society for the Psychological Study of Social Issues (New York: Henry Holt & Company, 1947), provided a base for the coalescence of the concerns of sociologists and psychologists interested in this field, so may we expect the present volume to contribute to the desired integration of the scientific and therapeutic approaches. The questions and challenges raised in the Introduction to the present series of papers must be confronted, along with many others. The reliance in this collection on the Western European tradition, and particularly on the English language publications, can be noted and understood, but still be deplored. Such sociocentrism cannot long be permitted to endure. In the "one world" of intellectual endeavor there must be no such barriers. It should be highly enlightening to see an analysis of readers' fantasies about the contents of a revised edition five or ten years hence.

The student of personality and the student of social psychology work at somewhat different levels of abstraction. The former attempts to identify and account for those aspects of the individual which characterize his activities in *all* his undertakings; the latter emphasizes the analysis of those aspects of the individual's behavior which derive from his membership in a structured society. Normally, the student of personality can be expected to offer but little to the examination of the *variable* responses of the individual as he plays his several roles in the course of a day. On the other hand,

653

the social psychologist, with his point of departure the complexly structured society, will make only a limited contribution to the understanding of the internal integration of the affective responses of the individual which defines his joys and sorrows, satisfactions and discomforts. The merging of the two emphases makes it possible to establish continuity between the two levels of study so that we can see the transformation of such "personality" attributes as needs and cognitive styles into concrete, manifest behavior; and conversely, it can account more adequately for the growing distress of an individual who is successfully fulfilling the requirements of a high status constellation of middle-class roles. The emergent synthesis is not easy to achieve, for we are each ego-involved in the disciplines in which we have been trained; we have our frames of reference which contribute to our selective perceptions of the available data, our ego ideals which provide us with models, our didactic experiences which have confirmed us in our approaches. However, the need is great, and with the superordinate goal requiring endeavors beyond that available within either group, we can confidently expect a coalition. New reference groups must be formed and cathected, new norms must emerge.

The hand of tradition seems to lie more heavily on the practitioner than on the academician; therefore it is the practitioner who must make the more strenuous efforts. It would be well for him to remember that Freud's analysis of groups derived primarily from his observations of the church and the army. He was well aware of the restrictions this imposed on his formulations and qualified his delineation of a psychological group by noting that this only held for groups having a leader. Today, of course, we would restrict it to groups with authoritarian leadership. Freud noted further that the conscience was the most common derivative from the ego, but that there were many other splits. Apparently the superego residual of the Oedipus complex is not the end of the development of internalized norms and self-regulating mechanisms. Later cathexes are also integrated. "Normally," wrote Freud, "the superego is constantly becoming more and more remote from the original parents, becoming, as it were, more impersonal." (*New Introductory Lectures on Psycho-Analysis* [New York: Carlton House, 1933], p. 92.) The analysis of groups as representing the family paradigm seems far less rigid in Freud's writing than in that of many of his followers.

The academician is far more ready to adopt new perspectives. The scientist has often been described as a faddist who embraces with enthusiasm new theories, new techniques, new terminologies. He will have difficulty, nonetheless, in accepting a formulation that suggests that the entire study of group process represents *merely* the elaboration of superego psychology. Perhaps it would be worth while searching for new terms in the more esoteric languages so that we may proceed with appropriate definitions unbeclouded by the connotations deriving from common usage.

The "mask" significance of persona, and the "indivisible" root of individual, both belie current conceptual significances. As we study group processes within the individual as well as in the interpersonal units, new dimensions should emerge, and we must be wary of having our understanding impaired by the channeling effects of inexact language.

Perhaps as a start we might address ourselves to the question of the extent to which group therapy really involves the *group* process rather than simply the concurrent analyses of the plural psychologies of a number of individuals. There is a tremendous difference between the functional interrelationships of individuals interacting to achieve a goal in common and a similar setting of individuals with common goals. The commonly cited illustration of a team whose members must win or lose together well illustrates the group with a goal in common. The ordinary college class shows none of the same sort of interdependence inasmuch as one student may, at the end of the term, get an A and his neighbor an F. Let the college instructor, however, announce a surprise quiz, and the class becomes a well-knit group of interdependent individuals whose success or failure in protesting the threat will blanket all equally. Note the great difference in reaction to events on the national and international scene, at the threat of thermonuclear war, between, on the one hand, the person who perceives his survival as a goal in common with that of potential enemies and thinks in terms of the interdependence of mankind and, on the other, the person who sees survival as a common goal but without a feeling for any interdependence. Where does the group of the group therapist fit in? Is it perceived by the participants as one in which their personal success, their cure, depends on the progress of their neighbors? Or do they have a sympathetic feeling for their fellow sufferers but essentially believe they are autonomous units? Either way, the group setting adds new dimensions to the therapy for the individual; but for the development of a sound and integrated theory we must know and understand what is transpiring in group process terms.

Let us approach another illustrative problem from the perspective of the practitioner. One of the first questions raised by the novice is, "How large should a group be?" What really *is* the optimal number of patients who may be formed into a group? For psychoanalytic group therapy, a very common answer, empirically derived, is "about eight to ten." The practitioner may be satisfied—he knows how to proceed; but the scientist would still want to know, "Why?" Let us consider the matter very briefly. What is the effect of size on a group? If we expect every individual to interact with each other individual, how many interactional bonds or units would there be in groups of different sizes? With two individuals, there is one bond between them; with three, two bonds; with four, six; with five, ten. The general formula, from elementary probability theory, would be the one for predicting the number of combinations taken two at a time from differently sized groups. If n equals the number of people in the group, the formula is: $n\,(n—1)/2$. Using this formula we can see that the interactional bonds within groups of various sizes increase as follows:

Number of people in group	Number of interactional bonds
6	15
7	21
8	28
9	36
10	45
11	55
12	66
13	78
14	91
15	105

Is the limit set at, let us say, eight because the therapist would have trouble keeping track of more than 28 interactional units? Or is it the patients who are so limited? With whose social perception span are we dealing? If the emphasis is on the patients' ability to maintain control over relationships, would we not expect this to be a variable depending on the kind and degree of the patients' pathology? If it is the therapist who is the limiting factor, would we not expect this factor to change as a function of experience? Are smaller groups less effective because they do not provide support or because they do not provide enough challenge and opportunity? To what extent ought the size of the group be varied during the progress of therapy in order to provide for increased therapeutic opportunities as the patients improve? Perhaps the decision about group size is primarily a matter of "practicality," the limit to the consumer's willingness to dilute his relationship to the therapist and still pay his fees; but might not this be related to the size of the family from which the patient comes? The relationship of group size to group processes is still a very real problem. Some laboratory studies of this problem have been undertaken, primarily with problem solving groups; are the results comparable to the findings (or observations) in therapy groups? The study of even small groups show consistent tendencies toward the development of scapegoating and supportive coalitions. Are such tendencies inherent in the group process, and how are they best integrated into the therapeutic theory and practice?

As we look forward to the continuing reciprocal enrichment of the studies and practice in the group process field, let us not overlook the need to retain our orientation toward the continued elaboration of the researches into the nature of motivation, of perception, and of the learning processes. Laboratory studies of traditional topics, as well as of such integrative concepts as coping and creativity, are making huge strides. For these tool concepts, unlike the advances in pharmacology, we do not have "detail men." We must do our own studying and appraising.

However, new knowledge does not come only from the laboratories. Clinicians in recent years have often noted that the pattern of presenting problems of patients coming for psychotherapy is manifesting a marked change. The classical symptomatology is far less frequently encountered now than formerly. Now patients are at a loss in their searching for identity, for meaning in life, far more often than before. But what new patterns of disorder will emerge tomorrow? Our age is characterized by a rate of acceleration in technological and social change hitherto unknown. The increasing tempo of this rate of change is bound to have profound effects on the human personality and its modes of adaptation —over and above the stresses of the threats of war and thermonuclear destruction. Whether cures will be found in surgery, pharmacology, psychotherapy, or milieu therapy, we can be fairly confident that there will be new forms of psychopathology to which we will have to address ourselves, new modes of adjustment to new kinds of problems which we will have to analyze.

If we are to meet the challenge of our field and our times, we must follow the precept of Gordon Allport to health workers and "develop skill as an *oculist,* training himself to look *at* his spectacles and not merely *through* them, and training himself to look both *at* and *through* the spectacles of the client with whom he deals." (The second Dorothy B. Nyswander Lecture, Berkeley, California, May 23, 1958.) Of both the scientist and the practitioner, the future demands no less.

INDEX

Note: To avoid duplication of entries, the terms "group psychotherapy" and "group therapy" have been combined in this index under the latter term. Other terms, however, which are not synonymous, such as "group analysis," "group psychoanalysis," "co-therapy," "multiple psychotherapy," are separately indexed.

Page numbers in italics indicate location of authors' papers in the text.

Abraham, Karl, 186, 498
Abrahams, J., 372
abreaction, 341, 470; ventilation and, 346
absences, group members' reactions to, 286, 439
acceptance, defined, 342; forms of, 343-344
Ackerman, Nathan W., 207, 228 *n.*, 250-260, 635
acting out, 233; analyst's fear of, 366; in coordinated meetings, 443-444; co-therapists and, 402; in group conflict, 257; group therapy as, 257; interaction patterns and, 192; vs. resistance, 433; suppression of, 259; therapist's control of, 444
acting-out characters, 418
actional factor, 347-348
"active control," of therapist, 215
activity, group life and, 72-73
activity catharsis (Slavson), 233
activity therapy, 409
adaptation, insight and, 256
Adirondack Cottage Sanatorium, 112, 118
adjunctive therapy, senile psychotics, 491
Adler, Alfred, 5, 36, 392

Adlerian psychology, group therapy and, 168-179; principles of, 168-173
administrative structure, organization of, 415-416
admissions, to group therapy, 214, 275, 329, 413-423; psychological testing for, 597
adults, group therapy with, 370-378
affect, hiding of by therapist, 316
affect-imagery, self-referent, 158
affective approach, group culture and, 75-76
affective exploration, 441-442
affecto-symbolic segment (Burrow), 158
aged, census data on, 487; group therapy for, 487-506; helplessness of, 495; home for, 494-495
age levels, family and, 640
aggression, in coordinated meetings, 444; vs. effiminacy, 298; phylic disturbance and, 156
aggressive child, 235
aggressiveness, acceptance of by therapist, 239
aggressive patient, exclusion of, 356
aging, psychology of, 488-489
Air Force bibliography, 18-19

659

alcohol, as drug, 622; as therapeutic agent, 620; in tuberculosis case, 117

alcoholic psychoses, group therapy for, 485

alcoholics, adjective checklist for, 512, 522-523; case histories of, 516-519; criticism of by wives, 515; depressive reactions in, 515, 520-521; drinking checklist for, 511-512; drinking expenditures of, 519; drugs for, 514; group meetings of wives, 510-524; group therapy for, 174, 176, 274, 276, 485, 510-524; guilt in, 522; here and now of, 522; history and characteristics of, 516-517; in hospital groups, 461; inadequacy feelings of, 521; irritability in, 520-521; marital difficulties of, 515-517; paranoid-schizoid pattern in, 512, 517; preparation of for therapy, 513; relatedness in, 517-518; satisfactions of from intoxication, 523; secret drinking of, 622; temporal orientation in, 514; transference in, 522; wife's implication in drinking, 522

Alcoholics Anonymous, 510; as group therapy, 179

alcoholism, 5; as disease, 146, 513; non-group treatment of, 510-511; symptom index in, 511-512; as "way of life," 516; see also alcoholics

Allan Memorial Institute of Psychiatry (Montreal), 496

Allport, Gordon, 657

aloneness, "horror" of, 164

Alpers, B. J., 489

alternate meetings, 437

alternating multiple therapy, 394-395

altruism, defined, 342; mechanisms of, 344

ambivalence, in alcoholics, 518, 521; negative, 371; valency pattern and, 75-76

American Group Psychotherapy Association, 7, 33 n., 124, 568

American Group Therapy Association, 250

American Indians, mushroom "drugs" of, 620-621

American Journal of Psychiatry, 415

American Orthopsychiatric Association, 7, 250

American psychiatry, pragmatism of, 3

American Psychoanalytic Association, 6, 154, 250

American Sociological Association, 2 n., 14

amylobarbitone, 632

analysis, contrasted with psychotherapy, 186; group method of (Burrow, 1927), 143-153; individual, see individual analysis; isolation and, 144; laboratory findings in, 149; see also psychoanalysis

Amgyal, A., 553

anger, 454

animal soul (Jung), 180

anonymity, in group membership, 278

Ansbacher, H., 36

ant colony, as organic group, 144

anthropology, philosophical (Buber), 504, 607

anticonvulsant drugs, 619, 629

antihistamines, in alcoholic psychoses, 514

antisocial behavior, 157; human nature and, 169

anxiety, alcoholism and, 512; "basic" (Horney), 196-199; chlorpromazine and, 630; defense against (Ackerman), 258; disruptive, 420; first appearance of, 190; in group, 202, 292, 417; group aggression and, 320; group culture and, 81; in hospital groups, 462; knowledge and, 627; as neurosis, 226, 454; Oedipal situation and, 377; psychotic patients and, 482; reduction of, 456; release of, 374; self-idealization and, 198;

at sexual material, 278; super-ego and, 234; in student therapists, 555-559; in teacher-training groups, 578; of therapist, 559, 563-564, 578; urge to "cure," 555; ventilation of, 346

anxiety neurosis, 226

anxiety-of-the-moment, 376

"anxious" patient (Wolf), 284

apothecaries' secrets, 621

"appropriate comment," defined, 480

Arapesh tribe, New Guinea, 625

Aristotle, 11, 169

army, psychiatric casualties in, 469-470

army life, isolation in, 473-474

Aronov, B. M., 396, 398

arrogance, 434

arsphenamine, 619

art, as nonverbal communication, 434

arteriosclerosis, cerebral, 489

Asch, Solomon E., 16, 42-51

"as if" function, 73

ataractic drugs, 629-634

attendance, group structure and, 408; voluntary, 214, 240, 479; *see also* absences

attention, detention and cotention in, 158

authoritarian groups, studies in, 39

authority figure, 441; avoidance of, 479; fear of, 439; therapist as, 219, 239, 479-480, 493

autistic image-bondage (Burrow), 157

autobiography, resistance through, 296, 326

autokinetic effect, 3

awareness of others, 184, 234, 332-334, 343, 460, 605

Axline, V. M., 535

Ayman, 127

Bach, G. R., 8, 396, 414

Baker, A. A., 464, 634

Bales, Robert F., 18, 105, 357

Balint, M., 567

Bannerjee, S., 623

Bartlett, F. C., 2, 16

Baruch, Dorothy W., 207, 261-272

basic anxiety (Horney), 198-199

basic assumption culture, concept of, 71-88

basic assumption leader, 87

Bass, B. M., 92

Bateson, G., 644

Beach, Margaret, 413-423

Beard, G. M., 4

bed-wetting, 384

behavior, biological principles of, 6; Bion's "valences" of, 10; goal-directed, 169; individual, *see* individual behavior; multidimensional, 615; symbolic level of, 615; teleoanalytical approach to, 170

behavior disorders, social aspect of, 154; social relatedness and, 6

behavior patterns, reactive, 196

"being and being," in patient-therapist relations (Mullan), 592

Bell, John E., 589, 635-647

Bellevue Hospital, New York, 6, 219

Bellevue-Wechsler test, 280

Bell's palsy, 429

belonging, vs. basic anxiety (Horney), 199; sense of (Adler), 167-170, 178

belongingness, 343, 457-458; in hospital groups, 456, 462; security through, 192; status and, 594

Bennett, C. C., 536

Bennington College, 39

Benoit-Smullyan, E., 62

Ben-Zeev, S., 90

Berenson, B., 600 *n.*

Berger, Milton M., 10, 209, 425-435, 553-557, 567

Bergson, Henri, 170

Berman, L., 567

Bernheim, H., 42

Betts, E. A., 534

Between Man and Man, 605

Beukenkamp, Cornelius, 543, 553-557, 567, 588, 614-616

"beyond-transference behavior," 567, 588, 614-616

biased apperception (Adler), 173

Bierer, Joshua, 7
Bills, R. E., 535
biographical material, patient's, 280, 422; as resistance, 296, 326; transference in, 304
biology, in Burrow's concepts, 158
Bion, W. R., 8-10, 31, 71, 87; theoretical concepts of, 72-74
biosocial unit (Ackerman), 253
Blackman, 477
Blanchard, P. J., 536
blocking, in psychotic groups, 483
Bock, J. C., 397
bodily functions, emotions and, 124, 547
body image, expression of, 220; history of, 222; in military neuroses, 470
body language, 428-430; *see also* nonverbal communication
Boenheim, C., 564, 566-567
Bordin, E. S., 514
Boston City Hospital, 126
Boston State Hospital, 129, 477
Boston University, 129
boys, delinquent, 63; from feminine environment, 235
boys' camp, group conflicts in, 52-60, 228
Bovard, Everett, 38
Bowen, M., 636
Bradford, L. P., 90
brain stem, drugs and, 622
brain syndrome, in aged, 492
Brawnthel, H., 567
Brehmer, H., 119
Breland, K., 29 n.
Breland, M., 29 n.
Brodey, W. M., 636
bromides, 550
Brompton Hospital Sanatorium, England, 118
Bross, R., 431
Brown, Donald T., 413-423
Brown, Lawrason, 112, 116
Bry, Thea, 377, 407
Buber, Martin, 209, 588; philosophy of, 604-613
Burns, James H., 129

Burrow, Trigant L., 5-6, 13, 109, 143-153, 211, 231, 355, 609; Lawrence's critique of, 162-167; psychoanalytic background, 155; stylistic complexity, 159; summary note on, 154-160
"buzz sessions" (Lewin), 357

Cabot, Richard C., 113, 122
California State Health Department, 95
Cameron, W. B., 2 n.
Campbell, Donald T., 529 n.
car-sickness, 643
Cartwright, Dorwin, 14, 357
Casella, Bernard, 381-390
casework, in parents' groups, 381-390
Cassirer, E., 600 n.
castration fears or anxiety, 222, 289, 296-297, 306, 317, 334
catalyst, patient as, 419; therapist as, 479; transference and, 336
catharsis, 341, 547; conflict and, 279; as element or fact, 354; ventilation as, 346; "vicarious," 392
"catharsis-in-the-family" (Wender), 216, 345
cathexis, 654
Catholic Church, brotherhood of, 34
Caudill, W., 92
Central Islip State Hospital, 490
central nervous system, drug action on, 622
central person, concept of, 87-88
Cerletti, A., 620
Chafetz, W. E., 372
chance probabilities, group methods and, 247
change, individual, 83-86
character disorders or neuroses, 226, 276; excluded from group therapy, 329
Character Education in a Democracy, 230
character structure, in nonverbal communication, 426
Charcot, Jean Martin, 42
Chasen, M., 372, 482, 485

chemotherapy, 328; *see also* drug therapy

Chicago, University of, 12, 31, 71, 110

child, parent counseling and, 381-390; therapist seen as, 303

child-centered parents' groups, 381-390

child development, 10; father's role in, 382

Childers, A. T., 228

child guidance clinics, 392

childhood experiences, as resistance, 296

childhood family, recreation of, 324

childhood memories (Horney), 197

child-parent relations, aging and, 489

child psychology, 8

child rearing, neuroses and, 253

children, denial and rejection in, 239; grade school teacher training and, 578; group therapy for (Slavson), 231-241, 635; permissive environment for, 236-237; problem groups in, 579; psychological tests for, 537; reading failures in, 534; reality testing in, 237; *see also* parent-child relationships

Child Welfare Research Station, University of Iowa, 14

Chinese, hexagram casting among, 621

chin stroking, 430

chlorpromazine, 491; anxiety and, 630

choice, sociometric, 77-78

Christ Church, N.Y., 114

Christian Science, 117, 183

chronicity, of symptoms, 644-645

church, brotherhood of, 34

Cincinnati, University of, 565

class differences, 322

class exercises, in group therapy program, 138

class hatred (Lawrence), 165

class meeting, Pratt's technique of, 117-118

classroom atmosphere, group experiments in, 38

class situation, 133

clergymen, in group therapy, 129

"client-centered therapy" (Rogers), 7, 355

clinical psychiatry, knowledge of, 572; training in, 568-569

clinical setting, outlined, 415-416

clique formation, 434, 483; in training school, 63

clinging, to neurotic pattern, 279

clusters, of neurotic behavior patterns (Horney), 197

Coe, George A., 39

cohesiveness, 482

Colburn, Donald L., 129

Coleman, James A., 17

collective counseling, 4-5

collective fear, 166

"collective therapy" (Dreikurs), 174

college classes, as groups, 35

Collegium Internationale Neuro-Psycho Pharmacologicum, 621

Columbia University, 17

Columbus Receiving Hospital (Ohio), 494, 497

Columbus State Hospital, Ohio, 564

Commager, Henry S., 597

"common feelings" (Scheidlinger), 355

Common Neuroses, The, 124, 126

common problems, discovery of as road to recovery, 323; self-exposure and, 323

communication, in democratic society, 462-463; "double bind" in, 644; group activities and, 464; in group therapy, 234; laboratory in, 92-104; nonverbal, *see* nonverbal communication; verbal, *see* verbal communication

communism (Jung), 184

community, transference to, 40

competition, group conflict and, 57-58

compulsive criticism, 296

compulsive missionary spirit, 294

concern, area of, 75

confidence, increased, 373

confidences, group, 283

conflict, acting out and, 257; instinct and, 156; projection of, 259; in psychotherapeutic process, 256 conflicting feelings (Horney), 198

conformity, vs. independence, 51; public vs. private, 65-66; striving and, 62

Consalvi, Conrad, 20, 31, 61-70

conscience, guilt and, 258

conscious personal action (Wolf), 310-312

consciousness, Lawrence on, 164; self-determination of, 170; "splitting" of (Lawrence), 163

"consciousness of kind" (Giddings), 213

consensual observation (Burrow), 158

consensus, need for, 51

conversions, suggestibility and (Jung), 182

Cooley, Charles Horton, 2 n., 11-12, 189

cooperation, vs. group conflict, 57-59

coordinated meetings, 437-447; affective exploration in, 441-442; initiation of, 438-439; resistance to, 442; theoretical concepts of, 440-441

Corcoran, D., 490-491

Coriat, Isadore, 123

Cornell Index, alcoholism, 512

Cornet, George, 119

Corsini, Raymond J., 4, 209, 340-348, 414

cotention (Burrow), 158

co-therapy, 391; advantages of, 399-400; co-therapists in, 396, 493; male and female leaders, 398; meetings in, 447

Cotzin, M., 526

couch technique, vs. face-to-face contact, 259

counterdependency members, 77

countertransference, 306, 345, 355, 364, 371, 374, 424; defined (Flescher), 377, (Wolf), 273; diluted, 399; with elderly patients, 504-506; hostile, 319; as nonverbal communication, 430-431; patient's skill in, 310-311; precaution on, 377

Cowley Road Hospital, England, 498

Cozin, L. Z., 496

creation, status and, 593

Creative Group Education, 230

Crowd, The, 336

Crutchfield, Richard S., 37

Cruvant, B. A., 466

Culpeper, N., 621

culture, faulty transmission of by parents, 598; impact of on personality, 2

culture preference (Stock and Thelen), 75-76

cyclothymic personality, 148

Dale, H., 621

Davis, 127

Day, Capt. George, 472

daydreams, discussion of, 287

day hospitals, for aged, 496-498

death, attitude toward, 222; fear of, 223, 503; meaning of, 220

death experience, overcoming of in insulin treatment, 624

decision making, sharing in, 462

deep insulin treatment, 623-626, 632

defecation, history of, 222

defective delinquents, group therapy for, 525-533; defined, 526

defense mechanisms (Adler), 173; resistance to, 295-296

defensive patterns, reorganization of, 354

Dejerine, Joseph Jules, 123-130

delinquent boys, training school for, 63

delinquents, defective, 525-533

delusions, in psychotic patients, 482

Demarest, Elinor W., 371, 397

democratic society, defined, 462

denial, rejection and, 239; of status in group, 591-603

dependency-counterdependency valence, 10

dependency culture, 73, 76, 82

dependency feelings, 89, 376

dependency-work culture (Bion), 73

depersonalization, 226; social fixity and, 238

depth factors, 357; in group analysis, 363-365

depression, in alcoholics, 515, 520-521; group therapy for, 213; suicide and, 226

desire to belong (Adler), 169

determinism, mechanistic, 170

Dewey, John, 39

Dewey, R., 2 *n.*

dexedrine, 514

diabetes, insulin treatment of, 629

diagnosis, for hospital groups, 478

diagnostic categories, 415-416

dialogue, Buber's philosophy of, 604-613

dictators, Jung on, 182

didactic groups, 328-338, 391-393, 457, 474, 477, 553-555, 560-561; *see also* training

disease, "moral" attitude toward, 146

dispute, absence of, 373

dissent, vs. majority opinion, 45-49

distance, vs. relation (Buber), 607-608

ditention (Burrow), 158

Dittes, J. E., 62

Dlin, B. M., 567

"do-gooder," 295

Domagk, G., 619

dominance, penis envy and, 317

doodling, 430

double bind, in schizophrenia, 644

drama, as mass psychotherapy, 3; *see also* psychodrama

dream analysis, 281, 346; rapport through, 283; use of, 220

dream symbolism, 287, 426

dreams, Burrow's theory of, 156; discussion of 287; as "factory of emotions" (Adler), 171; free association and, 283, 306, 311, 319, 325, 364, 424; group discussion of, 214-215; phenothiazine drugs and, 632; reporting of, 284-285; sexual content of, 290; status and, 593; ventilation through, 283

Dreikurs, Rudolf, 4, *168-179*, 347, 392, 394, 414, 635

drinking checklist, for alcoholic patients, 511-512

drugs, for alcoholics, 514; for elderly patients, 503; psychotropic, 588-589, 618-634

drug therapies, classification of, 619; history of, 620-622; placebo response in, 633

Dubo, Sara, 125

Durkheim, Emile, 10-11

"dynamic doctor's group" (Stein), 565

dynamics, group, *see* group dynamics; in therapeutic situations, 340-341

dynamism, "obsessional," 189

Dyrud, J. E., 394

eating habits, 222

economic status, therapy and, 248, 273; *see also* fees

education, biological meaning of, 331; reading disabilities and, 534; vs. therapy, 358

educational programs, psychotherapy in, 577-582

educational theory, 33

effeminacy, shyness and, 298

ego, defective, 233; reading and, 536; supportive, 233

ego building, growth of, 444-445

egocentricity, neuroses and, 164

ego concept (Klein), 9

ego frustrations, reality testing and, 344

ego ideals, 654; development of, 216; therapist and, 326; transference of, 614

ego increase, 183

ego integration, 381

ego involvement, 20

ego loss, in group (Jung), 181

ego splitting, 9

ego strength, 373, 465

ego structure, hostility and, 320

ego support, 341, 343

ego therapy, psychoanalysis as, 260

ego values, 29

Ehrlich, Paul, 619

elderly patients, case histories of, 499-504; cause of emotional disorders in, 498; day hospitals for, 496-498; frustration in, 502; in mental hospital, 490-494; physical illness in, 495; sexual problems of, 506; therapist's technique with, 498-499; transference and countertransference in, 504-506

electroshock therapy, 328, 619

embarrassment, feelings of, 263

Emerson, W. R. P., 329

Emmanuel Church tuberculosis class, 112, 114

emotional contact, fear of, 279

emotional dynamics, group culture and, 71-89; sociometric choice and, 77-78

"emotional illiterates" (Leopold), 426

emotional maturity, education as, 331

emotional processes, vs. intellectual, 225

emotional support, in group therapy, 354

emotions, acceptance of by patient, 271; bodily functions and, 124, 547; eye and face expressions in, 429; function of (Adler), 171; psychopathology of, 454; valency and, 74-75

empathic relatedness, 594

empathy, humaneness and, 178; of therapist, 265

encephalopathy, hypertensive, 497

"encouragement," therapeutic, 177

endorganismic patterns, 158

English psychiatry, 7-8, 31

English psychoanalysts, 9

English psychologists, 16

engrams, 171

enuresis, 384

epilepsy, 629

epistemology, of treatment, 374

equality, principle of, 169; in therapy group, 178

essential "we," 610; dialogue and, 604-613

E.S.T. (electroshock therapy), 328, 619

European group methods, 5

existential guilt, 604, 611-612

existentialism, 588

"existential psychotherapy," 109

experience, profiting by, 454; see also group experience

exploration, affective, 441-442

externalization (Horney), 198

extra-individual influence, 242

extramarital affairs, 263

eye expressions, 426, 428-429

facade, "penetration" of (Wolf), 289-290, 321, 323

facial expressions, 426, 428-429, 644; of therapist, 481

family, adult's reconstruction of, 637; aims and goals of, 639; "catharsis" in, 216; child's view of, 637; chronicity of symptoms and, 644; definitions of, 637-638; as group, 638-639; group as, 193, 208, 216, 277, 322-324, 365, 602; group formation in, 639-641; health and pathology in, 641-642; as institution, 638; intrapsychic relations in, 637; parent-child relations in, 640; as primary group, 11; psychoanalytic conception of, 34; revolt against, 365-366; social role and, 637; transitive actions in, 639; value changes in, 645

family change, motivation for, 645

family conflicts, 146-147

family constellation, 173

family group, 34, 638-639

family group theory, 397, 638-642; advances in, 635-647; criticism of, 636

family group therapy, as mechanism for change, 645-646

family history, of patient, 220; see also life history

family life, Freud on, 253

family problems, parent counseling and, 382-383

family process, 636-637

family relationships, drama and, 3

family situation, Burrow's work on, 155

fantasies, in deep insulin treatment, 623-624; in schizophrenia, 625; status and, 593

father, family and, 12; role of in child development, 382; sexual problems relating to, 222, 224

father image, co-therapists and, 403; patient as, 367; therapist as, 302, 307, 439

fear, 454; as disjunctive force, 459; knowledge and, 627

"feedback" (Lewin), 357; in quiet-vocal group studies, 101-102

Feeling of Rejection, The, 38

feelings, "asking" for, 374; contradictory, 198; language of, 426; manipulation of, 426

"feeling sensation," 158

fees, in group therapy, 139-140, 273, 656; discussing with patient, 281; flexibility in, 327; hospitalization and, 212; as of 1935, 131; setting of, 415

Fenchel, G. H., 62

Fenichel, O., 186

Fiedler, Fred, 110

field theory (Lewin), 357

fight-flight culture, 10, 73-75, 81, 88

films, in psychology courses, 38

financial factors, 212, 281, 327; *see also* fees

Findlay, G. M., 619

finger tapping, 430

Flescher, J., 377

flight member, 77

Flowerman, S., 431

focusing, of group discussion, 265

follow-up interviews, 217

food, complaints about, 492; sharing of, 433

Foulds, G. A., 632

Foulkes, S. H., 7, 312, 337, 375, 451, 469-476

France, dynamic psychiatry in, 13 *n.*; group studies in, 11

Frank, G. H., 398

Frank, Jerome D., 124, 355, 364, 377, 396, 451, 453-467, 510-524, 512

free association, 281, 298; "blank" reaction in, 295; dreams and, 283, 306, 311, 319, 325, 364, 424; in groups, 273; interpersonal, 288-293; limited, 257; of medical students, 582; on sexual material, 297; vs. suggestibility, 186; use of, 220

Freedman, M., 414

"freedom," as neurotic enslavement (Wolf), 318

French, John, 37

French, J. P., Jr., 441

Freud, Sigmund, 4, 6, 8, 20, 29, 37, 42, 151, 153, 155, 171, 186, 198, 208, 225, 336, 356, 451, 526, 654; concept of group, 242; on elderly patients, 502; on group psychology, 11-12, 151-152, 356-357; irritation with Burrow, 159; in Lawrence's critique, 162-167; personality concept of, 9; on primary group, 11; psychoanalytic theory, 188; on social psychology, 252; transference theory, 40, 148; "vicious unconsciousness" of (Lawrence), 165

Friedman, Maurice, 209, 543, 588, 604-613

frigidity, sexual, 294, 297

Frimley Sanatorium, England, 118

Fromm, Erich, 6, 593, 607, 609

frontier, disappearance of, 34, 39

frustration, 344, 454; in aged, 502; causes of, 291; reality testing and, 344; tolerance in, 239

full-term multiple therapy, 395-396

functional neuroses, defined, 454

Furst, William, 407-410

game theory, 16

gangs, in boys' camps, 54-56; conflict between, 52; formation of, 12

Gann, E., 534

Ganzarain, R., 567

Gates, A. I., 534, 536

Gates Advanced Primary Reading Tests, 537

Gaylord Farm Sanatorium, N.Y., 118

Geller, Joseph J., 411-412, 414, 566-567

Geller, M., 526

General Electric Company, Hawthorne plant, Chicago, 12

general hospital, neurosis treatment in, 124-125

general practitioner, neurosis treatment by, 124

German army, psychology of (Jung), 182

Germany, group studies in, 11; psychology in, 14; tuberculosis sanitoria in, 118-119

geriatric patients, 490-506

gerontologic group therapy, 490

Gestalt psychology, 14; Adler and, 172

Gibb, J., 90

Giddings, 213

Gifford, S., 477

Gitelson, M., 488

Glauber, Helen, 228 n.

Glatzer, Henriette, 409

Glenn, J., 567

Glidewell, John C., 91

Gliedman, Lester H., 510-524

goal-directed behavior (Adler), 169

goal-directedness (Mullan), 602

goals, alignment of, 174; basic (Horney), 172-173; "fictitious" (Adler), 173; patient's, 280; and uniqueness of individual (Adler), 172

God, concept of, 148

"going around" (Wolf), 325; see also free association

Golden, 127

Goldfarb, A. I., 495, 499

Goldman, George D., 188-194

Goldstein, Kurt, 154

Goodenough test, 280

grade school teachers, group therapy teaching of, 578

Gradolph, Ida H., 90

Gradolph, P., 90

graduate training, for group therapists, 565

Grauer, D., 372

Gray, W., 372

Greek dramatists, 3

Greek mythology, 625

Greek religions, 33

Greek Stoics, 169

Greene, James Sennett, 231

gregarious impulse (McDougall), 212

Grinker, R. R., 38

griping, cohesiveness and, 466-467; in hospital groups, 458

Grotjahn, Martin, 368, 377, 393, 505, 566

group, admission to, 214, 275, 329, 597; age and sex of, 214; "allies" in, 319; anonymity in, 278; anxiety in, 202, 292, 367, 417; attendance and, 408; biological principles of behavior in, 6; Burrow's definition of, 143; characteristics shared in, 440; cohesive forces in, 460; "combining with others" in, 74; communication in, 464; compatible, 92; "compulsion" in, 133; in day hospitals, 496-497; defined, 31, 143, 574; disintegration of, 314, 319, 420; as distinct being, 11; distinguishing features of (Mullan), 591-592; "effective" vs. "ineffective," 418-420; ego increase and (Jung), 183; emotional climate of, 322; enthusiasm in, 133; exposing neurotic character of, 314-316; as family or peer group, 193, 208, 216, 277, 322-323, 345, 365, 602; family as, 345, 638-639; formation of, see group formation; Freud's concept of, 242; as "gallery of mirrors" (Grotjahn), 368; goal-directedness of, 602; "good" vs. "poor," 482; group situation and, 72; heterogeneous, 193; "no hiding place" in, 367-368; homogeneous, 274-276, 407-410; impact of leader in, 15; impersonality of, 133; "incorporation" in, 444-446; vs. individual, 655; individual behavior and, 92; individual freedom and, 318; individual "role" in (Ackerman), 253-254; informal, 61-70; instinctual preoccupations of, 73; interaction in, *see* group interaction; interdependence in, 655; interpersonal nature of, 588; interrelatedness in, 591; intrapsychic needs in, 201; lowered morale of (Jung), 184; mature vs. immature, 82; as microcosm of society, 592; mutuality in, 199, 324-325; as natural state of man, 615; neurotic pattern exchange in, 200; number of in everyday life, 229-230; organic, 143-144; parents', 383-388; permissive atmosphere in, 236, 323-324; primary, *see* primary group; psychoanalysis of, 208, 362-369; quiet vs. vocal, 92-104; relatedness in, 594; roundtable, 466; sects and, 182; sex of, 275, 302; size of, 276, 411-412, 415, 479, 655-656; small, 11-16, 358, 411, 554; socialization and, 230; as social unit, 255; subtypes and subgroups in, 77-78; trainee's participation in, 565-566, 570-571; unfeeling attitudes of, 314; valency patterns in, 78-79

group acceptance, 343

group analysis, Burrow's use of term, 5; Wolf's use of term, 273-327; *see also* group therapy

group analyst (Wolf), 312-319; *see also* therapist

group anxiety, 202, 292, 367, 417

group approaches, growth through, 352

group atmosphere, 431

group behavior, defined (Scheidlinger), 356; dynamics of, 357; psychoanalytic approach to, 32; psychodynamics of, 251; valency pattern and, 75-76; "vocal" vs. "quiet" participation in, 92-104

group belongingness (Frank), 456

group-centered psychological teaching, 38

group cohesiveness, 344, 457, 463; psychotic patients and, 482; *see also* belongingness

group concept, clarification of, 574

group conflict, competition in, 57-58; cooperation and, 58-59; experiments in, 52-60; types of, 52

group counseling, with parents, 381-390

group culture, area of concern in, 75; Bion's categories of, 73; concept of, 83; culture preference and, 76; emotional dynamics and, 71-89; individual change and, 84-85; leadership and, 87-88; learning environment in, 86; sociometric choice and, 77-78; subgroup functioning and, 89; valency and, 73

group decision, social change and, 15

group dynamics, 229; in hospital groups, 458; group therapy and, 8-10; "laws" of, 31; massive emotional reactions and, 72; vs. patient treatment, 208; as "phyloanalysis," 6; study of, 1

group education, vs. group therapy, 358

group events, understanding of, 88

group experience, interpersonal vs. leadership concept in, 587-588; nature of, 256; personality and, 358; validity of, 597

group formation, dynamics of, 251; in family, 639-641; homogeneous vs. heterogeneous, 408; intellectual processes in, 30; princi-

group formation, *(cont'd)*
    ples of, 13; verbal output and,
    92-93
group growth, dynamics of, 81-83
group identification, 343; homogene-
    ous vs. heterogeneous, 408
group interaction, 213, 216-217, 255-
    256, 345, 356; aspects of, 82;
    Bales's system of, 18; bonds in,
    656
group interest behavior (Mullan), 598
group leader, therapist as, 262; *see also*
    leader; leadership
group learning, 39
group life, 17; cognitive and emotional
    factors in, 71; work aspects of,
    72
group meetings, alternate, 437; anxiety
    increase in, 292; coordinated,
    437-447; first, 282; frequency
    and length of, 214, 219, 276,
    285, 356, 415, 479, 514-515;
    in hospitals, 461-462; infor-
    mality of, 282; material of,
    214-215; in military hospitals,
    470-476; premeetings and post-
    meetings, 438; seating arrange-
    ments in, 478
group member(s), "acceptance" by,
    599; aggressive, 356; alcoholic,
    518-523; anxiety of, 376-377
    (*see also* anxiety); "anxious"
    type, 284; assimilation of, 281;
    attitude of on joining, 277; be-
    havior restrictions on, 481;
    characteristics shared by, 440;
    drop-outs among, 528; growth
    indications from, 271; hostil-
    ity of to therapist, 286-287; in-
    dividual culture of, 599; vs. in-
    dividuality, 186; mutual help
    of, 599; nonverbal communi-
    cations of, 425-435; parents
    as, 383-385; "penetration" ad-
    mitted by, 289; positive-negative
    feelings of, 77; provocative role
    of, 302-306, 320, 326; reaction
    of to absences, 286, 439; "real
    self" of, 598-599; relatedness

of, 192; same sex or mixed, 214;
    self-acceptance by, 271; sexual
    relations between, 320, 367; so-
    ciometry and, 13-14; status de-
    nial in, 592-594; statuses of,
    591-592; students as, 566; test
    for cure in, 318; therapist as,
    316, 556, 570-573; types of
    (Slavson), 236; verbal output
    of, 92-93
group methods, teaching of, 560; va-
    lidity of, 246-248
group mind, concept of, 30
Group Mind, The, 336
group needs, vs. patient's, 420-421
group norm, 3; formation of, 66
group resistances, 376
Group Situation Test, 10
group soul (Jung), 181
group structure, 10
group superego, 234
group phenomena (Bion), 72; individ-
    ual-centered, 9
group pressure, consciousness and, 186;
    individual change and, 16; in
    informal groups, 61-70; Jung
    on, 182; motivation and, 61-
    62; status and, 61-70; resist-
    ance to, 50; work productivity
    and, 12
group problem solving, 78-81
group process, analysis of, 653-657;
    class, 93; interpersonal difficul-
    ties and, 199; training and, 567
group process laboratory, 93
group psychoanalysis, challenge of,
    362-369; *see also* group therapy
Group Psychology and the Analysis of
    the Ego, 37, 336
group psychotherapy, *see* group therapy
group therapy, as "acting out," 257;
    Adlerian psychology and, 168-
    179; with adults, 370-378; ag-
    gression and anxiety in, 190,
    202, 292, 320, 417; for alco-
    holic patients, 174, 176, 274,
    276, 485, 510-524; alternate
    names for, 391; as American
    product, 4; analysis of tech-

niques in, 262-270; analyst's objections to, 363-364; antiquity of, 132; anxiety and, 190, 202, 292, 320, 417; application of, 211-217; ataractic drugs in, 629-634; "atmosphere" of, 136; basic assumptions of, 213; basic categories of, 245-246; bibliography of, 18-19; "candidates" for, 214, 275, 329; cases treated in (Marsh), 140-141; challenge of, 657; clergymen in, 129; clinical setting of, 414; cohesiveness as goal of, 457-458, 460; common elements of, 354, 370-372, 440; communication in, 463-464; constructive patterns in, 323-327; current research and theory in, 16-19; danger of (Jung), 185; for defective delinquents, 525-533; defined, 35, 352, 413, 424, 558; Dejerine's methods in, 123-130; "depth" in, 363-365; description of project in, 261-272; destructive patterns in, 319-322; development of, 453; didactic, 328-338, 391-393, 457, 474, 477, 553-555, 560-561; discovery of common problems in, 323; drugs in, 618-634; dynamic, 159; dynamics of, 211-217, 250; as educational process, 176, 184, 358-360; for elderly patients, 487-506; emotional factor in, 347; "encouragement" of patient in, 177-178; European, 5; expansion of, 1; experimental teaching of, 577-584; experiments in, 36-38, 247-248, 330; as family support, 35-36; fees in, 131, 139-140, 212, 273, 281, 327, 415, 656; fifth stage in, 300-310; first stage, 280-282; founder of, 109; fourth stage, 293-300; Freud on, 11-12, 356-357; future of, 41; gerontologic, 490; goal of, 20; goal-directed nature of, 602; grading in, 137; and group dynamics, 8-10; vs. group education, 358; growth of, 353; history of, 3-10, 109-203, 329, 391-393; homework in, 139; for hospital patients, 478-486; hour-to-hour happenings and, 599-600; indications and contra-indications in, 248; individual analysis in, 280-282; vs. individual therapy, 35, 176, 183, 208, 213, 218, 230, 242, 245-246, 278, 323-327, 354-356, 417, 445, 458, 498-504, 549, 561; "inside outward" movement of (Ackerman), 255; insight in, 175-176, 232, 324 (*see also* insight); insulin treatment in, 623-626; intellectual factor in, 347; intensity range of, 336; leaders in, 129; lecture course in, 135; levels of, 372-377; levels of achievement in, 370; literature of, 8, 340-342; LSD in, 626-629; Marsh technique of (1935), 131-142; mathematical approach to, 16-17; mechanism of, 340-348; for medical students, 547-552, 580-582; in mental hospitals, 453-467; vs. mental hygiene, 358-360; military factors in, 475-476; in military neurosis center, 469-476; mutual "treatment" in, 138; new trends in, 587-657; nonverbal communication in, 424-435; organization in, 137; origin of, 329 (*see also* history of); outside reading in, 137-138; principal types of, 477; process and dynamics in, 340-348; psychiatric clinic and, 131-141; vs. psychoanalysis (Ackerman), 250-260; psychoanalytic, 11-12; psychodynamics of, 340-341; psychotic episodes in, 366; for psychotics, 477-486; questions and answers in, 136; relation to other group influence

group therapy, (*cont'd*)
    attempts, 352-360; relationships in, 175; research in, 14, 19-21, 83; resistance in, *see* resistance; retarded readers and, 534-538; role-playing and, 14; satisfaction for therapist in, 601; schools of, 7; scientific foundations of, 242-248; second stage of, 283-288; self-learning and insight in, 175-176; seminars in, 560-561; in severe neurosis, 218-227; sexual material in, 326; as "shotgun" technique, 363; situational nature of, 232; sixth or final stage in, 310-312; small group research in, 11-16; social hunger in, 232-233; social neuroses and, 225; social rewards of, 323; society and, 33-41; sociocultural approach to, 35; status denial in, 591-603; stresses created by, 419; student therapist in, 547, 553-557; structuring of, 415-416; synonymous with group psychotherapy, 186; "teaching" vs. "treating" in, 136; teaching of, 391, 395, 547-552, 577-584; test for patient's discharge, 310-311; textbook use in, 336-337; theory vs. practice in, 353; theory and technique of, 207-447; therapist in, *see* therapist; third stage of, 288-293; trainee's need for experience as patient, 567, 570-571; training concepts in, 543-585; training literature in, 564-568; for tuberculosis patients, 112-120; types of disorders amenable to, 213-214; validity of, 246-248; wealthy vs. poor in, 248; *see also* cotherapy; group analysis; multiple therapy
group therapist, *see* therapist
group transference, 365-366, 387-388
Grunwald, Hanna, 381-390
Gruppengeist (Jung), 182

"guiding lines" (Adler), 173
guilt, existential, 611-612
guilt feelings, 263, 270, 454; of alcoholics, 522; existential theory of, 604-613; mitigation of, 258, 260; as "pretenses" (Adler), 171; sex drives and, 221
guilt patterns, 258
Gurri, J., 372, 485-486

Hadden, S. B., 377, 392, 545-552, 554, 566
Hagen, M., 566
Haigh, G., 393, 399
Haley, J., 644
hallucinating psychotics, 276, 482
hallucinations, 481; drug therapy and, 632
hallucinogens, 619
hangover, alcoholic, 521
Hardwick, R. S., 536
Harris, Herbert L., 130
Hartley, E. L., 32, 62, 653-657
Hartshorne, 220
Harvey, O. J., 20, 31, 52, 61-70, 208
Hastings Hillside Hospital, 211
Hata, Sahachiro, 619
Hauptmann, Alfred, 130
Hawes, John B., 112
Hawthorne plant, Chicago, 12
Hayward, M. L., 392, 394
"healing through meeting" (Buber), 609-610
hebephrenic patient, 394, 461
hedgehog metaphor, 458
Heintz, R. K., 441
Henry Phipps Psychiatric Clinic, 124, 465, 510
Heracleitus, 610
here and now (Horney), 197, 203; alcoholics and, 514, 522; therapists' status and, 603
herd instinct (Jung), 184, 187
Hermann, L., 360
heterogeneous groups, 274-276; vs. homogeneous, 407-410
Hilferding, Rose, 129
Hill, William F., 91
Hillel, Rabbi, 425

Hillside Hospital, New York, 560
Hinchley, R. G., 360
historical survey, 109-203
history, interpersonal reactions and, 315; as resistance, 296, 326; transference in, 304
History of Psychoanalysis in America, 6
Hitler, Adolf, 182
Hobbs, N., 355, 537
Hoffman, A., 620
holism (Smuts), 172
homeopathy, 621
homework, in group therapy, 139
homicide, 420
homogeneous group, defined, 407; vs. heterogeneous, 407-410
homosexuality, 149; banter about, 402; Burrow on, 156; fear of, 226; Lawrence on, 166
honesty, 291; "love" for, 322; need for (Lawrence), 167; of therapist, 316
Hood, William R., 52
Hospital of the University of Pennsylvania, 546
Horder, Lord, 126
Horney, Karen, 6; group psychotherapy concepts of, 195-203
hospital, military, 470-476
hospital groups, 453-467, 478-486; communication and democratization in, 463-466; drug therapy for, 633; geriatric, 490-506; teaching in, 562, 565
hospitalization, as "last resort," 211
hospital life, gregariousness in, 212
hostility, free expression of, 236; in hospital groups, 458
Howard, Tasker, 114
Hulse, W. C., 414, 564, 572
Human Dynamics Laboratory, University of Chicago, 71, 83
human equality, principle of, 169
humanness, of therapist, 193
Human Potentialities, 40
human solidarity (Jung), 181
Huntington, Robert, 52, 526
Hurst, Sir Arthur, 123

husband, alcoholic, 511; friction with, 381
hydrotherapy, 328
hyperactivity, 236
hypercriticism, 296
hypermanic patients, 276
hyperpyrexia, 328
hypnagogic reactions, 229
hypnosis and hypnotherapy, 219, 242, 330; suggestibility and, 42; therapist and, 244
hypochondriasis, 226
hypomanics, in group reactions, 284
hysteria, 129, 149, 226; Lawrence on, 165

I and Thou, 604
iatrogenetic behavior, 615
identification, as relationship with others, 343, 373
ideologies, "common" nature of, 221
id impulses, exposure of, 377
id transference, 614
ignorance, as "insulation," 332
Illing, Hans A., 110, 180-187, 398
illness, physical vs. mental, 146
"image-consciousness," 166
image fixation, in mother-child relations, 148
image substitution (Lawrence), 163
image symbols, "misuse" of (Burrow), 158
"imagining the real" (Buber), 608
immigration, industrialization and, 1
immobilization, in tuberculosis treatment, 116
impasse, therapeutic, 393-394
imperfections, acceptance of, 224
impotence, in aged, 504; social vs. sexual, 297
impulses, fear of, 237
inadequacy, feelings of, 354, 374, 377, 483; in alcoholics, 521
incentives, productivity and, 12
incest, awe of, 156; in group meetings, 320
incest motive (Lawrence), 163
independence, vs. conformity, 51

independent judgment, tests of, 45-47

individual, artificial separation of from group, 30-31; concern with, 1; "egocentric absolute" of (Lawrence), 164; vs. group, 34, 74-77, 186, 655 (*see also* group); "inalienable rights" of (Jung), 187; isolation of, 144; "movement" of (Adler), 172; "normal" vs. "neurotic," 148-149; as unit of analysis, 31

individual analysis (Jung), 183-185; *see also* individual therapy

individual behavior, vs. group culture, 74-77

individual-centered psychology, 38

individual change, group pressure and, 16; readiness for and characteristics of, 83-86

individual culture, of group meeting, 599

individuality, vs. group membership, 186; vs. social relationship, 327; supremacy of (Jung), 185; "unsound emphasis" on (Wolf), 318

individualism, neurotic, 327

individual personality, vs. group culture, 74-77

individual psychology, "crudity" of (Murphy), 36

individual psychotherapy, *see* individual therapy

individual therapy, for elderly patients, 498-504; vs. group, 176, 183-185, 208, 213, 218, 230, 242, 245-246, 250-260, 278, 280-282, 323-327, 354-355, 417, 445, 458, 498-504, 549, 561, 600; multiple therapy and, 400-401; patients not amenable to, 329; as training for group therapist, 569; variable responses in, 653

individual valency, 79-81

industrialization, group experience and, 39; immigration and, 1

Industrial Revolution, 33

industry, group organization in, 12-13

infant, ego growth in, 9; primary identification with mother, 155

infanticide, 420

infantile behavior, neuroses and, 239

inferiority feelings, 220, 374-375, 377; Adler on, 173; in group, 176; removal of, 177

informal groups, status and conformity in, 61-70

initiation ceremonies, 624-625

Inkeles, A., 2

inmates, penal, 526-532

"insane asylum," hospital as, 132, 134

insight, acquisition of in group therapy, 232; development of, 256, 270, 278-279, 289, 308, 324, 341, 368, 374-377; as final aim of psychotherapy, 219; fostering of, 457; group structure and, 408; in group therapy, 175-177; importance of, 354; intellectualization and, 215; need for, 457; overemphasis on, 222; in patient-therapist relations, 219; psychoanalytic, 219; social integration and, 313; social vs. sexual, 299

"instigators" (Slavson), 236

instinct, social conflict and, 156

instinct theory, Freud's, 8

institutions, penal, 526-532; social, 148

insulin coma therapy, 328, 460, 622, 632; death in, 624; future research in, 628-629; group therapy and, 623-626; for schizophrenics, 619

integrating patterns (Horney), 196

intellectualization, defined, 342; group, 213; mechanism of, 215, 346

intellectual processes, vs. emotional, 225

interactional bonds, number of, 656

interactions, defined, 343; dynamisms in (Sullivan), 191; in group, 213, 216-217, 255-256, 356; levels of, 615; mechanisms of, 345; self-system of (Sullivan), 189-190

interdependence, concept of, 655

intergroup relations, 57
"interhuman relations" (Buber), 606
interns, as "ghosts," 124; as therapists, 391
interpersonal dominance, 327
interpersonal free association (Wolf), 288-293
interpersonal reactions (Horney), 199; prior history and, 315
interpersonal relations, 356; acquisition of, 327; group system and, 411-412; Sullivan's theory of, 8
interpretations, character of, 87
intervention multiple therapy, 393-394
interviews, in first stage of treatment (Wolf), 280; heterogeneous groups, 409; *see also* admissions; psychological tests
intimacy, fleeing of, 77
intolerance, perfection and, 224
intrapsychic patterns and needs, 199-201
introjection, 9, 547
involution, in aged persons, 488
Iowa, University of, 14, 39
"I-persona" (Burrow), 157
IQ, "dialogue" and, 605; reading disabilities and, 537
"isolates" (Slavson), 236
isolation, analysis and, 144, 332; loss of, 341, 343, 354; resistance and, 151; secrecy and, 218; social clubs and, 457
"I-Thou," healing relation in (Buber), 609; and "I-it" relations, 604-605; patient-therapist relationship and, 609-610

Jackson, D. D., 644
Jackson, James, 125
jails, delinquent groups in, 526-530
James, William, 62
Janet, Pierre, 13 *n.*
Jelliffe, Smith Ely, 124
Jellinek, E. M., 511
Jewish Board of Guardians, 6, 230
Joel, W., 396, 398
Johns Hopkins Hospital, 124
Johnson, Adelaide, 635

Johnson, N. L., 392, 395, 397
Johnson, Paul E., 129
Jones, Ernest, 186
Jones, M., 464
judgment, effect of status on, 66-69
Jung, Carl G., 6, 110, 151, 154-155, 588, 625; letters on trends in group therapy, 180-187

Kadis, A. L., 209-210, 437-447
Kallman, F. J., 488
Kaplan, J. H., 127, 129
Kell, B. L., 393, 399
Kelley, H. H., 17, 62
Kelman, H. C., 512
Kenworthy, M., 566
Kevin, David, 413-423
Klapman, J. W., 328-338, 347, 457, 477
Klein, Melanie, 9, 536
Knopka, G., 564
knowledge, opinion and, 43; "futility" of in psychoanalysis, 153
Knutson, A. L., 32, 92-104
Kopel, D., 536
Kopp, Sheldon B., 391-403
Kotkov, Benjamin, 370-378, 567
Kowert, E. H., 566
Krehl, Rudolf, 126
Kugelmass, S., 564, 567

laboratory findings, analysis and, 149
labor unions, group studies by, 16
Ladd, Henry, 39
Landau, David, 129
Langer, S. K., 601 *n.*
language, "misuse" of, 158
large groups, 412
Lasley, P., 2 *n.*
Laughlin, H. P., 567
Lawrence, D. H., 6, 109; critique of Burrow by, 162-167
Lazell, Edward, 5, 329, 372, 477
leader, associate, 83; "basic assumption," 87; differential conformity of, 66-67; differential influence of, 63; Freud on, 654; griping and, 467; in hospital groups, 459; identification

leader, (cont'd)
with, 12, 451, 459; "independence" of, 51; influence of on group events, 86-87; interpretations of, 87; responsibility of, 76; vs. second-ranking persons, 69; status and, 62, 594; therapist as, 262, 556, 594; in training groups, 83; verbal fluency in, 103

leadership, function of, 587; group-centered, 441; in group discussions, 265-270; "natural," 87; participating, 441; in small-group situations, 102-103; as status of therapist, 556, 594; therapist's responsibility for, 262, 556; verbal fluency as mark of, 103; in vocal and quiet groups, 95

learning process, social definition of, 39; see also education; training

Leary, T., 8

Le Bon, G., 11, 208, 336

lectures, in group therapy, 135, 560-561

Leipzig, University of, 125

Leopold, H., 426

Leslie, Robert E., 129

Levy, D. M., 355

Lewin, Kurt, 8, 14, 39, 451; field theory of, 357

Leyton, S., 626

libido-binding activity, 234

Lichtenberg, J. D., 490

Liébault, A. A., 42

Lieberman, Morton A., 90

life history, of patient, 220, 280, 315; as resistance, 296, 326; transference through, 304

life span, status and, 595

life style (Adler), 170, 173, 334, 394; change of, 177

Lifwynn Foundation, 6, 154, 157

light flashes, distance-judging experiments with, 61-70

Linden, M. E., 397-398, 492-493, 504

Lippitt, Ronald, 14

lobotomy, vs. drug therapy, 634

Loeffler, F. J., 398

Loeser, L. H., 377, 407

logic, "private" (Adler), 171

Lonely Crowd, The, 34

"looking-glass" personality (Mead), 37

Lorand, S., 566

Lott, G. M., 393

Lourdes (France), cures at, 182

love, aggressiveness and, 239; concept of, 148; need for, 222

Low, A. A., 179

Lowrey, Lawson G., 207, 238-241

LSD (lysergic acid diethylamide), 618; group therapy and, 626-629; inhibited effects of, 623; mushrooms and, 620-621

Luce, R. D., 17

Lundin, W. H., 396, 398

lysergic acid, 620; see also LSD

McCann, W., 466

McDougall, William, 2 n., 212, 336

Mackenzie, J., 477

MacGregor, Douglas, 14

McPherson, Dorothy, 90

McPherson, J., 90

"magical solution," 259, 376

majority, individual vs. (Jung), 187; opinion of, 45-46

maladaptive patterns, 454

man, as social animal, 11, 169; holistic concept of, 172; interdependence of, 655; as "social organism," 152-153; "isolation" of, 152

mana, mushrooms as, 620, 622

manic depressive psychosis, 372

Manifestations Fonctionnelles des Psychonévroses . . . , 123

Mann, A., 526

Mann, James, 477

marital problems, 263, 381; alcoholism and, 511-512, 515-517, 520-521; transference and, 309

marriage, social concept of, 148

Marsh, L. Cody, 5, 109, 131-141, 329, 336, 372

Martin, P. W., 183

Maryland, University of, 39

masculinity, destructiveness and, 235
masochism, in elderly patients, 504
mass, individual vs. (Wolf), 327; Jung's views on, 185-186
Massachusetts General Hospital, 112, 114, 129
Massachusetts Institute of Technology, 14
mass communications laboratory, 93 *ff.*
masses, contempt for (Jung), 184-185
mass living, vs. solitary, 40
mass psychotherapy, drama and, 3; *see also* psychodrama
masturbation, 263-265, 270; history of, 222; neurosis of, 318-319
mathematical models, 16-17, 340
Mathematical Thinking in the Measurement of Behavior, 17
Mathis, A. G., 90, 93
matriarchy, dominance of, 332
Mayo, Elton, 13
Mead, George Herbert, 11-12, 37
medical schools, psychiatry in, 545
medical students, group therapy for, 580-582
medicine, neuroses and, 124-126
medieval guilds, 33
Meerloo, J. A., 488, 502-506
meeting, "healing" through (Buber), 609-610; living as (Buber), 607
meetings, coordinated, *see* coordinated meetings; group, *see* group meetings
memory, defective, 492
Menaker, Esther, 583
mental hospital, admission to, 460-461; elderly patients in, 490-494; group therapy in, 453-467
mental hygiene, courses in, 358-359
mental illness, drug treatment of, 618-634; "moral" attitude toward, 146; "punishment" for, 212; social aspect of, 154; stigma of, 243; Sullivan's definition of, 190; teaching of, 545
mental patients, intake and exit groups, 461; mutual distrust among, 459; relationship problems

among, 458; *see also* group members; patient
mephenesin, 514
Merchant, K. C., 566
mescaline, 620
Metrazol, 491
Metropolitan Life Insurance Company, 120
Mexican mushrooms, 621
Meyer, Adolf, 6, 189
Michigan, University of, 14, 31, 38
midbrain, drugs and, 622
middle-class roles, 654
military group therapy, 470-473
military neurosis center, group analysis in, 469-476
Miller, J. S. A., 566
Minnesota, University of, 360
Minor, Charles L., 112
minority opinion, tests of, 45-46
"missionary" type, 294, 367
Mitchell, Weir, 123
mob, concept of, 208; *see also* mass
"momism," 295
Monderer, J. H., 62
monologue, vs. dialogue, 605
Moore, Merrill, 126
moral codes, distorted values and, 155
morality, demands of, 221
Moreno, Jacob L., 4-6, 13-14, 39, 189, 207, 242-248, 347, 357, 392, 477, 566
Morgenstern, O., 16
morons, 276
Mosak, H., 394
mother, aging, 489; friction with husband, 381; primary identification with, 155; sexual problems and, 222
mother-child relationships, 381-390; neurosis and, 150; in social process, 148
mother-dependent feelings, 398
mother fixation (Burrow), 156
mother image, therapist as, 302, 307; transference and, 306
motivation, status system and, 61-62
motivational theory, 30
motor activity (Burrow), 156

Mount Sinai Hospital, N.Y., 229, 562
Mullan, Hugh, 210, 375, 565, 568, 587, 591-603
multidimensional behavior, 615
multidimensional therapy, 616
multiphasic behavior, 616
multiple psychotherapy (or therapy), 391-403, 494; alternating, 394-395; co-therapists in, 399-400; beginnings of, 392; full-term, 395; problems of, 401-403; in training programs, 581; treatment-centered, 393-397
Murphy, Gardner, 2, 22, 30, 33-41, 329, 335, 338
Murphy, Lois, 39
mushrooms, hallucenogenic, 620
Mussolini, Benito, 184
mutual difficulties, released, 373-374
mutuality, in group, 199
mutual revelation, 325
mycophila, 620
mystery religions, 33

name-calling, group conflict and, 58
narcissism, 156, 233
Nash, Helen T., 510-524
National Association for Study and Prevention of Tuberculosis, 115-118
National Education Association, 16, 90
National Training Laboratories, 16
need gratification, 376
Negro members, of defective delinquent groups, 527
Neighbor, J. E., 413-423
"nervous breakdown," 383
Neumann, J. von, 16
neurohumoral transmitters, 622
Neurons and Human Growth, 197
neuropharmacology, 622
neurophysiological interpretations (Burrow), 156
neurosis(-es), "age" of, 498; child-rearing concepts and, 253; clinging to, 279; defined, 454; egocentricity as cause of, 164; general practitioner and, 124;

"honesty" and, 167; Lawrence's views on, 166; and mother-child relationship, 150; as natural state of man (Lawrence), 166-167; as "old friend" (Rosenbaum), 368; reading disability and, 536; severe, 218-227; "social," 154-155; student observation of, 548
neurotic blocking (Horney), 196
neurotic patient, "relative" sickness of, 145; *see also* patient
neurotic reactions (Burrow), 155
neurotic symptoms, purpose of, 171
"neutralizers" (Slavson), 236
Newcomb, T. M., 39
Newstetter, W. I., 228
New York Association for Jewish Children, 230
New York City, tuberculosis class in, 113-114
New York State Training School, 39
New York University, 230
nicknames, in group conflicts, 54-55
Niles, Walter L., 114
nonrejection, inclusiveness and, 596
nonverbal behavior, 10, 234; group functioning and, 93; in schizophrenics, 372
nonverbal communication, 209, 424-435; defined, 424; in psychotic patients, 478; symptoms as, 642-643; of therapist, 432-433, 556
"normal" vs. "neurotic" individuals (Burrow), 148-149
normality (Lawrence), 164; as "neurosis of human race" (Burrow), 155
Norristown (Pa.) State Hospital, 492
note taking, 560
NVC, *see* nonverbal communication

Obendorf, Clarence P., 6, 155 *n.*
"observation" ward, 131
obsessional dynamism, 189
obsession-compulsion, in alcoholics, 512

obsession neurosis, 225
occupational therapy, 632; for senile patients, 491
O'Connor, N., 526
Oedipal situations or conflict, 334, 398; anxiety and, 377; Burrow on, 156; in elderly patients, 505; insight in, 308; projection of, 374; social meaning of, 220-221; superego residual of, 654
Oldsted, M. S., 17
old-age homes, 494-495
older persons, 487-506; *see also* elderly patients
opinion, psychological experiments in, 44-45; social pressure and, 42-51
orality, reading and, 536
Orange, A. J., 396, 401
organic groups, 143-144
organismic reorientation (Burrow), 158
Organization Man, The, 34
orgasm difficulties, 294
Osawatomie State Hospital, Kansas, 491
"other guy," ignoring of, 332-334
"otherness" (Jung), 184; acceptance of, 605
others, awareness of, 234, 460; identification with, 343
"ought," responsibility and (Buber), 606
Our Inner Conflicts, 197
outpatient treatment, 132, 562
Oxford day hospital, England, 496
Oxford Movement, 182-183

pain, psychic origin of, 127
pairing and counterpairing, 10
pairing culture (Bion), 73, 75, 79-80
Papanek, H., 566
paranoia, Rauwolfia and, 623
paranoid patients, 478
paranoid-schizoid position, 9
parataxes, defined, 191
parent, aging, 489; therapist as, 439, 446-447

parental types, 446-447
parent-child relationships, family and, 640; students in, 577
parents, family group therapy and, 635-647; faulty culture transmission by, 598; group counseling with, 381-390; as group members, 383-385; isolation of, 384-385; mutual help by, 385-386
Park, R. E., 12
Parloff, M. B., 512
patient(s), acting-out effects on, 366-367; anxiety of, 190; basic problems of summarized, 220; case histories of, 222-224; as "catalytic agent" (Wolf), 283, 419; common factors among, 440; "courage" of, in visiting psychiatrist, 334; defective delinquents as, 525-533; diagnostic categories of, 415-416; discovery of common problems by, 323; elderly, *see* elderly patients; "emotionally illiterate" (Leopold), 426; expansive, 426; as father image, 367; fear of hospitalization in, 211; goal and life plan of, 220; incorporation" of, 445-446; life history and reports required of, 220; military, 470-476; mutual help among, 345; needs of, vs. group needs, 420-421; preliminary interviews with, 280; provocative role of, 302-306, 320, 326; psychotic, *see* psychotic patient; qualifications of for group therapy, 214, 275, 329, 597; restricting of behavior of, 481; "role" of in group (Ackerman), 254; selection and screening of, 413-423; self-effacing, 427; student as, 580-581; "talking out" by, 549; test for "cure," 318; as therapist, 371; trainee as, 567, 570-571, 573; types of, 418; *see also* group member; mental patient

patient care conference, weekly, 565
patient-patient relationships, 197, 209, 215-216, 244, 341, 344-345, 371
patient-patient transference, 215-216, 345, 396
patient-student relationships, 547
patient-therapist relationships, 174, 209, 214, 218, 285, 341, 345, 365, 455-456, 499-500, 556; Ackerman's view of, 256; "being and being" in, 592; changing nature of, 598; common denominator in, 602; communications in, 465-466; in drug therapy, 627, 633; with elderly patients, 498-499; in first meetings, 282; in hospital groups, 462; "I-thou" relationship and, 609-610; "love" in, 294; with psychotic patients, 483; satisfaction in, 601; as symbolic experience, 600; teaching and, 551; transference analysis and resolution in, 300-310
Peabody, Francis W., 125
Peck, H. B., 228 *n.*
pedagogy, methods of, 336-338; transference and, 331
Pederson-Krag, G., 376
perfection complex, 224
penal environment, 528-529
"penetration of facade" (Wolf), 289-290, 321, 323
penicillin, 619
penis envy, 307, 317, 334
Pennsylvania, University of, 546
pentylenetetrazol, 491
perceptual satisfactions, 601
permissive atmosphere, 323-324, 344, 354, 417; in group meetings, 265; need for, 236; in sexual relations of group, 321
Perry, Ralph Barton, 29
Perry Point Veterans Hospital, 464
"person," growth of, 209
persona (Burrow), 157; "mask" of, 655
personal analysis, need for in therapist

training, 572; *see also* individual therapy
personality, as aspect of social process, 335; as biosocial unit (Ackerman), 253; cultural impact on, 2; functions and operations of, 253; as "generalized other," 37; "looking-glass" (Mead), 37; social role and, 254; unity of (Adler), 172
personality development, group experience in, 358
personality disorders, 416; *see also* character disorders
personality processes, multidimensional (Horney), 198
personality studies, social psychology and, 653
personality theory, psychoanalysis as, 252
personality variables, group life and, 17-18
"personal liberty," as social exploitation, 318
Pettigrew, T. J., 621
phallus worship, 317
phenobarbital, 550
phenothiazine drugs, 631-632
Philadelphia General Hospital, 545, 550
philosophical anthropology (Buber), 607
Phipps Neuropsychiatric Institute, 114, 124, 465, 510
phonemes, vs. paralinguistics, 209
phylic disturbance (Burrow), 156
"phyloanalysis" (Burrow), 6, 154, 158-159, 355
phylobiological studies, Burrow's, 158-159
phylopathology, 158
physical examination, need for, 140
physical illness, in aged, 495; vs. mental, 146
physicians, need for psychiatric knowledge in, 545
physiology, preconscious and, 156
Piaget, Jean, 10
pneumonia, 619

polarity concept (Beukenkamp), 614-615

Polatsek, I., 526

postmeetings, 438

Powdermaker, F. B., 355, 364, 377, 396

placebo, 632; in neurosis, 548

placebo effect, defined, 529

placebo groups, 527

placebo response, 619-620, 634

pragmatism, of American psychiatry, 3

Pratt, Joseph Hersey, 3-4, 13 *n.*, 109, 111-122, 123-130, 132, 329

preconscious (Burrow), 155-156, 164

prejudice, in group conflicts, 60; as nonverbal behavior, 433-434

premeetings, 438

pre-Oedipal needs, 382

Prescott, Daniel, 39

Preston, M. G., 441

pride system (Horney), 198

primal scene, voyeurism and, 295

primary group, concept of, 11; formation studies of, 12; *see also* family

primary identification, principle of, 149; with mother, 155

primary polarity, 615

prisoners of war, 472

privacy, "invasion" of, 277

"private" areas, problems of, 243

"private consultation," group therapy and, 139

"private logic" (Dreikurs), 392

private sanatorium, 132

problem children, special treatment for, 579

problems, basic, of patient, 220; discussion of, 284-285; social character of, 220; "working through," *see* working through

problem-sharing, 36, 213; constructive, 323

problem-solving, group, 18, 78-81, 357

progress card, 140

Progressive Education, 582

projection, 9, 374, 547

propaganda, social pressure and, 43; studies in, 37

propriocentive awareness, 156

"propriocentive reconstellation" (Burrow), 158

provocative personality of patient (Wolf), 302-306

pseudogroup situation, 148, 151

pseudosexual images, 149

psilocybin, 620

psychiatric clinic, group therapy in, 131-141

psychiatric residents, 560-561

psychiatrist, "courage" required to meet, 334; "five-dollar," 36

psychiatry, American, 3; clinical, 561, 568-569; derivation of word, 126; social, 154 (*see also* social psychology); teaching of, 547; training in, 567

psychoanalysis, appeal of to elite, 36, 218; classical, 29; contrasted with psychotherapy, 186; vs. group therapy, 250-260, 272-327 (*see also* individual therapy); high cost of, 218; group methods of, 149-150 (*see also* group therapy); hospitalization and, 212; insight through, 219; "knowledge" of, 153; meanings of (Ackerman), 251; origin of, 188; patient-therapist basis in, 218; as personality theory, 252; in severe neuroses, 218; Wolf's techniques in, 273-327

psychoanalysts, European, 5; objections of to group methods, 363; *see also* therapist

psychodrama, 6, 14, 243, 453, 457; "staff" in, 244; therapist in, 244; in training programs, 566

psychodynamics, Horney's concepts of, 202

psychological tests, 280; admissions and, 597; children's, 537

psychologists, nonmedical, 393

psychology, group-centered, 38; individual-centered, 38; teaching of, 38 "psychology hobby," avoidance of, 214

psychoneuroses, group therapy for, 213, 276; *see also* neuroses

psychopathic ward, 1935, 131

Psychopathology of Everyday Life, The, 172

psychopaths, exclusion of from groups, 276, 278, 368

psychoses, experience and, 454; student observation of, 550; *see also* psychotic patients

psychosomatic disorders, 418

psychotherapist, nonmedical, 393; *see also* therapist

psychotherapy, contrasted with psychoanalysis, 186; Dejerine's views of, 127; vs. education, 358-359; elements common to, 354; "existential," 109; final aim of, 219, 455; individual vs. group, *see* individual therapy; "locus" of, 242-243; vs. mental hygiene, 358-359; multiple, 391-403; teaching of, 545-552, 567; *see also* group therapy

psychotic episodes, 366-367

psychotic patients, behavior restrictions on, 481-482; group therapy for, 276, 393, 396, 477-486; prognosis for, 484-485; senile, 491; therapy stages for, 482

psychotropic drugs, 618-634

P.T.A., role of in child behavior, 40

public opinion, 37; social pressure and, 42-51

"punishment," hospitalization seen as, 212

purposiveness, 170

question-answer period, in group therapy, 136, 265

questionnaires, 222

quiet groups, vs. vocal, 92-104

racial instinct, 144-145

racial unity, 144

Rademacher, E. S., 228

Raiffa, H., 17

rank, competition and, 58; status and, 63

rapport, in group therapy (Wolf), 283-288

Rashkis, H. A., 633

rationalization, 547

Rauwolfia alkaloids, 623

reading, oral drives and, 536

reading courses, 137

reading failures, and related skills, 534

Readings in Social Psychology, 653

real, "imagining" of (Buber), 608

reality, distortions of, 324; group experience and, 221; inner vs. outer, 255; self-hate and, 198; social, 327; social images and, 148

reality testing, 341; in children, 237; defined, 342; as element or factor in therapy, 354; group structure and, 408; mechanisms of, 344; as psychotherapeutic goal, 455

"real self," behavior of, 598

rebirth, forms of, 625-626

recorder-observer, 560; training and, 565

Redl, Fritz, 87, 336, 375

Redmount, R. S., 535

Rees, T. P., 633

Reeve, G. A., 395, 397

regression, 547; in psychotic patients, 482

Reik, Theodore, 186, 367

relatedness, empathic, 594; of group members, 192; status and, 594

relation, distance and (Buber), 607-608

relationships, eye expressions in, 429; identification as, 373; as psychotherapeutic element, 354; *see also* patient-therapist relationships

"relationship therapy" (Levy), 355

religion, as group therapy, 132; psychiatry and, 4

remedial reading courses, 535

Rennie, A. C., 124

reorientation, of life style (Adler), 177

repetition, transference and, 300

repression, 547; image-preoccupation and, 156; social process and, 147

research, 14, 19-21, 83

resentment, 291

reserpine, 491; for alcoholics, 514

resident therapist, 391, 560

resident training, group resistance in, 596

resistance, 473; analysis of (Wolf), 293-300, 346; biography as, 296, 326; "bursting" of (Wolf), 325; centralizing of, 375-376; five types of, 375-376; generalized, 319; importance of, 355; isolation and, 151; as nonverbal communication, 427; patterns of, 258-260; in psychotic groups, 484; release and, 373; in student groups, 566; subgrouping and, 438; in therapist, 557

responsibility, idea of (Buber), 606

rest, in tuberculosis treatment, 115-116

retaliation, fear of, 289, 433

retarded readers, group therapy with, 534-548

reveries and daydreams, 287; *see also* daydreams; dreams

"reversed Oedipus constellation" (Grotjahn), 505

Rhoades, Winifred, 129

Rhoads, J. M., 567

rhythm bands, 457

Riecken, H., 102

Riesman, David, 34

Riley, M. W., 2 *n.*

Ringleheim, D., 526

Rioch, M. J., 394

Rogers, Carl R., 7, 347, 355, 537, 607, 609

role-divided therapy, 391, 395-396

role-playing, (Lewin), 14, 357; by therapist, 305

Rorschach test, 280, 309, 535

Rose, Sidney, 195-203

Rosen, I. M., 482

Rosenbaum, Max, 209, 362-369

Rosenberg, Bina, 209, 340-348

Rosenthal, David, 127, 510-524

Ross, Edward A., 2 *n.*

Ross, Mathew, 452, 487-506

Ross, T. A., 124, 126

Ross, W. D., 565-567

round-table groups, 466

Rutherford, Jeanne, 62

St. Elizabeth Psychiatric Hospital, 5, 477

St. George's Church, N.Y., 114

Sakel, M. J., 632

sanatorium treatment, tuberculosis cases, 118-119

Sandison, R. A., 588, 618-634

Sapir, Edward, 13, 21

Sarah Lawrence College, 39

satisfactions, sensual and perceptual, 601

scapegoating, 333

Scheidlinger, Saul, 209, 352-360, 564

Schilder, Paul, 6-7, 207, 218-227, 231, 273, 336, 347, 477

Schiller, Johann Christoph, 187

schizophrenia, ambulatory, 416; case history in, 335; deep insulin treatment of, 632; defenses in, 483; "double bind" in, 644; group therapy for, 213, 226, 234, 276, 398; hallucinogens and, 619-620; in hospital groups, 459; in women, 625

schizophrenic patients, communication among, 464; drug therapy for, 631; fear of therapist in, 465; participation of, 372

schizoid patients, 276, 291

Schonell, F. J., 534

school groups, 38; *see also* classroom; education; students

school teachers, group training of, 578

Schossberger, J., 564, 567

scientific foundations, 242-248

scientific movement, 33

Scott, R. D., 624

screening, of patients, 413-423; in heterogeneous groups, 408
Schwartz, E., 208, 409
seating arrangements, group therapy, 478
Sechrist, Lee, 525-533
secondary polarity, 615
self-acceptance, 223; in children, 237; security and, 232
self-aggrandizement, illusion of, 327
self-assessment, need for, 446
self-concepts, idealizing of (Horney), 197
self-confidence, 455
self-consciousness (Lawrence), 164
self-contempt, 202
self-creation, 593
self-destruction, 376
self-determination, 170
self-discipline, insight and, 215
self-disinterest activity (Mullan), 598
self-effacement, vs. hostility, 198
self-encapsulation, 612; removal of, 237
self-esteem, in elderly patients, 492
self-evaluation, in quiet and vocal groups, 99-100
self-expression, "dialogue" and, 607
self-fulfillment (Horney), 200
self-hate, 198-201
Self-Help (Low), 179
self-identity, questioning of, 154
self-idolatry (Lawrence), 164-165
self-image, conflicts with (Horney), 200; scapegoating and, 333
self-interest behavior (Mullan), 598
self-realization (Horney), 196
self-respect, from awareness of others, 460; in group therapy, 177; as psychotherapeutic goal, 455-456
self-seeking, 453; Lawrence on, 166
self-system (Horney), 203; Sullivan's, 189-190, 194
self-understanding, need for, 456; see also insight
Self You Have to Live With, The, 129
Seliger, R. V., 511
semantics, 340

seminar work, 560-561
Semrad, Elvin V., 372, 451, 477-486, 567
senescence, psychology of, 488-489
senescent behavior, character of, 498-499
senile groups, 490-500
sensations, social character of, 220
sensuous satisfactions, 601
separateness, sense of (Lawrence), 163
sex, complementary equality of, 317; of group members, 214, 275; self-seeking in (Lawrence), 166
sex dreams, of elderly patients, 503
sex drives, guilt and, 221
sex-repression (Lawrence), 163
sexual ability, LSD treatment and, 628
sexual conflicts, repression and, 147; social system and, 147
sexual development, patient's, 220
sexual difficulties, 263, 294
sexual fantasies, 146-147
sexual frigidity, in alcoholics, 515, 518
sexual insight, 299
sexual intercourse, 222; discussion of, 320-321; between group members, 320, 367; mutual gratification in, 319
sexual material, anxiety at discussion of, 278, 326; resistance in, 297
sexual outbursts, at coordinated meetings, 444
sexual problems, father and, 222; geriatric patients and, 506
sexual prowess, 317
Seymour, N. Gilbert, 114
Shakespeare, mass psychotherapy and, 3
Shapiro, D., 396, 398
sharing, in alcoholics, 518; in group, 278-279; mechanisms of, 347
Sheps, J., 499
Sherif, Carolyn W., 52
Sherif, Muzafer, 2, 16, 20, 30, 52-60, 208
Shields, C., 157
Shils, E. A., 105
shock therapy, see electroshock therapy; insulin coma therapy
Shulman, B., 394

sibling rivalry, 387, 397-398

sibling substitute, therapist as, 303, 307

silence, "conspiracies" of, 159; as non-verbal communication, 427-428; as resistance, 299; of therapist, 431

Simmel, G., 11

"sissy," epithet of, 235, 376

situational therapy (Slavson), 232

situation analysis, 355

skill, emphasis on, 33

Slavson, Samuel R., 6, 207, 228-241, 347, 375, 377, 398-401, 414, 564, 573

small group, 411; research in, 11-16; teaching through, 554

smiling, emotions and, 430

smugness, 434

Smuts, Jan C., 172

Snyder, Robert, 525-533

social animal, man as, 11, 169

social change, group decision and, 15

social clubs, therapeutic, 7, 417, 453, 457, 463

social clusters (Burrow), 149

social concepts, reality and, 148

social conflict, image preoccupation and, 156

social education, group theory as (Jung), 184

social equality, in therapy group, 178

social experience, vs. psychoanalytic relationship, 255

social fixity, 238

social hunger (Slavson), 232, 384

social images (Burrow), 157

social impotence, vs. sexual, 297

"social insanity" (Lawrence), 165

social insight, 299

social integration (Wolf), 310-312; insight and, 313

social interaction, personality and, 213, 254

social interest (Adler), 170

socialization, education and, 230

social living, "logic" of (Adler), 169

social mind, concept of, 152

social mobility, 238

social needs (Adler), 169

"social neurosis" (Burrow), 154-155, 225

"social neuters" (Slavson), 236

social participation, 372-373

social position, group conflict and, 57; status and, 596

social pressure, consensus and, 51; opinion and, 42-51

social process, personality and, 335; repressions and, 147

social psychiatry, Burrow's work in, 154

social psychologists, group studies by, 2

social psychology, beginnings of, 43; field of, 2; Freud on, 252; vs. personality studies, 653; research in, 14; small-group theory and, 29-104

social purpose (Adler), 170

social reality (Wolf), 327, 344

social relationship, establishing of, 327; group therapy and, 12

social resistance, shared nature of, 37

social role (Ackerman), 254

social sciences, teaching of, 554

social service agencies, 133

social suggestion, as transference, 148

social system, mental illness and, 146-147

social unconsciousness, 152

social workers, training of, 559

societal consciousness (Burrow), 166

society, communication in, 462; as group, 2; group psychotherapy and, 33-41; as "therapeutic community," 40; "weak" level of, 184

sociodynamic effect (Moreno), 247-248

sociograms, 14; chance vs. actual, 247; group conflict studies and, 56

sociologists, vs. psychotherapists, 2; at University of Chicago, 12

sociometric choice, group culture and, 77-78

sociometric methods, values and, 13-14, 244

sociometric questionnaire, 64

sociometric test, 357

Sociometry, 14

soldiers, psychiatric casualties among, 469-470

solidarity, human (Jung), 181

Solomon, A., 398

Solomon, H., 17

soul, nobility of (Jung), 185

spectator therapy, defined, 343; mechanisms of, 345

speech defects, 223

speech-with-meaning (Buber), 611

Spiegel, J. P., 38, 636

Spiker, Dorothy, 228 *n.*

Spitz, Herman H., 391-403

sports, intergroup conflicts in, 56-57

Spotnitz, H., 375, 566

stammering, 4-5, 223, 225

Standish, Christopher T., 451, 477-486

Stanford Achievement Test, 527

state hospital, outpatient department, 132

status, differential influence of in group norm, 66-67; of group members, 591-592; group pressures and, 61-70; leadership and, 594; motivation and, 62

status denial, 591-603; importance of, 592-594; method of, 594-596

status-equilibration hypothesis, 62

status-fixed state, 597

status-free state, value and, 600

status system, hierarchy in, 61

Stein, Aaron, 377, 466, 558-574

Stieper, D. R., 566

stigma, of mental illness, 243, 354

Stock, Dorothy, 10, 31-32, 71-89, 90, 93

Stogdill, Ralph M., 357

Strachey, J., 536

Strecker, Edward A., 124

striving, status and, 62

Strong, Isabel, 112

students, freshman and sophomore, 580-581; as patients, 581

student-teacher relationships, 577

student-therapist relationships, 547, 566

stutterers, 276; acting out and, 443

subgroups, discouraging of, 438; in family, 638; operation of in group culture, 77-78, 89; *see also* cliques

sublimation, 341, 547; social process and, 148

sudden noise, fear of, 222

suggestibility, as "heightened risk" (Jung), 186; social pressures and, 42-43

suggestion, effects of, 183-184; in group therapy, 216-217

suicidal patients, exclusion of, 420

suicide, depression and, 226; drug action and, 631

Sullivan, Harry Stack, 6, 8, 13, 451; theories of, applied to group psychotherapy, 188-194

Sundby, E., 62

superego, drug action on, 630-631; Freud on, 654; modification of, 370; reading and, 536; resistance of, 376; "shedding" of, 255; "suspension" of, 233; transforming of, 234

superiority feelings, 220

supervision, of training program, 572-573

supportive ego, 233

survival, interdependence and, 655

Sussman, Marvin B., 52

Sutherland, J. D., 567

Swarthmore College, 46

Sweet, B., 414

symptom, as form of communication, 642-643

symptom identification, 370

syntactics, 340

Syz, Hans, 6, 109, 154-160, 609

"talking out" by patient, 549; *see also* verbal behavior; vocal groups

Tarde, Gabriel, 43

task activity, 73

taxonomy, of group therapy mechanisms, 347

teachers' college, group therapy training in, 578

Teachers College, Columbia University, 9
teacher-student relations, 38
teaching, of group therapy, 558-574; responsibility of, 553; vs. "treating," 136
teaching methods, in group therapy, 336-338
technology, science and, 33
Teicher, A., 371, 396-397
teleological mechanisms (Adler), 170
tension, anxiety and, 456
tertiary polarity, 615
Texas, University of, 40
textbook, use of, 336-337, 347
Thelen, Herbert A., 9-10, 31-32, 71-89, 93
Thematic Apperception Test, 280
theoretical material, use of in meetings, 214
therapeutic change (Ackerman), 256
therapeutic group discussion (Baruch), 261
therapeutic impasse, 393-394
therapist, absences of, 439-440; acting out and, 366, 444; active or senior, 394; "active control" by, 215; aggressive vs. passive, 402; anxiety of, 559, 563-564, 578; approaches to role of, 397-399; "appropriate comment" of, 480; attachment to, 345 (*see also* transference); as *au courant* to developments in group, 439-440; as authority figure, 239, 439, 479-480, 493; body language of, 481; as catalyst, 479; character-structure limitations of, 238, 244, 265, 305, 312-313; in child-centered parents' groups, 388; clinical psychiatric training of, 568-569, 572; "counterattack" by, 289; countertransference in, *see* countertransference; cues from, 292, 432; dependence on, 326; "doctor" status of, 587, 593; dream interpretation by, 287; dual or multiple, 493-494; as

ego-ideal, 326; for elderly patients, 498-499, 505-506; "evolvement as therapist," 594; "exclusive possession of" (Wolf), 277; "expert" fantasy, 314; facial and eye expressions of, 481; "faith" in, 243-244; familial roles of, 302; in family group theory, 646-647; as father or mother image, 302, 307, 446; favoritism shown by, 432; fear of, 289, 363, 433; female, 493; goal of, 20-21; graduate training program for, 565; group attitudes toward, 285-286; as group member, 316, 366, 556, 600; helpful attitude of, 219; "heritage" of, 555; honesty of, 316; for hospital groups, 462; humanness of, 193; ignorance of, 557; importance of group work to, 600; increased leadership in, 526; individual therapy training for, 569; inexperience of, 560; influence of on group patients, 176; insensitivity to individuals, 314; insincerity of, 459; and interdependence of group, 655; interns and residents as, 391; interpersonal demands on, 318; isolation from group, 595; jealous reactions to, 484; judgment of, 195; as leader, 219, 587, 593-594; life-span relationship (Mullan), 595-596; love for, 294; LSD drug therapy and, 627; for military groups, 471-472, 476; modern views on, 568-571; multiple, 391, 398-402, 581; "need to lead" in, 556; need to participate in group, 570-573; neutrality of, 238-239; nonintervention role of, 371; nonverbal communication of, 431-433, 556; number of in group, 415; "omnipotent" role, 326-327; optimism of, 315; parent role, 302, 307, 446; as part of group,

therapist, (*cont'd*)
439-440, 570-573; passivity of, 265; as patient, 570-573; patient as, 371; personal analysis needed by, 572; personality of, 238, 244, 265, 305, 312-313; prime function of, 313; pseudowarm reactions to, 441-442; relationship with patient, *see* patient-therapist relationships; resentment and anger at, 286; resident, 560-561; resistance in, 557; retaliation from, 289, 433; in retarded reading groups, 537; role of, 302, 307, 312-319, 326, 397-399, 446-447, 462, 476, 481, 505-506, 537, 646-647; role-playing by, 305; "satisfaction" demand by (Mullan), 601; schizophrenic's fear of, 465; in school setting, 577; for senile patients, 491-493, 506; sex of, 303, 388, 398, 493; silence and, 428, 430-431; sincerity of, 480; "sitting near," 478-479; as "son" in aged group, 506; status denial in, 592-594; student, 553-557, 547; "suggestibility" of, 184, 186; suggestion by, 216-217; support from, 235; as teacher, 358; technique of, 278-279, 282, 432-433; training of, 476, 553-557, 558-574; transference in, 214-215 (*see also* transference); "tricking" of by elderly patients, 499-500; urge to "cure," 555
therapy, "agent" of, 243; locus of, 242-243; *see also* group therapy
Thibaut, J. W., 17
Thomas, Giles W., 7, 129
Thorndike, Edward L., 43
Thorpe, J. G., 632
thoughts, "common" nature of, 221
Thrasher, F., 12, 62
three-cornered therapy (Bock), 391
thumb-clasping, 430

toadstools, hallucenogenic, 620
tobacco, emotional content of, 629
togetherness, 343
tolerance, 343; vs. family prohibitions, 323-324; insecurity and (Jung), 187; transference and, 300
trainee, personal analysis of, 572; supervision of, 566, 572
training, experiment in, 577-584; of grade school teachers, 578; group experience in, 83, 567; in hospital groups, 562-564; literature on, 564-568; need for experience as patient, 567; present-day views on, 568-571
tranquillizers, 588, 619; sanctions on use of, 630
transference, 214, 243, 374, 424; acting out as, 433; in alcoholic, 522; analysis of, 300-310; Beukenkamp's concept of, 615; "beyond-transference behavior," 588, 614-616; in biographical materials, 304; case histories in (Wolf), 306-309; changes in, 366; checking of, 257; to community, 40; co-therapists and, 399-402; defined, 342-343, 375; and depth of analysis, 363-364; dilution of (Slavson), 354; vs. doctor-patient relations (Horney), 197; dynamics of, 341; ego ideal and, 614; in elderly patients, 504-506; fantasy of, 600; of group, 150, 365-366; Horney's theory of, 197, 203; hostile, 319; id and, 614; levels of, 396; mechanisms of, 345; in military groups, 475; multiple, 273-274, 285, 311, 324, 455; negative, 356; neurosis of, 615; nonverbal communication and, 430-431; in parents' group, 387-388; patient's "disposing" of (Wolf), 310; pedagogy and, 331 (*see also* teaching; training); positive and negative, 221, 336; resolution of, 300-

310; sex factors in, 302-303; social suggestion as, 148; socio-biological structure and (Burrow), 157; subgrouping and, 438; teaching and, 554; terror from, 321; undesirable, 371; unmanageable, 418; Wolf's theory of, 300-310; *see also* patient-therapist relationships
treatment, epistemology of, 374
Trends in Therapy, 228
tribal instinct, 144-145
"Troubled People Meet," 201
tuberculosis, aftercare of, 111; rest treatment of, 115
"tuberculosis class," Pratt's, 111-122
Tuberculosis Nurse, The, 119
Tulchin, S. H., 536

unanimity, majority and, 47
unconscious (Ackerman), 251-252; Burrow's view of, 155; explosive effect on, 324-325; Freud's theory of, 165; Jung's theory of, 180; social, 152
unconscious feelings, anxiety and, 376
unconscious material, shared, 325
universalization, defined, 342; mechanisms of, 344
unmasking, mutual, 324-326

vacillation, in coordinated meeting, 442-443
Vail, D., 526
valency, basic assumption culture and, 88; defined, 73-74; individual, 81; pattern in (Bion), 78; problem solving and, 78-81
value, status-free state and, 600
venereal disease, 146
ventilation, defined, 343; mechanisms of, 346
verbal behavior, index of, 104
verbal facility, group participation and, 95; as leadership characteristic, 103
Verdun Protestant Hospital (Montreal), 491
Veterans Bureau, 546

Vienna Child Guidance Clinics, 392
virility, exhibition of, 298, 317
virtue, concept of, 148
Visher, John S., 413-423
vocal groups, 92-104
vocal intonations, 429
Vorhaus, P. G., 536
Votos, A., 567
voyeurism, 277; resistance and, 295

Wagner, Ernest, 125
Wandlungserlebnis (Jung), 180
Warkentin, J., 392, 395, 397, 543, 577-584
Wasson, G., 620
Watson, J. B., 222
Wayne, G. J., 501
Weakland, J. H., 644
"We," of community, 610-611; "essential," 604-613
Wechsler Intelligence Scale for Children, 537
Weinstein, H. M., 399
Weltanschauung, Freud's, 225
Wender, Louis, 5, 7, 207, 211-217, 231, 273, 466, 566
Whitaker, Carl, 392, 394-395, 397, 567, 583
White, B. J., 52, 208
White, Ralph K., 15
White, William F., 12
Whyte, W. H., Jr., 34
wife, as target of alcoholic husband, 511
Wilcox, G., 526
Wile, Ira, 229
Winder, A., 566
withdrawal, 236; *see also* isolation
Witty, P., 536
Wolf, Alexander, 7, 20, 207-210, 273-327, 375, 409, 437, 564, 567-568, 612
Wolff, K., 492
woman, as ideal image, 625; psychological immaturity of, 625; schizophrenic, 625; senile or aged, 492-493
Wood, N. K., 113

Worcester, Elwood, 112

Worcester (Mass.) State Hospital, 133

work-dependency culture, 82

"work-emotionality" culture, 81-84, 88

"work-fight-flight" culture, 73

work incentives, 12

"working through," conflict and, 259-260; group therapy as, 371; by parents, 385; reality testing and, 344

workshop training, 565-566

World War I, 5, 39

World War II, army pilots' leadership groups in, 38; group therapy experience following, 1, 373; Lewin's studies during, 15-16; literature growth since, 7-8

worthlessness, feelings of, 483; *see also* inadequacy

Wortis, J., 619

Yogi philosophy, 215

Yonge, K., 526

Zander, A., 357